Hispanic Texas
A Historical Guide

HISPANIC TEXAS

A Historical Guide

Edited by
HELEN SIMONS
and
CATHRYN A. HOYT,
Texas Historical Commission

University of Texas Press, Austin

In memory of
John Edward Aiken

The publication of this volume was assisted by a gift from
Houston Endowment, Inc.,
to the Texas Historical Commission
in support of the commission's recognition of the
Columbus Quincentenary

Requests for permission to reproduce material from this work should be sent to
Permissions, University of Texas Press, Box 7819, Austin, TX 78713-7819.

∞ The paper used in this publication meets the minimum requirements of American National Standard for Information Sciences—Permanence of Paper for Printed Library Materials, ANSI Z39.48–1984.

Library of Congress Cataloging-in-Publication Data
Hispanic Texas : a historical guide / edited by Helen Simons and Cathryn A. Hoyt. — 1st ed.
    p. cm.
    Includes bibliographical references and index.
    ISBN 0-292-77662-4 (alk. paper)
    1. Historic sites—Texas—Guidebooks. 2. Hispanic Americans—Texas—History. 3. Texas—Guidebooks. 4. Texas—History, Local. I. Simons, Helen,
date . II. Hoyt, Cathryn A. (Cathryn Ann), date
F387.H56 1992
917.6404′63—dc20   92-320

FRONTISPIECE: *Hispanic Heritage of Texas* by José Cisneros.

Contents

Foreword

When in the course of my chairmanship of the Texas Historical Commission, staff members asked me for a go-ahead for a guidebook to Hispanic Texas as a Columbus Quincentenary project, this was one of the easiest decisions I ever had to make.

No matter that as yet there was no budget, no publisher, no dazzling array of committed contributors. It was a splendid idea, put forth as a labor of love as well as scholarship, and it was easy to believe that it would come to pass.

"Hispanic Texas" is a catchy but amorphous concept. It can mean many things. We, however, believe that there is a need to search out, identify, and survey all those things pertaining to the centuries-old and culture-rich Hispanic presence in our state and to make them, through this guidebook, more easily available to both Texans and the world. Two of the Texas Historical Commission's responsibilities are historic preservation and education—to preserve the *total* Texas heritage so far as we can capture it, and to inform Texans and others about that heritage.

These essays and guidebook fill a void too long neglected. But they are more than a mere guide, a travelogue to what remains of historic places and artifacts. They point out the present as well.

The Hispanic heritage of Texas is something that was, but it's also something that is. It's with us, independent of any interpretation of history. We are, I would hope, beginning to recognize that it is a misuse of the past to peruse it solely in search of heroes and villains, ideologies or anathemas, or to seek historical people either to identify with or dislike. History is a process that rarely "proves"; it happens, makes, shapes—and goes on.

For example, Italy has a heritage created by a mix of Iron Age peoples, Etruscans, Romans, Latins, Oscans, Greeks, Goths, Lombards, Byzantines, and Normans, all of whose presence and cultures impressed something of themselves in stone, language, or remembrance. Even those that left behind no living language or literature still exert subtle influences upon the modern, industrial state and nation.

The land of Texas has something of the same quality, successive peoples and cultures in successive eras, all creating a common heritage whether recognized or not.

The Hispanic heritage of Texas does not belong to Hispanics or the Spanish-speaking alone. It is a part of the continuing heritage of every Texan, whatever tongue we speak and from whatever continent we or our ancestors arrived. It is part of our common past, and it forms part of our present reality.

My own Texas land titles descend directly from eighteenth-century grants by the Spanish Crown. In 1941 the boundaries of one such property were defined by a Texas court relying on precedents in Castilian law compiled by King Alfonso el Sabio in the thirteenth century.

This is what I mean by living heritage, which is more than crumbling walls or dusty records or even the blood flowing in our veins.

I trust this book will make these things, from remaining artifacts to vivid place-names, more visible and understood by all Texans with an interest in our common past.

T.R. FEHRENBACH
Austin, Texas

Acknowledgments

The editors wish to express their deepest appreciation to members and staff of the Texas Historical Commission whose support and encouragement made this project possible from its inception. Special contributions were made by T.R. Fehrenbach, former chairman of the Texas Historical Commission, Curtis Tunnell, executive director of the commission, and staff members Jim Bonar, Nancy A. Kenmotsu, Patricia A. Mercado-Allinger, Hector Meza, Roni Morales, Ann Perry, Martha Peters, Anice Read, Frances Rickard, James W. Steely, and Deborah Smith. Robert J. Mallouf, state archeologist, made it possible for us to complete the project once begun, and we express our thanks also for his patience and understanding. Staff members Cindy Leo, James Bruseth, and Mario Sánchez, in addition to those named above, served on the project advisory committee. We also want to express again our indebtedness to Félix Almaráz, F. Jesús de la Teja, Joe S. Graham, Jack Jackson, Enrique Madrid, and Robert S. Weddle, who volunteered their contributions at a time when many other demands were being made on their generosity and expertise. Jane Ashley, Michelle Bridwell, Carmen Lomas Garza, Jesse Herrera, Diane H. Hughs, Sam McCulloch, Bob Parvin, Amado Peña, and Raúl Valdez, who contributed their artwork and photographs, have helped us to see what can at best be only suggested in words.

Our special thanks go to the Houston Endowment for the generous financial support that made possible this realization of the Texas Historical Commission's Columbus Quincentenary project.

Tom Alex, Al Davis, Stephen Fox, Dr. Clotilde P. Garcia, Joe S. Graham, Sheldon Hall, Mary Kay Shannon, Lela Standifer, W.H. Timmons, and Rose Treviño are among the old and new friends who helped by reviewing large sections of the guidebook and identifying additional significant resources. County historical commissions all across the state also reviewed sections of the guidebook and responded with helpful corrections and suggestions.

We wish also to acknowledge the contributions of the hundreds of other individuals and organizations who provided information used in this volume. Museums, Texas Family Land Heritage ranches, festival sponsors, churches, and institutions listed in the guidebook were contacted individually, and this volume would not have been possible without their participation. Listed below are individuals and organizations who also contributed, but whose names do not appear in the guidebook entries. There are undoubtedly individuals and organizations whose names were not recorded in the course of the many letters and phone calls required for compiling the guidebook. To everyone who helped, we express our sincere appreciation.

.Abilene Hispanic Chamber of Commerce; Alamo Center, Amarillo; Amarillo Parks and Recreation Department; Aransas County Historical Commission; Archdiocese of San Antonio; Archer County Historical Commission; Senator Gonzalo Barrientos' Office, Austin; Bexar County Historical Commission; Big Bend Natural History Association; Big Spring Chamber of Commerce; Brazoria County Historical Commission; Brewster County Historical Commission; Briscoe County Historical Commission; Bosque Memorial Museum, Clifton; Cameron County Historical Commission; Carrizo Springs Chamber of Commerce; Carson County Historical Commission; Joe Cavagnaro, Irving; Chambers County Historical Commission; Cherokee County Historical Commission; Andy Cloud, THC; Colorado County Historical Commission; Columbus Area Chamber of Commerce; Comal County Historical Commission; Martha Compean, Wichita Falls; Cooke County Historical Commission; Corpus Christi Hispanic Chamber of Commerce; Corsicana Chamber of Commerce; Courthouse Museum, Helena; Culberson County Historical Commission; Dallas County Historical Commission; Amy Dase, THC; Deaf Smith County Historical Museum; Denton County Historical Commission; DeWitt County Historical Commission; Dickens County Historical Commission; Edinburg Chamber of Commerce; Falfurrias Chamber of Commerce; Victor Flores, Abilene; Fort Bend County Historical Commission; Fort Stockton Main Street Program; Galveston County Historical Commission; Joe García, Laredo State University; Gillespie County Historical Society; Goliad County Historical Commission; Ventura Gonzales, Jr., Crystal City; Victor Gonzales, Corpus Christi; Gray County Historical Commission; Gregg County Historical Commission; Guadalupe County Historical Commission; State Representative Lena Guerrero's Office, Austin; Gulf Coast Portland Cement Company, Houston; Hardeman County Historical Commission; Harris County Heritage Society, Houston; Harris County Historical Commission; Harrison County Historical Commission; Hartley County Historical Commission; Hays County Historical Commission; Henderson County Historical Commission; Elvia Hernández, Midland; Hidalgo County Historical Commission; Gerron Hite, THC; Hondo Chamber of Commerce; Houston County Historical Commission; Betty Howell, Amarillo; Bruce Jensen, THC; Raymond Jiménez, Cameron; Jim Wells County Historical Commission; Karnes County Historical Commission; KCTI Radio, Gonzales; KDCY Radio, Cotulla; KDHN Radio, Dimmitt; Kerr County Historical Commission; KGUL Radio, Port Lavaca; KIBL Radio, Beeville; Kinney County Historical Commission; KNDA Radio, Odessa; KTXZ Radio, Austin; KVDA TV, San Antonio; Lamar County Historical Commission; Lavaca County Historical Commission; Liberty County Historical Commission; Limestone County Historical Commission; Llano Chamber of Commerce; Lubbock Chamber of Commerce; Lubbock County Historical Commission; Manuel Luna, Fort Stockton; Raúl Marcos, Big Spring; Henry Martínez, Dallas; Mason County Historical Commission; Polly Mays, Big Spring; Coco Medina, Amarillo; Medina County Historical Commission; Midland Hispanic Chamber of Commerce; Milam County Historical Commission; Joe A. Morales, Austin; Museum of East Texas, Lufkin; Nolan County Historical Commission; Nueces County Historical Commission; Sylvia Orozco, Mexic-Arte, Austin; Palo Pinto County Historical Commission; Avelina Pina, Rockport; Pioneer Memorial Museum, Harper; Port Arthur Public Library; Potter County Historical Commission; Presidio County Historical Commission; Ralls Historical Museum, Ralls; Randall County Historical Commission; Charles Richey, Amarillo; Patricia Riddlebarger, Hermann Hospital, Houston; Rincon & Associates, Dallas; J.A. Ríos, Hondo; Connie Robles, San Angelo; Runge Museum, Runge; Runnels County Historical Commission; Rusk County Historical Commission; Sabine County Historical Commission; Tony Salazar, Corpus Christi; Judith Sallee, Grand Prairie; San Antonio Arts and Cultural Affairs Office; San Antonio Public Library; San Augustine County Chamber of Commerce; San Augustine County Courthouse Archives, San Augustine; San Augustine County Historical Commission; San Benito Chamber of Commerce; San Marcos Hispanic Chamber of Commerce; San Patricio County Historical Commission; Nicole Smith, San Antonio; Wayne Smith, Lamesa; Washington County Historical Commission; Starr County Historical Commission; Swisher County Historical Commission; Tarrant County Historical Commission; Terrell County Historical Commission; Terry County Historical Commission; Texas A&M University, University Archives, College Station; Texas Association of Mexican American Chambers of Commerce, Austin; Texas Department of Transportation, Austin; Texas Folklife Resources, Austin; Texas Parks and Wildlife Department, Austin; Texas Press Association, Austin; Rosalie Pawelek Titzman, Gillett; Eliseo (Cheo) Torres, Texas A&I University, Kingsville; Abby Treece, Austin; State Senator Carlos F. Truan, Corpus Christi; Upton County Historical Commission; Uvalde Chamber of Commerce; Uvalde County Historical Commission; Val Verde County Historical Commission; Victoria County Historical Commission; Victoria Public Library; Marie Vigil, Amarillo; Washington County Historical Commission; Webb County Historical Commission; *West Texas Hispanic News,* Lubbock; Wichita County Historical Commission; Wilbarger County Historical Commission; Willacy County Historical Commission; Williamson County Historical Commission; Dennis Zamora, Dallas; Zavala County Historical Commission, Crystal City.

Texas Historical Commission Members

Dr. Brian Babin, Woodville; Maj. Gen. John M. Bennett, San Antonio; Mrs. Carrielu Christensen, Vice-chair, Austin; Mr. George E. Christian, Austin; Mr. Harold Courson, Secretary, Perryton; Mrs. Martha Crowley,

Richardson; Mr. Al Davis, Houston; Mr. T.R. Fehrenbach, San Antonio; Dr. Clotilde P. Garcia, Corpus Christi; Mrs. Willie Lee Gay, Houston; Mr. Sheldon Hall, El Paso; Mrs. Betty E. Hanna, Breckenridge; Mrs. Jean W. Kaspar, Shiner; Mr. Karl Komatsu, Chair, Fort Worth; Mr. Thomas E. Kroutter, Jr., Port Arthur; Dr. Archie P. McDonald, Nacogdoches; Mr. James S. Nabors, Lake Jackson; Dr. Dan Willis, Fort Worth.

Introduction

Country roads and modern highways have long since replaced the foot paths, ox-cart ruts, and horse trails of the sixteenth through nineteenth centuries. Beside these new roads in 1936, to celebrate its centennial, the State of Texas placed granite monuments as memorials to the people of the frontier—the early hunters and gatherers, the explorers and missionaries, traders and settlers, cowboys and miners, statesmen and heroes, men and women. Continuing that tradition, the Texas Historical Commission, the state agency for historic preservation, has since the 1950s placed hundreds of historical markers across the state. The familiar bronze plaques and medallions are located near archeological sites in rural areas and attached to buildings in the towns and cities to commemorate the people who built the state—the American Indian, Spanish and Mexican, Czech, German, Irish, French, and Polish, the African- and Anglo-American—Texans all.

The Quincentennial observance of Columbus' arrival in the New World offered a special occasion to single out one group of these Texans for special attention—the Hispanic Texans. As used here, Hispanic Texans include people of Indian-Spanish-Mexican descent, both those who have lived here since long before state lines were conceived and more recent immigrants from Mexico. We have used the word *Hispanic* for want of a better word that includes people of all of these cultures through time. When referring to modern Texans in particular contexts, the terms *Mexican-American* and *Spanish-speaking* are more appropriately used. As we single out these people, however, we find not a focus but a broadening of view, a realization that theirs is indeed a heritage in which all Texans share.

Hispanic influence permeates almost all aspects of contemporary Texas life. Its presence is felt not only in solidly material worlds such as architecture, ranching, and foodways, but in the more intangible universes of language, music, and folklore. So familiar are many of these influences that they are scarcely recognized as Hispanic in origin, but simply as comfortingly familiar and uniquely Texan.

A catalogue of all aspects of Hispanic heritage in Texas is beyond the scope of this volume, which focuses on historic sites and structures. Yet, a catalogue limited solely to places and buildings, even with the inclusion of brief historical descriptions of the individual sites and properties, could not express the depth and breadth of Hispanic heritage in Texas. The

American Indians, Spaniards, Mexicans, Anglo-Americans, and immigrants from many countries have left their mark on Texas. Texas Memorial Museum collections, photo by Bob Parvin.

Spanish Colonial missions, for example, arose from the period of exploration that preceded them and were part of Spain's effort to protect its New Spain holdings from the intrusion of other European nations. The Indians for whom the Spanish built the missions had lived in Texas for thousands of years before the explorers arrived, and their lives were changed drastically in the centuries that followed. Mexican immigrants of more recent times—the *pastores, vaqueros, braceros,* and railroad workers—have played an important role in the development of the modern state but are associated with few historic monuments. Because of the importance of historical context, this volume includes a collection of essays that set the scene for the major entries in the guidebook section.

Authors of the essays, both Texas Historical Commission staff members and other authors with special expertise in their fields, address specific topics that highlight the resources included in the guidebook. Although providing in part a chronological perspective, the essays also deal with geographical or topical subjects that overlap in time. For ease of reading, modern place-names are used as points of geographical reference, even when the places (such as Austin) had not yet been founded. All of the essays, regardless of approach, are presented with the general reader in mind—the Texan who has not studied Texas history since schooldays or the visitor who has missed out altogether on that fascinating, rewarding, and sometimes exasperating study.

Part I: *The Essays*

The essays begin with words and end with words, reflecting the spoken and written, as well as the historical and geographical, importance of the Spanish language in Texas. Félix D. Almaráz, Jr., in the first essay, traces Hispanic imprints on the Texas landscape from the time of exploration to the present. Spanish-derived place-names, both descriptive and commemorative, fixed to natural as well as political features on the map of the state, are both tangible and intangible aspects of our Hispanic heritage. Almaráz's tracing of place-names as they have been applied over the centuries also provides introductory glimpses of many topics that are discussed in the following essays.

Cathryn A. Hoyt presents an overview of Spanish exploration in Texas during the sixteenth and seventeenth centuries. For almost two centuries, exploration was motivated by the search for gold, despite each new expedition's failure to find much more than stories of the treasure to be found elsewhere. Many of these early routes today are remembered primarily through historical markers, since only documentary accounts of the expeditions remain.

Robert S. Weddle briefly recounts the history of Spanish Colonial missions and presidios in Texas, highlighting those that have survived the centuries. From East Texas to El Paso the missions—whether archeological sites, ruins, restorations, or original structures—are the best-known symbols of Hispanic heritage in Texas. The history of the mission period is the background against which the surviving structures in El Paso, San Antonio, and Goliad should be viewed.

Late eighteenth- and nineteenth-century cart roads and wagon trails in the Texas Panhandle were clues to the presence of *ciboleros* (buffalo hunters), *comancheros* (traders) and *pastores* (sheepherders) from New Mexico. Patricia A. Mercado-Allinger traces the evidence of Hispanic influence in the Texas Panhandle from the time of the New Mexican buffalo hunters through the end of the frontier. The end of the story also marks the beginning of the heyday of big ranches on the Texas plains.

The vast holdings of Anglo-American cattlemen like Charles Goodnight and Mifflin Kenedy are the best known ranches in Texas, but the state's cattle industry began with Spanish *ranchos* of the mission period. Jack Jackson reminds us that our most beloved mythical figure, the cowboy, owes much to his Spanish *vaquero* predecessor. The vaquero, his methods, and his language still play an important role in ranching in Texas.

Vernacular, or folk, construction in the South Texas ranching country provides an opportunity to view resources related not only to early land-owners but to the everyday lives of common people, who are so often neglected in both political and architectural history. Joe S. Graham examines the wealth of surviving architectural and other components of the built environment in South Texas that are little known to those outside the region and too often little appreciated by those living in the area.

Curtis Tunnell and Enrique Madrid provide another distinctly regional view of Hispanic heritage in Texas, in the West Texas borderlands. Along the Rio Grande in this sparsely settled region old traditions and occupations have survived. Candelilla wax making, rope braiding with lechuguilla fibers, folk healing, and a host of other activities reflect the ancient blending of Spanish, Indian, and Mexican cultures in Trans-Pecos Texas.

A more sophisticated aspect of Hispanic influence is examined by James W. Steely in his study of Spanish Mission Revival style in twentieth-century architecture. Popular interest in this architectural revival can be traced to the 1880s. Since that time architects have re-created the outstanding features of Spanish missions in impressive homes, churches, commercial buildings, theaters, and railroad depots in almost every major city in Texas.

The architectural and historical importance of Spanish Colonial mission churches often has overshadowed other historic Catholic churches in Texas. Helen Simons and Roni Morales present brief histories of major churches that are both architecturally significant and important as historic expressions of Hispanic Catholicism in Texas.

Ann Perry celebrates Hispanic festivals that are based on historic events and secular traditions. Cinco de Mayo, Diez y Seis de Septiembre, and Día de la Raza (Columbus Day) are celebrated almost as widely as the Fourth of July in Texas. Charros ride, mariachis play, Mexican food is consumed, and a good time is had by all.

The popularity of traditional Mexican foods and cooking styles represents the most widespread acceptance of Hispanic culture in Texas. Literally all ethnic groups—German-Texans, African-American Texans, Anglo-American Texans, and naturalized Texans of every ilk—adapt Mexican foods to their own home-cooking styles or satisfy their craving in restaurants. Helen Simons takes a Polish-Texan view of this remarkable and delicious phenomenon.

As we attempt to capture in words and pictures the essence of Texas' Hispanic heritage, Jesús F. de la Teja reminds us, in the final essay, that written words, as preserved in early documents, are not just research materials but historic resources in their own right. Major libraries and archives contain valuable collections of Hispanic documents from the time of the first exploration through the period of the Republic and beyond. And others preserve more recent materials relating to Mexican-American history and culture.

Part II: *The Guidebook*

Many different approaches have been taken in Texas guidebooks. A few dealing with the entire state and many dealing with only one region take a tour approach, leading the visitor from one place to another along a set route. Some guides that attempt the state as a whole simply list cities and towns alphabetically and allow visitors to find their own way around. We have adopted a compromise approach, dividing the state into seven regions, each planned around a major visitor center (such as El Paso, San Antonio, or Laredo). From these centers, which are presented first in the section, the visitor should be able to plan long tours or short side trips. Following the entries for the major center, other towns and cities in the region are listed alphabetically, and the map that accompanies each region can be consulted for locations.

Guidebook entries illustrate the topics discussed in the essays, as well as other aspects of Hispanic heritage. However, comprehensive coverage of any topic simply was not possible. Buildings, places, and sites that receive official historic designations are limited, generally, by a rule that they be at least fifty years old. In addition, historic buildings of the recent past often are selected for their association with important people or events or for the buildings' architectural significance. Thus, as is true for any ethnic group, there is a gap between the culture of the common folk and what is generally considered historic or significant, and the closer those resources are to the present, the broader the gap becomes. To bridge this gap, we have included in the guidebook a selection of Hispanic community churches, festivals, public art, and institutions that reflect both modern adaptations of Hispanic heritage and the culture of contemporary Mexican-Americans, who make up almost 26 percent of the state's population.

These "recent" selections, too, often are indeed samples and not comprehensive inventories. For example, festivals held in major cities, especially San Antonio, are nationally and even internationally known and attract hundreds of thousands of visitors each year. Celebrations in smaller cities and towns may be regional or even local in their attraction and are not widely publicized, although they are equally important as expressions of community identity. The inclusion of selected resources that are local in importance and recent in time assumes on the part of the reader a level of interest that goes beyond mere tourism. It is hoped that those who use the guidebook will be inspired by these entries to look around and discover other cultural treasures on their own. With the clues provided in the guidebook in hand, the visitor may find other adobe houses in West Texas, roadside shrines in South Texas, neighborhood parks and churches in Central Texas Hispanic neighborhoods, small-town fiestas, and interesting collections of artifacts in small museums off the beaten path.

We have also included a sample of parks and scenic drives that allow a glimpse of the historic environment once inhabited by the Indians of Texas and traversed by the early explorers and missionaries. Complementing these are places where buffalo and Longhorn cattle can be seen in non-zoo settings. While no large, free, wide-ranging herds remain, both of these hardy beasts have survived the threat of extinction and are living reminders of our Indian and Spanish past. One other living creature that played a vital role in the changes resulting from European contact is the horse, but no guide is needed for seeing this animal at work or at play wherever you travel in the state. And museums and art galleries offer a wide range of views of the roles that buffalo, Longhorns, and horses have played in the West and its myths.

Official state historical markers in Texas have been in place since the 1930s, and some private markers are even older. These early markers will reflect the scholarship of their era. The routes of the early explorers, especially, have been interpreted and reinterpreted many times since the first Texas Centennial marker was placed in 1936. While some of the markers may be in error, they are nevertheless important as expressions of community pride and as statements of our recognition of the importance of Texas' early history under the sovereignty of Spain and Mexico.

Many historic places and events in Texas, particularly those that were interpreted more than twenty or so years ago, often reflect a decidedly Anglo-American point of view. For this reason, some sites related to Indian wars or the Texas war for independence and the Mexican War have been excluded. To include them as multicultural resources, as they relate to either American Indians or Mexican-Americans, is pointless because the weight of historical interpretation is too decidedly Anglo-American. The exclusion of these places is not intended as an effort to gloss over the reality of the past, but rather as an admission that much of the past is still greatly in need of reinterpretation. It is hoped that this volume will contribute to the continuing resolution of this historical problem—and remind us once again that the Alamo is indeed the shrine of Texas liberty, but it is also a Spanish mission that once housed Texas Indians and that Mexican Texans also died there in the cause of Texas independence.

A guidebook such as this, while serving as an introduction to the best-known expressions of Hispanic heritage in Texas, can also be used as a means of evaluating what has been omitted from our inventories. It can be used indirectly to help us identify periods of history or kinds of things that are under-represented or missing entirely. And it can provide us with a good idea of the amount of work that still needs to be done before we can truly say that we have identified and preserved a representative sample of Texas' Hispanic past.

PART I

The Essays

Hispanic Imprints on the Texas Landscape

FÉLIX D. ALMARÁZ, JR.

Crisscrossed from north to south and east to west, the Lone Star State is replete with Hispanic place-names. Given the magnitude of Texas' geographic expanse, the Spanish legacy is all the more remarkable because of the widespread distribution of names applied to bays, canyons, counties, creeks, dams, escarpments, fords, forests, hills, islands, lakes, mountains, parks, rivers, roads, towns, valleys, and other landmarks. The evolution of these place-names began with the arrival of intrepid explorers in the sixteenth and seventeenth centuries, followed by pioneer immigrant colonists in the eighteenth century. Spanish rule in North America ended in the early part of the nineteenth century, but Mexican frontier folk were still here to embellish the landscape with Spanish place-names, some commemorative, a few possessive, and still others descriptive or incidental. In the twentieth century, although with lesser frequency, the trend has continued, reflecting the values and expectations of a new wave of immigrants uprooted by the social unrest of the modern Mexican Revolution and the ages-old human quest for a better life. The continuing tradition demonstrates how each generation has contributed its share to the changing kaleidoscopic pattern of Hispanic imprints upon the land. In this volume, as cultural origins are examined in the beginnings of exploration and colonization and in regional expressions of Hispanic heritage, the place-names, new and old, surviving and almost forgotten, will clearly reflect that legacy throughout the years and across the state.

A Legacy of Intrepid Explorers

Christopher Columbus' encounter with the New World (which he named *Las Indias,* the Indies) included the requisite act of possession by which he claimed the islands and adjacent lands, known and unknown, in the name of their Most Catholic Sovereigns, Isabel and Ferdinand. In the wake of the historic encounter, the age of aggressive conquest—typified in North America by the exploits of Hernán Cortés in the central Valley of Mexico—inspired venturesome explorers to probe the mystery of unknown lands. In the vanguard of exploration came Alonso Álvarez de Pineda, a mariner, who charted the Texas coastlands and made his generation of explorers aware of a *tierra incógnita* that lay to the north of Mexico.

Opposite: The Spanish exploration and settlement of Texas has left an enduring legacy of descriptive place-names, such as this creek named for the *tules* or bulrushes that grew along its banks. Modern scholars have found that many of the early Spanish place-names, such as *tule,* which is derived from a Nahuatl word, were simply translations of the original Indian names. Photo by Cathryn Hoyt, THC.

For over two centuries, Spanish explorers ventured into the unknown lands of Texas, mapping and naming the geographical features they encountered. Drawing by José Cisneros, courtesy of Félix D. Almaráz.

Not by design but by accident, as the result of a storm, Alvar Núñez Cabeza de Vaca and three companions became the first Europeans to travel through the interior of Texas. These early travelers, survivors of Pánfilo de Narváez's disastrous expedition in Florida, were more concerned with survival than exploration and contributed few names to the terrain. However, Cabeza de Vaca's account of their eight-year adventure in the wilderness piqued the interest of readers with vivid descriptions of *el cíbolo* (bison, or American buffalo) and *un río grande del norte* (great river of the north), two references that were later to identify specific features of the Texas landscape.

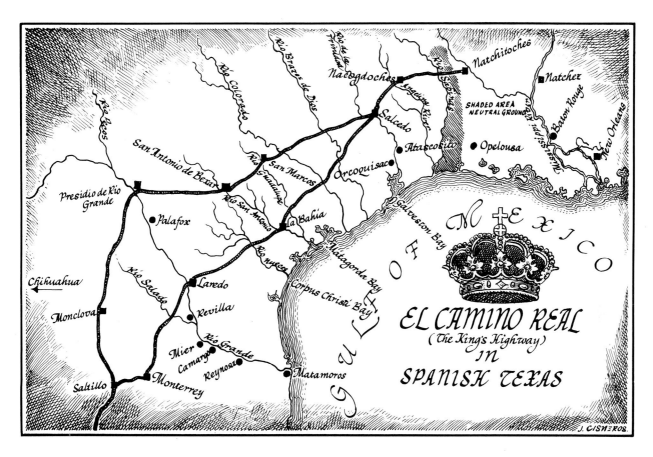

Domingo Terán de los Ríos led the expedition that blazed El Camino Real—and added a landmark name to Texas history. Map by José Cisneros, courtesy of Félix D. Almaráz.

Public interest in the northern mystery, generated by both the oral and written accounts of Cabeza de Vaca, culminated in the expedition of Francisco Vásquez de Coronado. Coronado's trek through the Texas Panhandle in 1541 resulted in the application of permanent place-names to the topography. First, the outstanding elevation and the flatness of the terrain prompted the chroniclers of the expedition to record the phenomenon of *el llano estacado* (meaning a "stockaded" plain) upon which they encountered vast herds of buffalo. Within that rugged environment, where knowledge of reliable sources of water often signified the difference between survival or catastrophe, these explorers found a series of *barrancas* (ravines), the most prominent of which they named El Palo Duro (for hardwood trees that grew there). With the conclusion of Coronado's expedition in 1543—and another entrada led by Hernando de Soto through the southeastern region of the continent—the age of aggressive conquest passed into history. The New Laws of 1543, a human rights document aimed at curtailing abuses committed against Indians, ended the Spanish practice of sending grand expeditions into the wilderness in the style of Coronado and De Soto.

For the remainder of the century, the line of Spanish colonization (consisting of mines, missions, presidios, haciendas, and towns) progressed slowly northward along a central corridor, bounded on the east and west by the Sierra Madre range. Toward the end of the sixteenth century, Juan de Oñate stretched the line of settlement even farther north into New Mexico. Capitalizing upon reliable knowledge acquired from prior expeditions, Oñate used the Rio Grande as an avenue of approach into the borderlands. At El Paso del Norte the governor and captain-general performed the requisite act of possession. By virtue of that ritual, and the founding later of Mission Nuestra Señora de Guadalupe in 1659, El Paso del Norte became a permanent fixture of the rugged Chihuahuan Desert landscape.

During most of the 1600s Texas remained outside the orbit of official Spanish interests in North America. Then, owing to the intercolonial rivalry that characterized most of the period, the competition between Spain and France intensified at mid-continent and in the Gulf of Mexico. This rivalry culminated in the encroachment of the Sieur de La Salle upon the Texas coastlands in the 1680s. Primarily to evict the French but also to explore the terrain, the viceregal government in Mexico City dispatched search patrols by both land and sea. Although the sea expeditions failed to find French intruders, the experience made Spanish mariners more knowledgeable about the contours of the coastlands, particularly around Matagorda Bay. The parties sent by land eventually were more successful in locating the ruins of La Salle's fort. Alonso de León, governor of Coahuila, conducted five expeditions that resulted in the founding of the first Franciscan missions in East Texas—and in the application of Hispanic names to much of the terrain.

As leader of the first official entrada to penetrate Texas since Coronado, Alonso de León carefully recorded the names ascribed to the landscape. An important legacy of his expeditions was the naming of every major river in Texas. The Nueces was named for the density of pecan trees along its banks. The Medina was so called in memory of Pedro de Medina, the governor's mathematics teacher in Spain. The Guadalupe, of course, was in tribute to Our Lady of Guadalupe, whom the soldiers had declared patroness of their entrada. The Brazos de Dios, now shortened to Brazos, was configured on a map in a way that resembled the outstretched arms of the crucified Christ. The Trinidad, now anglicized to Trinity, was so named for the three branches that come together to form the main body of the river. The name Sabinas, later Sabine, was inspired by the cypress trees once so abundant in the eastern timberland. And, in the tradition of explorers elsewhere in the borderlands, De León assigned his surname to a meandering creek in Central Texas.

In the final decade of the century, Domingo Terán de los Ríos, first governor of the province, led a relief expedition in support of the eastern Franciscan missions that resulted in two additional landmarks of place-name geography: the blazing of El Camino Real (the royal road) and the discovery of Río San Antonio de Padua. Now called simply the San Antonio River, this locale of so many important events in Texas history was

Coronado was the first European to record the phenomenon of *el llano estacado* and the rugged barrancas that cut into it. Photo by Bob Parvin.

Immigrant colonizers in South Texas left a legacy of descriptive place-names such as La Sal Vieja (the Great Salt Lake), a lake that was an important source of salt for the Indians as well as the later Spanish colonists. Photo by Bob Parvin.

named in honor of St. Anthony because it was on this saint's feast day, June 13, that the Spaniards first approached the river. In contrast to the cavalcades and pageants of earlier centuries, no doubt the later exploratory entradas in Texas lacked drama and fanfare. Nonetheless, in charting the terrain these explorers performed significant yeoman service that was vitally important to the colonization effort that was to follow. And they left a lasting legacy of place-names that have been repeated many times since in the names of counties, streets, and structures all across Texas.

Contributions of Immigrant Colonizers

The start of the eighteenth century, with the ascendancy of the energetic House of Bourbon on the Spanish throne, coincided with the inauguration of serious colonization in Spanish Texas. In rapid succession the entradas of Captain Domingo Ramón (1716), Governor Martín de Alarcón

(1718), and the Marqués de Aguayo (1720) not only reinforced Hispanic claim to the region, but added many familiar names to the roll of place-name geography. Beginning with the interior settlement of San Antonio de Béxar (Béxar in memory of a deceased relative of the incumbent viceroy), the list included numerous creeks and rivers. The Angelina River is said to have been named in honor of a Caddoan Indian girl who was educated at Mission San Juan Bautista on the Rio Grande and there baptized and christened Angelina. The name of the Colorado (Spanish for *red*) River is somewhat misleading because the waters of the river are clear and probably always have been. The Colorado may have been confused with the Brazos during the early period, but the present names of both rivers were well established by the end of the colonization period. The name of the Comal River comes from a Spanish word meaning a flat clay dish used for cooking, possibly derived from the valley through which the river flows. The Hondo and Salado creeks and the Frio River received descriptive names, respectively deep, salty, and cold. Garcitas Creek (actually *garcetas*), famed as the probable locale of La Salle's Fort St. Louis, signifies the sprouting horns of deer. Like the San Antonio River, the San Marcos River and San Pedro Creek were named for saints. Reflections of Catholicism also appear in coastal locales, such as Bahía de San Bernardo on Matagorda Bay.

By mid-century, with an increase of missionaries, soldiers and their families, and civil settlers, Hispanic imprints on the land became more noticeable. In the Hill Country Spanish place-names survive chiefly in rivers and creeks, but farther south, in the Nueces–Rio Grande watershed, an array of Spanish names dominate the region. The pioneer families commonly gave descriptive names to their *porciones* (land grants).

Along the Rio Grande between Laredo and El Paso eighteenth-century exploratory expeditions left a legacy of descriptive names for mountains, including the following sample: Barrilla (roughly meaning alkaline mountain); Chisos (perhaps the ghostly mountains, but probably named for the Chisos Indians); Cuesta del Burro (donkey ridge); Rosillos (clear red mountains); Sierra Blanca (white mountain range); Sierra del Carmen (red mountains, for the volcanic tuffs on the western slopes); and Sierra Vieja (old mountain). Later towns in the region also bear descriptive names: Paso del Águila (Eagle Pass); Presidio de la Junta del Río del Norte y Conchos (fort at the confluence of the River of the North and the Conchos River, now simply Presidio); and San Felipe del Río (the creek and springs of St. Philip, reportedly reached by the Spaniards on the saint's day, gave their name to the site of a future settlement, which is now known simply as Del Rio).

Around El Paso del Norte, reinforcing a fledgling community, Franciscan friars contributed to the place-name geography of the area with the founding of Missions Corpus Christi de la Ysleta del Sur (which gave its name to the Ysleta community, now part of El Paso), San Antonio de Senecú, and Nuestra Señora del Socorro (which gave its name to the present town of Socorro). To provide security to these settlements, the military constructed Presidio San Elizario in the vicinity, and this in turn became a

SOUTH TEXAS LAND GRANT NAMES

Between 1746 and 1755 José de Escandón established 23 settlements, two of them, Rancho de Dolores and Villa de Laredo, north of the Rio Grande. Besides the Escandón settlements, Spanish and Mexican land grants played a major role in the settlement and development of South Texas between the Nueces and the Rio Grande. Beginning in 1767 *porciones* were assigned to individuals with agricultural and ranching interests to encourage settlement of the as yet unappropriated lands of the Valley north of the Rio Grande, and even larger land tracts, suitable for large-scale ranching, were granted farther north. After 1821, when Mexico gained its independence from Spain, lands continued to be granted in the same manner. During the years from 1829 to 1836 residents were encouraged to immigrate into the country between the Nueces River and the Rio Grande, an area commonly known as Llanos de las Mesteñas, or Wild Horse Desert. Creeks of this heartland of ranching also received Spanish names, such as Aransas, Blanco Medio, Macorrera, Papalote, and Sarco. Many descriptive names designated the land grants assigned to pioneer families. Among the most prominent porciones with descriptive names were the following:

NUECES COUNTY:

Agua Dulce (sweetwater), granted by Mexico to Rafael García, 1834 (with lands also in Jim Wells County)

Casa Blanca (white house), granted by Spain to Juan José de la Garza Montemayor and his sons, 1807 (with lands also in Jim Wells County)

El Chiltipín (from *chiltipiquín*, meaning hot chili plant or fruit), granted by Mexico to Blás María de la Garza-Falcón, 1834 (with lands also in Kleberg County)

Los Sauces (the willows), granted by Mexico to Antonio Longorio, 1831 (with lands also in Jim Wells County)

Palo Alto (tall timber), granted by Mexico to Matías García, before 1836

Rincón de Corpus Christi (*rincón* means a cozy corner in a home or a small piece of land), granted by Mexico to Ramón de Ynojosa, 1832

settlement that still exists. To three mountain landmarks east of El Paso, local residents applied the names Cornudas (horned), Hueco (hole or hollow, for the natural stone basins that occur here), and Guadalupe (again, for the Virgin of Guadalupe).

Toward the end of the eighteenth century the rise of the cattle industry accelerated the establishment of *ranchos,* which were an important aspect of Spanish land-settlement patterns. In the vicinity of Nacogdoches, a few tributaries of the Angelina River ran through ranchos and bore Spanish names: Alazán (meaning sorrel or sandy in color), Botija (earthenware jug), Carrizo (reed or cane), Durazno (peach), La Nana (an affectionate term for grandmother), La Vaca (the cow), Loco (crazy), and Moral (black mulberry). Southwest of San Antonio de Béxar, surnames of leading families identified many of the ranchos in the region: Arocha, De la Garza, Delgado, Flores, Montes de Oca, Navarro, Pérez, Piscina, Rivas, Ruiz, and Seguín. Finally, south of the Nueces River, stemming from the porciones tradition, well-known ranchos continued the tradition of using descriptive terms, religious terms, and saints' names: Barranco Blanco (white ravine), Hacienda de Dolores, Las Animas (the souls), Melado (honey colored), Palo Blanco (white wood), San Leandro, San Diego, and Santa Gertrudis.

Alterations by Mexican Frontier Folk

Following the end of Spanish rule in North America, during the relatively brief period of Mexican sovereignty, a new generation of Spanish-surnamed pioneers, such as Martín de León and Plácido Benavides, made their contributions to place-name geography in the lands between the Guadalupe and Nueces rivers. De León's colony, the only one of the nineteenth-century colonies to be settled predominantly by Mexicans, was established at Guadalupe Victoria (later simply Victoria), named in honor of the first president of Mexico. Gonzales, founded as the headquarters of the DeWitt Colony in 1825, was named for Don Rafael Gonzales, then governor of Coahuila and Texas, who began his military career as a cadet at Presidio La Bahía in Goliad. Plácido (later Placedo) honors Plácido Benavides, who served as *alcalde* of Guadalupe Victoria and later played a prominent role in the war for Texas independence. Vital to the success of the De León Colony were the creeks and rivers where the empresario and his heirs watered their livestock. Besides the major rivers, the list of waterways with Spanish names included Aransas, Arenosa, Atascosa, Blanco, Coleto, and Medio creeks—minor waterways in an area that played a major role in the development of ranching in Texas. Slightly eastward two other rivers and a creek—Lavaca (the cow), Navidad (the Nativity), and Tres Palacios (in honor of José Félix Trespalacios, governor of Texas, 1822–23)—also aided the livestock industry of the region.

In the struggle for Texan independence, achieved through the efforts of both Anglo and Mexican Texans, several locations with Hispanic names became beacons of awareness in historical annals. Anahuac, a coastal garrison dating from 1821 and the scene of early rebellion, probably was

KENEDY COUNTY:

Barreta (small bar), granted by Spain to Francisco José Ballí, ca. 1804

Las Barrosas (muddy places), granted by Mexico to Irinéo Gómez, 1833

La Parra (the grapevine), granted by Mexico to Alvino and Domingo de la Garza, 1833

Rincón del Peñascal (craggy terrain), granted by Mexico to Rafael Ramírez, 1833

San Antonio de Encinal (oak cluster or grove), granted by Mexico to José Antonio Leal de León, 1833

San Juan de Carricitos (*carrizo* meaning small cane), granted by Spain to José Narciso Cabazos, 1792 (with lands also in Hidalgo and Willacy counties)

CAMERON COUNTY:

Concepción de Carricitos, granted by Spain to Bartolomé and Eugenio Fernández, 1789

La Feria (the fair, or market), granted by Spain to Rosa María Ynojosa de Ballí, 1777

Potrero del Espíritu Santo (*potrero* means colt, or colt pasture), granted by Spain to José Salvador de la Garza, 1781

Potrero de Santa Isabel, granted by Mexico to Rafael García, 1828

HIDALGO COUNTY:

El Encinal de San Fernando (*encinal* means oak grove)

Las Mesteñas (wild, unherded livestock), granted by Spain to Vicente Ynojosa, 1798 (with lands also in Cameron and Willacy counties)

Llano Grande (large plain, as in the Great Plains), granted by Spain to Juan José Ynojosa de Ballí, 1790

San Salvador del Tule (a tule is a type of bulrush common in wetlands), granted by Spain to Juan José Ballí, 1797 (with lands also in Brooks, Kenedy, and Willacy counties)

KLEBERG COUNTY:

Rincón de Santa Gertrudis, granted by Mexico to Juan Mindiola, 1832

named for an ancient word describing either the Central Valley of Mexico or the proximity of marshlike terrain. San Felipe de Austin, founded by Stephen F. Austin in 1823, served as the seat of the provisional government of the proclaimed republic and was burned following the Battle of San Jacinto. Both San Felipe and San Jacinto (the river and the plain on which the battle was fought in 1836) are named for saints. And, of course, some of the most famous place-names in Texas history bear Hispanic names: El Alamo (site of the former Mission San Antonio de Valero), Goliad (from rearranged letters in the surname Hidalgo minus the H), and Refugio (which derives its name from another Spanish mission, Mission Nuestra Señora del Refugio, the last conversion center built by the Franciscans in Texas, in 1793). These never-to-be-forgotten place-names were later to be joined by those given to honor heroes of the struggle, including Juan Seguín and Lorenzo de Zavala.

Beginning in the years of the Republic of Texas and continuing during statehood, at varying times of goodwill and tolerance, the government has paid homage to the Hispanic past by naming, for example, counties in deference to either an event, an individual, a principal town, or a river. Of 36 Texas counties with Spanish place-names (14.2 percent of the total of 254), most reflect names previously given to major rivers or creeks. Others duplicate the name of the county's principal city, leaving a distinct minority of counties whose legislative sponsors recognized the contributions of individuals to Texas history: El Duque de Béxar (a relative of Viceroy the Marqués de Valero), Rafael Gonzales (governor of the dual state of Coahuila and Texas, 1824–26), Miguel Hidalgo y Costilla (father of Mexican independence), Martín de León (Mexican empresario), Pedro de Medina (mathematics teacher in Spain), José Antonio Navarro (signer of the Texas Declaration of Independence), Colonel Antonio Zapata (Mexican federalist), and Lorenzo de Zavala (from Yucatán, ad interim vice president of the Republic of Texas).

Recent Place-Name Geography

In the modern period, countless names of Spanish origin have been added to an already lengthy checklist. Following the end of the United States–Mexican War, the Treaty of Guadalupe Hidalgo conclusively defined the Rio Grande as the international boundary. The watershed that previously had been a component of the Colonia of Nuevo Santander (changed in 1824 to the Mexican state of Tamaulipas) immediately came under American jurisdiction. El Paso del Norte, which in the colonial period was part of New Mexico, by virtue of the Compromise of 1850, shifted allegiance. In effect, the national legislation of 1850 vastly modified the configuration of the State of Texas, defining the state's present, familiar shape. Throughout the remainder of the nineteenth century and extending into the modern era, a host of towns and cities with Spanish names were established on the Texas landscape.

Not as numerous, but significant for their association with the Span-

State and national parks, recreation areas, and wildlife refuges, such as Laguna Atascosa (named for the marshy land surrounding the lake), have been given Spanish names in recognition of their association with the Spanish heritage of Texas. Photo by Bob Parvin.

ish heritage of Texas, are a few of the state parks and historic sites that are major recreational and tourist facilities, including Mission San Francisco de los Tejas, Port Isabel Lighthouse, the José Antonio Navarro House, and Palo Duro Canyon and Pedernales Falls state parks. Federal lands and national parks are relatively scarce in the state, but these, too, include Spanish names: Lake Falcon (for descendants of the South Texas colonizer Captain Blás María de la Garza Falcón) in Zapata County; Lake Amistad (for international friendship) near Del Rio; Chamizal (denoting a density of wild cane used for thatching) National Monument in El Paso; Guadalupe Mountains National Park, near Pine Springs in Culberson County; Padre Island National Seashore (for Padre José Ballí, who founded the first mission church in present Cameron County) near Corpus Christi; Palo Alto Battlefield, in Brownsville; the San Antonio Missions National Historical Park; and four national wildlife refuges—Anahuac, Aransas, Laguna Atascosa, and Santa Ana.

11

An important facet of Spain's legacy in Texas, spanning nearly five centuries, is clearly evident in the nomenclature of much of the landscape. Hispanic explorers, as they blazed trails into the wilderness, commenced the process of naming major rivers, creeks, and other natural landmarks. Successive waves of immigrant settlers gradually supplemented the earlier contributions by establishing missions, presidios, towns, roads, and ranches. Still later generations of newcomers, as they confronted the environment, continued the tradition of applying commemorative and descriptive names to the topography. In modern times, demonstrating sensitivity and awareness of the Hispanic culture, representatives of the state and national governments have extended the list of place-names.

Regardless of the form of expression, the *quinto centenario* of Columbus' historic voyage of encounter with America offers an opportunity for reflection and renewal, for commitment and dedication to rediscovering the best of our Hispanic heritage for all Americans. Beyond the celebration, the composite of what contemporary society learns of Spain's presence in America will become the legacy to be conveyed to the next generation.

Riches, Religion, and Politics
Early Exploration in Texas

CATHRYN A. HOYT

And after XXX days were past, they furiousely cryed out againste him, and threatened him that he shoulde passe no further. But he ever with gentle wordes and large promises, appeased their fury, and prolonged day after day, some time desireing them to bear with him yet a while, and some time putting them in remembrance that if they should attempte any thing against him, or otherwise disobey him, it would be reputed for treason. Thus after a few dayes, with chearful haartes they espied the land longe looked for. (Pietro Martire d'Anghiera, The Decades of the Newe Worlde or West India, *London, 1555)*

Columbus' arrival in the New World in 1492 resulted in one of the most consequential gold rushes in history. Woodcut from Columbus' 1493 letter describing his first voyage, from *Vita di Cristoforo Colombo* by Luigi Bossi (1818), courtesy of Benson Latin American Collection, General Libraries, University of Texas at Austin.

Columbus in 1492 did reach "the land longe looked for," but his voyage across the Ocean Sea has often been called a failure. His primary purpose was to find a shorter route to the riches of the Far East. According to chronicler Martire d'Anghiera, he promised the Spanish king and queen that this route would not only expand the Christian religion, but also enrich Spain "by great plenty of golde, pearles, precious stones, and spices, whiche might be founde there." Instead of China, however, Columbus ran into the islands dotting the Caribbean.

Columbus' initial reports of thick woods in which nightingales sang, peaceful natives and, most important of all, gold, led to one of the largest, longest-lasting and most consequential gold rushes in history. At first, most of the gold was obtained through looting of native burial mounds, ransom payments, trade, or conquest. The immediate result of this New World treasure hunt was that, within twenty years, the Spanish had siphoned off most of the gold the Indians had produced over the preceding 1,000 years. But rumors of plentiful gold persisted. There was more farther west, over the next hill, or just beyond that mountain range. The search for gold and riches spurred the discovery and exploration of North and South America, the discovery of a route to the Far East from the New World, and, eventually, the formation of a Spanish empire in which, quite literally, the sun never set.

We will probably never know the identity of the first European who set eyes on the coast of Texas, but the earliest record of the region comes from a map produced during the exploring voyage of Alonso Álvarez de

Pineda, undertaken in 1519 under the sponsorship of Francisco de Garay, governor of Jamaica. Garay had permission to explore the mainland coast for evidence of a strait connecting the Gulf of Mexico with the South Sea (the Pacific Ocean). He chose Pineda to serve as captain-general of the voyage and provided four warships and 270 men. Pineda spent approximately six months mapping the Gulf Coast from the northwest coast of Florida around to Tampico, Mexico. Pineda's voyage was a landmark in many ways: he was the first European to realize that Florida was not an island, the first to record the Mississippi (which he named the Espíritu Santo), and the first to accurately map the entire Gulf Coast. Garay was granted title over the land Pineda mapped, and the province was named Amichel.

Garay never knew the full extent of his province. He tried to establish a settlement on the Río Pánuco in Mexico, but internal conflicts and arguments with the neighbors, including the Huasteca Indians and Hernán Cortés, who preceded Garay in establishing a presence in the region, led to the eventual failure of the colony.

Although Pineda's map of 1519 is relatively accurate, it does not indicate that Pineda spent much time exploring the Texas coast. A few rivers are marked and the barrier islands are sketched in, but few other details are noted. In fact, the Spanish Crown would not know much about the land to the north until the year 1536, when Alvar Núñez Cabeza de Vaca and his three companions reached Spanish territory in Mexico after spending eight years wandering through southern Texas and northern Mexico.

The Lure of Riches

Cabeza de Vaca's story was remarkable. He and his companions were members of the ill-fated Pánfilo de Narváez expedition, which left Spain in June of 1527 to conquer and govern the provinces of Florida—then defined as stretching from the modern state of Florida around the Gulf Coast to the Río de las Palmas in Mexico. Landing on the west coast of Florida, Narváez made the first of many errors; he decided to explore inland while sending his ships and supplies around to the port of Pánuco, which his pilots assured him was only ten or fifteen leagues from their present location. The pilots were grossly mistaken. Pánuco was actually on the east coast of Mexico—over 600 leagues (1800 miles) from Florida.

Over the next three months, Narváez and his expedition struggled north until they finally reached the shores of Apalachee Bay, where the Florida coast begins to turn west. Many men died along the way from starvation, illness, and Indian attack. Not finding the supply ships waiting, the expedition members decided to build barges to sail back to Mexico. Again, fate took a hand. After 46 days at sea, Cabeza de Vaca and his shipmates were thrown ashore on the Texas coast, on an island they called Malhado. (Most recent historians identify this island with what is now a peninsula that parallels the mainland just west of Galveston Island.) Cabeza de Vaca, rescued by the Karankawa, spent the next eight years living among various

Opposite: Cabeza de Vaca described the South Texas landscape as one "so remote and malign, so destitute of all resource" that he could not recommend further exploration. Photo by Bob Parvin.

15

Indian groups and wandering through Texas and northern Mexico as a slave, a trader, and finally a healer. He eventually met up with the last three survivors of the Narváez expedition, Alonso Castillo Maldonado, Andrés Dorantes de Carranza, and Estevanico, a Moorish slave. Nine years after the expedition set sail, the four made their way back to Mexico.

Cabeza de Vaca's stories of his wanderings (*Adventures in the Unknown Interior of America,* translated by Cyclone Covey, 1983) and his official report to the king of Spain, written in 1542, heavily influenced the course of exploration and settlement in northern New Spain. Cabeza de Vaca did not think much of the country that was later to become Texas. The land was "so remote and malign, so destitute of all resource," the people so poor, that he could not recommend further exploration. However, the land to the east and west was a different matter. The harbor now known as Tampa Bay, Florida, he considered "the best in the world. It has six fathoms of water at its entrance and five near shore. It stretches inland seven or eight leagues. Its bottom is fine white sand; no sea breaks upon it or wild storm; and it can contain countless vessels. Fish is plentiful." And to the west, Cabeza de Vaca and his companions were told of "lofty mountains to the north, where there were towns of great population and great houses." They were given fine cotton blankets, beads made of coral from the South Sea, and fine turquoises from the north. And perhaps most importantly, they saw "undeniable indications of gold, antimony, iron, copper, and other metals" in the mountains through which they traveled.

The viceroy, Don Antonio de Mendoza, was intrigued by the tales of Cabeza de Vaca and his companions. Mendoza immediately organized a small expedition designed to investigate the lands they described. This expedition, under the leadership of Fray Marcos de Niza—accompanied by Brother Onorato, Cabeza de Vaca's former companion Estevanico, and about 300 Mexican Indians who had converted to Catholicism—headed north in March of 1539 and advanced to the area of the Zuñi pueblos in present western New Mexico. Although this expedition never entered Texas, it set the stage for later explorations.

Fray Marcos' expedition resulted in the death of Estevanico and most of the Indians accompanying him. Barely escaping with his life, Fray Marcos returned to Mexico with tales of the Seven Cities of Cíbola and a land that was undoubtedly the most promising of any yet discovered. The cities of this valley were built all of stone with many stories and flat roofs, the doorways decorated with turquoise. He also reported on another valley that contained seven fair-sized settlements where the natives had gold fashioned into ornaments for their ears and vessels from which they ate. For the viceroy, Fray Marcos took formal possession of the Seven Cities of Cíbola and the valley of Abra—neither of which he had actually entered—and returned to Mexico City.

Rumors of the Seven Cities of Cíbola spread quickly and became entwined with legends of the mythical Seven Islands of Antille. Fray Marcos' cities built of stone soon grew into immense walled towns. The fabled land abounded in gold, silver, and other wealth. So wealthy were these people of Cíbola that the women wore belts of pure gold. The animals reported from this land were equally wondrous. Unicorns, cows, sheep, camels, and partridges were plentiful, and the people rode upon strange beasts as yet unnamed.

So quickly did the rumors fly, so tantalizing was the prize, that 300 Europeans and 800 Indians gathered within a few days after Viceroy Mendoza announced his plans for an expedition to Cíbola. This expedition was to be led by Mendoza's good friend Francisco Vásquez de Coronado, a young man only thirty years old.

In 1540, after several months of gathering food, supplies, and people, Coronado's expedition began the journey north. Coronado's muster roll included over 300 Europeans, most of them young Spanish men, although at least three women and their children also accompanied the expedition. Also included were five Portuguese, two Italians, one Frenchman, one Scotsman, and one German.

Europeans were not the only ones struck by dreams of wealth in Cíbola. Several hundred Indians also volunteered to accompany the expedition north, serving the army as scouts, guides, personal servants, and stock handlers. Strict regulations stated that the Indian expedition members were to be treated well, were not to carry burdens other than their own personal gear, and were to be allowed to return to Mexico at any time after having received their share of the expected wealth.

The expedition must have provided a stirring sight as it rolled out of Compostela, on the western coast of Mexico. Franciscan friars were followed by over 250 men on horseback, several hundred foot soldiers and Indians, and almost 1500 horses, mules, and sheep. But as is often the case, barroom dreams make harsh reality. The roads soon proved much more difficult to traverse than Fray Marcos had led the travelers to believe, and scouting parties failed to bring back news of fabulous cities or gold-bedecked women.

After many hardships and increased muttering about Fray Marcos' promises, the expedition reached Cíbola. It was there that everyone came to the full realization that they had been misled—for what they found was just the opposite of Fray Marcos' descriptions. Rather than brick houses decorated with turquoise, the explorers found stone-and-adobe pueblos. What turquoise there was, as well as the women, children, and elders of the village, had been removed to a safe place, well away from the reach of the Spanish explorers.

Coronado was disappointed but still optimistic. Inhabitants of the region told of other villages east and west of Cíbola, and so Coronado sent out small exploring parties to gather more information. The most important of these for our story was led by one Captain Alvarado, who was taken to Cicúique (now known as Pecos, New Mexico) by two chiefs, Bigotes and Cacique. At Cicúique the Spanish were given an Indian slave whom they named the Turk. The Turk came from a region that he called Quivira, which lay to the northeast of Cicúique. Quivira, he promised the Spanish, was the golden land they sought. The lords of the province traveled in

MYTH OF THE SEVEN CITIES

When Coronado set out in search of the Seven Cities of Cíbola, he was pursuing a myth that was hundreds of years old. According to tradition, the Seven Cities were established on islands in the Atlantic by seven bishops who left Portugal in A.D. 734 when the Moors invaded their homeland. For hundreds of years, the Seven Islands of Antille, as they were then called, were prominently displayed on world maps. The islands were always located to the west, just beyond range of any ship.

In 1447 Antonio Leone, an Italian sea captain serving the king of Spain, reported that he had been blown to the Seven Islands of Antille during a terrific storm. The Portuguese-speaking inhabitants, he reported, lived on seven small, crescent-shaped islands and were divided into seven unbelievably wealthy communities. Each community had its own beautiful stone cathedral constructed of slabs of basalt cemented together with powdered shell and decorated with glittering gold. The rediscovery of the Seven Islands of Antille became a goal for any ship sailing west into the unknown.

When Columbus sailed the Atlantic and failed to locate the Seven Islands of Antille, the myth moved farther west. Having grown up with a belief in seven cities of gold somewhere to the west, the Spanish found it easy to transfer the myth from Seven Islands in the Atlantic to Seven Cities of Gold in Cíbola and, when that proved incorrect, to Seven Cities of Gold in Quivira.

The playa lakes, encountered by Coronado on the Llano Estacado, were described as being "rounded as plates, a stone's throw or more across, some fresh and some salt." Photo by Bob Parvin.

large canoes with golden eagles on their prows and slept under a great tree from which hung tiny golden bells to lull them to sleep. The villagers used dishes of wrought-gold plate and jugs and bowls of gold.

Under the guidance of the Turk, Coronado's army set out for the land of Quivira. Their path led them onto the great, flat plains of the northern Panhandle region of Texas, which they called the Llano Estacado. Pedro de Castañeda, one of the chroniclers of the Coronado expedition, gives a vivid description of the Panhandle, before irrigation and fences turned the land into farms and ranches:

> Several lakes were found at intervals; they were round as plates, a stone's throw or more across, some fresh and some salt. The grass grows tall near these lakes; away from them it is very short, a span or less. The country is like a bowl, so that when a man sits down, the

Opposite: Moscoso found the thick piney woods and swamps of East Texas to be a formidable barrier to exploration. Photo by Bob Parvin.

horizon surrounds him all around at the distance of a musket shot. (Hodge and Lewis, *Spanish Explorers in the Southern United States 1528–1543*, 1984)

The Spaniards were astonished not only by the vast expanse of the plains, but by the land's inhabitants. They encountered nomadic Indian groups, called the Querechos and Teyas, who used large dogs as pack animals and followed the great herds of buffalo. The buffalo were a source of unending amazement to the explorers. Castañeda, in his struggle to describe this beast, resorted to familiar images for an audience that would probably never see one. The buffalo had a beard like a goat and wool like a sheep that girdled the buffalo like the mane of a lion. The buffalo's hump was like a camel's but larger and, when running, he held his tail like a scorpion. Working from descriptions like these, it is no wonder that sixteenth-century artists had a difficult time rendering accurate drawings of a buffalo.

Coronado never found the golden cities that he sought. As with Cíbola, Quivira, in modern Kansas, was a bitter disappointment. The Turk had led them on with his tales of golden eagles and plates of wrought gold in order to return safely to his homeland, where he hoped to gather enough support to rid himself of the intruders. His plot failed and he was put to death for his deception, but the hopes of the Coronado expedition were crushed. The next mountain had been reached and still the gold and treasure were just an illusion.

Historically, Coronado's expedition was tremendously important. The various reports of the journey provided much new information about the geography of the interior, including the Grand Canyon of Arizona, and about the Indians of the American Southwest, including the Pueblo Indians in Arizona and New Mexico and the Plains Indians of the Llano Estacado. Yet the expedition did not provide the returns expected by its financial backers and was therefore judged a failure.

At the same time that Coronado was approaching Texas from the west, another group of Spanish explorers was entering from the east. This group, led by Luis de Moscoso, was the remnant of a large exploration and colonizing party which had set out for Florida under the leadership of Hernando de Soto. After exploring most of the southeastern coastal states, De Soto was killed on the banks of the Mississippi River. Moscoso was elected the new captain-general and, because the voyage by sea was considered too hazardous, decided to return to New Spain by marching west.

This route led Moscoso's people into what is now East Texas. They were disappointed to find very little maize or other food and described the country as being very poor. Finally, after having been led in circles by several Indian guides, and fearing that they were about to enter the land in which Cabeza de Vaca said that the Indians wandered like Arabs with little food to sustain them, Moscoso and his men decided to return to the Mississippi. Corn was abundant near the river, as were materials to build a boat to sail back to New Spain.

Sixteenth-century explorers resorted to familiar images to describe the buffalo: he had a beard like a goat, wool like a sheep, a hump like a camel, and held his tail like a scorpion when running. Woodcut from Francisco Hernandez Medico's *Nova Plantarium, Animalium, et Mineralium Mexicanorum* (1651), courtesy of Benson Latin American Collection, General Libraries, University of Texas at Austin.

The reports brought back by Cabeza de Vaca, Coronado, and Moscoso did not inspire the Spanish Crown to finance further exploration. Southern Texas, according to Cabeza de Vaca, was dry and inhabited by nomadic Indians subsisting on prickly pear. Eastern Texas, Moscoso reported, was poverty-ridden. The Panhandle region had food in abundance in the form of buffalo, but Coronado found neither mines to provide wealth nor sedentary Indians in villages that could provide the bases for settlements. In the meantime, the Spanish had found their way to the wealth of the Orient. Exploration of the American Southwest came to a grinding halt for almost forty years.

The Mexico frontier, however, kept being pushed northward as ranchers sought pastures for their livestock, miners sought precious metals, and missionaries sought souls for the Church. By the late sixteenth century, silver had been discovered in northern Mexico, and the mining communities of Santa Bárbara, Parral, and San Bartolomé were soon thriving. Gradually, interest in the golden cities of Quivira and Cíbola was revived as Indians reported large settlements to the north that had plenty of food, raised cotton, and worked gold. Although the explorers of this new generation knew of the Coronado expedition, they retained the hope that perhaps Coronado and his men simply had failed to search in the right places.

Expeditions again marched north. This time the route led down the Río Conchos to La Junta de los Ríos where the Conchos flows into the Rio Grande. From there, the explorers followed the Rio Grande north into New Mexico in search of the Pueblo Indians. Although these expeditions passed through the land that is now Texas, their primary goal was the exploration of New Mexico. This flurry of activity in the late sixteenth century culminated in the founding of the Province of New Mexico by Juan de Oñate and his followers in 1598.

The Influence of Religion

Over half a century was to pass before interest in the land north of the Rio Grande was renewed, and this time the interest was fostered by religious rather than military or financial sectors. As settlements and missions were established closer and closer to the Rio Grande, the missionary fathers began to receive requests from Indian tribes living north of the river who wished to be settled in missions. One such request made by Pablo, described as a chief of the Manosprietas and representative of other Indian groups along the Rio Grande, resulted in one of the first exploring expeditions into southwestern Texas. This expedition, led by Fernando del Bosque, set out in April of 1675 to investigate the situation among the Indians. Included on the expedition were two missionary fathers, Indians from the pueblo of San Miguel de Luna, and several soldiers.

Their journey took them generally north-northwest into the region that is now Edwards County. Along the way, Bosque made careful notes of the land and peoples he encountered. He was impressed by the fine pastures, the abundant fish found in the streams and rivers, and the number of buffalo that roamed the land. His expedition met several groups of Indians who expressed an interest in becoming Christians and settling in pueblos—perhaps more inspired by the need for protection from their enemies than by religious fervor.

Bosque, upon his return, recommended that three missions be established in the northern territories to accommodate the three nations of Indians found there. The Indians had begged Bosque to give aid to the groups separately, since they were enemies and would kill one another at the slightest provocation. In addition Bosque recommended that presidios (Spanish military encampments) be established near the missions to keep order. The result of the Bosque expedition was the establishment of four missions in the northern Mexico area to serve the Coahuiltecan Indians both north and south of the Rio Grande.

Other missionary expeditions were reaching into west-central Texas from the New Mexico settlements. Since the early seventeenth century, representatives of the Jumano tribes, with tales of a Lady in Blue who had begun their religious instruction, had been petitioning the missionary fathers in New Mexico to send padres east to instruct them. In response to the Indians' requests, several small expeditions were sent out to make contact with the Jumanos during the early to mid-seventeenth century. During these expeditions, the Spanish discovered pearls in the Concho River and learned of the kingdom and peoples of the Tejas in eastern Texas. Rumors of the fabulous kingdom of Gran Quivira, which lay on the other side of the kingdom of Tejas, were renewed.

By this time, 130 years had passed since Coronado's journey in search of Quivira, and men once again grew excited about the possibility of discovering a fabulously wealthy new land. In 1684 an exploration party was put together under the leadership of Captain Juan Domínguez de Mendoza and Fray Nicolás López. Their goal was to bring back samples of pearls from the Concho River and to gather information about the Jumano Indians. The Mendoza-López expedition made a broad sweep through west-central Texas following the Pecos River, the Middle Concho, and the Colorado as far east as its junction with the main body of the Concho River. Mendoza and López found the land fertile and the inhabitants willing candidates for religious instruction.

Political Motivations

Captain Mendoza and Fray López, upon their return, requested missionaries and soldiers to settle the newly explored area. Their petitions might have been granted had it not been for rumors that spread like wildfire in September 1685. Captured pirates told of a bold Frenchman by the name of René-Robert Cavelier, Sieur de La Salle, who had sailed down the Mississippi River into the Gulf of Mexico and then proceeded to establish a colony near Matagorda Bay. This blatant violation of Spanish territory led to renewed interest in the exploration of the Gulf of Mexico and the inte-

The American buffalo, called the "cattle of the plains" by early explorers, were the chief resource of the Plains Indians. Buffalo once roamed over most of Texas; Fernando del Bosque recorded seeing them as far south as Edwards County in 1675. Rock art in Brewster County, photo by Bob Parvin.

rior regions. Spanish exploring parties, four by sea and five by land, were sent to discover the location of the French colony, Fort St. Louis, and to drive the colonists from the land. By the time the Spanish found the colony, it had been destroyed by the Indians of the area. Continued rumors of French colonies in Spanish territory, however, eventually led to the establishment of Spanish missions in eastern Texas and the beginning of a new era in Texas history.

Historical Reminders

Legends and tales of Indian and Spanish gold persist to this day, yet very little physical evidence of the sixteenth- and seventeenth-century exploring expeditions has ever been found. The explorers rarely remained in one place for more than a few days at a time, and all traces of their camps have long been obliterated by time and weather. Occasionally, however, a Spanish spur or other object has come to light, reminding us of their passing. Although the vast lands crossed by the Spanish in the sixteenth and seventeenth centuries bear no material evidence of the explorers' presence, these early expeditions did leave a permanent legacy—the accounts of their journeys. Intended as official reports, the journals and diaries prepared by the early explorers are also wonderful sources of information about the land and peoples of Texas during the age of exploration. Many of these documents have been translated into English and are readily available in libraries and bookstores.

Little physical evidence remains of the passing of the Spanish explorers through Texas except accounts of their journeys, such as Cabeza de Vaca's *La Relación* (1542). Courtesy of Barker Texas History Center, General Libraries, University of Texas at Austin.

Cross and Crown
The Spanish Missions in Texas

ROBERT S. WEDDLE

Spanish Franciscan missions founded within the present boundaries of Texas from 1682 to 1793 have been estimated to number thirty-five to forty. Extending from El Paso to the state's eastern border, the individual missions lasted from less than a year to more than a hundred. Hardly ever were more than a dozen in operation at the same time.

The mission, as it operated in New Spain, was an agency of both church and state. Although religious and political aims at times were divergent, the Spanish government's official policy called for reduction and conversion of the native peoples to the Catholic faith. The missionaries' role was to assist in extending, holding, and civilizing the frontiers while converting the natives into useful Spanish subjects as well as Christians. The missionaries also served as explorers and diplomats, seeking to counteract the influence of other European nations on the Indians while keeping the natives peaceful. Yet, in the eyes of the church and their own, the missionaries' chief function was to spread the faith:

> Their zeal for the task often led them onto the frontier in advance of official orders and without military protection. The thought of "uncivilized" natives living in "paganism" without knowledge of Christianity stirred an ache within the apostolic breast. The missionary was impelled and dedicated to winning the Indian to 'the society of our Holy Mother Church and the obedience of His Catholic Majesty.' (Weddle and Thonhoff, *Drama and Conflict: The Texas Saga of 1776*, 1976)

The concomitants of such a calling were many. The missions, aside from giving religious instruction, schooled the Indians in industry and agriculture. After settling their subjects in a given location, the Franciscan padres sought to make them self-sufficient by teaching them a trade or putting them to work on farms and ranches established on lands provided by the Crown. In the mission village, a community patterned after the Spanish town, the Indians were given a measure of self-government. Instruction in such matters often was hampered by the language barrier. Many of the friars learned native dialects, but in certain localities there were so

Opposite: **Spanish missionaries founded more than thirty missions in Texas. Those that remain, like Mission San José in San Antonio, are monuments to the Spanish Colonial period. Photo by Bob Parvin.**

many that it was impossible to learn them all. An effort was made, therefore, to teach Spanish to the Indian children while communicating with the elders through native interpreters.

Fray Isidro Félix de Espinosa, president of the Querétaran missions in Texas from 1716 to 1722, describes in his *Crónica* of the missionary colleges the methods used for training the Indians for organized political life. Planting was done in community, the Indians assisted by a soldier who served as overseer. The missionary kept custody of the harvest, issuing provisions to his subjects weekly or daily, depending on the degree of demonstrated responsibility. The surplus was sold to the neighboring presidio or to Spanish civilians, the priest standing by while the trade was made to keep the Indians from being cheated.

Church services were held in the mission village each morning and evening. Baptized Indians assisted with religious instruction to the newly gathered. Only the ill were excused from attending services, and the absentee without such cause was given "four or five lashes" before the village populace. In such circumstances, the culprit was apt to feel himself beckoned by his former lifestyle and to take flight. The missionary—with or without military escort—was obliged to pursue and bring him back. Seldom did a mission have more than two priests to carry on its varied tasks, and many had only one.

The presidio (fort or garrison) worked in tandem—but not always in harmony—with the mission. It provided mission guards, mounted Indian campaigns, conducted supply trains, and explored the country. That many of the missions operated without a presidio to protect them is evident from the numbers. Texas had, within its present boundaries, only eight of these forts. Although a number of presidios on the right bank of the Rio Grande assisted missions on the other side, the number of forts was much too small to give more than token protection to all the missions founded in Texas.

The first East Texas missions (1690), for example, were left with a guard of only half a dozen soldiers, five hundred miles from the nearest Spanish settlement. The intermittent missionary effort at La Junta de los Ríos, at the juncture of the Rio Grande and the Río Conchos, went on for three quarters of a century before a presidio at last was established there (at Ojinaga, Chihuahua). The San Xavier missions, on the San Gabriel River in Milam County, existed for four years before the presidio came, and then the fort was more a hindrance than a help to the work of the religious. There was often conflict between the military and religious contingents, as the two groups held to different standards.

The first missions within present Texas boundaries were those at El Paso. Established on the right bank of the Rio Grande in the years following the 1680 Pueblo Indian revolt in New Mexico, the El Paso missions came to Texas by virtue of floods that changed the river's course. Initially, four missions extended seven leagues (about eighteen miles) along the right bank of the river. San Antonio de Senecú, first established two leagues (about five miles) below Ciudad Juárez in the spring of 1682, served the Piro Indians, former residents of the Senecú pueblo in New

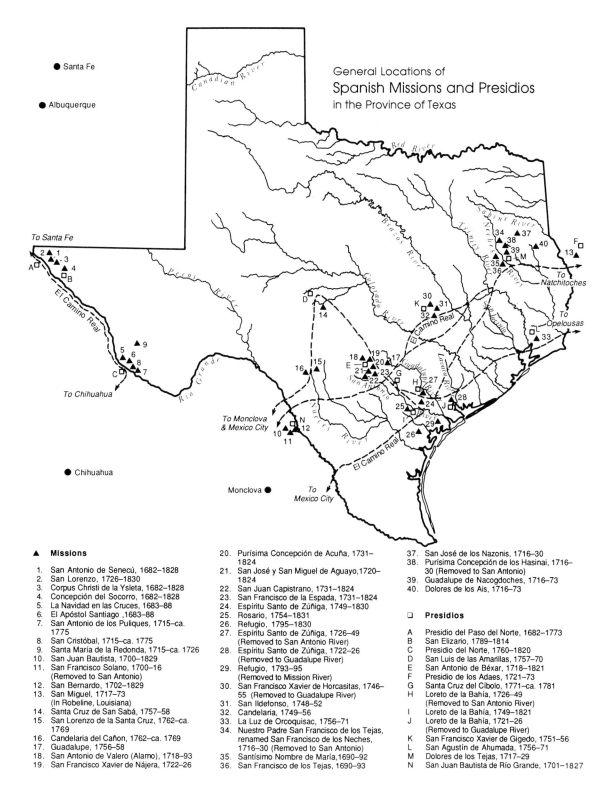

General Locations of
Spanish Missions and Presidios
in the Province of Texas

▲ **Missions**

1. San Antonio de Senecú, 1682–1828
2. San Lorenzo, 1726–1830
3. Corpus Christi de la Ysleta, 1682–1828
4. Concepción del Socorro, 1682–1828
5. La Navidad en las Cruces, 1683–88
6. El Apóstol Santiago ,1683–88
7. San Antonio de los Puliques, 1715–ca. 1775
8. San Cristóbal, 1715–ca. 1775
9. Santa María de la Redonda, 1715–ca. 1726
10. San Juan Bautista, 1700–1829
11. San Francisco Solano, 1700–16 (Removed to San Antonio)
12. San Bernardo, 1702–1829
13. San Miguel, 1717–73 (In Robeline, Louisiana)
14. Santa Cruz de San Sabá, 1757–58
15. San Lorenzo de la Santa Cruz, 1762–ca. 1769
16. Candelaria del Cañon, 1762–ca. 1769
17. Guadalupe, 1756–58
18. San Antonio de Valero (Alamo), 1718–93
19. San Francisco Xavier de Nájera, 1722–26

20. Purísima Concepción de Acuña, 1731–1824
21. San José y San Miguel de Aguayo,1720–1824
22. San Juan Capistrano, 1731–1824
23. San Francisco de la Espada, 1731–1824
24. Espíritu Santo de Zúñiga, 1749–1830
25. Rosario, 1754–1831
26. Refugio, 1795–1830
27. Espíritu Santo de Zúñiga, 1726–49 (Removed to San Antonio River)
28. Espíritu Santo de Zúñiga, 1722–26 (Removed to Guadalupe River)
29. Refugio, 1793–95 (Removed to Mission River)
30. San Francisco Xavier de Horcasitas, 1746–55 (Removed to Guadalupe River)
31. San Ildefonso, 1748–52
32. Candelaria, 1749–56
33. La Luz de Orcoquisac, 1756–71
34. Nuestro Padre San Francisco de los Tejas, renamed San Francisco de los Neches, 1716–30 (Removed to San Antonio)
35. Santísimo Nombre de María,1690–92
36. San Francisco de los Tejas, 1690–93

37. San José de los Nazonis, 1716–30
38. Purísima Concepción de los Hasinai, 1716–30 (Removed to San Antonio)
39. Guadalupe de Nacogdoches, 1716–73
40. Dolores de los Ais, 1716–73

□ **Presidios**

A Presidio del Paso del Norte, 1682–1773
B San Elizario, 1789–1814
C Presidio del Norte, 1760–1820
D San Luis de las Amarillas, 1757–70
E San Antonio de Béxar, 1718–1821
F Presidio de los Adaes, 1721–73
G Santa Cruz del Cíbolo, 1771–ca. 1781
H Loreto de la Bahía, 1726–49 (Removed to San Antonio River)
I Loreto de la Bahía, 1749–1821
J Loreto de la Bahía, 1721–26 (Removed to Guadalupe River)
K San Francisco Xavier de Gigedo, 1751–56
L San Agustín de Ahumada, 1756–71
M Dolores de los Tejas, 1717–29
N San Juan Bautista de Río Grande, 1701–1827

Map by Hector Meza, THC, with the assistance of Robert S. Weddle; adapted from a Texas Parks and Wildlife Department map.

**Corpus Christi de la Ysleta, founded in 1682, was the first mission
established within the present boundaries of Texas.**

Mexico. About the same time Corpus Christi de la Ysleta, for the Tigua,
and Nuestra Señora de la Concepción del Socorro, serving the Piro, Tano,
and Jémez Indians, were established farther downstream. A refugee camp
called San Lorenzo, founded immediately after the revolt, became a mission in 1726. Socorro was swept away about 1830 by one of the river's many
floods, and its church was rebuilt half a mile away on the Texas side of the
river. Subsequent changes in the river's course placed the other three missions on the left bank.

Second only to the El Paso missions in order of founding were those
at La Junta de los Ríos (near Presidio, Texas, and Ojinaga, Chihuahua),
dating from the 1683–84 expedition of Juan Domínguez de Mendoza and
Fray Nicolás López. The history of La Junta's missions, so often plagued
by Indian troubles and repeatedly abandoned, is difficult to trace. The four
established on the Texas side of the Rio Grande were forsaken within the
year in the face of an Indian rebellion. Renewed in 1686, the missions were

left again in 1688, possibly restaffed briefly in 1695 or 1696, and renewed in 1715 to be forsaken two years later. Military visitors to the location in 1747 found the ruins of San Antonio de los Puliques, opposite the mouth of the Conchos, and San Cristóbal farther downstream, as well as the ruins of an adobe mission church in the pueblo of the Tapalcomes and the abandoned site of the Cíbolo mission, Santa María de la Redonda, near Shafter. When the presidio—first established on the right bank of the river in 1760—was regarrisoned in 1773, the missionaries returned to La Junta. The missions on the Texas side had ceased to function by 1795, and there are no authenticated structural remains.

Mendoza and López, making an exploratory thrust among the Jumano Indians of the Edwards Plateau, sojourned six months at a place called San Clemente. To call this wilderness camp a mission, as some interpreters have done, is an overstatement. The site of this encampment, assigned variously to the Concho, San Saba, and Llano rivers, has not been determined. Expected results of the Mendoza-López effort, pointed toward the founding of missions in western Texas, were frustrated by other developments—notably, La Salle's landing at Matagorda Bay. The French incursion in 1685 shifted the focus of Spanish interest and, in view of the foreign threat to Spanish territory, the Trans-Pecos and Edwards Plateau regions were temporarily forgotten. While the Spaniards spent more than three years searching for the French colony, the intruders manufactured their own tragedy and thus nullified the Spaniards' labors.

The greatest effect of the La Salle episode lies in the Spanish reaction it caused. The Spaniards, to nail down their claim to the vacant territory, sent missionaries under Fray Damián Massanet to establish the first East Texas mission, San Francisco de los Tejas, on a Nueces River tributary in Houston County in 1690. A second mission, Santísimo Nombre de María, was founded among the Hasinai, or Tejas, Indians the same year. These missions, five hundred miles from the nearest Spanish settlement with only half a dozen soldiers to protect them, soon became untenable. Santísimo Nombre was destroyed by flood in January 1692. The missionaries unknowingly introduced European diseases for which the natives had no immunity. They so often baptized the dying victims that the Indians came to regard the baptismal water as fatal. Under threat of an Indian uprising, the missionaries withdrew to Coahuila in the fall of 1693, some in disillusionment and despair, but one with determination to return.

Fray Francisco Hidalgo engineered the return to the Tejas. His first step was to establish the mission San Juan Bautista on the Río de Sabinas, some miles south of the Rio Grande, near the crossing of the Camino de la Nueva Francia ("the road from New France"). A few months later he moved the mission to the Rio Grande, at Guerrero, Coahuila. At that location San Juan Bautista and two companion missions for the nomadic Coahuiltecans became the parent of virtually all the Texas missions founded later. It was Fray Hidalgo's initiation of contact with the French at Mobile and the resultant journey across Texas of the French trader Saint-Denis that at last goaded Spanish officials to action. Six missions—three pertaining to each of the two missionary colleges, Santa Cruz de Querétaro and

The rock art of Texas Indians records, in painted and engraved images, the arrival of Europeans. These images of a mission church and a man smoking a pipe are in Val Verde County. Photos by Bob Parvin.

29

Mission San Antonio de Valero (the Alamo), founded in 1718, was the first of the five Spanish missions established at San Antonio. Photo by Diane Hopkins Hughs.

Guadalupe de Zacatecas—and a presidio (Nuestra Señora de los Dolores de los Tejas) were established near the eastern Texas border in late 1716 and early 1717 to work among the Caddoan confederacies.

Two years later Fray Antonio de San Buenaventura y Olivares moved the mission San Francisco Solano from the Rio Grande to the San Antonio River in Texas. Given the new name of San Antonio de Valero, it grew near the second Texas presidio, San Antonio de Béjar. The new settlement served as a convenient way station on the road to the East Texas missions and marked the beginning of settlement where the city of San Antonio was to rise. Activity in this locality was expanded in 1719, when the East Texas missionaries withdrew under threat of French invasion at the outbreak of the War of the Quadruple Alliance. In 1720, the Venerable Fray Antonio Margil founded Mission San José y San Miguel de Aguayo a few miles south of San Antonio de Valero. A third mission, San Francisco de Nájera, begun a few years later, was short-lived and never had permanent buildings.

The East Texas missions were reestablished in 1721 by the Marqués de San Miguel de Aguayo. Aguayo also founded the Presidio de Nuestra Señora del Pilar de los Adaes, near the Mission San Miguel (at Robeline, Louisiana) to secure the eastern frontier against the French. This post served as the capital of the province of Texas for half a century. On Garcitas Creek at the head of Lavaca Bay, Aguayo established, on the site of La Salle's Fort St. Louis, Presidio de Nuestra Señora de Loreto de la Bahía to guard the coast and the neighboring Mission Nuestra Señora del Espíritu Santo de Zúñiga.

Economy measures advocated by Brigadier Pedro de Rivera y Villalón, following his 1727 inspection of the Texas frontier, nullified much of Aguayo's work. The oldest presidio, Dolores, just east of the Angelina River, was suppressed, and the three Querétaran missions were withdrawn from East Texas. After spending several months in passage near Barton Springs (at Austin), the missions landed in 1731 at San Antonio with the names San Francisco de la Espada, Nuestra Señora de la Purísima Concepción, and San Juan Capistrano.

Beginning in 1747, three missions were undertaken on the San Gabriel River in Milam County for Atakapan and Karankawan tribes living along the Trinity River and westward along the coast. Presidio de San Xavier de Gigedo was added in 1751. Disease and dissension between soldiers and missionaries plagued the effort. Drought dried up the river, and most of the Indians returned to their former lifeways. In August 1755, the garrison and the missionaries were removed to the San Marcos River. One of the missions, San Francisco Xavier de Horcasitas, later was located on the Guadalupe River near New Braunfels, where it remained until March 1758. That was the time of the San Sabá Mission massacre, the only instance of the outright destruction of a Texas mission by Indians. The San Sabá attack spread terror across the province of Texas and northern Mexico. The Guadalupe mission was withdrawn to San Antonio out of fear of another such occurrence.

The mission Santa Cruz de San Sabá, for the eastern Apaches, and a presidio designed to protect it, called San Luis de las Amarillas, were founded on the San Saba River near Menard in April 1757. The former San Xavier garrison made up a part of the San Sabá garrison, and the property of the San Xavier missions was transferred to the new Mission Santa Cruz. Although the Apaches never settled in the mission, the Norteños ("northern tribes"), comprising Comanche, Wichita, Caddoan, and Tonkawan affiliates, were resentful of the Spaniards' alliance with their enemies. On March 16, 1758, they sacked and burned the mission, killing at least eight Spaniards, including two priests. The mission was never rebuilt. To maintain Spanish honor, the presidio remained more than a decade, a lone ship, as it were, in a sea of Indian hostility. During that time the presidio commander joined with ministers from San Juan Bautista to establish two Apache missions on the upper Nueces River in Real and Uvalde counties.

Presidio de la Bahía and Mission Espíritu Santo, meanwhile, had undergone two moves from their original site on Garcitas Creek. After reposing on the Guadalupe River above Victoria from 1726 to 1749, they came finally to rest on the San Antonio River at Goliad. A second mission, Nuestra Señora del Rosario, was founded nearby in 1754 and placed under the protection of Presidio de la Bahía.

The arrest of a company of French traders near the mouth of the Trinity River about this time brought a flurry of Spanish exploration of that area and the ultimate founding of a presidio and mission. Presidio de San Agustín de Ahumada and Mission Nuestra Señora de la Luz, near Wallisville, Chambers County, spanned the years 1756–71. Their turbulent existence was afflicted by internal dissension and the governor's attempt to use them as a front for his own contraband trade operation.

The last Franciscan mission to be established in Texas was Nuestra Señora del Refugio, originally located in 1793 on Goff Bayou near the juncture of the Guadalupe and San Antonio rivers. Late in 1794 it was moved to a new site at Refugio.

Secularization—turning the mission jurisdiction into a self-sustaining parish administered by a parish priest instead of religious friars, with the lands divided among the converted Indians—was a mission's ultimate objective. Initially, it was expected that this milestone would be reached within ten years, but never in Texas was that timetable met. Most of the missions, in fact, had demised, for one reason or another, before secularization ever became a possibility. The remaining 1716 missions of eastern Texas and western Louisiana were terminated in 1773 with the frontier reorganization that followed France's cession of Louisiana to Spain.

The El Paso missions were first secularized in 1756 but reverted to mission status in 1771. Ysleta, at least, was still operating as a mission when the viceroy's general secularization order was issued in 1794, as were at least two of the missions at La Junta de los Ríos. San Antonio de Valero was suppressed in 1793, its equipment used in the new Mission Refugio. But its role in history was far from over. Afterward known as the Alamo, for the garrison from Alamo de Parras stationed there, it served as a military post for Spain, Mexico, Texas, the United States, and the Confederacy. The

Adina de Zavala, 1936. Courtesy of the Institute of Texan Cultures, *The San Antonio Light* Collection.

SAVING THE ALAMO
The Role of Adina de Zavala

Part of the complex that is known today as the Alamo owes its preservation to a granddaughter of Lorenzo de Zavala, a founder of the Republic of Texas. Adina de Zavala was born in 1861 in Harris County. As early as 1889 in San Antonio she organized a group of women committed to the preservation of Texas history. When the Daughters of the Republic of Texas (DRT) was founded two years later, she formed its De Zavala Chapter in San Antonio.

In 1904 she directed her attention to the Alamo. The mission church had been owned by the state of Texas since 1883, but parts of the original mission compound surrounding the church were being threatened with commercial development. De Zavala appealed to fellow DRT member Clara Driscoll, who provided a down payment for the property on which the buildings were located. Driscoll was reimbursed during the state's next legislative session, and the DRT soon was granted stewardship over the site.

Despite their original joint endeavor, De Zavala and Driscoll were by 1907 embroiled in a controversy over how the

other four San Antonio missions were partially secularized the following year, but the churches remained in the care of missionary priests who resided at Mission San José. Full secularization was not achieved until 1824. Mission Refugio, having just begun its work when the 1794 order was issued, continued to serve until 1830. The two missions at Goliad, Espíritu Santo and Rosario, were secularized in 1830 and 1831.

Following secularization, the missions fell victim to different kinds of use and abuse, some eventually to be reclaimed in various ways and in varying degree. Many of the mission sites scattered across the southern half of Texas are not precisely known. The 1936 replica of the first East Texas mission, in Mission Tejas State Historic Park near Alto, for example, is at the wrong place. A few other missions are represented in archeological sites not open to the public.

None of the sites today offers a complete picture of the mission as it existed in the eighteenth century. The most impressive visual remains are found in the San Antonio Missions National Historic Park, where the restored Mission San José gives the clearest indication of what it looked like in the original. The park also includes the remains of San Juan Capistrano, San Francisco de la Espada, and Nuestra Señora de la Purísima Concepción de Acuña. Each of the four mission churches serves an active Catholic parish. All are open to visitors seven days a week. San Antonio de Valero, or the Alamo, venerated more as a shrine of Texas independence than as a mission, is operated as a museum by the Daughters of the Republic of Texas. Free tours are provided seven days a week.

At Goliad, the church of Mission Espíritu Santo was reconstructed in 1936, using part of the original walls and foundations. It is the focus today of Goliad State Historic Park, which has been expanded to include the rather extensive ruins of Mission Rosario (which are not yet open to the public). Also at Goliad, the restored Presidio de la Bahía, which played such a vital role in both the Mexican and Texas revolutions, commemorates the frontier military post of Spanish Texas. The remarkable restoration of this fort was completed in 1967. It is open to public tours for a small fee, seven days a week. The presidio museum, which has collections of artifacts recovered prior to restoration, is operated by the Catholic Diocese of Victoria.

The only other extant example of a Spanish presidio in Texas is the ruins of Presidio de San Luis de las Amarillas (San Sabá) one mile west of Menard. The most visible ruins, however, are of a 1936 reconstruction of the main buildings, not the original structures.

At El Paso, three of the four mission sites are presently within the city. Only historical markers indicate those of San Lorenzo and Senecú. Ysleta has survived to be called "the oldest town in Texas," even though it lies within El Paso. Descendants of its Tigua Indian subjects still live there. The church is a partial reconstruction of the one built for the mission in 1744. An effort to smoke bats from the church belfry in 1907 started a fire that burned the timbers but left the walls standing. In a village of 350 persons, the rebuilt Socorro survives with only the vigas from the original mission church serving in the present one, built following the flood.

property would be interpreted. Driscoll wanted the remaining convento buildings removed to provide an area of parklike landscaping that would emphasize the eighteenth-century church. De Zavala insisted that the two-story stone walls remain so that part of the larger mission complex could be preserved. Soon even the top leadership of the state became involved in the controversy. In 1912, while the governor was out of the state, the lieutenant governor ordered the convento's top story demolished. Although neither side won a complete victory, time has justified De Zavala's position, and the remains of the convento are a reminder of the days when the Alamo was Mission San Antonio de Valero.

Adina de Zavala went on to found the Texas Historical Landmarks Society and to become one of 100 committee members who planned the 1936 Texas Centennial celebration. She also was a charter member of the Texas State Historical Association, and she continued to support the preservation of Texas history and landmarks until her death in 1955. She is remembered not only as a preservationist who understood the broad context of history, but also as a Hispanic Texan who connected her family's heritage directly with the creation of the modern state of Texas.

Several missions in Texas still serve active parishes, but only Mission Ysleta continues to serve descendants of the original mission Indians, the Tiguas. Photo by Bob Parvin.

To maintain Spanish honor, Presidio San Luis de las Amarillas was manned for more than a decade after the sacking of Mission Santa Cruz de San Sabá in 1758. The presidio fell into decay, little more than a pile of rubble, until a section was reconstructed in 1936. Photo by Cathryn Hoyt, THC.

Like the El Paso missions, Presidio de San Elizario began on the other side of the Rio Grande but was left on this side by a flood that changed the river course. Nothing remains of the post itself, but the El Paso County town of San Elizario marks the site.

The mission system on New Spain's northern frontier is generally regarded as a failure. Yet, while the missions fell short of their objectives, they represent a crucial step in the introduction of European civilization to Texas and the American Southwest. The Spanish influence on the region's culture, in its architecture, laws, customs, and language is out of all proportion to the meager numbers sent by Spain to convert the Indians of Texas and guard the frontier.

Opposite: Mission Espíritu Santo was located at its final site, Goliad, in 1749. The church was reconstructed in 1936 and is now the focus of Goliad State Historical Park. Photo by Kathryn Respess.

The valley of the Canadian River was a trail across the vast plains of the Texas Panhandle. Photo by Bob Parvin.

Hispanic Heritage on the High Plains
The Panhandle Perspective

PATRICIA A. MERCADO-ALLINGER

The landscape of the Texas Panhandle is dominated by vast stretches of level plains known as the Llano Estacado. The Canadian River has carved an east-west valley, with mesas scattered along its margins, across the northern reaches of the region. The Prairie Dog Town Fork of the Red River has eroded the eastern Cap Rock escarpment, exposing multicolored layers of rock from the region's geological past. Generations of Indians made their homes on these high plains, gathering the plant foods and hunting the animals the region had to offer. In recent centuries, many changes have occurred on the Llano Estacado, and the catalyst that set these changes in motion was Spanish exploration.

Today's traveler is met with many reminders of the Panhandle's unique Hispanic heritage. Historical markers commemorating important people, events, and routes of exploration and trade are scattered along the highways. Several Panhandle communities bear names that reflect a Spanish presence—Amarillo, Vega, Romero, Tascosa. Natural features and landmarks—playa lakes, Palo Duro and Tule canyons, Rita Blanca Creek—testify to Hispanic relationships. Exhibits at museums such as the Panhandle-Plains Historical Museum in Canyon and the Carson County Square House Museum in Panhandle display local materials derived from Spanish explorers, New Mexicans, and Mexicans in the region for over four hundred years. Even more clues to the Hispanic past lie buried in the land and in almost forgotten historical documents.

Commerce on the Plains

By the early eighteenth century the need for trade and communication routes between the growing Spanish Colonial centers of Santa Fe, New Mexico, and San Antonio was recognized. A major barrier to establishing these routes was removed when a treaty granting New Mexicans the right to trade with the Comanche Indians was approved by tribal representatives and New Mexican governor Don Juan Bautista de Anza in 1786. The exploration of direct routes between the two centers was commissioned and accomplished between 1786 and 1788 by Frenchman Pedro ("Pierre") Vial and Spanish corporal José Mares. Each of these exploratory excursions

Plains Indians with travois. Photo by Edward S. Curtis, courtesy of Amon Carter Museum, Fort Worth, Texas.

THE HORSE AND THE PLAINS INDIANS

By the eighteenth century, a cultural revolution was underway on the plains in response to a Spanish import—the horse. With the acquisition of the horse and horsemanship skills, the Plains Indians were able to follow the buffalo herds over a wider territory.

It was once thought that strays from the early Spanish expeditions were the ancestors of horses obtained by Plains tribes. While the Indians may have acquired strays in these early years, the horses were first viewed as another food source rather than as a mode of transportation. Archeological excavations at the Lubbock Lake National Historic Landmark have uncovered butchered horse remains, and there are undoubtedly other examples of similar meals still undiscovered on the Llano Estacado.

The horse, once its use for transportation was mastered, rapidly became a valued possession that expanded the Plains Indians' ranges for hunting, fighting, raiding, and trading. Early Spanish soldiers, attired in armor, soon found themselves being outrun and outmaneuvered by their Indian opponents and were forced to make changes in their tactics. By the nineteenth century, Indian raids on ranches and communities to obtain horses and other livestock had become commonplace occurrences and were so necessary to the Plains Indian way of life that they became special rituals "sanctioned by the spirits." The very names Apache and Comanche came to symbolize a mastery of horsemanship and warfare that will never be forgotten.

crossed the Texas Panhandle and may have crossed the paths traveled by the earlier expeditions of the sixteenth and seventeenth centuries.

Relative peace with the Comanches and a growing demand for buffalo hides, meat, and tallow enticed a few brave souls to venture from their New Mexican settlements onto the Llano Estacado to hunt. These people came to be known as *ciboleros* and were the first non-Indians to establish a regular presence on the Texas plains. Hunting excursions generally were undertaken in October, after harvest and before the winter storms. This practice allowed the men to maintain their homesteads for most of the year and to supplement the rewards of settled life with a bonus derived from hunting. The buffalo herds were in prime condition in the fall, and their annual migration brought them to the Canadian River Valley and points south. At the end of the hunting season, long wagon trains heavily laden with hides and meat headed back to New Mexico, and from there some of the cargo continued south to Mexico.

From historical accounts we know that ciboleros were mounted on horseback and favored the use of long metal lances, rather than firearms, against their prey. The guns they did possess have been described as obsolete and probably were kept on hand mainly for protection. The ciboleros occasionally used bows and arrows, which they had adopted from the Plains Indians who were highly dependent on the buffalo herds. Skill and bravery were required of the ciboleros. The hunter often had to use both hands to wield the lance, guiding his horse with subtle signals of touch and pressure. The danger of the hunt is revealed in a ballad composed for the tragic fate of one cibolero, Manuel Maes, who was thrown by his horse and impaled on his own lance. The rewards, however, evidently were worth the risk.

Little is known about the relationship between the ciboleros and the buffalo-hunting Indians, but their very presence on the plains argues that they coexisted in relative peace. Both groups were ousted from the plains by the American buffalo hunters, who arrived on the scene in 1874. Unlike the Indian hunters and ciboleros, the newly arrived hunters were interested primarily in hides. Buffalo carcasses were commonly left to rot, leaving piles of bone to bleach in the sun. Competition for the herds became fierce, and the decimation of the buffalo was the quick result. After only three or four years, according to some accounts of the period, the buffalo hunt ceased to be profitable.

The encampments of the ciboleros have long since vanished from the plains, and even descriptions of how the men lived while on the hunt are lacking in historical accounts. Many of their camps were undoubtedly temporary, leaving few physical traces, and so the archeological record is lacking as well. It is also possible that, in later years, the ciboleros joined their fellow countrymen, the *comancheros* (Indian traders) at semipermanent trading centers. Historical accounts mention settlements occupied by Mexican hunters *and* traders north and east of the Llano Estacado. On the Texas plains, evidence of the cibolero presence is limited to isolated lance-head finds, examples of which are on display at the Panhandle-Plains Historical Museum in Canyon.

Contemporaries of the ciboleros—and sometimes former ciboleros—the Indian traders known as comancheros also flourished on the plains following the 1786 treaty between the Comanches and the Spanish government in New Mexico. Permission was granted by the governor, Fernando de la Concha, to those who sought permission to trade in Comanche country. The governor hoped that the comancheros would acquire valuable information about the terrain and its water sources. Since prehistoric times Pueblo Indian traders had made trips to the east of their New Mex-

The American buffalo, as depicted in *The Herd on the Move*, by William J. Hays (1862), was the chief resource on the plains for Indians, ciboleros, and comancheros alike. Courtesy of Amon Carter Museum, Fort Worth, Texas.

ico homeland, seeking Indians who had buffalo hides and furs to barter. This practice was mirrored in the nineteenth-century trade, and the comancheros included in their number both Pueblo Indians and Hispanics. Although the term comanchero is found in Spanish administrative reports as early as 1813, business probably was not restricted to the Comanches but included other Plains tribes as well, such as the Kiowas and Kiowa-Apaches.

In the early years comanchero activities were described as unorganized, with traders wandering the plains—supplied with goods such as salt, blankets, strips of metal (valued for making metal arrowpoints), tobacco, trinkets, and bread—searching for Indians with goods to barter. By the time of their heyday in the 1860s and early 1870s, the comancheros were well organized and had established trading centers along well-traveled routes crossing the Llano Estacado. Comancheros generally maintained their permanent homes in New Mexico and operated from the trading camps on the plains at set times during the year. August and September were considered the peak trading months. Trade centers were located in Yellow House Draw, near Lubbock; at Las Tecovas or Sanborn Springs, on the Fort Smith road (where the headquarters for the Frying Pan Ranch was later established); at Mulberry Creek; and on the Río de las Lenguas (also referred to as the Tongue River, but noted as Los Lingos on today's county highway map), east of the Cap Rock escarpment in the Quitaque area.

Anglo-Americans who entered the region in the nineteenth century reported evidence of the presence of comancheros as early as 1820. In that year U.S. Army officer Stephen Long reported that a "well-beaten trail containing more than twenty parallel bridle paths followed the Canadian River eastward from New Mexico." The 1845 scientific exploration of the Canadian River led by Lt. J.W. Abert of the U.S. Corps of Topographical Engineers found a trail resembling a wagon road.

When United States jurisdiction was extended to the region following the conclusion of the Mexican War in 1848, an effort was made to stem the comanchero-Indian trade in stolen livestock by requiring the comancheros to apply to U.S. authorities for permission to trade with the Indians. Only a limited number of new licenses were issued but the tactic was unsuccessful, largely because the traders simply shared permits and continued business as usual. Lt. Amiel Weeks Whipple, during a reconnaissance across the region in 1853, observed evidence of the presence of the traders in adobe ruins and an *acequia* (irrigation ditch) in Hutchinson County. Comanchero José García even joined the Whipple expedition to serve as a guide.

Comanchero trade was at its height in the 1860s and early 1870s, when it took on a different dimension. Traders enlarged their stock to include restricted commodities such as guns, whiskey, and ammunition. Livestock and captives stolen from ranches and farmsteads in Texas and Mexico became regular offerings from the Indians. The vicinity of Las Lenguas trading station came to be known as the Valle de Lágrimas (the Valley of Tears) because bands of Indians congregated there with their captives.

American hunters, ranchers, and troopers in the seventies encountered increased evidence of the comanchero trade. In 1874 American hunters reported finding trade items, trinkets and beads, at the crumbling remains of an adobe north of the Canadian River, near what was to become the Adobe Walls trading post. Rancher Charles Goodnight later observed at least three main comanchero trails that led to western destinations.

In the 1870s troops under the command of Col. Ranald S. Mackenzie observed the remains of comanchero settlements and also had several encounters with active traders. The troops reported what they called "caves in the high banks or bluffs," which were unoccupied dugouts, composed of a wooden framework over which earth (possibly adobe) was placed. In 1874 Mackenzie's men also arrested prominent trader José Pieda Tafoya, who subsequently served as an army scout during Mackenzie's campaign to expel the remaining Indians from Texas. Tafoya later returned to the Texas Panhandle to raise sheep, and it is quite probable that his career was typical of many of these hardy Hispanic inhabitants of the frontier. They turned their hands to freighting, hunting, trading, sheepherding or any occupation that offered sufficient reward for hard work.

American buffalo hunter Frank Collinson wrote of seeing mud and rock houses on the Canadian River and along Las Lenguas in 1875. He de-

Comancheros bartered manufactured goods for buffalo hides, echoing the centuries-old trade between the pueblos and the plains. Mural by Ben Carlton Mead, courtesy of Panhandle-Plains Historical Museum, Canyon, Texas.

Casimero Romero brought several pastores families and three thousand sheep to the Texas Panhandle in 1875. From *Maverick Town: Story of Old Tascosa*, by John L. McCarty. Copyright © 1946, 1968, 1988 by the University of Oklahoma Press.

scribed Las Lenguas as a small settlement of adobe houses with an acequia leading from the creek to a field of corn and other vegetables, and he said that it was here that comanchero José Tafoya was taken prisoner by Mackenzie. A century later, archeologists excavated the remains of the comanchero settlement described by Collinson. The site, now known as the Merrell-Taylor Village, was discovered in Floyd County and found to contain a cluster of four dugouts built into a slope overlooking the confluence of two creeks. Traces of the irrigation system also were found, along with a variety of household goods, firearms, hardware, and other debris. Some of these materials are on display at the Museum of the Llano Estacado in Plainview.

Metal arrowpoints fashioned from strips of metal, glass beads, the remains of firearms, and other artifacts have been found at numerous Indian sites on the Llano Estacado and its environs. Such items bear witness to historic trade in the final years of Indian occupation of the plains—a trade which was terminated with the expulsion of the Indians in the mid-1870s.

Settlement on the Plains

As the comancheros and the Indians disappeared from the plains, the Texas Panhandle entered into a new era—explorers, hunters, and traders had had their day, and settlers soon began to arrive. The earliest of the settlers, *pastores* (sheepmen) from New Mexico, were prompted eastward by changes in the market for wool. Like the cattle industry in Texas, the sheep industry in New Mexico expanded tremendously in the latter half of the nineteenth century. Before the Civil War, sheep had been raised chiefly in the Rio Grande Valley and primarily for mutton, much of which was sold to mining settlements in northern Mexico. A number of factors, including the subduing of the Indians and the Civil War itself, brought

HARPER'S WEEKLY.

JOURNAL OF CIVILIZATION.

VOL. XVIII—No. 937.] NEW YORK, SATURDAY, DECEMBER 12, 1874. [WITH A SUPPLEMENT. PRICE TEN CENTS.

Entered according to Act of Congress, in the Year 1874, by Harper & Brothers, in the Office of the Librarian of Congress, at Washington.

SLAUGHTERED FOR THE HIDE.—[SEE PAGE 1022.]

From *Harper's Weekly* (1874), courtesy of Amon Carter Museum, Fort Worth, Texas.

EXTINCTION OF THE BUFFALO AND A WAY OF LIFE

From the sixteenth century onward, travelers on the plains reported encounters with nomadic, buffalo-hunting Indians. The buffalo offered the Indians meat and tallow for food, hides for clothing and shelter, and bone for tools. Several different Indian groups relied upon the buffalo and adapted their lives to the migrations of the herds. Indians pursued the animals on foot in prehistoric and early historic times, and on horseback in later years. The herds were immense—their numbers seemed countless. It was inconceivable that there would come a time when the buffalo would be decimated, and the Plains Indian way of life forever gone.

Had there been only two hunters on the plains, the Plains Indians and the New Mexican *ciboleros,* the great buffalo herds may have survived. Both groups made thorough use of their kills and did not generally kill more than was needed. But another hunter arrived on the scene—the American hide man. The hide men, often armed with Sharps rifles, were primarily concerned with the hides, which could be processed into leather. Their appearance on the plains of "No Man's Land" in the late nineteenth century was in direct violation of the 1867 Medicine Lodge Treaty, but the attractive prices offered for buffalo hides were too tempting to resist. The American buffalo hunters swept down the plains, wiping out herds at an alarming pace. They slaughtered thousands of animals and left skinned carcasses to rot. By the spring of 1874 buffalo were extremely scarce north of the Arkansas River. The hide men abandoned these depleted hunting grounds for the Texas Panhandle, where the herds were still plentiful, but the winter of 1874–75 offered these men the last profitable hunt in the buffalo's last stronghold. The Plains Indians, their livelihood destroyed, were soon subdued and placed on reservations. None remained in Texas.

Soon, even the bones of the destroyed buffalo were gone. The mounds of sun-bleached skeletons were gathered and shipped to distant markets, where the bones were ground into fertilizer. Few traces of the buffalo and the people that once depended on the herds remained when the twentieth century arrived.

about an increased market for wool and caused a shift in emphasis. The sheep of New Mexico, descendants of those introduced by Oñate, were noted for producing tasty meat and poor wool. The flocks were gradually improved by the introduction of Merino breeding stock and by the 1880s almost half of New Mexico's sheep were of the improved type. There was also a tremendous increase in sheep population. In the Spanish tradition, grazing land was free domain, so it is not surprising that the sheepmen of the eastern New Mexico plains expanded their lucrative operations into western Texas.

As the threat of Indian raids dwindled, several New Mexican pastores established themselves on the Llano Estacado, where the grasslands provided ample grazing for their stock. The pastores concentrated in the western Panhandle and congregated in communities, known as *plazas,* similar to the fortified towns favored in eastern New Mexico. Among the pastores were a number of comancheros who had returned to their former occupation of sheep raising. Men such as Colas Martínez, Casimero Romero, José Tafoya, and Juan Trujillo, once reliant on trade with the Indians, began to be known as the sheepmen of the plains.

Leading the migrants was Casimero Romero, who was a prominent and wealthy trader from the days of the comancheros. He brought his own family, 3,000 sheep, and the families of Henry Kimball and Agapito Sandoval to the Texas Panhandle in 1875. They settled on Atascosa Creek and there Romero built a large adobe home. Within the next few years other pastores arrived, including the Trujillos, Borregos, and Montoyas. A few Anglos also had flocks in the Panhandle at this time, and these men often married into the Hispanic pastor families. One of the Anglo-Americans, called "Padre" Green because he allegedly had been a priest, operated a big wool house and was considered one of the biggest sheepmen on the Plains.

Nearest the New Mexico–Texas boundary was the Salinas Plaza, which was located near Salinas Lake. To the east were the plazas of Boquilla, Trujillo, Manzanares, Joaquín, Chaves (sometimes called Charvez), Pescado, Ortega, Romero Springs, and Corsino (also known as Casino and believed to be the easternmost plaza). Many of the plazas bore the names of the founding families, while others like Boquilla (meaning irrigation canal opening) and Manzanares (apple orchards) may have been named for local features. The plazas varied in size from the large settlements at Tascosa, Trujillo, and Salinas, which included stores and saloons, to the small handful of structures clustered at Pescado.

The plazas established by the pastores, as well as the small farms they developed, generally followed centuries-old patterns from New Mexico. They were usually located near springs along tributaries of the Canadian River, and acequias were dug from these water sources to irrigate nearby fruit orchards and fields of beans, corn, grains, melons, and peppers. Houses were constructed of adobe bricks or stone slabs and often contained corner fireplaces of adobe in each room. The roofs of the structures were composed of layers of wood and dirt supported by poles placed on

the tops of completed walls. Local gypsum provided the raw material for whitewashing interior walls.

Social life in the plazas also followed patterns that can still be seen in many Hispanic communities in New Mexico and Texas to this day. Weddings among the prominent pastor families were major social events, featuring elaborate dinners and entertainment. *Bailes* (dances), games, and other diversions also were popular, and religious observances were central to community life even though the Texas Panhandle was far removed from church centers in both New Mexico and Texas.

The parish at Chaperito, New Mexico, was one of the first to send priests to pastor settlements on the Llano Estacado in Texas. Records for births of pastores children in the Panhandle settlements of Atascosa (later changed to Tascosa), Trujillo, Los Salinas, and Mobeetie can be found in the baptismal records from Chaperito. There was later an adobe chapel at Tascosa, but, unlike the Hispanic cattle ranches of South Texas, most of the scattered sheep ranches on the Llano Estacado did not have chapels, perhaps because the ranches and plazas existed for such a brief period of time. Instead, a room in the house of a prominent rancher was used for services when the priests visited. At the home of Casimero Romero a large central hallway was used, and people of all faiths gathered there for religious services, marriages, and infant baptisms.

Just as the pastores brought with them from New Mexico their own architectural and social customs, they also brought Hispanic traditions of sheep raising. The pastores' flocks usually consisted of 1500 sheep or more, and the herders spent months with their flocks on long, migratory circuits,

Adobe home of Casimero Romero as it appeared in 1941. THC photo.

often accompanied only by their sheep dogs. *Majordomos* (head shepherds) managed several flocks at a time, traveling from one flock to another to supervise operations. Many of the pastores were *partidarios*, who made agreements to care for the livestock of larger owners. According to Fabiola C. de Baca, who grew up on a sheep ranch on the Llano Estacado in New Mexico, the *partida,* or share system, evolved from an arrangement in which the partidario was expected to return double the number of stock at the end of five years to one in which the partidario paid the owner 20 percent of the stock each year. While the range was still free, some partidarios prospered, but the coming of the big ranches brought an end to both the migratory treks of the shepherds and the holdings of the wealthier sheep ranchers on the plains of the Texas Panhandle.

The era of the pastores began in 1875 and lasted for little more than a decade. When cattlemen entered the scene and claimed the Panhandle as their range, the sheepherders were faced with shrinking pastures for their flocks, and only a few pastores stayed on into the 1890s. Abandoned cemeteries, the ruins of plazas, temporary camp sites, stone walls, and sheep pens on isolated ranches are all that remain of the pastores today. In 1983 the Texas Historical Commission sponsored an archeological study to locate pastores sites in the Texas Panhandle. As a result of this study, pastores sites in Armstrong, Floyd, Hartley, Oldham, and Potter counties were carefully recorded and are now listed on the National Register of Historic Places.

A Region in Transition

The frontier town of Tascosa sprang up around the original plaza established by Casimero Romero, and for years the town boasted the only store and hotel to be found in the entire region. The growth of the cattle industry in the Panhandle helped to stimulate the growth of Tascosa and the eventual formation of Oldham County. Tascosa was inhabited by both Hispanics and Anglo-Americans, but the former group vastly outnumbered the latter in the early 1880s. When Oldham County was organized in 1881, two of the four county commissioners were Hispanics, as was the assessor and the first county clerk, undoubtedly a reflection of the fact that a majority of the voters were Hispanic. The county even had a Hispanic deputy sheriff, David Martínez, who was killed trying to intervene in a dispute after only one day of public service.

The 1880s brought many changes to the Texas Panhandle. According to the census rolls, only 22 percent of the total population of the region in 1880 were Spanish speakers. However, Hispanics outnumbered Anglo-Americans in Oldham and Hartley counties, where the pastores settlements were originally concentrated. Sheepherders were still listed in each county of the region, but Hispanics were also turning to other forms of employment, such as plasterer, freighter, laborer, stockman, and storekeeper. Even Casimero Romero, the "founder" of the pastores, abandoned sheepherding, established a store in Tascosa, and freighted goods to

46

Dodge City, Kansas, where he had a second residence. Romero finally sold his interests in Tascosa in 1897 and returned with his family to eastern New Mexico.

When Charles Goodnight and his fellow cattlemen arrived in the Texas Panhandle, sheep dominated the region. Goodnight himself estimated that there were about 75,000 to 100,000 sheep on the Canadian River in 1876. That the sheepherders rights to the land were recognized is evident in the fact that Goodnight negotiated an agreement with them to divide the rangelands. However, as the ranches grew and the Llano Estacado was subdivided with barbed wire fences, relations between the ranchers and the sheepherders became more and more strained. Personal grudges arose and shootings were not uncommon, with liquor often providing the final catalyst for gunfire.

Unfortunately, most of the New Mexican sheepmen had not filed formal land claims. Some of the pastores received compensation for their improvements from the ranchers and freely elected to return to their original homes in New Mexico and Colorado. Others were strongly "encouraged" to do so. Ranch hands recalled setting fire to the abandoned homes of pastores to discourage their return.

The railroad came to the Llano Estacado in the 1880s, offering jobs and bringing a new wave of Hispanic settlement to the Panhandle. Photographer Julius Born documented the lives of these people in the early 1900s. Courtesy of Panhandle-Plains Historical Museum Archives, Canyon, Texas.

Little remains of the early Hispanic presence in the Panhandle except scattered ruins such as the José Tafoya House in Hartley County. THC photo.

Some Hispanics decided to remain on the Llano Estacado and found work with the very ranches that ushered in the end of the pastores era, but history has recorded few details about these men and their families. Tantalizing glimpses appear in local sources, such as early photographs of XIT Ranch operations, which show Mexican cooks and cowboys with familiar surnames—Baca and Trujillo—listed in the captions. Juan Rodrigues, an employee of the JA Ranch, was listed in the 1890 census of Armstrong County as having served in the Civil War with the Union's 1st Texas Cavalry.

The 1880s brought not only large ranches but the railroad to the Llano Estacado. Construction of the railways across the Texas Panhandle offered employment to resident Hispanics and attracted laborers from Mexico. The Fort Worth and Denver City Railway was the first to enter the region, in 1880. The Santa Fe and Rock Island rail lines followed suit, with construction completed by 1910. Again, little is known about the labor force responsible for these historic accomplishments, although many images of railroad workers and their families have survived. These images, in photographs taken during the early 1900s by Julius Born of Canadian, Texas, show proud Hispanic men with their wives and children, dressed in their finest clothes, in the formal poses typical of the period. These treasures are on file at the Hemphill County Library in Canadian and at the Panhandle-Plains Historical Museum Archives in Canyon. The names of these people are unknown, but the photographs are testimony to their presence and of their contributions to the settlement of the region.

Many Hispanic families currently make their homes in the Texas Panhandle. Some may be descendants of the early families, but many more are recent arrivals, drawn to the region in the changing demographic patterns of post–World War II America. The future will reveal the role these people are to play in the continuing saga of the plains. Nor is the story of the past yet fully told. This brief essay is intended only to spark an awareness of the contributions Hispanics have made to the exploration and settlement of the region. And to remind today's travelers that they could be flying into the urban airport of Yellow (Amarillo) or visiting Hardwood (Palo Duro) State Park if it had not been for the unique series of events that have shaped the history of the Llano Estacado.

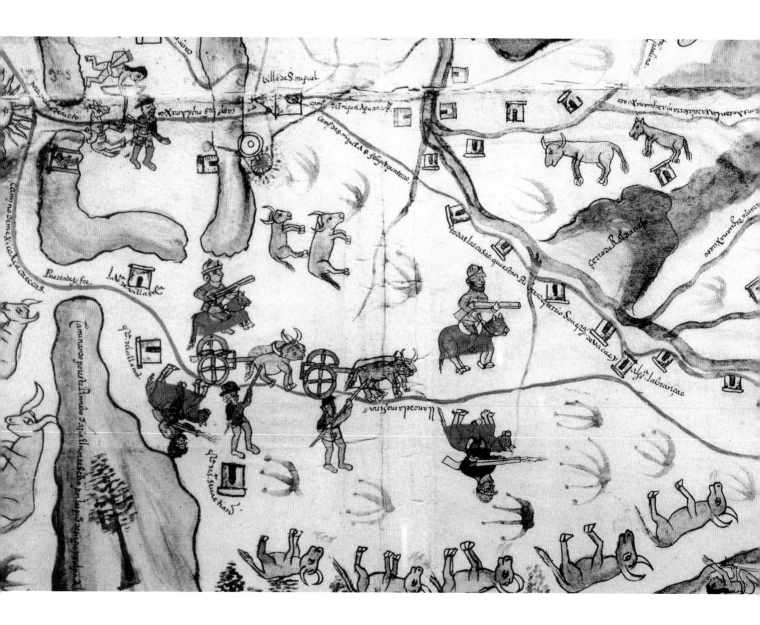

Spanish ranches, such as this one in the Río de San Miguel Valley (1580), were established in Mexico by the sixteenth century. The practices developed on these ranches and on the later 18th-century ranches in the Province of Texas have influenced the language, gear, and techniques used today. From *Mapas Españoles de América* (Madrid, 1951), courtesy of Benson Latin American Collection, General Libraries, University of Texas at Austin.

Hispanic Ranching Heritage

JACK JACKSON

Ranching in Texas had its beginnings in practices that Spaniards developed in the province during the eighteenth century. And what happened in remote Texas during this formative period can be understood only in a context that stretches back for two or more centuries in Mexico. The gear, techniques, land-tenure policies, and social dimensions of ranching in colonial Texas have their roots south of the border. These Hispanic influences had an impact on ranching long after Spain and Mexico passed from the scene politically, and did much to shape the stock-raising practices of Anglo-Texans in the nineteenth century.

A study of historical documents can tell us a lot about how Spanish ranching evolved in Texas, even though most of its vestiges have long since crumbled away. The Spanish expeditions to Texas in the 1680s, which commenced in response to rumors of French intrusion, brought livestock with them, both as transportation and for sustenance. Some animals escaped or were lost and remained to thrive in the wilderness when the soldiers and missionaries withdrew. These wild animals, both equine and bovine, came to be known as *mesteños* and were joined by stock that wandered away from the ranches just beginning to be established in northern Coahuila. The broad expanses of Texas were an ideal breeding ground, and the wild herds multiplied prodigiously, in time becoming a key factor in the development of ranching.

Stock raising was first practiced in Texas by the Franciscan missionaries who came to convert the native tribes. Sheep, goats, and cattle were important to the missions because these animals represented both a food supply and a source of income. The manpower needed to maintain the herds was scarce on the frontier, however, and it soon became necessary for the padres to teach the mission Indians the basic skills of stock tending. The Indians learned quickly to ride, rope, brand, herd, and do most of the other chores necessary to operate the mission ranches around San Antonio de Béxar. Even so, hostilities from other tribes like the Apaches and the Comanches—tribes that refused to become "reduced" to mission life—made ranching a risky business. The herds, though they increased rapidly, became semiwild and more difficult to manage. By mid-century, the priests acknowledged that their cattle were mostly out of control. The custodians of the missions felt lucky to brand even a small percentage of their annual calf crop.

Reconstruction of Rancho de las Cabras. Drawing by Jack Jackson, from *Los Mesteños: Spanish Ranching in Texas, 1721–1821* (1986), courtesy of the artist.

The wild herds, we may judge, acted as an incentive for the next phase of Texas ranching: the rise of private stockmen. Soon after the Spanish made peace with the Apaches (1749), small *ranchos* began to dot the San Antonio River valley between Béxar and Espíritu Santo (Goliad). As most of the land and cattle in this region were claimed by the missions, conflict was inevitable. Indeed, the squabbles between missions and private ranchers dominate the archival records of the period, continuing even beyond final secularization of the missions in the 1820s. It is through such records that we have reached our present understanding of exactly how ranching was conducted in Texas during the colonial period.

And a fascinating portrait it is! All the ingredients of the later, better-known trail-drive era are to be found in the Spanish period, although perhaps on a smaller scale. Roundups, in which thundering herds of wild cattle and mustangs were driven from the brush, were held just as they were in post–Civil War Texas. Cattle were trailed to markets in Louisiana and Coahuila, with the same hair-raising adventures that took place in the 1870s. Rustling, Indian attacks, droughts, the indomitable grit of the men and women who made ranching their way of life—they are all here, in Spanish Texas, just as Anglo-Americans experienced it a century later. The remarkable thing is how similar the Hispanic and Anglo experiences were, especially if one begins the comparison assuming that the two had little in common.

After a shaky start, the private ranchers in the San Antonio River valley grew in number and power, until their rivalry with the missionaries became an open confrontation. The priests accused the ranchers of rustling, of building their herds with stock stolen from mission pastures. In the Baron de Ripperdá the missions found a governor willing to press

RANCHO DE LAS CABRAS

The ranches established by the San Antonio missions were among the first in Texas. Rancho de Las Cabras, overlooking the San Antonio River in Wilson County, was established about 1745 by Mission Espada, and large-scale ranching was being undertaken by the 1750s. A 1772 inventory of Mission Espada described the ranch headquarters as being enclosed by a stone wall for the protection of the herdsmen. The enclosure had two entrances with gates. Inside were four *jacales* (houses built of wood and thatch), and in one was an altar, indicating that it was used for religious services. The ranch included a corral complex with barricades and gates for the livestock, which included over 500 horses, numerous mules and burros, about 1,000 sheep, 1,000 head of cattle, and other smaller animals, including pigs. The estimated number of cattle running wild in Espada's pastures was about 3,000 head. The ranch was one end of a supply system and the mission the other.

By 1784 Don Ignacio Calvillo, a Spaniard who had married into a Canary Islander family, was operating a ranch leased from part of the ranchlands of Espada. By 1814 he was living on the ranch with his family and there was an extensive ranching complex. Calvillo was murdered in a bandit raid led by his own grandson in 1814. The ownership of the ranch is unclear until 1828, when his daughter María del Carmen applied for title to the land and took over management of the ranch. By the time of her death in 1856 at the age of 91 she and Rancho de las Cabras had witnessed the major events in the evolution of the state of Texas—the end of the mission period, the Mexican and Texas struggles for independence, and the achievement of statehood. The Texas Parks and Wildlife Department now administers the site of the ranch. The Center for Archaeological Research of the University of Texas at San Antonio has undertaken extensive documentary and archeological investigations to trace the history of the ranch and the material remains of the ranching complex.

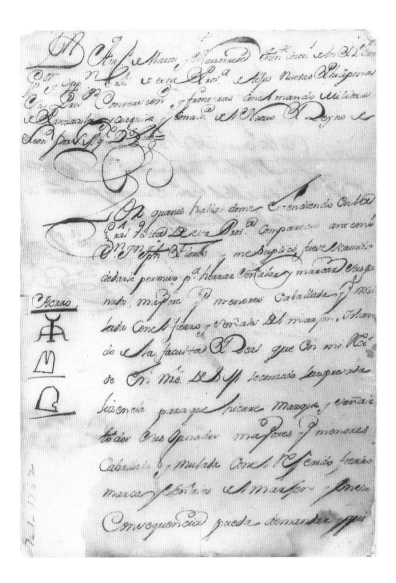

The practice of branding livestock was brought to the Americas by Spanish conquistadors. In the mid-eighteenth century brands for the private ranches dotting the San Antonio River Valley were registered at Béxar. Courtesy of Barker Texas History Center, General Libraries, University of Texas at Austin.

their claims. Twice during his administration, Ripperdá hauled the province's leading citizens into court and charged them with rustling.

The ranchers' opposition against church and state hardened during this prosecution (which the ranchers considered persecution) and entered a more strident phase during the term of Domingo Cabello, Ripperdá's successor. The situation was aggravated in 1778 when the new commandant general, Teodoro de Croix, visited Texas and declared all its wild livestock to be the king's property. Further, he imposed a tax on the exploitation of this resource, which the citizens and the missions claimed as theirs.

Thus a "private quarrel" became a public matter, and the stock raisers were forced to put aside their differences and unite against the enforcement of Croix's decree.

Several important memorials written during the 1780s were directed toward fighting the usurpation of the wild herds and the imposition of a tax thereon. These documents trace much of the ranching history of the province and give us insight into the institution and its day-to-day operation. While these protests were being considered by the king's representatives, the ranchers received a number of roundup and branding extensions. These "grace periods" were permitted so the ranchers, mission and secular, could separate their stock from the king's property, the wild herds. As may be imagined, the roundups conducted under such circumstances were as wild and woolly as any ever have been. Finally, in 1795, the ranchers won a victory of sorts: past tax debts were forgiven but, in principle, Croix's law remained on the books.

Such technicalities mattered little, because by that time the wild cattle herds had become severely depleted by two decades of intense exploitation. During the later 1790s, horses replaced cattle as the province's leading export, a trend that was to grow as Americans streamed westward into Louisiana. The efforts of enterprising traders like Philip Nolan to cater to this new market caused Spain to stiffen its grip on the northern frontier, but the change came too late. Others followed in Nolan's footsteps, until what began as mere smuggling for personal profit became politically directed moves against Spanish rule.

Throughout the turbulent filibustering period, 1800–20, the market for Texas mustangs remained constant. If these animals could be caught, broken, and driven to Louisiana markets, a man could make himself rich. Thus did the wild horse herds, said to abound in Texas, serve as a lure to the bold in spirit. Faced with the government's determination to shut off the horse trade, such men made good revolutionaries.

When Anglo empresarios like Stephen F. Austin brought colonists to Texas in the 1820s, there can be little doubt that these people already possessed a set of skills and attitudes that were applied to their stock-raising endeavors. These attitudes, which some authorities have traced back to the cowpens of the Carolinas, did not remain unaffected by the Hispanic "system" that Austin's colonists found at work in Texas. Whether it was the land and climate that forced the changes, or whether the Spanish way of doing things was judged superior to the Anglo, we can only speculate. But the fact is that, in only a short time, the Anglo colonists began to alter their approach to ranching to fit what the Tejanos were doing, and subsequent waves of colonists could not tell the difference between the two. This blending of traditions—with the Hispanic usages dominant for the most part—resulted in an institution and style of life that has come to be synonymous with Texas. We are fortunate to have had two such rich sources to draw upon in making our ranching heritage second to none.

What aspects of Spanish ranching heritage influenced Anglo-American ranching, and what still remains today? Let us start our inventory with the gear of a typical *vaquero* and see how it influenced that

used by cowboys. Apart from his horse, the three most important tools of the vaquero and cowboy alike were his saddle, rope, and branding iron. It is true that Anglo stockmen used all three before reaching Texas, but it is also true that these tools and the way they were used underwent a transformation when exposed to the Tejano variety. Anglo saddles sprouted horns (where the English riding saddle had none) and "Mother Hubbards" (covers patterned after the *mochila*, a removable housing typical of Mexican vaquero saddles). Anglo stirrups soon sported "taps" (from *tapaderas*, used to protect the foot from thorns and brush). By the 1840s "everyone in Texas" was riding on Mexican saddles, according to Prince Carl Solms-Braunfels; his German colonists began tanning leather and making saddles soon after their arrival. Their pattern was the Mexican stock saddle, and its popularity quickly spread beyond the borders of Texas.

The use of the lasso (*lazo*) or lariat (*la reata*) underwent a similar transformation once Anglo cowboys saw how effectively the Mexican vaqueros used it in working cows on the open range. Whips, preferred over ropes by the cowboys along the Atlantic coast, quickly gave way to the lasso in Texas. Roping became an essential part of the cowboy's working skills, acquired from his Spanish teachers. Some of the terms used in roping, like "dally" (from *da le vuelta,* to take a turn around the horn), betray

The Mexican stock saddle, lariat, and chaps are familiar western gear adopted by Anglo cowboys from their counterparts, the vaqueros. Photo by Bob Parvin.

55

The Longhorn, a descendant of the cattle introduced by Spain into the New World, is making a comeback among Texas growers. Photo by David Langford.

their Spanish origins. Indeed, many Spanish ranching terms entered the English language, so integral were they to the way in which Anglos learned to conduct stock raising: ranch (from *rancho*), rodeo, corral, chaps (from *chaparreras*), sombrero, poncho, serape, bandana, remuda, mustang (from *mesteño*), and bronco, to name a few.

Nor should we forget the Hispanic contribution to ranching *practices*, to the way that cattle came to be worked in Texas, as opposed to how they were tended "back East." In Texas, cows generally ran free and were subjected to an annual roundup (*rodeo* or *corrida*), in which they were separated according to owner. After the calves were branded, the herd was turned loose again to graze on the open plains. If an owner wanted to trail cattle to market, lesser roundups were conducted until he had a sufficient number corraled and marked with his road brand. The object of these cow-hunts was usually unbranded stock. Many a ranching dynasty was founded on the benefits of wild cattle, which could be found in South Texas until the late nineteenth century. Likewise, the cattle were of Spanish origin, the tough, stringy progenitors of our Longhorn breed, which—after near extinction—is making a comeback among Texas growers. Anglo contributions to the industry generally came in the post–Civil War period and consisted of things like the introduction of northern breeding stock (shorthorns), barbed wire fences, windmills, and market-oriented developments such as packeries, railroad shipment, and stockyard operations. As important as these innovations were, for the essence and true flavor of ranching we must look to an earlier era, before the Anglo cattleman crossed the Sabine and Red rivers.

Spanish and Mexican land grant policies also helped shape the dimensions of Texas ranching. Ranches were measured not in acres but in leagues—*thousands* of acres. Every married colonist who was admitted to Mexican Texas and declared his intent to engage in stock raising was en-

Even with technological advances in ranch management and stock breeding, the traditional skills of the vaquero remain an essential part of ranch life. Photo by Bob Parvin.

titled to a *legua,* or league, of land (4,428 acres). Prominent citizens, especially military veterans or their descendants, obtained more land without difficulty. Thus, as a legacy from the colonial period, ranching in Texas took on epic proportions and left its stamp on the way Texans perceive themselves and the way they are perceived by others. The mentality reflected in the movie *Giant* was a state of mind lifted from what the Anglos saw happening on the *haciendas* and *ranchos* of the northern borderlands; only the roles changed, not the play itself.

How did Anglos, once they had become masters of the land and inheritors of the Hispanic legacy, organize and run their ranches? According to the Spanish pattern, for the most part, especially if the ranch was located in the southern part of the state. But early ranches elsewhere in Texas soon got the hang of it. Also, many of the ranchers used Mexican hired hands and found it cost-effective to cater to their way of doing things. Thus the old *patrón* system was perpetuated—even into the twentieth century—as these laborers became attached to various estates, often working their entire lives for the same ranch.

The work itself was conducted much as it had been before ownership of the land changed. A *mayordomo* (foreman) directed daily operations, sometimes assisted by a *caporal*. As for the vaqueros, they managed to retain time-honored work habits, including traditions like afternoon snacks (*meriendas*), and a penchant for entertainments that they shared with the cowboys of Western legend—periodic dances (*bailes*) and drinking binges (*parrandas*). If they wound up in jail, the patrón would bail them out. For the most part they were honest, hard working, and fiercely loyal to their employers. It is no accident that now, in our modern era of technological advances in stock breeding and ranch management, the old skills are best practiced by Mexican hands recently come to Texas. Even in this age when we are trying to herd cows with helicopters, they still sit the saddle the way our ancestors did.

The Built Environment in South Texas
The Hispanic Legacy

JOE S. GRAHAM

South Texas, settled by Spanish colonizers beginning in 1750, offers a wealth of architectural and other components of the built environment little known to those outside the region and too often little appreciated by those living in the area. Of the significant Hispanic structures, most are associated with ranching, which was the basis of Spanish settlement in the region. Many of the early structures now lie in ruins, some are in serious need of preservation or restoration, but others remain in remarkably good condition. Both individually and together, these structures are best understood when viewed in their historical and social context—as material expressions of the Hispanic culture of the region.

The Spanish Settlement of South Texas

Although Spaniards had traversed the area now known as South Texas in the early 1500s, there was no successful attempt to extend Spanish control over the region until the mid-1700s. Fearing an incursion of French influence into the region known as the Seno Mexicano, in 1746 the Spanish king commissioned José de Escandón, a talented and successful military officer and colonizer, to organize a group of people to settle the region and take control of it for Spain. After inspecting the area in 1747, Escandón recruited ranchers and adventurers from the rural areas of Querétaro and farther north in Coahuila to organize a civilian colony, in contrast to the traditional religious and military colonies of earlier Spanish settlement. In 1748 over 3,000 settlers and soldiers left Querétaro, headed for what was relatively unexplored territories. By 1755 Escandón and his lieutenants had established 23 settlements with only 146 soldiers among the 8,933 settlers and an estimated 3,500 Indians. Unlike other colonizers, Escandón established no presidios, although 15 missions were founded among the settlements by the Franciscans.

The new province, Nuevo Santander, was settled by colonists who traveled overland with their household goods and livestock, in much the same fashion as the westward-moving Anglo-American pioneers who would settle the West over half a century later. Led by the promise of free land and other concessions from the Spanish government, these settlers

Opposite: **Many South Texas ranch houses had flat roofs. However a few, such as this example built of sillares on El Guajillo Ranch, were built with steeply pitched gabled roofs. Photo by Joe S. Graham.**

would become the foundation of a new society. The region was ideally suited for cattle and horse raising, and it developed as a center for raising livestock. The first *villas* (settlements) established near the Rio Grande included Camargo (1749), Reynosa (1749), Revilla (1750, later renamed Guerrero), and Mier (1752). In less than a decade, these settlements would become important ranching centers. On the Texas side of the Rio Grande, among the earliest ranch communities that later became towns were Nuestra Señora de los Dolores, later called Dolores Viejo, founded in 1750; San Agustín de Laredo, founded in 1755; and Rancho Davis, which was part of the lands belonging to the 1757 Rancho Carnestolendes and which later developed into the settlement named Rio Grande City.

In 1757, less than a decade after Escandón brought his colonists into Nuevo Santander, José Tienda de Cuervo reported more than 80,000 head of cattle, horses, and mules, and over 300,000 head of sheep and goats in the province. By 1781, nearly all available lands in South Texas were assigned through land grants from the Spanish government—and nearly all of these lands were ranches. By 1836 and the Texas Revolution, Nuevo Santander boasted over 350 *rancherías* (ranch headquarters) with over 3,000,000 head of livestock, and Matamoros, the largest city in the province, had a population of over 15,000 inhabitants. Cattle drives were being conducted from this region into Louisiana and south into Mexico well over a century before the famed post–Civil War cattle drives to the northern markets made history and captured the imagination of a nation.

Mexico's independence from Spain in 1821 produced little change in the everyday lives of the inhabitants of Nuevo Santander. Nor did Texas' independence from Mexico in 1836 have a great initial effect on the people of the region. The area between the Rio Grande and the Nueces River—much of what we now call South Texas—remained contested territory until the Mexican War of 1846, which brought a permanent U.S. military presence to the region and initiated changes that were to transform the culture, society, and social institutions forever. By the end of the war in 1848, the region was firmly in the control of the United States.

Immigrants seeking land came into the region from both the north and the south. The Anglo-Americans, however, had a decided advantage in that the political and legal systems were under their control, and their economic resources and technology were superior. Through a number of legal, extralegal, and illegal means, the Anglo-Americans acquired much of the land formerly owned by Tejanos. Many Anglo-Americans married into the wealthier Tejano families, and they remained prominent business and political figures for decades. South Texas had become a region in which the majority Tejano population was militarily, politically, and economically dominated by the Anglo-American minority. That pattern held until well beyond the turn of this century.

Although the region's towns were prosperous, most people lived in small, isolated ranch communities made up of extended families or clans. Over time the huge ranches of the early colonists were divided again and again among descendants. As the number of descendants grew larger, the land was often held in common rather than being divided. Owners lived in

The typical South Texas jacal, such as these early twentieth-century examples in San Ygnacio, was built of sticks and mud with a steeply pitched gabled roof thatched with grass. Blake Collection, courtesy of Barker Texas History Center, General Libraries, University of Texas at Austin.

small villages around what had been the ancestral home, and eventually everyone became related to almost everyone else. These tight-knit communities were geographically isolated from the outside world. By the turn of the century, communications had improved little. In 1904 the railroad connected Brownsville to the rest of Texas, but as late as the 1920s many parts of the old province were still relatively isolated. It was not until the 1940s that a paved highway connected Matamoros to the interior of Mexico.

The Hispanic Architecture of South Texas

Associated as the built environment was with ranching, most of its components in early South Texas were dwellings, structures to enclose land, and structures to hold or produce water. Of the many components of the built environment in the region, the most important, the most numerous, and the oldest are dwellings. Although no examples of some of the earliest types of structures, such as *jacales de leña,* remain from the period of eighteenth-century settlement, later examples do exist and apparently are close, if not identical, to the earlier structures.

When first the Spaniards and later the Mexicans came into Texas, they brought with them the idea of what a house should be, borrowed from the regions in Spain or Mexico whence they came. In South Texas, where timber was lacking, their ideas were expressed in the materials at hand—primarily sticks and mud, mud bricks (adobe), stone, and caliche blocks. There is no evidence that the Indians of South Texas contributed to Hispanic architecture in the region, although Indian resistance to settlement did influence the fortification of houses and arrangements that were made for the safety of communities. Hispanics in Texas had a very distinctive vernacular (folk) architecture; that is, an architecture built from local ma-

61

terials and without formal plans. Many of these house forms persisted into the twentieth century, and examples of most of them still stand in the region, even though they are no longer being built.

As one might expect, each social class among the early settlers had fairly distinctive house forms. While the wealthy class built *casas grandes* of hewn sandstone or *sillares* (caliche blocks cut from the earth), the poorer classes built and lived in jacals. The word *jacal* (from the Nahuatl *xacalli*) literally means "hut" but came to mean a specific kind of house form to those who used it. The typical South Texas jacal was a rectangular-shaped dwelling made of the region's most readily available materials—sticks and mud. In constructing the jacal, four corner poles (*horcones*) were partially buried in the ground at the bottom and forked at the top to hold the roof supports (*vigas*). Between these upright corner posts were placed smaller intermediate posts, their bases also buried a few inches in the ground. Horizontal sticks were fastened at intervals to the inside and outside of the upright posts, and these horizontal sticks formed a framework that held the wall materials in place. The walls, supported by the horcones and the horizontal sticks, were made from available materials, usually vertically placed brush and sticks, stones or rubble, or, most commonly in South

The massive stone *chiminea* almost overwhelms this jacal de leña kitchen on Rancho La Purísima, Zapata County. Photo by Joe S. Graham.

62

Texas, split mesquite laid horizontally. The jacal with split mesquite walls was called a *jacal de leña* (jacal of firewood) or sometimes *estilo de raja,* or raja-style jacal (a *raja* is a short piece of wood that reaches from one vertical wall post to another or, in the roofs of flat-roofed houses, from viga to viga). The use of rajas in jacal wall construction was common in Mexico, its probable place of origin, although this type of wall structure was also known in Spain. Some jacals had palisade, or vertical post, walls, and this type of construction also was common in both Spain and Mexico. When plastered inside and out with mud or lime mortar, the walls of most jacals were from six to ten inches thick, providing excellent insulation.

The roof style of the early jacals also was distinctive. The typical South Texas jacal had a steeply pitched gabled roof supported by a stout ridgepole resting in the forks of two long poles in the center of the narrow side of the house. The steep pitch was required to shed the torrential rains that sometimes occur in southern, as well as central and eastern, Texas. The roof was thatched with grass (usually carrizo, sacahuiste, or sacaton) tied in bundles, palmetto leaves, animal skins, *tule* rushes, yucca leaves, or other similar material tied to a framework of poles supported by the ridgepole and the vigas sitting atop the walls of the jacal. The roof had to be rethatched every three or four years, and some thatched roofs of South Texas jacals were eventually replaced with wooden shingles (*tejamanil*) or, later, with galvanized, corrugated metal roofing.

The size and finished appearance of the jacal were largely determined by the materials available in the environment. The South Texas jacal was normally from ten to twelve feet wide and eighteen to twenty-four feet long, most often consisting of one room, perhaps with a cloth divider making two rooms. The interior height at the center, determined by the ridgepole, was ten to fifteen feet from the floor. The typical floor consisted of packed and hardened dirt, but some were of *chipichil*—a mixture of lime, sand, and gravel. The jacal usually had a door in one gabled end and small windows on one or more sides. Once completed, the jacal was rarely enlarged, since the steeply pitched gabled roof made it impractical to add rooms to the building. When kept in good repair and whitewashed with lime inside and out, the jacal was a comfortable, attractive home that could last for decades.

Many of the early ranches that became settlements were made up of small clusters of jacals surrounding the *casas mayores,* or main ranch houses. By 1753 Vásquez de Borrego's ranch, which became the settlement known as Dolores Viejo, consisted of 23 families, 21 of them living in jacals. San Agustín de Laredo, established as a ranch headquarters by Tomás Sánchez, had a population of 185 by 1767. By 1789 Laredo boasted a population of 708, a new stone church, a few stone and adobe houses, and a large number of one-room jacals.

Jacals were found throughout Texas where Hispanics lived, and this house form was adopted by other groups as well, including the Germans in the San Antonio area and the Anglos of South Texas. In 1854, for example, when Captain Richard King brought his bride to what was to become the King Ranch, the headquarters consisted of a cluster of jacals and

a gray tangle of mesquite corrals (*corrales de leña*). Tom Lea, in *The King Ranch* (1957), quotes Henrietta Chamberlain King as saying, "When I came as a bride in 1854, the little ranch house then—a mere *jacal* as Mexicans would call it—was our abode for many months until our main ranch dwelling was completed. . . . I remember that my pantry was so small my large platters were fastened to the walls outside." She may not have realized that she was following a pattern set over a century before by the early Spanish colonists—using a jacal as a temporary shelter while waiting for the main house to be completed.

The main house of the landowner class usually was built of sillar, stone, or, in rare cases, adobe. Houses of hewn sandstone were common in the areas of earliest settlement, on both sides of the Rio Grande. The stone was usually quarried from locations near the building site, and there is ample evidence in the buildings themselves that skilled stonemasons plied their craft in the region. The earliest ranch structures built of hewn sandstone consisted of one- or two-room, rectangular houses with floors of chipichil and flat roofs supported by vigas. The lime used in the chipichil and for plastering jacals was produced in kilns built near the ranches and towns. (There are at least thirteen *caleras,* or lime kilns, on the outskirts of Mier, an early ranching settlement near the Rio Grande in the Mexican state of Tamaulipas.) These houses were often fortresslike, with walls that were two feet thick (or thicker) and as much as twelve to fifteen feet high,

The original ranch house on Rancho San Francisco, Zapata County, was made of hand-carved sandstone with a flat, chipichil roof. The original roof is now protected by a modern metal roof. Photo by Joe S. Graham.

designed for protection against the Indian raids that occurred in the region as late as the 1880s. Windows, which had no glass until the late nineteenth century, were provided with double shutters and wooden bars (and later iron bars, or *rejas*). The lintels over the doors and windows often were of hewn mesquite. The doors were most often French double doors of mesquite and cypress, furnished with hand-forged iron hardware. Some houses had massive stone fireplaces, though most apparently had separate kitchens of jacal construction.

In addition to the fortresslike walls, other aspects of construction also were influenced by the need for fortification. The main house at Dolores Viejo—South Texas' first ranch—included a watchtower. (This ranch was evacuated on several occasions because of Indian attacks, and finally was abandoned in favor of a safer location; only the foundations of the ranch structures still exist.) *Troneras,* which were gun ports in the walls or in parapets that often extended above the roofs two or more feet, were still being included in homes built as late as the 1860s. The gun ports were about two inches in diameter on the outside and expanded to about two feet by eighteen inches on the interior. The Jesús Treviño house (known as Fort Treviño) in San Ygnacio is an excellent example of this type of stone architecture.

Sandstone on the Texas side of the Rio Grande was available only in a fifteen- to twenty-mile-wide area bordering the river. Therefore, beyond this area, the building material of choice was sillar blocks, cut from the strata of caliche that covers almost the whole of South Texas, lying from six inches to three or four feet below the surface. Because of the ready availability of caliche blocks, the flat-roofed, rectangular structure of sillares was, except for the jacal, perhaps the most common type of early rural vernacular residence in South Texas. Working-class houses as well as *casas mayores* were built of caliche blocks. At Rancho Mota de Olmos, located about five miles east of Benavides and settled by the Bazán family in 1848, the original main house (dismantled about ten years ago) was an excellent example of sillar construction with troneras similar to those found in houses of sandstone construction. The two-room, rectangular structure had a flat roof. The walls extended up as parapets about five feet above the roof, and these walls had troneras to help protect against Indian raids. When Indians were in the area, the family would close the window shutters, bar the doors, climb through a hole in the roof, carrying water and food with them, and wait out the situation. Another, similar house, but without the parapet walls and the troneras, was built on the ranch at a later date and remains in good condition.

Flat-roofed, working-class houses of sillares can still be found in Bruni, Hebbronville, Benavides, San Diego, Alice, Kingsville, and other communities in the region, as well as on many ranches in the area. On El Guajillo, located in the same area as Mota de Olmos and settled in the 1860s by the Hinojosa family, one finds two examples of another style of house found in the area—the one-room house of sillares with steeply pitched gabled roof. The original roofs of the El Guajillo structures reportedly were thatched, but these were long ago replaced with roofs of

The first house built at Rancho La Mota de Olmos, Duval County, in the early 1850s was an excellent example of sillar construction. The house featured four troneras along the roofline and canales for draining the flat-roof. Courtesy of Joe S. Graham.

wooden shingles, which became available in the region in the 1870s. The sillar house type with steeply pitched gabled roof is far less common than the flat-roofed type.

While the dominant Mexican-American house form in West Texas is the flat-roofed adobe, ranch houses of adobe brick were rare in South Texas. Early records indicate that there were a few adobe dwellings in Laredo and in other South Texas communities, but they were the exception rather than the rule. No houses of adobe have been located on the ranches surveyed in the region. Some early travelers mistook sillar for adobe construction. One individual reported, for example, that the houses of Randado were built of adobe, when clearly they were of sillar. Culture, not environment, usually accounts for the house type in a given region, and, as Robert West has shown, the early settlers in South Texas came from areas of Mexico that had few if any flat-roofed adobes. Adobe dwellings in South Texas apparently were built for the wealthier classes living in towns, and these houses often had façades of handmade brick.

Flat-roofed, rectangular or L-shaped houses of brick or a combination of adobe and brick constitute another type of vernacular architecture in South Texas. Houses of this type are common in Starr County but far less common in Zapata County and in counties farther from the river. This is the predominant house type showing the influence of Mexican settlers in Roma and Rio Grande City. Such houses are also common in rural com-

COMMERCIAL ARCHITECTURE IN THE LOWER RIO GRANDE VALLEY

Commercial architecture in the Lower Rio Grande Valley originated with simple-one room adobe or jacal buildings containing both domestic quarters and commercial activities. Although more sophisticated emporiums segregated trade and living spaces in at least two rooms, it was not until the 1850s that buildings more readily recognizable as commercial establishments were being constructed in early settlement areas—such as San Ygnacio north of the Rio Grande and Old Guerrero south of the river. These buildings featured the use of coursed-stone, load-bearing walls, hewn wooden lintels and double doors, and shallow parapets concealing flat roofs that were drained by canales. The finer buildings sported decorative quoins, cornices, and, occasionally, wooden door molds. The preferred form was either an L-plan, enclosing a private area, or a rectangular plan, both with symmetrically placed double doors opening onto the street. The preferred location was a prime corner lot on the central plaza. The overriding cultural influences on the architectural style of these buildings derived from Spanish and Mexican building traditions.

By the late nineteenth century, commercial architecture had begun to reflect greater accessibility to industrially produced construction materials. The typical building featured load-bearing brick walls, machine-sawn wooden door and window surrounds, and a tall parapet concealing either a flat or hipped roof. While the preference for corner locations and the L-plan continued, the change from stone to brick as the major construction material allowed designers to build two-story structures and to define cornices and pilasters with corbelled brick. With the appearance of second stories came wrought-iron balconies, and the living quarters typically moved upstairs.

Late-nineteenth-century commercial buildings of the Lower Rio Grande Valley embody an artful confluence of Spanish, Mexican, and Anglo-American cultural traditions. The Spanish influence is reflected in the European practice of combining commercial and residential spaces under one roof. The Mexican is

Silvero de la Peña House and Store, built in 1886, Rio Grande City. Photo by Curtis Tunnell, THC.

demonstrated by traditional design responses to the local climate and by the use of local construction materials. And the Anglo-American is probably best shown in the architectural details of the buildings, which were derived from classical models in American-published pattern books or from nearby construction at Fort Brown and Fort Ringgold. Particularly fine examples of late-nineteenth-century commercial architecture are located in the historic district in Roma.

munities such as Escobares, Garciasville, and La Grulla, though less common on ranches in the area. Most of the brick (much of it handmade) in both Starr and Hidalgo counties came from the Mexican side of the river, although some was made on the Texas side.

Although brick construction became more common in towns from Brownsville to Laredo during the second half of the nineteenth century, the jacal long remained the typical house for most of the population of the region. However, as communities grew and cut lumber became more available and less expensive in South Texas, working-class Tejanos began to aspire to more socially prestigious house forms. Between the 1870s and the 1930s the jacal slowly gave way to a second-generation house type—the small, board-and-batten house (*casa de madera parada*). Ada L. Newton, conducting fieldwork for her master's thesis near Rio Grande City in the early 1960s, reported that "Today a cheap wooden structure is favored over this dwelling [the jacal] which would scarcely be larger than the jacal just abandoned. . . . A brick structure in any state of repair is better to the old citizen of the area than a well kept jacal; therefore, because of this feeling, the jacal is fast disappearing from the Rio Grande City landscape." Thus, the jacal did not disappear because it was not functional, for many were more functional than some modern structure types. It disappeared principally because it did not fit the changing esthetic and social demands or needs of its occupants.

The board-and-batten house usually began as a small one- or two-room structure built on a framework made of rough-cut 2 × 4 lumber and enclosed with 1 × 12s nailed vertically to form the walls. Smaller strips of lumber (1 × 4s) were then nailed over the cracks between the 1 × 12s

67

This house in San Benito shows the transition from first- to second-generation vernacular housing. The original jacal de leña section with its thatched roof is at right, while the later board-and-batten section, with its wooden shingle roof, is at left. The Institute of Texan Cultures, courtesy Mrs. Clara Zepeda, San Benito.

(hence the name board-and-batten, or box-and-strip). The typical early board-and-batten house had wooden floors and a gabled roof of wooden shingles, while later examples had roofs of galvanized, corrugated metal. As the family grew and as financial circumstances permitted, the family would add rooms to the back of the house and perhaps a porch to the front. The first addition was usually a kitchen, and the second, a bedroom. Many of these houses are still in use in South Texas, and as many as four additions have been made to some of the original structures. The board-and-batten house most likely evolved from the construction techniques used in building the jacal, rather than being borrowed from Anglo-American culture.

Small board-and-batten houses can be found on ranches and in communities throughout South Texas, including the largest cities (Laredo, Corpus Christi, Brownsville) and the smallest villages. Rows of such houses, for example, can be found lining the streets of the oldest sections of Laredo and in the working-class barrios of Brownsville. Starting in the 1930s and 1940s, these houses began to be replaced with small frame houses in the popular tradition. However, the tendency in South Texas is not to tear down older houses when new ones are built, but rather to convert the older structures to other uses, such as storage. Therefore, there are several ranches in the region where one can view the history of working-class architecture—from nineteenth-century house built of sillares, to early-twentieth-century board-and-batten house, then to the small frame house of the mid-twentieth century, followed by a small brick house or, more recently, a double-wide mobile home.

While early Hispanic vernacular architecture has had little impact on the region's modern popular and elite architecture, it still is a significant component of the built environment in South Texas. It remains as physical evidence of Hispanic history and culture in the region, so often denied—or at least ignored—in both popular and scholarly histories of Texas.

Dams, Wells, Watering Troughs, and Corrals

The availability of water, particularly drinkable water, has been critical to almost every aspect of life in South Texas since before the coming of the Spaniards. It was no accident that the early settlements in South Texas were located along the banks of the Rio Grande, where water was usually plentiful both for humans and animals. Many of the early houses built on both sides of the river featured elaborate water-collection mechanisms and cisterns. The farther from the river one lived, the more uncertain was the water supply. Raising livestock is especially dependent on water, and much of the pastureland in South Texas was essentially useless until the advent of the windmill in the early 1880s because there simply was no water available.

Ranchers who did not have access to the Rio Grande solved their water problems either by digging shallow wells or by building large dams across dry *arroyos* (gullies). Some ranches were located near flowing springs, but these were very rare. Although hand-dug wells were restricted to areas where potable water was only a short distance from the surface, examples can be found on many ranches and in communities throughout the region. The wells often were lined with whatever building material was available, usually brick, cut stone, or sillares. As a matter of fact, many ranch headquarters were located where they are precisely because water

The availability of water has been critical to every aspect of life in South Texas since before the coming of the Spaniards. Photo by David Langford.

69

was available at that place. In many areas of the region, drinkable water is as much as 2,000 feet and more below the surface. At present, water is still piped as much as twenty miles to areas without potable water. The quest for water continues to provide a challenge in some areas of Zapata, Webb, Starr, and Jim Hogg counties.

Old hand-dug wells exist in several locations in the region, including Rancho Randado, where the wells date to the 1830s. Few of these, however, have the *buques* or the long watering troughs that are characteristic of the oldest wells. Only two *norias con buque* have been documented in the area—one on the McAllen Ranch in Hidalgo County and another at San Isidro, a small ranching community in northeastern Starr County—that apparently date to the Spanish Colonial era (there has been no official documentation). The well of the noria con buque at San Isidro (believed by local residents to have been used by some of Santa Anna's soldiers on their way to the Alamo) measures about six by nine feet and is about 85 feet deep. It is lined with sillar blocks. The well and watering trough on the McAllen Ranch are made of stone set in lime mortar, rather than sillares. Both of these wells are accompanied by large watering troughs of Spanish design—significantly different from the standard tanks and troughs built later by Mexican-American and Anglo-American ranchers.

The buque structure of the well at San Isidro has one wall extending about four and a half feet above the ground level and two walls extending about eleven feet. Approximately eight feet above ground level, a large mesquite tree trunk was placed horizontally between, and set into, the two higher walls. This thick trunk was used to support the pulley system, and the large bucket was pulled by an ox, horse, donkey, or other animal. The water was brought to the surface and poured into two tanks, which hold about 6,000 gallons of water. These tanks feed into the attached watering trough. The watering trough, also made of sillar blocks, is about a hundred feet long. The trough is about fifteen inches deep and a foot wide, but it has a back wall about six feet high that prevented cattle from trying to climb over or into the trough. Water was drawn and stored in the tanks, then released into the trough as the cattle herds were brought in to water. This noria con buque is still in fairly good shape, but the mesquite trunk is gone, the walls are beginning to deteriorate, and the well itself is currently being used as a trash receptacle.

Other constructed sources of water in the region were reservoirs built to catch rainwater runoff. Two large dams built in the past century are still in use in the Zapata area: one on Rancho Randado in the western part of Jim Hogg County and the other on Rancho La Union, near San Ygnacio. Although only these two examples from the nineteenth century are known, there may be others as yet unrecorded. The earthen dam at Rancho Randado was built sometime between 1830 and 1850, and the exact method used in its construction is uncertain. The present owner, Rafael de la Garza (great-grandson of the founder of the ranch, Hipólito García), claims that the workers built the dam by loading dirt with shovels onto a steerhide, which was pulled by oxen. The dirt was dragged to the dam site and dumped, shaping the dam a little at a time, and packed by driving livestock over the dam. Beatriz C. Izaguirre records that the dirt was carried in hide containers carried by men rather than on steerhides pulled by oxen. She says that the workers used the *guaripa,* a four-handled cowhide container, and the *mecapal,* which was carried on a man's back and held by a strap across the forehead. Both sources agree that it took several years to build the dam, which was faced with sillares like those used to construct the buildings at the ranch headquarters. The dam reportedly once retained a five-acre body of water. Over time, floods have washed dirt into the dam and filled up the deeper parts of the original excavation in front of the dam. At present, the water covers about one acre.

The principal supply of water for Rancho La Union, owned by Guadalupe Martínez, is the water held by the dam on the arroyo that passes near the ranch headquarters. The dam is approximately thirty feet high, some two to three hundred feet long, and about twenty feet wide at the bottom. The front of the dam (facing the reservoir) is faced with cut sandstone set in lime and sand mortar. The stones were brought by wagon from a quarry about twelve miles away. Earlier, the dam had a spillway on one side, complete with a large, carved stone cup set on a base that bore an inscription giving the names of the builders, José María and Manuel María Uribe, and the date of completion 1874(?). When filled to capacity, the reservoir is between twenty-five and thirty feet deep and covers several acres. Like the dam at Rancho Randado, the dam at Rancho La Union was built by hand. Earth was moved from the excavation in front of the dam to the base of the dam on steerhides pulled by oxen. The earth was packed by driving livestock back and forth over it. The oldtimers in the area cannot remember the reservoir ever drying up, though a recent drought brought it to one of its lowest levels in memory—an estimated eight to ten feet deep.

The construction of earthen dams was made easier in the late nineteenth century, when earth-moving equipment of the type known as buck or fresno scrapers came into use. Dams built with this equipment, as well as more recent dams built with the heavy equipment of the twentieth century, have continued to play an important role in supplying the water needed by the ranches of South Texas, even though modern drilling equipment, windmills, and electric pumps have opened up supplies of good water far below the surface. The quest for a reliable supply of water— whether for drinking, agriculture, or industry—is still a problem in much of the region.

Unlike structures related to water sources, extensive fences are relatively recent on the ranches of South Texas. Before the coming of barbed wire to South Texas in the 1880s, the region was open range, with nothing but an occasional stone marker to divide the lands of the large ranches. Groups of ranchers held large roundups on the open range during branding and shipping times. Even in the days of the open range, however, fenced holding pens, or corrals, were a necessity. Corrals were an important component of every ranch. One of the most common types of corral, found on almost every ranch, was the corral de leña made of the region's abundant mesquite logs.

A roofed structure, storage tanks, and a long water trough are part of the old hand-dug well known as a noria con buque. This noria con buque near San Isidro is one of only two documented in South Texas. Photo by Joe S. Graham.

Before the advent of barbed wire, corrals were made of mesquite logs laid between upright posts. Photo by Joe S. Graham.

The corral de leña was constructed of parallel posts embedded into the ground about a foot apart and held together at the top with rope or other strong fibers or, later, with wire. The span between these sets of parallel posts varied from three to six feet, depending upon the size of mesquite trees available. Between these upright posts were laid horizontal mesquite limbs. The corrals varied in height from about five to as much as eight feet. Some were simple enclosures consisting of a single pen, while others were complex sets of corrals with several different pens. Rafael de la Garza states that his grandfather had as much as 15,000 acres enclosed in this type of fence on Rancho Randado. Diego Gutiérrez recently had two similar corrals built on his Rancho El Niño Felíz near Zapata. These are a combination of the old corral de leña and modern building materials—posts of steel pipe and heavy-gauge wire. In these recent corrals, as in many other small things of everyday life, the past and present are bound together in the ranching country of South Texas.

Conclusion

When José de Escandón and his followers came into South Texas almost two and a half centuries ago, they brought with them much more than the goods and possessions they carried in wagons and on horseback. They brought with them a culture deeply steeped in the ranching tradition of Spain and Mexico, a culture that had prepared them to cope with the many challenges of a harsh, arid, unsettled terrain where they had little access to the amenities of civilization. With them came craftsmen who would shape the built environment in the image of that which they had known in Spain and Mexico, adapted to new surroundings with different resources.

The same culture that helped the early colonists develop successful ranching practices also made it possible for them to take the materials at hand and fashion dwellings and other structures that would help establish a viable, productive community. It was no accident nor was it sheer genius that led them to fashion livable jacals and strong corrals from the abundant mesquite of the area; to quarry sandstone from the hills and riverbeds of the region and to discover and cut the sillar blocks that could be used to build safe, comfortable homes; to construct dams to collect reservoirs of water for large herds of cattle and the people who owned and worked them; to locate underground water and to dig wells that would permit them to inhabit the previously uninhabitable areas of South Texas.

We can read in the built environment left by these early Spanish settlers and their descendants the struggle to take possession of the land in the name of their God and their King and to bring civilization to the wilderness that was first known as El Seno Mexicano, then Nuevo Santander, and finally South Texas and Tamaulipas, Mexico. This built environment should—indeed, must—be preserved for future generations that they, too, may understand and learn from the contributions their biological or cultural ancestors made to the creation of a modern state.

Exploring the West Texas Borderlands

CURTIS TUNNELL and ENRIQUE MADRID

The Rio Grande flows southward from New Mexico, then southeastward to the Gulf of Mexico, forming a border but not a barrier between northern Mexico and Texas. In southwestern Texas, in the region known as the Trans-Pecos, the river meanders slowly through flat, desert-surrounded floodplains and rushes through deep, rocky canyons that it has tenaciously worn down through the centuries. The area where the river, finding its way through mountains and canyons, is forced into its sharpest and largest turn from south to north is known as the Big Bend. In this rough country, the Indians said, the Great Spirit dumped the stones and piled the unused earth left from the creation of the earth. This stony, arid, but majestic landscape reminds the visitor that the vast time scale of geological ages is the one that matters here, not the brief hours and minutes of man.

Spanish explorers crossed the Rio Grande and the Pecos River but avoided the interior they called *el despoblado,* the uninhabited land. The Spanish presence was limited to a handful of settlements such as those at El Paso del Norte and La Junta de los Ríos (where the Río Conchos joins the Rio Grande). After the passing of the Spanish empire, the Apaches and Comanches were left in possession of the lands west of the Pecos. During the nineteenth century the region served as a corridor for Plains Indian raids on settlements in Mexico, and the "Great Comanche War Trail" has become part of both the history and myth of the American West. During the period of Apache and Comanche domination, the remaining Indians of the villages along the Rio Grande probably were assimilated into the larger Mexican population along the river, both in Mexico and Texas. Only the Tigua Indians in El Paso, immigrants from New Mexico in the late seventeenth century, have maintained their ethnic identity.

In the West Texas borderlands American settlement occurred later than in other areas of the state for many reasons, the most important being the remoteness of the area from the urban supply centers of the eastern half of the state, the Indian raids in the area, and the aridity of the land itself. Following the Civil War, ranches were established—some of them, like Ben Leaton's, built as much like forts as ranch headquarters—but not until 1880, when the last of the Apaches led by Victorio were killed or driven from the area, were the great expanses of "free land" claimed by American ranchers and homesteaders.

The isolation and aridity of the Trans-Pecos has fostered the survival of some of the oldest elements of Spanish-Mexican-Indian heritage in Texas. Photo by Bob Parvin.

The isolation and the aridity that helped to delay Anglo-American settlement in this last Texas frontier have fostered the survival of traditions that are centuries, and even millennia, old: the use of wild plants for food, medicine, and fibers; the construction of dwellings and fences from available materials, like ocotillo and the earth itself; and the observance of religious and healing rituals that combine elements of Indian lore with Christian observances. All of these are to be seen in the small towns and villages that most modern guidebooks describe as "dusty," "remote," or even "primitive." For the visitor who wishes to see firsthand some of the oldest surviving elements of Spanish-Mexican-Indian heritage in Texas, and who has time to listen and observe, the small towns of the upper Rio Grande border are as rich a source as the famous Spanish Colonial centers of San Antonio and El Paso.

Desert Dwelling Places

Many structures in the border zone are made of locally available and inexpensive materials, and some of the construction techniques go back to early Spanish or even prehistoric times. After more than a hundred years of American settlement, the more affluent residents of the region have built fine buildings of stone or brick masonry, but wooden frame buildings are still rare because of the cost of shipping in lumber. For centuries perhaps the most common material used for vernacular architecture has been adobe, or sun-hardened mud bricks, which is much more common in this region than in the Lower Rio Grande Valley. Here one sees homes, commercial buildings, churches, and an occasional school built of durable adobe. Even the courthouse in Hudspeth County is built entirely of mud bricks, and it is believed to be the only government building made of adobe that is still in use in the region.

Although adobe was used in a few places in prehistoric America, the Spanish spread the use of this material throughout the arid lands of northern Mexico and the American Southwest. Using a few basic tools, the abundant materials at hand, and lots of hard work, one can still build a durable adobe at low cost. The thick mud walls also offer other advantages, being warm in winter, cool in summer, and easily repaired.

A relatively common sight in the desert region is an area covered with newly formed mud bricks drying in the sun. In the past, men mixed the mud, water, and straw with their feet in a broad, shallow pit. Now a cement mixer is commonly used to mix the mud to the proper consistency, but brick making for a new home still is often a family affair. A simple wooden mold, resembling a short ladder, is used to form three or four bricks at a time. The bricks are turned to expose alternate sides and dried for several days in the desert sun, until they become quite hard. They are then stacked until needed for construction of a new home or an addition to an older structure.

Mexicans and Mexican-American Texans have not been the only inhabitants of the borderlands to make use of mud bricks. The earliest

Mud, water, and straw are mixed to form adobe, then shaped in rectangular forms and dried in the hot sun. Photo by Bob Parvin.

Anglo-American ranchers, such as Ben Leaton and Milton Faver, made use of this indigenous construction material. Later ranchers, who came after the Indians were expelled from the region, also built with adobe. L.F. Buttrill established a ranch in the Rosillos Mountains in the late 1890s and housed his family in a traditional adobe. Although only ruins of his ranch headquarters now remain, they stand as mute testimony to the fact that Texas ranchers not only adopted Hispanic ranching practices, but Hispanic construction methods as well. The Buttrill ranch lands are now part of Big Bend National Park, where there are many examples of nineteenth- and early-twentieth-century stone and adobe buildings. Most of these buildings were constructed by Mexicans and Mexican-Americans, using locally available materials and traditional building methods. The buildings most easily accessible to visitors are those at Castolon, including the Alvino house, which is the oldest standing adobe structure in the park.

Homesteaders, too, found the building methods and assistance of their Mexican neighbors extremely useful. J.O. Langford, whose account of homesteading in the Big Bend is brief but perceptive, came to the Rio Grande in 1909 and was soon introduced by Mexican inhabitants to two ancient traditions that were witnessed by the first Spanish explorers—baking sotol hearts in pits and building houses of mud. Langford ate the sotol to be polite but found that building a home of mud bricks was a necessity, just as it had been for centuries of desert dwellers before him. Cleofas Natividad, a Mexican floodplain farmer "squatting" on the lands acquired by Langford, helped to build an adobe house and to acquaint the Langford family with other skills necessary to their survival in the borderlands.

In West Texas communities all the way from El Paso to the Pecos River examples of traditional, flat-roofed adobe houses still exist. At Fort Leaton State Historic Site, near Presidio, visitors can view Ben Leaton's

fortified adobe with its massive walls, reminiscent of the fortified ranchos of colonial New Spain and built to withstand both Indian and border-bandit raids. Yet another variation of adobe construction exists in Fort Stockton, where the Annie Riggs Memorial Museum is housed in a former frontier Victorian hotel, similar to the Territorial style homes of New Mexico.

Jacal construction is an even more ancient technique for making temporary homes and utilitarian structures. In general, the jacals still being built in the borderlands are less substantial than the early structures, like those in the Lower Valley, that were built as permanent homes. Usually, six or more mesquite posts are set upright to support an interwoven framework of ocotillo, sotol stalks, or river cane. This basic framework is sometimes hand plastered with mud both inside and out and allowed to dry in the sun. A thatch roof made of cane and grass completes the structure. One man using only a machete and bucket can quickly build an adequate jacal home for his family, a shed for his goats, or a corral for his horses. Jacals must be regularly patched and maintained, but they can last for years. However, they are becoming increasingly rare, even south of the border, as concrete blocks and other such materials become more readily available.

Another interesting construction technique seen in the border zone continues the tradition of using readily available materials, both natural

Jacals along the upper Rio Grande differ from their southern counterparts in their materials. Those of the Trans-Pecos are made with sotol stalks, river cane, or in this case, ocotillo stalks. Photo by Curtis Tunnell, THC.

and man-made. This recent construction type consists of a basic framework of posts and poles covered with sheets of steel and tin. The posts and roof beams are made of mesquite poles and large sotol stalks, much like those used in building a jacal, wired together into a sturdy frame. Sheets of steel made from flattened oil drums and corrugated sheet iron form a very durable wall when wired to the wood frame. Advantages of these structures include their ability to withstand hailstorms and the relative ease with which they can be disassembled and moved to a new site. The obvious disadvantage is that they are cold in winter and boiling hot in summer.

An observant traveler in the border zone will find many interesting examples of vernacular adobe, jacal, and sheet-iron construction. These structures are economical, functional, and often a source of pride to their owners. All of these human shelters are the material reflection of a long tradition of human adaptation to the arid lands of the Chihuahuan Desert in northern Mexico and western Texas.

Harvesting the Wilderness

Beauty is the chief utility of desert plants to modern West Texans, as anyone can attest who has ever visited the Chihuahuan Desert when the cacti are in bloom. The cactus family is indigenous to the Southwest, and over 100 species occur in Texas. The Chihuahuan Desert lacks some of the largest species, like saguaro, that dominate arid landscapes in other parts of the Southwest. Nevertheless, fields of cholla, pitahaya, and prickly pear provide their own spectacle when in bloom, adding vivid color to the austere desert scene. In addition to cacti, typical plants of the desert are yucca (the low-growing variety known as Spanish dagger, and two larger species), sotol, agave (including lechuguilla), ocotillo, desert willow, creosote bush, cenizo, and candelilla. Many of these plants have been utilized for thousands of years as sources of food, fiber, and construction materials.

Lechuguilla is one of the small, spiny agave plants prevalent throughout the Chihuahuan Desert. Spines of the plant can cause much discomfort and inconvenience by puncturing automobile tires or hikers' legs, and only javelina hogs attempt to get at the hearts of these prickly devils for food. The wise observer would, at first glance, judge the lechuguilla to be totally useless to man—but look again. In the desert nothing is wasted, not even the resources that are most difficult of access. Early Indians of the region devised ways of making sandals and other useful items out of the fibrous leaves of the lechuguilla. And in remote settlements along the border today are individuals who are skilled at turning lechuguilla fiber into a variety of useful articles, such as ropes, bridles, brushes, and brooms.

To fashion some items, only the more tender heart leaves of the plants are harvested. These are steamed in a bucket of water over an open fire until they turn amber in color. After the leaves are shredded by a sharp knife to remove pulp, the clean, white fibers are separated and spread to dry, usually on the flat roof of an adobe dwelling. When sufficiently dried, the fibers, which are very strong and durable, are gathered into loose bundles. Using a spinning device made from an old brake-drum or bicycle wheel, a skilled rope maker will spin long skeins that are then combined into tightly twisted ropes of varying diameters and lengths. These ropes are used for handling cattle and horses, tying bundles of candelilla and cane, and for a myriad of other purposes. Smaller-diameter fiber strings may be woven into durable bridles for horses and burros, or may be made into mesh bags for general utilitarian use. Some workers harvest the entire plant and remove the pulp from the fiber without boiling. After the bundles of fiber are washed, dried, combed, bound, and trimmed, the strong lechuguilla fiber makes good brushes and small brooms. In the desert, even the seemingly most noxious of plants can be converted into a valuable resource.

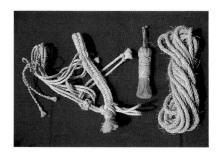

Lechugilla fibers, in addition to being made into ropes for cattle and horses, are also used in making bridles, bags, brushes, and small brooms. Photo by Curtis Tunnell, THC.

The candelilla plant yields a wax that few people in this country have heard of, and only a handful have seen the wax being produced, yet nearly everyone has had personal contact with this anonymous substance. If you have chewed gum, used cosmetics, worn shoes, fired a gun, ridden horseback, polished an automobile, typed a letter, played a phonograph record, or stepped onto a dance floor, you probably have encountered wax from candelilla plants.

Candelilla, a plant of the genus Euphorbia, grows on dry, limestone slopes in the border zone. Individual plants may have a hundred or more thin, gray-green, erect stems. The common name candelilla was applied to the plant because its smooth, vertical, wax-coated stems were thought to resemble candles. In remote canyons along the Rio Grande, men gather the wild plants, transport them in bundles on the backs of burros, and process wax from them in primitive, transient camps. The plants are processed in boiling vats, and the high-quality wax is skimmed off and cooled into caramel-colored blocks. Burro trains bring tons of wax out to ranches or villages where buyers acquire it for refining and marketing. Many people in the Chihuahuan Desert have survived by the back-breaking labor of extracting candelilla wax, and a few have grown rich from marketing it to large corporations.

A column of smoke in a remote canyon along the Rio Grande may lead one to a temporary camp of wax makers, where great mounds, containing tens of thousands of harvested candelilla plants, await processing. The men sleep in primitive, thatched shelters under mesquite trees and cook meager meals over open fires. After the "weed" has been boiled and its wax extracted, the remains will be dried and used for fuel to fire the vats. Hobbled burros graze around the camp until they are needed to help harvest more plants or to transport bags of wax out for sale. After remelting and further refining, the hard caramel-colored wax will be shipped out by the truck load to various manufacturers.

Among the most common products in which the wax has been used are chewing gum and breath mints, but it has also been used in a variety of other products, including floor wax, furniture polish, varnishes and lacquers, crayons, cosmetics, adhesives, and even lead pencils. During the

various wars of this century, candelilla wax was indispensable for water-proofing tents, tarpaulins, and clothing. Airplane parts were coated to lessen friction, and powder charges of naval guns were impregnated with the wax. Candelilla wax is also found in such diverse products as linoleum, plastics, rubber, ointments, dental castings, and molded figurines and toys.

Candelilla wax has more uses than any other product originating from a wild, uncultivated plant. However, all attempts to cultivate the plant have failed, and in this country attempts in the early twentieth century to industrialize wax production also failed. This wax has touched all our lives through a variety of products, but its primary production is still by means of hot, back-breaking labor and burro power.

Almost unrecognizable remains of early-twentieth-century wax-processing plants can still be seen in Big Bend National Park. At Glenn Spring in the southern part of the park, where one of the largest factories was established, little remains except half-dugouts that were the homes of Mexican workers. The factory at Glenn Spring was established in 1914 and was the scene of a notorious border-bandit raid in 1916. At McKinney Springs, in the eastern part of the park, ruins of stone walls and mounds of ash mark the location of another factory established by the owners of the Glenn Spring operation. At the end of World War I, wax prices dropped

Skimmers, usually handmade from tin cans, are used to transfer the foamy candelilla wax from the boiling vats into molds. Photo by Curtis Tunnell, THC.

The juice from sotol hearts, baked in stone-lined ovens, is fermented to produce an intoxicating and medicinal beverage. Photo by Curtis Tunnell, THC.

sharply, and all of the factories closed. Some of the West Texas factories reopened and prospered in the 1940s, but the only small factories still operating today are in the interior of northern Mexico. Transient wax camps have been the major source of production in Texas for decades, and archeologists have recorded numerous temporary wax camps along the border. These camps are one of the sights pointed out by guides in the course of the now-popular river trips through the canyons of the Rio Grande.

The maguey is the source of one of the best-known products derived from desert plants—tequila. A lesser-known liquor is made from the heart of the sotol plant and is still marketed here and there in the border zone. The sotol plant, a spiny pineapple of the Dasylirion genus, grows at higher elevations in the Chihuahuan Desert. The sweet hearts of these plants have long been used by desert dwellers to produce an intoxicating and medicinal beverage. Prehistoric Indians made a fermented brew by baking the plants in stone-lined earth ovens and then fermenting the juice. When the Spaniards arrived in the New World, they showed the Indians how to make the beverage even more potent through the process of distillation.

When U.S. troops were amassed along the border during the Mexican Revolution in 1916 and 1917, the sotol liquor business boomed. Then came the 1918 influenza epidemic, and it was widely believed that sotol, taken daily, would prevent infection. The demand for the tasty liquor skyrocketed and price was of no concern. The Volstead Act of 1919 made prohibition universal in the United States, contributing to the demand for sotol liquor. Through the 1920s, great numbers of people on both sides of the river were involved in producing and marketing it.

In addition to being an intoxicating beverage, sotol liquor is widely used as a medicine along the border. When a housewife or *curandera* (healer) acquires sotol for medicinal purposes, the liquor will be placed in a clay pot with various herbs, depending on the ailment to be treated. The liquid eventually becomes a rich amber color, and at the correct time the leaves and stems of the herbs are strained out and the medicine bottled. The potion is then ready for use by family members or the healer's patients. Medicinal sotol may be used internally in measured doses, applied externally as a liniment, mixed with grease as a salve, or combined with mud and made into a poultice.

The most common maladies treated with sotol-herbal brews are colds and influenza. A mixture of honey, lemon juice, and sotol is a cold remedy reminiscent of southern American home cures that use corn whiskey instead of sotol. Sotol and sugar are combined as a cough syrup for children, and a hot tea made from *yerba de vibora* and sotol soothes the symptoms of colds, grippe, and coughs in youngsters. A sotol and egg punch is also an effective treatment for colds and grippe, especially when sotol is also heated in a pan and rubbed on the throat and chest.

Sotol concoctions are also commonly used like rubbing alcohol or liniment. Camphor crystals dissolved in sotol make an effective lotion for skin rashes, and a plant called *guaco* is soaked in sotol to make a potent antidote for insect bites. Some cures recall the wondrous benefits that have long been claimed as justification for taking a little nip. For example, many believe that as long as you drink sotol you will never get sunstroke in the hot sun. Other medicines prepared with sotol have a less familiar ring— and undoubtedly a less efficacious result—including the mix of pulverized rattlesnake meat and sotol recommended for tubercular patients.

At a few remote places in the mountains of the Chihuahuan Desert there may still be found small *vinatas* producing this potent liquor. Hundreds of plant hearts are baked in rock-lined earth ovens and then chopped and fermented in wooden vats in the ground. The fermented soup is distilled twice in huge copper *peroles,* or kettles, over mesquite-wood fires. The final product is a clear liquor with a strong and distinctive flavor. While traveling in the border zone you may yet find a dusty bottle of sotol on the bottom shelf of a liquor store. If you do, use it wisely.

Faith and Folk Practices

The use of wild plants in medicines has been known in southern Texas since Alvar Núñez Cabeza de Vaca and his companions were living among the Texas Indians in the years following 1528. The Spaniards observed Indian medicine men using herbal preparations, bleeding, heat treatments, and other healing practices. Eventually the Spaniards were called upon to invoke the powers of their god through prayers and blessings in healing among the Indians. According to the Cabeza de Vaca narrative, many were healed and rejoiced.

This same combination of folk remedies, herbal medicine, and religious blessings is still used effectively by hundreds, or perhaps thousands, of folk healers known as curanderos. Healers may be male or female, young or old, and they are highly respected and frequently called upon in their communities. *Curanderismo,* the practice of folk medicine, is not limited to the western borderlands. Curanderos may be found all along the Rio Grande and throughout South Texas, in both rural areas and large cities. However, folk healing is particularly important in the isolated reaches of Trans-Pecos Texas and northern Mexico, where towns and doctors are few and far between.

Healers may be asked to treat all manner of illnesses, from croup and breech birth to headache and cancer. They may also be asked to free a child from an evil spell, help a person attract a lover, or bring good luck at bingo. A good healer will do his best to minister to everyone who seeks help. A wide variety of treatments may be used, including calling down the spirit of a saint to bless the patient, prescribing an herbal medication for a specified period of time, laying on of hands and massaging the afflicted area of a person's body, cleansing of a person with wands of herbs and religious crucifixes, preparing an amulet to be worn for a prescribed time, or burning a candle that has a particular prayer printed on the candle jar.

Prayers may be directed to a favorite saint or to a particular saint who is associated with a specific need. Popular Catholic saints in the border zone include Niño de Atocha, Saint Martín de Porres, Saint Joseph, and, of course, the revered Virgin of Guadalupe. In addition to these, there are two very important healers who are revered as folk saints. Don Pedrito Jaramillo is the famous "Healer of Los Olmos," who practiced near Falfurrias in the Lower Valley at the turn of the century. Statues and photographs of the bearded old man are common all along the border, and his shrine near Falfurrias is visited by thousands of devoted believers annually. Niño Fidencio Constantino was a famous young healer at Espinazo, Mexico, in the early twentieth century, and tens of thousands of pilgrims visit his shrine each year. Fidencista missions are found throughout South and West Texas, and his spirit is believed to continue to cure the ill through modern healers.

Contemporary healers differ from one another not only in the cures they use and the saints they call on, but in where and how they practice their art. Some healers work in their homes at carefully prepared home altars. A few may have small commercial healing centers, and still others practice their craft at special healing sessions held in the countryside. Some healers wear colorful robes and caps but most dress simply, in street clothes.

Curanderismo requires ready availability of many products such as blessed candles, packaged herbs, special soaps, incense, perfumes, and statues of saints. All of these supplies and a wonderful array of other amazing things can be found in *hierberías,* special shops found in all larger cities and some smaller towns across southern Texas. It is in these shops and in traditional Mexican markets that visitors will find evidence of folk healing practices. Many people throughout Texas and northern Mexico will attest to being healed through local practitioners of curanderismo. Folk medicine has served the people well for five hundred years and promises to continue for a long time to come.

The common folk, those who still build their homes of adobe, make lechuguilla rope, and use ancient herbal remedies, have until recently been

Curanderos use a combination of folk remedies, herbal medicines, and faith to heal all manner of illnesses. Photo by Bob Parvin.

almost entirely ignored in accounts of the history and heritage of Texas. Nowhere is there more poignant evidence of their lives than in the rural and small-town cemeteries of West and South Texas. Hispanic cemeteries, which are quite distinctive and beautiful, can often be recognized almost at a glance because of a profusion of elaborate and colorful decorations and distinctive grave markers.

There are differences in Hispanic cemeteries from region to region across the state, just as there are differences of class and wealth among people with Hispanic surnames, but all share common traits. The use of crosses, whether simple or elaborate, and the profusion of floral offerings are almost universal characteristics. *Nichos,* or niches, made of cement, tile, or wood to contain statues of saints adorn many graves. Hand-made but elaborate crosses may consist of timbers decorated with tacks, tile-covered cement, or cement set with glass marbles, or wrought-iron crosses made by a blacksmith. Grave markers may be given a bright coat of white or turquoise blue paint that gleams in the Texas sun. Graves may be covered with wreaths of home-made paper flowers, glasses filled with burning candles, religious statues, and toys or other personal belongings. Granite headstones are now more common, but these too are distinctive in decoration, often including ceramic photographs of the deceased or engraved decorations of favored possessions.

Plastic and silk flowers are beginning to replace those made of paper, but one still sees the traditional hand-made wreaths, known as *coronas,* in a wide variety of shapes and colors. Individuals will spend many hours making coronas for family graves, or occasionally for sale. In some remote communities along the border there are still families who subsist by making and selling beautiful paper cemetery wreaths. Colored crepe paper, paper napkins, and even aluminum cans are cut into various shapes and assembled into flowers attached to stems made of recycled electrical wire. The hoops on which the flowers are mounted may be made of strips of river cane or heavy electrical cords.

Although the arrangement of burials in Hispanic cemeteries may not emphasize family groupings, the closeness of family ties is reflected in the care given to the burial plots. Families often continue to clean and decorate family graves many decades after the people have died, and it is not unusual to see a baby's grave covered with flowers thirty or forty years after the infant was buried. Ancestors' graves may be maintained by third- or fourth-generation descendants who never knew the relatives they honor.

The well-maintained appearance and abundance of decorations in most Hispanic cemeteries is also in part a result of the traditional observance of Día de los Muertos (All Souls' Day) on November 2. On that day families gather at the cemetery and spend the day, and often most of the night, cleaning and decorating family plots and communing with their blessed dead. Older family members may sit pensively beneath hastily rigged sunshades while younger adults paint headstones, arrange flowers, cut weeds, sweep the ground, and light candles. Children also participate in the event, fetching and carrying brushes or other tools, buckets of water, and refreshments. Food and cold drinks bought from vendors are enjoyed by all, and there may be intervals of prayer and even singing. Mounds of fresh and artificial flowers cover graves throughout the cemetery for many days following this traditional observance. Graves may also be cleaned and decorated at Easter, Christmas, and on the birthday of the deceased, so there will always be some freshly adorned graves in every cemetery.

Terry Jordan, author of *Texas Graveyards,* has observed that Hispanic cemeteries are one of the last strongholds of folk customs in Texas, where popular culture has intruded but not yet conquered. These cemeteries, if we recognize their value and protect them from the incursions of urban development, will continue to be lasting memorials to the Hispanic heritage of Texas.

Adaptation and Conservation

Popular culture and mass-produced items may alter or even replace some folkways, but there is strong evidence that at least a few folk arts will merely absorb the new ideas or materials and survive, as healthy as ever. The tradition of piñata making has been changing ever since the custom of using plain clay jars was first adopted by the Spanish. A "teenage mutant ninja turtle" piñata recently seen in an Austin *hierbería* shows not that folk art is being changed by popular culture, but that folk art is alive and well, absorbing the new, using whatever it finds useful, and going about its way. For Hispanics in the Trans-Pecos using whatever is available and useful is a very old tradition indeed. Recycling of materials and resources is not a recent fad along the border. Conserving limited resources has long been a way of life in this vast and arid land.

Wood, one of the scarcest resources, is carefully used. In the adobe homes that are still common in the region, wooden roof beams may show signs of having been reused for decades or even centuries. In recent adobe buildings one may find irrigation pipes, discarded because of leaks, being used as a substitute for wooden roof beams. A wooden bow-top trunk can make an excellent beehive, and driftwood collected along the river is often fashioned into packsaddles for burros.

Metal, because of its durability, is particularly suited to adaptive reuse. A defunct automobile in someone's backyard is not perceived as junk, but rather as an almost endless source of useful objects. The body of the car may be used as a chicken coop or as a pen to protect baby goats at night. The back axle and wheels may be mounted under a wooden carriage to make a burro cart for hauling barrels of water. A section of the frame can serve as a rocking beam on a pump-jack for a water well. A leaf from one of the auto springs may be made into a fine machete by the local blacksmith. The smith can also cut and weld three or four car wheels into a long-lasting wood stove to heat the home. A brake drum may be mounted on a short post in such a way that it can be used to spin lechuguilla fiber into twine and rope. One of the most innovative examples of adaptive reuse was seen in a remote town where flat tires are a way of life and there is

Hand-made coronas, or wreaths, of brightly colored paper flowers are still being placed in borderlands cemeteries. Photo by Curtis Tunnell, THC.

no service station for miles. A local farmer salvaged the compressor from an old automobile air conditioner. With a little work it was converted into an air compressor that could inflate a flat tire in a few minutes time, and it had served him and his neighbors faithfully for years. Through the years an old car can thus be given new life in dozens of useful things around the desert homestead.

An old refrigerator lying on its back makes a good weather-proof tool box, and a hasp bolted to the side can be locked for security and safety. Many small homes have a kitchen stove made from a steel oil drum partially filled with sand and with a stoke hole cut in the side. A TV antenna can be made from a bicycle wheel, and a turkey cage can be fashioned of bed springs. And a popular, contemporary pleasure like "cooking out" can be achieved by refashioning a disc plow into a beautiful, curved steel stove called a *disco*. Materials like sheet iron, wire, and nails will be salvaged and straightened and reused time and time again.

In this region of sparse population and no cities, there may not be a local facility for recycling aluminum cans, but they will never go to waste. A can may find many uses other than being shaped into flowers for a wreath. With a twisted wire attached as a handle, a can hangs as a cup at the water barrel. Steel cans are commonly flattened, punched full of nail holes, and tied to a stick handle for use in skimming candelilla wax from a boiling vat.

Plastic and rubber items are especially useful, for the very quality that makes them such an environmental nuisance—they last for a long time. Bleach bottles that would be immediately discarded in a city will be used for years in desert villages. Hung on a saddle or a man's belt, a plastic bottle may serve for years as a water canteen. Along the river, bottles are also used as fishing floats. A penned pig eats his meals out of a plastic hard-hat from the oil fields. A yard fence can be constructed of plastic milk crates flattened and wired together into panels. Old tires can be cut in such a way that they form attractive planters for the front yard. Cut sections of tire treads may be made into soles for work sandals or hinges for a shed door. Old tires are also used to line interior corral walls to keep horses and riders from injuring themselves against the posts.

An important lesson can be learned by taking a close and appreciative look at how people in the borderlands use their limited resources. And, if there is ever any question of the relevance of anthropological and archeological study to the modern world, one has only to look to the Chihuahuan Desert. There adaptation to an arid environment and making the best use of limited resources are part of a continuum that is literally thousands of years old. What we learn about how prehistoric and historic people have lived and survived and changed there may well point the way for our own survival in an ever changing world.

Recycling is not a fad but a way of life along the border—here, three tire rims have been converted into a wood stove, and a trunk into a beehive. Photos by Curtis Tunnell, THC.

Spanish Mission Revival in Twentieth-Century Architecture

JAMES W. STEELY

The old mission buildings of El Paso and San Antonio, as well as scattered archeological evidence throughout Texas, are enduring reminders of the Hispanic culture's early foothold on our landscape. Our state's fabulous collection of Spanish and Mexican craftsmanship speaks to us of the builders' colonial intentions, their standard of living, and most especially their response to the geography of their remote assignments on the frontiers of New Spain.

The dominant features of Spanish Colonial architecture represent a skilled adaptation of Spanish architectural traditions to the needs and influences of life in the American Southwest. Plastered adobe or rough stone walls were a result of available building materials, and long, narrow porches formed by a series of round arches were a response to the climate. Elaborate ornamentation, although limited to larger buildings at their door and window surrounds, often represented a high degree of craftsmanship. The mission church ideally featured twin bell towers connected by a curvilinear parapet over the main entry. Flat roofs with ceiling poles, or *vigas*, projecting from the outside wall, a reflection of Puebloan Indian influence, are common in Texas and New Mexico. Tile-covered gabled roofs, a familiar solution from Mediterranean countries, are more common on original mission buildings in California.

A century ago this precious architectural and cultural legacy was threatened by neglect and outright destruction. An impatient new culture was busy exploiting the region's natural resources on an unprecedented scale, shoving aside the delicate evidence of earlier civilizations. But just as the settlement boom of the late 1800s seemed ready to erase the genuine past, a new appreciation for the region's Spanish heritage developed as a popular movement. By 1900 twin bell towers, baroque stone carving, barrel-tile roofs, and curved parapets were incorporated into the vast "revival" vocabulary of the era's builders and architects.

What we now call the Spanish Colonial Revival style of architecture was but one of many revival movements popular throughout the United States after the Civil War. The closely related, turn-of-the-century Mission Revival style is set logically within the longer-running Spanish Colonial movement. Also connected to these styles is the more encompassing Spanish Renaissance Revival, because the New World precedents from the fif-

Although the Alamo church had become an enormously popular tourist attraction by the time this photograph was taken (1912–1920), its influence on new architecture was not as strong as that of the other San Antonio missions or their California contemporaries. THC photo.

Opposite: San José Mission's famous Rose Window, carved from local San Antonio limestone in the late 1700s, is among the greatest works of Spanish Renaissance art in the New World. It has been reproduced on countless Mission Revival style buildings. Photo by James W. Steely, THC.

teenth- through nineteenth-century Spanish Colonial period were an extension of, and a source of wealth for, the general Renaissance of Spain itself. The climax of all this Hispanic revivalism in the United States occurred between the world wars, as most Spanish Colonial examples had been exhausted by architects, and direct precedents from Renaissance Spain were copied.

Other nineteenth- and twentieth-century revival styles—which led to the creation of "American colonial" homes, "classical" churches, "Romanesque" courthouses, and "Italianate" railroad stations—were based on precedents from somewhere else. By contrast the Spanish past of Florida, Texas, and the Southwest provided solid regional prototypes for new architecture, revealed not only in neglected mission complexes but in humble adobe residences and churches, stone presidios and pueblolike governmental buildings as well. By the 1920s from California to Florida various interpretations of "Spanish" characteristics were hugely popular for residences and institutional buildings, particularly small- to medium-size railroad stations.

Contributing to a popular revival of Spanish Colonial designs was the temperate climate of the southern and southwestern United States. In general the early Spanish builders had felt at home with this landscape and found familiar building materials—stone and good soil for sun-baked bricks—to create comfortable shelter in the region. The modern industrial culture's new building technologies made many of the original construction methods obsolete, but the efficiency, charm, and simple ornament of the Hispanic buildings were affirmed as appropriate to the geography (and importantly, the romanticized past) of the region.

The earliest popular interest in Hispanic precedents for modern building designs in Texas can be traced to the 1880s. The Alamo church became state property in 1883, but this early preservation effort grew more from an interest in the 1836 revolution than from the building's role as anchor of the eighteenth-century Spanish mission San Antonio de Valero. The Alamo church's design influence, spun around its distinctive curvilinear parapet, possibly was an early influence but would not be obvious in new buildings of the Spanish Colonial Revival for another thirty years.

In the 1880s builders and the new professionals calling themselves architects relied largely on pattern books and a growing list of periodicals for their inspiration. The building designer's real talent went into a durable structure and functional interior. The exterior was finished by craftsmen following the designer's and owner's attempts to make their building distinctive. Included in the wide range of published style choices based on historic examples were "Moorish" details. These appeared on San Antonio's First National Bank Building in 1886 in the form of horseshoe arches, a minaretlike corner turret, and arabesque reliefs carved in local limestone.

No research has yet proved that the bank's owner, G.W. Brackenridge, and New York architect Cyrus Eidlitz made a connection between San Antonio's heritage and the Moors' ancient influence on Iberian cultures. However, these same exotic details were employed momentarily by other

James Riely Gordon of San Antonio designed the State of Texas Pavilion at the 1893 Chicago World's Columbian Exposition. Drawing liberally from the eighteenth-century missions of his home town, he gave the structure twin bell towers and "rose windows." Courtesy of Architectural Drawings Collection, University of Texas at Austin.

builders around the state, on Houston's Federal Building (1888, gone), the mosquelike Texas Spring Palace in Fort Worth (1889, gone), and the Aransas County Courthouse in Rockport (1890, gone).

The Aransas County Courthouse was designed by young San Antonio architect James Riely Gordon. Gordon's maturing designs in the 1890s showed a keen understanding of Texas climate and building materials—much as his Spanish predecessors had—and he probably thought the Moorish examples appropriate to the region. By 1892 he was completing drawings for the new Bexar County Courthouse in San Antonio, continuing this theme with a "beehive" spire akin to the Brackenridge bank's turban-capped turret. As early as the year before, Gordon and his partner, D.E. Laub, were commissioned to design the state's pavilion at the planned 1893 world's fair at Chicago.

One year off the intended jubilee but grandly named the World's Columbian Exposition, the fair was a herculean effort to celebrate the 400th anniversary of Columbus' arrival on the continent. The monumental main buildings of the fair and its vast landscape manipulation caused a sensation in American decorative arts and urban planning, focusing mainstream commissions on Greek and Roman classicism for the next half century. Nevertheless, many state buildings represented an early recognition of

The soaring skylit ceiling and classical garlands lined with hundreds of lights reveal the impact of the Beaux Arts school on the interior of San Antonio's Southern Pacific Railroad depot. Photo by Cathryn Hoyt, THC.

"regionalism," and Gordon's Texas pavilion clearly acknowledged the missions of San Antonio in some details.

The Texas building erected at Chicago was in many ways a typical exercise in the most popular design approach of the time, known as the Beaux Arts after the French design school. Gordon's was a formal and imposing design, symmetrical and generally complicated with porches and towers. Yet these towers flanked the entrance much like the ideal Spanish mission church, such as Concepción in San Antonio. And the elaborate windows beside the entry doors were copied directly from the unique "Rosa's Window" (or Rose Window) at Mission San José.

The California building at the 1893 fair also mimicked that state's missions from early Spanish colonization. The state's exhibition hall, bigger than the Texas pavilion and a more sophisticated approach to adapting the historic mission church façades to a new building, exerted a much stronger influence on subsequent architectural trends than did Gordon's design, even in Texas. Waco's celebrated 1894 Cotton Palace (burned, replaced by a simplified version, gone by 1940) was a direct copy of the California building. Even Gordon soon embraced other revivals for his designs, successfully incorporating Romanesque and then Renaissance details into his several courthouses through 1900.

California Mission Revival in Texas

The Mission Revival in California soon became a very popular regional trend. In the two decades following Chicago's fair the movement inspired a wide range of interpretations there, including countless hotels, churches,

schools, apartment houses, and government buildings. And the best of these designs were picked up by publications and exposed to the rest of the country, including Texas. The handful of known Texas buildings reflecting the Mission Revival between 1893 and 1915, including Waco's Cotton Palace, Fort Worth's Livestock Exchange (1902), and Brenham's Blinn College main building (1906) ironically were closer to the churches at Carmel and San Luis Rey than to the Alamo and San José.

One of the best Mission Revival designs in Texas came directly from California and forecast one of the most prolific adaptations of Spanish design to a new building type. The Southern Pacific Railroad passenger station in San Antonio was designed in 1902 by the railroad's San Francisco office. This cathedral of transportation combines many Spanish and Mediterranean elements, such as arcaded porches and barrel-tile roofing, with other bold features such as broad Romanesque arches. Its huge curvilinear parapets at each end reaffirm the impact of the 1893 California pavilion at Chicago; this time-proven profile is repeated in bulkheads for the adjacent former restaurant and express-freight wings. Inside the main passenger waiting room, the even stronger impact of the Beaux Arts school is evident in a soaring skylit ceiling and classical garlands lined with hundreds of lightbulb sockets.

The Southern Pacific continued to build Mission Revival depots on its main line west to California and east to New Orleans for years to come, and there are several other surviving examples in Texas. Southern Pacific's

San Antonio's Southern Pacific Railroad depot was designed by San Francisco architect D. J. Patterson and was inspired by California's 1893 world's fair pavilion. Courtesy of Ed Kasparik, Texas Railroad Commission.

1905 Union Station in El Paso is an unusual composition with an interesting history. Its main concourse is a miniature Roman bath hall, reflecting the popular prototype for larger railroad terminals in the eastern and midwestern United States. Its startling "witch's hat" tower contrasts so obviously with the "bath's" Beaux Arts classicism that the railroad removed the spire in 1941 and painted the whole building white to resemble stucco. The occasional fine line between some Beaux Arts and Mission Revival designs of the period was crossed with this remodeling, causing the building to pass, from a distance, as a mission derivative. These alterations were reversed in a 1981 restoration of the red brick complex and its tower.

The El Paso terminal was designed by the Daniel H. Burnham Co. of Chicago, whose namesake had controlled building designs for the 1893 fair. In that capacity Burnham apparently was responsible for insisting that Texas and California submit state pavilion designs based on their "regional" Spanish missions. Yet just as the genuine Texas missions in San Antonio were largely ignored for the next fifteen years of the Mission Revival movement, so were El Paso's own Spanish missions neglected as inspiration for that city's 1905 Union Terminal design.

The Socorro Mission church, one of three founded near El Paso in the late 1600s, survives today much as it was last rebuilt in 1843, with a distinctive square *espadana*, or bell parapet, over the central entry. The churches along the Rio Grande at Ysleta and San Elizario by contrast have been rebuilt many times in the past two centuries, and their most recent rehabilitations benefitted—full circle—from the Mission Revival early in this century. Ysleta's current façade, rebuilt after 1907, is a near copy of the much imitated San Luis Rey mission church north of San Diego, California. The curvilinear parapet of San Elizario, probably dating from 1935, bears a close resemblance to that of the 1893 California pavilion at Chicago!

Expanding Mission Revival Influences

San Antonio's final railway terminal construction, built in what was an obligatory style for that city and Texas railroads by 1917, was at last based on local mission prototypes. The entry pavilion to the Missouri, Kansas & Texas (Katy) Railway depot (gone), designed by New York architect Frederick Sterner, took fairly precise measurements from the façade of Mission Concepción's twin-towered church. The depot's elaborate main door surround was inspired by that of Mission San José. Parapet gables at the sides of the building, however, were typical California curvilinear arches, again from 1893 in Chicago, that adapted so well to the waiting rooms and train sheds of this building type.

The Katy depot in San Antonio, though built in a style becoming quite familiar to local citizens, was a result of the next great phase for the Spanish revivals. The 1915 Panama-California Exhibition in San Diego created an entire complex (now Balboa Park) of buildings on the theme of Spanish Colonial and Spanish Renaissance designs. Once again a large international exhibition caused a strong national reaction in architectural

The last major railroad depot project in San Antonio, the Missouri, Kansas & Texas depot, finally recognized the presence of Spanish missions in the city. Courtesy of Ed Kasparik, Texas Railroad Commission.

trends. (The Panama-Pacific International Exhibition, held the same year as the "world's fair" in San Francisco, received higher attendance, but its eventual architectural influence did not match that of the San Diego event.) Soaring towers encrusted with carved details, colorful low domes, and the extensive planting of palm trees on the surrounding landscape excited the previously restrained trend of mission inspirations. San Diego's elaborate exhibit hall designs, many by architect Bertram Goodhue, went beyond the historic mission prototypes of the American Southwest, taking cues from more elaborate churches in Mexico City, Central and South America, and Spain. This broad examination of Latin America and Europe reflected the fair's purpose of celebrating the 1914 opening of the long-awaited Panama Canal. But in addition, a growing awareness before World War I of historic Spanish buildings outside the United States indicates how the earlier Mission Revival led various periodicals to photograph and study an ever widening range of examples.

In addition to a fresh burst of Mission Revival depots, another new building type became associated with Spanish decoration after 1915. Theater interiors, particularly elaborate projects spanning the transition from stage entertainment to movie projection, were designed to transport the customer to a brief exotic vacation, and a Mediterranean or Caribbean paradise was a popular "destination." The Majestic Theater in San Antonio, designed in 1927 by renowned "atmospheric theater" architect John Eberson, is the state's best example of such an interior fantasy. The lobby ceilings are incredible plaster creations duplicating the richly textured woodwork of *Mudejar* (Moorish) craftsmen. The auditorium walls are lined with backlit architectural vignettes of mission façades and towers, complete with palm fronds and tropical birds. The ceiling is pierced with tiny lights in star patterns; originally vaporizers sent clouds billowing across the "night sky." Several other theaters in Texas survive from this golden age following the San Diego fair when entertainment and tropical Spanish decorations were synonymous.

During the general economic boom of the 1920s in Texas, not only theaters but city halls, hotels, retail businesses, homeowners, and churches found an appropriate identity in Spanish Renaissance prototypes. Oil discovery towns in particular—from Beaumont, Kilgore, and Longview to Eastland, Cisco, and Big Spring—all feature various buildings from this popular trend well into the Depression of the 1930s. The power company West Texas Utilities built a series of office buildings across their service area during this time, with examples surviving in Ozona and Fort Stockton. National and regional publications continued to be the vehicle for this widespread popularity; wherever the railroads went and mail was delivered, even the most remote town could keep up with the latest innovation from California, Florida, and the Midwest. Prefabricated architectural details made this stylistic proliferation possible as well, so that cast-stone solomonic columns or colorful terra-cotta arabesque reliefs made in St. Louis or Chicago could be shipped to any building site in the nation near a railhead.

The ornate Southern Pacific Railroad depot in Brownsville, built in 1928, is an excellent example of the surviving Mission Revival railroad depots in Texas. Photo by Cathryn Hoyt, THC.

The Majestic Theater in San Antonio, designed in 1927 by John Eberson, is the state's best example of the lavish "atmospheric theaters" from the golden age of Spanish Revival architecture. Vignettes of Spanish mission façades line the auditorium walls. Courtesy of Las Casas Foundation.

Arcaded walkways, such as this one at Texas Tech University, are characteristic of Spanish Revival buildings and are particularly suited to the Texas climate. Photo by James W. Steely, THC.

ST. FRANCIS ON THE BRAZOS
A Mission San José Replica in Waco

The Church of St. Francis in Waco was conceived as a memorial to the first Franciscan missionaries in Texas and to the return of the Franciscan Fathers to Texas in 1924, after an absence of more than one hundred years. The famous Mission Church of San José in San Antonio, dating from 1768, was selected as an appropriate model to honor the Franciscans. The Waco church is dedicated to St. Francis, under whose patronage Mission San Francisco de los Tejas, the first church dedicated to Christian worship to be built in the Spanish province of Texas, was constructed in 1690.

Roy E. Lane, the architect for St. Francis, began plans for the Church of St. Francis in 1928. He made several trips to San Antonio to familiarize himself with the original Mission San José and completed numerous sketches, but he did not attempt to slavishly copy the original. His stated goal was to preserve the atmosphere of the original in its exterior appearance. Because of the differences in terrain between the two sites, he carefully studied the perspective and foreshortened vistas and proportions to give a similar impression of the outline and mass of the original. Therefore, the tower of St. Francis is different in proportion and is reversed from that of San José. However, the ornamental stone façade is the same size and proportion as the original, and the famous Rose Window is duplicated on the side wall of the baptistry transept. In designing the interior, Lane used a modern adaptation of Spanish Renaissance style. He described this approach as allowing an interesting composition of Roman, Moorish, and Spanish Gothic motifs in the ornamental details.

The cornerstone of the Church of St. Francis was laid on March 15, 1931, and the church was dedicated on Thanksgiving Day, November 26, of that year. The church is located at 301 Jefferson in Waco.

St. Francis on the Brazos Catholic Church, Waco. Photo by Cathryn Hoyt, THC.

Dozens of congregations built new Mission Revival churches in this period. St. Francis Catholic Church in Waco, completed in 1931, is a reasonable facsimile of San Antonio's Mission San José. Many small Catholic churches, including examples at Crockett and Nacogdoches, chose to copy the diminutive chapel at Mission Espada. Other Catholic congregations hired San Antonio architect Leo Dielmann to design their sanctuaries in abstracted Spanish derivatives, including those at Brenham and Abilene. Many churches other than Roman Catholic also opted for Mission Revival style. The Alamo Methodist Church in San Antonio, which features twin towers flanking an arched parapet, reflects Spanish Colonial and Mission Revival styles. The Central Christian and English Lutheran churches in Austin both mirror the era's regional identity with its romanticized Spanish past.

Among the largest architecture commissions, and some of the best examples, of the Spanish Renaissance Revival in Texas came from university building programs. The University of Texas at Austin continued during a twenties and thirties construction boom with its design theme begun before 1910 and based on Italian and Spanish Renaissance precedents. Several imposing buildings of limestone and buff brick, with shady roofs of red tile and typical decorations from the Spanish Revival, were built during this period. When the Texas Technological College began planning its new campus at Lubbock in 1923, much comment was made about the appropriate selection of Spanish examples. They related both to the state's early history and to the "great table lands of west Texas . . . [which] have likeness in color and character to the table lands of central Spain," according to their concept architect William Ward Watkin. The resulting Main Building at Texas Tech owes its proportions and stone details directly to the University at Alcalá de Henares in Spain.

Outshining even the university projects of the period, the construction (begun in 1929) of Randolph Field for the Army Air Corps north of San Antonio created a huge planned community, all in Spanish Revival. Housing, hangars, a chapel based on the local missions, and other support facilities are all stuccoed and topped with red-tile roofs. The main building, nicknamed the Taj Mahal by early flying cadets, is a sprawling structure at the center of the complex. Rising from its administrative wings is a massive "Moorish" tower, disguising a 500,000-gallon water tank, topped by a shallow dome painted in yellow and blue zig-zags. Here the occasional fine line between late Spanish Revival buildings and Art Deco is easily perceived.

Still another new building type, the shopping center, embraced the Spanish Revival movement between the wars. Suburban commercial strips in Dallas and Oak Cliff, Amarillo, Corpus Christi, and San Antonio dress up their storefronts with Alamo parapets, false roofs of red tile, miniature niches and iron balconies, and other familiar details. Highland Park Shopping Village of 1931, one of the first planned shopping centers in the nation, was designed by Dallas architects Fooshee and Cheek after a trip to Barcelona to study the historic Renaissance and world's fair examples directly.

The close of this heyday of Spanish architectural revival in Texas came fittingly with major restoration projects for most of the historic mission complexes themselves. Long neglected throughout the century following their secularization, even during the Mission Revival of the 1920s, these missions found relief through local and federal public works programs during the 1930s Depression. In San Antonio the Alamo church received a stone interior floor and a wall around the compound, San José's entire church roof was rebuilt and its old courtyard reconstructed, and the ruins of Espada and San Juan were investigated and stabilized for public enjoyment through New Deal programs. In El Paso the chapel of San Elizario was rebuilt after a fire in 1935. At Goliad the church of Mission Espíritu Santo was reconstructed. And Spanish archeological sites were investigated in several locations. Public officials and their constituents wholeheartedly supported these church restorations, perhaps because the more recent Spanish Revival buildings around them had presented a subconscious and persistent history lesson.

Although World War II ended the popular revival trends in American architecture, the Spanish presence in Texas still provides a strong sense of regional identity. Fortunately the San Antonio and El Paso missions are still the subjects of restoration and interpretation projects. And their contemporaries are still an occasional inspiration for new designs. From a bar in Austin with its façade featuring the entire Alamo church front and Taco Bell food joints with their trademark *espadana* parapets, to more subtle uses of patios and earthen finishes in modern motels, offices and homes, the revival, and the legacy, are still with us.

Churches, Chapels, and Shrines
Expressions of Hispanic Catholicism in Texas

HELEN SIMONS and RONI MORALES

In the last two decades of the seventeenth century, with the establishment of the Spanish missions of El Paso del Norte and the early missions of East Texas, the Spanish colonization effort and Catholicism were formally initiated in the part of northern New Spain now known as Texas. From the 1680s until secularization of the missions began in 1793, the Franciscan fathers were the stabilizing element of Catholicism in Hispanic Texas. When the missions were secularized—converted to parish churches—the missionaries departed to other fields of service and Catholicism passed into the hands of the diocesan priests.

During the Spanish Colonial period, in addition to the well-known missions, secular parishes had been established in San Antonio, Laredo, La Bahía, San Juan Bautista on the Rio Grande, and El Paso (then part

Missions San José, Concepción, Espada, and San Juan Capistrano still serve as active parish churches. Mariachi masses are held on Sundays at San José and draw many visitors to this centuries-old mission church. Photo by Bob Parvin.

Opposite: San Agustín Church, a Gothic Revival structure with a five-story tower and spire, dominates San Agustín Plaza in Laredo. Photo by Bob Parvin.

of New Mexico). In 1810, when Mexico began its struggle for independence from Spain, a long period of turmoil began, disrupting the expansion of the church. By 1830 there were only two Franciscans remaining in Texas, one in Goliad and one in San Antonio, and by the end of 1834 there were none.

When Texas declared its independence from Mexico, the old missions were confiscated by the new republic, and during the years of the republic communications between Mexico and the remaining Catholic churches in Texas were hampered by continued hostilities. Nevertheless, the Catholic hierarchy directed renewed attention to Texas in 1838, and reorganization of the Catholic Church in Texas began in 1840. In 1847, following the United States War with Mexico, the status of the church's jurisdiction in the state of Texas was raised, and the first diocese, the Diocese of Galveston, was created. In geographical extent, this was a very large diocese indeed, but part of its territory was still disputed. The Treaty of Guadalupe Hidalgo, in 1848, accepted the Rio Grande as the Texas-Mexico boundary, but Texas continued to argue with the U.S. government over the extent of the state's territory to the north and west. The disagreement was finally ended by the Compromise of 1850, settling not only the size of the state but of the new Catholic jurisdiction in Texas.

Although the establishment of the Diocese of Galveston began a period of renewed growth of the Catholic Church in Texas, it also created new problems. Many of the newly installed, non-Spanish-speaking clergy were strangers to the area as well as to the people and their customs. The anti-Mexican and anti-Catholic attitude of post-independence Texas continued into the early statehood period, adding to the difficulties of the church. And the extreme poverty of many Hispanic communities was a barrier to the construction of new churches. Nevertheless, in the ranching area of South Texas, many traveling missionary priests were uncommonly dedicated and sensitive to the needs of the region's Spanish-speaking people. They also were instrumental in establishing many churches that are now considered not only architectural but historical treasures of the late-nineteenth century.

In the early years of statehood, Texas recognized the claim of the Catholic Church to several of the mission churches, and the active life of these historic structures was renewed. Most of these centuries-old buildings continue to serve as active parish churches today, and their congregations include members who are descendants of the original Native American and Spanish inhabitants of the mission settlements. Spanish Colonial missions, more than any other historic site or artifact, symbolize Hispanic heritage in Texas. The mission churches and presidio chapels of San Antonio, El Paso, and Goliad are not only inseparable from the early history of the state, they also bear witness to the Catholic heritage that still is central to Mexican-American community life. These churches and chapels are of national historical importance, and their dramatic histories and architecture have overshadowed other churches whose historic roles are set in more local scenes.

CHURCHES, CHAPELS, AND SHRINES

Historic Churches

Most of the hundreds of Catholic churches in Texas' Mexican-American communities postdate the period of statehood, but there are several historic churches whose structures or congregations reflect the long continuum of Hispanic heritage in Texas. The oldest parish church in Texas, San Fernando Cathedral, is a historical contemporary of San Antonio's Spanish missions. As part of a short-lived Spanish plan to populate the province of Texas, sixteen families were sent from the Canary Islands to San Antonio in 1731. The Canary Islanders formed the first formally organized civil government in Texas and founded the Villa of San Fernando de Béxar. The people of the villa attended church at Mission San Antonio de Valero (the Alamo) for a short period, then built a temporary chapel in the presidio. In 1738 they began construction of their first permanent church on the west side of the town plaza. San Fernando, which opened in November 1749, was the first parish church in San Antonio and is one of the oldest in the Southwest.

Many leading Texans of the Spanish, Mexican, and early Texas periods were baptized, married, or buried at San Fernando. Heroes of the Texas Revolution associated with the church include both Mexican-Texans such as Juan Nepomuceno Seguín, who was baptized there on November 3, 1806, and Anglo-Americans such as James Bowie, who married Ursula María de Veramendi there on April 22, 1831. However, neglect of the church, which began with secularization of the missions, escalated during the early nineteenth century, when the structure was damaged by floods and fire. Then came the confusion and turmoil that prevailed in San Antonio during the struggle for Texas independence, and by 1839 San Fernando Church was reported to be almost in ruins.

Fortunately for the survival of this important link with the Spanish Colonial period, a long series of renovations and enlargements of the church began in 1840. By 1863 the population of the parish required a larger building, and extensive additions were made to the original church. Architect François Giraud designed a classical Gothic Revival building to be built over the old church, with the old transept becoming the sacristy of the new church, and reconstruction was completed in 1873. When the Diocese of San Antonio was created in 1874, San Fernando became a cathedral. The twin bell towers of the cathedral were part of Giraud's design, but the second tower was not added until the early twentieth century. During this period stained glass windows also were added, a communion rail and marble altar were installed, and tile and terrazo floors were laid. In 1926 San Antonio was elevated by the Catholic Church to an archdiocese, headed by a bishop. Renovations were again undertaken in 1974–76, and the cathedral was rededicated in 1977. The church has existed under four different dioceses—Guadalajara, Linares, Galveston, and San Antonio—and five governments—Spain, Mexico, the Republic of Texas, the Confederacy, and the United States. Despite floods, fires, revolutions, and re-

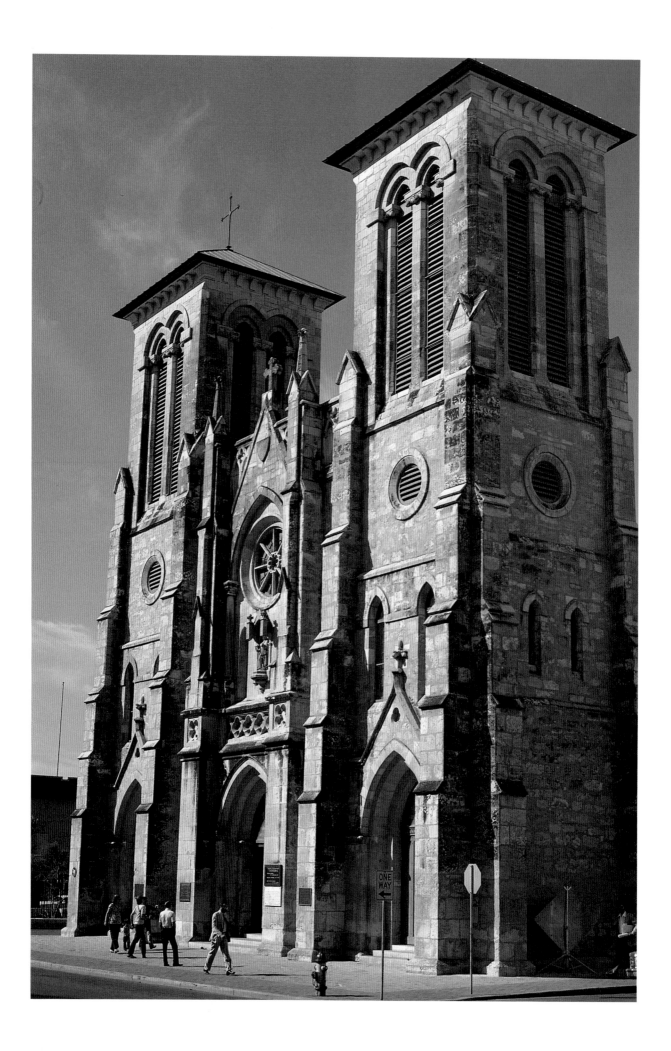

constructions, the church of San Fernando remains as a historic reminder of life in old San Antonio and a significant expression of Hispanic Catholicism in Texas.

In Losoya, in the greater San Antonio area, stands the bell tower of an 1877 church that is a poignant reminder of the last years of the Spanish Colonial period. At this site in 1817 the original mission chapel of Nuestra Señora del Carmen was erected as a memorial to the heroes of the Battle of the Medina, fought nearby in 1813. The encounter was an unsuccessful attempt by Anglo, Mexican, and Indian Texans in the Republican Army of the North to free Texas and Mexico from Spanish rule. The 1877 church, the third structure at the site, was built over the site of the crypt of the original church. The 1877 church was replaced in 1967, but its bell tower still stands between the new El Carmen Catholic Church and the old parish cemetery.

Not only San Antonio but all of South Texas was affected by the secularization of the missions and the end of the Spanish Colonial era. In the late 1830s there was only a handful of priests to serve the entire Rio Grande Valley. Although the Mexican Church continued to provide priests along the Rio Grande throughout much of the 1800s, many priests during the latter half of the century were Oblates. The Missionary Oblates of Mary Immaculate were attracted to the region in the 1840s, following the end of the United States–Mexican war. One of these early missionary priests, Father Pierre (Peter) Yves Keralum (1817–72) was ordained in France, in 1852, where he had also studied architecture. That same year he came to South Texas and began a life of service that was to affect both the tangible and intangible expressions of Catholicism in South Texas. Father Keralum designed several important churches, but he was known as "El Santo Padre Pedrito" for his dedicated missionary work. Evidence of his architectural skill can be seen at San Agustín in Laredo, the Cathedral of the Immaculate Conception in Brownsville, the Church of Our Lady of Refuge of Sinners in Roma, and Our Lady of Visitation Church, near Harlingen.

Like San Fernando in San Antonio, San Agustín Church in Laredo is the focal point of an area that reflects a historical continuum from the colonial period to the present. Laredo was founded in 1755 by Tomás Sánchez de la Barrera y Gallardo as part of José de Escandón's settlement of the Lower Rio Grande Valley. In its early years the settlement had no missionary or priest, but depended on the minister at Revilla. In 1767 the village of San Agustín de Laredo was formally settled and laid out, and the first resident secular pastor was sent to the Laredo-Dolores area in the early 1860s. San Agustín Church has its roots in the adobe church built in this period. This parish is the second oldest in Texas to be administered by diocesan (or secular) priests, and it too has survived through revolutions, counter-revolutions, and several relocations. The present church structure was designed by Father Keralum and built in the late nineteenth century. A masonry, Gothic Revival structure with a five-story tower and spire, the church dominates San Agustín Plaza and forms the nucleus of historic Laredo.

Opposite: **San Fernando Cathedral was established by colonists from the Canary Islands and is the oldest parish church in San Antonio, and one of the oldest in the American Southwest. Photo by Bob Parvin.**

Roma, located on a high bluff above the Rio Grande in Starr County, was founded on *porciones* (plots of land) allotted to residents of the Escandón settlement at Mier, south of the river. Members of the Salinas and Sáenz families established ranches on their plots in 1757. The lands around the ranching settlement that was to become Roma apparently changed hands, and for a while the town was known as Garcías. In the 1840s, entrepreneur Richard Stillman purchased land from the Garcías, and the town became known as Roma. The first chapel in Roma was built about 1840 by volunteer labor on a donated site, of contributed materials, and is still standing (it is now a museum). Secular priests from Mier served the chapel until Oblate fathers arrived in 1853.

Roma flourished during the era of steamboat trade on the Rio Grande, and the Oblate Fathers described it as one of the most picturesque towns along the river. On September 18, 1854, the cornerstone for Our Lady of Refuge Catholic Church was laid at the east end of the town plaza, on land given to the Oblates by the García family. The structure, designed by Father Keralum, was not immediately completed, and the church was not active until the late 1860s. At that time Roma, located halfway between Laredo and Brownsville, became the center of a parish equal in territory to the largest dioceses of many more metropolitan areas. The tower of the present church remains from the 1850s building, a reminder of the architectural and missionary legacy of Father Keralum.

More recent than the Roma church or San Agustín in Laredo, Immaculate Conception in Brownsville is important not only for its architectural significance but for its role in the history of American Catholicism. Four priests of the Oblates of Mary Immaculate came to Brownsville from Canada in 1849 and built a chapel at the site of the later permanent church. This chapel was the first permanent settlement of the Oblate Fathers in the United States. The Immaculate Conception church was completed in 1856–59. Designed by Father Keralum, this stuccoed brick structure with its central entry-bay bell tower is a fine early example of the Gothic Revival style, which was not widely popular in Texas until the 1880s. Although a single-story structure, its walls are 40 feet in height and the entrance tower rises to an imposing 88 feet. Thirty-eight stained glass windows grace the cathedral. The interior features a floor of green terrazo and a rib-vaulted ceiling panelled with blue-painted canvas lined with gold leaf. The rectory, built in 1861, was the site of the first Oblate Seminary in the United States, and it also served as a haven for priests fleeing the turmoil of revolutions in Mexico. Immaculate Conception became a cathedral in 1874, but its status was revoked after only eight months, when the bishop moved to Corpus Christi. The Diocese of Brownsville was established in 1965, and restoration of the cathedral occurred in that year and again in 1970, following damage by fire. Designed by a French priest for a largely Hispanic population in a town named for an Anglo-American soldier, Immaculate Conception Cathedral truly reflects the multicultural heritage of South Texas.

Santa Maria, near Harlingen, is located in an area that was settled in the eighteenth century by colonists from the Escandón settlements. Our

Lady of Visitation Catholic Church has served the residents of Santa Maria, Bluetown, and other communities for over a hundred years. Built from plans drawn by Father Keralum, the Gothic Revival church was dedicated June 29, 1882. The building was constructed of locally made bricks, and many of the original furnishings, including the altar, pews, and confessional, are still contained in the church.

In the ranching country of South Texas, chapels that served extended families or the communities that grew up around ranch headquarters were common, and several architecturally and historically important examples have survived. One of the best known is La Lomita Mission, south of the town of Mission in Hidalgo County. The original adobe chapel here was built in 1865 on a rise of land that contrasts with the surrounding plain, giving the chapel its name, which means "little hill." The chapel was visited by horseback-riding Oblate missionary priests who served the ranches midway between Brownsville and Roma. Late-nineteenth-century floods destroyed the first chapel, and a second was built in 1899. This small, twelve-by-twenty-foot, stuccoed stone building has a small bell tower topped by a simple cross, reflecting the austere and modest lives of the missionaries who served here. The small scale and simplicity lend to the charm and intimacy of the interior, where interesting features include the original pews and railings, and the exposed framing and open truss work of the ceiling.

The chapel was neglected somewhat after the Oblates relocated their main church in Mission, and it was further damaged by hurricanes in the 1920s and 1930s but was restored in 1949, the 100th anniversary of the arrival of the Oblates in South Texas. The complex at La Lomita also includes other historical reminders of the Oblates, including the surrounding land that was used for farming and ranching, a convent, and St. Peter's Novitiate, a training center for priests. Both the convent and the novitiate continued in use until the late 1950s. The two-story novitiate is a brick structure in Spanish Revival style, featuring twin towers, arches, and a low-pitched, tile roof.

One of the most beautiful ranch chapels of South Texas is found on the Toluca Ranch in the vicinity of Progreso in Hidalgo County. Founded by Florencio Sáenz in 1880 on lands that were part of the Llano Grande land grant of 1790, Toluca is one of the few South Texas ranching complexes to survive intact, still owned by the founding family. The complex consists of four buildings, the church of St. Joseph the Worker, the ranch house and store, and the schoolhouse. The earliest of the four buildings is the church, built in 1899. It is a handsome Gothic Revival design, with a tower placed at the main entrance. The tall doors, with lancet-shaped panels in their upper sections, are set in a lancet-arch opening. The main body of the church is cruciform in plan. Interior decoration is largely confined to the chancel, which has a fine wooden altar rail across its width. The altar is arranged in four tiers, with statues of St. Joseph, the Virgin Mary, and the Sacred Heart of Jesus, each framed by a lancet arch in the end wall. The surfaces of the ceiling vaults are formed by canvas, painted a deep blue.

The simplicity and charm of La Lomita Chapel is reflected in the interior, which still contains the original pews and railings. Photo by Cathryn Hoyt, THC.

113

Only a few towns that derive from ranching settlements of the brief Mexican national period (1821–36) in Texas have survived. Victoria, on the central coastal plain, was founded in 1824 by Martín de León, one of the most successful of the Mexican-Texan colonizers. He and his sons also are credited with being among the most significant instigators of profitable, large-scale cattle ranching, an industry that was vital to the growth and development of nineteenth-century Texas. One of the first acts of De León's Victoria colonizers was the establishment of a church, but many of these families fled to Mexico for safety after 1836. The church was reorganized in 1840, and in 1863 a new brick structure was built on land donated by De León's widow. St. Mary's, the successor of Victoria's first church, is a Gothic style building constructed in 1902–04. Other Catholic parishes have since been formed in Victoria, generally along ethnic or cultural lines. Our Lady of Lourdes was built in 1875 for a predominantly German parish, while the twentieth-century church Our Lady of Sorrows was established to serve a predominantly Mexican-American congregation. St. Mary's, however, has continued to serve the descendants of the early Mexican, Irish, and Italian settlers of Victoria.

Throughout South Texas there are recent structures that are the successors of much older churches. Our Lady of Refuge Church in Refugio, for example, had its beginnings in the 1793 mission Nuestra Señora de Refugio. Part of the old mission was converted into a chapel at the site in 1845, and in 1866 a stone church was built. The third church at this site, the present frame structure, dates only from 1901 but its historic beginnings are commemorated in the bell from the mission that is on display in the church.

East Texas also boasts at least one church whose beginnings go back to the Spanish Colonial period. The history of St. Augustine Catholic Church, the oldest church in San Augustine, dates to the establishment of Mission Dolores. When the Catholic Church was reorganized after the Texas Revolution, this church became a mission within the Sacred Heart Parish of Nacogdoches. The first church building at the present location was built in 1881 and replaced in 1937. In August 1975, after 259 years as a mission, the church became a vicareate seat.

In far West Texas, as in San Antonio, more recent churches are dominated by the mission churches of the Spanish Colonial period, located in the El Paso area at Ysleta and Socorro. The Ysleta Mission church still serves the Tigua, for whom it was founded in the 1680s. In the Presidio, Texas–Ojinaga, Mexico, area, some residents may trace their ancestry to the Indian villagers of the upper Rio Grande for whom missions also were established in the 1680s. More typical of the region are the St. Joseph's Catholic churches in Fort Stockton and Fort Davis, adobe structures that date from 1876. Early settlements grew up around the forts, but most of the region attracted few settlers until the late nineteenth century. Well into the twentieth century, the small towns of the Big Bend were still being served by priests from Fort Davis. This still-sparsely settled area boasts few imposing structures, but there are a number of simple churches that reflect the persistence of tradition in the small towns of West Texas. The churches

in Fort Davis, Marfa, and Marathon are noteworthy because they combine Gothic Revival influences, popular at the turn of the century, with indigenous adobe construction. In this region also are a few surviving ranch chapels, as well as houses and buildings of adobe and stone, that reflect the endurance of a Hispanic population whose ancestors were there when the first Catholic missionaries arrived.

Located on a private ranch near Lajitas, this small adobe chapel has survived the ravages of time. Photo by David Alloway, courtesy of Fresno Ranch.

Twentieth-Century Churches and Shrines

The Virgin of Guadalupe has become a common denominator of Catholicism among Hispanics of the American Southwest, and she is the patron saint of hundreds of twentieth-century churches in Texas that bear her name. The revering of Nuestra Señora de Guadalupe dates from the early Spanish Colonial period in Mexico. In December 1531 in the hills north of Mexico City, the vision of a woman dressed in robes of turquoise blue is said to have miraculously appeared to Aztec Indian Juan Diego. Speaking to him in his native tongue, she offered to all of the inhabitants of the land her love and protection and requested that a temple be built at the site. As proof of his vision, Juan presented to the bishop his *tilma*, or cloak, on

115

which was imprinted in brilliant colors the image of Our Lady. The tilma, now enclosed in glass, is enshrined in the Basilica of Our Lady of Guadalupe in Mexico City. Miracles were soon attributed to the Virgin of Guadalupe, and her appearance to Juan Diego is credited with having brought about the conversion of more than seven million Indians within a few years. By the time of Spanish exploration into Texas, a significant portion of the native population of Mexico, Spaniards as well, had embraced the brown-skinned madonna.

Our Lady of Guadalupe churches are to be found not only in predominantly Hispanic areas such as San Antonio and South Texas, but across the state. Not surprisingly, many of the early Hispanic Catholic churches in the Panhandle were established for communities made up largely of railroad workers. For example, Our Lady of Guadalupe in Amarillo was constructed to serve the city's Hispanic community in 1920, although the present brick, Mission Revival style church was built in 1949. The church's statue of Our Lady, retained from the old church, was originally purchased in 1916 with funds donated primarily by Spanish-speaking railroad workers. In Central Texas, the name Our Lady of Guadalupe immediately distinguishes Hispanic community churches from those of other ethnic groups, such as Czechs, Poles, and Germans, that are also common in the region. Our Lady of Guadalupe in Austin is an imposing American Federal style church originally built in 1907 and restored in 1953. However, its architectural significance, like that of the numerous churches that share its name, is secondary to the role it plays in community life.

Our Lady of Guadalupe in San Antonio is an excellent example of an urban, twentieth-century church that plays a major role in Hispanic community life and in the preservation of cultural traditions. Established in 1911, the church now occupies a structure completed in 1926. Under the Jesuit fathers, who took over the parish in 1923, efforts were made to preserve the traditions of the Mexican-Americans in the parish, and the presentation of religious dramas such as Los Pastores, Las Posadas, and Las Mañanitas was encouraged. The Guadalupe Players of San Antonio have become the state's best known performers of Los Pastores. Particularly important to all of the churches dedicated to Our Lady of Guadalupe is December 12, the annual feast day of the Virgin of Guadalupe. Observances, especially in the larger churches like those in Austin and San Antonio, include as many as ten special masses during the twenty-four hour period, the singing of morning serenades, and special prayers. Folklórico dancers wearing brilliantly colored costumes and flowered or feathered headbands, mariachis in their traditional garb, and charros displaying daring feats of horsemanship may also be part of special events held throughout the week, and Protestants as well as Catholics gather to enjoy the festival and share in its message of hope and cultural continuity.

Hispanic Catholics in Texas still undertake pilgrimages to sacred sites to fulfill a promise, give thanks, or request a great favor. The favored destination of the devout is the Basilica of Our Lady of Guadalupe in Mexico City, but Texas has two shrines that attract pilgrims from throughout the state and from Mexico as well. The most elegant of the two is the Shrine of

Images of Our Lady of Guadalupe, the patron saint of Mexico, can be seen on and in countless Hispanic Catholic churches in Texas. Photo by Cathryn Hoyt, THC.

HOME ALTARS

The Virgin of Guadalupe, her image depicted in paintings or statues of wood or plaster, is a popular figure in the home altars of many Mexican-American families. Less common today than they were three or four decades ago, home altars are still a traditional Mexican-American religious expression. In isolated rural areas, especially in Mexico, where access to churches is limited, such altars are especially important to the devout. Home altars, often placed on a table or the top of a chest in a bedroom, contain collections of sacred images, crucifixes, candles (often in glass jars depicting an image of a holy figure), incense, *medallitas* (saints' medals), flowers, family photographs, and other personal items arranged on an altar cloth. In addition to the Virgin of Guadalupe, other favored images are those of the Virgin of San Juan (or La Milagrosa), the Sacred Heart of Jesus, and El Niño de Dios, although prayers may be addressed to other saints, depending on the need expressed in the prayer. Each altar is unique to the person who created it, usually a woman, and is the center of the family's spiritual life. The home altars of folk healers, or *curanderos,* may be especially elaborate and often contain images of the popular "folk" saint and healer Don Pedrito Jaramillo.

Home Altar. Photo by Jane E. Levine.

In San Antonio, the first public presentation of Los Pastores, a Christmastime folk drama depicting the struggle between good and evil, was presented in 1932. Courtesy of the Institute of Texan Cultures.

117

Our Lady of San Juan of the Valley, in San Juan, Hidalgo County. This beautiful structure, built with 24-inch-thick limestone walls, features terrazzo floors and faceted glass windows. It houses a replica of Our Lady of San Juan de Los Lagos of Jalisco, Mexico, an eighteen-inch statue revered by migrant farm workers. The statue is set in a ceramic altar backdrop that was created in Barcelona. The shrine serves as a point of pilgrimage for Catholic worshippers from both Texas and northern Mexico. On a simpler scale, and more closely allied to folk practices, is the shrine dedicated to Don Pedrito Jaramillo, near Falfurrias. One of the most famous of all *curanderos,* Don Pedrito was a healer of the late 1800s who is credited with many miraculous cures. The shrine contains a lifesize, seated statue of Don Pedrito, and in the chapel are numerous mementos of cures attributed to him and petitions for his help. This shrine is still visited by believers and descendants of those who knew him, and he has achieved folk-saint status in the borderlands.

Most Mexican-American Texans continue to embrace the Catholic faith, but no ethnic group is a monolith, even in its most significant characteristics. Many Mexican-Americans are members of Protestant faiths, and their churches range from the simplest small-town chapel to elegant structures in major cities such as El Paso and San Antonio. Nevertheless, the material expressions of Hispanic Catholicism in Texas are among the richest aspects of the state's multicultural heritage. The ancient dignity of the Spanish missions, the majesty of San Fernando Cathedral, the charm of La Lomita Chapel, and the simplicity of the adobe churches of West Texas appeal to Texans of all classes, and ages, and faiths.

Decades after the death of Don Pedrito Jaramillo, believers still travel to Falfurrias to visit his shrine and leave momentos of cures attributed to the South Texas folk saint. Photo by Curtis Tunnell, THC.

119

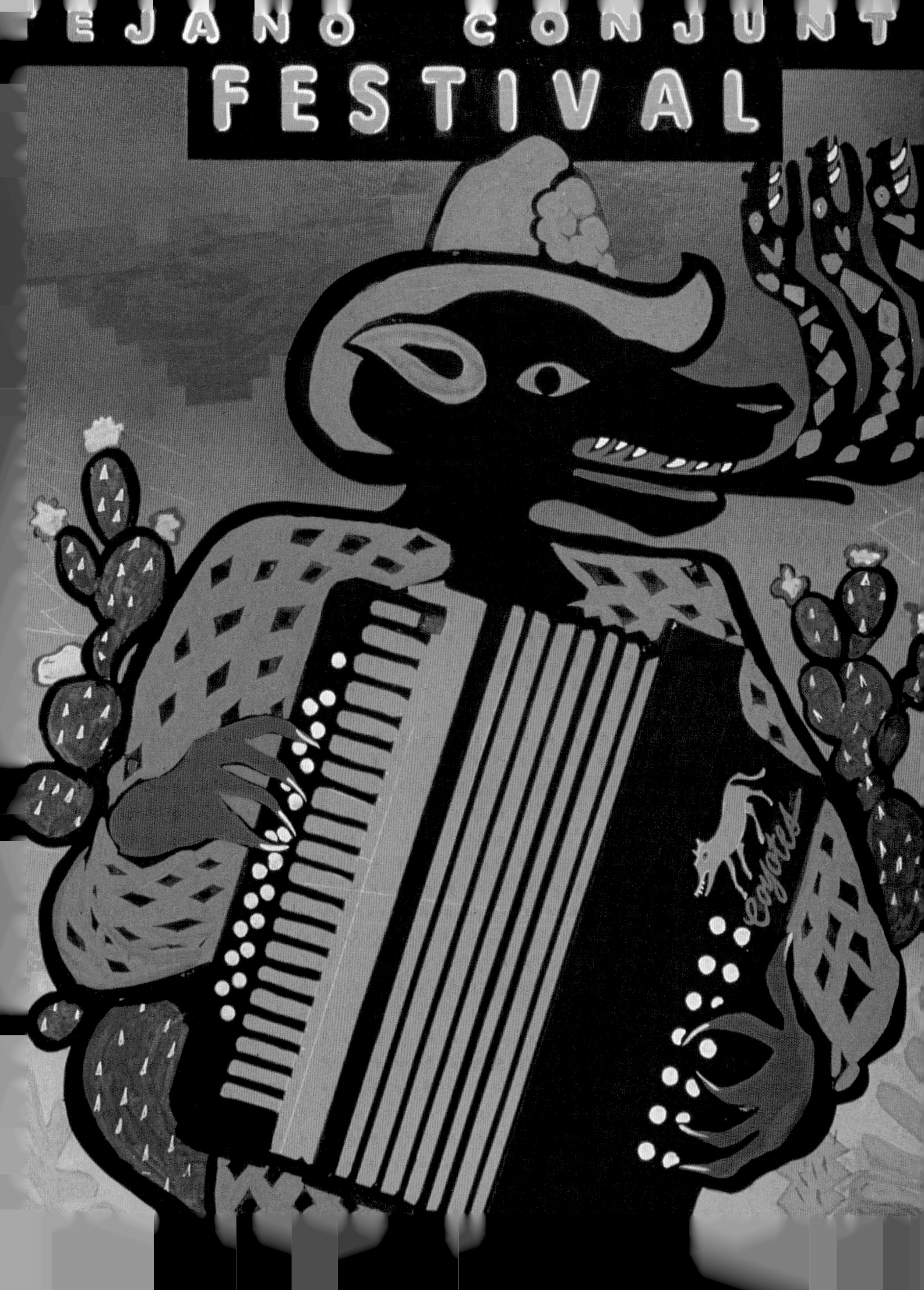
EJANO CONJUNT
FESTIVAL
Coyotes

Tejano Festivals
Celebrations of History and Community

ANN PERRY

Festivals that celebrate Hispanic history and culture are enjoyed by Texans of all ethnic backgrounds, all across the state. Swinging piñatas, spiraling folklórico dresses, spicy tamales, and strolling mariachis are but a few elements of the lively and colorful Mexican-American fiesta tradition. Promoting goodwill between sister-cities along the border, commemorating the anniversaries of historic events, and recognizing and perpetuating Hispanic folklife are but a few of the excuses to *echar todo por la ventana y divirtirse*—to "throw everything out the window and enjoy oneself."

Three festivals in particular, El Día de la Raza, Diez y Seis de Septiembre, and Cinco de Mayo have acquired such renown that Texans of diverse ethnic backgrounds find themselves commemorating Columbus, thrilling to Padre Hidalgo's stirring words, and cheering Zaragoza annually. Yet, despite the long history of Hispanics in Texas and their growing demographic presence, many lifelong residents of the Lone Star State respond only with sheepish grins when asked to explain the historical significance of even these well-known festivals, much less the social signifi-

Texans of all ethnic backgrounds enjoy the color and pageantry of Tejano festivals. Photo by Jesse Herrera.

Opposite: San Antonio's Tejano Conjunto Festival is the largest of its kind in the world, attracting music lovers from as far away as Japan. Poster by Jesse Almazan, courtesy of Guadalupe Cultural Arts Center, San Antonio.

cance these and other festivals hold for Mexican-American communities. Hispanic festivals—from the Valley's widely known Charro Days to the regional Olton Mexican Festival in the Panhandle—are important components of Tejano (Texas Hispanic) folklife. They are significant to their host communities because festivals are a means of transmitting history and values, perpetuating traditional arts and crafts, and renewing community bonds.

Columbus Day (October 12), known as El Día de la Raza (the Day of the Race) to the Spanish-speaking world, commemorates the arrival of Columbus in the "New World"—and the beginning of *mestizaje,* the blending of Spanish and Native American cultures. Houston, with its large Mexican-, Central, and South American population, hosts the largest Columbus Day festival in Texas. The Institute of Hispanic Culture presents El Día de la Raza Festival Folklórico, bringing together dancers, musicians, and international Hispanic stars from over fourteen Latin American countries. Farther south, in the predominantly Mexican-American town of Falfurrias, Columbus Day is a time to celebrate the city's *mexicanidad* (Mexican-ness). To Gustavo Barrera, founder and organizer of the local festival, El Día de la Raza "makes us aware of our diverse Mexican cultural heritage, gives us pride in preserving Hispanic history and ways of life, and provides an excellent opportunity to promote Hispanic heritage throughout our community."

Diez y Seis de Septiembre (September 16) and Cinco de Mayo (May 5) are *las fiestas patrias,* the patriotic festivals of Mexico and Mexican-American Texans. Diez y Seis de Septiembre commemorates the anniversary of Padre Miguel Hidalgo's impassioned call for social justice, the famous "Grito de Dolores" (Cry from Dolores), during Mexico's war for independence from Spain. At about 2:00 A.M. on September 16, 1810, Padre Hidalgo rang the bells of his church in Dolores, Guanajuato, and shouted to his impoverished Indian parishioners, "Will you free yourselves? Will you recover your lands? Will you not defend your religion and your rights? Long live Our Lady of Guadalupe! Death to bad government!" Although Padre Hidalgo was eventually executed for his beliefs, his words inspired those who continued the struggle for equality and continue to inspire those who fight for social justice today.

Cinco de Mayo, a celebration of Mexican national sovereignty, commemorates the victory of General Ignacio Zaragoza and his 3,000 troops over 5,400 invading French troops at Puebla on May 5, 1862. The French invasion ultimately succeeded and led to a brief period of occupation (1864–67), but Zaragoza's initial victory strengthened Mexican national pride. Today, Zaragoza's victory is celebrated annually all across Texas, but nowhere as joyfully as in Goliad, the general's hometown. The Sociedad de Ignacio Zaragoza, formed to honor Goliad's native son, has sponsored Cinco de Mayo fiestas at the general's birthplace since 1948, staging a Battle of Puebla reenactment that is the only one of its kind in the United States.

The patriotic festivals are the most widely observed among Mexican-Americans in Texas, but scores of other events with Hispanic themes are

Father Miguel Hidalgo's famous "Grito de Dolores" is commemorated during one of the fiestas patrias, Diez y Seis de Septiembre. Courtesy of the Institute of Texan Cultures.

held around the state. San Antonio alone offers at least fifteen throughout the year, and the city's Christmastime Las Posadas, along the scenic River Walk, is one of the most famous Christmas celebrations in the United States. The candlelit procession is based on an old Spanish religious pageant depicting the Holy Family's search for an inn. From El Paso to Brownsville, festivals express and preserve cultural ties that transcend the international boundary between Texas and Mexico. In Laredo observances of July 4, as Borderfest, and Washington's Birthday are unique expressions of the cultural mixture along the lower Rio Grande.

Mexicanidad is celebrated not only through the historical and cultural significance of these festivals, but also through traditional music, dance, games, sports, and arts and crafts. Mariachi, Mexico's most prestigious music genre, is one of the best-known types of ethnic music in Texas and can be heard at every Tejano festival. Mariachi music, originally a folk genre played exclusively on stringed instruments, gained its name during Maximillian's short reign in the 1860s, when French culture swept Mexico.

Mariachis have been an integral part of Hispanic festivals for many years. These mariachis performed at Brownsville's Charro Days in 1939. The Institute of Texan Cultures, courtesy Corpus Christi Public Library.

123

The name *mariachi* is thought to derive from the French *mariage* (marriage), associated with the musical ensembles because they so often played at weddings. About 1940 a "commercial" mariachi style, characterized by the addition of the trumpet to the stringed instruments, began to develop in major Mexican cities. It is almost exclusively this type of mariachi that is found in Mexico today. However, mariachis playing only stringed instruments and singing their romantic songs may still be found serenading the diners in Mexican restaurants in Texas and strolling among the evening crowds at traditional festivals.

The sweet sounds of the mariachis are often followed by the foot-stomping rhythms of *conjunto*. Also known as *norteño* music (from the north, between Monterrey and San Antonio), conjunto originated in late-nineteenth-century Mexico, blending Mexican rhythms with German and Austrian polkas and schottisches brought to Mexico by European industrialists during the presidency of Porfírio Díaz. Working-class Mexicans adopted the accordion as their own, soon realizing how much cheaper it was to hire one accordionist than an entire orchestra, especially since an accordion could simulate nearly as many instruments. Today the accordion is usually accompanied by the *bajo sexto*, an amplified twelve-string guitar, as well as the electric bass and drums.

Foot-stomping rhythms, complex footwork, and colorful costumes have made ballet folklórico a perennial favorite at Tejano festivals. Courtesy of Office of State Senator Gonzalo Barrientos.

In 1925, Hector Carillo and Jessie Magnon performed the Jarabe Tapatio at the Mexican Blue Cross Convention in San Antonio. Courtesy of the Institute of Texan Cultures, *The San Antonio Light* Collection.

By the early twentieth century, a unique style of conjunto music had developed in South Texas. Known as *Tejano conjunto*, this music is now nearly synonymous with the conjunto style. Three regional variants have evolved: the San Antonio, a fast-paced style with simple accordion fingering; the Coastal Bend (or Corpus Christi) style, featuring slower tempos but complex accordion fingering; and the Valley, a Mexican-influenced style featuring a slower tempo and vocal duets. In recent years, Tejano conjunto has gained national and international recognition. Flaco Jiménez's 1987 Grammy award, the Grammy nominations of Santiago Jiménez and Steve Jordan, and the commercial production of Jordan's namesake accordion, the "Tex-Mex Rockordeon," all attest to the growing acceptance of conjunto within the music establishment. Conjunto, long an important part of the entertainment offered at almost every Tejano festival in Texas, is now itself the focus of an annual celebration. Established in San Antonio in 1982, the Tejano Conjunto Festival has grown so popular that it now offers more than 40 hours of live performances and attracts over 30,000 visitors from around the world.

The sounds of a festival are often accompanied by crowd-pleasing dancers, who, with their colorful skirts, lace, ribbons, and petticoats, appear to onlookers as swirling, spinning blurs during the fast steps of a well-executed dance. Mexican folk dance, or ballet folklórico, is a living tradition whose roots may be traced to such diverse sources as the Jewish and Arab foot-stomping dances brought to Spain through historic migrations; the tempos of the waltz, schottische, and varsovienne brought to Mexico by European immigrants; and even the rhythms of Africa and the Caribbean.

Two of the most popular folklórico dances are La Bamba, a *huapango* from the state of Veracruz, and the Jarabe Tapatio, of Jalisco, Mexico's national folk dance. During the performance of La Bamba, two dance partners execute complex steps to transform a sash lying on the floor into a bow. The Jarabe Tapatio is a courtship dance known to most Americans as the Mexican hat dance. The highlight of the dance is a couple dancing around a sombrero in courtship. When the woman picks the hat up and places it on her head, their engagement is confirmed, and the couple, dancing arm in arm, turn to face a cheering audience.

Hispanic festivals are family events, and games for all ages are an important part of any celebration. The piñata is the most popular and best known of these games. The origins of the party game lie in sixteenth-century Italy, where blindfolded participants wielding sticks attempted to smash a pineapple-shaped clay pot filled with sweets and small favors. This Renaissance custom had reached Spain by the mid-1600s, and was brought to Mexico by Spanish colonists. However, an Indian version was already present in the New World. Used by the Aztecs to symbolize the struggle between good and evil, feather-covered clay piñatas were broken at the foot of idols during commemorations of the birth of the god Huitzilopochtli.

Piñatas continued to be made with clay jars until the mid-twentieth century, when increased demand by American tourists led to the use of papier-mâché, a faster construction method. Modern piñatas, decorated with brightly colored tissue paper, can be found in the shape of animals, stars, fruits, vegetables, and other fanciful forms. Piñatas are most commonly associated with children's birthday parties or school celebrations, but Hispanic festivals still provide adults with the chance to take a swing. "Piñatas are broken by the old as well as the young," says Vicki de la Garza of Teatro de Artes de Juan Seguín, organizer of Seguin's Fiestas Patrias Mexicanas, where there is even a special senior citizen piñata game.

A special event during some fiestas is the *charreada,* or Mexican-style rodeo. *Charrería,* the art of the charro and the national sport of Mexico, developed from Old World equestrian practices that evolved into a distinctly Mexican style in response to the rigorous demands of cattle-ranching. Vaqueros, who usually were of mixed Spanish and Indian ancestry, developed stylized ways of carrying out chores such as rounding up

Colorful piñatas are a favorite at the annual Texas Folklife Festival in San Antonio. Photo by Cathryn Hoyt, THC.

cattle, branding livestock, and judging horses. Though vaqueros valued speed and ease during the workday, after work they polished their styles, strove to achieve more difficult feats, and often competed informally to show off their skills.

In the early twentieth century, charro associations were formed to perpetuate the traditional equestrian skills in a formal competition setting. Members compete not for prize money (none is offered in competition), but rather to experience the glory and honor of charrería. In Texas today, this art is fostered by more than twenty charro organizations, some composed largely of descendants of those hacendados (landowners) or vaqueros who originally defined charrería. Charrería enthusiasts—none of them professional charros or charras—passionately devote evenings and weekends to the sport and to collecting and using the traditional costume and tack associated with it. San Antonio, Houston, El Paso, Midland, Dallas, and many more Texas cities are home to charro organizations that present breathtaking exhibitions of Mexican equestrian heritage at fiestas all over the state. These displays of the art of Mexican horsemanship, in which both men and women take part, are not to be missed by any lover of tradition, spectacle, rodeo, horses, or excitement.

Both the process of festival organization and how festivals are celebrated can reveal much about the relationships between members of the community that host an event. Anthropologist Stanley Brandes has argued that in Michoacán, Mexico, festivals, rather than being chaotic affairs where inhibitions are forgotten, are events where orthodox behavior and relationships are reinforced. Preparing the festival is a community effort in Michoacán, and the process serves to reinforce the reputations of individuals in the community by testing their reliability, be they donors assuring that all expenses are shared, *encabezedos* (persons in ad hoc positions who collect money from the community), food preparers, or dancers. The fiesta reinforces the interdependence between individuals and the village.

In Texas, Hispanic festivals continue to be organized much like those in Mexico. From the mid-1920s through the 1970s the San Angelo Mexican-American community elected a Comité Patriótico Mexicano (Mexican Patriotic Committee) to organize their fiestas patrias. The committee solicited donations from business firms and other supporters and redistributed the proceeds from the fiestas to the community to make physical improvements in the barrio. Similar organizational structures are seen in other communities. In Austin the Comité Cinco de Mayo is composed of Tejano representatives from the League of United Latin American Citizens, the Austin Hispanic Chamber of Commerce, and the Austin Parks and Recreation Department. They raise funds, coordinate volunteer participation, and distribute the fiesta proceeds equally among five local recreation centers in Austin's predominantly Hispanic south- and eastside neighborhoods. Thus, planning the festival becomes as much of a community event as the festival itself.

Hispanic festivals—particularly Cinco de Mayo, Diez y Seis de Septiembre, and El Día de la Raza, but also dozens of other community celebrations—continue to be an integral part of Mexican-American folklife.

LOTERÍA MEXICANA

Lotería mexicana is a nineteenth-century Spanish form of bingo still avidly played by many Hispanic Texans of all ages. Similar to bingo, lotería differs from its northern counterpart in its use of pictures rather than numbers and in its incorporation of humorous and witty rhymes, riddles, and puns during the calling of the figures. Lotería has been a favorite pastime of Mexicans in both high social circles and modest pueblos since the Spaniards first brought the game to Mexico soon after translating it from the Italian original in 1830.

Lotería playing pieces consist of a deck of fifty-four cards, each with a different, commonly known figure such as *el diablo* (the devil), *la campana* (the bell) or *el pájaro* (the bird). The deck is accompanied by players' forms, each containing sixteen figures arranged in a square pattern (four across, four down). The game requires at least three players: one *cantador* (caller), who picks the cards and "sings" the names of the figures, and two players who, marking their forms with small objects like dried beans, race to be the first to complete a horizontal, vertical, or diagonal line, or to completely cover a form.

Most contemporary editions of *lotería* contain many of the same figures as the original Italian and Spanish editions, such as *el sol* (the sun), *la luna* (the moon), and *la estrella* (the star), but the calling of the cards incorporates Mexican-American lore. The caller, instead of quickly revealing a card's figure, teases the players with hints and clues in rhyme, riddle, pun, or verse form. These calls are spontaneous and colloquial, varying from place to place and even between groups in a community.

An experienced caller might use elaborate rhymes, while a less serious caller might opt for a simple rhyme such as "Diana-la-rana" (Diana the frog), teasing one of the female players. Riddling—such as "el farrol de enamorados: la luna!" (the lantern of lovers: the moon), "el que todos van a ver, cuanto tiene que comer: el nopal!" (that which all are going to see when they have to eat: the cactus), and "los de San Pedro: los llaves!" (those of St. Peter: the keys)—is another common form of call. Usually a call is unique to the caller, time, and place, with riddles reflecting local image associations, and rhymes and double-meanings poking fun at players.

Charros execute the daring Paso de Muerte. Courtesy of *TEXAS HIGH-WAYS Magazine.*

Through them, Tejano communities celebrate their history, perpetuate folklife, and reinforce solidarity and pride among community members. "Many of our parents and relatives were born in Mexico, but most members of our Mexican-American community have never been there," explains Henry Pérez, an organizer of the Mexican Fiesta in Olton, near the Oklahoma border. "We started the festival in 1982 to keep our culture and history alive for our children—and those adults who have forgotten." Similarly, festivals like Fiesta Ranchera in Falfurrias "preserve our food and music, and help us promote our way of life to the younger generation," notes organizer Gustavo Barrera. According to Vicki de la Garza of Teatro de Artes de Juan Seguín, "Seguin was over 50 percent Hispanic, yet there were no festivals or activities that Hispanics were involved in [together]. We brought back the traditional Diez y Seis to fill the void of Hispanic culture and traditions. It has been very successful."

The sights and sounds of Hispanic festivals are a well loved part of the heritage of Texas, enjoyed by Texans of all backgrounds. After all, everyone needs an excuse to *echar todo por la ventana y divirtirse* occasionally!

EVENTS OF
LA CHARREADA

Transport yourself across time and space to life "allá en el rancho grande" at a *charreada*—a thrilling, Mexican-style rodeo—featuring traditional Hispanic horsemanship. Charros perform nine *suertes* (translated literally as "luck," but meaning "feats") in a *lienzo,* a frying pan-shaped arena consisting of a round ring with an adjacent long chute.

In the first event, the *cala del caballo* or "test of the horse," the charro qualifies for competing in the day's events by proving his control over his horse in an exercise traditionally used to demonstrate a horse's worth for sale. Horse and rider gallop at full speed into the arena and come to a screeching halt before a drawn line—then calmly execute precise quarter, half, and full turns. Next, during *el terna en el ruedo,* audiences marvel at the speed and coordination necessary to catch or "head and heel" a bull before branding or castration. Three charros and one wild bull enter the arena. One charro drives the bull toward the other two, then the other two charros simultaneously lasso the bull's horns and hind legs—exhibiting fancy tricks with their forty-meter ropes to earn extra points—and effortlessly secure the animal by dallying their ropes around their saddlehorns.

Some events of the charreada originated purely for fun. The sole women's event, the *escaramuza charra,* began in the 1950s as a way for women to take part in the sport and exhibit their own equestrian mastery. Not to be outdone by their male counterparts, the women's teams—dressed in colorful costumes and riding sidesaddle at full speed—execute a series of intricately braided formations. The grace of the escaramuza is contrasted by another daring event called *el coleo,* "the tailing," from which few steers or bulls emerge with pride intact. The mounted charro chases the animal down the chute at full speed and, when he catches up to it, in the blink of an eye salutes the judge, slaps the animal's rump, then throws the animal around the rear of his horse (still galloping) a full 180 degrees, sending it tumbling across the chute.

The most thrilling and daring suerte of the day is the last, the *paso de muerte* or "death pass," and certainly, the literal translation of suerte—"luck"—is not lost on the competitors. The event begins with three mounted charros chasing a wild mare around the edge of the arena. One charro, the competitor, emerges from the trio to make the "death pass." He leaps from his galloping horse to the running, bareback mare, with only its mane to hold. If he falls, he risks being trampled not only by these two horses, but also by the two running behind him.

Corn for tortillas was traditionally ground with the mano and metate, the same stone tools used by American Indians for thousands of years. *Olla Series: La Preparación*, by Amado Peña, courtesy of the artist.

The Tex-Mex Menu

HELEN SIMONS

The first European to enjoy Texas hospitality was Cabeza de Vaca, who landed on the coast of Texas in 1528. There he was served a breakfast of fish and roots by his hosts and rescuers, the Karankawa Indians. The coastal Indians in whose company he later began his journey into the unknown interior were hunters and gatherers, and among the foods they favored were mesquite beans and prickly pear. At times during his eight years and thousands of miles of wandering he went hungry because no food was available and at other times he went hungry because he found the unfamiliar foods unpalatable.

While Cabeza de Vaca was dining sparingly among the Indians of Texas and northern Mexico, the menu in other parts of the New World at the same period was much more sophisticated. A Franciscan friar, Bernardino de Sahagún, recorded Aztec life in great detail, including foodways. His sixteenth-century account, *General History of the Things of New Spain,* shows that most of the variations of Mexican food today are descendants of Aztec recipes, in which corn and chiles in several variations were basic foods. The *tlaxcalli,* a flat corn bread that was a staple of the Aztec diet, was being called *tortilla* (the Spanish word for omelet) by the 1570s and is still known by that name more than four centuries later.

In addition to corn, the New World contributed many other important foods to the Old World and, eventually, back to European settlements in North America. Peppers (including the familiar jalapeño), potatoes, tomatoes, beans, pumpkins and other squashes, sweet potatoes, peanuts, pineapples, and avocadoes as well as chocolate and vanilla, are among the many "discovered" foods that we eat or cook with today. The complete list of New World foods is much longer, but these are the most important. And of these, the most important to North American Indians were corn, squash, and beans.

Beans and squash were the earliest foods to be cultivated by Native Americans, about six or seven thousand years ago. Chiles were then brought into the garden, and in a few thousand years wild corn was tamed. Gradually over thousands of years these food plants dispersed from the agricultural centers in the south to North America. During the time known to archeologists as the Late Prehistoric, which began in Texas about 1,000 years before the arrival of the Spanish, agriculture was being practiced by

Cabeza de Vaca reported traveling with Indians to the South Texas prickly pear fields in the 1530s, making the fruits of the prickly pear one of the oldest recorded foods in Texas. A twentieth-century harvesting of the plant is shown in *Abuelitos Piscando Nopalitos* (Picking Nopal Cactus), by Carmen Lomas Garza, courtesy of the artist.

village-dwelling Indians in northeast Texas, the northern Panhandle, and along the Rio Grande. Village life and the cultivation of crops brought new tools and new lifeways to these Texas Indians, but some very ancient tools, the *mano* and *metate* (a hand-held grinding stone and grinding basin or slab, used somewhat like a mortar and pestle) were found to be very useful in processing domesticated plant foods. The Mexican and Indian inhabitants of Texas were still grinding corn by the mano and metate method well into historic times.

Cabeza de Vaca, in his long trek through Texas and northern Mexico, finally encountered the farmers along the Rio Grande, who offered him squash and beans. They also grew corn, but drought had destroyed their plantings. They said that the real corn country lay to the north and west—in the land of the pueblos. Later explorers in Trans-Pecos Texas, en route to the pueblos in search of another kind of golden treasure, also encountered *rancherías* (agricultural settlements) on the Rio Grande. At La Junta de los Ríos (in the area of Presidio, Texas) the Spanish eventually established six missions, four of them on the Texas side of the river. By the mid-1700s a settlement had grown up at La Junta, and fewer than a hundred families formed the nucleus of a community that has persisted for over two hundred years. Joe Graham, an astute observer of border folkways, has said that the merging of Spanish and Indian cultures is nowhere more apparent than in the foodways of these early Mexican pioneers. To the native Indian foods both domestic and wild—including prickly pear, chiles, corn, squash, and beans—the Spanish settlers added new sources of meat such as pigs, goats, cattle, sheep, and chickens, as well as new plant foods from other areas of Mexico. Here the traditions of northern Mexico and Texas continue to blend to this day, as they do along the entire Rio Grande border. It is this blending of traditions and cross-cultural borrowing that gave rise to the style of cooking known as Tex-Mex.

Until recently serious scholars have paid scant attention to the foodways of Mexican-Americans. As with folk arts and crafts, the focus of attention has been on Mexican, rather than Mexican-American, traditions, although there are encouraging indications that change is underway. Oral history techniques are increasingly being used to record vanishing Texas lifeways. Folklife festivals, such as the one sponsored by the Institute of Texan Cultures in San Antonio, include foods along with traditional crafts and music. These often emphasize foods prepared in Mexican-American homes, which are much more varied than those that appear on restaurant menus. The family traditions involved in the making of dishes like *tamales*, the blending of Indian and Spanish foods, the preparation of foods for special celebrations (such as *bizcochitos* and tamales at Christmas, and figurine-shaped breads for El Día de los Muertos), traditional planting practices and beliefs in rural areas—all are topics for deeper study. The foods considered here are those Tex-Mex dishes that are prepared in the homes of Texans of all ethnic backgrounds, and in numerous restaurants across the state, yet are still distinctly Spanish-Indian-Mexican in character. The popularity of these foods represents the most widespread acknowledgment and acceptance of Hispanic culture in Texas.

Corn. Adapted by Hector Meza, THC, from a Florentine Codex drawing.

CORN BECOMES A CROP

The domestication of corn was a dramatic event in the history of the New World. The ability to store food, in the form of dried corn, meant that people could settle in permanent locations. Freedom from the constant struggle to survive created time for other endeavors, and some people became political and religious leaders, architects, artists, and artisans. Thus do beginnings in humble villages, through many changes and over many centuries, become the complex societies of the Southwestern Puebloan Indians, the Caddoans of the Southeast, and the great civilizations of the Mayans, the Incans, and the Aztecs.

Maize, or corn as it was dubbed by Europeans, was domesticated about 5000 years ago in south-central Mexico. Archeological evidence suggests that this important food source came from the Tehuacan Valley, but scholars disagree about how it was dispersed. Either domestication occurred simultaneously in several locales or the practice and the plant dispersed rapidly throughout the area from one central location. Over the centuries, corn became the single most important staple for the Indians of the Americas. The practice of cultivating corn had spread to Texas by the early years of the first millennium A.D.

Because corn was domesticated during

The traditional foods prepared in Mexican-American homes are much more varied than those that appear on the Tex-Mex restaurant menu. Family scene by Amado Peña, courtesy of the artist.

prehistory, no written records describe the process. When Europeans arrived in the New World, the folklore and mythology of the native peoples, especially those with highly organized societies like the Aztecs and the Incas, included many allusions to maize. Important religious ceremonies, like the corn dances of the Puebloan Indians, were directed toward ensuring a bountiful harvest. Most Indian myths attribute the origins of corn to some supernatural agency or to another, ancient race of people. The actual process probably involved the cross-pollination of several native grasses of the south-central Mexico region, several of which have been identified. Among these are wild plants of the genus *Tripsacum L.*, whose range extends from the south-central United States to Paraguay and southern Brazil.

Before ordering from the Tex-Mex menu, the newcomer to Texas should first be aware of what this food is *not*. Despite the northern Mexico influence, it is not Mexican food. Visitors who are fond of the foods of Mexico, including the traditional Spanish dishes of the interior or the seafood specialties of the coastal regions, may find themselves, like Cabeza de Vaca, on *tierra incógnita* in Texas. Neither is Tex-Mex the same as New Mexican or Californian Mexican foods, although together these are all part of a Mexican-American system that can be distinguished from the cooking of Mexico as a Southwestern North American style. However, in comparison with Tex-Mex, the traditional foods of New Mexico rely more on fresh green chiles and refined green tomatillo sauces. Green-corn tamales, made with a filling of grated young corn, green chiles, and cheese, are a good example of the delicious foods of New Mexico. California Mexican food reflects yet another style, featuring the lavish produce of the state, especially lots of avocado, garnished with sour cream and Spanish olives.

Chili

Chili is an appropriate dish to place first in a definition of what Tex-Mex food *is,* since it is distinctly Texan and is, in fact, recognized as the Official State Dish (adopted in 1977). The spelling *chili* distinguishes the dish from the pepper, spelled *chile.* The novice cook should remember this distinction, since it is possible to purchase both chili powder (which is a blended mixture of all the seasonings needed to make the dish) and chile powder (which is the ground, hot pepper ingredient in chili powder). Having mastered this simple distinction, the adventurous chef, diner, historian, or folklorist is ready to proceed with a more detailed examination of the subject.

The true beginnings of chili are obscured by time and legend. A few writers have claimed that chili in some form was probably made by the Aztecs, who cultivated its basic ingredient, the hot little pepper called chilipiquín. This assertion has been challenged by Indians of the American Southwest who are certain that chili derives from a kind of pemican, dried meat ground with wild peppers, made long before the Aztecs established their great civilization and developed tortillas. However, the first recipe for chili is said to have been given to West Texas Indians in the seventeenth century by the helpful apparition of a Spanish nun known as "the Lady in Blue." (The appearance of the Lady in Blue among the Jumano Indians of West Texas is an authentic folktale, but the chili-recipe variant is definitely suspect.) Some western historians, debunking both the prehistoric and seventeenth-century accounts as myth, believe that chili is actually a mid-nineteenth-century concoction, first made on trail drives by cow-camp cooks, probably using a deviled beef mixture related to the pemican made by Indians but adding water to form a kind of stew. Other historians have asserted that chili was originally cooked up in San Antonio at least as early as the 1830s by "chili queens" who worked as laundresses during the day and sold chili, made in their washtubs, in the evenings on Military Plaza. A story also has been told that chili resulted from a visiting Englishman's failed attempt to make curry using Texas Mexican ingredients. However, those who accept only the written word in the form of a bona fide recipe assert that chili was not eaten by anybody until the 1880s, when it suddenly appeared in San Antonio. In the last analysis, the honor probably really does belong to the mid-nineteenth-century cooks of San Antonio, an honor that is recognized in the city's many fiestas, when vendors in costume once again sell chili from stands in the plazas during the evenings.

The only argument about the ingredients of chili should be the central, great debate: to add beans or not to add beans to the basic meat and seasonings mixture. The meat (preferably lean beef or venison) should be chopped or coarsely ground, but many a delicious pot of chili has been made with hamburger. The only other basic ingredients besides chili powder are water and salt, but many cooks add chopped onion, garlic, and canned tomatoes. Otherwise, if it looks like chili (red) and tastes like chili (hot), it's chili. Make your own from the many recipes that are to be found in Texas newspapers, magazines, or church-group cookbooks, and keep trying till you find the one that tastes right to you. Or buy chili mix with the instructions written on the package. Do not go to a chili cook-off in search of the best chili and take all of the fixings seriously. Some entrants in these events have been known to include old leather boots in their secret recipes!

If chili is eaten as a soup or stew, with crackers, it may arguably be called simply a Texas dish. If used as a sauce, as on enchiladas, it is an authentic Tex-Mex food. From the spicy mixture sold in the plazas of San Antonio to the chuck-wagon versions served in nineteenth-century cow camps or the Helen Corbett version served at Neiman Marcus in the twentieth century, more native and naturalized Texans probably have eaten chili than any other Tex-Mex food. We take it very seriously and not seriously at all. Chili cook-offs are part of many annual festivals in Texas, and there are major competitions, like the ones at Terlingua and San Marcos, where the cook-off is the festival. Humor and showmanship abound at the cook-offs, and their popularity has encouraged supporters of other traditional foods to organize cook-offs of their own—for *menudo* (tripe soup) and *frijoles* (pinto beans).

Tamales

The tamale, unlike chili, is unquestionably Mexican and does not have a cow-camp origin myth. (The singular is sometimes given as *tamal* in Spanish but usually *tamale* in Texan.) Like chili, this dish deserves special attention because the version eaten in Texas is uniquely Tex-Mex, yet its origins are ancient. An early version probably was made by the Aztecs, and the corn and corn shucks that are indispensable in making tamales are definitely New World contributions. However, the Tex-Mex version depends

By the mid-19th century, chili was being sold from stands on the plazas of San Antonio by women known as "chili queens." The Institute of Texan Cultures, courtesy Dr. Thomas Cutrer.

on a stuffing of pork or beef from the cattle and pigs that were introduced by the Spaniards. And unlike the tamales of Mexico, which are prepared with a variety of fillings including sweet ones, the tamale on the Tex-Mex menu is stuffed only with a spicy meat filling. The traditional stuffing of Christmas tamales, which are prepared as a sort of seasonal open-house treat, is ground pork from a boiled hog's head. Processed cornmeal called *masa harina* is used to make the *masa* (dough) for stuffing (the cornmeal may also be called simply masa). Spiced broth from the boiled meat, salt, and a little chili powder season the masa, which is cooked and then worked with lard. The masa is spread thinly on prepared corn shucks and spread with the ground meat mixture, then the shucks are rolled up and the tamales are steamed till done (a half hour or more). Making dozens of tamales is an assembly-line process and is best undertaken, like a quilting bee, as a social occasion.

The time and effort involved in making tamales, plus the fact that really good ones have long been available from vendors (and now from the local grocery store), is an aspect of the tamale's unique place on the Tex-Mex menu: tamales are eaten almost as commonly as chili, but most cooks who are not Mexican-Americans do not make their own at home. (Important exceptions to this rule, and a testament to the multicultural heritage of Texas, are the many African-American Texans who have been tamale chefs par excellence.) As the population becomes more mobile and fewer people live near their extended families, and as more women enter the work force, more Mexican-American cooks also prefer to buy rather than prepare tamales.

The Mexican Plate

Among the combination dinners on the Tex-Mex restaurant menu should be one called the Mexican Plate. It contains chili-covered enchiladas or tamales (or both), refried beans, and Spanish rice. A Tex-Mex enchilada consists of a chopped onion and grated cheese mixture rolled in a tortilla and covered with chili (sometimes topped with more cheese); this is heated in the oven till the cheese melts and is then served immediately. Lots of melted cheese is a primary characteristic of Tex-Mex cooking. Refried beans (*frijoles refritos*) are cooked pinto beans mashed, seasoned, and refried in lard. Spanish rice is seasoned with tomato paste, chili powder, and cumin.

Tostadas (fried corn tortillas) and salsa (or picante sauce) may be served before the main course begins. Heated corn tortillas have traditionally been served with Tex-Mex food, but flour tortillas are rapidly surpassing the original flat corn breads in popularity, even in such traditional places as the Presidio area. Tacos, chalupas, chile con queso, and guacamole are acceptable side dishes, and either a pecan praline or sherbet may be offered for dessert. These are the dishes that can be found in many "home cooking" cafes around the state, along with other standard fare such as chicken fried steak, fried chicken, fried catfish, and barbecue. These are also the foods most commonly prepared in non–Mexican-American homes.

The typical Tex-Mex menu, like many other regional aspects of American life, has been affected by the increased movement of the population and the communications explosion that has occurred since the 1940s. The development of national chain restaurants, especially fast-food chains, has, ironically, fostered both change and standardization. As more Americans eat Mexican food in a chain restaurant in New York or Chicago, the more they expect Mexican food in the Southwest to taste like what they are used to. And if a burrito is garnished with ripe olives in California, so should it be in Texas. Milder chili and chile sauces are even being served in many places in Texas because so many palates have been educated elsewhere.

Despite these pernicious influences, not all of the changes occurring in the Tex-Mex menu are the result of nontraditional intrusions. Some of the "new" dishes have long been cooked in Mexican-American homes but were not necessarily found in restaurants. Good examples of this phenomenon are burritos and fajitas, both now familiar items across the state. Burritos are simply soft tacos made with flour tortillas. Favorite fillings include a scrambled egg and chile mixture, egg and potato, refried beans, and carne guisada.

Fajitas, soft tacos filled with strips of marinated and grilled flank

The "Mexican Plate" will include many of the dishes shown here— and always the enchiladas. Photo by Bob Parvin.

Making tamales, as shown in Carmen Lomas Garza's *La Tamalada*, becomes a social occasion. Courtesy of the artist.

steak, are a reflection of the economic choice that has given rise to many excellent home-cooked meals around the world: choose a cheaper, and usually tougher, cut of meat and find a delicious way to cook it. Today, fajitas have become one of the most popular—and expensive—items on the Tex-Mex menu. They have become so popular that national food chains have even developed fajita offshoots such as the chicken fajita (a contradiction in terms, since fajita refers to the flank steak) or the fajita pita which substitutes Middle Eastern pita bread for the tortilla.

Of course, there have long been restaurants in the larger Texas cities that serve a much broader selection of traditional dishes than the "Mexican Plate." Some common items on these extended menus are chile relleno, chicken con mole, and carne guisada. And, in Hispanic neighborhoods, there are the many restaurants that offer Hispanic "home cooking," where one finds dishes like menudo (a tripe soup made with either *pozole*-type corn or hominy) and even *cabrito* (young goat), baked in the oven (*al horno,* for the traditional outdoor oven) or cooked on a spit over coals (*al pastor,* or as the shepherds cooked it).

Bread and Breakfast

Wheat flour, one of the Old World foods imported to the New World, has been put to good use by Mexican-American cooks, not only in flour tortillas (now being made in a whole wheat version) and delicious crusty rolls called *bolillos,* but also in delicious sweet rolls. The term *pan dulce* (literally *sweet bread*) describes several sweet rolls that are great for breakfast with café con leche. Wherever you find a good Mexican bakery (*panadería*), you will find the pan dulces, *empanadas* (little fried pastries stuffed with fruit

The blending of Old and New World foods is the key to Tex-Mex cooking. Tortillas, made of corn since Aztec times, now have popular white and whole wheat flour versions. Photo by Cathryn Hoyt, THC.

Above left: Fruit drinks called aguas frescas have long been popular at carnivals and fiestas. Photo by Jesse Herrera.

preserves or pumpkin), and several kinds of cookies. The favorites of children usually are the pig-shaped gingerbread cookies called *marranitos*. *Buñuelos* (fried, sweet flour tortillas, sprinkled with cinnamon and sugar) are related to *sopapillas*, which are now common in restaurants. Sopapilla pastry is fried so that it puffs up rapidly and steam forms a hollow shell in the center, ideal for holding the honey that is usually served as an accompaniment.

Those who like a heartier, less continental breakfast will find the Tex-Mex egg dishes more filling: *huevos rancheros* (eggs served with a tomato and pepper sauce, very hot), *migas* (eggs scrambled with corn tortillas, cheese, and onions), and *huevos con chorizo* (eggs scrambled with Mexican sausage). The Spanish omelet, however, should be viewed with suspicion by those in search of traditional dishes, since it is usually indistinguishable from a creole omelet or an American version sometimes called a Western omelet. Much more in keeping with the Tex-Mex tradition is the simple practice of pouring chili over scrambled eggs or simply covering fried eggs with picante sauce. Hearty Tex-Mex egg dishes are especially popular for weekend brunches, rather than as early morning breakfasts.

Memories

Many people who have grown up in Texas share fond memories associated with their favorite Tex-Mex foods. A simple dish of tamales may serve as a reminder of almost forgotten neighbors and their offerings of friendship on Christmases past. Conjunto music on the radio may stir memories of Diez y Seis carnivals and *aguas frescas*—cool, fruit-flavored drinks served from large glass-jar dispensers. The mechanized tinkle of an ice-cream truck may recall to older Texans a time when *la raspa* (fruit-flavored, shaved ice, like a snow cone) could still be purchased from ancient horse-drawn ice-cream carts. Then there were little neighborhood grocery stores in almost every block, many of them just small shops in the fronts of peoples' homes, and they sold chorizo and bologna, penny candy and the red, green, and white striped coconut candy from Mexico. The spicy aroma of food booths at a fiesta may once again transport us back to those days of our childhood, recalling the vivid spring green of *nopalitos* and grass and the laughter of childhood friends. Or those memories may be sparked by the vivid blues and greens of a painting of nopalito harvesting by Carmen Lomas Garza, remembered from her South Texas childhood. The memories we share are part of the heritage we share.

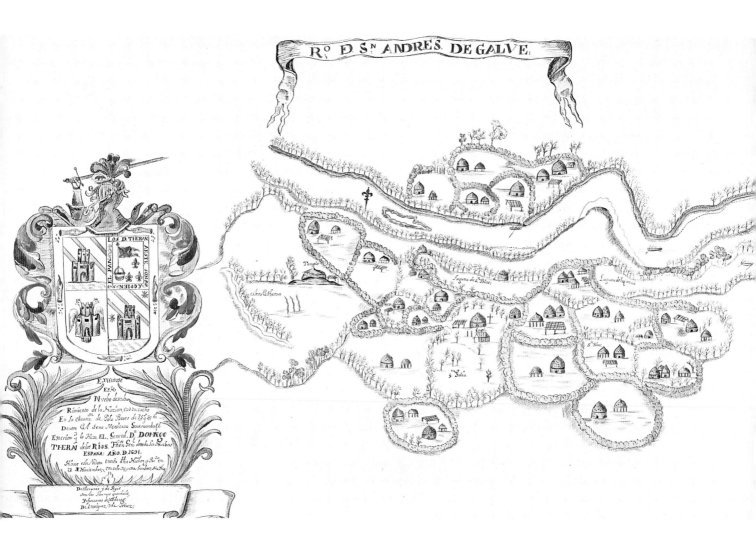

The Written Word

JESÚS F. DE LA TEJA

It is deeply to be regretted that those venerable archives could not have been preserved and protected, alike from ignorant, wanton vandalism, and the marauding speculator. The loss from these sources of destruction, to the early history of our State, will never be fully appreciated. The fragments left serve only to admonish us that [the loss] has been great and irreparable.

Thus wrote Texas Supreme Court Chief Justice Abner Smith Lipscomb in 1851 regarding the disappearance of San Antonio's founding documents, which townspeople had preserved from 1731 until the onset of the Texas War of Independence. His comments point to the unique place of the written word in early Texas history. No painting, sculpture, music, or dance created in Texas during the Spanish or Mexican periods has come down to us. Architectural artifacts—the ruins of missions, *acequias,* and presidios—have been supplemented by modern reconstructions that may or may not wholly reflect the spirit of the original. Yet within Texas, in Mexico, and in Spain a rich written record remains, enabling archeologists, folklorists, historians, architects, and other scholars to reconstruct a panoramic view of what Texas was like during Spanish and Mexican rule.

We find documentary sources for early Texas history in a number of formats—originals, transcriptions, photocopies, microfilm—throughout the state. However, three archival collections associated with the eighteenth-century settlements of San Antonio, Nacogdoches, and Laredo contain the lion's share of original documents. These collections share a number of features, including not being located in the cities for which they are named, containing more than just city records, and being readily available on microfilm.

The Bexar Archives is the largest and most varied of the three collections. Transferred to the University of Texas at Austin by the Bexar County Commissioners Court in 1899, the collection is now housed in the Eugene C. Barker Texas History Center. The Bexar Archives consists of 80,000 documents and over 250,000 manuscript and printed pages. A small part of the original archives, considered to have permanent legal value to the county, were kept by the county clerk's office.

Opposite: The rich written records of our state reflect a panoramic view of what Texas was like during the years of Spanish and Mexican rule. Bexar Archives, courtesy Barker Texas History Center, General Libraries, University of Texas at Austin.

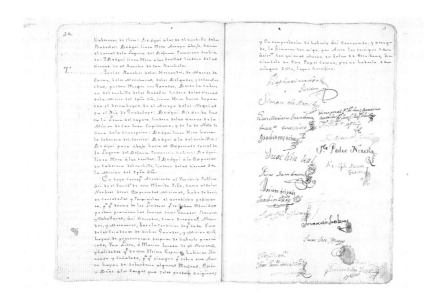

This 1787 testimonial regarding cattle rights is the earliest known history of San Antonio. Bexar Archives, courtesy Barker Texas History Center, General Libraries, University of Texas at Austin.

Manuscripts in the Bexar Archives include documents of governors, military commanders, and provincial political bodies, as well as San Antonio's city records. Law suits, criminal proceedings, and a few examples of private correspondence provide a wealth of detail on everyday life. Among the most interesting documents is a 1787 testimonial by the town's citizenry regarding rights to cattle; it is, in effect, the earliest, locally written, full history of San Antonio. And, for sheer physical impression, there are a large number of royal and viceregal printed decrees, orders, and instructions boasting imposing seals and undecipherable autographs.

Though much smaller, the Nacogdoches and Laredo archives compete in informational importance with the Bexar Archives. As the only other surviving archives of colonial Texas, the Nacogdoches material also shares the distinction of being housed in Austin, in the Archives Division of the Texas State Library. Originally transferred to the Texas secretary of state's office in 1850, the Nacogdoches Archives came to include a number of documents from San Antonio that had also been transferred to the state government for safekeeping. As in the Bexar County case, the Nacogdoches County clerk's office retained records considered of legal importance to the Nacogdoches area.

The documents in the Nacogdoches Archives reflect that settlement's status as the administrative center of Spanish East Texas. Records from its predecessor settlement, Los Adaes, date to the 1730s and include end-of-term reviews for early governors who were based there. During the Mexican period Nacogdoches was the entry point for many immigrants, and the collection contains numerous documents detailing Mexican efforts to control Anglo-American immigration. Even records from subordinate East Texas settlements established by the newcomers, such as Attoyac, San Augustine, and Liberty, may be found in the collection.

The Laredo Archives, now housed at St. Mary's University in San Antonio, led an even more precarious existence than the Bexar or Nacogdoches archives. The Spanish- and Mexican-period records of Laredo were abandoned in the basement of the Webb County Clerk's office until 1934, when as a result of remodeling work they first surfaced. Sebron S. Wilcox, an avocational historian interested in local history, was alerted to the records and subsequently found the rest of the surviving Spanish documents in 1936. Sometime in the 1950s, Wilcox acquired personal possession of the records and after his death in 1959 his wife donated them to St. Mary's University.

The Laredo Archives chronicles the history of the only permanent Spanish settlement on the north bank of the Rio Grande. Covering the period between 1768 and 1868, it includes the same types of records—censuses, governmental communications, legal proceedings—as the Bexar and Nacogdoches archives. Unlike them, however, the Laredo Archives as it passed into private hands retained many of the types of records that had been culled from the Bexar and Nacogdoches archives and kept in those county clerks' offices. Consequently, the Laredo Archives includes a substantial number of wills and probate proceedings and land records.

While the number of records retained by the Nacogdoches County Clerk's Office is rather limited, the volume and scope of material held in San Antonio deserves special attention. The Spanish Mexican Records (1737–1836) in the Bexar County Archives is a collection of approximately 2,500 documents dealing with lands, wills and estates, contracts, legal proceedings, postal and customs administration, and government communications. Some documents concern lands in other parts of Texas, including Victoria, Goliad, San Patricio, and Nacogdoches, as well as the San Antonio and Refugio missions.

Parts of the Bexar and Nacogdoches archives also found their way into the Spanish Collection at the Texas General Land Office. As the repository for original land grant documents, the Land Office has one of the largest collections of Spanish- and Mexican-period records in the Southwest. Documents include over 4,000 land grants, most of them dating from the 1820s and 1830s, legal proceedings, laws, and correspondence. The Land Office is also the custodian of the original founding documents for Mission San José y San Miguel de Aguayo. The manuscript, dating to 1719–20, is on extended loan from the Moody Foundation, Galveston.

Aside from the vast number of original records that have remained in the state, scholars during the past century have routinely traveled to Mexico and Spain to bring back copies of Texas-related materials. Among the most prominent researchers to bring back materials was Carlos E. Castañeda, author of the seven-volume history *Our Catholic Heritage in Texas*. Beginning about 1930, Castañeda made a series of trips to various cities in Mexico, where he had made photostatic copies and transcriptions from governmental and religious archives. Copies of these materials, which date from the sixteenth to the early nineteenth centuries, may now be found in the Barker Texas History Center and the Catholic Archives of Texas in Austin.

Indeed, church records are among the most important sources of information for early Texas. Until well into the nineteenth century the church, through sacramental records, was the only recorder of births, marriages, and deaths. The surviving records are valuable genealogical, demographic, and social-history tools. Unfortunately, wars, natural disasters, and carelessness have taken a heavy toll on these records.

The Archdiocese of San Antonio has originals of many parish registers dating to the town's founding in 1731. The diocesan archives also hold a number of registers from the neighboring missions. Original parish sacramental records are also to be found at Laredo in San Agustín Church. Other Laredo records, as well as local books, are to be found in Mexico, in the parish church of Camargo, Tamaulipas. The parish church of Reynosa, Tamaulipas, also has a number of early sacramental books covering families living north of the Rio Grande. Likewise, Our Lady of Guadalupe Church in Ciudad Juárez is the repository for many records dealing with the missions on the Texas side of the Rio Grande near El Paso.

The Catholic Archives of Texas, in the chancery building of the Diocese of Austin, has copies of many of the above records, including photostatic copies of the Laredo and San Antonio records. Also in the archives are photostats of the Nuestra Señora del Refugio Mission records, which were taken to Matamoros during the Texas War of Independence. Among the photostats of other mission records to be found in the Catholic Archives are parts of those from the Franciscan missionary colleges that operated in Texas, Santa Cruz de Querétaro and Guadalupe de Zacatecas, and the Franciscan mother house in Mexico City, San Francisco El Grande. Copies of records from the dioceses of Guadalajara and Monterrey relating to Texas are also to be found in the Texas Catholic Archives.

The University of Texas System includes a number of special collections containing important Spanish- and Mexican-period materials. The Special Collections Department at the Arlington campus holds a number of manuscript collections regarding the Mexican period, particularly the Robertson Colony Collection. Its Cartographic History Library contains an exceptional collection of historic maps including Spanish- and Mexican-period charts of Texas and the Southwest. The El Paso Special Collections Department has made an effort to collect Spanish- and Mexican-period archival reproductions; more than 1,600 reels of microfilm include archives from Chihuahua, Ciudad Juárez, Durango, and Janos, Mexico, as well as early mission and parish records from the region. The John Peace, Kathryn Stoner O'Connor, and Texana collections housed in the Special Collections Department of the San Antonio campus are of considerable importance. Among the more interesting items are military diaries kept by Mexican officers during the Texas War of Independence.

In Austin, the Barker Texas History Center has a very large collection of photostatic and transcript copies from archives in Spain and Mexico. For the Mexican period, the Barker is particularly rich in manuscript collections, most importantly the papers of Stephen F. Austin. Next door to the Barker, the Benson Latin American Collection has microfilm copies of major portions of the Mexican National Archives (Archivo General de la

The Catholic Archives of Texas,
housed in the Diocese of Austin, is
one of several major libraries in the
capital city that contain records
related to Spanish Texas. Photo by
Cathryn Hoyt, THC.

Marriage manual, ca. 1789, at
Mission San Juan, San Antonio.
Photo by Sam McColloch.

145

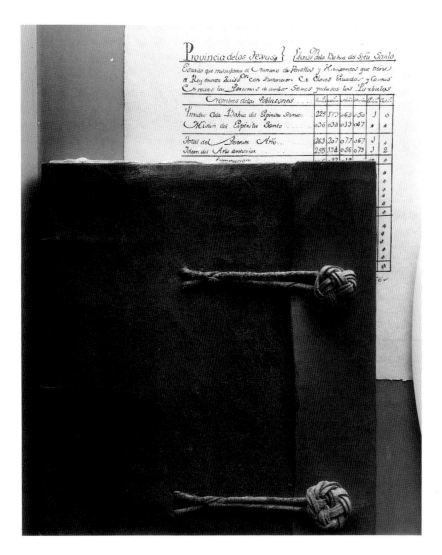

María Luisa Villalongín, actress daughter of Carlos Villalongín, ca. 1917. Carlos Villalongín Dramatic Company Collection, 1848–1945, Benson Latin American Collection, General Libraries, University of Texas at Austin.

Historical documents are themselves examples of material culture, reflecting the craftsmanship of their makers. This mission census and dispatch pouch are on display at Mission Espíritu Santo in Goliad. Photo by Sam McColloch.

Nación de México), and unsurpassable early Mexican newspaper holdings, many of which document affairs in Texas. Among the handful of manuscript collections that emphasize Texas and the Southwest is the Archives of the Presidio of Janos, which includes documentation for the El Paso area in the eighteenth and nineteenth centuries. Both the Barker and the Benson maintain large cartographic collections, including originals and reproductions of early Spanish and Mexican maps of the region.

A number of regional and local repositories around the state also have interesting and important holdings relating to Texas's Spanish and Mexican heritage. The Bastrop County Historical Society, Gonzales Historical

NETTIE LEE BENSON LATIN AMERICAN COLLECTION
Mexican American Library Program

Early maps made by explorers, diaries and accounts of expeditions, and Spanish Colonial manuscripts are all part of the Hispanic heritage of the New World, and examples of all of these are to be found in the Latin American collection of the University of Texas Libraries in Austin. The internationally known collection here began in the early 1920s with the acquisition of the Genaro García library, which brought to the university 25,000 published works and 250,000 pages of manuscripts relating to Mexico. Since

Museum, and Victoria County Library have records dealing with the original settlement of those areas during the 1820s and 1830s. Major repositories for East and Southeast Texas are the Rosenberg Library in Galveston, with its fine map collection, the Houston Metropolitan Research Center of the Houston Public Library, the Sam Houston Regional Library and Research Center in Liberty, and Special Collections at Stephen F. Austin State University in Nacogdoches.

For West Texas, important collections are housed at the Southwest Collection of El Paso Public Library and the Archives of the Big Bend at Sul Ross State University. The Dallas Historical Society, with documents dating back to 1590, and the DeGolyer Library at Southern Methodist University are major collections in North Texas. Strong in San Antonio-related materials, the Daughters of the Republic of Texas Library in San Antonio contains a broad range of materials for early Texas history, including the papers of several prominent local families.

For those interested in delving more deeply into the Spanish and Mexican archival and manuscript heritage of Texas, two books offer a good starting point. The first, Henry Putney Beers' *Spanish and Mexican Records of the American Southwest* (Tucson: University of Arizona Press, 1979), includes a long and detailed section specifically on Spanish and Mexican Texas. *A Guide to the History of Texas* (Westport, Conn.: Greenwood Press, 1988), edited by Light Towsend Cummins and Alvin R. Bailey, Jr., is a bibliographical overview of Texas history, over half of which is devoted to archival and manuscript institutions around the state.

that time coverage has expanded to include all of Latin America, as well as Spanish-speaking peoples in the United States.

In 1974 the importance of systematically collecting and preserving current materials was realized. The Benson Latin American Collection formally initiated the Mexican American Library Program to strengthen and develop Mexican-American materials and research sources at the university. Published books and periodicals on Mexican-American topics, as well as archives and manuscripts are included in the library. Some archival collections, such as the Carlos Villalongín Dramatic Company Archives, the journal of Catarino Garza, and the personal papers of Carlos Eduardo Castañeda were acquired before the formal organization of the program. The personal and professional papers of influential Mexican-Americans, such as George I. Sánchez and Julian Samora, also have been acquired. Since 1974 a vigorous, ongoing acquisition program has brought to the library such prime sources as the literary manuscripts of Rolando Hinojosa-Smith and the archives of the League of United Latin American Citizens (LULAC). Many collections contain photographs, slides, and other visual documentation. Taped conferences, lectures, and interviews also are part of the collection, as are memorabilia such as campaign buttons, bumper stickers, and flags. The Mexican American Library Program is building a storehouse of information and represents a major effort to collect and preserve materials relating to the history and culture of Mexican-Americans.

All materials are available to university and nonuniversity users, although some materials are limited to building use only. Copying of materials is permitted, and reader assistance is available at all times. The Benson Latin American Collection is located in Unit 1 of Sid Richardson Hall on the University of Texas at Austin campus.

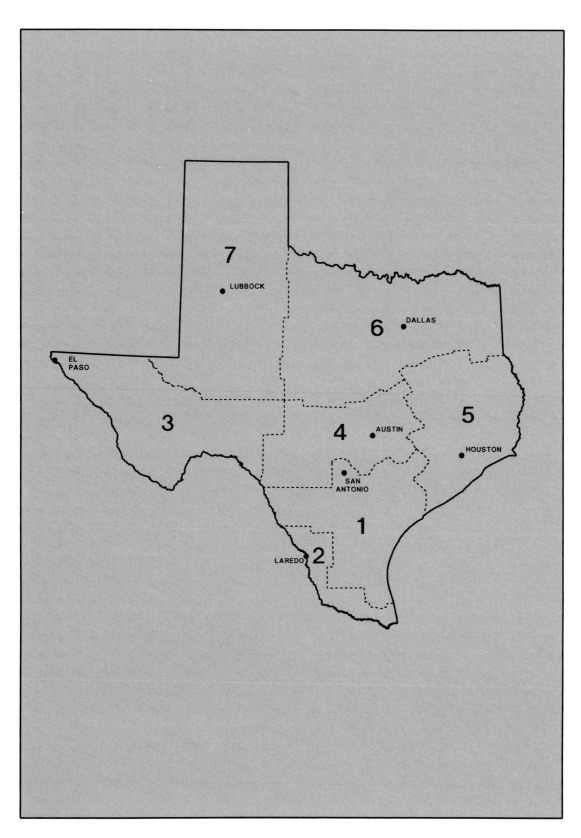

The map of guidebook regions.
Map by Greg Miller.

PART II

The Guidebook

Compiled by

Cathryn A. Hoyt
Ann Perry
Helen Simons
Deborah Smith

REGION I

San Antonio and South Texas

San Antonio, once Spain's major Texas outpost, lies in a region that is rich in Hispanic heritage. At the time of European contact, much of this large region was occupied by groups of nomadic Indians later known as Coahuiltecans. By the late 1700s, the Apaches of the Plains were being pushed farther south by the incoming Comanches. The introduction of the horse, as well as guns and metal tools, and interaction with Europeans caused territorial and cultural changes among the tribes. The beginnings of American settlement in the early 1800s initiated an era of struggle that resulted ultimately in the expulsion of all major Indian groups from Texas. Forces that were set in motion by the first explorers thus affected the indigenous population until the beginning of the modern period. The long history and tragic end of Indian occupation in this region is commemorated in the Spanish missions, in numerous historical markers, and in many museum exhibits, from the smallest county museums to those in the largest cities.

The story of Texas as part of New Spain, which is central to this region's history, is told primarily in the missions of San Antonio and Goliad. Mission San Antonio de Valero was founded in 1718, and eventually five missions were located along the San Antonio River in the area now encompassed by the city of San Antonio. San Antonio was a major stop on El Camino Real, and about 1720 the King's Highway from San Antonio to Goliad was established as "El Camino Real a la Bahía del Espíritu Santo." Goliad was home to two missions and a presidio founded in the 1740s and 1750s: Mission Nuestra Señora del Espíritu Santo de Zúñiga, Mission Nuestra Señora del Rosario de los Cujanes, and Presidio de la Bahía.

The last Spanish mission built in Texas, Mission Nuestra Señora del Refugio, was relocated near Refugio in 1795. One other mission, although not located within the present boundaries of the state, played an important role in the Province of Texas: Mission San Juan Bautista, known as the "Gateway to Spanish Texas." San Juan Bautista is located in Guerrero, Coahuila, Mexico, about 30 miles from Eagle Pass, Texas.

The missions of San Antonio and Goliad have left a lasting legacy, not only in architectural style, but in the development of ranching in Texas. By the mid-18th century, all of the San Antonio missions had well-established ranches. The Goliad missions at the peak of their success also possessed huge herds of cattle, and Espíritu Santo supplied both its own needs and

Opposite: **Mission San Antonio de Valero (the Alamo), San Antonio. THC photo.**

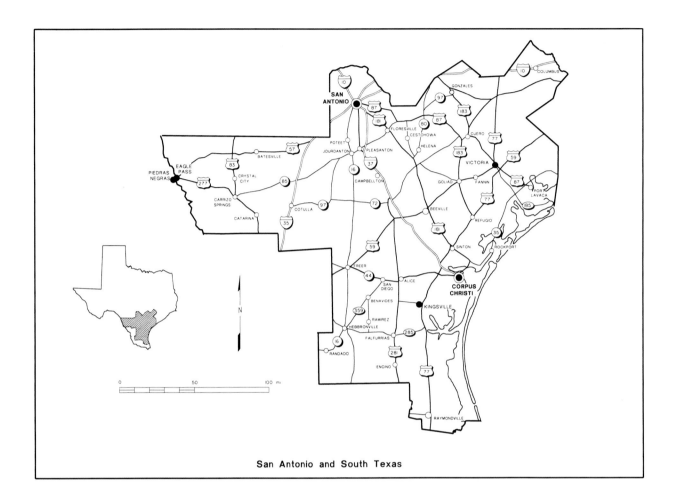

San Antonio and South Texas

those of other Spanish colonial settlements. Canary Islander settlers from San Fernando de Béxar (San Antonio) soon began settling along the San Antonio River near the mission ranches. After the secularization of the missions at the end of the 18th century, the Canary Islanders remained in the area as farmers and ranchers, some of them taking over the former mission ranches.

Although the mission ranches along the La Bahía Road were the earliest in Texas, it was in the South Texas Brush Country that ranching took on epic proportions and left its stamp on Texas forever. In the southern portion of the region, especially Brooks, Duval, Jim Hogg, Kenedy, and Willacy counties, are to be found the locales of many Spanish and Mexican land grants dating from the late 18th and early 19th centuries, as well as several ranches still owned by the descendants of the original landholders.

The early 19th century also marks the beginning of Mexico's struggle for independence from Spain and the initiation of the brief period of Mexican sovereignty in Texas. The first stirrings of revolutionary fervor in Mexico were scarcely felt in the remote reaches of Texas, but major clashes occurred at Goliad and San Antonio in 1813. Following independence from Spain, Mexico's brief hold on Texas was marred by struggles between sup-

Guidebook Region I. Map by Greg Miller.

porters of the Mexican Constitution of 1824 and supporters of Santa Anna's government. The end result of the political disagreements and the pressures brought to bear by new colonists during this period was Texas' declaration of independence from Mexico. Both San Antonio and Goliad were the scenes of major events in the Texas war for independence, which brought an end to Hispanic government in Texas.

From the establishment of the Republic of Texas until well into the 20th century, the history of many Mexican-American Texans has been one of a long struggle for economic and social equality. Yet, from a cultural viewpoint, this period also has been one of significant contribution and achievement. In this region one can experience widespread acceptance and influence of Hispanic heritage—in architecture and the built environment, language and place-names, ranching practices, food, entertainment, and many other aspects of daily life.

SAN ANTONIO AND VICINITY, Bexar County

San Antonio (pop. 935,933). On the feast day of St. Anthony, June 13, in 1691, an expedition led by Governor Domingo Terán de los Ríos arrived at a village of the Payaya Indians and named the place San Antonio de Padua. In 1718 Fray Antonio de San Buenaventura y Olivares, with an expedition led by Martín de Alarcón, established Mission San Antonio de Valero (the Alamo) on San Pedro Creek. On May 5 the governor named the settlement Villa de Béjar and established the presidio, San Antonio de Béjar (later spelled Béxar). Although earlier explorations and settlements occurred elsewhere in the vast land that was to become Texas, it was here that colonization and civilian government began. In 1731 the Villa of San Fernando de Béxar was established by colonists from the Canary Islands. The capital of Spanish Texas was moved from Los Adaes (Robeline, Louisiana) to San Antonio in 1773. After the Mexican state of Coahuila and Texas was formed in 1824, San Antonio was no longer the capital but remained the chief Mexican stronghold within the present boundaries of Texas until Texas in turn gained its independence in 1836.

At the beginning of the Mexican period, San Antonio was on the western edge of Anglo-American settlement in Texas. Following Texas independence, Bexar County was formed in 1836. As late as 1858 the area around San Antonio remained sparsely settled, a reflection of the continued importance of ranching in the surrounding countryside. Although German, French, and Anglo-American immigrants have added to the original Spanish, Mexican, and American Indian character of the city, San Antonio remains one of the most charmingly Mexican of all Texas cities. Even with guidebook in hand, the visitor who sees all of the historic sites listed may still miss much of the charm and cultural wealth of San Antonio and its Hispanic citizens. The neighborhoods where the variety of Mexican-American yard art can be seen, homes where *capillas* (outdoor yard shrines) and home altars honor special saints, the community churches on feast days, the backyard picnics where tacos are served and conjunto music plays on the radio—these are the heart of Hispanic San Antonio.

Information Centers

San Antonio Chamber of Commerce. 602 E. Commerce at Alamo St. More business-oriented than the Visitors Bureau, the chamber has various guides and media lists. Open Mon.–Fri. 8–5.

San Antonio Convention and Visitors Bureau. 317 Alamo Plaza. Provides information on San Antonio attractions and events, free maps, directions, literature, and information on accommodations and dining. Open daily 9–5:30.

San Antonio Hispanic Chamber of Commerce. 110 Broadway, Suite 50. The oldest Hispanic Chamber in the United States, the San Antonio Hispanic Chamber of Commerce was chartered in 1929. Although the chamber is not a major tourist information center, the friendly staff is always happy to assist visitors. Open daily 8:30–5:30.

San Antonio Missions National Historical Park. 2202 Roosevelt Ave. Provides information on the missions and on special events held at the missions. Contact the park (at the address above, San Antonio 78210) for information on Los Pastores, Mission Fest, and Open House at the Missions (*see* Festivals entries).

Historic Sites

Alamo. *See* Mission San Antonio de Valero.

Alamo Plaza. Downtown on Houston St. The plaza was originally the courtyard of Mission San Antonio de Valero. Much of the mission compound was destroyed after the famous battle of 1836, but archeological excavations have revealed the original walled perimeters of the mission complex. These perimeters are now indicated by paving stones laid in front of the Alamo church. When the U.S. Army established a quartermaster depot in the remaining stone buildings of the mission in 1847, trade was drawn to the area and soon hotels and mercantile establishments bordered the open plaza.

Alderete-Caile House. *See* La Villita Historic District.

Bexar County under Nine Governments. Marker, county courthouse, 100 Dolorosa St. The administrative government of Bexar County, the oldest in Texas, has served under nine governments, including six different Spanish and Mexican regimes, from 1718 through return to U.S. statehood following the end of the American Civil War. *SM 1967.*

Canary Islanders. Marker, NW corner of courthouse lawn. The earliest civilian colonists of San Antonio were brought here by the Spanish government from the Canary Islands. Sixteen families (56 people) arrived at Presidio San Antonio de Béxar in March 1731 and formed the first organized civil government in Texas. The colonists founded the Villa of San Fernando de Béxar, at the site of Main Plaza. They also built the church that was to become San Fernando Cathedral. Many descendants of these original settlers have played important roles in the development of Texas. Among the heroes of the Texas war for independence were several descen-

Chapel of Miracles, San Antonio.
THC photo.

dants of the Canary Islander settlers, including Ambrosio Rodríguez, who
fought at San Jacinto under Juan N. Seguín. *SM 1971*.

Casas Reales Site. Marker, Main Plaza. This site was chosen in 1731
for "government houses" by the people of San Fernando de Béxar. The
buildings served as municipal headquarters under Spanish, Mexican, Republic of Texas, and American regimes, but were vacated in 1850 by the
city. The site is now occupied by commercial structures. *SM 1971*.

Chapel of Miracles. 113 Ruiz St. This small, stuccoed stone structure
was built by Juan Ximenes in the 1870s as a private family chapel. One of
the only such chapels remaining in San Antonio, the Chapel of Miracles
has been maintained by Ximenes' descendants, who still live nearby. The
chapel is furnished with crude benches and *prie-dieus* (kneeling benches),
two small side altars, and a larger, stepped altar set into the rear wall. A
Spanish Colonial crucifix, known as "El Señor," hangs above the altar,

dominating the interior of the shrine. The crucifix is said to have come from the church at Mission San Antonio de Valero and miracles are attributed to it. The statue of Our Lady of Sorrows is from the same period as the crucifix. The Gothic windows and low steeple were added in a 1946 renovation. *NR 1980. See also* San Fernando Cemetery No. 1.

Chihuahua Road. Marker, intersection of Acme and Castroville Rds. Following an old Indian route, the Chihuahua Road (also called Chihuahua Trail) originated in northern Mexico, entered Texas at Presidio and passed the Horsehead Crossing on the Pecos, then proceeded through Uvalde and Castroville en route to San Antonio and the coast. It was a major route of the 19th-century Mexican silver trade. A much older road, El Camino Real from Chihuahua through El Paso to Santa Fe, also is known as the Chihuahua Trail. *SM 1965.*

General Cós House. *See* La Villita Historic District.

Melchior de la Garza House. 100 S. Laredo St. Built about 1800, this stuccoed, caliche-block cottage has a three-bay façade and a shed addition at the rear. The gabled roof reveals wood shingles under the newer asbestos shingles. This house is the one remaining example of the type of homes that ringed Main and Military plazas during the Spanish Colonial period and well into the 19th century. Most of these houses were replaced by commercial and local-government structures during the post–Civil War boom. *NR 1979.*

Domínguez-Micheli Houses. 228 Arciniega St. The first house (1811) at this location was built by Cayetano Domínguez, whose rebellion against Spain led to the confiscation of his home. Vincente Micheli, a merchant, bought the old structure, added to it, and in 1844 built the associated two-story home. *RTHL 1964.*

El Camino Real. Marker, Nacogdoches Rd. and Loop 410. El Camino Real stretched 1,000 miles from Mexico to Louisiana. Domingo Terán de los Ríos, first governor of Texas, blazed the central section of the road in 1691. Called the "Trail of the Padres," it linked Monclova, Mexico, with the Spanish missions of East Texas. San Antonio was a major stop on El Camino Real. *SM 1979.*

El Carmen Church (Our Lady of Mt. Carmel Church). Off US 281S, in Losoya. In 1817 the original mission chapel of Nuestra Señora del Carmen was erected as a memorial to the heroes of the Battle of the Medina. By 1854 a rectory had been added and the chapel enlarged into a church. This structure was almost completely destroyed by fire in 1872, but by 1877 it had been restored in a location directly over the original crypt. In the 1870s the church was the center of a settlement known as La Villa del Carmen, where cattle drivers halted on their way to the railhead in San Antonio. The church was damaged again by fire in 1904 and, although restored, it weakened through the years and was replaced with a new structure in 1967. However, the bell tower of the historic building remains as a memorial to Texans who took part in Mexico's struggle for independence from Spain. *See also* Enrique Esparza; Gutiérrez-Magee Rebellion.

El Cuartel Site. Marker, 418 S. Alamo St. El Cuartel (also spelled Quartel), the barracks or quarters for the militia, was built in 1810. Here in

1811 Capt. Juan Bautista de las Casas recruited forces for the first overthrow of Spanish rule in Texas. Juan Zambrano, who led the counterrevolutionary force, also recruited here to overthrow the Las Casas regime. El Cuartel de San Antonio de Béxar apparently was destroyed during the Texas Revolution. *SM 1967.*

El Mercado. Market Square, Santa Rosa and Commerce Sts. The traditional, Mexican-style market features farm produce, local handicrafts and Mexican imports, and several restaurants in more than 50 shops. The largest of its kind in the United States, the 150-year-old market has undergone many changes during its history, but its Hispanic heritage remains undimmed. El Mercado also is the scene of celebrations throughout the year, featuring music, food, and entertainments (*see* Festivals entries).

Enrique Esparza. Marker, Mt. Carmel Cemetery, 6 mi. S of San Antonio via FM 1937, in Losoya. Enrique Esparza was the son of Alamo defender Gregorio Esparza and one of the few survivors of the 1836 siege of the Alamo. His eye-witness story later became an invaluable account of the historic battle. *SM 1967.*

Goliad Road. Marker, on the "Burnt Oak" at Pecan Valley Country Club, 4711 Pecan Valley Dr. Established about 1720 as "El Camino Real a la Bahía del Espíritu Santo," the King's Highway to Goliad, this route served for 150 years as a major emigrant, military, and trade road and became a segment of the Chihuahua Road, which connected the Texas Gulf Coast and Mexico. *SM 1968.*

Grass Fight. Marker, IH 35 frontage road near San Antonio stockyards. Near here occurred what may have been one of the most disappointing victories in the Texas war for independence. On November 26, 1835, Texas forces, composed of both Anglo- and Mexican-Texans, were camped near San Antonio waiting for a chance to engage the army of the Centralist regime stationed there. At this site the Texan forces captured a pack train bound for Béxar. After the battle they discovered that the animals were not carrying silver to pay the garrison but hay for the Mexican troops' livestock. *SM 1982.*

Gutiérrez-Magee Rebellion. This rebellion was instigated by José Bernardo Gutiérrez de Lara, a revolutionary refugee from Mexico, with the support of Augustus William Magee, an American army officer. Gutiérrez established himself in Nacogdoches and gained the support of American adventurers and frontiersmen, many of them recruited by Magee. Their Republican Army of the North, made up of Mexican, Indian, and American rebels, crossed the Sabine and entered Nacogdoches in August 1812. The force also captured Goliad, but Magee died there of a fever. The rebels took San Antonio in March 1813 but were ousted later that year. Three battles in this struggle for Mexican independence from Spain occurred in the San Antonio area.

> **Battle of Rosalis.** Marker, intersection of W.W. White and Hildebrandt Rds., 3.5 mi. S of San Antonio. At the Battle of Rosalis the Republican Army of the North, led by Bernardo Gutiérrez de Lara and Samuel Kemper, defeated Royalist Spanish forces on March 29, 1813. *CM 1936.*

Battle of the Alazán. Marker, 2300 W. Commerce. On June 20, 1813, the Republican Army of the North engaged Spanish Royalists in this vicinity. Gutiérrez led his men through the very center of the Spanish camp, whose forces were led by Col. Ygnacio Elizondo. *CM 1936; SM 1967.*

Battle of the Medina. Marker, 14 mi. S of San Antonio on FM 1937 at Losoya, off US 281S. At the Battle of the Medina, August 18, 1813, an army of Spanish Royalists commanded by Gen. José Joaquín Arredondo defeated the Republican Army of the North, commanded by José Álvarez de Toledo. José Menchaca commanded the Mexican division of the republican army at the battle and was killed in the engagement. Thus ended the Gutiérrez-Magee Rebellion, an attempt to free Texas and Mexico from Spanish rule. *CM 1936.*

Old Houston Road. Marker, Lincoln Park on E. Commerce St. The Old Houston Road, the link from old Spanish Texas to the Austin Colony, ran near this site. *SM 1965.*

La Quinta de las Piedras. 223 W. Gramercy. Miguel Menchaca, descendant of prominent Canary Islanders who came to Texas in 1731, built this house in the 1850s. The stone villa was constructed with gun slits in its thick rock walls for observation and defense. A spring under the house supplied water in times of siege. *RTHL 1962.*

La Trinidad Iglesia Metodista Unida. 300 San Fernando St. This is one of the oldest Spanish-language Methodist congregations in the United States. Because of the long tradition of Catholicism among Hispanics, Protestant churches made few early efforts to establish Spanish-language churches in the United States. In the late 19th century, evangelical work by Methodists was undertaken in South Texas, and a mission known as La Trinidad was organized in 1876 in San Antonio. The mission first met in private homes, then in rented rooms near El Mercado. The church, during the years of the Mexican Revolution, served as a refuge for many leaders involved in the revolutionary movement. The first church was built in 1886 at the corner of Pacos and San Fernando, a second church was built in 1921, and a third, at the present location, in 1967. The church has been known by several previous names, including, in chronological order, Mission Mexicana, La Iglesia Metodista Mexicana, and La Iglesia Metodista La Trinidad.

La Villita Historic District. Complex along river downtown, bounded by S. Alamo, Navarro, and Durango Sts. and the San Antonio River. The 27 structures in this National Register Historic District (*NR 1972*) are examples of vernacular construction reflecting Spanish, Mexican, European, and 19th-century Anglo-American influences. The buildings were in ruins when restoration began in 1939 as a public works project. Restored structures, including authentic early adobe houses, provide a Mexican village atmosphere to the complex, which includes small restaurants and arts and crafts shops. La Villita is one of the locales favored for fiesta events (*see* Festival entries). The following are major examples of structures that reflect Hispanic construction methods and styles:

General Cós House, San Antonio.
Photo by Cathryn Hoyt, THC.

Alderete-Caile House. 526 Nueva St. The two houses on this property, located on land that originally belonged to Mission San Antonio de Valero, are interesting examples of traditional Hispanic building techniques. The structure in the rear, built about 1818, was made by lacing vertical poles together to form walls that were then plastered with mud. This house is thought to be the home of Dolores Alderete, the widow of Ygnacio Gil, who had earlier received the site as a grant from the Spanish government for the military service of her husband. The second structure is a caliche-block home built by Robert Caile soon after he bought the property in 1857. *RTHL 1966.*

Caxias House. 416-B Paseo de la Villita. The one-story, stuccoed house reflects Mexican vernacular style.

General Cós House. 503 Villita. An example of Old San Antonio architecture, the house was the scene of the signing of the Articles of Capitulation by Gen. Perfecto Cós after Texans captured San Antonio from Mexican forces in 1835. *RTHL 1962.*

Díaz House. 206 Arciniega. This stuccoed stone, vernacular residence was built about 1840. The small windows and thick walls help to keep the house cool during hot Texas summers. The house was restored in 1980 and is now part of the Four Seasons Hotel complex.

Staffel-Elmendorf-Tyler House. 220 Arciniega St. This stuccoed double house with center chimney was built about 1850. German immigrants often combined their own house styles with details copied from local structures, such as the pedimented porch on this surviving example. The house was restored in 1979 and is now a part of the inner court of the Four Seasons Hotel.

Manuel Yturri House. 327 S. Presa. The one-story section was built of limestone about 1817. The Victorian front was added in 1881.

Main Plaza. Downtown, separated from Military Plaza by San Fernando Cathedral. Laid out in 1731 and known as the Plaza de las Islas, this was part of the Canary Islander settlement called Villa de San Fernando. The old plaza has been the site of many significant events in the history of San Antonio. Together with Military Plaza, it is included in the Main and Military Plaza Historic District, which includes thirteen blocks of downtown San Antonio surrounding Main and Military plazas, with San Pedro Creek and the San Antonio River forming the east and west boundaries. This National Register of Historic Places District illustrates San Antonio's evolution from Spanish stronghold in the 18th century, to 19th-century cowtown, to modern commercial center. In addition to the two historic plazas, the district includes the Spanish Governor's Palace, San Fernando Cathedral, and the Melchior de la Garza House (each listed separately). Examples of Spanish-influenced architecture also are present in the district, including the Chee Kunh Tong Chinese Free Masons building and the Kallison Block (listed under Spanish Revival Architecture below). *NR 1979.*

Market Square. *See* El Mercado.

Matamoros Road. Marker, intersection of Ashley, Roosevelt, and S. Flores Sts. About 330 miles long, the route of Matamoros Road varied with seasons and conditions. The trip from San Antonio to Matamoros, Mexico, took six to eight weeks if no major delays occurred. This route was used by Indians and Spaniards before it became a major 19th-century road. *SM 1965.*

Milam Square. At Santa Rosa and Houston Sts. The east end of the park served as the cemetery for the Canary Islander colonists and San Fernando Church until the mid-19th century. The park is dedicated to this now-vanished historic cemetery in which many of San Antonio's early settlers were buried. Symbolic headstones were placed in the cemetery area in the 1970s and bronze plaques list the names of those originally buried there.

Military Plaza (Plaza de Armas). Downtown, separated from Main Plaza by San Fernando Cathedral. The Presidio de Béxar was relocated here in 1722 from its original site farther north. This plaza served as the drilling ground for troops stationed at the presidio. The area is one of the oldest permanently settled locales in Texas. *SM 1971; NR 1979.*

Mission Concepción (Nuestra Señora de la Purísima Concepción de Acuña). 807 Mission Rd. This mission was first established in East Texas, moved to the Austin area in 1730, and moved to San Antonio in 1731. At its permanent site in San Antonio, Concepción was under construction for more than 20 years and was built of locally quarried tufa and limestone. The massive church, in Spanish-Mexican Baroque style with carved stone detail, twin bell towers, and vault and dome, was completed in 1755 and is the oldest unreconstructed stone church in the United States. The adjacent cloister arcade is partly reconstructed. Colorful geometric designs once covered the exterior surfaces of the church but the patterns have long since faded. However, original interior paintings of the Spanish Colonial period still remain at Concepción. Some are religious symbols, while others are

decorative architectural embellishments. *RTHL 1964; NHL.*

Mission Espada (San Francisco de la Espada). 10040 Espada Rd. Mission Espada was moved from East Texas in 1729 and established in San Antonio in 1731. The present church was completed in 1756. The southernmost of the San Antonio chain of missions, Espada served the needs of Coahuiltecan Indian groups until secularization in 1793–94. The mission declined following secularization, and vandalism, weather, and neglect contributed to its abandonment. Efforts were made to reconstruct and repair remaining structures in the mid-19th century, and restoration occurred again about 1935 as a public works project. In addition to the church, remaining early structures include the southeast bastion, or fortified tower (the only mission fortification left intact in San Antonio), the walls that once surrounded the mission compound, the foundations of a granary, and part of the original mission waterworks. *RTHL 1962; NR 1972.*

Mission Espada Dam, Ditch, and Aqueduct. Marker, near the aqueduct on Mission Rd. The Espada aqueduct is believed to be the only remaining Spanish structure of this type in the United States that is still in working use. Built from 1740 to 1745, this Romanesque construction of locally quarried limestone was once part of an integrated irrigation system that served the five missions in the San Antonio area. The dam still directs water from the San Antonio River to the *acequia* (ditch), which in turn carries water to the aqueduct. The aqueduct carries the water over San Pedro Creek and has survived floods of as much as eight or ten feet over

West side of Main Plaza, San Antonio, in 1849. Painting by William Samuel. Courtesy of San Antonio Museum Association, San Antonio, Texas. On loan from Bexar County.

161

Interior of Mission Concepción, San Antonio. Photo by Sam McColloch.

the structure. Despite floods and time, the dam and aqueduct have carried water every day since Spanish Colonial times to many users along the irrigation ditch. Aqueduct lands were purchased by the San Antonio Conservation Society in 1941. *RTHL 1962; NHL.*

Mission San Antonio de Valero (the Alamo). Downtown, Alamo Plaza at Houston St. Established in 1718, this was the first of five Spanish missions to be founded in San Antonio. The mission was moved to its present location in 1724. The original church, begun in 1744, was destroyed, and construction of a second church, the structure now known as the Alamo, was begun about 1755. Built from heavy limestone quarried in the vicinity, the Alamo's façade was originally designed to have twin bell towers, but these were apparently never finished. The mission was secularized in 1793, the church was closed in 1812, and in 1814 the convent began to be used as a hospital. In 1836 the most famous battle of the Texas war for independence was fought here. Eight Mexican-Texans were among those who died defending the Alamo: Juan Abamillo, Juan Antonio Badillo, Carlos Espalier, Gregorio Esparza, Antonio Fuentes, Toribio Losoya, and Andrés Nava of San Antonio, and José María Guerrero of Laredo. The mission was almost totally destroyed following the 1836 battle, but in 1849 the U.S. Army repaired the church and other buildings to use as warehouses. It was not until 1850 that the Alamo's now-familiar parapet was added to the building over the original church's unfinished façade. Eventually rescued by state and private efforts, the Alamo is now a museum administered by the Daughters of the Republic of Texas. Open Mon.–Sat. 9:30–5; Sun. 10–5:30. *RTHL 1962; NHL. See also* Museums, Libraries, and Cultural Centers: Daughters of the Republic of Texas Library.

Mission San Antonio de Valero *Acequia Madre.* Marker, inside HemisFair Park. This *acequia madre* was one in a network of irrigation ditches begun by the Spanish and their Indian charges at the founding of Mission San Antonio de Valero in 1718. The hand-dug *acequia* diverted water from the San Antonio River through fields belonging to the mission. Irrigation was the key to growth of both the mission and the town. This section of the *acequia* was reconstructed in 1968. *SM 1968.*

Mission San Francisco Xavier de Nájera Site. Marker, at Mission Concepción, Mission Rd. This mission was established in 1722, but no permanent buildings were constructed. The Indians at the mission were relocated to Mission San Antonio de Valero in 1726. Land belonging to the San Francisco mission was later granted to Mission Nuestra Señora de la Purísima Concepción de Acuña, which was reestablished in this vicinity in 1731. *CM 1936.*

Mission San José (San José y San Miguel de Aguayo). 6539 San Jose Dr. Established in 1720, the mission was relocated to its present site in 1740. San José is known as the "Queen of Missions." Constructed of locally quarried limestone with elaborate carved detail, the domed church was built between 1768 and 1782. Its most famous feature is the sculpted sacristy window known as the Rose Window. The fine detail of this legendary feature demonstrates the high level of craftsmanship among the artisans who worked on the missions. The entire mission compound has been restored,

Reconstruction of the Mission San Antonio de Valero acequia madre, San Antonio. Photo by Diane Hopkins Hughs.

including the outer wall with Indian quarters, the granary, and workshops. Inside the restored granary is a model of the mission as it looked in the 1700s. Outside the north wall is an old mill built about 1790, the first flour mill in Texas. Like other mission churches, the one at San José still functions as a parish church. A modern feature of San José is the Sunday-noon mariachi mass. The mariachis, dressed in traditional costumes, play from the choir loft, their inspiring performance attracting crowds of visitors. *RTHL 1962; NHL.*

Mission San Juan Capistrano. 9101 Graf Rd. Mission San Juan Capistrano, founded in 1731, was the successor to the East Texas Mission San José de los Nazonis (1716) and was established in San Antonio for the Coahuiltecan Indians. The church, convent, and granary of local limestone date from 1756. The chapel and some other structures survived secularization in 1794, but much of the complex eventually fell into ruins. In the course of a public works project in 1934, the Indian quarters and remains of a large church were located. The chapel, priest's quarters, and other structures were rebuilt in the 1960s. Archeological remains at the site include the unfinished church, jacals, and other structures. The entrance gate at San Juan is typical of the Romanesque arches found in the San Antonio missions. The little chapel, featuring an open bell tower, still serves the community of Berg's Mill (now part of the city). The restored missionary residence displays artifacts from the Spanish Colonial period. *RTHL 1962; NR 1972.*

Celso Navarro House. Witte Museum Grounds, 3801 Broadway. Celso Navarro was a descendant of Canary Islander settler Ángel Navarro. The limestone house, built in 1835, was reconstructed on the museum grounds in 1948.

José Antonio Navarro State Historic Site. 228 S. Laredo St. José Antonio Navarro was a San Antonio native, a statesman, and a founder of the Republic of Texas. He was one of the signers of the Texas Declaration of Independence, helped write the Constitution of the Republic of Texas, and served in the republic's congress. Three structures that were his home, office, and separate kitchen, dating from about 1850, make up the historic site, which reflects Mexican, German, French, and pioneer styles. Contents include personal memorabilia and authentic period furnishings, providing a glimpse of life in a Texas-Mexican home during the mid-1800s. The Navarro House was restored by the San Antonio Conservation Society in 1962 and donated to the Texas Parks and Wildlife Department in 1975. Open Tues.–Sat. 10–4. *RTHL 1962; NR 1972.* A marker commemorating Navarro also has been placed in San Fernando Cemetery No. 1. *CM 1936.*

Our Lady of Guadalupe Church. 1321 El Paso St. The original church of this parish opened its doors in 1911, but by 1920 the church was too small for the growing population, and a new church was completed in 1926. Jesuit fathers took over the parish in 1932 and encouraged preservation of Mexican-American traditions, including the presentation of religious dramas such as Los Pastores, Las Posadas, and Las Mañanitas. The Guadalupe Players are Texas' best-known performers of Los Pastores, a Christmas drama based on the shepherds' visit to the Christ child. The church also is noted for its celebration of the feast day of Our Lady of Guadalupe. Guadalupana events start at 4 a.m. on December 12, and masses and special events, such as mariachi and charro performances, continue throughout the day. *See also* Festivals: Los Pastores.

Pajalache Acequia. *See* Yturri-Edmunds Home and Mill.

Paseo del Rio. *See* River Walk.

Plaza de Armas. *See* Military Plaza.

Plaza de Las Islas. *See* Main Plaza.

River Walk. Downtown, along the river; access from Alamo Plaza and city streets S. Alamo, S. Broadway, Presa, Navarro, St. Mary's, Market, Commerce, and Crockett. The River Walk passes through a historic area of Old San Antonio, part of it on land granted to Ambrosio Rodríguez, a Canary Islander descendant who served under Juan Seguín at the Battle of San Jacinto. Landscaping along the river in downtown San Antonio was undertaken in 1938–41 as a public-works project, and beautifully lush plants complement the walk's manmade attractions. Designed by architect R.H.H. Hugman, the landscaped stone paths were intended to invoke a Spanish atmosphere. Access to the River Walk, now a major tourist attraction, is by stairways from graceful stone bridges that arch over the San Antonio River in the downtown area, and the walkway leads to historic La Villita and the Arneson Theater. Water taxis and dining barges cruise the river, and hotels, art and gift shops, restaurants and side-walk cafes, boutiques, and cabarets line the walk as it wanders several miles through the heart of the city. In the evenings music of all kinds, including mariachi, emanates from the clubs along the River Walk, but the best time to hear traditional Mexican music is during one of the many festivals held here throughout the year (*see* Festivals entries).

Col. José Francisco Ruiz. Marker, Dolorosa St., S side of Main Plaza. The marker commemorates Ruiz as a founder of the Republic of Texas. *See also* Ruiz House; San Fernando Cemetery No. 1.

Ruiz-Herrera Cemetery. Somerset Rd. between Loop 410 and Medina River. The Ruiz-Herrera Cemetery, started in the 1840s, is still used by the founding families. Graves include those of Texas patriots Francisco Antonio Ruiz, whose father and uncle signed the Texas Declaration of Independence, and Blás Herrera, who alerted the Alamo defenders to Santa Anna's approach. *SM 1967.*

Ruiz House. Witte Museum grounds, 3801 Broadway. The José Francisco Ruiz house was built about 1745. The front room became the first public school in San Antonio, in 1803. The house, which formerly stood on the south side of Military Plaza at 420 Dolorosa St., was dismantled in 1942 and moved to the Witte Museum gardens for reconstruction. The five polychromed-wood bas-relief panels hanging on the walls of the Ruiz house are the work of Roberto de la Silva, Mexican primitive artist. *RTHL 1962. See also* Ruiz-Herrera Cemetery; San Fernando Cemetery No. 1.

Salado Valley. Marker, on Clubhouse of Pecan Valley Country Club, 4711 Pecan Valley Dr. Named by Spanish explorers in 1709, Salado Creek became the town boundary of San Fernando de Béxar after the arrival of the Canary Islands colonists. The valley was a well-known watering spot between San Antonio and all points east. Major 19th-century roads crossed the valley, and Santa Anna traveled through here in 1836. The valley also was the locale of more than one battle during the Texas war for independence. *SM 1968.*

San Antonio Missions National Historical Park. Four of the five missions of San Antonio are now included in a national park and are listed on the National Register of Historic Places as the Mission Parkway Historic-Archeological District (*NR 1975*). The district also includes prehistoric and historic archeological sites in the area. The San Antonio Missions National Historical Park was authorized by Congress in 1978 and was opened to the public in 1983. The mandated purpose of the park is to preserve, restore, and interpret the Spanish missions and related historic irrigation systems in San Antonio. *See also* Mission Concepción; Mission Espada; Mission San José; Mission San Juan Capistrano.

San Fernando Cathedral. Main Plaza, downtown between W. Market and W. Commerce Sts. San Fernando Cathedral, the first parish church of San Antonio, was established in 1738 by the Canary Islands colonists. The original church, built of rough limestone, was constructed on a cruciform plan with a crossing dome. From 1828 to 1868 the structure faced a long series of disasters, including fires and bombardment. In 1868 the church was enlarged, incorporating part of the original structure and adding the present Gothic Revival façade. In 1926 San Antonio was elevated by the Catholic Church to an archdiocese (headed by a bishop). The church was restored in the mid-1970s, revealing the original 18th-century walls and crossing dome. Bishop Patrick F. Flores, the first Mexican-American bishop in the United States, became a resident of the cathedral in 1970. *PM 1924; RTHL 1962; NR 1975.*

San Fernando Cemetery No. 1. Veracruz and San Marcos Sts. San Fernando Parish cemetery originally was located near the church but was moved to a site about one mile southwest in the 1830s. Many descendants of old San Antonio families are buried in this historic cemetery. San Fernando Cemetery No. 2 was established in 1922 at Cupples and Castroville roads. Historical markers have been placed in Cemetery No. 1 for the following individuals who helped to establish the Republic of Texas:

Plácido Olivarri. Olivarri served as a guide to the Texas Army in 1835. Born in San Antonio in 1815, Olivarri died in 1894. *CM 1936.*

Capt. José Antonio Menchaca. Menchaca was a native of San Antonio and a hero of the Texas war for independence. He participated in the Siege of Béxar in 1835 and served in Juan N. Seguín's company at the Battle of San Jacinto. He later served several terms as an alderman of San Antonio and as mayor pro tem in 1838. *CM 1936.*

José Antonio Navarro. *See* José Antonio Navarro State Historic Site.

José de Jesús Rodríguez. Rodríguez, a veteran of the Texas war for independence, participated in the Storming of Béxar on December 5, 1835. *SM 1962.*

Col. José Francisco Ruiz. Ruiz, native San Antonian, signed the Texas Declaration of Independence and served as a senator of the Republic of Texas. He was one of two native Texans (one of three of Hispanic descent) who signed the declaration and helped found the Republic of Texas. His house is preserved on the grounds of the Witte Museum. *CM 1936; SM 1973. See also* Ruiz House.

Juan Ximenes. Ximenes was a veteran of the Texas war for independence and one of the storming party at Béxar in December 1835. *SM 1962. See also* Chapel of the Miracles.

San Pedro Springs Park. San Pedro Ave. Inhabited since prehistoric times, San Pedro Springs influenced the decision to locate Mission San Antonio de Valero and the villa of San Fernando de Béxar in the vicinity. The springs area was designated a public space in 1729 by King Philip V of Spain. The park area contains both prehistoric and historic archeological remains. *SM 1965; NR 1979.*

Erasmo Seguín. Marker, south yard, Bexar County Courthouse, 100 Dolorosa St. Erasmo Seguín, a native San Antonian, helped establish the first public school in the city and, in 1821, served as alcalde of Béxar. A friend of Stephen F. Austin, he supported Anglo-American colonists in their demands for local self-government. His ranch near Floresville was well known as a stopping place for early Texas travelers and became a supply station for Texas troops during the war for independence. Seguín worked after the war to reestablish civil government in San Antonio and to prevent conflicts between Anglo-American immigrants and Mexican-Texans. *SM 1973.*

Spanish Governor's Palace. Military Plaza, 105 Plaza de Armas. This structure, completed in 1749, was the *Comandancia,* or home, of the captain of the Presidio de San Antonio de Béxar. The captain of the presidio also served as governor of the territory, and his headquarters thus came to represent the seat of civil government after the Villa of San Fernando de Béxar (now San Antonio) became the capital of the Spanish Province of Texas in 1773. The ten-room, walled adobe structure, with its carved doors, low-beamed ceilings, and courtyard, is typical of early Spanish architecture in San Antonio. José Ignacio Pérez bought the building in 1804, and in 1929 the City of San Antonio purchased the structure (only the main walls were then intact) from his descendants. It is the only building of the Spanish Colonial period remaining at Military Plaza. Restored by the city, the Governor's Palace is now a museum exhibiting Spanish Colonial and Mexican furnishings, art, and household items. Open Mon.–Sat. 9–5; Sun. 10–5. *PM; RTHL 1962; NHL 1970.*

Storming of Béxar. Marker, NE corner of Main Plaza. The takeover of San Antonio by Texan troops on December 5–9, 1835, is commemorated here. Supported by a contingent under Juan N. Seguín, Ben Milam led Texan volunteers in the storming of Béxar, expelling the Centralist army and setting the stage for the siege of the Alamo, February 23–March 6, 1836. Native Texans among the troops included Juan Ximenes and José de Jesús de Rodríguez. *SM 1971.*

Texas' First All-Spanish Radio Program (The International Goodwill Program). Marker, 2700 Cincinnati Ave. In 1928, KGCI (later KMAC) initiated a two-hour nightly program entirely in Spanish. The station's owner, Sam Liberto, persuaded Julian F. Lozano to produce and announce the program, and Lozano continued to promote the cause of international understanding until his death in 1951. In the tradition established by this program, San Antonio radio stations schedule many hours of programs in Spanish each day. *SM 1972.*

Walsh Ranch. 11 mi. S of San Antonio. The original ranch was founded about 1800 by José Ignacio Pérez, son of a Canary Islander, who served in 1817 as governor of Spanish Texas and was owner of the Spanish Governor's Palace after 1804. A descendant, Casimira de la Concepción Walsh, sold the Governor's Palace to the City of San Antonio in 1929. The Walsh Ranch, which includes part of the original Pérez holding, is still owned by descendants. Private ranch, not open to the public. *TFLHR.*

Yturri-Edmunds Home and Mill. 257 Yellowstone St. This home and mill is typical of the small farmsteads that once lined the banks of the San Antonio River. The complex was built about 1840 on the Pajalache Acequia (*CM 1936*), on lands formerly part of Mission Concepción. The complex furnished food to early settlers and served as a resting place for travelers en route to Béxar from the missions. The house, built of adobe bricks made of mud mixed with goat hair, has recently been restored. Open to the public.

Arneson River Theater, San Antonio. Photo by Cathryn Hoyt, THC.

Spanish Revival Architecture

Alamo Methodist Church. 1150 S. Alamo St. Built in 1912–13, the brick structure with cast-stone and corbeled-brick detail reflects Spanish Mission Revival influences. The building features a façade of twin towers flanking an arched parapet, tall chimneys on a gable roof, and art-glass windows. It is one of many Protestant churches in Texas whose architecture is patterned after the Catholic mission churches of New Spain. *NR 1979.*

Arneson River Theater. In La Villita area. Outdoor musical presentations, including ballet folklórico performances, are frequent at this Spanish Revival style theater on the River Walk, especially during the summer and on the occasion of the many fiestas held in the city. *See* Festivals entries for more information.

Aztec Theater. 104 N. St. Mary's St. Built in the 1920s, the theater portrays a Pre-Columbian impression of sacrificial temples, Aztec gods, and the meeting of Cortez and Montezuma. To create this fantasy, the architect studied Mayan and Aztec ruins in Mexico. San Antonio's other Art Deco movie theaters of the 1920s include the Majestic and the Texas (only the façade of the Texas remains).

The Bushnell (Apartment Building). 240 Bushnell St. This seven-story, reinforced concrete building with stuccoed exterior and cast-stone details exhibits Spanish Revival elements. It was built in 1916 by the Kelwood Co. *NR 1982.*

Chee Kunh Tong Chinese Free Masons. 117 W. Nueva. Spanish influence in the architectural style of this early 1920s, two-story brick structure is evident in the elaborate stone decoration at the end bays and the *canales* (roof drains) piercing the parapet. The building was constructed to serve the city's Chinese population, which greatly increased after General John J. Pershing's expedition into Mexico searching for Francisco ("Pancho") Villa just before World War I. Chinese railroad workers in Mexico fled to the United States, and many remained in San Antonio's Chinese community after they were granted special citizenship by the U.S. Congress. *NR 1979.*

International & Great Northern Railroad Station (later Missouri and Pacific). Medina and Houston Sts. Architect Harvey Page designed this great Mission Revival style rail depot for the city's west side in 1907. The two-story, brick-veneer structure has a steel-frame central rotunda clad with plaster-on-lath details; the rotunda dome originally was covered with copper. The copper Indian atop the dome, as well as the elaborate art-glass windows, were restored in a recent rehabilitation, and the building now houses commercial offices. *NR 1975.*

Thomas Jefferson High School. 723 Donaldson Ave. This two- and three-story, Spanish Revival style, rambling complex with brick veneer and cast-stone detail features an elaborate Baroque entry and four-story domed tower. *RTHL 1983; NR 1983. See also* sidebar: Thomas Jefferson High School.

Kallison Block. 101–125 S. Flores. Dating from about 1920, this row of two-story, brick commercial buildings reflects mission influence in its classical Spanish detailing at the second-level window moldings, tile roof, and elaborately detailed, angled entrance. The first level has been altered. *NR 1979.*

McNay Art Museum. *See* Museums entry.

Majestic Theater Building. 214 Houston St. Built in 1929, this 18-story theater and office building in Spanish Revival style was designed by renowned "atmospheric theater" architect John Eberson. The Majestic is the state's best example of the fantasy theaters of the 1920s. The theater occupies the equivalent of six stories of the building and has two ornamented balconies and an auditorium that seats 4,000. This theater in the grand style has an elaborate Baroque plaster interior featuring architectural façade vignettes and sculptural (*Mudejar*) ceilings, with decorations of clouds and twinkling stars creating an "outdoor theater" effect. Rehabilitated in 1983 and later, in 1990, for use as the San Antonio Symphony Hall. *NR 1975.*

Municipal Auditorium. 100 Auditorium Circle. Built in 1926, this three-story, reinforced-concrete structure with a two-story steel-truss auditorium dome is Spanish Revival in style and features carved-stone details and decorative tiles. The main entry arcade is flanked by domed towers. The building was rebuilt and renovated following a fire in 1979. *NR 1981.*

Our Lady of Sorrows Church. 3107 N. St. Mary's. The original small church was constructed in 1915 for Mexican-American families in the area around Valdez St. In the mid-1930s the church was enlarged, but its simple Mission-influenced façade was retained.

Randolph Air Force Base. Originally a major air corps training center, Randolph Field was constructed in 1928–31 on a 2,300-acre tract 18 miles

Thomas Jefferson High School, San Antonio. THC photo.

THOMAS JEFFERSON HIGH SCHOOL
Gem of Spanish Renaissance Architecture In San Antonio

In 1929 the citizens of San Antonio passed a $3,700,000 school bond proposal to build a new high school on the north side of San Antonio. The new school, designed by the architectural firm of Adams and Adams, was a monumental Spanish Renaissance complex with intricate cast-stone detailing inspired by Spanish and Mexican-American-Indian designs. Cost estimates for construction of the school ran as high as $1,250,000—and school officials were constantly criticized for their extravagance during the hard economic times of the Depression.

Despite the criticism, plans progressed for the building and a 33-acre site was chosen for construction. Again school officials faced an uproar as people complained that the site was so far away from the populated areas of the city that only students in the outlying areas would be able to attend. There was some truth to these objections. The architect and the school district superintendent had to ride to the site on horseback to check on progress as there were no roads out that far.

Soon the field of weeds and mesquite became a beehive of activity. Eight mule-

170

northeast of San Antonio. All of the original buildings were in Spanish Revival style and were laid out around the centrally located Administration Building. The Spanish Revival theme, although simplified, is still maintained in the base's permanent buildings.

Administration Building (Building 100). Nicknamed the "Taj Mahal" since its construction in 1930–31, the Administration Building has a Spanish Revival style base and Modernistic-inspired tower. The two-story main building, a reinforced concrete structure with stucco finish and tile roofs, has corner pavilions with hip roofs and central bays with semicircular arches. The blue-and-gold-chevron pattern tilework on the tower derives from 19th-century churches in Mexico. *NR 1987.*

Base Chapel. Located to the left of the Administration Building, as one approaches from the main gate, is the base chapel. This beautiful Mission Revival style structure is decorated with cast-stone detailing reminiscent of the Mission San José façade.

drawn rigs were used to dig the 35-foot-deep holes for the foundation. Local artisans Hannibal Pianta and his son Eugene were hired to cast the ornamental concrete work that adorns the main entrance of the school, and Tony Lozano and Larry Peña of Redondo Tile were contracted to make the decorative tile that was used throughout the building.

The school incorporated many "firsts" into its design: it was the first school in San Antonio to have tile floors instead of wooden ones and the first to have its own gymnasium, lockers that were built into the walls, indoor firewalls, and its own specially designed coat-of-arms. The cluster of buildings, linked by arcades and courtyards, was completed in 1932.

Soon, the school was both nationally and internationally renowned for the beauty of its architecture and the spirit of its student body. In 1937 *Life* magazine chose Jefferson High School as the most outstanding high school in America and ran features on it in the March 1938 issue. By 1939 the school had been featured in *Life, American Weekly,* several European publications, and *National Geographic* and had been used as the setting for two Hollywood movies.

In 1983 Thomas Jefferson High School was designated a Recorded Texas Historic Landmark by the Texas Historical Commission and listed on the National Register of Historic Places. The school is located at 723 Donaldson Avenue in San Antonio.

Randolph Air Force Base Chapel, San Antonio. Photo by Cathryn Hoyt, THC.

St. Anthony Hotel. 300 Travis St. Built in 1909–10, this ten-story masonry and steel-frame structure with tile roof and Spanish Revival detailing incorporates four towers into one building with a common façade and lobby. Two of the four towers were added to the building in 1935, and the fourth in 1941. Two entries on the side of the main façade are capped by segmental, stepped parapets, and the arcade spans the central section. Distinctive detailing includes the *rejas,* or grilles, on the top floor. Restorations of 1981–83 highlight the 1935 historic period, when the refurbishing and expansion of the hotel played a role in the transformation of San Antonio into a major urban center. *NR 1986.*

St. Anthony of Padua Church. 102 Lorenz Rd. This church was established in 1925 to care for about sixty families, mostly Mexican-Americans, living in a community known as Cementville. The community received its name from the fact that all of the people living there were employees of the Portland Cement Company, located off Broadway. Housed in an old frame building, the first church was dedicated to St. Anthony, the patron saint of San Antonio. The structure of the present church, dedicated in 1957, reflects the lines of the Alamo.

St. Gerard's Church. 1617 Iowa St. Twin bell towers and ornamental stonework can be seen in this attractive example of mission-influenced architecture. St. Gerard's was built in 1912.

St. Henry's Church. 1619 S. Flores St. In 1902 the original frame church of St. Henry's Parish was constructed for the predominantly German-speaking residents of the southwestern part of San Antonio. Since that time several parishes have been created from the extensive territory of St. Henry's Parish. The present mission-influenced structure with its twin bell towers was built in 1929.

San José Burial Park Chapel. On Mission Rd., S of SW Military Dr. The cemetery's Spanish Mission Revival style chapel was built about 1930.

Southern Pacific Depot. 1174 E. Commerce St. Built of brick and adobe, in 1902, the two-story, stuccoed structure, with ornate cast-stone details, is an excellent example of Mission Revival style. Beaux Arts influence in the interior is evident in a soaring skylit ceiling in the main passenger waiting room and in the use of classical garland decorative motifs. *NR 1975.*

Southwestern Bell Telephone Building. 105 Auditorium Circle. The first three floors of this Spanish Revival style building, constructed in 1931, are adorned with intricate terra-cotta decoration inspired by Mission San José.

Temple Beth-El. 211 Belknap. This synagogue reflects the Spanish heritage of San Antonio with its use of white stucco and ornate terra-cotta façade. The line of scalloped shells that form the cornice are particularly reminiscent of Spanish design.

Museums, Libraries, and Cultural Centers

Archdiocese of San Antonio, Archives of the Chancery. 2718 W. Woodlawn. The holdings of the Archdiocese, which include parish registers and marriage, birth, and death records, are primarily of interest to historical researchers. For information contact the Archdiocese at P.O. Box 28410, San Antonio 78228.

Community Cultural Arts Organization. *See* Public Art: Murals.

Daughters of the Republic of Texas Library. At the Alamo, Alamo Plaza at Houston St. The holdings of the DRT library focus on Texas history, including the Spanish Colonial period. Collections are primarily of interest to historical researchers. For more information contact the library at P.O. Box 2599, San Antonio 78299.

Guadalupe Cultural Arts Center. 1300 Guadalupe. The center showcases local visual and performing artists, and offers art exhibits, films, concerts, and classes in art and drama. It also sponsors annual festivals, including CineFestival, an international Latino film festival. *See also* Festivals entries.

Hall of Texas History and Wax Museum. At Lone Star Brewery, 600 Lone Star Blvd. Of particular interest is a collection of life-sized dioramas depicting major events in Texas history, from the Spanish mission period through the period of the Republic. Open daily 10–5.

HemisFair Park. *See* Institute of Texan Cultures; Instituto Cultural Mexicano; Universidad Nacional Autónoma de México.

Institute of Texan Cultures. In HemisFair Park. Exhibits are devoted to the many ethnic and cultural groups that have contributed to Texas' heritage. The emphasis is on people—including their foods, crafts, costumes, tools, toys, and music—rather than historic persons or events. The exhibits present a hands-on approach to history. The Mexican area, for example, includes opportunities to grind corn or read about vaqueros, the first American cowboys. The institute's libraries contain an extensive collection of books, documents, microfilms, and more than two million photographs relating to the ethnic history and traditions of the many peoples who have settled Texas. The institute sponsors an annual Texas Folklife Festival in early August. Open Tues.–Sun. 9–5.

Instituto Cultural Mexicano. 600 HemisFair Park. The institute features changing exhibits of Mexican art, and also offers occasional conferences and music or drama performances. Reproductions of Mexican monumental art from prehistoric through Spanish Colonial times decorate the exterior and grounds of the institute.

McNay Art Museum. 6000 N. New Braunfels Ave. at junction with US 81. The museum is housed in a Spanish Revival style house built in 1928 for Marion Koogler McNay, on whose collection the museum is based. Some of the decorative tilework of the passageways was done by well-known San Antonio artisan Larry Peña. The museum formally opened to the public in 1954. Although emphasis is on modern art, international collections include works of Diego Rivera and El Greco. Selections from Mrs. McNay's collection of furniture, textiles, pottery, jewelry, and carved and painted votive images of the greater New Mexico area are on exhibit in the Southwestern Gallery. Open Tues.–Sat. 9–5; Sun. 2–5.

Mexican-American Cultural Center. 3019 W. French Pl. The center conducts dance and music workshops and sponsors the local company of

Instituto Cultural Mexicano, San Antonio. Photo by Cathryn Hoyt, THC.

ballet folklórico.

Mexican Cultural Institute. *See* Instituto Cultural Mexicano.

Old Spanish Missions Historical Research Library. Our Lady of the Lake University, 411 SW 24th St. The library includes special collections relating to missions and the Spanish Colonial period in San Antonio and has on microfilm thousands of Spanish documents relating to the missions. Open Mon.–Fri., 8–5 or by appointment. Contact the library at the street address above, San Antonio 78207-4666.

St. Mary's University, Academic Library. One Camino Santa Maria. The Laredo Archives are housed in the university library's Special Collections.

San Antonio Museum of Art. 200 W. Jones Ave. off Broadway. Located in a renovated historic brewery complex of six buildings (dating from 1883), the museum focuses on art of the Americas, including Pre-Columbian, American Indian, and Spanish Colonial, as well as 18th- to 20th-century American painting and sculpture, photographs, furniture, and decorative arts. Open Mon.–Sat. 10–5; Sun. noon–5.

Universidad Nacional Autónoma de México (National University of Mexico). 600 HemisFair Park. This branch of the University of Mexico offers courses in Spanish and Latin American art, history, and anthropology taught by instructors from Mexico. It also offers occasional special programs on Mexican topics.

University of Texas at San Antonio, John Peace Library. University campus. A major emphasis of the university library's holdings is the Spanish Colonial period. While the library is open to the public, its collections are primarily of interest to historical researchers.

Witte Memorial Museum. 3801 Broadway. Focusing on natural history and archeology, the museum also features slide presentations about San Antonio history. The José Francisco Ruiz and Celso Navarro houses have been reconstructed on the grounds of the museum. Open Mon.–Sat. 10–5; Sun. noon–5.

Public Art

Faux bois (simulated wood, concrete and steel constructions), by Dionicio Rodríguez and Máximo Cortez. In Brackenridge Park (3800 Broadway). Rodríguez and Cortez sculpted cement to resemble wood, especially in the form of the intertwined tree limbs seen in the ornamental pedestrian bridge in the park. They also created the bus stop at Broadway and Patterson and the entrance to the Sunken Gardens (near Brackenridge Park). Cement sculpting, especially scoring and painting cement to create a wood effect in objects such as stepping stones, is still practiced by Mexican-American artisans in San Antonio. (The park also offers picnic spots and bridle paths; open daily 8–11.)

Lady Bird Johnson Fountain. 1974. Intersection of Bonham and Crockett. The fountain was modeled on the ornate public fountains of Mexico.

Murals. Hundreds of murals by Hispanic artists or with Hispanic themes can be found in San Antonio. The following is a sampling of representative works, most of them located in conveniently accessible places.

Community Cultural Arts Organization murals. Anastacio Torres initiated a murals program in 1978 that is now funded through the Arts and Cultural Affairs Office of the City of San Antonio. Numerous murals on topics ranging from social problems to political, social, and cultural subjects can be seen at Cassiano Homes, Menchaca Homes, and Mirasol Homes. Artists include Rudy Limón, Mark Méndez, and Samuel Pinales.

Confluence of Civilizations, by Carlos Merida. 1968. Eastern end of Henry B. González Convention Center, 200 E. Market St., inside.

Confluence of Civilizations, by Juan O'Gorman. 1968. Lila Cockrell Theatre for the Performing Arts (within Henry B. González Convention Center complex), 200 E. Market St., west side, exterior.

Images of My Town, by Jesse Treviño. 1982. Kelly National Bank, 707 Castroville Rd.

La Historia Chicana, by Jesse Treviño. 1974. Our Lady of the Lake University, Student Lounge.

St. Elizabeth, by Sergio Ruiz. 1988. Resurrection of the Lord Catholic Church, 7990 Military Parkway West.

San Antonio River, by Roland Rodríguez. 1988. Walkway between Alamo Plaza and Losoya St.

Untitled (depicts market scene), by Armando Sánchez. 1986. Farmers' Market Association of San Antonio, 612 W. Commerce St., southwest corner.

Untitled (depicts struggle against drug addiction), by Alex Rubio. 1988. North wall of Palmer Drug Abuse program's southside center, 1406 Fitch St.

Faux bois picnic table, Brackenridge Park, San Antonio. Photo by Cathryn Hoyt, THC.

Untitled (tile), by Jesse Treviño. Dagen Bela Art Gallery, Dolorosa St. side, in Market Square.

Victory and Triumph, by Roland Rodríguez. HemisFair Arena.

Virgin of Guadalupe, by Candelario Espinoza. 1987. Annie's Lounge, 901 N. Zarzamora St.

Sculpture

Carmen, Luna y Canto, by Victor Gutiérrez. Market Square. Bronze statue of a seated female figure.

Father Hidalgo. 1941. In Plaza Juárez, La Villita area. Bronze statue of Father Hidalgo bearing a banner with the image of Our Lady of Guadalupe.

St. Anthony de Padua. 1950s. On Bexar County Courthouse grounds, 100 Dolorosa St. Statue of St. Anthony, erected by the Order of Alhambra; St. Anthony is the patron saint of San Antonio.

Toribio Losoya, by William Easley. 1986. Losoya St., across from the Hyatt Regency Hotel and near the Alamo. Life-sized bronze statue of Toribio Losoya, located on the street that also bears his name. The statue commemorates one of eight native-born Texans who died at the Alamo in 1836.

Festivals and Events

Ballet Folklórico de San Antonio. June through August, at Arneson River Theater. The Ballet Folklórico de San Antonio was founded in 1965 to preserve Mexican and Spanish culture through the art of dance. In 1981, with the support of the city of San Antonio, the ballet launched the city's first professional folkloric dance company and upgraded and expanded its academy. Ballet Folklórico de San Antonio presents Spanish and Mexican dances and music Sunday evenings during the summer months at Arneson River Theater. Performances can also be seen at other events and festivals, including the Texas Folklife Festival. For additional information, contact the ballet at P.O. Box 1263, San Antonio 78295.

Charreadas. *See* Day in Old Mexico.

Cinco de Mayo. Weekend nearest May 5, at Market Square. Sponsored by the Mexican-American Cultural Center, the festival features live music, dance, and Tex-Mex foods. For information contact Market Square/El Mercado, 514 W. Commerce, San Antonio 78207.

Cine Festival. Late January or early February, at Guadalupe Cultural Arts Center, 1300 Guadalupe. North America's oldest and largest international Latino film exhibition.

Diez y Seis de Septiembre. Weekend nearest September 16, at various locations. Speeches, concerts, fiestas, and parades throughout the weekend. Charreadas and the celebrations at El Mercado, La Villita, and Arneson River Theater are especially popular.

Fiesta de las Luminarias. Weekend before Christmas, on the River Walk. For this fiesta the River Walk is decorated with thousands of lights and luminarias. Consisting of candles in paper sacks, luminarias sound

Statue of Father Hidalgo, La Villita area, San Antonio. Photo by Cathryn Hoyt, THC.

prosaic but are truly beautiful, traditional Christmas lights. The festival of lights follows a tradition begun in the 1500s that represents lighting the Holy Family's way to Bethlehem. Sponsored by the Paseo del Rio Association, the lights provide a breathtaking background for the city's famed Las Posadas procession.

Fiestas Navideñas in El Mercado. Mid-December, at El Mercado. Christmas is celebrated at El Mercado with music, folk dances, and traditional holiday foods. Events for children include piñata parties, blessing of the animals, and talking with "Pancho" Claus.

Fiesta Noche del Rio. June through August, at Arneson River Theater on the River Walk. Mexican and Spanish folk dances are featured Tues., Fri., and Sat. evenings at 8:30 during the summer months.

177

Fiesta San Antonio. In April, during a ten-day period including San Jacinto Day (April 21), at various locations in the downtown area. This major citywide celebration, established to honor veterans of the Texas war for independence, has been held since 1892. The fiesta has expanded from the initial commemoration and now celebrates the city's rich and diverse cultural history. The ten-day festival features more than 150 events, and over 3 million people participate. For information contact Fiesta San Antonio Commission, Inc., 1145 E. Commerce, San Antonio 78205.

Day in Old Mexico and Mexican Charreada; Fiesta Charra. In April (date varies), during Fiesta San Antonio, at San Antonio Charro Ranch, 6126 Padre Dr. (off S. Roosevelt St.), adjacent to Mission County Park. The *charreada* is an equestrian competition stemming from traditional hacienda ranching practices in Mexico. *Charros* (horsemen) compete and *charras* (horsewomen) perform daredevil events, a ballet folklórico performance is part of the festival, and traditional food and drink are available. Also during Fiesta San Antonio, the Fiesta Charra presentation is held at the Convention Center Arena. Since 1983 the crowning of Miss Charro, staged by the Confederation of Charros, has included orquesta and mariachi music, ballet folklórico, and a charro roping exhibition. Charreadas also are a feature of several other festivals throughout the year, especially Diez y Seis de Septiembre.

Fiesta del Mercado. In April (date varies) during Fiesta San Antonio, at El Mercado. Fiesta del Mercado, founded in 1983, is a ten-day celebration featuring continuous live entertainment (ballet folklórico, conjunto, and mariachi performances on five stages), Tex-Mex foods at over 45 booths, and special indoor events presented by the Farmer's Market Tenants Assn. This event is jointly sponsored by the Market Square Dept., the El Mercado Merchants Assn., and the Market Square Assn. and attracts more than 500,000 visitors annually.

Mariachi Festival. Four consecutive evenings in April (dates vary) during Fiesta San Antonio, along the River Walk. Since 1973, the annual Mariachi Festival has brought the best young mariachi talent in South Texas to San Antonio for four consecutive nights of music. Each evening, from barges on the river, traditionally dressed musicians from area churches and schools serenade visitors with this best-known Mexican music form. Sponsored by Paseo del Rio Assn. and Pace's Picante Sauce.

Night in Old San Antonio. Four days in April (dates vary) during Fiesta San Antonio, at La Villita. Known as San Antonio's biggest block party, Night in Old San Antonio draws crowds of about 25,000 each evening. The festival features music, food, and entertainment at culturally diverse theme areas in La Villita. At the Mexican Market and South of the Border areas visitors can sample a variety of foods and enjoy breaking *cascarones* (confetti-filled eggs). Held since 1947; proceeds go to the sponsor, the San Antonio Conservation Society, to aid the preservation of historical sites and structures in San Antonio.

Rey Feo Fiesta Reception and Parade. In April (date varies) during Fiesta San Antonio, in downtown San Antonio. El Rey Feo (the ugly king) Reception is an annual celebration for Hispanic fiesta royalty. The evening, filled with traditional Mexican music, dance, and food, is highlighted by the new-member induction ceremony of the Royal Order of the Cabrito, led by El Rey Feo. The annual Fiesta Flambeau Rey Feo parade, sponsored by the local LULAC Council, salutes El Rey Feo and his court, the queen of La Feria de las Flores, and other fiesta royalty in an illuminated night parade featuring over 175 floats, clowns, marching bands, and other amusements.

Las Posadas. In December, on a Sunday before Christmas, on the River Walk. This old Spanish religious pageant depicts the Holy Family's search for an inn. In this reenactment, held since 1966, the procession is led by mariachis, children in costume, and a choir singing traditional Posada songs and Christmas carols in both Spanish and English. The candle-bearing procession winds along the River Walk to Arneson River Theater, then adjourns for refreshments, folklórico dancing, and a piñata party for the children. Held in conjunction with the Fiesta de las Luminarias and sponsored by the San Antonio Conservation Society, San Antonio's Las Posadas is one of the most famous Christmas celebrations in the United States and has been listed in *Traveler* Magazine as one of the world's top ten Christmas attractions.

Los Pastores. In December (date varies), at Mission San José. A religious pageant, Los Pastores was developed by the Franciscan friars to instruct neophytes in the Christian religion. In particular, as performed in the frontier missions, Los Pastores integrated many Indian motifs as it told the story of the shepherds' trip to see the infant Jesus and the attempts of Lucifer and his devils to prevent their journey. The modern version of this traditional Christmas celebration, which symbolizes the ages-old conflict between good and evil, has been performed in San Antonio for decades. Traditional foods are sold before the performance. Performed in Spanish (with English interpretation) by the Guadalupe Players on the grounds of Mission San José. Sponsored by the San Antonio Conservation Society and the National Park Service.

Mission Fest. Third weekend of October, at Mission San José. Mission Fest, established in 1986, is held to increase understanding of the Spanish Colonial period of American history and of the lifestyles of the American Indians who came under Spanish influence. The festival has evolved into a presentation of traditional crafts and skills of the 18th-century Spanish frontier missions. Sponsored by the National Park Service and Los Compadres de San Antonio Missions National Historical Park.

Open House at the Missions. On a Sunday preceding August 25, at Missions Concepción, San José, San Juan, and Espada. August 25 is the anniversary of the establishment of the National Park Service. Open house at the missions celebrates both the missions and the National Park Service, which administers historical and cultural sites around the United States.

Return of the Chili Queens. Annually in May, on Memorial Day weekend, in downtown San Antonio. In this annual celebration of chili, vendors replicate the "chili queens" of old San Antonio and sell chili from stands in the plazas during the evenings.

San Antonio Festival. During 17 days in June, at various locations. Since 1983, the San Antonio Festival has brought nearly a month of international music and dance to San Antonio. Although acts vary from year to year, the festival includes a significant Hispanic component. Previous entertainment has included Bolivian, Peruvian, Ecuadorian, Brazilian, Puerto Rican, and Cuban music, a conjunto carnival, Cuban-American dance, and a show on Mexican sculpture. For featured entertainment contact San Antonio Festival Assn., 339 S. Presa, San Antonio 78205.

Tejano Conjunto Festival. Four to seven days in May (dates vary), at Rosedale Park (340 Dartmouth) and the Guadalupe Theater (1300 Guadalupe). Sponsored by the Guadalupe Cultural Arts Center, the festival is intended to preserve and promote Tejano conjunto music, a folk music genre unique to South Texas. Founded in 1982, the festival now features more than 42 hours of live performances by more than 30 different groups. Other events include films and videos about conjunto music, master accordion workshops, a poster contest, and the annual induction ceremony into the Conjunto Music Hall of Fame. Over 30,000 fans come from all around the world to dance, enjoy the music, and sample the traditional foods that are part of the festivities. For information contact Xicano Music Director, Guadalupe Cultural Arts Center, 1300 Guadalupe, San Antonio 78207.

Texas Folklife Festival. First full weekend in August, on the grounds of the Institute of Texan Cultures and HemisFair Park. Initiated in 1972 by the Institute of Texan Cultures, the festival provides an entertaining and educational setting where traditional folklife activities are demonstrated. Special emphasis is placed on the preservation and demonstration of traditional customs, crafts, and activities of ethnic, cultural, or national groups. The festival has a significant Hispanic component, with about one out of every forty events or booths relating to Mexican-American or Latin American culture. Musical performances, arts and crafts demonstrations, and ethnic foods are among the attractions, and over 100,000 people attend the festival each year. For information contact Institute of Texan Cultures, P.O. Box 1226, San Antonio 78294.

ALICE AND VICINITY, Jim Wells County

Alice (pop. 19,788) area settlement began with the Charco de los Presenos land grant in 1831. During the early 1830s the Mexican government continued to encourage Mexican and European settlement in the region. Early communities in the area included Los Presenos, Lara, Palito Blanco, La Trinidad, and Amargosa, some of which still retain their early names. The oldest structure in Jim Wells County, Casa Blanca was built in the 1750s using *sillares* (caliche blocks cut from the earth). The structure, which once was used as a "sub-mission," was included in the 1806 Spanish land

Hand-carved wooden bench by Agustín Castillo, in a traditional crafts demonstration at the Texas Folklife Festival, San Antonio. Photo by Cathryn Hoyt, THC.

Vaquero from Beeville, ca. 1900. The Institute of Texan Cultures, courtesy Ida Treviño.

180

grant (with lands also in Nueces County) of Juan José de la Garza Montemayor. In 1875 the property was purchased by John Wade, whose descendants still own the land (the ruins of the site are located on private property, not open to the public). Alice was founded in 1888 as a depot on the San Antonio & Aransas Pass Railway. Now a petroleum and ranching center, Alice is the county seat of Jim Wells County.

South Texas Museum. 66 S. Wright St. The museum focuses on the history and traditions of this part of South Texas, from prehistory to the present. Emphasis is on pioneer ranch and household artifacts, including some items from the Spanish Colonial and Mexican periods. Open Tues.–Fri. 1–4; Sat. 10–2.

BATESVILLE AND VICINITY, Zavala County

Batesville (pop. ca. 200), first settled about 1870, became the county seat when Zavala County was organized in 1884. The county seat was moved to Crystal City in 1927, and Batesville is now primarily a farming and ranching center.

First Zavala County Courthouse Site. Marker, Batesville Plaza, intersection of Bates and Main Sts. The courthouse marker also commemorates the naming of Zavala County for Lorenzo de Zavala, a veteran of the Battle of San Jacinto. *SM 1984.*

Scenic Route. From Batesville E on SH 57 to IH 35. Roadside crosses, Spanish ranch names, and a fine example of a traditional *corral de leña* fence (approx. 3 mi. E of Batesville) along this route are graphic reminders of the rich Hispanic heritage in South Texas.

BEEVILLE AND VICINITY, Bee County

Beeville (pop. 13,547) marks the beginning of the South Texas brush country, the homeland of Hispanic vaqueros and Longhorn cattle. The city had its beginnings as a town named Maryville, in an area settled by Irish colonists in the 1820s. The town was renamed Beeville when it became the county seat in 1860. Traditional yard art, including painted tire planters, Virgin of Guadalupe figures, flowers, and wrought-iron work can still be found in the Mexican-American neighborhoods of Beeville. Yard art, like home altars and other folk traditions, is becoming increasingly rare, even in South Texas.

Medio Creek. Marker, E side of Medio Creek near its intersection with US 59. The name of this creek, applied by Spaniards about 1800, signifies its midway position between the San Antonio and Nueces rivers. The creek was crossed by explorers, padres, soldiers, and settlers as they traveled on three early ox-cart roads that led from Mexico to Mission La Bahía at Goliad. The mesquite brush that thrives along the creek is said to have grown from mesquite beans used as feed for the Mexican carters' teams. *SM 1967.*

Our Lady of Victory Catholic Church. North Ave. and W. Carter Sts. This predominantly Hispanic church is a modern, white brick structure with a bell tower showing Mission Revival stylistic influence.

BENAVIDES AND VICINITY, Duval County

Benavides (pop. 1,788), in south-central Duval County on the Texas-Mexican Railroad, is named for Plácido Benavides, who donated the land for the townsite. Although still a trade center for the surrounding oil, cattle, and farming area, the town has declined in importance since 1950, when its population had reached 3,000.

Barroneña Ranch. E of Benavides, about 27 mi. S of Freer on SH 16. The Barroneña Ranch, a reminder of early South Texas ranching, was part of a larger tract owned by Diego Hinojosa, who received a 42,072-acre land grant, known as San Rafael de los Encinos, from Mexico in 1835. The ranch has been owned since 1905 by the Bennett family. The property includes a 19th-century adobe house, reportedly a stage stop between Goliad and Laredo. A native rock wall (about one mile in length) and a rock water trough also are early structures. Private ranch, not open to the public. *SM 1989.*

Duval County Park. 4.7 mi. W of intersection of US 359 and FM 2295, just N of Texas-Mexican Railroad tracks. This 40-acre county park provides recreational and picnicking facilities under shade trees along Agua Poquita Creek. The cattle-dipping vat, cypress water tank, and feed troughs remain from the Driscoll family ranch at the locale once known as Norway Community. The community was a stop on the Tex-Mex Railroad as well as a ranch, and the dipping vat, near the tracks, is one of only a few that remain in the county, and the only one on public property. Thousands of head of cattle were put through dipping vats like this one by the vaqueros of the brush country in the effort to eradicate the tick-spread cattle disease known as Texas fever.

The Park. Hackberry and Depot Sts. This park is a typical Mexican-style plaza with walkways radiating out from the central bandstand and cast-cement benches facing the street around the perimeter of the plaza. The park serves as a social gathering place for the residents of Benavides.

San Pedro del Charco Redondo Ranch. In Ramirez, southern Duval County on FM 1345. The San Pedro del Charco Redondo grant was originally settled by Simón Ramírez, who petitioned Spain for the land in 1808. After Simón's death, his son-in-law Rafael Ramírez continued to cultivate the land until about 1836. The ranch was reestablished in 1852 by Rafael and Zinfuriana Ramírez when their ownership was confirmed by the Texas Legislature. The ranch was stocked with Longhorn cattle and Merino sheep brought from Spain. In addition to cattle and sheep raising, the ranch eventually included orchards and farming operations, a church, school, grocery, and hardware store. The ranch is still owned by descendants of the original founder. Private ranch, not open to the public. *TFLHR.*

The Park, Benavides. Photo by Cathryn Hoyt, THC.

Santa Rosa de Lima Catholic Church. Hackberry and Depot Sts. This white, stuccoed church, with its twin bell towers, reflects California Mission revival influence. The church was built in 1940. In the manner of traditional Mexican towns, the church faces a plaza, known simply as "the park."

CAMPBELLTON, Atascosa County

Campbellton (pop. ca. 300) was founded by John Campbell, an Irish immigrant who moved to Atascosa County in 1857 and established a store near his ranch. The store became a relay station for mail from San Antonio and Oakville and points south. By 1874, the town had one school, two churches, and a post office. Today the economy is based primarily on ranching, with some oil activity.

Sacred Heart Church. On St. Francis St. and Campbellton Blvd. Land for the first Catholic church was donated in 1897 by Campbellton's founder. For almost 30 years the church was served by a priest who made the trip by horse and buggy from Floresville. In 1928 a San Antonio parish took over the care of the mission church, whose parishioners were predominantly Spanish-speaking people. The first church, a frame building, served the community until 1939, when the present stone, mission-style church was dedicated. In 1948 the church at Campbellton was attached as a mission to St. Andrew's Parish in Pleasanton.

CARRIZO SPRINGS, Dimmit County

Carrizo Springs (pop. 5,745) was established in 1865 and named for the reeds (*carrizos*) that grew around the spring. Cattle raising was the only industry until 1890, when the discovery of artesian wells made irrigation farming possible. The town was incorporated in 1913 and is now the county seat of Dimmit County.

Our Lady of Guadalupe Church. 1004 N. 6th St. From 1881, Carrizo Springs was served by priests who traveled by horseback from Eagle Pass. The first church, a thatched-roof structure, was built in 1904. A more permanent frame church, constructed in 1910, was demolished by a storm in 1943. For several months, until the parish hall was completed, mass was offered in a theater owned by the Benito Silva family. Construction of the permanent church was delayed by lack of funds, even after the cornerstone was laid in 1949. The new church, modeled on Santa Barbara Mission in California, was completed in 1952. The façade features a stained-glass image of Our Lady of Guadalupe above the main entrance. Carrizo Springs was formally established as a separate parish in 1962.

Brush Country Days. In late October or early November, at the rodeo grounds. The Hispanic component of this regional celebration includes traditional foods, music, and dance. For information contact Carrizo Springs Chamber of Commerce, 107 W. Nopal, Carrizo Springs 78834.

Sacred Heart Church, Campbellton. Photo by Cathryn Hoyt, THC.

CATARINA, Dimmit County

Catarina (pop. ca. 45) was established in 1925 as a model city for the Winter Garden Farms Corporation. San Antonio investors who foresaw the agricultural boom in South Texas purchased land in the area and laid out palm-tree-lined streets with curbs and sidewalks, and brick-pillared gateway entrances on the main street. Farm plots were sold to investors, who were told that they could not possibly fail because of the area's rich soil and abundant water supply. By 1929 Catarina had about 2,500 residents, but by 1930 Catarina Farms was failing rapidly. By 1940, only 400 people still resided in the area. Insufficient water, poor farm-management practices, and lack of financing caused most of the farms to fail.

Royal Palm Hotel. SH 83. The Royal Palm Hotel was built to house prospective landowners who came to Catarina on the train. Spanish Revival in design, the rose-pink stuccoed hotel is U-shaped with small stepped parapets flanking the main entrance. The central courtyard, with its pond and lush tropical plants, enhances the Spanish effect. The hotel is one of the few remaining original buildings from the model city built by the Winter Garden Farms Corporation.

Valenzuela Ranch Headquarters. 10 mi. SW of Catarina. Begun in the 1870s by Thomas Kearney and James A. Carr, this became one of the area's largest ranches. Carr retained the western half after Kearney sold his share in 1884, and the western portion became known as Valenzuela. In 1894 Carr sold to Edward Kotula. The Hispanic-inspired architecture of the house features a thatched roof, stepped buttresses, and stuccoed sandstone walls. Private ranch, not open to the public. *NR 1985; RTHL 1987.*

CESTOHOWA, Karnes County

Cestohowa (pop. ca. 110), on FM 3191 in northwestern Karnes County, is overwhelmingly Polish- and Czech-American in current population, but a Spanish outpost was located here in the 18th century.

El Fuerte del Cíbolo. Marker, at Nativity of the Blessed Virgin Church; FM 3191, W of SH 123. In 1758 a Spanish fort called El Fuerte del Cíbolo, then the only outpost between San Antonio and Presidio la Bahía, was built near here to protect the presidio horses from Comanche raids. Later, Spanish cowboys from this fort assisted Governor Barnardo de Gálvez, who led Spanish forces against the British along the Gulf of Mexico at the time of the American Revolution. *SM 1991.*

COLUMBUS, Colorado County

Columbus (pop. 3,367). An Indian village named Montezuma is thought to have existed near here during the Spanish period. The Colorado County area was crossed by Alonso de León's fourth expedition to East Texas in 1689 and by the Marqués de Rubí in 1767. The Atascosito Road, established by the Spanish before the mid-18th century, crossed the

Colorado River near Columbus. Anglo-American occupation dates from the Mexican period, with an early settlement called Beason's Crossing. The Baron de Bastrop and Rawson Alley platted the town in 1823, and by 1835 the village on the Colorado was known as Columbus. During the Texas war for independence Santa Anna and Sam Houston camped on opposite banks of the river at Columbus, and the Texan army burned the town to keep the buildings from being occupied by Mexican forces. After the war Columbus began rebuilding and became the county seat of Colorado County. In May 1989 the Texas Legislature named Columbus the Official Columbus Quincentenary Town of Texas.

Alley Log Cabin Museum. 1234 Bowie. This small museum has a few Spanish Colonial and Mexican materials on permanent exhibit. Open 1st and 3d Thurs. of each month and 3d weekend in May.

Dilue Rose Harris House Museum. 602 Washington St. The permanent exhibits of this small museum include a few Spanish Colonial and Mexican materials. Open 1st and 3d Thurs. of each month and 3d weekend in May.

CORPUS CHRISTI AND VICINITY, Nueces County

Corpus Christi (pop. 257,453), one of the most charming coastal cities in Texas, is located on Corpus Christi Bay, from which the city received its name. The bay was first explored by Alonso Álvarez de Pineda in 1519. It was named San Miguel Arcángel in 1747 by Joaquín Orobio y Basterra and was renamed Corpus Christi by Diego Ortiz Parrilla in 1766. Mexican-Americans are believed to have settled here as early as 1837, but Anglo-American settlement dates from the Mexican War period of the 1840s. Corpus Christi became the county seat of newly formed Nueces County in 1846. The old Hispanic area of the city, known as The Hill (located off Leopard in the Waco St. area) has long been the heart of the Mexican-American community of the city. Ben Garza, a local businessman of the area, was the driving force in the establishment of the League of United Latin-American Citizens (LULAC) in 1929. Ben Garza City Park (1800 Howard at 300 Culberson) is named for him. Another influential national Hispanic political organization, the American G.I. Forum, also was founded here.

The city became a major port in the 1920s and is also the gateway to the northern tip of Padre Island. The island, which stretches south along the coast to Brownsville, is one of the longest barrier islands in the world. In addition to the tourist attractions of the island, the city offers a number of areas in which visitors can view a wide range of structures, from cathedrals to modest residences and modern shopping centers, that have been influenced by Spanish Revival architectural styles. The Westside is now the predominantly Mexican-American sector of the city. In this neighborhood can be seen several Hispanic Catholic and Protestant churches, shops such as *panaderías* (bakeries) and *hierberías,* small cafes, orchestra ballrooms, yard shrines and other yard art, flea markets, and other cultural expressions of the Mexican-American community.

Order of Sons of America, Council No. 4, Corpus Christi, Texas, 1927. Members took part in a Flag Parade with the local chapter of Elks. Later, through the efforts of this Council, three Organizations were merged, and LULAC was created on February 17, 1929.

Order of Sons of America (1927), one of three groups that merged to form LULAC. Courtesy of Benson Latin American Collection, General Libraries, University of Texas at Austin.

In May 1989 the Texas Legislature named Corpus Christi the Official Columbus Quincentenary City of Texas.

Information

Corpus Christi Visitors Center. Exit 16 on IH 37. Open daily, 9–5.

Historic Sites

Casa Blanca Land Grant Site. Marker, NW corner of FM 666/FM 624 intersection, 6 mi. N of Banquete. Casa Blanca, granted in 1798 to Juan José de la Garza Montemayor and his sons, was the first Spanish land grant awarded in Nueces County. Located between Penitas Creek and the Nueces River, it consisted of 70,848 acres and received its name from nearby Casa Blanca Fort. The property remained in the Montemayor family until 1849. Lands once included in the grant now lie in Nueces (44,042 acres) and Jim Wells (26,806 acres) counties. *SM 1988.*

League of United Latin American Citizens (LULAC) Site. Marker, Lipan St. between Carrizo and Artesian Sts. Obreros Hall, once located here, was the site of the founding of LULAC in 1929. This organization has since become a major voice advocating social and educational programs for Hispanic-Americans. *SM 1981.*

Padre Island and Padre Nicolás Ballí. Marker, Padre Ballí Park, Park Rd. 22, 5 mi. SE of Corpus Christi. First called Corpus Christi Island or Isla Santiago, Padre Island was finally named for Padre José Nicolás Ballí. In 1800 Padre Ballí applied to Spain for 11.5 leagues of land on the island in order to establish a ranch and mission. His petition was granted and, with the help of his nephew, he established the first settlement on the island in 1804. *SM 1979.*

Alonso Álvarez de Pineda. Marker, Cole Park, Ocean Dr. at Oleander St. Alonso Álvarez de Pineda was commissioned in 1519 to explore the Gulf Coast and succeeded in mapping 800 miles of coastline from Florida to Vera Cruz, Mexico. This expedition encouraged further exploration along the Gulf Coast that eventually led to colonization by Spaniards and other Europeans. Pineda charted Corpus Christi Bay, but it was 300 years before a settlement was begun here. *SM 1983.*

Rincón del Oso Land Grant Site. Marker, corner of S. Staples and Leopard Sts. The Rincón del Oso Land Grant was awarded to Capt. Enrique Villarreal in 1831 by the Mexican government but had been used by Villareal as ranch land since 1810. The 42,840-acre grant included much of the land that now constitutes Nueces County. When Henry Lawrence Kinney established his trading post where Corpus Christi was later to develop, he did so on land that was part of the Rincón del Oso grant. Kinney came to own all of the grant after Villareal's death in 1846. *SM 1986.*

Santa Petronila Ranch. Marker, SW of Corpus Christi near intersection of US 77 and FM 665, at Driscoll. Capt. Blás María de la Garza Falcón established an outpost and way station near here in 1764. By 1766 he had moved his family, friends, and herds of livestock to what was called Rancho de Don Blás or Santa Petronila Ranch. The ranch served as headquarters for exploring expeditions led by Falcón and his son. Both men played an important role in settling towns along the Rio Grande and Nueces River as well as Padre, Mustang, and St. Joseph's Islands. *SM 1978.*

Spanish Revival Architecture

Corpus Christi Cathedral. 500 block of N. Upper Broadway at Lipan St. The cathedral, designed by L. L. Monnot of Oklahoma, is the city's largest and best-known church constructed in Spanish Mission Revival style. Built in 1940, the church features asymmetrical bell towers with painted terra-cotta domes, a cast-stone façade, and the traditional red tile, arches, and wrought-iron details. *RTHL 1991.*

Wynne Seale Junior High School. 1707 Ayers St. Constructed in 1935–36, this was the first junior high school in Corpus Christi. The ornately detailed Spanish Revival school was designed by the architectural firm Hamon and Griffith, and was built as a public works project by the federal government. The brick structure has a red tile roof and features cast-stone and tile details. *RTHL 1986.*

Museums, Libraries, and Cultural Centers

Art Museum of South Texas. 1902 N. Shoreline Dr. The museum schedules about 20 exhibitions each year, featuring the art of all cultures, past and present. Several exhibitions each year celebrate the achievements

of Latin American artists. The museum also serves the community as a cultural center, presenting film viewings, lectures, literary readings, and concerts. Inquire locally or write for information on current programs and exhibits. Open Tues.–Sat. 10–5; Sun. 1–5.

Corpus Christi Museum of Science and History. 1900 N. Chaparral. Artifacts from a 1554 Spanish shipwreck off the coast of Padre Island are on permanent display. Historic artifacts from the shipwreck include a large wrought-iron anchor, silver coins and gold ingots, rare navigational instruments, armaments, and personal items. The materials are displayed in a 16th-century dockside setting. Open Tues.–Sat. 10–5; Sun. 2–5.

Corpus Christi Public Library. 805 Comanche. The library has holdings that focus on South Texas and northern Mexico, and the Local History Room contains genealogical information and files on Mexican-American topics.

Multicultural Heritage Center. 1581 N. Chaparral. Located in Heritage Park and administered by the City Parks and Recreation Department, the center is dedicated to the recognition and appreciation of the city's multicultural heritage. The center is housed in the historic French-Galván House (*RTHL 1986*). Built in 1907-08, the house was acquired in 1942 by Rafael Galván, a founder and charter member of the League of United

Wynne Seale Junior High School, Corpus Christi. Photo by Ann Perry, THC.

189

Corpus Christi Museum of Science and History, Corpus Christi. Photo by Pat Mercado-Allinger, THC.

Latin American Citizens (LULAC). Included in the park complex are the headquarters of several culturally or ethnically based organizations, including LULAC.

Weil Gallery. Corpus Christi State University, 6300 Ocean Dr. Occasional exhibits of Mexican art and folk arts and frequent exhibits of Mexican-American art are held at this gallery. Inquire locally for exhibits information. Open, during exhibitions, Mon., Wed., Thurs. 10–4; Tues. 10–7; Fri. 10–3.

Public Art

Alonso Álvarez de Pineda, bronze sculpture, by Sherman Coleman and his daughter, Kathleen Coleman. In De Pineda Plaza, the Westside community park.

American Indian Figures. Bronze sculpture (untitled), by Sherman Coleman, Main Lobby of Nueces County Courthouse. *Carancahua,* bronze by Dennis Silvertooth, in Natural History section of the Corpus Christi Museum. Pre-Columbian style copper and cement sculpture at interchange, Cooper's Alley and Mesquite Sts.

Christopher Columbus. Sculpture, Port of Corpus Christi Cargo Dock 1 (across the street from the Corpus Christi Museum of Science and History), under the Harbor Bridge.

King Charles III of Spain. Bronze sculpture, Main Lobby of Nueces County Courthouse. King Charles III, who aided the American cause against the British during the Revolutionary War, is commemorated with this sculpture, which was a gift to the city from King Juan Carlos I of Spain.

190

Festivals and Events

Bayfest. Last weekend in September or first in October, along Shore-line Dr. Bayfest, begun in 1976 as an American Bicentennial celebration, is held to promote and fund the visual and performing arts. Nearly 40% of the activities relate to Hispanic heritage, including ballet folklórico presentations, mariachi and conjunto music performances, and educational exhibits from the Institute of Texan Cultures. Traditional foods, including a seafood tampiqueño specialty, are available. Approximately 250,000 people attend each year. For information contact Bayfest, Inc., P.O. Box 1858, Corpus Christi 78403-1858.

Diez y Seis de Septiembre. Annually, weekend closest to September 16, at Multicultural Center in Heritage Park. The focus of the celebration is on mariachi music; traditional foods are available. For information contact Multicultural Center, 1581 N. Chaparral, Corpus Christi 78401.

Feria de las Flores Scholarship Pageant. In August (date varies). Each of the contestants in the pageant, in appropriate costume, performs the traditional dance of a state in Mexico. For information contact LULAC Council No. 35, P.O. Box 5135, Corpus Christi 78405.

Fiesta de Corpus Christi. In June on weekend nearest Feast Day of Corpus Christi, around the Watergarden at Bayfront Plaza. The city initiated the Fiesta de Corpus Christi in 1989 to commemorate Alonso Álvarez de Pineda's discovery of Corpus Christi Bay in 1519 and the naming of the bay on the feast day of Corpus Christi. Featured events include a procession along scenic Shoreline Drive, in which over 3,000 local and area parishioners and members of the Knights of Columbus participate, singing in Spanish and English and accompanied by the Charros La Paloma carrying Mexican and U.S. flags. Other highlights of the event are a commemorative tribute to Pineda and Columbus, a boat parade and blessing of the fleet, and a charreada. Mariachi and salsa music are performed, and traditional foods are offered at the fiesta's mercado area. For information contact Corpus Christi Area Convention and Visitors Bureau, 1201 N. Shoreline, P.O. Box 2664, Corpus Christi 78403-2664.

Folklife Festival. In October (date varies), at Heritage Park. This multicultural festival includes a variety of music and dance performances and arts and crafts demonstrations by members of various ethnic groups, including Mexican-Americans. For information contact Multicultural Heritage Center, P.O. Box 9277, Corpus Christi 78469-9277.

COTULLA, La Salle County

Cotulla (pop. 3,694) is located in the brush country, where herds of mustangs once roamed. Once a wild west town, it is now a livestock and hunting center and the county seat of La Salle County.

Brush Country Museum. On Front St. The permanent exhibits of the museum include a small collection of documents, photographs, and other materials relating to Mexican and Mexican-American heritage in Texas. Open Mon.–Fri. 10–2 and 1–3.

CRYSTAL CITY, Zavala County

Crystal City (pop. 8,263), which is associated with the beginnings of the Raza Unida political party in the 1970s, is the setting of a number of structures and events reflecting the Hispanic heritage of South Texas. Public artwork includes murals, a statue of Benito Juárez (given to the people of Crystal City by the Mexican government), and a "statue of three faces," depicting the confluence of Spanish, Indian, and *mestizo* ancestry. The City Library contains exhibits relating to local history and heritage, and both Cinco de Mayo and Diez y Seis de Septiembre are celebrated with festivals featuring traditional music and foods. In this area people look north for work and south for ties with family in Mexico. Made up of ranch and farm lands (in the farming country known as the Winter Garden district), the area has long been a winter home for migrant families. Crystal City is the county seat of Zavala County.

Sacred Heart Church. 618 E. Zavala St. The first Oblate priest came to Sacred Heart Parish in 1907. The first frame church in Crystal City burned in 1922, and services were held in a barber shop until the new brick and tile church, exhibiting simple Spanish Mission stylistic influences, was constructed in 1925.

CUERO AND VICINITY, DeWitt County

Cuero (pop. 6,700) is located in an area once inhabited by nomadic Coahuiltecan Indians, and Cabeza de Vaca may have crossed this way in the 1530s. Early Spanish expeditions in the area were those of Alonso de León in 1689, Martín de Alarcón in 1718, and Pedro de Rivera in 1727. The first Anglo-Americans settled on DeWitt grant lands in this area in 1825. Following the Texas war for independence, German immigration began, and by 1860 Germans made up the majority of the county's population. A post office named Cuero (the Spanish word for hides) existed by 1846, and the town of Cuero, four miles to the south of the original settlement, became the county seat in 1876. The Cuero I Archeological District (*NR 1974; SM 1979*) in the vicinity reflects the area's multicultural heritage in mission-period contact sites as well as prehistoric sites and 19th-century farmsteads (protected-location sites, not open to the public).

Charles Cook House. 103 E. Sarah. This one-story frame dwelling exhibits Spanish Revival stylistic elements. The stucco veneer structure features a clipped gable roof, inset-entry portico, and stone surround with carved detailing. *NR 1988.*

St. Mark's Lutheran Church. 400 N. Esplanade. This California Mission influenced church was constructed in 1939 by refugees from Indianola after a hurricane devastated the port town in 1886. *SM 1972.*

EAGLE PASS AND VICINITY, Maverick County

Eagle Pass (pop. 20,651) is located at the Rio Grande crossing of El Camino Real, the old road from Mexico City to San Antonio. (The crossing, known as El Paso del Aguila, is located about three miles below Eagle Pass.) About 30 miles south of the river on this historic route was Mission San Juan Bautista (1700–1829), known as the Gateway to Spanish Texas. U.S. settlement began with the establishment of Camp Eagle Pass during the 1846 Mexican War, and in 1849 a permanent post, Fort Duncan (now a historical museum), was founded. The military road from Fort Duncan north to San Antonio attracted merchants and traders and encouraged border trade. In the 1850s, immigrants to California, drawn by the gold rush, would camp north of the fort for safety. Over the years this camp developed into the small settlement that was to become Eagle Pass. During the American Civil War, Eagle Pass was an important trade outpost for shipments from Mexico to the Confederacy. Today the town is the county seat of Maverick County and a point of entry into Mexico through Piedras Negras.

Aztec Theatre. Main at Jefferson Sts. This unusual theater is an example of eclectic design at its best. The overall appearance of the theater is Spanish Revival, with the two flanking towers and the arched parapets;

St. Mark's Lutheran Church, Cuero. Photo by Cathryn Hoyt, THC.

Aztec Theatre, Eagle Pass. Photo by
Dick Ryan, THC.

195

however, the influences of both Moorish and Mayan design can be seen in the detailing of the façade.

Kickapoo Indian Reservation. 8 mi. S of Eagle Pass. A 125-acre site is under development as a federal reservation for the Kickapoo Indians, a tribe that for years had special border-crossing privileges. The Kickapoo, originally a branch of the Algonquin, gave up their northern lands in the early 19th century, and part of the tribe settled in East Texas. Denied land by both Mexico and the Republic of Texas, they participated in the 1838 Córdova Rebellion and were expelled from Texas. A small group then settled at Piedras Negras, across from Eagle Pass.

Our Lady of Refuge Catholic Church. 812 Ceylon. The first church of Our Lady of Refuge Parish was an adobe structure, built in the 1860s. The original church was replaced in 1882, and in 1884 the Oblate Fathers were placed in charge of the parish. During the years from 1927 to 1929, when the Catholic Church in Mexico was caught up in political turmoil, many Catholics from Piedras Negras and other towns in northern Coahuila came to Eagle Pass for baptisms and marriages. Several refugee priests settled in the Texas town, and Our Lady of Refuge flourished. The present church was constructed in a new location in the late 1970s. The new brick church, although of modern design, reflects Spanish mission stylistic influences in the bell tower and the use of arches. The spacious interior is open and contemporary in design, with beamed ceilings, but, in recognition of the church's predominantly Hispanic congregation, traditional images of saints with places for burning candles have been retained in the atrium. Our Lady of Refuge, an early church in this region, has played an important role in the history of Hispanic Catholicism in southwestern Texas.

Tile panel, Our Lady of Guadalupe Church, Falfurrias. Photo by Curtis Tunnell, THC.

Border City

Piedras Negras (pop. ca. 33,000). Following the establishment of Fort Duncan, a Mexican military post was established across the river. The settlement that grew up around the post became Piedras Negras, which is named for the black rocks found along the Rio Grande. Modern Piedras Negras offers handcrafted items in many shops and a traditional Mexican market area, restaurants, and entertainment. In Piedras Negras US 57 connects with Mexico 57, which leads to Monclova, Saltillo, San Luis Potosí, and Mexico City. Portions of this route pass through spectacular scenic areas of the Sierra Madres.

FALFURRIAS AND VICINITY, Brooks County

Falfurrias (pop. 5,788) lies in an area that was Mexican ranchland in the 19th century. Among the major land grants in Brooks County was the San Salvador del Tule, granted by Spain to Juan José Ballí in 1797; 21,768 acres of this 315,391 acre grant were in Brooks County. Other large grants included the Loma Blanca grant of 22,142 acres to Francisco Guerra Chapa in 1831; La Encantada grant of 29,855 acres to José Manuel Chapa and Luciano Chapa in 1831; and 18,756 acres of the 27,812-acre San Antonito grant to José Antonio Morales García and Apolinario Morales García in 1835. Indian resistance to settlement of the region brought about the end of the ranches, and Falfurrias did not prosper until the arrival of the railroad and the establishment of a creamery (famous for its butter) in the early 20th century. Falfurrias, like Kingsville, is a stepping-off point for the vast ranchlands to the south that are heavily populated by Mexican-Americans. Though historic monuments are few, the region is rich in Hispanic folklore and traditions. Falfurrias is the county seat and major trade center of Brooks County.

Brooks County's Catholic Heritage. Marker, Blucher and Caldwell Sts. This area remained in the Diocese of Monterrey, Mexico, until the Diocese of Texas was formed in 1847. In 1904–05 the mission of San Ysidro was founded in Falfurrias, and the Chapel of Saints Peter and Paul was built nearby in 1916 for English-speaking communicants. In 1925 the mission merged with the church of Saint Isadore to form Sacred Heart Church, now on Garza St. and renamed Our Lady of Guadalupe. Also commemorated in the marker are other Catholic churches of the area. *SM 1976.*

Garza Ranch. Rural Brooks County, in the Encino area, S of Falfurrias. This ranch is still owned by descendants of Matías Ramírez, who founded the ranch in 1808. Private ranch, not open to the public. *TFLHR.*

Don Pedro Jaramillo Shrine. On FM 1418, off SH 285. Among the most famous of all *curanderos*, Don Pedro Jaramillo was credited with many miraculous healings. The shrine contains a lifesize, seated statue of Don Pedrito, and in the chapel are numerous mementoes of miraculous cures attributed to him. This shrine is still visited by believers and descendants of those who knew him. He has achieved the status of unofficial saint. Open to the public. *SM 1971. See also* sidebar: Don Pedrito Jaramillo.

Los Braziles Ranch. 18 mi. W of Falfurrias. José Anastacio Barrera and his wife, Rafaela Hinojosa, came from Mier, Tamaulipas, Mexico, in 1878 to work about 19,000 acres that originally were part of an 1808 Spanish land grant inherited by Juan Manuel Falcón. Here they raised cattle, horses, sheep, goats, corn, beans, and cotton. Their brand, the shoe sole, probably was brought with them from Mier and is still being used today. The main building, a two-room house constructed of locally made adobe, is still standing and in use, although the original grass roof was replaced long ago, and several additions have been made to the structure. Hand-dug wells also remain from the early days, and descendants of the founder still own the ranch that includes part of the original holding. Private ranch, not open to the public. *TFLHR.*

Los Olmos Site. Marker on US 281 at FM 1418, 0.5 mile N of Falfurrias. Los Olmos, the first permanent settlement in Brooks County, was located at the southwest corner of El Paisano land grant, given to Ramón de la Garza about 1830. The village served a region settled originally by ranchers from northern Mexico, and the schoolhouse was the site of services conducted by traveling priests. As the town of Falfurrias grew, Los

Don Pedrito in 1894. Estate of James and Scottie Roddy Pirie, courtesy of Institute of Texan Cultures.

DON PEDRITO JARAMILLO
A South Texas Folk Saint

Generations of South Texas residents have been touched by the healing power of a humble man who settled at Rancho de los Olmos (near Falfurrias) nearly a century ago. Today, decades after his death in 1907, the influence of Pedro Jaramillo, "the Faith Healer of Los Olmos," continues to be felt in the ranches and towns of South Texas.

Don Pedrito, as he came to be known, was born in Guadalajara, Mexico, in 1827. He spent the first part of his life working as a poor laborer. The story of his beginnings as a healer says that one day, while he was riding horseback through the brush, he was hit in the face by a tree limb. To ease the pain, he covered his injuries with mud from a nearby pool of water. Finding that the pain was relieved, he repeated the treatment for three days. Then, as he was sleeping, a voice awakened him and told him that he was to become a healer.

In 1881 Don Pedrito came to South Texas, an area with which he had long

197

Olmos began to decline, but descendants of the founders still reside in this area. *SM 1976.*

Fiesta del Campo. Weekend nearest October 12, at Mary and Ed Lasater Park in Falfurrias. Falfurrias residents celebrate Columbus Day, or El Dia de la Raza, at Fiesta del Campo. The festival features team roping and a charreada, other sports events, polka and bolero dance, conjunto and mariachi music, and traditional arts, crafts, and foods. A chili cook-off is a major event, and the fiesta draws about 7,000 visitors each year. For information contact Falfurrias Chamber of Commerce, P.O. Box 476, Falfurrias 78355.

Fiesta Ranchera. Weekend nearest May 5, in Mary and Ed Lasater Park in Falfurrias. Founded in 1982 to focus attention on Tejano history, particularly General Ignacio Zaragoza and the events of Cinco de Mayo, the festival features a charreada, trail ride, team roping, other sports events, traditional dance and music performed by Hispanic artists, and traditional arts, crafts, and foods. A carne guisada cook-off is a special attraction. For information contact Falfurrias Chamber of Commerce, P.O. Box 476, Falfurrias 78355.

FANNIN VICINITY, Goliad County

Fannin (pop. ca. 100), a small community in the east-central part of Goliad County, developed because of its location on the Texas and New Orleans Railroad. Its population 50 years ago was about the same as it is today.

Battle of El Perdido. Marker, FM 2987, N of Fannin. During the 1810–19 efforts to expel Spain from Texas, a battle occurred here on June 19, 1817. Spanish forces defeated a Mexican Republican army invasion led by Col. Henry Perry and Maj. James H. Gordon. *SM 1967.*

FLORESVILLE AND VICINITY, Wilson County

Floresville (pop. 5,244) derives its name from Francisco Flores de Abrego, who established a ranch on a Spanish land grant about six miles to the northwest in 1832. Another early rancher in this area was Erasmo Seguín, who was one of the first landowners to experiment with growing cotton in Texas. Erasmo, father of Juan Seguín, supported the idea of a separate state government for Texas and later supplied horses and cattle to the Texas army. In 1883 Josefa Augustina Flores de Abrego Barker, a descendant of Flores de Abrego, donated land to establish a county seat at Floresville. Two years later, Floresville officially became the county seat of Wilson County.

Canary Islanders Cemetery. Marker, US 181 near NE edge of Floresville. Canary Islanders established the first organized civil settlement in Texas at San Fernando de Béxar (San Antonio). The Spanish missions of San Antonio had established *visitas*—outposts for the Indian herdsmen who worked the mission ranches—along the San Antonio River Valley,

been familiar and in which there were few doctors. There he built himself a jacal and began practicing his gift. He traveled between San Antonio, Laredo, and Corpus Christi, visiting the sick and prescribing *recetas,* or cures. Don Pedrito, emphasizing that his gift was to help people release their own healing power through faith, would prescribe simple treatments, such as bathing in tepid water, and he charged nothing for his cures.

Patients often tried to give Don Pedrito donations, but the gifts were rarely accepted. He did, however, accept a gift of 100 acres of land, on which he lived and raised corn, watermelons, garbanzo beans, and garlic. When he was away, he would leave these foods at his home so that patients who came to see him from a distance would not be hungry while they awaited his return. At times when he returned home, there would be as many as 500 people waiting to see him. When a post office was established at Paisano, he began to send *recetas* by mail, and he sometimes received 200 letters a week. When the railroad was expanded to the then new town of Falfurrias, more people than ever were able to visit the healer.

Don Pedrito is credited with having healed thousands of South Texans during the last 26 years of his life in Los Olmos. After he died, at the age of 77, people who had known him continued to share his *recetas* with others. Now, decades later, his grave, beside the site of his jacal, is a shrine where people come to ask his spirit for aid and to thank him for healing received. As a folk saint, his photograph is commonly found beside statues of Catholic saints on home altars throughout the region. In honor of the influence that Don Pedrito Jaramillo had on generations of South Texans, the citizens of Brook County dedicated an Official Texas Historical Marker in 1971 at his gravesite near Falfurrias.

Woman from Tenerife, Canary Islands, ca. 1834. From d'Urville Dumont, *Voyage pittoresque autour du monde* (Paris 1834). Courtesy of Institute of Texan Cultures.

and the Canary Islanders began settling along the river near the visitas. This cemetery predates the nearby chapel at Rancho de las Cabras, which was built in 1732. Following secularization of the missions in 1794, the Canary Islanders remained in the area as farmers and ranchers. *SM 1967.*

Casa Blanca Ranch Site. Marker, on Bus. 181, W of Floresville, ca. 0.1 mi. W of Seguin Branch. The historical marker commemorates the site of a ranch complex built by Erasmo Seguín in the early 1830s. In addition to being known for his support of Texas independence, Seguín brought Stephen F. Austin into Texas and represented Texas at the Mexican national congress that created the Federal Constitution of 1824. *CM 1936.*

Flores de Abrego Family and Floresville. Marker, courthouse lawn. The Flores de Abrego family came from Spain during the 18th century and established ranches along the San Antonio River. The head of the family was Francisco Antonio Flores de Abrego II. His son José Joaquín Flores de Abrego grew up on the San Bartolo Ranch (in Karnes County), and his grandsons fought on the Texan side during the war for independence from Mexico. Descendant Josefa Augustina Flores de Abrego Barker later donated land for the Wilson County seat, Floresville. *SM 1986.*

Pointed D Ranch. 11 mi. W of Floresville. This ranch was founded by Santiago and Juan Smith Tarín, grandsons of Erastus ("Deaf") Smith, Texas patriot who served as a scout in Sam Houston's army. Juan's wife, Otilia Rodríguez, was a descendant of one of the Canary Islanders who settled San Antonio in 1731. Santiago and his wife, Ángela, built an adobe house that is still in use today. Private ranch, not open to the public. *TFLHR.*

Rancho de las Cabras Site. Marker, on SH 97, 2 mi. S of Floresville. Rancho de las Cabras, situated at an important ford on the San Antonio River, was a subsidiary ranch for Mission Espada. In 1732 a chapel was constructed for the herdsmen at the ranch. After secularization of the missions in 1794, Espada's former ranch was owned by Ignacio Calvillo, and the chapel remained in use until the 19th century. The ruins of the complex consist primarily of sandstone-block walls, although archeologists have found evidence of jacal constructions. The ranch site is now administered by Texas Parks and Wildlife Dept. *SM 1970; NR 1973.*

Sacred Heart Catholic Church. 1009 Trail. Sacred Heart, located in a predominantly Hispanic parish, is a community-oriented church. Fiesta Guadalupana (annually on December 12), which features a traditional procession, is the major devotional and popular celebration of the year. The church also sponsors an annual barbecue.

Wilson County Museum. 1140 C St. on the courthouse square. Museum exhibits include Spanish Colonial, Mexican, and Mexican-American materials. Open Fri. 12–5; Sat. 10–4; other openings for local events and special requests.

GOLIAD AND VICINITY, Goliad County

Goliad (pop. 1,946) is one of the oldest municipalities in Texas. In 1749 Mission Espíritu Santo and Presidio La Bahía (Fort of the Bay) were moved to the site of an Indian village called Santa Dorotea by the Spanish. Soon, merchants and other tradesmen were drawn to the area and a small settlement known as La Bahía grew up around the presidio. After Mexico won its independence from Spain, the town was officially recognized and given the name Goliad, a phonetic anagram of Hidalgo (for Father Miguel Hidalgo y Costilla, the hero of the Mexican Revolution). Several military actions related to Mexican and Texas independence occurred here, including the famous Goliad campaign of 1836. Goliad was incorporated by the Republic of Texas in 1840 and is the county seat of Goliad County.

Historic Sites

Goliad State Historic Park. *See* Mission Nuestra Señora del Espíritu Santo de Zúñiga; Zaragoza Birthplace.

Mission Nuestra Señora del Espíritu Santo de Zúñiga. In Goliad State Historical Park, 0.25 mi. S of Goliad on US 183. First founded on Lavaca Bay as La Bahía del Espíritu Santo, this mission reflects its former site in its popular name "La Bahía." The mission was reestablished at Goliad, its third site, in 1749. The mission was granted jurisdiction over all land between the Guadalupe and San Antonio rivers as far north as modern Gonzales and soon established a huge ranching operation. At the peak

of its success the mission possessed over 40,000 head of cattle that supplied both its own needs and those of other Spanish settlements as far away as Louisiana. The mission was secularized in 1830 and fell into ruin. The mission complex was partially restored as a public works project in 1933–41, with reconstructions undertaken by a Civilian Conservation Corps work force under National Park Service supervision. Now administered by the Texas Parks and Wildlife Dept., the site offers excellent interpretive displays relating to the Spanish Colonial and Mexican periods of Texas history and to the historic Indians of the mission area. Craft demonstrations, slide and film presentations on the history of the area, and special seasonal events also are held here. Camping and picnicking facilities are available in the park. Mission open daily 8–12, 1–5. *CM 1936; RTHL 1969; NR 1977.*

Mission Nuestra Señora del Rosario de los Cujanes Ruins. Ca. 6 mi. W of Goliad off US 59. The mission was founded in 1754 for Ka-

Mission Nuestra Señora del Espíritu Santo de Zúñiga, Goliad. THC photo.

rankawa tribes, but missionization of the Karankawa was never successful and Rosario was abandoned in 1807. In 1830 its lands were distributed to Spanish settlers. Foundations of the stone walls were excavated during a public works project in 1940–41, and additional archeological investigations were undertaken in 1974 by the Texas Parks and Wildlife Dept., which administers the site. *CM 1936; SM 1969; NR 1972.*

Presidio de la Bahía (Nuestra Señora de Loreto de la Bahía). US 77A and 183, 1 mi. S of Goliad. Presidio la Bahía was established here (at its third site) in 1749 to protect Espíritu Santo Mission. The fort has a turbulent history, including a siege by the Gutiérrez-Magee expedition in 1812–13 and occupation by revolutionary forces during the Texas war for independence. In 1835 the Goliad Declaration of Independence was read here to the people of Goliad. Among the signers of the declaration were Mexican-Texans José Miguel Aldrete and José María Jesús Carbajal. The presidio was the scene of a major event of the Texas revolution, the 1836 Goliad massacre, which resulted in the largest single loss of life in the cause of Texas independence. Following a battle in which Col. James Fannin's men were defeated by superior forces under Gen. José Urrea, Santa Anna ordered the execution of the captives. Only 28 of the Texans held prisoner here were spared, despite Urrea's orders that the captives be treated with consideration. Some of these survivors owed their lives to the pleas and assistance of Francisca Álvarez, the Angel of Goliad. Among those who were freed was drummer boy Franklin Hughes, and it is largely from his later accounts that the story was recorded. A mural depicting the Angel of Goliad is in the headquarters building at Goliad State Historical Park. The presidio was restored in 1963–67 to its 1836 appearance, including the officer's quarters, barracks, guardhouse, and bastions at the quadrangle corners. Church services are now held in Our Lady of Loreto Chapel, which is located within the walls of the presidio. Of particular interest in the chapel is a statue of Our Lady of Loreto that was placed there in 1749 and a lovely mural painted by Antonio García in 1946. Open daily 9–4:45 except major holidays. *NHL 1967; RTHL 1969.* For additional information on the various festivals held here (*see* Festivals entries), contact the presidio at P.O. Box 57, Goliad 77963.

Scott's Texas Longhorn Cattle Ranch. 0.2 mile off US 77A/183 on FM 2441. This is a private working ranch, but the roadside pasture often holds Longhorns, providing visitors an opportunity to view these descendants of Spanish cattle in their natural setting.

Zaragoza Birthplace. 0.5 mi. S of Goliad on US 183 at Presidio la Bahía. Ignacio Zaragoza was born at this site in 1829. Educated in Mexico, he joined the Mexican army and achieved the rank of general. Zaragoza is famed for having led poorly armed Mexican soldiers to victory over a superior French intervention force at the Battle of Puebla, May 5, 1862. This victory gave Mexico and Mexican-Americans the great national patriotic anniversary, Cinco de Mayo. The site includes a heroic statue of the general and a reconstruction of his birthplace. Exhibits focus on Zaragoza's life and career and related Goliad and Mexican history, and a bilingual historical marker commemorating Zaragoza has been placed at the site. Administered by the Texas Parks and Wildlife Dept. and included in Goliad State Historical Park. Open. Fri.–Sun. 9–5. *SM 1967.*

Festivals and Events

Celebration of American Cultures. On or near July 4, at Goliad State Historical Park. This event celebrates America's multicultural diversity, with the focus on American Indian, Hispanic, African-American, and other ethnic cultures. Music (including conjunto and mariachi), traditional dance with performers in costume, and craft demonstrations are featured. For more information contact the park at P.O. Box 727, Goliad 77963.

Christmas at Goliad. First Saturday in December. This celebration features a traditional reenactment of Las Posadas; participants gather at dusk on the square for a mile-long candlelit procession to Presidio la Bahía.

Cinco de Mayo. *See* Fiesta Zaragoza.

Fannin Occupation of Fort Defiance and Goliad Massacre Memorial. Late March or early April (near Palm Sunday), at the presidio. This living history demonstration, sponsored by Presidio la Bahía and the Catholic Diocese of Victoria, is the only event in Texas that portrays the Federalist Texas Hispanic struggle against the Centralist Mexican Government during the Texas war for independence. Featured events include a living history demonstration, candlelight tours of the presidio, battle reenactments, and a memorial service. Texas Revolutionary period military music is performed, with many performers dressed in period costumes, including those of the Cuautla Dragoons, Yucatán Battalion, and Mexican Infantry.

Fiesta Zaragoza. May 5, at Zaragoza Birthplace. Established in 1948 and sponsored by the Zaragoza Society, this fiesta commemorates Zaragoza's victory at Puebla, known as Cinco de Mayo. The fiesta is notable for the only reenactment of the Battle of Puebla in the United States, with performers dressed in native Mexican, Mexican military, and French Zouave costumes. The celebration also includes a memorial mass, performances of ballet folklórico, arts and crafts, and traditional music and foods.

Gutiérrez-Magee Siege of 1812–13. Second or third weekend in January (date varies), at the presidio. This living-history event recreates the Gutiérrez-Magee siege of 1812–13 and is the only commemoration of this event in Texas. The Battle of the White Cow is reenacted by performers wearing traditional period costumes. Over 2,000 visitors attend the event annually.

La Bahía Awards; Texas Frontier Rendezvous; Las Posadas Pageant. Usually first weekend in December, at the presidio. The presidio and the Catholic Diocese of Victoria sponsor these events, which relate to Spanish, Mexican, Mexican-American, and other Hispanic cultures. Weekend events include musical performances of Mexican liturgical Mañanitas,

Portrait of Ignacio Zaragoza. From *Album de las glorias nacionales, 1862–1866* (Mexico City, n.d.). Courtesy of Institute of Texan Cultures.

Choros, and Diegenos; participants dressed in early Tejano costumes; and Mexican and Tejano foods. About 2,000 visitors attend the festival each year.

GONZALES, Gonzales County

Gonzales (pop. 6,527) was founded as the headquarters of the DeWitt Colony in 1825. The town was laid out in the traditional Mexican pattern, with five central squares, or plazas, and was named for Rafael Gonzales, then governor of Coahuila and Texas, who began his military career as a cadet at Presidio la Bahía in Goliad. Gonzales is the major town and county seat of Gonzales County, and the courthouse complex now occupies the town's original central plaza.

Military Plaza. Marker, St. Louis St. The 1825 town plan of Gonzales followed a typical Mexican town layout, and Military Plaza, at this locale, was one of the five main plazas. The original streets of Gonzales, like St. Louis, were named for saints. *SM 1966.*

Scenic Area. Palmetto State Park, 10 mi. N of Gonzales via US 183 and FM 1586 to Park Rd. 11. The 178-acre park offers a wide variety of plant life in a heavily timbered swampland set in the midst of surrounding prairie. This unique area has been known since the Spanish period, and legends say that people have lost their lives in the bogs near the river. The park, however, is now crossed by safe and scenic trails, and camping and hiking are permitted.

HEBBRONVILLE, Jim Hogg County

Hebbronville (pop. 4,465) is located on land originally in the Noriecitas grant, given by Spain to Simón de Hinojosa in 1740. Hinojosa's heirs took possession of the land in 1858 and sold their shares in 1890. One of the buyers was James R. Hebbron, who platted the town of Hebbronville on his land. The original railroad station, La Peña, which ran east of Hebbron's property, was moved 1.5 miles to the new town. The early economy was based primarily on raising Longhorn cattle, but a drought from 1892 to 1894 caused many residents to lose their ranches. The town declined until oil was discovered in the region in 1924. Hebbronville was designated county seat of the newly created Jim Hogg County in 1913.

Hotel Viggo. 205 N. Smith Ave. (SH 16). The Spanish Revival style Hotel Viggo was built in 1913–15 to serve the needs of visitors to the new county seat.

Our Lady of Guadalupe Catholic Church. 500 block of E. Santa Clara St. Part of the Scotus College complex, this beautiful California Mission Revival style church was built in the 1940s. The building's front towers are decorated with colorful black and white tile roofs, and the side and rear domes are decorated with blue, pink, and white tiles. The altars inside the church, donated by the Kenedy and Guerra families, are made of fine, carved cedar from San Luis Potosí in Mexico.

Scotus College. 500 block of E. Santa Clara St. The seminary at this site was established in the 1920s by Franciscan priests from Mexico. This impressive Mission-style structure was designed by José Alvarez, and construction began in 1940. However, the Franciscans then returned to Mexico, and the building was not completed until 1944. Scotus College now serves students from South Texas and Mexico.

JOURDANTON VICINITY, Atascosa County

Jourdanton (pop. 3,220) was founded nearly overnight when two area ranchers paid the Artesian Belt Railway $50,000 to locate through the area. Lots were sold to the public in a three-day sale, and the town soon prospered as a shipping point for livestock and cotton. Today Jourdanton is the county seat of Atascosa County, and the economy is based chiefly on oil and gas.

Atascosa County. Marker, roadside park, 3 mi. NE of Jourdanton, SH 97. As early as 1722 El Camino Real from the Rio Grande to San Antonio was well established in this area. The Spanish word *atascosa*, denoting boggy ground that hindered travel, gave the region its name. José An-

Scotus College with Our Lady of Guadalupe Church in the background, Hebbronville. Photo by Cathryn Hoyt, THC.

tonio Navarro, whose 1831 claim was the first grant recorded in the area, gave land in 1857 for the first county seat, Navatasco. The county seat moved to Pleasanton in 1858 and to Jourdanton in 1911. *CM 1936; SM 1969.*

Atascosa County Courthouse. Intersection of SH 16 and SH 97. This is the fifth Atascosa County Courthouse, but the first in Jourdanton. The Spanish Revival building, with its twin towers and ornate detailing, was designed by H.T. Phelps and constructed in 1912.

KINGSVILLE, Kleberg County

Kingsville (pop. 25,276) is located on lands that originally were included in the 15,500-acre Rincón de Santa Gertrudis land grant that was made to Juan Mendiola by Mexico in 1832. Mendiola held the land until 1836, when his heirs sold the ranch to Richard King, developer of the King Ranch. Kingsville is the last town of any size before the highway south enters the vast reaches of the King Ranch, where vaqueros, among Texas' most skilled cowboys, still work cattle in the brush country. Visitors who plan to proceed south to Raymondville will see a virtually empty stretch of over 70 miles of ranchland. Kingsville is the county seat of Kleberg County.

John E. Conner Museum. Texas A&I University Campus, Santa Gertrudis Ave. The museum has extensive collections relating to the Spanish Colonial and Mexican periods (Escandón settlements), Mexican-American culture, and Spanish ranching heritage in South Texas (including almost a thousand branding irons). Collections are displayed in both permanent and changing exhibits. In addition, the museum's holdings include taped oral histories and more than 2,000 slides of architectural sites, artifacts, and folk crafts of South Texas. The museum has recently completed a traveling exhibit entitled Tejano Folk Arts and Crafts. The Caesar Kleberg Hall of Natural History, through lifelike dioramas enhanced with nature's sounds, explores the natural beauties and dangers of South Texas and Northern Mexico ecosystems. Open Mon.–Fri. 9–5, Sun. 2:30–5.

Charles H. Flato Junior High School. Santa Gertrudis and 3d Sts. The school was built in 1924 to serve as the elementary school for Kingsville. The Spanish Revival structure has beautiful tile detailing and cast-stone work.

King Ranch. Kingsville vicinity, off US 77 on SH 141. The King Ranch was founded by Richard King in 1853 when he purchased 75 acres of land on Santa Gertrudis Creek. The ranch now encompasses hundreds of thousands of acres in Kenedy, Kleberg, Nueces, and Willacy counties. King sold a half interest in his early ranch to Mifflin Kenedy, but this partnership was dissolved in 1859. King retained the Santa Gertrudis division, which is the basis of the modern ranch. Originally based on Texas Longhorns, the ranch led in the introduction of purebred cattle into the state. Since the beginnings of the ranch, Mexican and South Texas vaqueros have been part of the colorful history of this huge ranching enterprise. Tom Lea's history of the ranch (1957) reports that the first houses on the ranch were jacals, the original stock and horses for the ranch were bought from the Flores brothers, and most of the names on the early payroll records are Spanish. During a widespread drought in the early years of the ranch, a village in Tamaulipas, Mexico, sold all of its cattle to King. Seeing that there was nothing left in the village, he relocated the entire community to his Santa Gertrudis ranch. The inhabitants of this village became some of the finest vaqueros ever to work on the King Ranch. In 1912 the original ranch headquarters burned, and the present house was built on the same site in 1912–15. The elegant three-story structure is a blend of Mexican and California mission styles and was designed by Max Frederick and Carleton Adams, of the Adams and Adams architectural firm in San Antonio. This firm designed several important Spanish Revival style buildings in Texas, including Thomas Jefferson High School in San Antonio. Guided tours daily, 10–3. *NHL 1961; SM 1965, 1977, RTHL (Ranch HQ) 1981.*

Henrietta M. King High School. Kleberg Ave. and 3d St. Funded by Henrietta M. King, wife of King ranch founder Richard King, this two-story brick structure is Spanish Mission Revival in style with Romanesque Revival elements. The 1909 building was known locally as the School of Three Missions because the designer combined elements from the Alamo, Mission Concepción, and Mission San José in the façade. The Alamo parapet is seen in the center, the left tower replicates the tower at San José, and the right tower is patterned after the Concepción tower. These missions were chosen as models for the school because of their strategic role in Texas history. *RTHL 1981; NR 1983.*

Old Kleberg Public Library. W. Yoakum and 3d Sts. The old public library, built in 1927, was designed by B.E. Giesecke and A.W. Harris of Austin in Spanish Revival style. The library served the citizens of Kingsville for thirty years before a modern facility replaced it. *RTHL 1981.*

St. Martin's Catholic Church. E. Ella and 8th Sts. St. Martin's, built in 1946 to serve the city's Spanish-speaking population, is an interesting adaptation of regional and Spanish Revival styles. The rounded buttress on the right corner of the church is a type commonly seen on vernacular adobe Spanish Colonial buildings in the Rio Grande Valley. The buttress on St. Martin's has been elongated and nicely balances the single bell tower on the opposite corner of the building.

Texas A&I University. Established in 1925 as South Texas State Teachers College, the institution's name was changed to Texas College of Arts and Industries in 1929. Texas A&I became a university in 1969. The main campus buildings, appropriate to their South Texas setting, are fine examples of Spanish-influenced architectural style. The university was the first in the country to offer a credited course in mariachi performance (in the Music Dept.), and it also offers a credited folklórico dance course (in the Health and Physical Education Dept.). University mariachi and folklórico performances each spring are open to the public; contact the appropriate departments of the university for further information; Texas A&I University, Kingsville 78363. *See also* John E. Conner Museum.

Las Posadas. In mid-December; procession begins at the courthouse

Henrietta M. King High School, Kingsville. Photo by Cathryn Hoyt, THC.

St. Martin's Catholic Church, Kingsville. Photo by Cathryn Hoyt, THC.

and continues about one mile to the Community Education Building. An evening event, the traditional Las Posadas procession—a reenactment of Mary and Joseph's search for lodging—features colorful costumes and music, and culminates with caroling. Las Posadas is one of three weekend events in the city's Christmas celebrations.

LA VERNIA, Wilson County

La Vernia (pop. 639), a small town in northwestern Wilson County, was settled by Anglo-American, Polish, and German immigrants in the second half of the 19th century. The first settlement occurred in the 1850s, perhaps drawn here by the presence of the Old Chihuahua Road trade route.

Old Chihuahua Road. Marker, US 87. The Old Chihuahua Road was a major trade route from central Mexico to the Texas coast at Indianola. After 1835, the route was important to the gold and silver trade with Mexico. *SM 1967.*

PLEASANTON, Atascosa County

Pleasanton (pop. 7,678) was established in 1858 but the locale was a much earlier center for Spanish, Mexican, and Anglo-American ranching. The town calls itself the "Birthplace of the Cowboy."

Longhorn Museum. SH 97 W on N end of town. This small museum focuses on the vaquero and cowboy, from the 1500s to the present, and also has exhibits devoted to Longhorns and mustangs. Open Tues.–Sat., 9–5.

José Justo Rodríguez Ranch. 4 mi. N of Pleasanton. The ranch was founded in 1878 by José Justo Rodríguez of Zaragoza, Coahuila, Mexico. A house of red sandstone was built here about 1895, but only a portion of the walls now remain. Hand-dug wells on the property, as well as an old barn, also were constructed in the early days of the ranch. Rodríguez, with the assistance of Enrique and Manuel Esparza—sons of Gregorio Esparza, a hero of the Alamo—helped to build a church in the community, known then as San Augustine, and school also was held in the church. A barn, still in use, was built in 1912 from lumber once used as a dance floor at Diez y Seis de Septiembre celebrations in Pleasanton. Descendants of the founder still own and operate the ranch that includes part of the original holding (now operated as three separate properties). Private ranch, not open to the public. *TFLHR*.

St. Andrew's Catholic Church. SH 97 and Market St. A mission church dedicated to St. Anthony was built in 1913 in what was to become St. Andrew's Parish. Because of flooding by the Atascosa River, the church was moved to North Pleasanton and the name changed to St. Andrew's. The structure was destroyed by fire in 1946, and services were held in a tent and then in a theater until the parish center was completed in 1948. The present building, dedicated in 1949, exhibits simplified Mission Revival influences. St. Andrew's serves a predominantly Mexican-American congregation.

PORT LAVACA AND VICINITY, Calhoun County

Port Lavaca (pop. 10,886) is located on the coastal plain, once home to the Karankawa Indians. Although Spanish explorers visited the area, permanent settlements did not exist here until after Anglo-American colonization. The original community was called La Vaca (the cow) and served as a shipping point for South Texas and northern Mexico. It was the county seat from 1846 to 1849 and became county seat again in 1886, following the destruction of the port town of Indianola. The presence of a significant contemporary Hispanic population is reflected primarily in churches (Our Lady of Victory Catholic Church on Austin St. and Central Baptist Church on West Main).

Indianola Site. West shore of Matagorda Bay, ca. 13 mi. SE of Port Lavaca via SH 238 and SH 316. Indianola is best known historically as the natural port through which German immigrants, led by Prince Karl of Solms–New Braunfels, entered Texas in 1843. The port was selected as a townsite later in that decade, and Indianola was incorporated in 1853. The locale, however, has a much earlier history, for it was on this shore that La Salle is thought to have landed in 1685. The French explorer's presence was the catalyst that initiated the establishment of Spanish missions in East Texas. Later, the thriving port was the terminus of the historic Chihuahua Road. In 1850 a federal commission met in Indianola to fix the boundary between the United States and Mexico under the treaty of Guadalupe Hidalgo. In 1875 Indianola, with a population of 6,000, was struck by a disastrous hurricane. The completion of the railroad from Galveston to San Antonio further diminished the port at Indianola, and another hurricane in 1886 caused the city to be abandoned. A solitary, monumental statue of La Salle remains to remind the visitor of the long-ago period of conquest and colonization. The county maintains Indianola County Historic Park at the site. *CM 1936.*

POTEET VICINITY, Atascosa County

Poteet (pop. 3,206), in the north-central part of the county, is famous primarily for strawberries.

José Antonio Navarro Ranch Headquarters Site. Marker, 3.4 mi. W from Poteet on FM 476, then 2.2 mi. S on FM 1333 (2.3 mi. SSE of site). The Navarro ranchlands were originally allocated in the 1700s as a ranch for Mission San José but remained unsettled in the 1820s. Navarro, a signer of the Texas Declaration of Independence, received a grant for this land on the Atascosa River in 1831 but may have occupied the ranch before that date. The ranch acreage remained in the Navarro family until his son sold the old ranch home in 1894. *SM 1986.*

RANDADO, Jim Hogg County

Randado. On SH 16 ca. 21 mi. SW of Hebbronville. The Randado settlement was founded on land granted by Mexico to Antonio García in 1836 and is still owned by his descendants. The Randado ranch is believed to have received its name from the beautifully crafted lassos that were made there in the mid-19th century. The ranch itself consisted of 45,000 acres of land on which cattle, horses, and mules were raised and marketed in San Antonio and Mexico. Of the original settlement, the old chapel, built in the 1830s, and the family burial ground survive, and a few hand-dug wells and a 19th-century dam remain of the ranching structures; these are located on a privately owned ranch, not open to the public.

RAYMONDVILLE AND VICINITY, Willacy County

Raymondville (pop. 8,880) is located on lands originally in the San Juan de Carricitos land grant—601,657 acres in Willacy, Kenedy, and Hidalgo counties—granted by Spain to José Narciso Cavazos in 1792. This area is part of the South Texas ranching country that gave rise to the Texas cattle industry, but today's environment also reflects modern agricultural development. Known as the "Gateway to the Lower Rio Grande Valley," Raymondville is the county seat of Willacy County.

La Becerra Ranch. Rural Willacy County. The original Cavazos ranch, La Jarita, was founded in 1792 on land granted to José Narciso Cavazos. In the mid-1800s disruptions along the Rio Grande caused the family to move from the area until 1861. The ranch was reestablished in 1872. La Becerra Ranch, which includes part of the 1872 holding, was formed in 1923 and is still owned by descendants of the founder. One of the family branding irons, a triple S believed to have been given to the ranch's founder in Spain, was exhibited at the Texas Centennial Exposition in 1936. Private ranch, not open to the public. *TFLHR*.

La Sal Vieja (The Great Salt Lake). Marker, 8.4 mi. W of Raymondville, on SH 186. La Sal Vieja is one of two historically important salt lakes in the region (the other, El Sal del Rey, is located in Hidalgo County). La Sal Vieja probably was used during prehistoric times by one of the many nomadic Indian groups later known as Coahuiltecans. The Spaniards were the first Europeans to trade with the Indians for salt, which may well be one of the earliest trade items offered by the indigenous populations. After the arrival of the Europeans, La Sal Vieja supplied salt to early area residents and to northern Mexico as well. The lake was on lands in the Las Mesteñas Petitas y las Abra grant secured by Rosa María Hinojosa for her son Juan José Ballí in 1794. In 1804, the land passed to Juan's brother, Padre Nicolás Ballí, for whom Padre Island is named. As late as 1920, salt was being commercially extracted from the lake. *CM 1936*.

Raymondville Historical and Community Center. 427 S. 7th St. at Harris. The center contains materials relating to early Willacy County and South Texas history. Featured are collections from the 1862 Corpus Christi home of Mifflin Kenedy and his wife, Petra Vela de Vidal. Open Wed. and Fri. 2–5.

San Juan de Carricitos Land Grant. Marker, 12 mi. E of Raymondville on SH 186 right-of-way. Over one-half million acres, this Spanish land grant was the largest in South Texas. The land was awarded to José Narciso Cavazos in 1792, and he took formal possession of the land, seven miles north of this site, in 1793. His heirs later sold most of the land, but some descendants still live within the grant boundaries. *SM 1988. See also* La Becerra Ranch.

Portrait of María Ygnacia Cavazos, founder of La Becerra Ranch. Courtesy of Mrs. Jane Guettler, Brownsville.

REFUGIO, Refugio County

Refugio (pop. 3,158) was founded in 1834 at the site of Mission Nuestra Señora del Refugio, which had been relocated here in 1795 and was the last Spanish mission built in Texas. The Mexican government allowed development of the Power-Hewetson Colony in this area to promote Irish and Hispanic settlement. The colonial government was established in 1834 with the arrival of the Irish settlers. During the Texas war for independence in 1836, the mission church was destroyed in the Battle of Refugio. Refugio is now the county seat of Refugio County and a center for the oil, ranching, and farming region.

Copano Bay. Spanish settlement in the area began in the 1790s, but the coast was the scene of an earlier Spanish presence. Near Bayside, on Copano Bay, Copano was established in the mid-18th century as a supply port for the Goliad mission and presidio. In the 19th century Irish immi-

grants entered through this port and settled in South Texas. Only faint traces of old Copano remain, and the site is on private land.

Our Lady of Refuge Church. On US 77S. In 1845 part of the old mission was converted into a chapel. Later, in 1866, stone from the old mission was used to build a church. The present frame structure, completed in 1901, is the third church at this site. The bell from the mission is on display in the vestibule, along with a model of Mission Nuestra Señora del Refugio.

Refugio City Hall. 613 Commerce St. The city hall was built in 1935 or 1936 on the original public square, which was platted for the townsite by the Mexican government. The building reflects modest Spanish Revival influence. *RTHL 1990.*

Refugio County Museum. 102 West St. This small museum has exhibits of local and pioneer history, including archeology and prehistory. A few Spanish Colonial and Mexican items, including artifacts from the mission, are on permanent exhibit. Open Mon.–Fri. 10–5 (summer 11–6), Sat.–Sun. 1–5.

Our Lady of Refuge Church, Refugio. THC photo.

Refugio Theatre. Commerce and Ygnacion St. This 1920s theater features an ornate window onto the projection booth, with the twisted columns and cast-stone work typical of Spanish Renaissance Revival style. Flanking the window are quatrefoils containing fleur-de-lys, an unusual decorative motif for a Spanish Revival building.

ROCKPORT, Aransas County

Rockport (pop. 4,753) was established as a cattle-industry shipping point in 1867. Now a fishing and tourist center, Rockport is the county seat of Aransas County.

Texas Maritime Museum. Off SH 35 in Rockport, near the harbor. The Texas Maritime Museum explores the full scope of Texas' maritime history, beginning with the discoveries of the early Spanish explorers. Open Wed.–Sat. 10–4; Sun. 1–4. *See also* sidebar: Rockport's Texas Scow Sloop.

Fiesta en la Playa. Annually, usually the first weekend in September, in Rockport and the Aransas County Festival Grounds. Fiesta en la Playa, founded in 1988, commemorates Rockport's Hispanic heritage with performances of mariachi music, Aztec dances, and various competitions such as a piñata-breaking contest, jalapeño-eating contest, and best-looking sombrero contest. Traditional foods and arts and crafts are available. For more information contact PODER, P.O. Box 464, Rockport 78382.

Scenic Area. Aransas National Wildlife Refuge, about 35 mi. NE of Rockport via SH 35 N, FM 774 E, and FM 2040 S. In addition to migratory and native waterfowl, waders, and shorebirds, including the famous whooping cranes, the refuge is home to wild turkeys, white-tailed deer, javelinas, and alligators. Wildlife refuges like Aransas provide a glimpse of the wide variety of resources that were available to coastal Indians during prehistoric and historic times.

SAN DIEGO AND VICINITY, Duval County

San Diego (pop. 4,983), the Duval County seat first known as Perezville, was established by Mexican settlers in the early 1850s. Several stone structures in the area of Padre Pedro Park date from this period, including the house at the northwest corner of the park, which was still occupied as late as 1985 by descendants of the 1850s settlers. The Hispanic heritage of this area is evident in the fact that all but two towns and most of the creeks in the county bear Spanish place-names.

Sepulveda Ranch. 6 mi. W of San Diego. Founded in 1877 by Ramón and Plácida G. Sepulveda of Mier, Tampico, Mexico. Ramón's grandson, Valentino G., served as a Duval County deputy sheriff from 1922 until his death in 1943. The ranch is still owned by descendants of the founder. Private ranch, not open to the public. *TFLHR.*

ROCKPORT'S TEXAS SCOW SLOOP

The Texas scow sloop is a shallow-draft, sail-powered, wooden fishing vessel ideally suited to the shallow waters of the Gulf Coast bays and lagunas. These efficient fishing craft, their design unaltered for at least a century, worked along the Texas coast from about 1850 to 1950.

The scow sloops operated in pairs with a net strung between the two boats, harvesting the bounty of the inland waters. They were perhaps too efficient for their own good, and new U.S. fishing regulations brought about their abandonment in Texas in the 1950s. Many vessels from Texas ended up in the inland waters of Mexico, where some still operate. The efficient, tough little boats even weathered Hurricane Gilbert, but their days are numbered as a result of increasingly strict Mexican regulations.

Fortunately for the preservation of Texas' maritime heritage, a fortuitous set of circumstances has led to the construction of a Texas scow sloop as a special project of the Texas Maritime Museum in Rockport. The museum learned about Miguel Garza, who built these vessels in the 1930s and 1940s. He learned from his father, who built them in the 1920s. And his grandfather sailed in them as a fisherman before that. The Maritime Museum was immediately interested in Garza's skills, and in April 1990 the construction program was begun.

Garza served as master boat builder and project advisor for the museum, and 25 to 30 volunteers donated their weekends to construction. There were no written plans for the vessel, and the project proceeded on Garza's memory and skills as an artisan. The boat was launched in the fall of 1990, successfully preserving an almost lost aspect of Texas coastal history.

The Texas Maritime Museum in Rockport, established in the late 1980s, is a new and important member of the preservation community. Because of the many other fascinating and colorful aspects of Texas history—conquistadores, cowboys, frontier forts, and pioneers—the preservation of almost 500 years of maritime history has long been neglected. Many items relating to our rich coastal history have vanished or found their way to markets in the eastern states. The passage of the Texas Antiquities Code in the late 1960s has protected important coastal shipwrecks from looting

213

SINTON AND VICINITY, San Patricio County

Sinton (pop. 5,549) began as a cattle loading station in 1886 when the Calmon-Fulton Pasture Co. built cattle pens where the railroad crossed Chilipin Creek. The area remained sparsely settled until a post office was established in 1888 and the first residents of Sinton arrived. The town prospered and Sinton replaced San Patricio as the county seat in 1894. Sinton is now an oil and agribusiness center.

Our Lady of Guadalupe Church. Sodville Rd. at Maldonado. This red brick structure exhibits Mission Revival influences in its tower, arches, cast-stone details, and fountain. A shrine to Our Lady of Guadalupe is located nearby at 609 Maldonado, in the yard of Our Lady of Guadalupe Convent.

Our Texas Heritage. Mural, US 181 at S. McCall St. Sinton's Bicentennial mural depicts two hundred years of Texas history, including panels on the Spanish Colonial and Mexican periods.

Sinton Public Library. 212 W. Sinton St. The public library was moved to this location and remodeled in 1976. The building's modern adaptation of Spanish Revival style is evident in the arched windows, bright tilework around the door, and red tile roof.

Welder Wildlife Refuge. N of Sinton off US 77. The wildlife refuge was created on acreage of the former Welder Ranch, which was originally established from a Spanish land grant. It is the largest (7,800 acres) privately endowed wildlife refuge in the nation. The museum contains exhibits of the area's natural history and Karankawa Indian heritage. Tours of the refuge are offered on Thursdays at 3.

VICTORIA AND VICINITY, Victoria County

Victoria (pop. 55,076) had its beginnings in 1824 when the Republic of Mexico granted a large tract of land on the lower Guadalupe River to Martín de León. De León brought 41 families to the newly established town of Nuestra Señora de Guadalupe de Jesús Victoria. De León laid out the town according to Mexican colonization laws that specified setting aside areas for a church, trade, public buildings, and a school. The central plaza, known as Constitution Square, was surrounded by a grid of streets running north-south and east-west. In 1829 De León sought to expand the colony and to bring in an additional 150 families. Permission was granted but he died of cholera in 1833 and his plans were never completed. De León's colony was the only 19th-century Texas colony to be settled predominantly by Mexicans. The town's name was shortened to Victoria following Texas' independence from Mexico. Victoria was one of the first three towns incorporated by the Republic of Texas. Today it is an important South Texas center and the county seat of Victoria County.

Martín de León Homesite. Marker, Market Square, 300 block of S. Main St. Born at Borgos, Mexico, in 1765, De León was appointed captain in the Spanish Army in 1790 for bravery displayed in battle. He founded Victoria in 1824 and died there in 1833. *CM 1936.*

and destruction. Now both vessels like those of the 1554 fleet—whose artifacts are housed in the Corpus Christi Museum of Science and History—and the humbler but no less important Texas scow sloop are finding a permanent home port.

De León Plaza. 100 block N. Main. This plaza, originally known as Constitution Square, was the center of Nuestra Señora de Guadalupe de Jesús Victoria and has long been an important social and civic gathering place. The beautiful bandstand in the center of the plaza, built about 1885, originally stood near Constitution St. but was moved to this location in 1923. The bandstand is located on the foundation of the city's old standpipe, or water tower. The plaza and bandstand are favorite gathering places for rallies, concerts, and other events.

Diocese of Victoria, Chancery Museum. 1505 Mesquite. The Chancery Museum houses artifacts from the Spanish Texas period. Open Mon.–Fri. 9–4.

Evergreen Cemetery. 1800 block of N. Vine. Evergreen Cemetery was established in the early 1850s, and many graves were moved here from Victoria's original cemetery on Memorial Square. Markers commemorating several De León family members have been placed in this historic cemetery. The Martín de León family suffered in one of the bleaker episodes following the Texas war for independence from Mexico. They were supporters of Texas independence, but following the revolution members of the family were falsely accused, arrested, and forced to abandon most of their land. The historical markers commemorate Martín de León's wife, Patricia de la Garza, and their sons (Agapito, Félix, Fernando, and Silvestre) as pioneer colony developers and Texas patriots. The burial place of Martín de León is uncertain. *SM 1972.*

McNamara Historical Museum. 502 N. Liberty St. Collections include Spanish, Mexican, and early Texan documents and artifacts. Open Tues.–Sun. 1–5.

Market Square. 300 block of S. Main St. Now the site of the city hall, Market Square was platted by José M. J. Carbajal, surveyor general of Martín de León's colony, in accordance with Mexican colonization laws.

Memorial Square. 400 block of E. Commercial. Memorial Square was laid out in 1824 as the public burial ground. However, many people disliked the location of the site and Evergreen Cemetery was established in the early 1850s. Many graves were moved from Memorial Square to the new cemetery. *See also* Evergreen Cemetery.

St. Mary's Catholic Church. 100 W. Church St. The De León colonizers' original church, located just across the street from this locale, was dedicated to the Virgin of Guadalupe and served by priests from La Bahía. Following the Texas war for independence, most of the settlement's original Mexican families returned to Mexico. The parish was resurrected in 1840 as Our Lady of Guadalupe and a new brick church was built at the corner of Bridge and Church streets on land donated by the widow of De León. The parish through time became known simply as St. Mary's. The present Gothic Revival style church was dedicated in 1904. *RTHL 1962; NR 1986.*

Victoria's First Church. Marker, Market Square, 300 block of S. Main St. The original Catholic church was erected by Martín de León soon after his arrival in 1824. The church was restored in 1840 by the Rev. John Mary Odin, the first Catholic Bishop in Texas. In 1850 the church was removed to the northwest corner of the lot later occupied by Nazareth

Martín de León, founder of Victoria. Courtesy of Institute of Texan Cultures.

Convent. Today's St. Mary's Catholic Church is the successor of Victoria's first church. *CM 1936.*

Victoria Public Library. 302 N. Main. The library has records dealing with the original settlement of the Victoria area during the 1820s and 1830s, including ledgers, correspondence, and photographs relating to descendants of Martín de León. In addition, the library is an excellent source of brochures and maps for the Victoria area.

Ballet Folklórico Cuicuilco. Performances in late June. The Catholic Youth Organization of Our Lady of Sorrows Church annually presents Ballet Folklórico Cuicuilco, a Mexican folk dance troupe, which performs traditional dances from the Mexican states of Campeche, Chiapas, Chihuahua, Jalisco, Nayarit, Veracruz, and the Yucatán. Also included in the production is a staging of a Latin American carnival celebration. For information contact Catholic Youth Organization, Our Lady of Sorrows Church, Victoria.

Martín de León Symposium on the Humanities. Saturday before May 5, in Victoria College Johnson Symposium Center. Focusing on His-

De León family plot, Evergreen Cemetery, Victoria. Photo by Cathryn Hoyt, THC.

panic contributions to the humanities, the symposium is open to the public.

Noche en México. May 5, in downtown Victoria. This celebration of Cinco de Mayo and Mexican culture includes traditional dances, arts and crafts, and food.

Victoria Vicinity

Anaqua Site. Located on N bank of San Antonio River. The history of the Victoria area dates from the earliest days of Spanish exploration. Anaqua, on the San Antonio River in the southern part of Victoria County, may be the locale described by Cabeza de Vaca as the site of an Anaqua Indian habitation. In the 1820s a rancho and chapel were built at the site. The community thrived through the period of Anglo-American settlement but was bypassed by the railroad and by the mid-20th century had almost vanished.

Mission Nuestra Señora del Espíritu Santo de Zúñiga Site. Victoria area. Two important Spanish Colonial archeological sites in the area are included on the National Register of Historic Places but are protected-location sites, not open to the public. One is the dam and *acequia* site associated with the second location of Mission Nuestra Señora del Espíritu Santo de Zúñiga (*NR 1980*). The other, known as the Tonkawa Bank site, may have been a *ranchería* (small village) or *visita* (country chapel) associated with the mission (*NR 1981*).

REGION 2

Laredo and the Rio Grande Valley

The Rio Grande Valley region includes five counties—Webb, Zapata, Starr, Hidalgo, and Cameron—bordering the Rio Grande from Laredo to Brownsville. During the years of Spanish exploration, the area along the river was inhabited by nomadic Indians who survived by hunting, fishing, and gathering plant foods. As European contact began in New Spain, Indian groups were displaced throughout Mexico, and many of the bands that were pushed northward settled along the Rio Grande. Most of those that inhabited southern Texas were known as Coahuiltecans. The Karankawa, a culturally distinct group, lived along the coast but moved inland at times according to the season and the foods that were available. They were the first Indians encountered by Cabeza de Vaca in 1528.

Several Spanish expeditions visited the region in the 16th and 17th centuries, but permanent settlement did not begin until the 1740s, under the direction of José de Escandón. Escandón, contrary to the usual Spanish practice of military-church governed settlements, founded civil towns that were largely responsible for their own defense. By 1755 he had established 23 settlements, two of them, Rancho de Dolores and Villa de Laredo, north of the Rio Grande.

Besides the Escandón settlements, Spanish and Mexican land grants played a major role in the settlement and development of the region. Beginning in the 1760s *porciones,* or land grants, were assigned to affluent individuals with agricultural and ranching interests to encourage settlement of the as yet unappropriated lands of the Valley north of the Rio Grande. Mission, Hidalgo, McAllen, Pharr, Edinburg, and San Juan, all in Hidalgo County, occupy lands originally assigned under these early land grants. Larger land tracts, suitable for ranching, were granted to the north, in the locations of Alamo, Weslaco, Mercedes, and Raymondville. After 1821, when Mexico gained its independence from Spain, lands continued to be granted in the same manner. When Texas gained its independence from Mexico, the Republic of Texas claimed the Rio Grande as its southern boundary, but the Mexican government still claimed the Nueces River as its northern boundary. The region between the rivers remained in dispute until the Rio Grande was recognized as the official boundary following the United States War with Mexico (1846–48). The end of the war and the

JOSÉ DE ESCANDÓN

José de Escandón, the colonizer responsible for the first permanent European settlements along the Rio Grande, was born in Spain in the year 1700. By the age of 15 he had come to America and joined a company of mounted men known as Los Caballeros Encomenderos. His distinguished military career culminated in 1746 when he was commissioned to survey the country between Tampico and the San Antonio River. He sent seven divisions into the area in 1747 and submitted a colonization plan to the king in 1748. Eventually he was made governor and captain-general of the area known as Nuevo Santander and began making land grants to individuals and families interested in establishing settlements in the Valley. Only two of his permanent settlements, Laredo and Dolores, were north of the Rio Grande. Several of the others—Revilla, Mier, Camargo, and Reynosa—were strung along the south bank of the river, and the settlers crossed the river to farm and ranch. Today, many of the Mexican-Americans living in the Laredo to Brownsville corridor are descendants of the first settlers in the Valley.

Opposite: Garlic vendor in Nuevo Laredo. Photo by Michelle Bridwell.

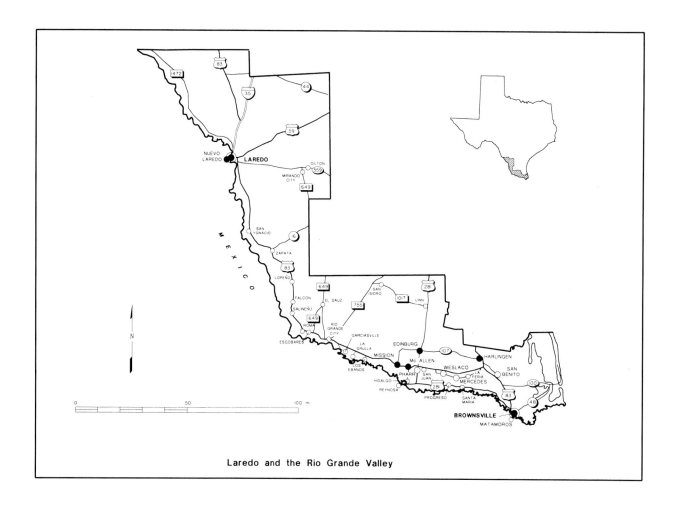

Laredo and the Rio Grande Valley

settlement of the boundary problem lured Texans and Americans into the region. Land disputes soon erupted, and a succession of revolutionaries, including the famed Juan Cortina, fought a number of skirmishes with U.S. troops in the period before the Civil War.

During the Civil War, because of Union blockades of southern shipping ports, the Rio Grande became an important trade area, particularly for the export of cotton. The last battle of the Civil War was fought near the mouth of the river, at a place called Palmito Ranch, on May 13, 1865. After the war, ranching replaced trade as the major economic factor in development of the region. By the beginning of the 20th century, railroads had arrived, and towns developed and grew rapidly along the rail routes. Agriculture, particularly citrus crops, is still a mainstay of the fertile, irrigated lands along the Rio Grande that were first claimed by the Escandón settlers more than two centuries ago.

As you drive through the Valley, take time to note the many fine examples of vernacular architecture that still exist. Drive slowly through the towns, and when possible, walk through the historic districts. Look up and step back. The builder often lavished great detail on the cornices and rooflines. In many downtown sections, the lower levels of buildings have

Guidebook Region 2. Map by Greg Miller.

been modernized and you must look beyond these alterations to appreciate the original form of the building. And finally, take the time to look closely. The workmanship of many buildings is extraordinary. Note the handmade doors and window frames, the decorative brickwork and carved stone ornaments, and the adaptations that were made to make life easier in an often harsh environment.

Board-and-batten residences and jacals were typical of the Rio Grande Valley during the early 20th century. John Wildenthal Family collection, courtesy of Institute of Texan Cultures.

LAREDO AND VICINITY, Webb County

Laredo (pop. 122,899) was founded in 1755 when Tomás Sánchez de la Barrera y Gallardo, under the authority of José de Escandón (*see* sidebar: José de Escandón), established a small settlement on the Rio Grande and named it San Agustín de Laredo. The settlement was designated a villa in 1767, and by 1789 the community had grown from the original 185 settlers to a population of about 800. Most of the villagers lived in jacals built of cane until stone and adobe buildings were constructed in the 1800s. Laredo served as a center of operations for Mexico's war of independence from Spain in 1810 and 1821 and in 1840 was the capital of the short-lived

221

Republic of the Rio Grande, which existed for only 283 days. In 1846 Zachary Taylor led U.S. troops into Laredo and declared the area to be part of the United States. The Treaty of Guadalupe Hidalgo, which ended the United States–Mexican War, was signed in 1848, and Mexico accepted the Rio Grande as its northern boundary. Today, the Hispanic influence and culture of the past and present are evident in the lifestyle and architecture of Laredo. Laredo is now the county seat of Webb County and a gateway to Mexico.

Information Centers

Laredo Convention & Visitors Center. 2310 San Bernardo, P.O. Box 790, Laredo 78040. The center provides information on local attractions, maps of Laredo, and information on crossing the border.

Texas Travel Information Center. IH 35, about 6 mi. N of Laredo. This is one of 12 centers that are located at key highway entrances to Texas; open daily except for major holidays.

Historic Sites

Benavides Brothers. Marker, San Agustín Plaza, San Agustín and Zaragoza Sts. The historical marker commemorates the Benavides brothers, who served in the Confederate Army during the American Civil War. *SM 1976. See also* San Agustín Laredo Historic District: Casa Vidaurri.

San Agustín Laredo Historic District. Bounded on the north by Iturbide St., on the east by Santa Ursula St., on the west by Convent St., and on the south by Water St. The historic district embraces the nucleus of the original city, which was founded in 1755 and officially surveyed and laid out in 1767. The town radiated outward from the central plaza and church. Although none of the structures in the district dates to the original Escandón settlement, they reflect the historical continuum of local development. The homes along Zaragoza Street, south of the plaza, have a particularly international flavor, as the families who built them in the second half of the 19th century were a mixture of Spanish, American, French, and Italian descent. *NR 1973.*

Capitol of the Republic of the Rio Grande Museum. 1009 Zaragoza, on San Agustín Plaza. This small, stone and adobe, L-shaped building, constructed before 1840 (perhaps as early as 1834), served as headquarters for the Republic of the Rio Grande in 1840. The republic was an unsuccessful attempt on the part of the Rio Grande colonies to break with the government of Santa Anna and either reinstate the 1824 constitution of Mexico or become an independent republic. Antonio Canales, chief of military forces for the republic, and his troops were defeated at Saltillo, in Mexico, bringing about the end of the republic. Today, the headquarters building houses a museum that commemorates the brief period when Laredo served as the capital of the Republic of the Rio Grande. The museum features one

Interior courtyard of the Casa
Ortiz, Laredo. THC photo.

of the larger collections of Mexican, Mexican-American, and Indian
artifacts in the region, including examples of tools, furniture, clothing, household items, musical instruments, toys, decorative arts, and
ranching equipment dating from the 1800s. Open Tues.–Sun. 9–4.
SM 1970.

Casa Ortiz. 915 Zaragoza St. This house was built between 1830 and
1872 by José Reyes Ortiz, a one-time resident of Palafox and merchant
and go-between for Mexico and Texas. The back part of the house
dates to the original 1830 structure, while the front (facing Zaragoza
St.) and the second floor were added in 1872. The spacious U-shaped
house, built around a central courtyard, has been home to five Ortiz
generations. *RTHL 1964.*

Casa Vidaurri. 202 Flores Ave. (west side of San Agustín Plaza). This
stuccoed stone house was built in 1874 by Santos Benavides. During

the American Civil War, Benavides rose to the rank of colonel in the Confederate Army, the highest rank achieved by a Mexican-American. His brothers, Cristóbal and Refugio Benavides, served under him as captains. Casa Vidaurri was sold in 1883 to Eulalio Benavides and is still owned by his descendants. *RTHL 1964.*

Old Cayetano de la Garza Home. Flores Ave. This two-story stone house with its cornice of molded brick is one of three buildings in San Agustín Plaza that date from the 1860s and 1870s. The building is now used as a hotel.

Edgardo Gonzales Residence. Santa Ursula and Grant Sts. This residence is a particularly fine example of a common building type in the area. The L-shaped house is situated almost flush with the street and opens onto a courtyard. The body of the house is constructed of hewn sandstone blocks that have been plastered. A cornice made of molded brick was added at a later date.

Alfonso Leyendecker Home. 204 Flores Ave. The Leyendecker home is the third of the large stone houses built in the 1860s and 1870s around San Agustín Plaza, the nucleus of old Laredo.

San Agustín Plaza. Marker, in the plaza bordered by San Bernardo Ave. and Zaragoza St. The plaza, named for Laredo's patron saint, San Agustín, was the heart of the original settlement. The city was laid out in 1767 around the first San Agustín Church. The plaza is now a park, with central bandstand, in the style that became popular in Mexico in the late 19th century. Statues of Ignacio Zaragoza and San Agustín can be seen in the plaza.

San Agustín (St. Augustine) Church. 215 San Agustín between Grant and Zaragoza Sts. The first church in Laredo, a small chapel built in the 1750s, was described a decade later as a poorly made jacal that was open to the elements. By the late 1790s, the hut chapel had been replaced with a stone church and sacristy on the east side of the plaza. This church served the people of Laredo and the surrounding area until the 19th century, when the present church was built under the direction of Father Peter Keralum, an Oblate missionary who had trained as an architect in Paris before coming to the Americas. The masonry Gothic Revival structure with its five-story tower and spire dominates San Agustín Plaza. Extant church records constitute a major historical archive for the area. Among the many devotional celebrations of the church is the Day of the Holy Cross, May 3. On this day parishioners dress in Roman and biblical costumes and re-create the events leading to that day. *RTHL 1963.*

Statue of Ignacio Zaragoza, San Agustín Plaza, Laredo. Photo by Cathryn Hoyt, THC.

Vernacular and Spanish Revival Architecture

El Azteca Neighborhood. The El Azteca, or El Ranchero, neighborhood is bordered by Hidalgo St. on the north, IH 35 on the west, the Rio Grande on the south, and Zacate Creek on the east. Most structures in the area are small one- or two-story houses, positioned close to the sidewalk and surrounded by small yards.

Mexican Colonial Brick House. 201 Iturbide. The one-story brick house, with its beautifully detailed brick cornice on the parapet walls, corbelling, dentils, and frieze, was built about 1890. The house closely reflects the stylistic tradition of earlier stone structures in the area.

Stone Cottage. 401 Grant. This one-story, one-room, stuccoed stone cottage with gabled parapet walls is similar to early houses in Roma and San Ygnacio. The original wooden shingles of the cottage are visible under the metal roof. Built about 1900, the structure is the best example of its type in Laredo.

Hamilton Hotel. 815 Salinas St. The Hamilton Hotel, a rectangular-plan, masonry structure with a flat roof, is Spanish Revival in style and was designed by the San Antonio firm of Atlee Ayres and his son Robert. Atlee Ayres practiced in San Antonio and in Mexico from 1894 until 1921, beginning his own firm in 1900. He was the author of *Mexican Architecture* (1926), and his familiarity with Mexican architecture, as well as the availability of Mexican craftsmen in the Laredo area, contributed to the fine decorative tile and stucco work of the Hamilton Hotel. Interior detailing of the building, particularly the first floor lobby, also reflects Spanish Revival design elements. *NR 1992.*

The Heights and Other Laredo Neighborhoods. The original Heights neighborhood was bounded on the north by Guerrero St., on the east by Urbahn St., on the west by Cedar St., and on the south by the railroad. Development of the area was first proposed in 1888 by the company responsible for the construction of Laredo's streetcar system. Many of the earliest structures in the Heights were built on large corner lots, with the adjoining lots being used for gardens and yards. The coming of the Tex-Mex Railroad in the late 1890s resulted in the construction of small, board-and-batten cottages for the work crews. This important type of vernacular architecture can still be seen in the older sections of Laredo.

Board-and-batten houses. On Convent, Cortez, and Garza Sts. Two single-story, board-and-batten houses with gabled, tin-covered roofs can be seen at 1417 and 1419 Convent St. Two examples of the cottages built for Tex-Mex Railroad workers in the 1890s are located at 216 and 218 Cortez St. At the northwest corner of Garza and San Jorge Sts. is a one-story, board-and-batten house with a corrugated-tin roof and a porch supported by wrought-iron columns.

Heights Elementary School. 1208 Market St. The Spanish Revival style school was built about 1923.

Our Lady of Guadalupe Church. 1718 San Jorge. Our Lady of Guadalupe Church began in 1897 as a mission chapel served by San Agustín Church. By 1920 the original chapel was too small and the present Spanish Revival church was constructed. The chapel continued to be used as a parochial hall until 1949, when the Guadalupe School was constructed on the chapel site. An outstanding feature of the interior of the present church, above the main altar, is an oil painting of Our Lady of Guadalupe that was donated to the church by a family in Guadalajara, Mexico.

Spanish Revival Houses. Cortez, Garfield, and Fremont Sts. At 1201 Cortez St. is a two-story, brick house with flat roof and a gallery with wrought-iron balustrades. The houses at 1220 Garfield St. and 1402 Fremont St. demonstrate interesting adaptations of Spanish Revival stylistic elements. Several houses similar to the two-story brick on Fremont were built in this neighborhood during the early 1900s.

Old Mercado District. Bordered by IH 35/US 83 on the east, the rail-road tracks on the north, Santa María Ave. on the west, and the river on the south. The Old Mercado District began to develop at the end of the 19th century when the Laredo City Hall was built in this area. The rear of the city hall was used as a market, where most of the townspeople did their trading, buying, and selling. Within a few years, the area became known as the Mercado. Gradually other businesses and services moved into the area. The Old Mercado District is particularly interesting today for the various architectural styles of the buildings in the area. Some structures are typical of the Victorian era, while others reflect traditional Spanish-Mexican build-ing forms, but many are a combination of both—traditional Mexican ver-nacular form with Victorian details. Watch for this graphic blending of cultures as you visit the Old Mercado District. Yard shrines, such as a fine example in the 500 block of Farragut St., like yard art, home altars, and other folk traditions, are becoming increasingly rare with each succeeding generation but can still be seen in Laredo and other cities along the border.

Adobe residence. 1308 Grant St. Although the construction date of the house is unknown, the style of this one-story, stuccoed adobe in-dicates that it was built before 1900.

Guadalupe-Treviño Grocery. 517–519 San Agustín. One of the earli-est surviving buildings in the area, the stuccoed stone structure was built about 1875.

Above: **Our Lady of Guadalupe Church, Laredo. Photo by Cathryn Hoyt, THC.**

Above left: **Board-and-batten house, Laredo. Photo by Cathryn Hoyt, THC.**

International Cleaners. 815 Hidalgo. This simple structure is an excellent example of the plain Mexican vernacular building style of the 1870s. Made of rubble stone with a stucco finish, its intact survival is amazing.

Laredo City Hall. 1110 Houston St. Built in 1883–84, the city hall served as the center of the city's business district during the late 19th century. The rear of the building originally served as a Market House where meats, produce, and other items were sold to the townspeople. Alterations in the 1930s and 1950s have changed the original design, and the structure now reflects Spanish Revival stylistic influences. *SM 1991.*

Mexican vernacular building. 409 San Bernardo Ave. This large one-story structure built about 1912–15 is an excellent example of the combination of building forms prevalent in the Old Mercado District. The main building, with its brick detail and flat roof, is typical Mexican vernacular style; however, the front porch is supported by Greek columns more often associated with classical architecture.

St. Peter's Plaza Neighborhood. Bounded by Zaragoza St. on the south, Santa María on the east, and the railroad tracks on the west and north. St. Peter's Plaza neighborhood is a quiet, turn-of-the-century area of the city. Most of the residences were built between 1884 and 1917, after the coming of the railroad. Included are architectural gems in Spanish Revival and Mexican vernacular styles. Even the "Anglo-style" structures, built of brick and often covered with stucco, exhibit a regional interpretation.

Board-and-batten houses. 300 block of Davis. Rows of board-and-batten houses were once common in Laredo but are now fast disappearing. The four houses surviving in this block were built about 1900.

Bonugli Buildings. 1520 Hidalgo and 1601 Hidalgo. These two structures were built in 1906–07 by C.A. Bonugli, an Italian immigrant and merchant, and they are typical of the Mexican commercial building style in this area. The building at 1601 Hidalgo is particularly interesting because of the use of three different construction materials: stone, ashlar, and brick.

Goodwin House. 1604 Houston. This two-story Spanish Revival residence was built about 1910.

Harding Jr. High School. 1701 Victoria St. This two-story brick school, built in 1923, is an example of the Mission Revival style that was popular during the early 20th century.

Mexican Consulate. 1612 Farragut. The consulate, built in 1930, is Art Deco in style with clear Mexican influences.

St. Peter's Plaza. The focal point of the area is St. Peter's Plaza, a landscaped square that covers a full city block and is still an actively used public area.

Santa Fe Depot. Santa Isabel St. The Santa Fe Depot, built in 1910, is a handsome interpretation of Spanish Revival style.

Edward Tarver House. 1903 Victoria St. This simple, one-story, stuccoed brick structure is vernacular in style and dates from the

1870s. It is believed to be one of the oldest houses in the St. Peter's Plaza neighborhood.

Wright House. 413 Davis. The turned posts and pilasters and gingerbread trim of this two-story residence are typical of the late-19th-century Victorian era. However, Hispanic influence is reflected in the building material chosen—stuccoed adobe.

Festivals and Events

Borderfest. Weekend closest to July 4, in Laredo at Civic Center Grounds. Borderfest was founded in 1980 by professors and community leaders of Laredo State University, Laredo Independent School District, and the International Bank of Commerce to promote the cultural and historical heritage of the border. The majority of Borderfest's activities directly relate to Spanish, Mexican, and Mexican-American cultures, and most of the performers are Hispanic. A mariachi competition is held on Friday night (the winner performs on Sunday), and Tejano music is played throughout the weekend. Ballet folklórico groups from Mexico, Eagle Pass, and other communities perform Indian and Mexican dances in traditional costumes. Also part of the festivities is an arts and crafts show, including demonstrations of blanket weaving, quilting, basket weaving, leatherworking, blacksmithing, and tortilla-making. A wide variety of Tex-Mex and Mexican foods are prepared, including tortas, sausage, tortillas, tacos, tripitas, and gorditas. Over 22,000 people attend the three-day event. For more information contact the Laredo Convention and Visitors Center.

"El Grito" Diez y Seis Festival. Mid-September, in Laredo and Nuevo Laredo. Mexican Independence Day is celebrated in various locations in both cities.

Las Posadas. In December, at various locations. Las Posadas processions recreate Joseph and Mary's journey to Bethlehem and their search for shelter. Each night singers ask for *posada* (lodging), at different homes. They are finally allowed to enter, where they find a party with food, drinks, and piñatas waiting.

Los dos Laredos Winter Texan Festival. January 26–28, at El Mercado. The weekend of Mexican-style festivities and family fun features lively mariachis and folklórico dancers, traditional Mexican arts and crafts, and games. For more information contact the Laredo Convention and Visitors Center.

Los Pastores. In December, at various locations. In Los Pastores, or shepherds plays, the devil is always vanquished and Christianity and goodness always win. These plays, with their unique and charming costumes, have their origin in medieval Spain and Italy and are a traditional part of the Christmas season.

Taste of Los Dos Laredos. October, at Civic Center Ballroom. Restaurants from both sides of the border show off their best culinary achievements. For more information contact the Laredo Convention and Visitors Center.

Participants in the Jalapeño Eating Contest during the Washington's Birthday Festival learn the meaning of hot. Photo by Michelle Bridwell.

Washington's Birthday Celebration. During week of February 22, at various locations in Laredo, including Civic Center Auditorium and Ballroom, Laredo Country Club, Lake Casa Blanca, and area around Laredo International Airport. The Washington's Birthday Celebration is a unique expression of Laredo's cultural mixture. The celebration was first held in 1898 and featured a burlesque play, mock battle, band concerts, and a parade described in a local newspaper as "a pageant which in size, variety and dazzling grandeur compared with all the other parades, processions, or pageants ever witnessed in this city." The two-day celebration ended with a reenactment of the Boston Tea Party of American Revolutionary fame. Today, the celebration has expanded into a 10-day event, starting on the Friday before February 22 and ending the following Sunday. Included in the festivities are the Colonial Pageant and Ball, the Jalapeño Street Festival—featuring everything from fajitas and tacos to hamburgers and hot dogs—parades on San Bernardo Ave., the International Water Race, and Noche Mexicana, a Mexican style variety show. For those in need of working off the fajitas, a 5K run follows the parade route in reverse. For information contact Washington's Birthday Celebration Association of Laredo, Inc., P.O. Box 816, Laredo 78042-0816.

Laredo Vicinity

Corral Fences. On W side of Las Tiendas Rd., approx. 17 mi. from FM 1472, and on the San Antonio Ranch, S side of Pita-Mangana Rd., approx. 5 mi. W of Jennings Rd. Traditional mesquite corral fences like these were once commonly seen in the area.

La Cruz Ranch. W side of Las Tiendas Rd., approx. 6 mi. N of FM 1472. The three ranch houses, two masonry buildings, and one jacal form an important group of traditional vernacular forms typical of the area. The masonry buildings are made of stucco-covered stone. The jacal was constructed by placing two rows of posts vertically in the ground, tying them loosely together with wire, and laying smaller posts horizontally between the vertical rows; the entire structure was then daubed with a sandy mud. Private ranch, not open to the public.

Las Tiendas Ranch. E side of Las Tiendas Rd., approx. 18.5 mi. from FM 1472. The ranch house is a very interesting early building form, possibly made of adobe, with later board-and-batten additions. Private ranch, not open to the public.

Pilotos Ranch. E side of FM 1472, approx. 34 mi. N of Laredo. The one-story T-shaped house is made of thick, stuccoed sandstone blocks. The thick walls and general character of this building suggest that it may be very early. An early water tower also is present on the property. Private ranch, not open to the public.

Velenzuela Trail (Piloncillo Ranch). 3 mi. W of US 83 and 1 mile N of Rancho Espejo Rd. This one-story, stone and adobe structure, built in the 1830s, is the only known stagecoach stop in this area. The building is constructed in a long rectangle made up of five adjoining rooms, four of which have stone fireplaces with stone-and-adobe chimneys and gunports. All five rooms have packed dirt floors. The roof is an interesting example of early construction techniques. The ridge pole is made of pin oak, and elm saplings serve as rafters. Carrizo cane was then nailed across the rafters, and the roof was then covered with local grasses. Private ranch, not open to the public.

Border City

Nuevo Laredo, Mexico (pop. ca. 240,000), and Laredo share a common history. Laredo's sister city caters to visitors throughout the year and has numerous gift shops offering jewelry, glassware, pottery, leathergoods, and other handicrafts. The following events, held in Nuevo Laredo, are attended by Laredo visitors as well as international tourists:

Expo-Mex Fair and Exposition. In September, at Fair Grounds adjacent to La Junta Park in Nuevo Laredo. Go south on Guerrero for approximately 20 blocks and watch for the Expo-Mex sign; turn left until dead end, left again. The week-long festival features concerts by famous Mexican musicians, as well as arts and crafts, industrial, and agricultural exhibits.

Festival Internacional de la Raza. May 1–5, in Nuevo Laredo. The festival seeks to bring Mexicans and Mexican-Americans together in public forums where a different theme is pursued each year. Music, dance, poetry, and other events are included.

Laredo's Arte—Los dos Laredos. In November, in Nuevo Laredo. At this time Nuevo Laredoans observe El Día de los Muertos, the Day of the Dead. *See* sidebar: El Día de los Muertos.

EL DÍA DE LOS MUERTOS

Laredo's Arte—Los Dos Laredos is celebrated from November 1 through 5 each year. At this time *El Día de Los Muertos* (the Day of the Dead) is observed with the typical humor of the Mexican people, who laugh at death and yet do honor to their departed family members. Altars of Remembrance are constructed—their size determined by the family's means—each containing representations of the four elements—water, fire, wind, and earth. Institutions, such as the Nuevo Laredo television studio, construct elaborate and beautiful altars where food is offered to the *difuntos* (deceased) and also shared with the public. The food offered can be elaborate or simple, but a special bread called Pan de Muerto is obligatory. Hot chocolate, sugar skulls, candy skeletons, and tamales are other typical offerings. Among the elements of this tradition that date from Pre-Columbian times is the use of the flower known as *Flor de Muerto* (Cempoalxochitt) in cemetery and altar decorations.

On the days of observance, music and dance are performed, and art exhibits are held on both sides of the border. *Calaveras*—anonymous, rhymed, satiric quatrains written supposedly as epitaphs for tombstones—are published in the newspapers and read at gatherings and on the radio. The ideal targets of the verses are politicians, who, because of their calling, are easy to satirize and instantly recognizable. Using the rapier of wit and words, *calaveras* are used to deflate vanity and pomposity. *Calaveras* can also be funny, bittersweet, tragic, and even cruel. These anonymous, satiric verses probably were first used as a way for people to voice their opinions without fear of retribution from those in power.

BROWNSVILLE, Cameron County

Brownsville (pop. 98,962) was founded in the mid-19th century, but its European settlement history reaches back 100 years before that date. The land around Brownsville was part of the Espíritu Santo land grant, a tract of land consisting of about 261,000 acres. José Salvador de la Garza settled on the north bank of the Rio Grande in 1781 and used the land for grazing and farming. After the Republic of Texas was annexed by the United States in 1845, controversy over the international boundary contributed to the Mexican War and the growth of the city of Brownsville around Fort Brown. Located near the mouth of the Rio Grande, Brownsville grew into an important shipping port with a cosmopolitan population. Spanish, French, Irish, English, German, and American merchants established businesses in the town. The unique character of Brownsville is due in large part to the intermingling of European customs and culture with those of the Spanish culture that was already well established in the area. Today, Brownsville, the county seat of Cameron County, remains an important shipping port for international trade, and its fair weather and close proximity to the Gulf of Mexico make it a popular resort city.

Information

Brownsville Visitors Center. 650 FM 802. Open daily, 9–5.

Historic Sites

Alonso Building (Los dos Cánones). 510–514 St. Charles St. Rare example of the old French-Spanish vernacular style buildings. Built in the late 1800s by Manuel Alonso, a native of Santander, Spain, the building was originally a retail grocery store specializing in fancy groceries and dry goods. The upper story, with its airy balcony and beautiful wrought-iron railing, was used as living quarters.

Cavazos House. 608 E. Adams. Fannie Seward Cavazos moved from Ohio to Bagdad, Mexico, during the American Civil War. She came to Brownsville in 1870 with her husband, Wenceslao Cavazos. After 1882 Fannie began a successful business dealing in Mexican-style, drawnwork lace. She also helped establish the Mexican Presbyterian Church in Brownsville. The Cavazos House is a late Victorian cottage with decorative woodwork. *RTHL 1984.*

Augustine Celaya House. 504 E. St. Francis St. The Celaya House is an eleven-room, two-story, masonry residence built in 1904 for Augustine Celaya, a prominent lawyer in the area. The bricks used in construction were hand-made by local labor; all walls are 13 inches thick, and outer surfaces are covered in natural cement. This construction provides insulation in both winter and summer. The design of the various wings and arched windows was developed by the owner to take advantage of the slightest tropical breeze. The movable vented shutters of the Celaya House are typical of homes of the period and the climatic location. An interesting complement of brick out-buildings is found behind the house. *SM 1989; RTHL 1988.*

Convent of the Incarnate Word and Blessed Sacrament (former site). Marker, 714 E. St. Charles St. America's first colony of sisters of the Incarnate Word and Blessed Sacrament, a cloistered teaching order, arrived here from France in 1853. The convent served as a boarding and day school for girls. For their bilingual (Spanish-English) pupils, the sisters were compelled to translate from French and to print textbooks on a small hand press. The sisters moved to Villa María, a modern educational center, in 1967. *SM 1972.*

Cueto Building (La Nueva Libertad). 1301–1311 E. Madison. The Cueto store, also known as La Nueva Libertad, reflects the prosperity of Brownsville at the turn of the century and is an outstanding example of 19th-century Rio Grande Valley commercial architecture. The store was built in 1893 by Andrés Cueto, a prominent businessman of Spanish birth, whose descendants still retain ownership of the structure. Cueto dealt in both wholesale and retail grocery and hardware items and supplied merchandise to Roma and Rio Grande City in Texas as well as Ciudad Victoria, Reynosa, and Monterrey in Mexico. The store reflects the strong tradition of Spanish building practices in the Rio Grande Valley. The lower floor was used for commercial purposes, while the upper floor, originally surrounded by a cast-iron veranda, served as the residence of the Cueto family. The masonry roof-construction system, consisting of two layers of brick set on top of wood decking and beams, is a type commonly used in the Spanish Caribbean colonies and a traditional form of vernacular construction in Spain itself. At the turn of the century, buildings such as the Cueto store were quite common in Brownsville, but only a few survive intact today. *NR 1984; RTHL 1985.*

Immaculate Conception Cathedral. 1218 E. Jefferson St. The cathedral was built in 1859 by Father Pierre Keralum (*see* sidebar: Pierre Yves Keralum). The bricks used to build the church were made as tithes by the parishioners and were each stamped with the letters OMI (for Oblates of Mary Immaculate). The parishioners also made a number of bricks for a parish hall; however, before construction could begin, Union troops landed in Brownsville and appropriated the bricks to build portions of Fort Brown. The church's rectory was the site of the first Texas Oblate Seminary and served as a haven for priests fleeing revolutions in Mexico. The church became a cathedral in 1874. *RTHL 1962; NR 1980.*

La Madrileña. 1002 E. Madison. Adrian Ortiz built this structure in 1892 to house his mercantile operation, La Madrileña (native of Madrid), an important community business for over 60 years. The Ortiz store sold groceries, hardware, clothing, and special items such as wine, dried codfish, and other goods imported from Spain. La Madrileña developed into a gathering place for neighbors that was managed under the watchful eye of Ortiz until his death in 1957. The architecture of the structure displays many of the characteristics of late-19th-century commercial buildings along the Rio Grande. The most noteworthy architectural features are the tall sculptural parapets with nine ornamental brick pinnacles, the corbeled

PIERRE YVES KERALUM— EL SANTO PADRE PEDRITO

Pierre Yves Keralum (often abbreviated to Peter Kalum and also known as "El Santo Padre Pedrito" and as "the Lost Missionary") was born in Quimper, Brittany, on March 2, 1817. After completing his secondary education, he became a cabinetmaker and later studied architecture in Paris. Following some success as an architectural practitioner in Paris, he made his profession as an Oblate of Mary Immaculate and was ordained in 1852 at age 35. Because of his architectural skills, he was sent to Texas, where the Oblates had become active in the 1840s. In addition to designing the church at Roma in 1854, Father Keralum designed and supervised Immaculate Conception Church in Brownsville in 1859 and assisted in the construction of St. Augustine Church in Laredo in 1872.

Father Keralum's strenuous activity for twenty years along the Rio Grande—including personal restraints that were injurious to his health—caused him to age prematurely. As a missionary priest, he went from ranch to ranch on extended horseback journeys. On November 9, 1872, Father Keralum, by then almost blind, left Brownsville to begin a circuit scheduled to last until after the New Year. On November 12 he arrived at the Tampacuas ranch, four miles north of Mercedes, and from there departed for the ranch of Las Piedras, eighteen miles northward. He did not arrive at Las Piedras, and several days later his horse was found unfettered but dragging a lariat. Immediately search parties were sent to find the priest, but no trace of the lost missionary was found.

In 1882 a rancher from Las Pitates went into the thick chaparral to disentangle two cows and found the skeletal remains of Father Keralum—identified by his Oblate cross, the chalice and paten, a holy oil stock, an altar-bread box, a holy water bottle, a piece of a rosary, an altar bell, a watch, and eighteen dollars in silver. It was surmised that he had lost his way and might have been bitten by a rattlesnake while resting, or that he had succumbed from natural causes as a result of his many personal privations. Father Keralum, whose vow of poverty was strictly observed in his lifetime, left a lasting legacy in many fine churches still being used in the Rio Grande Valley.

Cueto Building (La Nueva Libertad), Brownsville. Photo by Cathryn Hoyt, THC.

La Madrileña, Brownsville. Photo by Cathryn Hoyt, THC.

brickwork, and the paneled doors with transoms. After the death of Ortiz, the building was left to deteriorate for 30 years. In 1987 it was completely restored and now serves as a source of pride for the people of Brownsville. *RTHL 1988; NR 1988.*

Land Grants in the Brownsville Area. Lands between Olmos Creek, 100 mi. N of Brownsville, and the Rio Grande. Unlike the area to the west that was divided into small land grants and settled, the land near Brownsville was not considered for town settlements during the Spanish period. Rather, the land was distributed in large tracts to wealthy cattle owners and Spaniards of "reliability." Some of the land grants, such as the Espíritu

Santo, the San Juan Carricitos, and the San Salvador del Tule, were quite large, ranging in size from 250,000 to 500,000 acres each.

Mural. Jacob Brown Auditorium at the Fort Brown Memorial Center. This untitled mural depicts the early history of Brownsville.

Public Market and Town Hall. 655 E. 12th St. The public market and town hall were authorized in 1850 on land deeded forever for this purpose. Butchers and other vendors moved in during 1851. The second floor of the market was lost in a high wind in 1867, but the building was restored in 1868 and has since been remodeled twice, in 1912 and 1948. The original foundations and walls still survive in the modern market. *RTHL 1965.*

Tijerina House. 333 E. Adams St. Tomás Tijerina, a descendant of 18th-century Rio Grande settler Blás María de la Garza Falcón, moved to this site in 1904. The original frame house was moved to the back of the lot in 1912 when the present brick home was built. Tijerina designed the residence and his neighbor, Teodoro Pérez, served as the general carpenter. The house features fine brick detailing and unusual buttresses, designed by Tijerina so that the house could withstand hurricane winds. *RTHL 1979.*

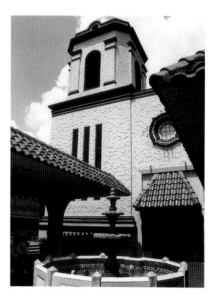

Public Market and Town Hall, Brownsville. Photo by Cathryn Hoyt, THC.

Spanish Revival Architecture

Church of the Advent. 104 W. Elizabeth. The Church of the Advent, founded in 1851, is one of the earliest Episcopal churches organized in Texas. The original church building was destroyed in a hurricane in 1867 and was rebuilt in 1926–27. The Mission Revival style structure was designed by Scottish architect Thomas McLaren and features a domed tower, barrel tile roof, and curvilinear parapet. *RTHL 1988.*

Southern Pacific Railroad Passenger Depot. 641 E. Madison St. The expansion of the Southern Pacific Railroad into South Texas in the late 1920s resulted in the construction of several fine Mission style depots in the region, including those in Edinburg, McAllen, and Brownsville. The Brownsville depot, built in 1928, is a particularly beautiful example of Spanish Revival architecture with its light-colored stucco and ornate cast-stone ornamentation at the major entrances, the cornice, the coped parapet at the gabled end, and the chimney and its adjacent parapet. The interior is finished with tile floors and wainscoting, plaster walls, stenciled beams in the waiting room, and decorative tile around the drinking fountain. The building was used as a passenger depot until 1952. *NR 1978; RTHL 1985. See also* Historic Brownsville Museum.

Museum

Historic Brownsville Museum. 641 E. Madison St. Housed in the historic Southern Pacific Railroad Passenger Depot, the Museum contains a "walk through time" that highlights the development of Brownsville and South Texas from Spanish times to the end of the 19th century. The Brownsville Heritage Education Center features the Mary Yturria Education Gal-

Southern Pacific Railroad Passenger Depot, Brownsville. Photo by Cathryn Hoyt, THC.

lery, which offers special programs, lectures, school tours, and exhibits. Open Tues.–Sat. 10–4:30. *See also* Southern Pacific Railroad Passenger Depot.

Festival

Charro Days. In February, at various locations in Brownsville and its sister city across the river, Matamoros. Charro Days was founded in 1938 to educate both citizens and winter visitors to the Brownsville-Matamoros area about Mexican culture. Today, Charro Days, Inc., continues to organize the festival, which focuses on the Mexican state of Tamaulipas and its historical influence on Spanish ranching techniques, especially those of the charros (the wealthy, landowning horsemen). The festival also features music, food, and customs of the South Texas border area. Major attractions are a charreada and a costume review of Pan American traditional dresses—a local collection that may be the largest of its kind in the world. Many Charro Days participants dress in authentic Mexican costumes as they enjoy performances of mariachi, conjunto, and marimba music, ballet folklórico, and live demonstrations and window displays of folk arts and crafts. All of the fiesta's performers are Hispanic. Young participants may celebrate at a special preschool fiesta complete with piñatas. Over 150,000 visitors participate in Charro Days each year.

Statue and historical marker commemmorating Padre José Nicolás Ballí, Brownsville vicinity. Photo by Cathryn Hoyt, THC.

Brownsville Vicinity

Padre José Nicolás Ballí. Marker, located on Park Rd. 100, at E approach to causeway, 3 miles E of Port Isabel. Ballí received a land grant of 11.5 leagues of Padre Island from Spain and, in 1804, started the first settlement, Rancho Santa Cruz, on the island. With his nephew, Juan José Ballí, as a partner, Padre Ballí ran large herds of cattle, sheep, and horses on the land. Ballí also founded the first mission church in Cameron County, and Padre Island is named for him. *SM 1983.*

Rancho Viejo. Marker located on US 77, 4.8 mi. N of Brownsville. Rancho Viejo was the site of the first European settlement in Cameron County. The area was settled by José Salvador de la Garza, who built his ranch, El Espíritu Santo, here in 1771. *CM 1936.*

Scenic Area. National Audubon Society Sabal Palm Grove Wildlife Sanctuary, 10 mi. SE of Brownsville off FM 1419. Originally part of the old Rabb Plantation, the Wildlife Sanctuary preserves the last portion of the virgin native-palm forest left in this area. Visitors to the sanctuary can appreciate the environment as it appeared to the original Indian inhabitants and first European explorers.

Border City

Matamoros, Mexico. Hosts of visitors from the United States cross the bridge to Matamoros throughout the year to enjoy the city's restaurants, night life, and gift shops. The city's market offers bargains in pottery and other traditional handicrafts.

EDINBURG, Hidalgo County

Edinburg (pop. 29,885), founded in 1908, was named Chapin after the original promoter of the townsite, but the name was changed to Edinburg in 1911. Now a center for citrus agriculture, Edinburg is the county seat of Hidalgo County.

Hidalgo County Historical Museum. 121 E. McIntyre. Museum exhibits record the history of the Valley from the prehistoric period and early Spanish exploration through ranching, farming, and the coming of the railroad. The museum emphasizes the blending of Anglo and Hispanic cultures that give the Valley its unique flavor. The museum is housed in the Old County Jail, which was in use between 1910 and 1922. The brick structure's white stuccoed walls and red roof tiles are typical elements of Spanish Revival architecture. Open Tues.–Fri. 9–5; Sat. 9–4; Sun. 1–5.

Padre Miguel Hidalgo y Costilla. Marker, Hidalgo Plaza, 100 N. Closner St. A bust and marker honor Miguel Hidalgo y Costilla (1753–1811), for whom the county of Hidalgo is named. Father Hidalgo is known as "the father of Mexican independence." His call to arms on September 16, 1810, began the revolt that ultimately led to Mexican independence from Spain in 1821. Mexico's independence was, in turn, a first step toward Texas statehood. Father Hidalgo continues to be honored for his leadership throughout Mexico and the Southwest and his call to arms is celebrated as the annual Diez y Seis de Septiembre festival, also known as Father Hidalgo Day. *SM 1983.*

Rio Grande Folklore Archive. Pan American University, 1201 W. University Dr. The archive specializes in Mexican-American materials from the Lower Rio Grande Valley. Collections include questionnaires, videotapes, and student papers on topics such as folk speech, folk medicine, and folk beliefs.

Fiesta Hidalgo. Last weekend in February, at the Bobcat Stadium parking lot, National Guard Armory, and Activity Center. Fiesta Hidalgo, sponsored by the Edinburg Chamber of Commerce, celebrates the establishment of the Hidalgo County seat in Edinburg in 1908. Many festival events relate to Mexican and Mexican-American cultures. Fiesta Hidalgo features ballet folklórico by performers dressed in Aztec and traditional Hispanic costumes, mariachi and conjunto music, and Mexican and Tejano foods (including fajitas, gorditas, sausage, nachos, and barbecue). Approximately 20,000 people attend the fiesta each year.

Las Posadas. In December, in Hidalgo Plaza. Luminarias around Hidalgo Plaza lend added charm to Las Posadas, the reenactment of the journey to the inn and the birth of Jesus. The celebration also features caroling and dancing, lively mariachis, home-baked goods, and crafts.

Pan American Days. Mid-April. Pan American Days is held as a salute to the 22 republics of this hemisphere.

Edinburg Vicinity

El Sal del Rey Archeological District. 22 mi. N of Edinburg, 4 mi. E of US 281 on SH 186. El Sal del Rey has been a source of high-quality rock salt for at least 3,000 years. José de Escandón's exploration parties in the early 18th century encountered native American salt traders from Nuevo León and Coahuila who were mining salt at Sal del Rey and other salines in the area and were taking it to Mier. An ancient road led from the ford at Los Ebanos to the site. The Spanish salt trade began sometime before 1747 when salt was collected and sold to the colonists in Escandón's Camargo settlement. The mineral rights belonged to the king, who received one-fifth of the proceeds, hence the name El Sal del Rey (Salt of the King). The Sal del Rey location was included in the San Salvador del Tule grant given to Juan José Ballí in 1794, and these lands later passed to the Cárdenas family. Until well after Texas was annexed to the Union, public ownership of the mineral rights was contested by the landowner, who wished to commercially exploit the salt. Private ownership of rights to the salt was not recognized until 1937—and salt was mined commercially only three more years. *RTHL 1964; NR 1979.*

Laguna Seca Ranch. Marker, located on local road off US 281, 12 mi. N of Edinburg. The Laguna Seca (Dry Lake) ranch was settled by Macedonio Vela in 1865. In 1871, his daughter, Carlota, grew the first orange trees in Hidalgo County. By 1892, the ranch had increased in size to 80,000 acres. A school was built there in 1892, the Delfina Post Office was opened in 1893, and a Catholic church was established in 1894. The Laguna Seca ranch is still owned by the Vela family. Private ranch, not open to the public. *SM 1975; TFLHR.*

San Juanito or McAllen Ranch. In Edinburg vicinity, Hidalgo County. The San Juanito Ranch, one of the oldest ranches in the area, was founded in 1797 when José Manuel Gómez purchased the Santa Anita grant, a 21.5-league tract of land. Gómez raised sheep, cattle, goats, and horses. The ranch has been continuously owned and operated by his descendants for almost 200 years. Hand-dug water wells and traditional cattle corrals can still be seen on the ranch lands. The main ranch house is riddled with bullet holes, attesting to the sometimes difficult life on the borderlands. Private ranch, not open to the public. *TFLHR.*

San Manuel Farms. In Edinburg vicinity, Hidalgo County. In 1876, Manuel Chapa and his wife, María Luisa Flores, early settlers in the South Texas region, gave 480 acres of their original 4,428-acre ranch to their son Félix and his new bride, Agustina Montalvo. Félix and Agustina named their ranch San Manuel in honor of Félix's father. Félix Chapa raised goats, sheep, horses, and cattle as well as small crops of cotton, corn, and beans. He also helped his father mine salt from El Sal del Rey. Today, San Manuel Farms is owned by the great-great-grandsons of Félix and Agustina Chapa and cattle, horses, and cotton are still produced here. Private ranch, not open to the public. *TFLHR.*

EL SAUZ VICINITY, Starr County

El Sauz (pop. ca. 90), a small rural community, serves as a supply center for ranches in the area. The name is Spanish for "willow."

Vernacular stone residence. On E side of FM 649, just S of El Sauz Creek. This one-story, mud and stone residence was built about 1900 and is typical of ranch outbuildings that were built of inexpensive, locally available materials.

ESCOBARES, Starr County

Escobares (pop. ca. 220), a small ranching community located east of Roma-Los Sáenz, shows the range of vernacular building styles typical of the early 20th century in the region.

Francisco Barrera House. Located one block E of town square on NE corner of the intersection. A very nice example of early-20th-century, brick vernacular architecture, the Barrera House was built around 1917.

Tomás Escobar House. Located diagonal to town square on SW corner of the intersection. This simple, one-story, board-and-batten house was built about 1916.

Severo Martínez Store. Located just E of SE corner of intersection across from town square. This brick vernacular structure, built about 1920, was used as a general store that served the Escobares area and also sent goods, such as kerosene, across the river to Mexico. Of special interest are the two sets of handmade, wooden double doors on the front of the building.

FALCON, Zapata County

Falcon (pop. ca. 50), a tiny community in southern Zapata County, was created in the 1950s after Lake Falcon had submerged the original townsite.

Falcon State Recreational Area and Lake Falcon. Entrance located approx. 2 mi. from Falcon Dam off Park Rd. 46. Falcon State Recreational Area is the largest recreational area in this part of the country and encompasses 572 acres of gently rolling hills covered with native vegetation. The lake is well known to fishermen for the black and white bass, catfish, crappie, and stripers caught there. Two hundred years before the creation of Lake Falcon, Spanish colonists settled the area between Zapata and Rio Grande City. Today, the ruins of these stone, adobe, and jacal buildings can be seen around the lake. The drive across the dam leads to Nuevo Guerrero in Mexico.

Old Falcón Site. Marker, US 83 right-of-way, Falcon. The village of old Falcón was one of the first towns submerged by the rising waters of the Falcon Dam. The area was originally a ranch settlement named Ramireño. Founded in the late 1700s by José Eugenio Ramírez, the site became a village in the early 1900s, and the name was changed to Falcón in honor of Ramírez's wife, María Rita de la Garza Falcón, in 1915. *SM 1983.*

GARCIASVILLE, Starr County

Garciasville (pop. ca. 100), located on FM 1430 east of Rio Grande City, developed in the late 19th century as a supply point for ranchers in the area. Named after an early settler, Garciasville is now a market center for vegetables grown in the surrounding area.

Board-and-batten house. 2 mi. E of FM 1430, on S side of road. This typical board-and-batten house was constructed about 1916. Of particular interest is the associated wooden cistern made of vertical planks held together by metal bands and built on high stilts. The cistern is a good example of a necessary feature in this dry area.

Garciasville Mission Church. Located 0.2 mi. E of Santo Domingo Rd., on S side of road. Although now abandoned and deteriorating, the structure is an interesting example of the typical form and detail of early churches in the Rio Grande Valley. Built about 1886, this brick church features a gable roof and frame bell tower, now in ruins. The church was named San Ygnacio de Loyola in honor of Ygnacio García, who donated land for the church site.

HARLINGEN, Cameron County

Harlingen (pop. 48,735) was the vision of Lon C. Hill, who built a house, 20 miles of telephone lines, and 10 miles of graded road at the location in 1901. However, the townsite remained undeveloped until the railroad came through in 1905. Harlingen is today the crossroads for two major highways and two major railroads and serves as a transportation center for the southern tip of Texas. It is the second largest town in Cameron County.

Information Centers

Mexican-American Chamber of Commerce. 712 N US 77 Sunshine Strip, Suite 3 (El Mercado Mall), P.O. Box 1587, Harlingen, TX 78551. The chamber can provide tourist information for the Rio Grande Valley and Mexico.

Texas Travel Information Center. US 83 and US 77. This is one of 12 centers that are located at key highway entrances to Texas; open daily except for major holidays. The center offers information on road conditions, sightseeing, and hotel accommodations as well as a slide show in Spanish and English that introduces the visitor to points of interest in the area.

Historic Sites and Museums

Bowie Elementary School. 309 W. Lincoln. This beautiful Aztec Revival school is nicknamed La Escuela de Las Víboras (the School of the Snakes) because of the snake motifs used in the cast concrete façade. In 1928, sculptor Luis López Sánchez was commissioned to make the molds and mix the paint pigments for the concrete castings. He produced a design that is a blend of Mexican art forms—from the Mayan works at Chichén-Itzá to the feathered headdresses of the Toltecs and the speech glyphs of the Aztecs—that emphasized snake figures. The snake, associated with knowledge and wisdom in many Mexican and American Indian cultures, is a particularly appropriate decorative motif for a school.

Santos Lozano Building. 112–115 W. Jackson. Built in 1915, the Santos Lozano Building is the oldest existing brick building in Harlingen. Designed and built by Baltazar Torres of Brownsville for the mercantile business of Santos Lozano, the structure also served as a community center, providing upstairs space for bilingual school classes and special events. *RTHL 1980.*

Rio Grande Valley Museum. Boxwood St., Industrial Airpark. The museum seeks to portray the bicultural heritage of the Lower Rio Grande Valley through educational and cultural exhibits. Displays include prehistoric artifacts from Karankawa and Coahuiltecan Indians through Spanish dominion, the Mexican Republic, and the Republic of Texas to the present day. Open Tues.–Fri. 9–12, 2–5; Sun. 2–5.

Festivals

Cinco de Mayo Celebration. Weekend nearest May 5, in Lon C. Hill Park. The three-day celebration features mariachi and other traditional music, ballet folklórico dancing, food and game booths, exhibitions of arts and crafts, and a celebration dance culminated by the coronation of Señorita Cinco de Mayo.

Diez y Seis de Septiembre. Weekend closest to September 16, in Victor Park. The Harlingen Mexican-American Chamber of Commerce has sponsored Diez y Seis de Septiembre since 1980. The celebration features ceremonies with visiting dignitaries, ballet folklórico performances, concerts of conjunto and mariachi music, arts and crafts exhibits, and a variety of Tex-Mex foods.

Harlingen Rio Fest. Early April, in Fair Park. Rio Fest is an international celebration of the arts and culture. Families come from both sides of the border to enjoy music, dance, drama, and art in this education and entertainment festival. Performers are predominantly Mexican and Mexican-American. Crafts, food, and drink are also featured. Between 25,000 and 30,000 visitors attend this event each year.

HIDALGO AND VICINITY, Hidalgo County

Hidalgo (pop. 3,292) was inhabited as early as 1774 under Escandón's colonizing efforts. Originally, the town was known as La Habitación, and, later, as Rancho San Luis and San Luisito. A ferry operated from Hidalgo to Reynosa until the construction of the international bridge. In 1852, the town was renamed Edinburgh and was made the county seat of the newly formed county of Hidalgo. The city name was changed to Hidalgo in 1861. The town retains much of its early appearance and its very strong Hispanic heritage.

Historic Sites and Museums

Father Hidalgo Statue. 5th and Esperanza at entrance to Hidalgo Municipal Park. The statue honors Father Miguel Hidalgo y Costilla (1753–1811), for whom the county of Hidalgo is named. Father Hidalgo is considered "the father of Mexican independence." His call to arms on September 16, 1810, which began the revolt that led to Mexican independence from Spain in 1821, ultimately was a first step toward Texas statehood. Father Hidalgo's call to arms is celebrated as the annual Diez y Seis de Septiembre festival, also known as Father Hidalgo Day.

Hidalgo-Reynosa Bridges. Marker, on US 281 spur at its terminus at the Rio Grande. In the late 19th century an irregular ferry service operated between Hidalgo and the Mexican side of the river. In 1910 the ferry was acquired by Crisoforo Vela and operated on a regular schedule until 1926, when the first Hidalgo-Reynosa bridge was constructed across the Rio Grande. For over six decades the Hidalgo-Reynosa bridges, the latest of which was completed in 1988, have facilitated transportation and fostered friendship between Texas and Mexico. *SM 1989.*

Mission San Joaquín del Monte Site. Marker, in City Park, First St. and Texano Dr. San Joaquín del Monte was a *visita*, or sub-mission, established in 1749 to serve the settlement at Reynosa; by 1750 there were five groups of Coahuiltecan Indians here. In 1887, floodwaters washed away all remnants of the mission. *CM 1936.*

Old Hidalgo County Courthouse. Flora and First Sts. The complex includes the former Hidalgo County Courthouse, which was constructed of handmade Mexican brick from Reynosa and built by mason Juan Ríos in 1886. The building served as the Hidalgo County Courthouse until 1908, when the county seat was moved 14 miles north to Chapin (now called Edinburg). The original second story and cupola of the courthouse were destroyed by fire in 1910. The courthouse complex was restored in 1984 by its current owner, the Border Bank. *RTHL 1963; NR 1980.*

Old Hidalgo County Jail. Flora and First Sts. The old Hidalgo County Jail, part of the Hidalgo County Courthouse complex, was built in 1886 and served the county during a turbulent period when bandit raids were still occurring. Built by Juan Ríos, the two-story structure features

handmade brick and a corbeled cornice along the roofline. The jail continued in use until 1908. *RTHL 1984.*

Post Office. NE corner of Flora and First St. This one-story brick building, with intricate brick detailing around the cornice, was built in 1889 to serve as a general merchandise store and post office. It served as the Hidalgo Post Office until 1913. *RTHL 1965.*

Vela Building. 220 S. Bridge St. In 1904, Crisoforo Vela and his wife, Florinda de la Vega Ballí, moved to Hidalgo from Santo Domingo Ranch in Starr County. Six years later, Vela acquired the ferry that connected Hidalgo with Reynosa, Mexico, and he operated the ferry until 1926. Vela lived in this beautiful two-story brick house, with its intricate wrought-iron balconies, until his death in 1932. Descendants of Vela still own the house. *SM 1984.*

Vela Building, Hidalgo. Photo by Cathryn Hoyt, THC.

Festival

Hidalgo Border Fest. Early March, at City Pavilion. This international celebration pays tribute to the diversified cultures of the Rio Grande Valley. Thousands of people join in the three days of fun, and events include a carnival, parades, craft demonstrations, and entertainment. An important feature of the celebration, usually on Friday, is the traditional *abrazo* (friendship embrace) between officials from Hidalgo and Reynosa.

Hidalgo Vicinity

Santa Ana Wildlife Refuge. Entrance 0.4 mi. E of US 281–FM 907 intersection, 7.5 mi. S of Alamo. The refuge is a 2,000-acre remnant of subtropical forest where indigenous plants such as the *tepeguaje* (leadwort), *granjeno* (scaly hackberry), bluewood, and Texas ebony still grow. The refuge also contains the largest remaining stretch of virgin chaparral in the Valley. This chaparral caused one early visitor to note with disgust that everything in the country sticks, stings, or stinks. Also to be seen here are the green jay and the pheasant-size game bird called *chachalaca,* both more common in Mexico. The land, originally part of the Santa Ana land grant, retains the characteristics of the brush country as it was when first viewed by the early explorers. Descendants of the Leal family, the original owners of the Santa Ana land grant, are buried in a 19th-century cemetery on the refuge.

Border City

Reynosa, Mexico (pop. ca. 250,000), was founded in 1749 as Nuestra Señora de Guadalupe de Reynosa. The salt trade was of early importance to this Spanish outpost, which was the second Escandón settlement on the Rio Grande. Mexican *carretas* (hauling wagons) and ox trains brought salt here from La Sal Vieja and El Sal del Rey. From Reynosa this valuable trade item was sold throughout the Nuevo Santander colony. Modern Reynosa offers restaurants and gift shops that cater to U.S. visitors, and handcrafted items can be found in both the tourist area and in the traditional market in midtown. Reynosa's Fruit and Vegetable Market (on Hidalgo at the railroad station, 10 blocks south of the plaza) is a traditional food market featuring chiles, herbs, and strands of braided garlic. Difficult-to-find ingredients such as chiles anchos, avocado leaves, Mexican chocolate, pumpkin seeds, and braided Oaxacan cheese can be found at the Astra Supermercado (on Hidalgo and P. Balboa; take Mexico US 40 toward Monterrey). Before buying produce, check with border officials about fruits and vegetables that can be brought back.

LA FERIA, Cameron County

La Feria (pop. 4,360) is located on land surveyed in 1777 for a Spanish land grant to Juan Hinojosa and José María Ballí, ancestors of the priest for whom Padre Island was named. Cattle, sheep, and goats were raised on the original ranch. By the 1790s a fairground had been established for fiestas and races that gave rise to the name La Feria. The modern townsite of La Feria was platted in 1906. A marker (*SM 1971*) commemorating the town is located on old US 83, near the American Legion Hall on the east side of La Feria.

Rosalio Longoria House. 223 Magnolia St. The Longoria House, the oldest residence in La Feria, was built in 1909 by local carpenter Felipe Pérez for Rosalio Ponce Longoria. Longoria was a contractor who cleared land for developers to build railroads and other Rio Grande Valley improvements. The board-and-batten house originally had two main rooms, two small bedrooms, a porch, and a kitchen. The additions date to the 1950s. *RTHL 1974.*

St. Francis Xavier Catholic Church. 213 W. Magnolia. The architecture of this charming church is an interesting combination of Anglo-American and Spanish influences. The placement of the dominant, central tower is typical of Protestant churches, while the style of the tower itself is derived from Mission San José in San Antonio.

St. Francis Xavier Catholic Church, La Feria. Photo by Cathryn Hoyt, THC.

LA GRULLA, Starr County

La Grulla (pop. 1,335) was founded in the late 1800s, but an earlier Mexican settlement extended along both sides of the river at this location. The town was named for the cranes that are common on the lake near the town. Today, La Grulla is a center for vegetable farming. Several interesting late-19th-century brick vernacular buildings can be seen in the southwest end of town, nearest the river.

Holy Family Church. The first church at La Grulla was Capilla de San Roque, built in 1849 by the Oblates. The present church is a rectangular, brick structure built in the early 20th century. This church reflects the Mexican influence that is evident in structures throughout the region. The beautiful brick detail seen on the church can also be observed on several of the crypts in the local cemetery.

LINN VICINITY, Hidalgo County

Linn (pop. ca. 450), although located in an area of early-19th-century settlement, is a 20th-century community established in 1927 as a railway station.

La Noria Cárdeneña Ranch. Marker, 2.7 mi. S of Linn on US 281 right-of-way. This ranch is the focus of two Spanish land grants: San Juan de Carricitos, granted to José Narciso Cavazos; and San Salvador del Tule, granted to Juan José Ballí. The Cárdenas family acquired Ballí land in 1828 and established a ranch in 1829. When the Cárdenas and Cavazos families intermarried, the property was combined to form a large ranch. A small cemetery, begun in 1835, a mid-19th-century main ranch house, and a church built next to the cemetery in 1944 still remain on the ranch. Private ranch, not open to the public. *SM 1988.*

LOPEÑO, Zapata County

Lopeño (pop. ca. 100) was relocated to this site in the 1950s following the creation of Falcon Reservoir.

Old Lopeño. Marker, US 83 right-of-way, in Lopeño. Old Lopeño was founded in 1749 on land originally granted to Ysabel María Sánchez, the widow of Joseph López, an early settler and rancher. In the early 1800s, part of the land passed to the Ramírez family, founders of the nearby Falcón settlement. In 1821 Benito Ramírez built a combination home, fort, and chapel that became known as Fort Lopeño. A general store and post office were established in the early 1900s. When Falcon Reservoir was created in 1952, the village of Lopeño was relocated to this site. *SM 1984.*

LOS EBANOS, Hidalgo County

Los Ebanos (pop. ca. 100), although located on an old crossing site, has developed as a community primarily since the second decade of the 20th century.

Los Ebanos Ferry. From US 83 take FM 886 S to Rio Grande River Ferry Crossing. Los Ebanos Ferry was established on an ancient ford site; the first recorded usage was by José de Escandón in the 1740s. A trail led from here to El Sal del Rey (40 miles northeast), an important salt source from prehistoric times through the mid-20th century. Los Ebanos Ferry is the last hand-powered, three-car ferry over the Rio Grande to Mexico and is the only international ferry operating on U.S. borders.

McALLEN, Hidalgo County

McAllen (pop. 84,021) was promoted as a townsite by the railroad in 1904. The introduction of irrigation made vegetable farming possible in the area and soon the town had a hotel, a grocery store, a Presbyterian church, a bank, and a weekly newspaper. The population increased rapidly in 1916, when 12,000 soldiers were stationed in McAllen to help restore order during the period of border disturbances. McAllen, now the largest town in Hidalgo County, has grown into a winter resort and gateway to Mexico.

Archer Park. N. Main St. across from Casa de Palmas. A typical Mexican style plaza, Archer Park features a bandstand, dated 1933, that is a fine example of the *faux bois* artform.

Casa de Palmas (Doubletree Club). 100 N. Main St. The hotel, originally built in 1918, features a central patio, red tile roof, and twin towers—all characteristics of Spanish Mission Revival architecture. The hotel burned in 1973 but was rebuilt in the original style. *RTHL 1979.*

Lamar Junior High mural, by Lamar Junior High students, directed by Raúl Valdez. 1980. 1009 N. 10th St. The panels of this mural feature images, such as palm trees and lowriders, that the students chose as being representative of their Valley lifestyle.

McAllen International Museum. 1900 Nolana. The arts and sciences museum has a large number of Mexican clothing items, masks, decorative arts, toys, dolls, and a few musical instruments and textileworking tools. Collections include items from at least eight states in Mexico. Open Tues.–Sat. 9–5; Sun. 1–5.

McAllen Post Office. 301 S. Main. This Spanish Revival structure features a baroque frontispiece around the front door, corbeled cornice, and a red tile roof. The Post Office, built in 1935, served the citizens of McAllen until 1957. *RTHL 1986.*

Quinta Mazatlan. 600 Sunset. Quinta Mazatlan, one of the largest adobe homes in the state, was built in the late 1930s by Jason Matthews, a composer, writer, and adventurer. The adobe blocks used in the construction were made at the site. The house has been carefully restored by its current owners. Not open to the public. *SM 1985.*

Southern Pacific Depot. 100 S. Bicentennial. This passenger depot, opened in 1927, served the San Antonio & Aransas Pass Railroad. The depot is stuccoed and detailed in Spanish Revival style. Passenger service ceased in 1952, and the building was used by public agencies until 1985. The depot was restored in 1986–87 and now serves as law offices. *RTHL 1986.*

Hotel (BPOE Hall), Mercedes.
Photo by Cathryn Hoyt, THC.

MERCEDES AND VICINITY, Hidalgo County

Mercedes (pop. 12,694) is located in an area that was originally part of the Llano Grande land grant, settled by ranchers in the late 1700s. In 1904 the town of Mercedes was established on the St. Louis, Brownsville, and Mexico railway.

Hotel (BPOE Hall). 236 Missouri Ave. Built as a hotel in the 1920s, the structure was designed to look as if the plaster were peeling from the brickwork, thus lending an air of age or "instant tradition" intended to be reminiscent of mission ruins. The designer's skill in using this technique is best illustrated in the whimsical pattern of the brickwork. Romanesque Revival influence is evident in the classic receding arches around the front entrance.

Relampago Ranch. Marker, 4 mi. S of Mercedes on US 281 right-of-way. Originally part of the Llano Grande land grant, the community of Relampago (lightning) lay along the stage and military route from Rio Grande City to Brownsville. In 1852 Thaddeus Rhodes acquired acreage here. He and José María Mora, who bought the adjoining land a few years later, helped bring economic stability to the region. Mora and his son Melchor (who served as a sheriff and Texas Ranger), farmed, ranched, and operated the only general store in the area. Descendants of the Mora family still live here. Private ranch, not open to the public. *SM 1980.*

MIRANDO CITY VICINITY, Webb County

Mirando City (pop. ca. 600), located in south-central Webb County, is the second largest town in the county. The city was founded by Oliver W.

Killam in 1921, after the discovery of oil deposits nearby, and named after Nicolás Mirando, recipient of an early Spanish land grant. Before the discovery of oil, the area around Mirando City was the site of several early Spanish ranches.

Los Ojuelos Ranch Historic District. In the vicinity of Mirando City off SH 359. The Los Ojuelos Ranch complex, centered around a vigorous artesian spring, was built between 1855 and 1857. Thirteen sandstone houses and numerous ruins remain, many representing the *casas de terrado* style with flat caliche-covered roofs. The Guerra brothers—Dionicio, Juan, and José María—raised cattle, horses, sheep, and corn here. Private ranch, not open to the public. *NR 1976.*

Casa de Palmas, McAllen. Photo by Cathryn Hoyt, THC.

MISSION AND VICINITY, Hidalgo County

Mission (pop. 28,653) was established in 1907–08 by developers John J. Conway and J.W. Hoit. First called Conway, it was renamed Mission in 1908 when the post office was moved there from nearby La Lomita. The mission church at La Lomita was established by the Oblate Fathers in 1865. An orange grove planted by the priests is believed to have been one of the

first attempts to raise citrus in the Valley. Their experimental orchard led to a major Valley industry.

Granjeno Ranch Cemetery. Follow FM 494 5 mi. S of intersection with Bus. 83 to Granjeno. This historic cemetery was established in 1872 with the burial of Antonio Garza. Interred in the cemetery are many of the early settlers of the region and their descendants, including veterans of the Civil War, World War I, and the Vietnam War. The cemetery has served families on both sides of the Rio Grande and is a reflection of the history of the area's small working-class villages. *SM 1985.*

La Lomita Historic District. 3.5 mi. S of Mission on FM 1016. The historic district includes 122 acres of the original Oblate Fathers ranch; the stuccoed stone La Lomita Chapel, built in 1899; the two-story frame convent, built in 1912; and the two-story, brick, Spanish Revival St. Peter's Novitiate, also built in 1912. The Oblate complex served as a rural mission until about 1960. *NR 1975.*

Capilla de la Lomita Historical Park. 3.5 mi. S of Mission on FM 1016. The park was established by the Mission Bicentennial Committee in 1976. Structures in the park include the original well, baking oven, and chapel (see below) for the mission complex. Interpretive signs point out the sites of additional adobe outbuildings and houses that were razed in 1949. A shrine to the Virgin Mary was placed here during the Year of Our Immaculate Mary (1956).

La Lomita Chapel. 3.5 mi. S of Mission on FM 1016. The first chapel of La Lomita Mission, built in 1865, was used by horseback-riding priests who served the ranches midway between Brownsville and Roma. The present chapel, constructed in 1899, has been restored several times and is now part of the Mission City Parks Department. Open weekdays 8:30–4:30. *RTHL 1964; NR 1975.*

Above: Grave marker at Granjeno Ranch Cemetary, Mission. Photo by Cathryn Hoyt, THC.

Above left: Nineteenth-century *casa de terrado* on Los Ojuelos Ranch, Mirando City. THC photo.

La Lomita Chapel, Capilla de la Lomita Historical Park, Mission. Photo by Cathryn Hoyt, THC.

La Lomita Farms. Marker, 3.5 mi. S of Mission on FM 1016, at St. Peter's Novitiate. The Catholic Oblate Order was given several hundred acres of land on the northern bank of the Rio Grande by René Guyard, a French merchant living in Reynosa, in 1861. A portion of the tract, commemorated by this marker, was set aside for the Order's farming and scholastic programs. *SM 1981.*

St. Peter's Novitiate. 3.5 mi. S of Mission on FM 1016. St. Peter's Novitiate, a training center for priests, was built in 1912. Both the nearby convent and the novitiate continued in use until the late 1950s. The two-story novitiate is a brick structure in Spanish Revival style, featuring twin towers, arches, and a low-pitched, tile roof. *NR 1975.*

Our Lady of Guadalupe Catholic Church. 6th and Dunlap. As the first mission of the La Lomita church, this parish is significant in the context of Hidalgo County's religious history. A congregation was established at least by 1899. The original sanctuary, destroyed by fire, was replaced with the current structure in 1927. The façade of the Mission Revival influenced structure features an elaborate door surround, arched windows, mission parapets, and a four-story tower. Our Lady of Guadalupe Church is an eclectic regional expression of Spanish Mission Revival design in ecclesiastical architecture. *RTHL 1990.*

Río Theatre. 516 Doherty. Originally called Teatro La Paz, this structure was built in 1912–15 by Juan Bautista Barberá, a bricklayer from Spain. On the theater's stage were presented internationally famous films, lecturers, actors, and musicians. Enrique Flores bought the property in 1945 and changed the name to Río Theatre. The building, a fine example of vernacular commercial architecture, has undergone general restoration and retains the original exterior façade. *RTHL 1982.*

Texas Citrus Festival. Late January and early February, in Mission and vicinity. Events include the coronation of citrus royalty, arts and crafts exhibits, mariachi music, ballet folklórico dancing, a parade, and tours of historic sites.

OILTON, Webb County

Oilton (pop. ca. 450), originally a station on the Texas-Mexican Railroad, was called Torrecillas (little towers) for two nearby rock formations. The name was changed to Oilton in 1922 following the discovery of oil in the area.

Leo's Texaco. On SH 359. This vernacular building was constructed of local stone by Mexican stonemasons in the 1930s. According to the current owners, its mission façade reflects the original owners' admiration for the Alamo. The arcaded wing walls that extend from the façade also are Spanish Revival stylistic features and give an impression of greater size to the tiny building.

PALAFOX HISTORIC DISTRICT, Webb County

San José de Palafox Historic and Archeological District. 31 mi. N of Laredo on FM 1472. The villa of San José de Palafox was founded along the north bank of the Rio Grande in 1810 by Antonio Cordero y Bustamente, governor of Coahuila. From its settlement, the village was a target for Indians who resented further intrusion onto their lands. By 1813 Governor Cordero had advised the settlers to move their families and all their possessions to Laredo. For seven years, from 1817 to 1824, San José de Palafox lay abandoned but not forgotten. In early 1824 the governor was petitioned to resettle the village with 31 families who had formerly resided there and 16 new families. Permission was granted, but by 1829, as noted on Stephen F. Austin's map of Texas, Palafox had been destroyed by Indian attack. Today, the stone ruins of at least six buildings and a cemetery mark the village site. The ruins indicate that these buildings were constructed of stone rubble mortared with lime. Two buildings had flat roofs supported by beams, while another small, one-room residence had a roof with gable ends supported by a ridge pole. The buildings probably were plastered on the exterior. Both of the vernacular styles represented here are still popular in the area. An early, undated map of the village indicates that there were probably a number of other buildings in the area. On private ranch, not open to the public. *RTHL 1972; NR 1973.*

PEÑITAS, Hidalgo County

Peñitas (pop. ca. 150) is located south of US 83 on FM 2062. According to tradition, six of Cabeza de Vaca's surviving shipmates settled in an Indian village that originally occupied the site of Peñitas in the 1530s, but this has not been substantiated. Regardless of its claim to being one of the oldest towns in Texas, Peñitas is rich in historical associations. Peñitas

Left: Leo's Texaco, Oilton. Photo by Cathryn Hoyt, THC.

Below: St. Peter's Novitiate, Mission. THC photo.

(little pebbles) Ranch (date of founding unknown) was located in the Town Commons of Reynosa, the second Escandón settlement, established in 1749 directly across the Rio Grande. A ferry was licensed here by Hidalgo County in 1852. A historical marker (*SM 1970*) commemorating Peñitas is located 7 mi. SE of the village in Bentsen Rio Grande State Park.

PHARR, Hidalgo County

Pharr (pop. 32,921), established in 1909 by Henry N. Pharr and John C. Kelly, became a shipping point on the St. Louis, Brownsville, and Mexico Railroad in 1911. The city is now a center for winter vegetables, citrus, and cotton.

Buell School. 218 E. Juarez. The Buell School was constructed as the Mexican Ward School in 1927. *RTHL 1990.*

Pharr Kiwanis Building. Park Ave. and Bluebonnet St. This handsome Spanish Revival style building was constructed in 1928. The Pharr Kiwanis building has the distinction of being the first meeting place of the Kiwanis International organization to be owned by a local club. *RTHL 1981.*

PROGRESO, Hidalgo County

Progreso (pop. 1,951) was the planned townsite (1926–27) and citrus-growing area of Progreso Development Company of Houston. After the 1949–51 freezes, sugarcane became an important crop in the area. Earlier settlement at this location centered around Toluca Ranch, about two miles to the southeast, and a post office was located there from 1906 to 1915.

St. Joseph's Church, Toluca Ranch. A family chapel built in 1899, St. Joseph's Church is located next to the Sáenz homestead on Toluca Ranch. The church is a handsome Gothic Revival design, with a tower over the main entrance and lancet-shaped windows and doors. In the interior, the surfaces of the ceiling vaults are formed by canvas, painted a deep blue. *SM 1982; NR 1983.*

Toluca Ranch. Marker, 3 mi. E of Progreso on International Bridge (FM 1015). The complex of three ranch buildings, the Florencio Sáenz homestead, the store, and the church (*see* separate entry for St. Joseph's Church), were built between 1899 and 1908. The buildings, particularly the house and church, show an interesting blend of styles—Victorian woodwork and towers combined with local materials and decorative brickwork cornices. The homestead served as the headquarters for the Toluca Ranch, which once stretched 17 miles north from the Rio Grande. Sáenz operated a mercantile store and promoted cattle ranching and river farming as successful business ventures for the Valley. Private ranch, open to the public by appointment. *RTHL (homestead) 1965; SM (ranch complex) 1982; NR 1983.*

Mexican freight carts were frequently seen on the streets of Rio Grande City in the early 20th century. Roy Wilkinson Aldrich Papers, courtesy Barker Texas History Center, General Libraries, University of Texas at Austin.

RIO GRANDE CITY, Starr County

Rio Grande City (pop. 9,891) was established on land that was originally part of the Carnestolendas Ranch, a land grant made to Capt. José Antonio de la Garza Falcón in 1767. In the 1830s a young Kentuckian named Henry Clay Davis came to the Rio Grande Valley to buy horses. There he met and married María Hilaria de la Garza Martínez, a descendant of De la Garza Falcón. Davis and his bride settled on the ranchland on the Texas side of the river. In 1848 Davis laid out a town with the business district built on the riverbank. This town, known as Rio Grande City, was an important stop for the steamboats that once plied the Rio Grande. About a year after its founding, the little town received an additional boost from the establishment of Fort Ringgold. Today, many of the original buildings constructed during Rio Grande City's prosperous years can still be seen. These buildings, with the fronts close to the roads, the upper floor balconies, and the combination of living and commercial quarters, reflect the Mexican vernacular style that is common throughout the Valley. Rio Grande City is now the county seat of Starr County.

Historic Structures

Silverio de la Peña Drugstore and Post Office. 423 E. Main St. at Lopez. The Silverio de la Peña Drugstore and Post Office was built in 1886 and is now recognized as one of the best preserved and most sophisticated of builder Enrique Portscheller's structures. According to local tradition, the interior walls were once resplendent with stencilling; still visible inside a cabinet is the remnant of a mortar and pestle design drawn especially for

the druggist by the architect. The intricate detailing and handsome proportions make it one of the Valley's outstanding 19th-century buildings, a unique type with Spanish and other stylistic antecedents adapted to local conditions. At the time of the building's construction, Silverio de la Peña's business was the only wholesale and retail drugstore between Laredo and Brownsville. The drugstore was in operation until 1914. At that time the adjoining post office expanded into the main office and remained until 1950. Since that time, the building has served as a political-campaign headquarters, a bookstore, and a Methodist church. *NR 1980.*

Juan Gonzales House. 104 E. Main St. This one-story, stuccoed brick residence, built in 1853, was the first hotel in Rio Grande City. It also served as the law offices of Edward H. Horde, a distinguished statesman, and as a meeting place for political groups. *RTHL 1964.*

Fred Guerra House. 800 block of E. Main St. Spanish Revival in style, the house was built for the owners of the First State Bank of Rio

Silverio de la Peña Drugstore and Post Office, Rio Grande City. THC photo.

Grande City in the late 1920s. It is an excellent regional example of the finer homes of that era.

Immaculate Conception School. 300 block of Britton Ave. Built about 1885, this three-story brick building with one-story wings shows the brickwork and design features typical of Enrique Portscheller's work.

Kelsey-Bass Home. 101 Washington St. This large brick structure was built by John P. Kelsey, a merchant originally from New York State. In 1860, Kelsey and his wife, Union sympathizers, moved to Camargo, Mexico, where they established a prosperous mercantile business. The Kelsey-Bass Home post-dates Kelsey's return from Camargo in 1877. The brick used in the construction of the building was made in his brickyard west of town and the lumber was pulled from sunken river boats.

Mifflin Kenedy Warehouse. 203 Water St. This two-story brick building with a one-story balcony across the second level served as the Starr County Courthouse in the 1850s and may be the oldest standing courthouse in Texas. The building was later used by Mifflin Kenedy as a warehouse.

Lázaro López–Tijerina House. 302 E. Mirasoles St. The Lázaro López–Tijerina house may be one of the oldest buildings in Rio Grande City. The original structure is believed to have been a one-story, stone house, built as early as 1830. A second story was added to the house about 1860. The old stone wall, which can be seen from Main St., also dates from the early period. A board-and-batten shed has been added to the side and rear of the house. *See also* Tijerina Wall.

Ringgold Hotel. 601 E. Main St. *See* sidebar: Ringgold Hotel.

Crisoforo Solís Building. 403 E. Main St. This two-story brick building with its double doors and balcony with wrought-iron railing is a fine example of Mexican Colonial commercial building style.

Tijerina Wall. 400 block of Main St. Made of varying sizes of rock, this rubble wall is said to be the oldest wall in town, perhaps dating to the original Rancho Davis. The door in the wall is framed in brick with a wooden lintel. *See also* Lázaro López–Tijerina House.

Villarreal-Scott House. Main and Avasolo Sts. This brick house was built in 1870 for Isaac Villarreal to be used as a home and store. Of particular interest are the patio gate and wall, which copy those found in many fine homes in Mexico.

Churches and Shrines

First United Methodist Church. 301 E. Third St. At the request of Henry Clay Davis, the first Spanish-speaking Protestant minister was assigned to Rio Grande City in 1875. For seven years, Protestant services were held in private homes until a small, temporary church could be built. Six years later, in 1888, the present brick church was constructed.

Santa Cruz Cross. Visible from US 83 about 4 mi. E of Rio Grande City. The cross, originally erected in 1900, was an offering from Domingo Peña, a local landowner. In 1892 a severe drought caused Peña and his sons

RINGGOLD HOTEL RECONSTRUCTION

The Ringgold Hotel was originally built in the late 1890s as a residence and store for François La Borde, a French immigrant and Rio Grande City merchant. Although the house was designed by a Parisian architect, it was an adaptation of the typical Spanish-Mexican townhouse that usually faced onto the street and combined both residential and business uses. In response to life on the frontier, the building was laid out in a U-shaped plan that provided both privacy and protection. The double galleries of the residence, decorated with Victorian gingerbread trim, provided a cool refuge from the heat. Local influence also is seen in the structural and decorative use of brick from a Camargo, Mexico, brickyard.

In 1917 La Borde decided to open a hotel, and he hired a San Antonio architect to put a second floor on his residence-store. The La Borde House, as it was known then, functioned as a hotel for over 60 years but gradually fell into a state of disrepair. By the 1970s the exterior woodwork was rotten, the roof was worn out, and the whole building was sagging. Larry Sheerin, a San Antonio businessman, nevertheless saw potential in the old building. He purchased the hotel in 1979 and embarked upon a $1 million restoration program, which was completed in April 1982.

Old photographs and original records were used to ensure the authentic restoration of the La Borde House. The Victorian gingerbread trim was recut and matched to existing trim by local craftsmen, the wooden galleries were replaced with beaded boards, and replacement bricks were obtained from the Camargo, Mexico, brickyard that provided the original brick for the hotel.

The furnishings, including armoires, round-back chairs, nightstands, and bed frames, were all chosen for their historical authenticity. Bright Oriental rugs and English Axminster carpets were used to cover the wooden floors after old ledgers from the La Borde house were found and provided evidence of the purchase of similar carpets for the original hotel.

A visit to the La Borde House takes the guest back to the turn of the century, when Rio Grande City was an important riverboat landing. *NR 1980.*

to carry water from the Rio Grande, about 4 miles away, in order to keep their livestock alive. After several years of drought, Peña vowed that he would build a cross on a hill when the drought ended. After the rains came, Peña hewed a cross out of a mesquite log and erected it on the hill above his house. Several years later he added a Christ figure to the cross. In 1957 Peña's son replaced the original with another handmade cross with Christ figure. Three generations of Peñas have attended their evening prayers at the cross.

ROMA–LOS SAENZ, Starr County

Roma–Los Sáenz (pop. 8,059), located on a high bluff above the Rio Grande, was founded in the 1760s by settlers from the nearby Escandón colonies. Originally the town was named Buena Vista, but the name Roma–Los Sáenz was adopted in the mid-19th century. Local tradition attributes the name Roma to a Major Richard Roman who served in the area and distinguished himself in the Mexican War, while Los Sáenz is in honor of a Spanish captain, Miguel Sáenz, who received a Spanish land grant in 1767. In the 1800s, when the Rio Grande was still navigable, Roma was an important shipping point for steamboats carrying cotton and other goods downstream. Mercantile enterprises flourished until river traffic was replaced by railroads and highways. The era between the Mexican War and the Civil War brought growth and prosperity to the community. During the post–Civil War period, the smuggling of contraband became a highly organized, if not completely respected, business that brought in hundreds of thousands of dollars. With this prosperity came an influx of revolutionary bandits, among them Abram García and Juan Nepomuceno Cortina. The fortunes gained in the contraband business financed the construction of many fine homes and warehouses. Today, the charm and character of the town result largely from these homes and stores, many of them designed and built by Enrique Portscheller. *See* sidebar: Heinrich ("Enrique") Portscheller.

Roma Cemetery. The Roma Cemetery contains several brick tombs designed by Portscheller. Basically rectilinear in form, the tombs have classical detailing, such as molding, pilasters, and pediments, similar to that seen on Portscheller buildings in town. The tombs date to about 1885.

Roma (Roma–Los Sáenz) National Register Historic District. Located one block W of US 83 on Convent St. The historic district encompasses parts of 15 blocks with some 43 historic commercial, residential, and religious structures, most dating to the 1800s. Included in the district are several architecturally significant structures designed and built by Portscheller, as well as stone and adobe buildings typical of the Rio Grande Valley. Roma's main plaza is bounded by the Church of Our Lady of Refuge of Sinners and the Old Convent. *NR 1972.*

Noah Cox House. On the Plaza. This two-story, stuccoed stone residence was built by John Vale in 1853. The gable roof is a later addition.

First Chapel in Roma (Roma Historical Museum). Estrella and Lincoln Sts. The chapel was built by volunteer labor about 1840. Secular

HEINRICH ("ENRIQUE") PORTSCHELLER

The Rio Grande Valley is dotted with buildings designed by Heinrich Portscheller, a German mason and architect who traveled and worked in the area during the second half of the 19th century. Portscheller was born in Germany about 1840. As a young man he spent some time in the Prussian army, but presumably deserted with a fellow soldier. Ultimately, the two found themselves in the port of Vera Cruz in 1865, where they were immediately impressed into the Imperial Army of Maximillian. A brief stint with the counter-guerrilla forces evidently did not agree with Portscheller, and by early 1866 he had deserted to fight with Maximillian's enemy, the Liberals.

Portscheller's whereabouts after 1866 until the late 1870s are unknown. Records show that in 1879 he was in Mier, a Mexican town near Roma, where he married Leonarda Campos. Portscheller probably developed his skills as a brickmason during this period. He had moved across the Rio Grande to Roma by 1883, and there he became known as "Don Enrique" and began building structures known for their elegant lines and finely wrought details.

In Roma, Portscheller, in partnership with men named Margo and Pérez, established a brickyard that manufactured large, buff-colored, sand-struck bricks. Local masons considered it quite an honor to work for Portscheller, and he was never without an abundance of apprentices. According to one mason who worked with him for three years, Don Enrique was personally involved in construction as well as design. He would prepare the building plans and make templates for the moldings, and then the other masons would rub or cut the bricks to the profiles determined. Most of the patterned work, as well as the intricate moldings or friezes, would be laid up by Portscheller himself, with the fill-in work executed by the other masons.

Portscheller lived and worked in Roma until 1894. He then moved to Laredo, where he remained until his death in 1915.

priests from Mier served the chapel until Oblate fathers arrived in 1853 and built Our Lady of Refuge Catholic Church. The chapel now houses the Roma Historical Museum. Museum exhibits depict various aspects of Roma's heritage, education, culture, religion, literature, farming, and ranching. Open Mon.–Fri. 10–4. *RTHL 1973.*

Leocadia Leandro García House. SE Corner of Convent St., 1 block S of Portscheller St. This house was built in 1857 by John Vale for a widow with children who were refugees from Mexico. The house is constructed of sandstone blocks covered with a splatter-finish coating of lime stucco painted olive green and gold. Originally, the lower floor was used for commercial space while the upper floor consisted of living quarters. The upper floor was later remodeled into one large space to allow *bailes* or fandangos to be held.

Manuel Guerra Residence and Store. Convent and Portscheller Sts. Manuel Guerra, a successful merchant during the golden age of the border trade, contracted with Portscheller for the construction of a two-story house and store in 1884. The result was one of the finest Portscheller-built structures in Roma. The building has commercial retail space on the first floor and residential space above. To the rear of the building, adjacent to Hidalgo St., is a long, one-story building that was probably a warehouse for the store. The finely proportioned architectural embellishments and superior craftsmanship of the structure reveal Portscheller's uniquely personal style, which utilizes classical orders similar to elements used in the early Renaissance period. *RTHL 1973.*

Old Convent. Convent and Estrella Sts. This one-story brick convent, built around 1880, has bayed ends, a porch across the main façade, a diminutive wooden cupola, and the fine brickwork and architectural detailing that characterize Portscheller's work.

Our Lady of Refuge Catholic Church. Convent and Estrella Sts. Roma, halfway between Laredo and Brownsville, was chosen as the site of the first permanent church of the Oblates. Our Lady of Refuge Catholic Church was designed by Father Pierre Keralum, who acted as the stonecutter and mason as well. The cornerstone was laid on September 18, 1854, on the feast of the Octave of the Nativity of the Blessed Virgin Mary. Today, only the church tower remains of the original church. *RTHL 1973.*

Ramírez Hall. Corner of Portscheller St. and Plaza. Built between 1850 and 1880, the building served as a commercial structure with a family home upstairs. Portscheller personally laid the brick around the windows and doors of the building. Three generations of the Ramírez family have now occupied Ramírez Hall. *RTHL 1973.*

Manuel Ramírez House. Convent and Estrella Sts. Home and office of Roma's first lawyer, Edward R. Hord, this two-story, stuccoed brick structure was built in 1853. The house was located on the original thoroughfare of the Camino Real and was two blocks away from the Roma steamboat landing. During the American Civil War, the house served as a military headquarters. The building is now the Manuel Ramírez Memorial Hospital. *RTHL 1965.*

Brick tomb in the Roma cemetery. THC photo.

Pablo Ramírez House (Knights of Columbus Hall). Estrella and Zaragoza Sts. This two-story, stucco-covered-brick structure, showing the fine detail work characteristic of Portscheller's designs, was built in 1884. *RTHL 1963.*

Rafael García Ramírez House. SE corner of Portscheller St. and Plaza. Two one-story brick buildings form an L at the corner of the street. Built by Portscheller in 1880, the buildings feature interesting doors in herringbone pattern and wood lintels over the transoms.

Roma Historical Museum. *See* First Chapel in Roma.

Antonia Sáenz House. Portscheller St. between Plaza and Juarez Alley. Portscheller designed this one-story brick house, noted for the interesting brickwork around its doors and windows.

Nestor Sáenz Store. Portscheller between Juarez and Bravo Sts. This outstanding structure, designed and built by Portscheller in 1884, is an excellent example of Rio Grande molded brickwork. Of special historical interest is the underground basement, which was used to hide refugees fleeing from the Mexican Revolution.

Vernacular Architecture. Several noteworthy buildings in Roma reflect the vernacular architectural styles of the area but are not included in the historic district. One type consists of two one-story houses (usually of stuccoed stone, but sometimes of adobe) grouped together to form what is known as a double house. The gable of one roof peaks over the parapet of the shed roof of the other house. Several examples survive in the area. Another important vernacular type showing the influence of Mexican settlers in Roma and Rio Grande City is a simple structure of brick or brick facing over adobe. The Rodríguez Store, at the corner of Juarez and Portscheller Sts., is a good example. The small, stuccoed brick and adobe building was constructed in 1886.

SALINEÑO, Starr County

Salineño (pop. ca. 150) is a rural community near the Rio Grande in the southwestern part of the county. Settlement here dates at least from the late 19th century.

Manuel Hinojosa House. N corner of town square. The small, one-story building was originally a jacal. Some of the mesquite and mud walls have now been covered by board-and-batten. This house is a good example of a typical type of construction used in this area and also demonstrates the traditional practice of building additions as the need and chance arose.

Guadalupe Ramós House. On NW side of the main street, one block SW of the town square. This one-story, stone block building, built in 1898, is one of the earliest houses in this ranch community.

San José Church. Behind new church on the town square, facing the Rio Grande. This church, built in 1910, exhibits the typical vernacular, stucco-covered stone construction found in the area.

Detail of south door, Rodríguez
Store, Roma. THC photo.

SAN BENITO, Cameron County

San Benito (pop. 20,125). Highway traffic signs here are in both English and Spanish, an essential in this bilingual region. Resaca de los Fresnos, a former channel of the Rio Grande, meanders through the community and provides some of the Valley's most beautiful scenery. Bougainvilleas bloom year round, but are particularly beautiful in April. Visitor information is available at the Chamber of Commerce, 210 E. Heywood St., San Benito 78586.

St. Benedict's Catholic Church. Bowie and W. Powers Sts. St. Benedict's became a parish in 1912, and the original church of 1910 was destroyed by fire in 1923. Built in 1925, the present structure features Mission Revival and Romanesque Revival stylistic elements. The brick and concrete building, with domed bell tower, was designed by architect J.E. Walsh of Mission.

San Benito Bank and Trust Company. 100 E. Robertson. This Spanish Revival structure of stucco-covered brick was completed in 1910. Its white walls and gold-domed towers glitter in the South Texas sun. In its early days the building served an important community role. As a local gathering spot, its arcades (removed in 1956) provided shade for street vendors selling *raspas* and *dulces,* and flags were flown from the top of the building to warn farmers of impending severe weather. The bank's location is on land originally in the 1789 land grant of Eugenio and Bartolomé Fernández. Known as Concepción de Carricitos, the grant derived its name either from *carrizitos* (little cane), from the small cane growing along regional waterways, or from the Carrizo Indians of the South Texas coastal zone.

Christmas in San Benito. In December, in downtown pavilion. The celebration features a street bazaar, food booths that offer a wide array of ethnic foods, piñata games, arts and crafts, and a lighted nighttime parade. With fun for all ages, this colorful holiday entertainment reflects the bicultural heritage of the region.

SAN ISIDRO, Starr County

San Isidro (pop. ca. 130) is a farming and oilfield community in northeastern Starr County. Settlement here dates at least from the late 19th century, and the ruins of several buildings from that period can be seen in the area.

Blás G. Peña House. N side of FM 1017, just W of FM 2294. This one-story board-and-batten house was built by Blás Peña, an important local carpenter, about 1900.

San Isidro Catholic Church. Off FM 755 and FM 1017. The old San Isidro Church dates to the late 1800s and has been preserved through the efforts of the local citizens.

San Isidro Community Well. S side of FM 1017, down private road approximately 1.5 mi. W of the intersection with FM 2294. The water well, built of limestone and mud, is made in four sections, with the tallest section being the well itself; from there the water spills to a second section, which is for human consumption; the third section is for washing; and the fourth section is for animal use. This is one of three such wells built in the community during the period of late 19th-century settlement.

SAN JUAN, Hidalgo County

San Juan (pop. 10,815) is an agricultural center located in the south-central part of Hidalgo County near Pharr and Alamo. Its name honors both the saint and John Closner, who organized the community in 1909. *SM 1984,* at Fifth and Standard streets.

San Juan Hotel. 125 W. Fifth. The hotel, completed and opened for business in 1920, is the social center of the area. The original structure had

little architectural ornamentation. The Mission Revival details, including a red-tiled parapet along the roofline and a curvilinear parapet over the entryway, were added in 1928. The building has been restored by its current owners. *RTHL 1985.*

Shrine of Our Lady of San Juan of the Valley. At Raul Longoria and US 83. This beautiful shrine, constructed with 24-inch-thick limestone walls, has terrazzo floors and faceted glass windows. The shrine houses a replica of Our Lady of San Juan de Los Lagos (a town in Jalisco, Mexico), an 18-inch statue revered by migrant farm workers. The statue is set in a ceramic altar backdrop that was created in Barcelona. The original shrine, built in 1954, was destroyed by an airplane crash in 1970. The edifice was rebuilt in 1979 and now serves as a point of pilgrimage for Catholic worshippers from Texas and Mexico. The chapel of the shrine can seat 1800. Open daily 6–9.

Above: **Shrine of Our Lady of San Juan of the Valley, San Juan. Photo by Cathryn Hoyt, THC.**

Above left: **San Benito Bank and Trust Company, San Benito. Photo by Cathryn Hoyt, THC.**

SANTA MARIA, Cameron County

Santa Maria (pop. ca. 200) is located in an area that was settled in the 18th century by colonists from the Escandón settlements.

Alonso de León Expeditions. Marker, in roadside park on US 281, 8 mi. E of Santa Maria. Among the first systematic explorations of East Texas, De León led five expeditions between 1686 and 1690, spurred by the presence of La Salle in the region. De León burned the ruins of La Salle's Fort St. Louis and established the first Spanish mission in East Texas, San Francisco de los Tejas. De León's successes stimulated Spanish colonization of Texas. *SM 1968.*

Our Lady of Visitation Catholic Church. US 281, 0.5 mi. E of Santa Maria. Designed by Father Pierre Keralum, the Gothic Revival church was constructed of bricks made at the nearby Rancho de Santa María. The church is located on lands originally in the La Feria grant, given to Rosa María Hinojosa de Ballí in 1777 after the death of her husband, José María Ballí. The cornerstone was laid during a blinding snowstorm in 1880 and the church was dedicated June 29, 1882. The altar, pews, and confessional and the statues of Our Lady of Visitation and of the Guardian Angel are all originals in the church; the prie-dieu and stations of the cross were added in later years. For over 100 years the church has served the residents of Bluetown, Santa Maria, and neighboring communities. *RTHL 1977*.

Rancho de Santa María. Marker, 1 mi. E of Santa Maria on US 281. This ranch was part of Spain's 1777 La Feria grant (12.5 leagues), which was partitioned in the 1850s. It served as a subpost of Fort Brown and Fort Ringgold in the 1850s and as a U.S. Army headquarters during the 1916 border troubles. *SM 1968*.

Our Lady of Visitation Catholic Church, Santa Maria. THC photo.

SAN YGNACIO AND VICINITY, Zapata County

San Ygnacio (pop. ca. 900), located south of Laredo off US 83, is a ranching community founded in 1830 by Jesús Treviño and his extended family. Jacals probably were the earliest homes, but the Treviños and other settlers soon began building houses of square-hewn sandstone blocks with flat, caliche-covered roofs, several of which can still be seen in San Ygnacio. Soon after its founding, the town became a regional center and an important port of trade. Thousands of head of cattle and other livestock passed through the town destined for the interior cities of Mexico. In exchange, wagonloads of *piloncillo* (brown sugar), beans, flour, and corn were brought north.

Main entrance of Delfino Lozano House, San Ygnacio. THC photo.

Historic Sites

La Paz Museum. At A.L. Benavides Elementary School in San Ygnacio. The museum is housed in a century-old, native sandstone building located on the school campus. The museum's collections include many local Mexican-American items and some Mexican and Spanish artifacts. The Regional Heritage Resource Center, located in the museum, contains books, family genealogies, and other documents of interest, such as a 1757 census and old land grant settlements. Open Mon.–Fri. 8–12.

San Ygnacio Historic District. Most of San Ygnacio is included in the San Ygnacio Historic District, listed on the National Register of Historic Places. The district is bounded by the Rio Grande on the west, US 83 on the east, Mina St. on the north, and Matamoros St. on the south. This historic district is particularly important because San Ygnacio is the only South Texas community that still retains a large number of the once-common sandstone structures built in the mid- to late 19th century. The historic district includes 36 buildings, many of which are outstanding examples of Spanish-Mexican vernacular architecture. As you drive or walk through the district, note the hand-wrought grilles covering the windows, the *palisado* construction of the barns and sheds, and the detailing applied to the stucco exterior of the houses. *RTHL 1972; NR 1973.*

> **Delfino Lozano House.** Uribe St. The Delfino Lozano House is a typical, flat-roofed, rectangular stone residence. A large chimney visible from the exterior marks the presence of a large cooking hearth, a feature common in older residences in the community and throughout South Texas. A construction date of May 7, 1873, is carved over the main entrance.
>
> **Nuestra Señora del Refugio Church.** Laredo St. The one-story, plastered-stone church was built in 1850 by the Oblate Fathers.
>
> **J.M. Sánchez Estate.** On Uribe St. Originally a schoolhouse, the one-story, stuccoed adobe building has distinctive, decorative applied plaques at the frieze. The same plaques were used as quoins. One of the beams inside is inscribed "La Paz De, Jesucristo Sea Con Nosotros * * Enero 30 De 1875."

Stuccoed House, Unnamed. Uribe and Benavides Sts. The main entrance of this one-story, stuccoed stone house has double doors with the inscription "MAYO 10 de 1873" on the lintel.

Jesús Treviño House–Fort. NE corner of Uribe and Benavides Sts. Initial construction of the complex began in 1830 with a simple one-room residence on the north side. Over the next 20 years several additions were made and the entire complex was walled-in, forming a fortified square covering most of one city block where the settlers could gather to defend themselves. Stone *gárgolas* (projecting rain spouts, also called *canales*) line the entire front of the building, and unusual corner detail has been incorporated into the northwest corner of the building. Carved on one of the beams spanning the interior is the motto "Paz y Libertad Obremos" (Let us work for peace and liberty). The sundial over the carriage entrance on the north side was placed there in 1851. *RTHL 1964.*

Manuel Benavides Treviño House. Corner of Laredo and Hidalgo Sts. An ornate carved cornice, unusually beautiful window and door detailing, and original grilles and hardware enhance the historical and architectural value of this house, built in 1887. The house was constructed of sandstone blocks with large, square hewn blocks at the corners. All of the hardware on the interior is handwrought and of high quality. The doors are handmade, pegged, and beveled. Additional rooms have been added on the east side of the main structure.

San Ygnacio Vicinity

Corralitos Ranch. Off US 83, N of San Ygnacio. Two *casas de terrado,* Mexican Colonial style ranch houses built about 1890, are located 100 yards east of the Rio Grande. The single-story structures are rectangular in plan with thick (about 30 inches) walls made of dressed sandstone bonded with lime mortar. Remnants of the whitewashed plaster can still be seen on the interior and exterior walls. One of the buildings, divided into two rooms, is made of *chipichil* (a kind of plaster) with sandstone cobbles and large amounts of aggregate. Tie rods, with escutcheon plates made from old plow parts, have been added to stabilize the buildings. *Vigas* (roof beams) and part of an earlier flat roof are evident in the interior, but the house is now covered by a corrugated-tin shed roof. The south door is of hand-made, pegged construction with beveled mesquite panels. Both buildings have *troneras* (gunports) at the parapet level that were apparently included in the structures to aid in defense against revolutionary bandits of the 1870s and 1880s. Ranch houses of this type were once common along the border in Texas and are still present in large numbers on the Mexican side of the border. Private ranch, not open to the public. *NR 1977.*

Dolores Arroyo. The arroyo crosses US 83 in the San Ygancio vicinity. The limestone blocks for the structures at the Dolores settlement were taken from a quarry site along Dolores Arroyo (creek). The scars from the

Jesús Treviño House-Fort in the 1920s, San Ygnacio. R.B. Blake Collection, courtesy Barker Texas History Center, General Libraries, University of Texas at Austin.

Ranch house on Corralitos Ranch, San Ygnacio vicinity. THC photo.

bars and picks used to quarry the stone can still be seen on the face of the arroyo.

Dolores Nuevo. About 24 mi. N of San Ygnacio or 19 mi. S of Laredo on US 83. Dolores Nuevo, a small ranching community, was founded in 1859 by Cosme Martínez as an extension of Dolores Viejo, located 1.5 miles to the south. The ruins of seven stone houses, a cemetery, and a well can be seen at this site. The most prominent building is a large, rectangular residence believed to be the home of Cosme Martínez. The house was built in 1860 of carefully dressed sandstone blocks with a flat roof spanned by horizontal beams that support the decking. Additional insulating material made up of a concrete-like substance formed of lime, caliche, and an aggregate (*chipichil*) covers the roof. The exterior and interior of the building were both plastered and whitewashed. An addition with a pitched roof and parapeted gable ends has been added to the south of the main residence, and a large, deep cooking hearth was added to the west. Another structure of interest is located directly across from the main building. Although in ruins, the house still retains a feature that is frequently seen in the indigenous architecture of the region—a forked log that serves as a ridge pole support. In this case the log has been incorporated into the wall itself and emerges at the peak of the gable. The wall construction of the house is unusual in that it appears to be of rubble rather than the finely dressed stones seen in the other buildings. On private ranch, not open to the public. *NR 1973.*

Dolores Viejo. About 20 mi. N of San Ygnacio, or about 23 mi. S of Laredo, off US 83. Of the 23 settlements Escandón and his lieutenants eventually established, only two, Dolores and Laredo, were located on the north bank of the Rio Grande. José Vásquez de Borrego was given the lands north of the river to establish the ranching community of Dolores in 1750, and for a time the settlement flourished. By about 1760 the ranch headquarters consisted of a stone house, commonly referred to as a fort, and other stone buildings that housed the ranch workers. By 1767 a ranch inspector noted a population of 123 people, 5000 horses, and 3000 head of cattle. The house, now in ruins, is strategically positioned on the bank of the Dolores Arroyo near its juncture with the Rio Grande, a location that allows a clear view of the river and creek to the south and the flat plains to the north and northeast. Still discernible in the ruins are the four *troneras* (gunports) in the walls of the house and the remnants of a circular corner bastion on the northwest corner of the main ruins. The bastion is detached from the main structure, and local legend reports that a secret tunnel connected the two structures. The foundations for other stone buildings, presumably houses for the ranch workers, can still be seen. José de Borregos' land grant specified that he was to "construct, at his own expense, two ferry boats for the crossing of soldiers, priests, and pilgrims en route to Goliad and the missions near San Antonio de Béxar and that he was not to charge for the service, but to render it free to all crossers." The ruts from the road leading down to the ferry crossing can still be seen. On private land, not open to the public. *CM 1936; NR 1973.*

Old Ramireño. Marker, 5 mi. SE of San Ygnacio on US 83 right-of-way, in Ramireño Community. The historical marker notes the location of Old Ramireño, an early settlement located on land granted to José Luis Ramírez. The home established here by Ramírez and his family in the late 18th century soon became the nucleus of the community. In 1953 Ramireño was relocated to a site two miles from the original Ramírez ranch because of flooding caused by the creation of Lake Falcon. Old Ramireño was eventually covered by the rising waters of the reservoir. *SM 1988.*

San Francisco Ranch. US 83 approx. 1.5 miles N of San Ygnacio. The remains of two whitewashed sandstone *casas de terrado,* built between the 1840s and 1870s, can be seen on this early ranch. The houses feature mes-

Whitewashed *casas de terrado* on the San Francisco Ranch, San Ygnacio vicinity. THC photo.

quite lintels, shaped stone quoins, carved sandstone *canales* (used to drain the original, flat roof) and *troneras* (gunports). The larger of the two buildings has ten *troneras* spaced around the perimeter, four on each of the long sides, and one on each of the short sides. Four-inch-square mesquite lintels span the openings, which are 20 inches from the floor. The *troneras* taper from a wide opening on the interior building to a small hole, the size of a rifle barrel, in a hewn mesquite board at the exterior wall. There are no windows in either of the buildings. The hipped roofs were added as later additions. Private ranch, not open to the public. *NR 1977.*

WESLACO AND VICINITY, Hidalgo County

Weslaco (pop. 21,877), located in the irrigated agricultural area of southern Hidalgo County, was developed by Ed Couch and Robert E. Reeves in 1919. Weslaco is an acronym for W.E. Stewart Land Company, from whom the developers purchased the townsite. The city is still an agri-business and food-processing industries center.

Charro Arena. West Rd. and Sugar Sweet Ave. This is the Valley's only charro arena. On weekends charro practice and Mexican-style horse-manship exhibitions are held. Check with the Rio Grande Valley Chamber of Commerce, Weslaco, for schedules.

City Hall. S. Kansas Ave. and Fifth St. This Spanish Revival style building, constructed in 1928, is decorated with mosaic tiles and ornate cast-stone sculpture. The architect, Newell Waters, is said to have dropped the molds for the stone sculptures into the Rio Grande when the project was completed so that the designs could not be duplicated. The stairway

City Hall, Weslaco. Photo by Cathryn Hoyt, THC.

just inside the front door is set with Moorish polychrome tiles imported from Spain. *RTHL 1978.*

Gibson Park. 301 S. Border. Within the park is a 5.5-acre nature area maintained by the Valley Nature Center that contains mesquite, cacti, trees and shrubs, and wildlife native to the Rio Grande Valley. The Nature Center offers exhibits and programs for schoolchildren and adults. Open Mon.–Sat. 9–1; closed Sundays and holidays.

Weslaco Bicultural Museum. 515 S. Kansas Ave. Museum exhibits illustrate the dual culture and history of the Weslaco area. Of particular interest is a collection of rocks, minerals, and gemstones from Mexico. Open Wed.–Thurs. 1–3; Fri. 10–12, 1–3; closed in August.

Weslaco Public Library. 525 S. Kansas Ave. Weslaco's public library, one of the finest in the Valley, is housed in a building that reflects Spanish and Mexican stylistic influences, particularly in its open courtyard and wall fountain set in a colorful, blue tile surround.

ZAPATA AND VICINITY, Zapata County

Zapata (pop. 7,119), originally called Carrizo, was settled about 1770 by residents of the Escandón settlement at Revilla (Guerrero), Mexico.

268

The name of the town and the county honors Col. Antonio Zapata, a pioneer Mexican rancher who was executed for his support of the Federalists in 1838–40. Zapata is now the county seat of Zapata County. A historical marker (*CM 1936*) commemorating Zapata County has been placed 5 miles northwest of Zapata on US 83.

Bustamante Ranch. Rural Zapata County, in Zapata vicinity. In 1802, Pedro Bustamante, of Ciudad Guerrero, Tamaulipas, was given a land grant of 22,000 acres by the Mexican government. Bustamante and his family raised peanuts, cattle, sheep, and goats on the land. Today, the great-great-grandson of the founder still owns 41.8 acres of the original ranch. Since acquiring title to the land in 1952, the owner has rebuilt a water pond originally put in by his grandfather and continues the family ranching tradition. Private ranch, not open to the public. *TFLHR.*

Colonization of the Lower Rio Grande Area. Marker, in Central Plaza by the courthouse in Zapata. Commemorates the work of José de Escandón, chief colonizer for the Lower Rio Grande Valley. *SM 1985. See* sidebar: José de Escandón.

Rancho El Niño Feliz Jacal. Thirteen mi. E of Zapata on SH 16, on private ranch. A small *jacal de leña,* which once housed ranch hands, can be seen from SH 16.

REGION 3

El Paso and Trans-Pecos Texas

Trans-Pecos Texas is the name applied to the rugged land that is roughly defined by the Pecos River on the east, the Rio Grande on the south and west, and the New Mexico state line on the north. Also included in this guidebook region is Del Rio and its surrounding Lower Pecos area.

American Indians succeeded in adapting to the harsh environment of the Trans-Pecos thousands of years ago. The earliest appearance of prehistoric architecture was in the El Paso area where, at the time of Spanish contact, the Indians were building multi-roomed pueblos of adobe. In the La Junta de los Ríos district (near Presidio) village-dwelling Indians built pit-houses similar to early structures of the El Paso area. The arrival of Spanish explorers marked the beginning of the historic period, but the early expeditions charted the region as *el despoblado* (the unpeopled place) and avoided the arid interior away from the rivers.

Antonio de Espejo, in 1583, led the earliest Spanish explorations of the Pecos River through this region. The Lower Pecos received its first European visitor in 1590, when Castaño de Sosa crossed the area on his way from Monclova, Mexico, to New Mexico. Juan de Oñate in 1598 led an expedition north to claim and colonize the New Mexico region. Upon reaching the El Paso area, Oñate claimed for Spain all of the land drained by the Rio Grande. The expedition then proceeded north to found the Province of New Mexico, bringing Spanish rule to the American Southwest and establishing the route later known as El Camino Real.

Most of the native inhabitants of the early historic period, including the settled farmers who lived in villages along the Rio Grande at El Paso and La Junto de los Ríos, were displaced by intruding Plains Indians. In the 17th century Apachean groups began to establish themselves and to make the Guadalupe Mountains area their heartland. They inhabited the mountainous areas between the Pecos and the Rio Grande until their final subjugation late in the 19th century. From Fort Stockton to the Big Bend, US 385 closely follows the route of the historic Comanche War Trail, a Plains Indian route through Texas into northern Mexico. The Chihuahuan Desert regions of Texas and northern Mexico were ruled by Apaches and Comanches until the late 19th century. With their defeat, thousands of years of Indian occupation ended and the period of Anglo-American dominance began.

Opposite: Rock art, Hueco Tanks State Historical Park. THC photo.

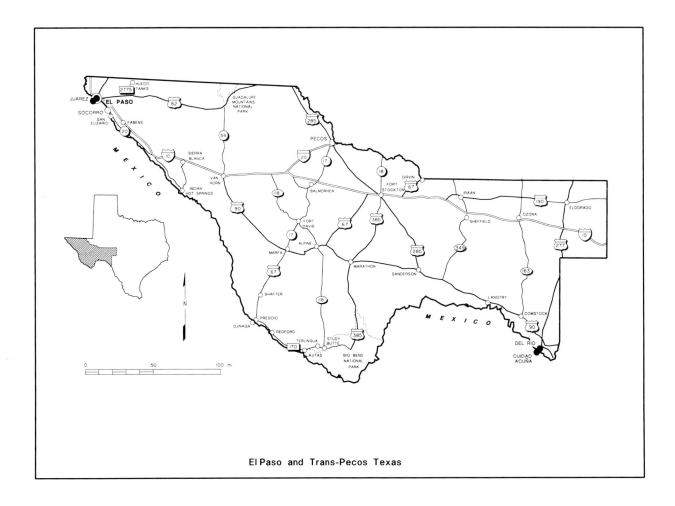

El Paso and Trans-Pecos Texas

The mission and early trading settlements that were to form the modern city of El Paso, at the western extreme of the Trans-Pecos, were isolated from the eastern centers of population in the state. The El Paso region thus formed close cultural ties with Mexico and New Mexico that still persist. Hispanic and Anglo-American settlement occurred later in the interior of the Trans-Pecos than along the Rio Grande floodplain. Traders and settlers, and soldiers to protect them, entered gradually into far western Texas, and early towns grew around the frontier forts. Areas of splendid isolation eventually yielded, little by little, to ranching and commerce. By the 1890s the frontier period was over and the taming of the wilderness had begun in earnest. The coming of the railroad, oil exploration, and mercury mining brought about the establishment of new settlements and the formation of modern counties. Like human attempts throughout the history of the region, some of the settlements succeeded and others failed. The failures are marked by stone and adobe ruins that typify the indigenous regional architecture. Both old and new adobe houses can still be seen in the small towns that dot the region, reflecting a continuum of cultural relationships that has persisted since prehistoric times.

Guidebook Region 3. Map by Greg Miller.

272

EL PASO, El Paso County

Ocotillo in Big Bend National Park.
Photo by Martha Peters, THC.

El Paso (pop. 515,342), the westernmost city in Texas, has had strong cultural ties with both New Mexico and Mexico since prehistoric times—ties that are easily explained by the fact that Mexico lies just across the river and Albuquerque is closer than Austin, Amarillo, or Houston. El Paso, under both Spanish and Mexican governments, was administered as part of New Mexico, and not until the Compromise of 1850 was the city located within the current boundaries of Texas.

The earliest Spanish settlement at El Paso del Río del Norte was a mission established south of the river in 1659. By 1670 about a thousand people were living in the El Paso area. A decade later an influx of population resulted from the arrival of Spaniards and Indians fleeing from the Pueblo Revolt in New Mexico. Four missions, including Corpus Christi de la Ysleta and Nuestra Señora de la Concepción del Socorro, were established along the river and eventually came to be located in Texas through floods and changes in the river's course. Settlements grew up around Ysleta and Socorro that still exist today.

273

Several communities that developed in the area eventually merged to form the city of El Paso. One was a community that grew around a hacienda built in 1827 by Juan María Ponce de León. After De León sold the property in 1848, the settlement was named Franklin. The name Franklin was changed to El Paso in 1859. The establishment of Fort Bliss in 1854 began a long military tradition in the city, and the arrival of the railroad in 1881, providing new opportunities for trade and communication, contributed to the growth of the modern city. In 1883 the city became the county seat of El Paso County.

The period of the Mexican Revolution was one of the most colorful eras of the city's history, as political and military leaders of both sides congregated in El Paso. Among the most famous were Porfírio Díaz, William Howard Taft, Francisco Madero, Francisco ("Pancho") Villa, and General John J. ("Black Jack") Pershing. During the period from 1910 to 1920, the population of the city increased from about 40,000 to 78,000, largely as a result of refugees fleeing from Mexico. In south El Paso an area between Paisano Drive and the Rio Grande became home to many of the refugees and became known as Chihuahuita, "Little Chihuahua." The southeastern part of the town is still predominantly Mexican-American.

El Paso is now the largest U.S. city on the Mexican border, and the combined population of El Paso–Juárez is about 1.5 million. In 1955 the El Paso city boundaries were extended beyond Ysleta, and this ancient Indian town became part of the modern city.

Information Centers

El Paso Tourist Information Centers. Locations: (1) IH 10E and Avenue of Americas; (2) in the El Paso International Airport; and (3) in the Civic Center Plaza. Each provides information on the El Paso area, but the Civic Center Plaza location is the central information center.

Texas Travel Information Center. Take IH 10E, Exit 0 to Anthony. Provides detailed information about El Paso and the state. This is one of 12 centers that are located at key highway entrances to Texas; open daily except for major holidays.

Historic Sites

Alderete-Candelaria House. *See* Ysleta.

Chamizal National Memorial. 800 S. San Marcial (at Paisano Dr. and San Marcial). The memorial was established in 1966 on a portion of land acquired from the Republic of Mexico after the Rio Grande changed its channel, thus creating a new international boundary. The memorial complex, consisting of a visitor center and surrounding park, marks the Chamizal Settlement of 1963, which amicably ended a longstanding border dispute between Texas and Mexico. The visitor center includes exhibits and films, in Spanish and English, on Chamizal and border history. Collections cover the period from about 1800 to the present and include materials from the U.S.–Mexico Boundary Survey of 1848–50, posters, survey maps, documents, and Mexican and Mexican-American artifacts. Open daily 8–5. *PM; NHM.*

Cristo Rey (the cross on the mountain). *See* Public Art entries below.

El Camino Real. Markers, placed on the route of El Camino Real at the following locations in El Paso: San Jacinto Plaza (*CM 1936*); 5800 Doniphan Dr.; 1720 W. Paisano Dr.; entrance to Socorro Mission on FM 258; and entrance to Tigua Arts and Crafts Center (119 S. Old Pueblo Rd.). This section of the Spanish road system known as El Camino Real reached from Mexico City to New Mexico and was first traveled by Juan de Oñate in 1598, little more than a century after Columbus reached the New World. Oñate's rate of travel through this rugged country has been estimated at 40 miles in 15 days. Commonly known as the Chihuahua Trail, this branch of the Camino Real became a major route for transporting goods from Mexico City and Chihuahua to Santa Fe and Taos. The trail joined the river near San Elizario and went west from there to Juárez, where it crossed the river at El Paso del Río del Norte, then followed the river north along modern IH 10 to Las Cruces and IH 25 to Santa Fe.

El Paso del Río del Norte. Marker, US 80A, just S of Hart's Mill site, 1720 W. Paisano Dr. This pass through the mountains, an important crossing on the Camino Real, is the lowest, snow-free feasible route from the Atlantic to the Pacific through the Rocky Mountains. Named El Paso del Río del Norte by Juan de Oñate on May 4, 1598, the city of El Paso perpetuates the name. W. Paisano Dr. provides scenic views of the Pass, the river, *Cristo Rey* (the cross on the mountain), and the outskirts of Juárez. *CM 1936.*

First Meeting of Presidents. Marker, SE corner of Main and Oregon Sts. In 1909 the first meeting between U.S. and Mexican presidents occurred. William Howard Taft met with Porfirio Díaz at the Juárez Customhouse just a year before the Mexican Revolution ended Díaz's long hold on power. The historical marker designates the site of the old St. Regis Hotel, where President Taft stayed during the meeting. *PM.*

Fort Bliss. *See* Old Fort Bliss; Fort Bliss Replica Museum, under Museums entries.

Franklin Canal. The canal, replacing El Paso's original *acequia madre* (the main irrigation ditch, which was constructed before 1845) channels water from the Rio Grande along a 31-mile course through El Paso County. Completed in 1891, the canal was acquired by the U.S. Dept. of Reclamation in 1912 from the Franklin Irrigation Company. Before completion of the Franklin Canal, each community had its own *acequia* system. The modern canal feeds lateral canals that, in turn, feed the irrigation ditches to communities as far away as Fabens.

Hart's Mill. 1720 W. Paisano Dr. A water-powered grist mill was built in 1849 or 1850 by Simeon Hart and his wife, Jesusita Siqueiros. The mill, also called El Molino, supplied flour and cornmeal to the military and early settlers throughout the area. A small settlement grew up around the mill and was one of five communities that later expanded and merged to form the city of El Paso. Hart's son, Juan, was one of the founders of the

El Paso Times. The Hart house, now occupied by a restaurant, is adjacent to the ruins of Old Fort Bliss. *RTHL 1981*.

Magoffin Home State Historic Site. 1120 Magoffin Ave. This Territorial-style hacienda was built in 1875 by Joseph Magoffin. The single-story structure is thought to be similar to an earlier Magoffin home, built in 1849 by Joseph's father, James Magoffin. The house has adobe walls over 2 feet thick, and the stucco on the outer walls is scored to resemble stone courses. Italianate details decorate the wooden window and door framing. James and his wife, María Gertrudis Valdez de Veramendi, were among the founders of El Paso. Magoffinsville, the settlement that grew up around the original Magoffin home, was one of several settlements that merged into the city of El Paso. Joseph also became an important citizen of El Paso, serving as a military officer, businessman, banker, and local public official. His home, like his father's, became the center of El Paso social life. The Magoffin family owned the house until it was acquired by the Texas Parks and Wildlife Dept., which restored the building in 1979–80. Many of the furnishings in this historic site are original; some were shipped overland from St. Louis, and some were made by local craftsmen who combined Victorian and Mexican motifs. The house is one of a few remaining examples of Territorial style architecture in Texas. *RTHL 1962; NR 1971*.

Mission and Pueblo of San Antonio de Senecú. Marker, 1.5 mi. NW of Ysleta, at the corner of Alameda and Valdespino Sts., on US 80. The marker commemorates the approximate site of the mission and pueblo of San Antonio de Senecú, established by Antonio de Otermín and Francisco Ayeta in 1682 for Piro and Tompiro Indians. *CM 1936*.

Mission Trail. The Mission Trail begins in El Paso at the Zaragosa exit off IH 10 and ends at FM 1110 (the Clint–San Elizario Road). The route is clearly marked with signs indicating the mission locations (see individual entries below). The trail also runs through El Paso's oldest Mexican and Indian communities and is lined with shops that specialize in Mexican and Southwestern arts and crafts and antiques. Many of the shops are open only on weekends.

Old Fort Bliss. 1800 block of W. Paisano Dr. This was the first permanent site of Fort Bliss, established in 1848. The fort was named in 1854 for Col. William Wallace S. Bliss and served as the base for several 19th-century Indian campaigns, including the 1885–86 pursuit of Geronimo. The fort at this location was abandoned in 1893. Remaining adobe structures include two-story officer's quarters on cut-stone basements (at 1838 and 1844 W. Paisano Dr.) and the former guardhouse (at 1932 W. Paisano Dr.). *CM 1936; RTHL 1963; NR 1971*.

Pioneer Plaza. Marker, corner of Mills, El Paso and San Francisco Sts. Pioneer Plaza, the center of public activity in early El Paso, is characteristic of the plazas to be seen in Spanish-influenced town layouts. A large tree in the plaza served as a bulletin board where announcements were posted and where anyone could—and did—voice his opinions about one or more of his fellow citizens. Originally, the *acequia madre,* or main irrigation ditch (later to become the Franklin Canal), ran directly through the plaza, but it has now been covered over. *SM 1986*.

Pioneer Plaza, El Paso. Photo by
Cathryn Hoyt, THC.

San Elizario. *See* separate community listing for San Elizario.

San Jacinto Plaza. Oregon and Mill Sts., in the center of downtown.
El Paso's first city square is said to be the site of an Indian pueblo garden
described by Oñate in 1598. Designated "the Plaza" by the city in 1889, it
was officially named San Jacinto Plaza in 1902. Its shade trees and benches,
reminiscent of those found in traditional Mexican plazas, provide a pleasant rest area for downtown visitors. Located here are a number of markers
commemorating events in El Paso's history. *PM*.

Silver Dollar Cafe. 1021 S. Mesa St. This one-story, brick structure is
built on an L-plan and has a low-pitched hip roof. While the building is

not architecturally striking, the floor and site plan are typical of South Texas–Northern Mexico structures of the 1875–1925 period. The building originally comprised 14 individual dwellings and a corner store. Located close to the Mexican border, it was built as tenement housing for Mexican immigrants driven from their homes by the Mexican Revolution. The Silver Dollar Cafe replaced the corner grocery about 1930 and was later converted to an apartment. *NR 1986.*

Socorro. *See* separate community listing for Socorro.

Ysleta, which claims to be the oldest town in Texas, now lies within the city limits of El Paso. Some of the earliest sites and structures in the El Paso area are located in Ysleta.

Alderete-Candelaria House. 120 S. Old Pueblo Rd. This adobe structure is believed to have been built, with the help of neighboring Tigua Indians, for Benigno Alderete in the 1870s. Alderete served as a Texas Ranger, county commissioner, and town mayor. The house became known as Candelaria house after Alderete's granddaughter, Ester, married Alex Candelaria. The building has housed several different businesses and was once the temporary El Paso County Courthouse. This historic house also formerly served as a Tigua community center and currently houses a restaurant. *SM 1984.*

Tigua Indian Reservation (Ysleta del Sur Pueblo). Adjoining Ysleta Mission; headquarters at 119 S. Old Pueblo Rd. The Tiguas came from the Puebloan heartland of New Mexico to the El Paso area along with Spaniards and other Indians fleeing from the Pueblo Revolt of 1680. A 1751 Spanish grant gave the Tiguas 20,000 acres, but time and encroaching development almost led to cultural oblivion. By 1871 their holdings had been reduced to about 300 acres. Only about 65 acres, some of which has been continuously cultivated since 1682, now remain in Indian hands. The city limits of El Paso eventually surrounded the Ysleta community, and by the 1930s only about 100 Tiguas remained. Finally, in the late 1960s state and federal governments officially recognized the Tiguas, and a people whose history extended for almost 300 years in Texas and over a thousand years in New Mexico were formally identified as American Indians. Through the help that was thus made available to them, private grants, and hard labor they completed a new pueblo structure in 1975. The Tigua have preserved substantial parts of their culture through the centuries and are the oldest identifiable ethnic group remaining in Texas. Tigua history and traditions can be seen at a living history pueblo and in their Arts and Crafts Center, which also houses a gift shop. Traditional dances are performed only on special occasions, but pottery making, weaving, and bread baking take place year round. Bread baked in adobe ovens called *hornos* is a Tigua specialty. The reservation also includes two restaurants. Open 9–6 through October, 8:30–5:30 during the winter. *See also* Festivals entry, Tigua St. Anthony's Day.

Ysleta Mission. 131 S. Zaragoza St. Originally known as Corpus Christi de la Isleta del Sur, the Ysleta mission and pueblo (the first in Texas), was founded by Antonio de Otermín and Francisco Ayeta in

Mural depicting the Ysleta Mission and Tigua Indian pueblos, El Paso. Photo by Cathryn Hoyt, THC.

Ysleta Mission, El Paso. THC photo.

1682 for the Tigua Indians, refugees of the Pueblo Revolt in New Mexico. The present chapel, which dates from 1851, has been rebuilt several times and contains materials from the mid-18th, mid-19th, and early 20th centuries. The walls and bells are from the 1744 building. The structure reflects a New Mexican interpretation of the Spanish Colonial style. The mission, also called Church of Our Lady of Mt. Carmel, still ministers to the Tigua Indians. *RTHL 1962; NR 1972.*

Spanish Revival Architecture

Hotel Cortez. 300 N. Mesa St. Built in 1926, this eleven-story, brick-veneer hotel, designed by Trost and Trost, is an excellent example of Spanish Revival style. *NR 1980.*

Manhattan Heights Historic District. Memorial Park (parts of 47 blocks plus 43-acre city park). Located on the former site of a smelting plant, Manhattan Heights developed after 1912 as a residential addition. Several houses in the district reflect Spanish Revival style: see examples at 3017 and 3144 Wheeling; 3000 and 3009 Silver; 3933 and 3038 Federal; 3147 Copper; 1718, 2905, 3010, and 3100 Gold; and 3023 Angora. *NR 1980.*

Palace Theater. 209 El Paso St. This three-story, brick veneer, Spanish Revival style structure was built in 1914. *NR 1980.*

Plaza Theatre. 125 Pioneer Plaza. Built in 1929–30, this Spanish Revival style theatre is of steel-frame, brick-veneer construction. The flat roof and stepped parapet are typical of the style. The auditorium rises four

Ornate detailing highlights the interior of the Plaza Theatre, El Paso. THC photo.

280

Hotel Cortez, El Paso. THC photo.

stories, but the entrance is two-story and has only a modest façade. Ornate artwork, metal railings, and fixtures in the lobby enhance the Spanish architectural features. The auditorium seats 1,410 and has three levels. The stepped roof line, foliage, cloud and bird machines, and twinkling pin ceiling lights were used to create an outdoor effect. The large proscenium arch stage is accented by twisted, textured columns. The Plaza Theatre is the only extant grand movie palace in El Paso and one of the few remaining in Texas. *NR 1987.*

Singer Sewing Machine Co. 211 Texas Ave. This two-story, concrete structure with stucco veneer, built in 1928, exhibits Spanish Revival influences. *NR 1980; RTHL 1983.*

Sunset Heights Historic District. The historic district is bounded by IH 10, N. Oregon St., Heisig Ave., and a continuation of River Ave. An early 20th-century neighborhood built on a rocky escarpment above the Rio Grande, Sunset Heights began to decline as a residential area in the 1930s but restorations have been undertaken in recent years. The district includes several Spanish Revival style residences. *NR 1988.*

Palmore Academy (now an apartment building). 519 Prospect. A small residence, built in 1907, makes up the front portion of the present building. Spanish Revival stylistic influence is evident in the stuccoed walls, red tile roof, and courtyard with fountain. The structure was purchased in 1917 by Professor Servando Y. Esquivel, who had directed schools in Chihuahua, Mexico, before the Mexican Revolution forced him to move to El Paso. The two-story addition to the residence was used as dormitory and classroom space for Palmore Academy, which he operated until 1952, when the structure was converted to apartments. Through his students, Esquivel had a profound influence on the cultural and intellectual environment of the region. In recognition of his accomplishments, he was awarded the Gold Medal of Mexico by Mexican President Adolfo López Mateo in 1959.

Wallace Apartments. 120 Randolph. These Spanish Mission Revival style luxury apartments were built in 1908 and designed by Edward Kneezel, one of El Paso's earliest architects. *RTHL 1985.*

Joseph Williams House. 323 Rio Grande. Joseph Williams, then mayor of El Paso, built this house in 1905. It is one of the earliest Spanish Revival style residences in the district. Meetings between Pancho Villa and U.S. General Hugh Scott were held here in 1915.

Museums and Cultural Centers

El Paso Centennial Museum. Campus, University of Texas at El Paso, at University Ave. and Wiggins Rd. Collections cover archeology, anthropology, geology, and history from about 1680 to the present. Materials include Spanish, Mexican, and Mexican-American items and Southwestern and regional Indian artifacts; archival holdings include some oral histories. Open Tues.—Sat. 10—4.

El Paso Museum of Art. 1211 Montana Ave. The museum has four permanent galleries and one wing of exhibits that are changed monthly. The annual El Paso Art Association exhibition is held here, as are frequent one-man shows by outstanding living artists of national and international reputation. The museum houses the famous Kress collection of works by European masters and also has holdings of traditional and contemporary Mexican and Southwestern art. In addition, Mexican Colonial works adorn many of the interior walls. Open Tues.—Sat. 10—5; Sun. 1—5.

El Paso Museum of History. 12901 Gateway West. Hispanic materials in the museum's collections include charro costumes and saddles, as well as Spanish, Mexican, and Mexican-American clothing, personal adornments, and ranching equipment. Area history, including early Spanish exploration and the founding of the missions, is depicted in dioramas. Historic Indian materials include Southwestern Indian pottery and some Apache items. Open Tues.—Sun. 9—4:50.

El Paso Public Library. 501 N. Oregon. The main library's Southwest Collection focuses on the history of El Paso and Trans-Pecos Texas. Included in the collection are books, periodicals, documents, maps, photographs, and other items.

Fort Bliss Replica Museum. Bldg. 600, Fort Bliss, Pleasanton Rd. and Sheridan Dr. The museum buildings are a scale replica of Fort Bliss as

Detail of a 19th-century *bota de ala* in the collections of the El Paso Museum of History. The *bota de ala* was a wing-shaped covering that tied below the knee and extended to the ankles and was used to protect the lower legs from thorny brush. Photo by Jim Ward, courtesy of El Paso Museum of History.

it appeared in 1854–68. The external appearance of the replica was based on drawings made by a soldier stationed at the fort in the 1850s. The replica of the fort is built of adobe, as the original was, and was dedicated by the citizens of El Paso on the 100th anniversary of the fort's founding. The buildings are maintained as a museum of the frontier military era. The grounds exhibit local desert flora, much as the scene might have appeared in 1854. Open daily 9–4:30.

University of Texas at El Paso. *See* El Paso Centennial Museum; University of Texas at El Paso Library.

University of Texas at El Paso Library. The library's Special Collections and Archives include 1,600 reels of microfilm containing early mission and parish records from the region and from northern Mexico. Other library holdings also focus on the history of the Southwest and Mexico. Nonstudents may use materials in the library.

Wilderness Park Museum. N of El Paso, 1000 Transmountain Rd. Human adaptation to the regional desert environment is portrayed in exhibits and dioramas in this 17-acre indoor-outdoor museum at the eastern edge of the Franklin Mountains. Replicas of a pueblo ruin, kiva, and pithouse can be viewed on the Nature Trail. Open Tues.–Sun. 9–5.

Public Art

Aztec Calendar Stone. Kansas St. and San Antonio Ave. The Aztec Calendar Stone, also called the "Stone of the Sun," has become an international symbol of Mexico. This replica reflects the close ties between El Paso and the land across the river.

Cristo Rey (the cross on the mountain), by Urbici Soler. 1937. IH

10W and Sunland Park exit to Doniphan Rd. Soler, a native of Spain, came to El Paso in 1937 to begin work on the statue *Cristo Rey,* a massive monument of Christ on the Cross that is similar to the statue overlooking Rio de Janeiro in Brazil. Built of Cordova cream limestone quarried near Austin, the statue stands on the peak of Sierra del Cristo Rey (the Mountain of Christ the King) overlooking El Paso. The boundaries of Texas, New Mexico, and Mexico meet within a few feet of the statue. On the last Sunday in October, the feast day of Christ the King, pilgrims climb to the 4,576-foot summit on a four-mile trail (strenuous climb, recommended for groups only). A historical marker (*SM 1983*) commemorating Soler and his monumental work has been placed in the Evergreen Cemetery, 4301 Alameda.

Murals. There are over 100 murals in the El Paso area. Centrally located examples include the following:

Acosta mural, unnamed, by Manuel Acosta. Campbell St. at the Border Highway. Depicts a Hispanic family, a charro, and images of Mexican-American culture.

Callejo mural, unnamed, by Carlos Callejo. Sante and Fourth Sts. Depicts theme of Hispanic youth and education.

Entelequia, by Carlos Rosas. West wall of El Paso Boys Club, 900 block of Campbell St. Depicts the evolution of the Mexican-American.

Pass of the North, by Tom Lea. El Paso Federal Courthouse, on San Antonio St. between Kansas and Campbell. Depicts a Spanish conquistador and various events and peoples that have contributed to the history of El Paso.

Southwest Landscape, by Tom Lea. El Paso Public Library, main library downtown. Depicts a typical Southwestern landscape.

Festivals and Events

Ballet Folklórico Cristo Rey. This professional dance troupe consists of children ages 4 to 17. Founded in 1982, the troupe performs traditional dances of Mexico as a way to entertain, educate, and instill pride in Mexican-American culture. The troupe presents an annual performance, in the spring or early summer, at the El Paso Civic Center Theater. For information contact: Director, Ballet Folklórico Cristo Rey, 601 Cresta Alta, El Paso 79912.

Border Folk Festival (Fiesta Chamizal). Held for 3 to 6 days, second week in October at Chamizal National Memorial. Begun in 1973, the music festival is dedicated to the preservation of folk music and dance. The celebration features international performers, including Mexican and Mexican-Americans; traditional music, foodways, folk arts and crafts; and workshops and concerts. Much of the focus is on traditional music.

Diez y Seis de Septiembre. September 15–16, at various locations in El Paso and Juárez. Music and a charreada usually begin this Mexican Independence Day celebration at Chamizal National Memorial on the 15th, and a parade and other events are held in Juárez on the 16th.

Fiesta de las Flores. Weekend preceding Labor Day, at Washington Park. The four-day (Fri.–Mon.) festival is a family affair, held since 1952, and features both Mexican and Mexican-American performers. Activities include traditional music (mariachi and conjunto) and ballet folklórico, as well as games (including a Huacha Tournament). The fiesta also features folk arts and crafts and traditional costumes of the various Mexican states. The event draws about 100,000 visitors. For more information contact LULAC Council #132, 4110 Alameda, El Paso 79905.

Festival de la Zarzuela. In August (date varies), at Chamizal National Memorial. Spanish folk dances celebrate both the United States' and Mexico's coming of age.

Juan de Oñate "First Thanksgiving" Festival. Last weekend (Fri.–Sun.) in April, at Chamizal National Memorial, at San Elizario Plaza in San Elizario, and at other locations in El Paso. A pageant of men, women, and children costumed as 16th-century conquistadores, soldiers, and grandees and their ladies commemorates a feast celebrated by the Oñate expedition on April 20, 1598—the first Thanksgiving celebration in North America—as well as the claiming of the land for Spain. Features of the

Young dancers from the Ballet Folklórico Cristo Rey model traditional costumes from Veracruz. Photo by "Francisco" (Frank Barron).

festival are a reenactment of the arrival of Oñate's colonizing expedition at the Rio Grande and the celebration of the first thanksgiving, local crafts and historical displays, tours of the El Paso missions and other historic sites in El Paso and Juárez, and charreada contests. Traditional foods are available, and performances include music, dance, and drama. The festival is sponsored by the El Paso Mission Trail Assn. and the Junior League of El Paso for the purpose of furthering knowledge and appreciation of Spanish heritage in America.

Siglo de Oro Drama Festival. In March (date varies), at Chamizal National Memorial Theatre. Companies from Latin America, Spain, and the United States bring classic Spanish plays to this annual Chamizal International Spanish classical drama competition.

Tigua St. Anthony's Day. June 13, at Tigua Indian Reservation. The celebration commemorates the patron saint day of the Tiguas. The Tigua mission was originally established under the name Mission de Corpus Christi de la Isleta del Sur, changed later to San Antonio, and still later to Nuestra Señora del Carmen. San Antonio was also the name of the original mission of La Isleta del Norte, in New Mexico. Thus, by custom and tradition, the Tiguas consider San Antonio, or St. Anthony, their rightful patron, and his feast is one of their special tribal commemorations. The Tiguas honor their patron saint with special ceremonies, dances, and ethnic foods.

Viva! El Paso. Thursdays–Saturdays, June through August, at McKelligon Canyon Amphitheater, McKelligon Rd. Outdoor, musical pageant depicting the colorful history of the El Paso area, from Indians and conquistadores to cowboys and cavalry. The canyon is also open to hikers and campers and for picnics.

Emiliano Zapata Charro Association. Arena on North Loop (FM 76) in SE El Paso. Charreadas (Mexican rodeos) are held at the arena on most Sunday afternoons. The charros also perform for the Border Folk Festival and other celebrations during the year.

A costumed member of the First Thanksgiving pageant surveys the landscape for signs of the Rio Grande. Courtesy of the *El Paso Times.*

Scenic Drives

Scenic Drive. Scenic Drive, accessible from Richmond St. on the east and Rim Rd. on the west, follows the southern edge of the Franklin Mountains, providing excellent views of El Paso and Juárez.

Transmountain Road (Loop 375) cuts through the mountains from east to west and provides scenic mountain and desert views at several points.

Border City

Juárez is Mexico's fourth largest city and largest city on the U.S. border. The earliest settlements at El Paso del Río del Norte, including Presidio del Paso del Norte (1682–1773) were south of the Rio Grande. Juárez was still called El Paso del Norte until 1888, when the name was changed in honor of Benito Juárez. Today, three bridges link the city with El Paso, and tourists enjoy a wide variety of shopping, dining, entertainment, and accommodations. Several points of historic interest are described below. In addition, on Avenida Lincoln is the only standing Lincoln Memorial statue outside the United States. The Chamizal settlement is commemorated at Parque Comemorativo Chamizal at the foot of the Avenidas de las Américas Bridge; the park also contains replicas of several of the most famous sites in Mexico, including Uxmal, Chichén-Itzá, and Teotihuacán. Charreadas are held on most Sundays in the summer at the Lienzo Charro Adolfo López Mateos on Avenida del Charros. El Día de los Muertos, the November 2 observance of All Soul's Day, is celebrated citywide with parades, religious and dramatic performances, and the special food offerings that are unique to this traditional event. The Feast of Nuestra Señora de Guadalupe, on December 12, also is observed with parades and festivities, including performances by Indian groups.

Mission Nuestra Señora de Guadalupe. Follow Juárez Ave. south; located next to the Cathedral in the old city square. The Franciscan mission of Nuestra Señora de Guadalupe was the first settlement in the area. Built in 1668, this mission is one of the foremost historic sites of Juárez. It also is the repository for many records dealing with the missions on the Texas side of the Rio Grande.

Mercado Juárez (Juárez City Market). No. 103 Avenida 16 de Septiembre, near downtown. Numerous booths contain a wide variety of merchandise and traditional foods; music is usually being played. Open sun-up to sundown daily.

PRONAF Center. In Juárez via the Córdova bridge, near intersection of Avenida 16 de Septiembre and Lincoln. An impressive government-sponsored, modern shopping area offering museums, accommodations, and a variety of shops selling arts and crafts from all over Mexico. The Museo de Arte y Historia has an excellent collection of pre-Columbian art, as well as historic and contemporary art and artifacts, all exhibited by period (open Tues.–Sun. 11–7). The Centro Artesanal (National Arts and Crafts Center) also is located in the center (open 10–7 daily).

First Methodist Church, Alpine.
Photo by Cathryn Hoyt, THC.

ALPINE, Brewster County

Alpine (pop. 5,637), established before 1882, developed as a ranching center in one of the last open-grazing-land areas in Texas. Known as a "cowtown," it was the home or shipping point for local cattlemen. Still a ranching center, Alpine is also a tourism center for the Big Bend region and the home of Sul Ross State University. Houses made of adobe are common in Alpine and are still being commercially constructed here. They reflect not only the presence of the many Mexican-American families who have long made their homes here, but the economic advantages and environmental suitability of adobe construction. Alpine since 1888 has been the county seat of Brewster County, a vast mountainous area that is the largest county in Texas.

First Methodist Church. E. Sul Ross Ave. and N. Third. Built in 1889, this Spanish Revival style adobe church was the first Protestant church in Brewster County. *RTHL 1965.*

García-Valadez House. 108 W. Avenue F. The García-Valadez House was built in 1890 by ranch hand Trinidad García. The original structure had adobe walls 27 to 33 inches thick. A social center for many years, the house has been the home of Thomas Valadez, leading local merchant, and his family since 1926. The house has been expanded over the years and now has eight rooms. *RTHL 1968.*

Museum of the Big Bend. On Sul Ross State University Campus. Exhibits illustrating the history of the region include artifacts representing thousands of years of prehistoric occupation in the Big Bend region.

Our Lady of Peace Catholic Church. 102 W. Ave. G. Like other small towns in the region, Alpine was included in the parish of St. Joseph's in Fort Davis after that parish was established in 1876, and residents here were served by missionary priests. Regular monthly masses were held in Alpine as early as 1892, and in 1902 the first permanent church, Our Lady of Guadalupe, was dedicated. The first resident priest came in 1916. The new church, Our Lady of Peace, was built in 1941, and the church's shrine to Our Lady Queen of Peace was dedicated in 1949.

Sul Ross State University, Bryan Wildenthal Memorial Library. The library's Archives of the Big Bend contain important collections that relate to Hispanic heritage in West Texas. *See also* Museum of the Big Bend.

Shrine of the Virgin of Guadalupe, Balmorhea. Photo by Cathryn Hoyt, THC.

BALMORHEA AND VICINITY, Reeves County

Balmorhea (pop. ca. 600) was established in 1906 as an irrigated-farming center supplied by San Solomon springs. Nearby is Brogado, a small farming community founded in the mid-19th century by Mexican farmers who grew corn, grain and vegetables, and raised livestock to supply the soldiers at Fort Davis.

Balmorhea State Park. 4 mi. SW of Balmorhea off US 290. The park, known as the "Oasis of West Texas," is built around San Solomon springs, which have provided water to area residents for thousands of years. The name San Solomon was given to the springs by Mexican farmers who settled in the area and used the water for irrigating crops. The canals that run through the park were first dug by these farmers and were later expanded by the Civilian Conservation Corps in 1935 as part of the park facilities. The San Solomon Springs Courts, an adobe complex constructed by the CCC in 1940, offer visitors a rare opportunity to experience life in an adobe dwelling. The waters of the springs now form the major attraction of the park—the world's largest spring-fed swimming pool.

Shrine of Virgin of Guadalupe. SH 17. This attractive and well-known roadside shrine is dedicated to the Virgin of Guadalupe. Built of local materials, the shrine is constructed of cemented creek rock and has a statue of the Virgin of Guadalupe enshrined in the niche. Travelers en route to Mexico often stop here to light a candle and pray for a safe trip.

The shrine is maintained by Christ the King Catholic Church, located nearby, which serves the Brogado area.

Labor Day Festival. Saturday of the Labor Day weekend, in September, in Balmorhea. Festivities in the downtown area include a frijole cook-off, day-long musical entertainment, dances, and games. Besides frijoles, many other traditional foods are available. Country-Western music is usually featured for the Saturday evening dance, but mariachi music typically can be heard during the course of the festivities.

BIG BEND NATIONAL PARK, Brewster County

Big Bend National Park encompasses over 800,000 acres, and its diverse scenery ranges from the majestic canyons of the Rio Grande and the river's lush floodplain through desert and mountain country. In the park, visitors can experience the plants and animals of the Chihuahuan desert, typical of the type of landscape in northern Mexico and far western Texas through which the early Spanish explorers passed en route to New Mexico. Evidence of Spanish-Indian-Mexican cultural adaptations to this arid environment can be seen throughout the park, which contains over 450 historic structures and ruins. Of the many sites, 54 are on the National Register list of classified structures or are listed in the National Register of Historic Places. The majority of these structures were built by Mexicans and Mexican-American Texans using traditional methods and techniques. Local vernacular architecture reveals a unique Hispanic adaptation and utilization of natural resources. Historic locales in the area include the sites of two 18th-century presidios (south of the river, not in the park proper), 19th- and 20th-century farming and ranching operations, 20th-century mining and commercial endeavors, Mexican border conflicts, and military history. Accommodations, camping facilities, and picnicking areas are available; advance reservations for lodging are strongly recommended throughout the year. Information, maps, and literature are available in the lobby of Park Headquarters at Panther Junction; open 8–6 in summer, 8–5 in winter.

Historic Sites and Collections

Alvino House. Located in Castolon Historic District. *See* sidebar: The Alvino House.

Big Bend National Park Study Collections. BBNP Study Collections consist of over 5,000 items including Mexican and Mexican-American furniture, clothing, personal adornments, agricultural and food-preparation tools, dishes, toys and dolls, and ranching equipment. Only a few objects are on display in visitor centers, but access to collections for study can be arranged by contacting the park's curator.

Boquillas–Rio Grande Village–Hot Springs area historic sites. In 1883 mining activities began in Mexico's Del Carmen Mountains, and related settlements grew up at Boquillas, Mexico, and Rio Grande Village

THE ALVINO HOUSE

Built by Cipriano Hernández in 1901, the Alvino House is the oldest known adobe structure in Big Bend National Park. Hernández lived in the house, farmed the land, and operated a store on the east side of his home until 1918. The land then changed hands twice before being purchased by Wayne Cartledge. In 1924, during the Cartledge era, the house was occupied by Alvino Ybarra and family, hence the name. The Alvino house was abandoned following U.S. government acquisition of the Cartledge land in 1961. Although the Park Service tried to stabilize the structure in the mid-1980s, lack of funds in the following years brought continued deterioration. Several expert adobe masons living in the nearby village of Santa Elena, Chihuahua, Mexico, offered their help, but there seemed to be insurmountable problems in accepting volunteer assistance from across the border. Finally concerned park rangers took the lead in investigating legal requirements that would allow the masons to lend their expertise. The cultural exchange initiative was made possible by cooperation from the Mexican Government in an international cultural-exchange program.

Working under the Volunteer-in-the-Parks Program, the adobe masons began their repairs, employing techniques still in use in the northern border states of Mexico. Adobe bricks were manufactured on the site, and useable adobes from a nearby stockpile made several years before also were utilized. In making new adobes, the master mason used traditional methods designed to retain, as near as possible, the original appearance and stabilization of the adobe building. Other replacement materials also matched the originals, including cottonwood for the vigas and river cane and leather ties for the *latías*. The preservation work on the Alvino House is the result of cooperation between several federal agencies, the Big Bend Natural History Association, and the volunteer artisans from Mexico. Here people divided by nationality, language, and a river have united to preserve their common heritage.

Agave, typical of the vegetation of the Chihuahuan Desert, growing at Big Bend National Park. Photo by Martha Peters, THC.

in Texas. The small smelter near Boquillas closed about 1900. Historic structures and ruins in this area exemplify regional use of traditional construction materials and methods. The structures at Rio Grande Village and Boquillas, across the river, include the Daniels Farm House, Barker Lodge, and the Graham house. The Daniels house (*NR 1989*), built about 1920, is a two-room adobe, with stone foundations, plastered walls, and a mud and river-cane roof. It is representative of early settlement and the development of floodplain farming along the Rio Grande. Barker Lodge is associated with the early settlement of Boquillas. The Graham house is a three-room adobe with rock foundation. The Hot Springs site centers around the early 20th-century resort development of J.O. Langford and includes one adobe ruin and three stone structures: the post office–store, the motel, and the house. Langford's recollections, in *Big Bend: A Homesteader's Story* (University of Texas Press, 1955), include an account of his friendship with local farmer Cleofas Natividad, who made the adobe bricks for the Langfords' house.

Castolon Historic District. Castolon Historic District contains structures, some in ruins, from Old Castolon and the Castolon Army Compound. Cipriano Hernández, the first permanent settler of Old Castolon, came from Camargo, Mexico, in 1901, built an adobe home (now known as the Alvino House), and established a farm. He maintained a small supply store in his house, and a nearby store was operated by Patricio Márquez. The army compound, also known as Camp Santa Elena, served as a garrison for U.S. Army troops from 1910 to 1914, during the Mexican Revolution. The permanent structures remaining from the army compound were built in 1919–20; these include the barracks, officers' quarters, noncommissioned officers' quarters, and the tack room, granary, and corral complex. Unrest along the border quieted in 1920 and withdrawal of troops began before the new compound was occupied. Wayne Cartledge and Howard Perry, operators of quicksilver mines in nearby Terlingua and owners of land near Castolon, acquired the army buildings and used them for stores and residences for their La Harmonia Company. Stockpiles of left-over adobe bricks of the type used in the three structures added during this period can be found near the officer's quarters. Border trading posts like the one at Castolon were lively trade centers that brought together people from both sides of the border and also served as important border points for U.S. forces during the Mexican Revolution and both world wars. Since 1961, La Harmonia store has been operated as a concession establishment within the park. The other structures, some of which are used by the park service, are preserved as an important part of Big Bend's past. *NR 1974.*

Central park area historic sites. In the central area of the park are Homer Wilson's Blue Creek Ranch and the Sam Nail ranch house, a one-room adobe. The Homer Wilson Ranch (*NR 1975*) represents ranching during the period 1890–1940 in the Big Bend and the attempts of settlers to "make do" with what was available in the remote and sometimes hostile frontier, including indigenous construction materials such as adobe brick. The Homer Wilson Ranch includes a bunkhouse, kitchen, corral, and dipping vat and chute. It is accessible from the road to Castolon (a 0.25-mile hike).

Comanche Trail. Marker, Persimmon Gap Visitor Center. This historic trail was blazed by Comanche Indians and their allies en route from the plains into the interior of Mexico. Comanches are believed to have acquired horses, introduced by Spaniards, as early as the 1600s. By 1705 Comanches were in New Mexico and before mid-century were militarily in control of much of the Southern Plains. In the 19th century they made annual raids, usually in September, through the Trans-Pecos into Mexico.

Battling Spaniards, Mexicans, Texans, and Americans, they were the last American Indians to surrender to U.S. domination. *CM 1936.*

Glenn Spring area historic sites. Glenn Spring lies on a branch of the Comanche Trail, but flint chips and bedrock mortar holes are evidence that earlier American Indian groups used the water stop long before the Comanches conducted their raids into northern Mexico. The area is named for the first Anglo settler, H.E. Glenn. In 1914 a factory was built near the spring to produce candelilla wax, employing 40 to 60 Mexican workers who lived across Glenn Draw from the spring. Despite the presence of nine U.S. soldiers stationed at Glenn Spring, a border bandit raid in 1916 destroyed much of the factory and left several people dead or injured. The military presence there was increased and the village persisted for three years, but a decline in the price of wax added to the factory's problems, and the property was sold in 1919. The property, as part of ranch lands, changed hands several times before it was acquired by the State of Texas and donated to the federal government for a national park. A few stone and adobe house ruins survive in the Mexican workers settlement on the west side of Glenn Draw. On the east side of the draw are foundations of the residences, store, and wax factory that relate to the commercial development of Glenn Spring, as well as foundations of cavalry outpost structures, parade grounds, and perimeter defensive fortifications that relate to the military occupation following the Glenn Spring raid. The historic site is accessible by high-clearance 4-wheel-drive vehicle.

Gomez Spring area historic site. In this area only one adobe structure remains, identified as Gomez Spring area house #1. The one-room adobe had rock foundations and two windows on the east and west walls. This site is accessible only by a 1.5-mile cross-country hike.

Luna's Jacal area. Located on Maverick Rd. Luna's jacal (*NR 1974*) was built about 1900 by Gilberto Luna near the Comanche War Trail. It was originally a partial dugout structure, with a sod roof and wood, stone, and adobe walls. Restoration of the structure included replacing the sod roof with concrete. Another stone ruin, 0.5 mile south of Luna's on the Maverick Road, was the residence of Tomás Hernandes. Both structures are associated with floodplain farming along a tributary of the Rio Grande.

Mariscal Mine. Ruins include stone, adobe, concrete, and brush structures related to the Mariscal Mine, which was an active mercury mine from about 1900 to 1923. The Mexican mine workers packed in water and wood by burro from distances as far as 5 to 20 miles for both mining operations and community use. Mine shafts and furnace ruins can still be seen here. *NR 1974.*

Rancho Estelle Ruins (Sublett Farm). Located between Castolon and Santa Elena Canyon. The stone and adobe structures, all now roofless except for the farmhand's *casita*, mark the site of the ranch first owned by L.V. Steele, who inherited the land from a wealthy Mexican rancher, a member of his wife's family. The site is associated with floodplain farming along the Rio Grande. The ranch was purchased by James Sublett and E.W. Dorgan in 1918. *NR 1974.*

Luna's jacal, Big Bend National Park. Photo by Tom Alex, courtesy of Big Bend National Park.

Events and Scenic Drives

Rio Grande Village: International Good Neighbor Day Fiesta. Mid-October in Rio Grande Village, 20 miles E of park headquarters. This celebration of international goodwill draws participants and entertainers from both sides of the Rio Grande. The fiesta features arts and crafts, traditional foods, cultural and educational programs, and a variety of games and entertainments.

El Camino del Rio (FM 170). This scenic drive extends from the western edge of the park to Lajitas, Redford, Presidio, and beyond. A well-traveled highway, it is one of the most spectacular drives in the nation and offers an opportunity to view areas of this rugged country that have remained largely unchanged since prehistoric times.

DEL RIO AND VICINITY, Val Verde County

Del Rio (pop. 30,705) grew from a settlement on the Rio Grande established by Spanish missionaries in 1635 and originally known as San Felipe del Río. The mission lasted only briefly, but the name survived until the late 1800s. The permanent community of San Felipe del Río was founded when the San Felipe Agricultural, Manufacturing, and Irrigation Co. (organized in 1869) promoted settlement by giving land along San Felipe Creek as wages to its employees. Further growth was spurred by the arrival of the railroad in 1880 and 1884, but sheep and goat ranching are still a primary industry in the area. The name of the community was shortened to Del Rio in 1883. Del Rio is the county seat of Val Verde County.

Historic and Cultural Resources

Amistad National Recreation Area. Headquarters on US 90 at the northern edge of Del Rio. Offers recreational facilities and campgrounds, administered by the National Park Service, and centered around Amistad International Reservoir. The dam that created this reservoir on the junction of the Devils, Pecos, and Rio Grande rivers was a joint U.S.-Mexico project and takes its name from the Spanish word for friendship. Overlooking the lake from the Mexican side is a massive stone statue of Tlaloc, the rain god. Also impressive is the international boundary marker at Amistad, which includes bronze statues of both the American and Mexican eagles. Panther Cave, one of the most spectacular prehistoric rock art sites in Texas, is located on the edge of Lake Amistad (access by boat only). Headquarters open Mon.–Fri. 8–5.

Brown Plaza. Cantu St. Brown Plaza, dedicated on Cinco de Mayo, 1908, has served as a gathering place for the community and the scene of many musical concerts, political rallies, and formal promenades. The plaza, with its beautiful bandstand and *faux bois* benches, was restored in 1969.

Cementerio Loma de la Cruz. Near SW city limits of Del Rio; take Garza St. W off US 277 (Margarite Ave.), S on Artega, then W on Noriega to Puerta Colorado and over bridge. Early land developer Paula Losoya Taylor Rivers gave land for this cemetery in 1884 to be used by Del Rio's Mexican colony. The Rev. Ramón V. Palomares, first pastor of Del Rio's Mexican-American Methodist Church, is buried here. Use of this cemetery was discontinued in 1933. *SM 1987.*

Chihuahua Road. Marker, on US 90, 8 mi. E of Del Rio, at E end of bridge. The Chihuahua Road connected Chihuahua, Mexico, with the Texas port of Indianola. Opened to exploit trade in Mexican silver and gold, it was an important trade route until the railroad came to San Antonio in 1877. *SM 1968.*

Del Rio Plaza. Bounded by Greenwood, Griner, and Garfield Ave. This classic plaza was given to the city by the Women's Civic League and dedicated to the American soldier in 1918. The plaza features a bandstand and *faux bois* benches.

First Methodist Church. Spring and Pecan Sts. The First Methodist Church, built in 1930, is a beautiful example of Spanish Revival architecture. The elaborate detailing of the façade was influenced by the Cathedral in Mexico City and the Alamo in San Antonio.

Paula Losoya House (Taylor-Rivers House). At Hudson and Nicholson Sts. The oldest house in Del Rio, this one-story adobe residence was built in the 1870s for James H. Taylor, one of the five founders of Del Rio, and his wife Paula Losoya. After Taylor's death, Paula married Charles Rivers and later operated the home as a boarding house. She became a benefactress for the city's Mexican community, contributing land for a school and cemetery, and she also is credited with having introduced irrigation and the growing of grapes to the Del Rio area. The house, originally a walled hacienda, remained in her family until 1939. *SM 1982.*

Our Lady of Guadalupe Church. 509 Garza St. This parish was

Brown Plaza, Del Rio. Photo by Cathryn Hoyt, THC.

Paula Losoya House, Del Rio. Photo by Cathryn Hoyt, THC.

Above: Roswell Apartments, Del Rio. Photo by Cathryn Hoyt, THC.

Above left: Historic photograph of the Val Verde Winery, Del Rio. Courtesy of Whitehead Memorial Museum.

founded in 1906 to meet the needs of Catholics in the Barrio de San Felipe section of Del Rio. The original frame church was replaced with one made of adobe, and the present brick church was built in 1918. The church was renovated in 1935, but the sanctuary, sacristy, and façade remain from the 1918 building. In 1966 stained glass windows were added and new pews were installed.

Roswell Apartments. Garfield Ave. at Griner St. This six-story, blonde-brick apartment building, built in the 1920s, features an arcade that is a wonderful mixture of Gothic, Spanish, and Mayan Revival styles. The columns and faces within the cast-stone detailing are derived from the Gothic, the framing of the faces shows strong Mayan influence, and the arches are Spanish.

San Felipe Springs. Marker, grounds of City Water Commission Building. San Felipe Springs is the third largest spring in Texas and feeds over 90,000,000 gallons of pure water into San Felipe Creek each day. The springs have a long recorded history as an oasis for explorers, soldiers, and freighters. In 1675 priests named the seven springs for the king of Spain. In the 18th century Comanches camped here on their war trail into Mexico. In 1808 a mission was established three miles downstream on San Felipe Creek. By the 1850s the springs were an important water source on the Chihuahua Road trade route. After settlers came in 1864, an *acequia madre* for irrigation was dug, parts of which are still in use. *SM 1966.*

Val Verde Winery. 100 Qualia Dr.; access via Pecan St. south. An Italian-American family enterprise in its fourth generation, the winery was founded in 1883. Grapes had been grown in the area since 1825, but the winery introduced other varieties from Spain, America, and Mexico. Tommy Qualia, the third-generation Qualia to operate the winery, has said that his grandfather got the original Lenoir grapes from Paula Losoya Tay-

International Chapel at the Whitehead Memorial Museum, Del Rio. Photo by Cathryn Hoyt, THC.

Raúl Valdez mural at Brown Plaza, Del Rio. Photo by Cathryn Hoyt, THC.

lor Rivers and her husband, and that the root stock at the winery is descended from these historic plants. The Lenoir grape, also known as the Black Spanish grape, was introduced into Texas from Mexico. The thick-walled adobe structure that housed the original winery is now the tasting room and is open to the public Mon.–Sat. 9–5. *SM 1971.*

Whitehead Memorial Museum. 1308 S. Main St. The museum complex is made up of several structures. The Perry Mercantile building, built in 1870, was once one of the largest mercantile establishments between San

Antonio and El Paso. The Hacienda building, which retains the original sales desk and registration unit, now contains Mexican-American exhibits. A recently completed chapel also is part of the museum complex and is dedicated to the area's Spanish heritage. The museum's permanent exhibits include items relating to the Spanish Colonial period, Mexico, Mexican-Americans, and American Indians. Open Tues.–Sat. 9–11:30 and 1–4:30.

Public Art

Amistad sin Fronteras, by Raúl Valdez, principal artist, assisted by local students. 1980, restored 1990. Intersection of Las Vacas Rd. and Ware St. This 8×24-foot, outdoor mural painted on concrete depicts themes of international friendship, as indicated in the title, which means "Friendship without Borders."

Brown Plaza mural, by Raúl Valdez, principal artist, assisted by local students. 1980, restored 1990. In Brown Plaza, Cantu St. This 8×24-foot mural on outdoor duraply panels features images chosen by the students as representative of their personal experiences in growing up on the border. Images include justice and injustice, corn, lowriders, and the death of a Hispanic Viet Nam veteran.

Sculpture. *See* Amistad Recreation Area entry.

Festivals

Cinco de Mayo Celebration. Weekend nearest May 5, at Brown Plaza. Festivities include traditional music and foods. Sponsored by Brown Plaza Association and City of Del Rio. For information contact City Manager's Office, 109 W. Broadway, Del Rio 78840.

Diez y Seis de Septiembre. Weekend nearest September 16, at Brown Plaza. Diez y Seis de Septiembre has been celebrated in Del Rio since the early 1900s. Saturday evening festivities include music, dancing, games, and food. The traditional Grito and speeches are presented on Sunday. Sponsored by Brown Plaza Association and the City of Del Rio; for information contact City Manager's Office, 109 W. Broadway, Del Rio 78840.

Fiesta de Amistad. Mid-October, at various locations. The citywide fiesta celebrates friendship between Del Rio and Ciudad Acuña, Mexico; events include parades, pageants, and an arts and crafts show. Sponsored by International Good Neighbor Council.

Border City

Ciudad Acuña, Mexico. Offers restaurants and shopping for handmade crafts and souvenirs. Most shops offering crafts and souvenirs are clustered on Hidalgo St., near the International Bridge and within walking distance of parking areas on the Del Rio side. Fiesta de Amistad, celebrated on both sides of the bridge, is held annually in October.

ELDORADO, Schleicher County

Eldorado (pop. 2,019) is located on the Edwards Plateau where lack of water discouraged settlement until wells were first drilled in the early 1880s. The sale of school lands at the turn of the century brought in other settlers and ranchers, and Schleicher County was organized in 1901, with Eldorado as the county seat. A livestock and wool center, Eldorado was established in 1895 and is the only town in the county.

Schleicher County Museum. US 190 just E of US 277. Collections include ranching items such as saddles, branding irons, and barbed wire. Open Mon., Wed., and Fri. in summer.

FABENS, El Paso County

Fabens (pop. 5,599) is located on land that originally was part of the San Elizario grant, but the town dates from the 20th century. It was laid out in 1911 and was named for a railroad company official. Although not an early settlement, Fabens offers opportunities to see examples of the adobe houses that characterize Hispanic vernacular architecture in far western Texas.

Our Lady of Guadalupe Catholic Church. SH 20 and W. 1st St. This church, with its unusually detailed, offset bell tower, was inspired by the architecture of the California missions. Above the front entrance of the church is a fine mosaic depicting Our Lady of Guadalupe.

FORT DAVIS AND VICINITY, Jeff Davis County

Fort Davis (pop. ca. 1,000) grew around, and is named for, the famous frontier fort established in 1854. The town managed to survive when the fort was abandoned in 1891, and the local economy is now largely based on tourism relating to Fort Davis and the Davis Mountains. Adobe houses, which still exist on the unpaved back streets of the town, and the historic old adobe church provide additional attractions. Fort Davis is the county seat of Jeff Davis County.

Chihuahuan Desert Visitor Center. SH 118, 3.5 mi. S of Fort Davis. The vast, arid Chihuahuan Desert includes northwestern Mexico and most of the Trans-Pecos. Visitors interested in the region and its plants as it was when the first explorers encountered the American Indians who lived here should contact the Chihuahuan Desert Research Center at Sul Ross in Alpine for access to the center's lands.

Davis Mountains State Park. 6 mi. W of Fort Davis, SH 118 and Park Rd. 3. Another excellent source for nature study in the region, the park also offers hiking, camping, picnicking, dining room, trailer facilities, and rest rooms. Indian Lodge, the park headquarters, was built by the Civilian Conservation Corps in the mid-1930s and is constructed of adobe in Puebloan Revival style. The adobe walls of the 39-room lodge are 18 inches thick, and many of the original furnishings from the 1930s still are in use.

Left: Indian Lodge, Davis Mountains State Park. Roy W. Aldrich Papers, courtesy Barker Texas History Center, General Libraries, University of Texas at Austin.

Below: Adobe Officer's Quarters, Fort Davis National Historic Site. THC photo.

Fort Davis National Historic Site. 4 mi. W of town of Fort Davis via SH 118. The original fort was established before the Civil War to wage war against the Comanches and Mescalero Apaches. The fort was re-established in 1867, and 53 historic structures, both ruins and restorations of adobe, stone, and wood, date from the second era (1867–91). Reconstruction of the post–Civil War fort began in 1867 under Lt. Col. Wesley Merritt. The first buildings were of stone, but the need for economy soon caused a change to adobe. Restored structures, such as the 1885–86 Officers' Quarters, are excellent examples of the use of indigenous adobe bricks in frontier fort construction. The fort was acquired by the National Park Service in 1963, and periodic reconstruction continues. Archival holdings, not on exhibit, include photos and documents related to Mexican families who were connected with Fort Davis. *CM 1936; NHL.*

Músquiz Ranch Site. Marker, SH 118, 6 mi. SE of Fort Davis. The marker commemorates the adobe homesite of Manuel Músquiz, a pioneer who settled here in 1854. The homesite was abandoned because of Indian resistance to settlement in the area but was used intermittently in the early 1880s as a ranger station. *CM 1936.*

St. Joseph's Catholic Church. SH 17 across from Fort Davis. St. Joseph's parish was established in 1876 and the church was built in 1892. St. Joseph's parish once included all of the Big Bend west to Van Horn, north to Balmorhea, and east to Marathon. Chapels in the small towns of the region were served by missionary priests. St. Joseph's Church is an adobe structure in Gothic Revival style, an intriguing example of the popular religious architectural style of the turn of the century expressed in indigenous construction materials and construction techniques. Many of the parishioners are descendants of soldiers who once served at Fort Davis, married here, and remained in the community.

FORT STOCKTON, Pecos County

Fort Stockton (pop. 8,524) is located at the crossing of the Old San Antonio Road and the Comanche War Trail. A major West Texas crossroads, the town developed following the establishment of the fort in 1859 and is now the county seat of Pecos County.

Historic Sites

Adobe Structures in St. Gall area. The St. Gall area, in the southeast part of Fort Stockton on Comanche Creek, is the oldest section of the town, and adobe structures are common here. Many are stuccoed and painted in bright colors, while others are bare adobe brick. In addition to those included in the Fort Stockton Historic District, there are several houses that have been recognized as historic structures. Look for private historical markers identifying the Albert Valadez Home—which predates the Riggs Museum building—the Will Rooney House, and the Anna Achterberg House. The house (unnamed; *RTHL 1966*) at 201 W. Sherrer

St. was built before 1859 and is the oldest residence in Fort Stockton. This adobe house, which originally had a thatched roof, is the only structure remaining from the original St. Gall townsite. *See also* Fort Stockton Historic District.

Comanche Springs. Springs Dr. at entrance to Rooney Park. Now the site of a swimming pool, Comanche Springs was once among the largest springs in Texas. Famous for its location on the Comanche War Trail, this area also lies on the projected routes of early Spanish explorers such as Cabeza de Vaca (1530s), Espejo (1583), and Mendoza (1684).

Fort Stockton Historic District. Area of older part of the city, generally lying E of Water St. and S to Springs Dr. In addition to the remains of Old Fort Stockton, this National Register District includes a number of buildings that were either directly related to the fort or to the history of the old part of the city during the frontier fort period. All of the historic buildings included here are adobe structures that reflect the use of indigenous, traditional construction materials and methods. *NR 1973.*

Annie Riggs Memorial Museum. 301 S. Main St. The building that houses the museum is an excellent example of the use of adobe brick in frontier Victorian construction. Buildings of this type, known as Territorial style, are more common in New Mexico than in Texas. Exhibits include Mexican woven saddle blankets, serapes, and crafts of the region. *RTHL 1966.*

Old Fort Stockton. E. Third and Rooney Sts. At the juncture of the Old San Antonio Road and the Comanche War Trail, Fort Stockton (established in 1859) was one of the many frontier forts established in West Texas during the struggle between Indians and the U.S. Army for control of the West. During the Civil War the fort was occupied by Confederate forces, and federal troops did not return until 1868, when permanent building was begun at the present site. The reactivation of the fort and the presence of troops there until 1886 provided the stimulus for the growth and development of the town. Originally, the fort consisted of 35 buildings, only 2 of which were built of limestone blocks. All others were made of adobe. Remains of the fort include a stone guardhouse, 3 officers' quarters of adobe construction on stone foundations, and stone foundations of what is believed to have been barracks. One of the officers' quarters has been restored to its 1870s appearance with the exception of one room that was left bare of the plaster finish so that visitors could examine the adobe construction. The historic cemetery used as the burial grounds for both the troops and the civilian population is located at Water and 8th Sts. *CM 1936; RTHL 1966.*

Grey Mule Saloon. 219 S. Main St. Built in the 1880s, this saloon is constructed of stucco-covered adobe. It was once frequented by troopers as well as hotel guests. *RTHL 1966.*

Rollins-Sibley House. Second St. and Springs Dr. Located at the site of the post hospital, this Victorian house is a stuccoed adobe structure with a gallery across the front (south) façade.

St. Joseph's Catholic Church. 403 S. Main St. In 1872 the first priests

St. Joseph Catholic Church, Fort Stockton. Courtesy of St. Joseph Catholic Church.

assigned to Fort Stockton held services in a chapel near the river. In 1874 the donation of three acres for a church near Comanche Springs was registered, and a permanent church was built in 1877. It was described as an adobe building with stone foundation and a flat roof of mud and tule. The beams for the roof were brought by mule from San Antonio. Unfortunately, the original roof proved too weak for the size of the structure and caved in after only two years. By the 1880s the church itself was in danger of falling into ruin. In the 1890s a new roof was placed on it, and new doors and windows were provided. For many years the church was served by visiting priests until the Fort Stockton parish was established in 1916. Improvements made between 1917 and the 1940s included replacing the roof, repairing the north and south wings and adding windows, moving the bell tower to its present position and altering the original simple façade. Other additions included stained glass windows and a chapel for Our Lady of Guadalupe. Many interior improvements have since been made, but the original adobe walls remain, making St. Joseph's one of the oldest adobe churches in the Trans-Pecos region. Major devotional celebrations during the year include St. Joseph's Day (March 19), those of the

Easter season, and the feast day of Our Lady of Guadalupe (December 12). *RTHL 1966. See also* Fiesta de San Juan.

Young's Store. 207 E. Gallagher St. Established in 1876, the F.W. Young Store, an adobe structure, served as both store and residence for the former post sutler. *RTHL 1966.*

Festivals and Events

Chili Cook-off. Labor Day weekend, in September, at Menudo Acres on Pecos Hwy. Offers a weekend of fun, music, dancing, and plenty of red-hot chili. Traditional Mexican music usually is included in the musical entertainment offerings.

Cinco de Mayo. May 5 or closest weekend, at 122–200 block of Main St. This Cinco de Mayo festival in Fort Stockton was initiated in 1988 and includes ballet folklórico performed by local schoolchildren dressed in traditional costumes, conjunto music, arts and crafts displays, and traditional foods. For information contact Main Street Project, Box 1000, Fort Stockton 78735.

Fiesta de San Juan. Weekend closest to June 24, at St. Joseph's Church. The fiesta began in 1959, when Fort Stockton celebrated its centennial. One day of that week-long event was assigned to the Mexican-American population of the town—June 24, the feast day of San Juan de Bautista—and the sponsoring committee thus named the day Fiesta de San Juan. The organizations of St. Joseph's Church began sponsorship of the fiesta in 1969. Events of this family-oriented celebration include a parade, queen and tiny tots contest, mariachi music, a barbecue, and dances. For information contact St. Joseph's Catholic Church, P.O. Box 1024, Fort Stockton 79735.

Menudo Cook-off. Memorial Day weekend in May. The menudo cook-off is a popular and well-attended Hispanic community event in Fort Stockton. Festivities include traditional foods and music, games and contests, and a Saturday (and sometimes Sunday) night dance.

GIRVIN VICINITY, Pecos County

Girvin (pop. ca. 30), a small local trade center dating from the turn of the century, is the nearest community to the historic locale known as Horsehead Crossing.

Horsehead Crossing on the Pecos River. Marker, on FM 11, 10 mi. N of Girvin in eastern Pecos County. The canyons of the Pecos were a barrier to exploration and settlement of the Trans-Pecos. Horsehead Crossing was one of only three crossings where explorers and settlers moving west could enter the region. A point on the Comanche War Trail, it is also remembered as a landmark on the Chihuahua Road and the Goodnight-Loving cattle trail. The stretch of the river on which the crossing was located is on private property, not open to the public. *SM 1974.*

GUADALUPE MOUNTAINS NATIONAL PARK,
Culberson and Hudspeth Counties

Guadalupe Mountains National Park. Main entrance, US 62/180 near Pine Springs. This park, which encompasses over 75,000 acres, includes the southernmost reaches of the Guadalupe Mountains. In the 17th century Apachean groups made the Guadalupe Mountains their stronghold, and they inhabited the mountainous areas between the Pecos and the Rio Grande until their final subjugation in the 1880s. Rare mixtures of plant and animal life can be viewed in the park, which offers a wide range of environmental zones. The mountains, which are penetrated by canyons, support forests that are in marked contrast to the surrounding desert. The park offers over eight miles of hiking trails, camping facilities, water, and rest rooms. Frijole Visitor Center is located on US 62/180 near Pine Springs.

Guadalupe Peak. Marker, on E side of US 62/180 in rest area at foot of El Capitan, Culberson County. Guadalupe Peak is the highest mountain in Texas at 8,751 feet. Stories of hidden gold in this area go back to Spanish days. Conquistadores who rode north from Mexico wrote about fabulous gold deposits, and Apaches later contributed to the myth, as did prospectors of the 1880s. Legends of Spanish treasure, though intangible, are an essential element of Texas' Hispanic heritage, and many a tale-telling session and frontier story would be the poorer without them.

Salt War. At the western base of Guadalupe Peak, near the small community of Salt Flat, Hudspeth County, are the salt deposits over which a bloody dispute known as the Salt War took place in the 1860s and 1870s. The disagreement arose over ownership of mineral rights, which in the Hispanic legal tradition were the property of the state. Following the Civil War, the state government introduced the concept of private ownership of mineral rights, and the local people soon were embroiled in a fight over rights to the salt. The salt trade was important to the economy of Mexicans and Mexican-Americans in the towns along the Rio Grande, especially in dry years when crops failed. However, businessmen in El Paso, including both Anglo- and Mexican-Americans, also viewed the salt as an economic opportunity. Before the dispute was over, it involved U.S. and Mexican citizens, the law and the military, and murder and assassination. Today Salt Flat, the small community that grew up near the surface salt deposits, has a population of fewer than 40 people. Some of the salt deposits may still be seen today from US 62/180, and a historical marker is located on the highway. *CM 1936.*

HUECO TANKS, El Paso County

Hueco Tanks State Historical Park. Off US 62/180 24 mi. E of El Paso, then 8 mi. N on FM 2775. The park is named for natural cisterns, or *huecos,* that trap rainwater. For centuries Hueco Tanks was a major watering place for Indians, emigrants, and travelers. Near here the Apache challenged those who wished to pass through their country. Also famous as an

Indian rock art site, Hueco Tanks contains over 2,000 pictographs dating from 8000 B.C. to 19th-century Apache, including early historic Indian depictions of horses. The Tiguas of El Paso claim association with some of the rock art of the historic period, and their pottery reflects designs found at the site. In 1858 a Butterfield Overland Mail station was established here, and its stone and adobe remains can still be seen. Permanent settlement came only at the turn of the century, when Silverio Escontrias established a ranch in 1898. The family ranch continued until 1956, and some of the buildings and a dam remain. Acquired by the state in 1969, the 860-acre park offers facilities for picnicking, hiking, climbing, and camping. Administered by Texas Parks and Wildlife Dept. *CM 1936; NR 1971.*

Adobe guest house at Indian Hot Springs resort, Indian Hot Springs. THC photo.

INDIAN HOT SPRINGS, Hudspeth County

Indian Hot Springs. On the Rio Grande, off FM 1111, S of Sierra Blanca. This locale was the scene of final skirmishes between U.S. forces and Victorio's Apaches in the early 1880s. The main building of the resort, built in the early 20th century, with its stuccoed walls and flat roof, reflects regional Southwestern architectural styles. The resort centers around a series of thermal springs that have been a locale for human occupation since prehistoric times. The residence was once occupied by a local Anglo practitioner of traditional Mexican healing practices. A border crossing formerly existed here, at a footbridge leading to the settlement that lies across the border. Privately owned and isolated. *NR 1990.*

IRAAN, Pecos County

Iraan (pop. 1,322) is an oil town that dates from the mid-1920s.

Iraan Museum. Alley Oop Park at W city limits. The permanent exhibits of this small museum include some Hispanic materials dating from the Spanish Colonial period to the present, as well as Historic Indian artifacts. Open Wed.–Sun. 2–6.

LAJITAS AND VICINITY, Brewster County

Lajitas (pop. less than 100), on FM 170 about 20 mi. from the western edge of Big Bend National Park, obtained its name (from a Spanish term meaning "little flags") from prominent, flat rock outcroppings in the area. The village is located at the San Carlos crossing of the Rio Grande, where the Comanche War Trail crossed the river. There had long been a Mexican settlement here, but most of the residents moved into the interior of Mexico, seeking protection from the Plains Indians who raided along the trail in the 19th century. Mexicans, as well as Mexican-Americans from the Presidio and Shafter areas, returned to the area in the early 20th century. The village grew when an army post was established to protect the Big Bend area from raids led by Francisco ("Pancho") Villa and when

H.W. McGuirk began farming activities that provided jobs. McGuirk, an Irish Catholic, married Josefa Navarro, a descendant of José Antonio Navarro, and was instrumental in the construction of the first Catholic church here in 1901. The original trading post at Lajitas is still a gathering place for local workers and is full of interesting historic relics of the region, such as burro packsaddles. A modern resort has been developed here and caters to tourists year round. An interesting attraction of the "new town" is a mission-style chapel. The surrounding area is an excellent locale for viewing typical Chihuahuan Desert scenery, including plants such as yucca (the low-growing variety known as Spanish Dagger, and two larger species), sotol, cholla, agave (the century plant is the best known of this species), ocotillo, desert willow, creosote bush, ceniza, candelilla, and numerous varieties of cactus. Many of these plants have been utilized for thousands of years as sources of food, fiber, and construction materials. Remember, however, that many desert plants are both rare and fragile, and should be loved and left.

Big Bend Ranch State Natural Area. Access to tours from Lajitas or Fort Leaton State Historic Site, Presidio. The 260,000-acre natural area, recently acquired by the Texas Parks and Wildlife Dept., is located just west of Big Bend National Park. Long noted for its environmental uniqueness, the natural area is also a rich preserve of both prehistoric archeological sites and historic sites associated with ranching in the area. There are several adobe ruins and structures in the park, including the original ranch headquarters. Quarters for vaqueros as well as fencework and stockpens reflect traditional Hispanic construction materials and techniques. In order to protect the area's fragile environment, access to the park is limited to guided tours, controlled back-country hiking, and permitted river use. The visitor center (*see* Barton Warnock Environmental Education Center below) is located in Lajitas.

El Camino del Rio (the River Road). Popular name for FM 170 that stretches from near Big Bend National Park, NW through Presidio to Candelaria. Upriver from Presidio the highway skirts the southern edge of the Chinati Mountains. The most scenic stretch of the road lies between Lajitas and Redford, a small community to the west in Presidio County. The highway follows the twisting bed of the Rio Grande through a scenic vista of rugged mountains and canyons. Between Presidio and Redford lies the area of the Rio Grande where Antonio de Espejo visited the Indian groups popularly known as the Jumanos in the late 1500s. Cabeza de Vaca also is thought to have passed through this area in the 1530s. Past Presidio, visit the villages of Ruidosa and Candelaria, which both offer adobe buildings and ruins. Watch for the old cemeteries along the road, see the adobe church ruin in Ruidosa, and visit the village store in Candelaria before returning to Presidio.

Barton Warnock Environmental Education Center (formerly Lajitas Museum and Desert Garden). FM 170 E of "downtown" Lajitas, near Terlingua. Displays focus on the archeology, geology, history, and wildlife of the region. Big Bend wildlife comes to life in three-dimensional dioramas. Historic materials cover the Spanish Colonial period to the present, as well as Southwestern Indian items. The garden features a wide variety of Chihuahuan Desert and regional plants. The center also serves as the Visitor Information Center for Big Bend Ranch State Natural Area. Open daily 9–5.

Paso Lajitas. Across the river from Lajitas is a small Mexican village, and boat rides across the Rio Grande are available. Drinking *cerveza* and eating border-style Mexican food are the two main entertainments offered.

LANGTRY VICINITY, Val Verde County

Langtry (pop. ca. 150) is located in the area visited by Capt. José Berroterán in 1728 in his unsuccessful search for a presidio location in the Lower Pecos region. The town was established when the railroad was being constructed through the region in the 1880s. Significant examples of adobe construction remain in the town, but Langtry is best known as the locale of Judge Roy Bean's saloon and courtroom, in which this colorful individual ruled as the "Law West of the Pecos" in the late 1800s. Statewide travel information and literature is available at the Judge Roy Bean Visitor Center, which is operated by the Texas Dept. of Transportation.

Small historic cemeteries, such as this one in Ruidosa, can be seen along El Camino del Rio. Photo by Dan Utley, THC.

After crossing the Pecos River Bridge, visitors traveling west are officially in the beautiful Trans-Pecos region. Photo by Cathryn Hoyt, THC.

Seminole Canyon State Park. US 90, 20 mi. E of Langtry. Seminole Canyon State Park contains plants and animals native to the Texas Hill Country, the Tamaulipas Thorn Scrub, and the Chihuahuan Desert. The rugged limestone terrain offers sparse vegetation and deep canyons, Seminole Canyon being one of the more spectacular. Prehistoric remains in the area extend back to at least 8,000 years ago. In this part of the state, where the Pecos River meets the Rio Grande, steep banks were undercut to form shelters in which early inhabitants lived. As well as archeological remains, these people left visual records on the stone walls of their desert homes. Manlike figures, plants, animals, and abstract designs are depicted. The Park Headquarters Visitor Center contains exhibits depicting the lifeways of prehistoric people based on artifacts and rock art and traces the history of the region to modern times. Exhibits include Spanish Colonial, Mexican, and Mexican-American materials, as well as photographic examples of the rock art of Lipan and Mescalero Apaches. Fate Bell Shelter in Seminole Canyon is accessible by guided tour (Tues.–Sat. 10–3); strenuous hiking is involved. The park also offers other hiking trails and picnicking and camping facilities. Headquarters open 8–5 daily.

Scenic Overlook. US 90, ca. 18 mi. E of Langtry. A roadside park overlooking the Pecos River provides a spectacular view and insight into the importance of historic crossings on the Pecos River, such as Horse-head Crossing (*see* Girvin). The steep canyon of the Pecos River was a formidable barrier to travel between the Trans-Pecos and the rest of the state in the days before railroads and modern bridges.

MARATHON AND VICINITY, Brewster County

Marathon (pop. ca. 800), a ranch country town, is the gateway to Big Bend National Park via US 385.

First School House in Brewster County, Marathon. Photo by Cathryn Hoyt, THC.

First School House in Brewster County. San Antonio St. This adobe school house, built in 1888, is the oldest surviving building in Brewster County. The windows and chimney are framed by beautiful native stone inlays. *RTHL 1965.*

Gage Hotel. Ave. C and US 90. Texas and Mexican antiques and Southwestern atmosphere can be found in this charming historic hotel, built in 1927. In 1991 a pueblo-style adobe addition was constructed west of the hotel. *RTHL 1981.*

Leoncita Springs. Marker, 42 mi. NW of Marathon. The first recorded use of the springs was in 1684 when Juan Domínguez de Mendoza camped here. The locale was later the site of a stagecoach stop on the San Antonio to El Paso route through Musquiz Canyon. *CM 1936.*

St. Mary's Catholic Church. 211 W. San Antonio. This simple, stuccoed Gothic Revival adobe church was built about 1915. A tilework shrine to the Virgin Mary can be seen on the wall directly in front of the church.

MARFA, Presidio County

Marfa (pop. 2,424), a ranching town, is famous for the Marfa Lights that appear 9 miles east of town off US 90. The lights reportedly have been sighted since the 1800s, and their source is still a mystery. Adobe buildings are common in Marfa, and excellent examples of small, vernacular adobe and wood-frame houses, as well as other structures such as the adobe compound wall on US 90 and Kelly St., can be seen around town. Marfa is the county seat of Presidio County.

El Paisano Hotel. N. Highland and W. Texas Sts. This two-story, U-plan structure is built of stuccoed, reinforced concrete and features finely cast Spanish Baroque "cartouche" work. Trost and Trost were the architects for this 1928 Spanish Revival style building. *NR 1978; RTHL 1979.*

Courtyard of El Paisano Hotel, Marfa. Photo by Cathryn Hoyt, THC.

309

Marfa and Presidio County Museum. 221 N. Mesa. County history, from prehistoric times to the present, is the focus of this small museum. Mexican-American materials are occasionally exhibited. Open Wed. 2–5.

St. Mary's Catholic Church. On US 90 and Austin Sts. The church is an adobe structure in modified Gothic style, with lovely stained-glass windows. From 1876 until the establishment of the parish here in 1899, Catholics in this area were included in the parish of St. Joseph's Church in Fort Davis. Movie buffs and lovers of obscure Texana items will be interested in the fact that a scene from the movie *Giant* was filmed here.

OZONA AND VICINITY, Crockett County

Ozona (pop. 3,181) was named county seat in 1891, although the town was then only an oil-well site. The first settlements in the county were outposts on the Chihuahua Road and stage stops along the route to California. Ozona, now a ranching and oil-industry center, is the only town in Crockett County.

Chihuahua Road and Escondido Water Hole. Marker, in the parking area, Fort Lancaster State Historic Site, about 35 mi. W of Ozona on US 290 Scenic Loop. A small part of the Chihuahua Road along the nearby Pecos River was followed by Gaspar Castaño de Sosa in 1590. By 1850 the route was extended to connect the city of Chihuahua and the Texas Gulf Coast, by way of San Antonio. Heaviest use came during the mid-1870s when freighters transported silver and copper from Chihuahua for shipment to the eastern United States. Escondido Water Hole was a landmark along the route in this area. *SM 1976.*

Crockett County Museum. 404 11th St. (US 290) in Ozona. Local and regional history exhibits include materials from the prehistoric period, historic Fort Lancaster, and tools of the working cowboy. This small museum has exceptionally fine interpretive exhibits in its Indian Room. Open March–October 10–6; November–February, 1–5.

Fort Lancaster State Historic Site. Sheffield vicinity, about 35 mi. W of Ozona on US 290 Scenic Loop. Stabilized ruins of adobe walls and limestone chimney remains from the frontier fort dating to the pre–Civil War period are the focus of this historic site. Museum displays include materials from the nearby Live Oak Creek Archeological District. The 70 sites in this National Register district span thousands of years of human occupation and include burned-rock and ring middens, rockshelters, and rock art, as well as Fort Lancaster. The district encompasses sites in Crockett, Pecos, and Terrell counties. *NR 1971.* Modern visitor-interpretive center open Wed.–Sun. 8–5.

Cinco de Mayo. In Ozona, in early May, at Parish Hall grounds, Our Lady of Perpetual Help Catholic Church (302 Vitela). For many years the church has sponsored a local celebration of Cinco de Mayo. The annual, two-day event features, on the first day, the crowning of a queen and an evening dance. The next day features a traditional Mexican dinner, and during the day games and food booths offer family fun.

West Texas jacal near Presidio in 1936. Courtesy of Institute of Texan Cultures.

PECOS AND VICINITY, Reeves County

Pecos (pop. 12,069) developed as a station on the Texas and Pacific railway in 1881. Pecos is the largest town in, and county seat of, Reeves County. The earliest settlers in the county were Mexican farmers who settled near the Pecos River and dug canals to irrigate their crops. Historic events, such as Cinco de Mayo, are observed in the community or marked by special exhibits at the West of the Pecos Museum (First and Cedar Sts.).

Spanish Explorers. Marker, 5 mi. E of Pecos at junction of FM 1450 and US 285 and at the West of the Pecos Museum, First and Cedar Sts. The marker relates Spanish exploration of the Pecos River: Antonio de Espejo, in 1583, was the first to explore the river, which he called Río de las Vacas for the buffalo in the area; and Castaño de Sosa, in 1590, was the first to travel the river's full length. *SM 1966.*

Diez y Seis de Septiembre. Mid-September, at Santa Rosa Church. Mariachi music performed by local groups, traditional foods and dance, as well as a parade, are the main events of this local, family-oriented celebration. For information contact: Santa Rosa Church, 620 E. 4th St., Pecos 79772.

PRESIDIO AND VICINITY, Presidio County

Presidio (pop. 3,072) grew from an early Spanish settlement once protected by a fort, or presidio, hence its name. The modern town on the Texas side of the river was established by 1858, but settlement in this area began in prehistoric times. Here the earliest Spanish explorers encountered Indians who lived in permanent villages and cultivated crops. The area became known as La Junta de los Ríos, and the numerous archeological sites that remain, dating from prehistoric through Spanish Colonial times, are now a designated historic district (*NR 1978*). The missions at La Junta de los Ríos were established on the Texas side of the Rio Grande in 1683–84 but were abandoned within one year. They were reoccupied intermittently until about 1717. The original inhabitants had disappeared by the time Presidio was established on the Chihuahua–San Antonio Road in the 19th century. The town developed as a trading center, supplying goods to Chihuahua, then an important mining town. During the days of the Mexican Revolution, Ojinaga, across the river, changed hands between federal and revolutionary troops five or six times, and Presidio was a lively place where both refugees and troops purchased supplies. Presidio is still the trade center for Ojinaga residents. Not for the tourist interested in shops and night life, nevertheless the Presidio–Ojinaga area offers much to the visitor who appreciates the grandeur of the area's desert scenery and its colorful human history. Adobe buildings are still common here, as they are in the nearby village of Redford and across the border in Ojinaga, and the influence of Spanish architectural style can be seen in buildings such as the public school and St. Teresa Catholic Church. The arid, rugged, but often spectacular terrain that confronted early explorers and settlers can be viewed from the scenic El Camino del Rio route (FM 170).

Big Bend Ranch State Natural Area. *See* Lajitas and Vicinity.

El Fortín de San José. Marker, Fort Leaton State Historic Site, FM 170, 4.5 mi. E of Presidio. A fortification was established here about 1773 by the Spanish garrison at Presidio del Norte to protect local farmers. It was abandoned about 1810, but a small settlement of farmers and goat herders remained in the area. After Ben Leaton acquired property in the area in 1848, the community came to be called Fort Leaton. Leaton's fortress is all that remains of the old settlement. *SM 1978.*

Fort Leaton State Historical Park. On El Camino del Rio (FM 170), 4 mi. SE of Presidio. In 1848, frontiersman Ben Leaton built a massive adobe fortress at this strategic site on the Chihuahua–San Antonio Road. Formerly in the pay of the governments of Chihuahua and Sonora to help eradicate Indians in the area, Leaton, ironically, began trading with the Apaches and Comanches. He was accused of encouraging Indian raids so that the Indians would have goods to trade, and, as a result of having played both ends against the middle, is remembered locally as *un mal hombre*. He died in 1851, survived by his wife, Juana Pedrasa, and three children. The site was donated to the state in 1968, and the Texas Parks and Wildlife Dept., using adobe bricks made near the site, has carefully restored 25 of the original 40 rooms. Fort Leaton, one of the largest standing adobe structures in the state, was built around a patio and the structure is roofed with cottonwood vigas and rajas (split cottonwood), sheathed with adobe. Exhibits cover the story of the area's violent past as well as prehistoric and historic settlers, including the agricultural Indians who farmed the floodplains at La Junta de los Ríos and the later Spanish, Mexican, and Anglo-American farmers and ranchers. Featured is a full-sized replica of a Chihuahua cart, the huge two-wheeled vehicle that plied the early trade routes of the region. Open daily, 8–4:30. *NR 1973.*

Kleinmann Store Ruins. Near the river in Presidio. Located in the sandy bottom area amid salt cedar and mesquite and near other defunct commercial structures, a roofless stone tower and scattered rubble are the remains of a store that supplied troops across the river in Ojinaga during the years of the Mexican Revolution.

Adobe chapel at Fort Leaton, Presidio. THC photo.

Mission del Apóstol Santiago Site. Marker, at Fort Leaton, 4.5 mi. E of Presidio on El Camino del Rio (FM 170). Site of one of the four missions on the Texas side of the Rio Grande established in the Big Bend country by Fray Nicolás López and Juan Domínguez de Mendoza in 1683–84, for Jumano, Julimes, and other Indians of this area. *CM 1936.*

Mission San Francisco de los Julimes Site (San Antonio de los Puliques). Marker, at Fort Leaton, 4.5 mi. E of Presidio on FM 170. Mission San Francisco de los Julimes was one of four missions established on the Texas side of the Rio Grande in the Big Bend country by Fray Nicolás López and Juan Domínguez de Mendoza in 1683–84 for Jumano, Julimes, and other Indians of this area. *CM 1936.*

St. Teresa Catholic Church. Santa Teresa de Jesús, a mission church established in the 1870s, was the predecessor of the present Catholic church in Presidio. Mission Revival influence is seen in the curved parapet and twin towers of the stuccoed adobe building.

Border City

Ojinaga, Mexico. Across the border from Presidio, Ojinaga is thought by some to be the site of an Indian village described by Cabeza de Vaca as he passed through this region in the 1530s. The town had its beginnings in Presidio del Norte (1760–1820), established here to protect the missions of the La Junta de los Ríos area. The name of the settlement was changed to Ojinaga in the mid-19th century. Milton Faver, an early Trans-Pecos rancher made famous by the TV series *Rawhide,* operated a store and freighting operation in Ojinaga during the 1870s. Many adobe houses remain along the main road and dead-end crossroads of the town. This is one of the least touristy of Mexico's border towns, but it offers a few good restaurants and bakeries that should not be missed. The old adobe church and cemetery are expressive of the long history of Hispanic Catholicism in this remote area of northern Mexico. A local legend says that Spanish priests imprisoned the devil in a mountain cave above Ojinaga, and each spring residents reenact a pilgrimage to the site; however this ancient ritual finds fewer participants each year for the strenuous trek up the mountain.

REDFORD, Presidio County

Redford (pop. ca. 110), a farming community near Presidio, originally was known as San José del Polvo. Although established on the site of one of the La Junta de los Ríos Indian villages, modern El Polvo did not begin until 1869. At that time Governor Richard Coke initiated a policy to encourage people from across the border to settle in Presidio County. El Polvo is believed to have been officially founded by the new colonists in 1871. There are a number of adobe buildings in Redford, and traditional lifeways are maintained.

Madrid Store. Here Lucia Rede Madrid established a library for the children of the Redford-Ojinaga area. The store where the library is located has been run by the Madrid family for several decades and is a center of community life in Redford. For Mrs. Madrid's contributions to education she was elected to the Texas Women's Hall of Fame in 1990. Adjacent to the store is a stone *nicho*, or yard shrine, dedicated to the Virgin Mary.

Old El Polvo Church. Ca. 1 mi. S of FM 170 (El Camino del Rio), on unpaved road. Now considered part of Redford, this locale is the site of the original Polvo settlement. The vernacular stone and adobe church was built at the turn of the century and is distinguished by its offset stone bell tower with a low hip roof. An ocular window is centered on the main façade and a semicircular transom window is placed above the wood paneled entrance doors. The church is now privately owned but may be viewed from the road.

RUIDOSA, Presidio County

Ruidosa (pop. 50) was established in 1874 when William Russell established a farm in the area to supply feed to the cavalry at Fort Davis. The town is believed to have received its name, the Spanish word for noise, because of the sound the water made falling over a dam and into an irrigation canal.

Adobe Church. This late 19th-century adobe church is considered a major landmark in West Texas for its historical significance as well as its architecture. The central entrance, with semicircular transom window and stone steps, is flanked by two hipped towers with corrugated metal roofing.

Old El Polvo Church, Redford.
Photo by Curtis Tunnell, THC.

Remains of adobe church, Ruidosa.
Photo by Dan Utley, THC.

SAN ELIZARIO, El Paso County

San Elizario (pop. 4,385), unlike Ysleta and Socorro, which were founded for religious purposes, was established as a presidio, or military garrison, to protect the missions of the El Paso del Norte area. Named for the French Saint Elcear, the presidio of San Elizario was moved 37 miles up the Rio Grande in 1789. When Mexico won its independence from

Spain in 1821, this location became a part of the state of Chihuahua. The presidio served as a nucleus for the development of the town of San Elizario, which by 1841 had a population of more than a thousand. With the outbreak of war between the United States and Mexico in 1846, American forces under Col. Alexander Doniphan found the presidio, including the chapel, in complete ruins. In 1848 the settlements of Ysleta, Socorro, and San Elizario became part of the United States, and San Elizario became the county seat of El Paso County. The county government remained here until 1873, when it was moved first to Ysleta and then to El Paso in 1883. The most famous episode in the American history of San Elizario is the Salt War of 1877. In that year so-called private interests in El Paso acquired a legal claim to the salt deposits that lay about one hundred miles to the east, and for the first time those who came for salt were charged a fee. The fee controversy was the immediate issue that brought forth a bloody racial conflict involving mob violence and a breakdown of law and order for months before peace was restored. In 1877 the railroad came to El Paso, bypassing San Elizario and leaving it a quiet, peaceful, picturesque farm community, in marked contrast with the turbulence of yesteryear. A marker in San Elizario Plaza (*SM 1985*) commemorates this historic community.

Casa Ronquillo. S and E of Los Portales, behind San Elizario Church. The house was built about 1821 as the home of wealthy merchant Ignacio Ronquillo, who served several times as village mayor. Originally constructed in the Mexican hacienda tradition, with elaborate viga ceilings, the complex was surrounded by a high adobe wall that separated the main house from the orchard and fields. Today only one wing with five rooms remains.

El Camino Real. Marker, San Elizario Plaza. The historical marker commemorates the passage of El Camino Real (the Chihuahua Trail to New Mexico) through the San Elizario area. *SM 1983*.

Espejo-Beltrán Expedition. Marker, San Elizario Plaza, FM 258 (Socorro Rd.). Fray Bernardino Beltrán formed an expedition to search for missionaries of the Rodríguez-Chamuscado expedition who had remained in New Mexico. Members of the Espejo-Beltrán expedition (1582–83) were the first explorers in the region from the Pecos River valley to La Junta de los Ríos. The explorers reached the El Paso area by January 1583. *SM 1981*.

First Thanksgiving. Marker, San Elizario Plaza. The marker commemorates the First Thanksgiving that was held after the Juan de Oñate expedition reached the San Elizario region in 1598. *PM. See also* El Paso: Juan de Oñate "First Thanksgiving" Festival.

Los Portales. W side of San Elizario Plaza. Built as a family home by Gregorio Nacenseno García about 1855, the structure's Territorial style features milled wood detailing and is reminiscent of New Mexico buildings such as the Governor's Palace in Santa Fe. The name Los Portales derives from its distinctive inset gallery, or portal. The structure served as the first El Paso County Courthouse, and then as a schoolhouse from the 1870s till 1922. The first teacher was Octaviano Larrazola, later Governor of New Mexico and a U.S. Senator. In 1965 the structure was purchased by El Paso Landmarks, Inc., and rehabilitated. *RTHL 1962*.

Los Portales, San Elizario. THC photo.

Old Molino. Opposite San Elizario ball park and fire station. The construction date for this old structure is unknown, but it is said to be more than 100 years old. Oxen were used here to power the mill that produced flour for the San Elizario area.

Juan de Oñate Expedition. Marker, San Elizario Plaza, Socorro Road (FM 258). Oñate was commissioned to lead an expedition north to claim and colonize the New Mexico region. Upon reaching the El Paso area in 1598, Oñate claimed for Spain all of the land drained by the Rio Grande. The expedition then proceeded north to found the Province of New Mexico, bringing Spanish rule to the American Southwest. *SM 1981.*

Presidio de San Elizario Site. Marker, US 80 in San Elizario. The Presidio de Nuestra Señora del Pilar y Glorioso Señor San José was established near Mission de Nuestra Señora de Guadalupe in El Paso del Norte (Ciudad Juárez), Mexico, by Domingo Jirónza Petriz de Cruzate in 1683. The presidio was relocated on this site in 1773 and named Presidio de San Elizario. *CM 1936.*

Rodríguez-Chamuscado Expedition. Marker, San Elizario Plaza, FM 258 (Socorro Road). Agustín Rodríguez, a Franciscan priest, led a missionary expedition in 1581 to explore the vast region from western New Mexico to the Texas Panhandle. This is believed to have been the first Spanish expedition to use the Pass of the North. *SM 1981.*

Salt War. Marker, San Elizario Plaza. The Salt War erupted in 1877 over political conflicts in El Paso County and from controversies over control of the salt lakes east of El Paso. For centuries the lakes had been a free source of salt for local residents, and attempts to exert private ownership were resisted with violence. San Elizario was the scene of some of the

Angel candelabra in San Elizario
Church, San Elizario. Photo by
Cathryn Hoyt, THC.

San Elizario Church, San Elizario.
THC photo.

bloodiest events in the conflict, which led to the reestablishment of Fort Bliss in 1878. *SM 1984.*

San Elizario Church. S side of plaza. The small church built here in 1853 proved to be inadequate for the growing town, so in 1883 a larger structure was completed. Restored after fires in 1935 and 1944, it is a stuccoed adobe structure that is less austere than the styles of the older Ysleta and Socorro missions. Statuary adorns the entire interior, and religious symbols decorate the stuccoed walls. According to the El Paso Chapter of the American Institute of Architects, the San Elizario church is an outstanding example of late adobe church architecture in the West Texas and New Mexico tradition. It reflects the influence of Spanish Mission architectural style, while the adobe walls and buttresses catch the Southwestern sunlight at its best. A shrine to the Virgin Mary can be seen next to the church. *CM 1936; RTHL 1962; NR 1972.*

San Elizario Jail. On Main St., 1 block NW of San Elizario Plaza. This adobe construction may have been built as a private residence as early as 1821. It became the first county courthouse and jail when El Paso County government was established in March 1850, with San Elizario as the county seat. The structure is a one-story, stuccoed adobe with a flat roof and traditional flat parapet and vigas. After it became a jail, two steel and wrought-iron cage cells were installed. The building served as the official county jail until 1873, with the exception of a one-year period in 1867–68 when Ysleta was the county seat. The county seat was again moved to Ysleta in 1873, where it remained for ten years until it was permanently moved to El Paso in 1883. The jail in San Elizario continued in use, and in 1876 it was, according to old timers, the scene of a notorious event. In that year Billy the Kid is said to have liberated his friend and sidekick, Melquiades Segura, from one of the iron cages of the jail. Billy, according to the story, arrived in the night, announced himself as a Texas Ranger, relieved the guards of their guns, and released Segura. The jailers were then locked up and the outlaws escaped into Mexico. In the following year, the bloody Salt War occurred, and the old jail probably was used to its fullest extent during this violent period. The jail was used until the 1940s and has been restored by the El Paso Mission Trail Association. *RTHL 1970.*

SANDERSON, Terrell County

Sanderson (pop. 1,128) developed about 1882 as a community called Strawbridge on the Texas and New Orleans Railroad, but the name was changed almost immediately to Sanderson. It became the county seat when Terrell County was formed from Pecos County in 1905. Sanderson also is the trade center of a ranching area in which Mexican *pastores* (sheepherders) have played an important role.

El Buen Pastor Church. Built by a congregation of 20 members in 1908, El Buen Pastor Church is constructed of adobe and plaster with brick quoins. The symmetrical one-story building has a small bell tower. El Buen Pastor is the only Protestant church in the area that holds services in Spanish. *RTHL 1962.*

Gothic Revival adobe church,
Shafter. Photo by Curtis Tunnell,
THC.

St. James Catholic Church. Second St. at Hackberry. The first
Catholic church here was a small adobe, built in 1922, but it has since been
replaced by the new St. James Catholic Church. St. James is a simple, rock-
faced structure showing Spanish Revival stylistic influences.

SHAFTER AND VICINITY, Presidio County

Shafter (pop. ca. 40) lies alongside US 67 forty miles south of Marfa.
The town sprang up in 1884 when the Presidio Mining Company was organized to extract and process ore mined in the Chinati Mountains. Said
to be the largest silver-producing mine in Texas, Shafter was a boom town
by 1888. Most of the workers came from Mexico, built homes in Shafter,
and remained until the mines closed in 1942. Many of the workers then
moved to Marfa and Presidio, and fewer than 50 people now reside there.
Shafter is one of many small communities in the region in which adobe
construction predominates.

Fortín de la Ciénega. 15 mi. NE of Shafter on Cienega Creek. This
adobe compound, partly in ruins, is thought to be the first Anglo-American
ranch in the Big Bend region. The ranch, established by Milton Faver,
dates from about 1857. Part of the compound has been restored and is now
a private ranch home, not open to the public. *NR 1976.*

Fortín del Cíbolo. In 1857 Milton Faver and his wife, Francisca
Ramírez, moved their family, vaqueros, and cattle over the Mexican border
into Texas, where they established a ranch in the mountain country near
Shafter. The Favers built their headquarters, described as a rectangular
adobe castle with huge mud towers at two corners, around a spring on
Cibolo Creek. From his ranch Faver supplied nearby Fort Davis with mutton, beef, vegetables, grain, and a particularly fine peach brandy. Faver's
empire disintegrated with his death in 1889. El Fortín del Cíbolo, which is
privately owned, is currently being reconstructed.

Hudspeth County Courthouse, Sierra Blanca. Photo by Cathryn Hoyt, THC.

Shafter Church. This modest adobe church, built about 1900, has Gothic Revival elements including lancet windows, a small central bell tower with a louvered lantern, and a short spire and cross finial.

Shafter Historic Mining District. In and around Shafter. Approximately 40 historic buildings and ruins of adobe and stucco remain from the 1886–1942 silver-mining and smelting activities. The mines employed as many as 300 workers, many of them Mexicans, before 1931. Use of wood by the inhabitants and the mine works had denuded the surrounding mountains of trees by 1910. In the nearby cemetery can be seen grave markers that the miners made from drill pipe and drill bits discarded from the mining operation. *NR 1976.*

SIERRA BLANCA AND VICINITY, Hudspeth County

Sierra Blanca (pop. ca. 700), named for the nearby Sierra Blanca Mountains, was established in 1881 with the coming of the railroad. Today the town is a ranching center and tourist stop on US 62/180 and serves as the county seat of Hudspeth County.

First United Methodist Church. FM 1111, N of railroad tracks. This adobe church, built by local citizens and ranchers in 1909, was the first Protestant church in Hudspeth County. Typical of many churches in the area, it features Gothic windows and a crenellated bell tower. *RTHL 1968.*

Fort Quitman. IH 10, 18 mi. W of Sierra Blanca. The authentic adobe replica of Fort Quitman houses displays of regional history from prehistoric times to the present.

Hudspeth County Courthouse. W of FM 1111, N of railroad tracks. This adobe courthouse with white stuccoed walls is thought to be the only in-use government structure made of adobe in Texas. *RTHL 1962; NR 1975.*

Scenic Drive. FM 1111, N 43 mi. to US 62/180. In the early spring, usually during March and April, giant yuccas bloom profusely, in huge clusters of white blossoms. The fibers of this typical desert plant once provided Indians of the region with material for making a wide array of utilitarian objects, including sandals, matting, and baskets. The skill of making rope from both yucca and lechuguilla fibers is still practiced in remote areas of the Trans-Pecos and in northern Mexico.

SOCORRO, El Paso County

Casa Ortiz, Socorro. Photo by Cathryn Hoyt, THC.

Socorro (pop. 22,995) developed around the mission established here in the early 1680s. Socorro and Ysleta are among the oldest continuously occupied settlements in the state.

Casa Ortiz. 10,167 Socorro Rd. Legend says that Casa Ortiz, also known as the Bosque Trading Post, was built before 1800. The house was owned in the 1840s by José Ortiz, a cart-train freighter, who also had been a comanchero, *salinero* (salt trader), and cibolero. Francisca Lujan, widow of Epifanio Ortiz, was the last to occupy the house, in the 1940s, as a family home. Casa Ortiz—with its thick adobe walls, cottonwood and willow vigas and latías, and dirt roof—is a fine example of New Spain's frontier architecture. The casa is now a small center for antique shops and art galleries. *RTHL 1973.*

Mission Socorro (Mission Nuestra Señora de la Purísima Concepción del Socorro). Moon Rd. and FM 258. Mission Socorro was established in 1682 by Antonio Guerra for the Piros Indians, refugees from Old Socorro, New Mexico. The original site was about eight leagues south of El Paso in Mexico, but after only one year at that site the mission was relocated to the Rio Grande, one league from Ysleta. An early-19th-century flood changed the course of the river and left the village and mission on the Texas side. The successor of the original mission church, the present church dates from the 1840s. The structure exhibits Indian influence on basic Spanish Mission style: whitewashed adobe brick walls, which are several feet thick; a stepped parapet; and an espadana campanile, or belfry parapet. Some of the structural elements, such as hand-hewn roof beams, are believed to date from the 1740s structure. The hand-carved wooden statue of St. Michael that graces the chapel is the subject of a local story: the statue was supposed to have been transported from Mexico to a church in New Mexico in 1845, but when it reached Socorro it suddenly became too heavy to transport and was thus acquired by the mission chapel. *CM 1936; RTHL 1963; NR 1972.*

Socorro Mission Rectory. Directly behind the Socorro Mission. The more recent rectory also is an interesting example of Spanish-influenced architecture, built with an interior courtyard and traditional flat roof.

Tienda de Carbajal Site. Old Socorro–San Elizario Rd. Site (partially reclaimed) of a 19th-century walled hacienda, which is recorded on an 1852 map as being located near the San Elizario Road crossing of the *acequia madre*. By 1873 parts of the building had been razed, but surviving

sections were occupied by a store, run by Juan Carbajal, and municipal offices. *SM 1972.*

STUDY BUTTE, Brewster County

Study Butte (pop. ca. 120) is located on SH 118 at the western edge of Big Bend National Park. In territory that once was the domain of Comanches and Apaches, non-Indian settlement came slowly and not always permanently. Mercury was discovered here in 1900, and the mining town of Study (pronounced Stoo-dy) Butte grew up around the Big Bend Mine, which closed in the 1940s. Here, as at other mines in the region, Mexican workers provided the labor force, and the old stone and adobe structures reflect their traditional construction methods and materials. A few of the houses are now occupied. The visitor may absorb the past among the remains at Study Butte, take the scenic drive along El Camino del Rio (FM 170), or inquire locally for information on river trips, which provide an opportunity for hardy spirits to view the region from the canyons of the Rio Grande.

TERLINGUA, Brewster County

Terlingua (pop. ca. 25), located between Lajitas and Study Butte near the western edge of Big Bend National Park, was a prosperous town in the early 20th century but is now a ghost town, marked mostly by ruins and a historic cemetery. Terlingua was the location of the Chisos Mining Com-

Above: Hand-carved statue of St. Michael in the Mission Socorro chapel, Socorro. Photo by Sam McColloch.

Above left: Mission Socorro, Socorro. THC photo.

Ruins of the mining town of Terlingua. Courtesy of *TEXAS HIGHWAYS Magazine.*

pany's mercury-mining operation and once boasted a store, post office, jail, hotel, and school in addition to workers' homes and a mansion built for the company president, Howard E. Perry, in 1906. Mexicans provided the major labor force for all early mining activities in the Trans-Pecos, and, as at most mining communities, the houses of Terlingua reflect indigenous construction styles and methods. Some of the town's rock and adobe houses have recently been restored and occupied, and a trading company, offering souvenirs and crafts, is located in the original Chisos Mining Company building off FM 170. Information can be obtained in Terlingua or at Lajitas on Rio Grande float trips. Terlingua also is the site of the annual World Championship Chili Cook-Off, held each year in November.

Perry Mansion. Influenced by Spanish country architecture, this two-story adobe residence was built in 1906 by Howard E. Perry, a Chicago industrialist. He was the founder of the Chisos Mining Company, which was the largest producer of mercury in the United States by 1921. The long, narrow design features an arcaded loggia along the front façade.

Perry School. The Perry School was built in 1930 to educate the children of miners working for the Chisos Mining Company. Pueblo and Mission Revival influences are demonstrated in this simple plastered adobe structure built on concrete footing walls. The school is distinguished by a stepped parapet and a gabled entry portico supported by adobe piers.

St. Agnes Catholic Church. The church, constructed about 1914, is built of adobe on a raised stone foundation. It has a gabled roof and a wood-frame open lantern and spire. Interior features include painted adobe walls, a beaded ceiling, and a pine floor. The church was the focal point of the company town.

Terlingua Theatre. Constructed of adobe, the Terlingua Theatre building is adjacent to the Old Chisos Mining Company Store. The galvanized tin roof is a modern addition to prevent further deterioration of the adobe walls.

St. Agnes Catholic Church,
Terlingua. THC photo.

El Capitan Hotel, Van Horn. Photo
by Cathryn Hoyt, THC.

VAN HORN AND VICINITY, Culberson County

Van Horn (pop. 2,930), originally a stage stop, grew into a town
with the coming of the railroad in 1881. The last resistance efforts of the
Apaches, led by Victorio, occurred in this area, before Victorio's final defeat and death in Mexico in 1880. Van Horn is the county seat of Culberson County.

Culberson County Historical Museum. In historic Clark Hotel,
intersection of US 80 and US 90, downtown. Exhibits include depictions
of talc and silver mining, which were the basis of the early Van Horn
economy. Van Horn also was a way station on the Old Spanish Trail from
San Antonio to California. The museum also contains artifacts relating
to prehistoric and historic Indians of the region. Open Sun. 2–4 or by
appointment.

El Capitan Hotel (Van Horn State Bank Building). US 80 at US 90.
The El Capitan Hotel, constructed in 1936, is a beautiful example of Pueblo
Revival style architecture. The hotel was a favorite resting place for travelers on the most southern transcontinental route in the United States. Today, the hotel serves as the Van Horn State Bank. Visitors are welcome to
view the interior, where the original Spanish tile floor and overhead beams
have been preserved.

First Presbyterian Church. Fannin and 3d Sts. Built in 1902, this
church, like many historic churches of the Trans-Pecos region, is constructed of adobe. The stuccoed walls of the church were once scored to
resemble stone. *RTHL 1964; NR 1978.*

San Antonio–California Trail. Marker, roadside park, 3 mi. W of
Van Horn on US 80. The historical marker commemorates the San Antonio–California Trail, which passed through this area about three miles
south of the marker location. *SM 1968.*

REGION 4

Austin and Central Texas

This Central Texas region encompasses most of the area commonly known as the Hill Country, as well as some of the prairie lands to the east. The Tonkawa, among the early historic peoples of the region, once roamed as far north as the Red River, following the buffalo herds, but during the 1700s they were located primarily in Central Texas. In 1758 they joined with the Norteños (Comanches and allied groups) in the destruction of the San Sabá mission, which had been established only the year before for the Apaches. Several major archeological sites in the region have been identified with the Tonkawas, but the presence of the Comanches and the Apaches was relatively brief and is noted primarily in the historical record.

In the western part of this region, mission and presidio sites are reminders of both the Spanish presence and of their largely unsuccessful efforts to missionize the Apaches. Santa Cruz de San Sabá (1757–58) and the fort built for its protection, Presidio San Luis de las Amarillas, were located near Menard. Partially reconstructed ruins of the presidio still exist. In Uvalde County, Mission Nuestra Señora de la Candelaria was established in 1762. In Milam County, near the tiny community of San Gabriel, were three mid-18th-century Spanish missions, located there in a failed attempt to establish a link with Nacogdoches. In 1730 Missions Concepción, Espada, and San Juan were temporarily located in the Austin area as they were being moved from East Texas to San Antonio. Despite these mission efforts, there were no permanent Spanish settlements in the region.

In 1808 the village of San Marcos de Neve was established on El Camino Real in Hays County, but Comanche raids and the brewing Mexican Revolution led to the abandonment of the villa in 1812. One of the early private ranches in this region was El Capote, founded about 1805 by José de la Baume on land granted for his services in the Spanish army. Several other early ranches were established on Mexican land grants, including that of José Antonio Navarro on Geronimo Creek. The town of Bastrop, platted in 1832, dates from the Mexican period and was named Mina from 1834 to 1837, when the town was chartered by the Republic of Texas.

Despite these early settlements and ranches, in most areas of the region contemporary Mexican-American populations are largely the result of 20th-century immigration. The southwestern part of the region, although geographically related to the Hill Country, has strong cultural ties

Opposite: **Old San Fernando Church, Alamo Village, Brackettville. Photo by Cathryn Hoyt, THC.**

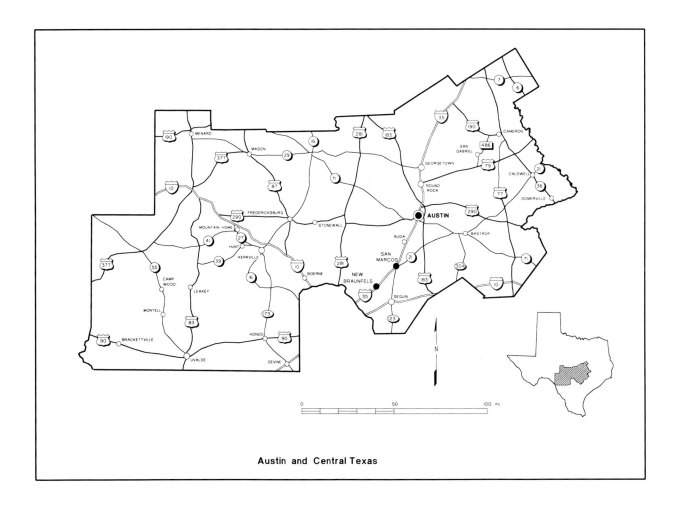

Austin and Central Texas

with South Texas and has been home to a significant Hispanic population since the 19th century. Central Texas with its rolling hills, ranching and farming country, and urban center in Austin is a particularly inviting region in which to enjoy Texas' multicultural heritage.

Guidebook Region 4. Map by Greg Miller.

AUSTIN AND VICINITY, Travis County

Austin (pop. 465,622) is located on the edge of the Edwards Plateau and is divided by the Colorado River, one of the major rivers named during the Spanish Colonial period. Several Spanish expeditions crossed the area in the late 17th and early 18th centuries. In 1730 Missions Concepción, Espada, and San Juan were temporarily located at the site of Barton Springs as they were being moved from East Texas to San Antonio However, there was no permanent Spanish or Mexican settlement in the area. Anglo-American settlement in the county began in the early 1830s. The town of Waterloo was selected as the capital of the Republic of Texas in 1839 and was renamed Austin. The city, as the state capital, the county seat of Travis County, and the home of the University of Texas at Austin, remains a governmental and educational center. Austin has become a mecca for historians, archeologists, genealogists, and other researchers because of its centrally located state and university libraries, archives, and museums. Tourists are attracted by the State Capitol and other historic sites in the area, as well as the man-made Highland Lakes. In Austin there are many neighborhoods, churches, restaurants, art galleries, and businesses associated with the city's Mexican-American community. Predominantly Hispanic neighborhoods in East and South Austin are also home to delightful *panaderías* (bakeries) and traditional grocery stores that stock Mexican herbs and spices and a variety of other hard-to-find items.

Information

State Capitol. Congress Ave. at 11th St. Tourist information is available in the Capitol rotunda.

Historic Sites

East Austin Historic Resources. East Austin was sparsely settled during the early years of Austin, and the historic French Legation was the most prominent building east of the Capitol until the 1870s, when German and Swedish immigrants began building homes in the area. Around the beginning of the 20th century, African- and Mexican-American families began moving into East Austin, occupying many of the late-19th-century homes. The ethnic history of this part of the city is commemorated in the Historic Resources of East Austin National Register District (*NR 1985*). Among the important Mexican-American resources in the district are the following:

Briones House. 1204 E. 7th St. *See* sidebar: The Briones House.

Community Center. 1192 Angelina St. The Community Center appropriately reflects the multicultural heritage of East Austin neighborhoods. Plans for the center, constructed during 1929–30, began in 1927 when seven Negro federated clubs united to form the Community Welfare Association and recognized the need for a meeting place and community center. The building's simplified Mission Revival style is uncommon in East Austin.

Guerrero Produce Company. 1001 E. 6th St. The one-story, plastered brick building features a curvilinear Alamo-style parapet. Built about 1905, the building, now vacant, was used for its original commercial purpose for more than 70 years.

Our Lady of Guadalupe Church. 1206 E. 9th St. Established in 1907, Our Lady of Guadalupe Church was first located at the corner of 5th and Guadalupe Sts. In 1926 a second church was built on a new site in East Austin, where most of the new Mexican-American families in the city were locating. By the early 1950s it was too small for the increasing number of Catholics in East Austin, and in 1954 the present church, an impressive American Federal style building, was com-

Briones House, Austin. Photo by Cathryn Hoyt, THC.

THE BRIONES HOUSE

The Briones House, at 1204 E. 7th St. in Austin, is a rare example of modern folk architecture in Central Texas. The style of molded and tinted concrete construction represented by the Briones House was introduced from Mexico in the 1920s, and it is most often practiced in cities with large Mexican-American populations. The best known examples in Texas are the cement constructions produced by craftsmen Dionicio Rodríguez and Máximo Cortez at Brackenridge Park in San Antonio (*see* San Antonio: Public Art entries). Other fine examples of this type of work are extremely rare.

Genaro P. Briones, creator of the Briones House, began work at age 14 as a bricklayer, apprenticed to his uncle in El Paso. A decade later, in Memphis, he learned to mold and tint plaster and concrete from a craftsman who had been trained in Mexico City. As part of this training Briones was taught the special formula and techniques he later used in tinting the concrete for the exterior and interior of his home in Austin. During his lifetime, Briones worked and traveled

pleted. The church is a center of Mexican-American community life in Austin.

Santiago del Valle Grant Site. McKinney Falls State Park, 7102 Scenic Loop Rd. The park lies in the center of an early Texas land grant that originally fell within the empresario contract of Ben Milam. Ten leagues of land were transferred in 1832 to Santiago del Valle, at that time Secretary of the Mexican Government of Coahuila and Texas. Del Valle sold the land in 1835. The southern portion of the original grant remained largely rural and is preserved in this state park; a marker (*SM 1984*) commemorating the grant has been placed at the Visitor Center. Although the Visitor Center at the park focuses on the history of Thomas F. McKinney, for whom the park is named, there are materials related to the Santiago del Valle land grant and a diorama depicting historic Indian lifeways in the area. The park also offers camping and picnicking facilities. Visitor Center open Wed.–Sun. 9–5.

Espinosa-Olivares-Aguirre Expedition. Marker, 3001 S. Congress at St. Edward's University. The historical marker was placed at the approximate turnaround point of the 1709 expedition up the Colorado River. Capt. Pedro de Aguirre and 14 soldiers escorted Fray Isidro de Espinosa and Fray Antonio de San Buenaventura y Olivares to this area, sent an invitation to the East Texas Indians to visit them on the Rio Grande, then turned back. *CM 1936; SM 1967.*

Wild Basin Preserve. On Loop 360, 1.25 mi. N of Bee Cave Rd. (FM 2244). This 220-acre preserve west of Austin provides four miles of hiking trails through scenic Hill Country wilderness. A self-guided tour booklet, *The Trail of Old Time Texas*, identifies 15 plant species seen on the easy-access loop and explains how each played a part in the lives of the men and women who were here before us, from the American Indians to the Spanish explorers and more recent settlers. Open daily sunrise to sunset.

Spanish Revival Architecture

General Examples. In addition to those listed below, there are a number of structures in Austin that are Spanish Revival in style. The Central Christian (1110 Guadalupe) and First English Lutheran (3001 Whitis) churches are excellent examples, and there are numerous Spanish Revival–influenced homes, especially in the older residential neighborhoods in the south-, north-, and west-central areas of the city.

Laguna Gloria. 3809 W. 35th St. Built in 1916, Laguna Gloria was designed by San Antonio architect Harvey L. Page, who combined Spanish and Italian elements in this Mediterranean style villa. The window to the right of the east entrance is a faithful copy in plaster of the Rose Window of Mission San José in San Antonio. Laguna Gloria was built by Clara Driscoll Sevier and her husband, Henry Hulme Sevier. The couple named their home Laguna Gloria in part after a Driscoll family ranch, known as La Gloria, in Duval County. Henry Sevier, a journalist, later became a legislator and U.S. ambassador to Chile. Clara Driscoll Sevier is best remem-

throughout Texas, Tennessee, California, and Mexico.

The Briones House was designed and constructed by Briones and his wife over a period of about 14 years. The primary feature of the eclectic, two-story house is its molded and tinted concrete surfaces that have been treated to look like stone and wood. Colorful pictorial details such as flowers and stars blend with the implied wood and stone. Columns at the first and second stories terminate in sculptured and painted blossoms and buds. The porch ceiling at the second floor is painted with a bold, geometric star design. The interior also is thickly plastered with tinted concrete. Two outstanding interior features are a wall niche lined and framed by gnarled trees (in the living room) and a gilt wall shrine (in the master bedroom). The Briones House, well known to the Austin Hispanic community, has served as the focal point of tours of barrio art, and it is often called the Casa de Sueños, or House of Dreams.

Although not open to the public, the house and its decorative yard furniture are clearly visible from the street.

Blessing of the Animals, Our Lady
of Guadalupe Church, Austin.
Photo by Jesse Herrera.

Laguna Gloria Art Museum, Austin.
Photo by Cathryn Hoyt, THC.

bered for her efforts to preserve the grounds surrounding the Alamo in San Antonio, and a carved fireplace mantel in the villa was made from a beam from the Alamo. In 1943 she donated Laguna Gloria to the Texas Fine Arts Association. The building now houses a museum dedicated to American art of the 20th century. *NR 1975; RTHL 1983.*

Rather House. 3105 Duval. This two and one-half story residence, built in 1910 for Charles Taylor Rather, includes Spanish Revival elements. The house was deeded in 1952 to the Episcopal Seminary of the Southwest, which also houses the diocese's Center for Hispanic Ministries. *NR 1979.*

Reuter House. 806 Rosedale Terrace. Built in 1934 for Louis and Matilde Reuter, the house offers a spectacular view of the city. It is a rambling, one- and two-story stone house that reflects Spanish Revival stylistic influences in its cast-stone detailing and red barrel-tile roof. *RTHL 1986; NR 1987.*

San Francisco Catholic Church. 9110 US 183 S. This lovely little country church was built in 1941 of fieldstone. Mission Revival stylistic influence is evident in the façade, which is reminiscent of San Antonio's Mission Espada. A grotto, also of rock construction, graces the hillside on the church grounds. The church serves a close-knit community of Hispanic families and offers mass in both English and Spanish.

San José Catholic Church. 2435 Oak Crest. San José is one of three churches established by the Community of Holy Cross in 1940–41 to serve Mexican-Americans in Austin and vicinity (*see* San Francisco Catholic Church above, and Buda: Santa Cruz Church). San José, which recently celebrated its 50th anniversary, is now housed in a new, Spanish style, stuccoed church built in the late 1980s. San José offers mass in both Spanish and English and is one of the major Mexican-American community churches in Austin.

University of Texas at Austin. Main entrances from Martin Luther King Blvd., Guadalupe St., Red River St., and 26th St. Before World War I, architect Cass Gilbert was university architect in charge of developing a master plan for university construction. He designed Battle Hall, built in 1911, in a style described as Spanish Renaissance. Only one other building, Sutton Hall, was actually built according to Gilbert's plan. However, several other buildings dating from the 1930s reflect the distinctive Beaux-Arts–Southwestern style initiated by Gilbert. These limestone buildings with terra-cotta ornamentation are easily identifiable and center around the Tower, or Main Building, constructed in 1936.

Museums, Libraries, and Cultural Centers

Austin Children's Museum. 1501 W. 5th St. The museum has holdings that include Mexican art and folk art, and sponsors occasional exhibits relating to Hispanic and other ethnic groups in Texas. Inquire locally for current exhibits and programs. Open Wed.–Fri. 10–5; Sat. 10–5; Sun. noon–5.

Barker Texas History Center. University of Texas campus, Sid Richardson Hall, Red River St. Barker is perhaps the single most important

San Francisco Catholic Church, Austin. Photo by Cathryn Hoyt, THC.

resource center for the study of Texas history. Established in 1945, the center is named for historian Eugene C. Barker, who, among his other accomplishments, is noted for having helped debunk the myth that all of the wrongs and causes of the Texas Revolution and the Mexican War were attributable to Mexico. The library has extensive documentary and photographic, as well as print collections, relating to Texas history from Indian and Spanish Colonial times to the present. Selections are displayed in changing exhibits. Included among the Spanish and Mexican archival holdings are the Bexar Archives, important records of Spanish and Mexican administration in Texas. Newspaper resources date back to the first Texas newspaper, the *Gaceta de Texas,* printed in Nacogdoches in 1813. Open Mon.–Sat. 8–5.

Benson Latin American Collection. University of Texas campus, Sid Richardson Hall, Red River St. This specialized research library focuses on materials from and about Latin America and on materials relating to Spanish-speaking people in the United States. The collection includes over 530,000 books, periodicals, and pamphlets; two million pages of manuscripts, 19,000 maps, about 20,000 microforms, and various other materials. Materials are available to non-university users but may be limited to building use only. Open Mon.–Fri. 9–6 and during evenings and weekends when the university is in session.

Catholic Archives of Texas. Congress Ave. at W. 16th St. Located in the chancery building of the Diocese of Austin, the Catholic Archives of Texas is the repository for copies of many records relating to the Spanish Colonial period. It is also an excellent source of information on the history of Catholic churches in Texas in general, as well as those that were established to serve predominantly Mexican-American communities.

Humanities Research Center Art Collection. University of Texas campus, Peter Flawn Academic Center, Guadalupe St. Collections, as well

Above: Apache Indian group from collections of the Eugene C. Barker Texas History Center. Courtesy of Barker Texas History Center, General Libraries, University of Texas at Austin.

Above left: Sutton Hall, University of Texas at Austin. THC photo.

333

as frequent exhibits, include Spanish Colonial and Mexican art and crafts. The center also has Mexican-American, Southwestern, and historic Indian materials in its permanent collections. Open weekdays 8–4:45.

Archer M. Huntington Art Gallery. University of Texas campus. The Huntington's contemporary Latin American art collection, with over 500 works, is considered one of the most extensive representations of contemporary Latin American art in the United States. Permanent collections are housed in the Harry Ransom Center (21st and Guadalupe), and temporary exhibitions are shown in the gallery of the Art Building (23d and San Jacinto). Open to the public; inquire locally for current exhibits.

Lyndon Baines Johnson Library. 2313 Red River St. The collections of the presidential library include Mexican and Latin American objects that were gifts from heads of state and reflect examples of regional crafts, a few Pre-Columbian items, and a still life by Diego Rivera. These impressive Latin American items are not on permanent display, so inquire locally for information on current exhibits. Open daily 9–5.

Mexic-Arte Gallery. 419 Congress Ave. The gallery features multicultural programming, including art exhibits, concerts, plays, and poetry readings. On permanent display is a photographic exhibit entitled History and Humanities of the Mexican-American Community in Austin. Among the gallery's annual special events is the Día de los Muertos (Day of the Dead) commemoration on the first weekend in November. Open Tues.– Sat. 11–6 and evenings for special events. *See also* Festivals: Día de los Muertos.

Museo del Barrio de Austin. 1402 E. 1st St. The museum focuses on Mexican-American and Latino art and participates in community observances, such as those for Día de los Muertos. Open Mon.–Fri. 9–5.

Texas Department of Agriculture. 9th Floor, Stephen F. Austin Bldg., 17th St. and Congress Ave. The Dept. of Agriculture sponsors the Texas Family Land Heritage Registry program, which recognizes properties in continuous agricultural usage and owned by the same family for a century or more. Numerous properties owned by Hispanic families, especially in South Texas, are included on the registry.

Texas General Land Office. 1700 N. Congress Ave. The Archives and Records Division preserves and makes available official land records for the State of Texas, dating from the Spanish Colonial period to the present, including maps of early land grants. The Spanish Collection, which begins with the 1720 land grant for Mission San José in San Antonio, is the oldest set of documents in the General Land Office Archives. Open Mon.–Fri. 8–5.

Texas Historical Commission. 1511 Colorado St. The official state agency for historical preservation, this agency maintains files on prehistoric and historic structures and sites, including National Register and historical marker properties, across the state. Publications covering a broad range of historic preservation and archeological topics are available from the commission. The Texas Antiquities Committee, which is housed with the commission, also distributes archeological reports, including the definitive work on the Spanish fleet wrecked off Padre Island in 1554. Both agencies can be contacted for further information at P.O. Box 12276, Austin, TX 78711. Open Mon.–Fri. 8–5.

Texas Memorial Museum. 2400 Trinity St. Collections include materials from the prehistoric period to the present. Especially significant are the Lazar Collection of over 1700 20th-century toys and other objects from Guanajuato, Mexico, and the Pérez Collection of 170 20th-century masks, most of which are from Oaxaca, Mexico. Items from both collections are included in occasional exhibits. Open Mon.–Fri. 9–5; Sat. 10–5; Sun. 1–5.

Texas State Library and Archives. Lorenzo de Zavala State Library and Archives Bldg., Brazos between 12th and 13th Sts. in the Capitol complex. The building that houses the Texas State Library and Archives is named for the ad interim vice-president of the Republic of Texas, and the east and west façades of the building display the seals of the nations whose flags have flown over Texas, including Spain and Mexico. In addition to the important Nacogdoches Archives, the library's collections relating to Texas history and genealogy are extensive. Library exhibits contain facsimiles of the Texas Declaration of Independence as well as other historic documents. Open Mon.–Fri. 8–5.

University of Texas at Austin. *See* Barker Texas History Center; Benson Latin American Collection; Humanities Research Center Art Collection; Archer M. Huntington Art Gallery; Texas Memorial Museum.

Public Art

Seals of the Nations. Terrazzo floor design. Texas State Capitol, center of Capitol complex, downtown Austin. In the center of the Capitol rotunda floor is a large, composite terrazzo design known as the Seals of the Nations. The Seal of the Republic of Texas forms the center of the pattern and between the points of the lone star are the coats of arms of each of the five nations of which Texas has been part: Spain, Mexico, France, the Confederacy, and the United States. Mexico's distinctive seal displays the famed eagle and snake of Mexican legend. Open 6–11 daily; free guided tours at 8:30 and 4:30. *See also* Texas State Library and Archives.

Raúl Valdez Murals. Over the past 15 years, Raúl Valdez, often assisted by local residents and school children, has created numerous murals depicting themes or historical events relevant to the communities in which the artwork is located. The majority of Valdez's murals are located in Austin, but his work also appears in Dallas, Del Rio, and McAllen. *See also* sidebar: The Murals of Raúl Valdez in Austin's Mexican-American Community.

Becker Elementary School Library mural. 906 W. Milton. Images in this 16 × 4-foot mural depict children with microscopes, books, and telescopes. These images stress the importance of learning about the smallest and biggest of things, and all things in between.

Education . . . Liberation of the Mind. 1984. Brooke Elementary School, 3100 E. 4th St. A 20-foot-high, freestanding steel structure shaped in the form of a bird in flight holds the panels of the mural.

Pan American Stage mural by Raúl Valdez, Austin. Photo by Cathryn Hoyt, THC.

The mural depicts the struggle of Mexican-American children to find role models in today's society. Images of life in a modern city, for example, contrast with the image of an elderly man teaching a youth how to plant.

Ollin. 1984. 1600 E. 1st St. Painted in collaboration with Carlos Lowry and Ramón Maldonado, this 25 × 69-foot mural consists of panels supported by a steel frame. The mural contains many images first painted by Valdez in his Juárez-Lincoln mural, which was destroyed when the building on which it appeared was razed in the early 1980s. Over 500 local residents consulted with Valdez on the images in *Ollin,* and about 80 residents participated in the painting. The central image depicts a girl breaking through a brick wall, surrounded by contrasting images of life and death.

Oral Tradition. 1977. 2300 block of E. 2d St. This 10 × 66-foot mural expresses the importance of the oral transmission of *mexicanidad* (that which makes one Mexican) from generation to generation.

Pan American Stage mural. 1978, restored 1991. 2100 E. 3d St. Created with the assistance of neighborhood residents and Zavala Elementary School students. Measuring over 3,000 square feet, the mural includes images of Mexican historical events and figures, as well as modern Mexican-American cultural images such as folklórico dancers and car clubs. Some graffiti signatures have been retained in the restoration and are viewed as dynamic parts of the mural in its function as public art.

Sanchez Elementary School Library mural. 1990. 73 San Marcos St. On the central panel of the mural, figures around a campfire sing *corridos* about events in Mexican-American history. This 1,000-square-foot mural depicts images of prehistoric American Indian lifeways,

PUBLIC ART
The Murals of Raúl Valdez in Austin's Mexican-American Community

To most Texans, the term *public art* brings to mind images of art in public places—statues on the grounds of the Capitol or the local county courthouse, paintings in a city hall, or sculptures in a public park. In this state's capital city, muralist Raúl Valdez and East Austin residents believe that it takes much more than a public space to create public art. Valdez, who teaches art at Austin Community College and is the former artist-in-residence for Austin Independent School District, has been awarded commissions to paint many public spaces, including elementary school libraries and park recreation centers. He believes that public art should not only be easily accessible to the public, but should reflect a community's history, values, and identity. To accomplish this, he believes, the members of a community must be included in all stages of the mural-painting process.

Early on in the designing and sketching stages, Valdez commonly finds himself literally "out in the neighborhood knocking on doors," asking residents for ideas of images for their mural. Though not every image will be incorporated, Valdez often will find patterns of images

Spanish contact and its consequences, and Mexican-American children in the 20th century.

Ignacio Zaragoza mural. Zaragoza Park, Pedernales at 7th St. in East Austin. The central image in the mural is General Ignacio Zaragoza, the hero of the Battle of Puebla that is commemorated in the celebration of Cinco de Mayo. Zaragoza Park, in which the mural is located, is one of the centers of Hispanic community life in Austin.

Festivals

Ballet Folklórico. Austin is the home of at least one professional folklórico dance group, Roy Lozano's Ballet Folklórico de Texas. The ballet has performed at many festivals and schools in Austin and also gives dance performances at local theaters.

Día de los Muertos (Day of the Dead). First weekend in November (Day of the Dead is November 2); events and exhibits at Mexic-Arte Gallery, 419 Congress. This important Mexican and Mexican-American memorial observation has its roots in Pre-Columbian Mexico. Breads baked in special shapes (such as male and female figures, and cruciforms) and the decoration of graves with flowers, as well as religious services, commemorate this special day.

Diez y Seis de Septiembre. Several Diez y Seis de Septiembre celebrations are held annually on the weekend closest to September 16. Events include El Grito ceremonies, conjunto music, ballet folklórico and special events for children. The Zaragoza Park Recreation Center sponsors a celebration at Zaragoza Park (Pedernales at 7th St. in East Austin), which features a special award presentation for "Amiga de la Comunidad Mejicana." All proceeds go toward projects, equipment, and scholarships for the Austin Parks and Recreation Dept. Austin's annual community-wide Diez y

or themes repeated by different people. Once the mural is designed, local residents and schoolchildren are invited to participate in the painting. In some cases, over a hundred people have been involved, and, notes Valdez, "we even had kids trying to skip school—we had to turn them away and send them back until after school." Once completed, the mural is already part of the community; in a sense, the finished mural does not so much make a statement about the community as much as it *restates* one that the community has already made.

While some murals are left untouched by spray painters, others may become almost totally obscured. Valdez has recently restored the Pan American Recreation Center Stage murals in Austin, but not to their original state. He has sacrificed some areas to preserve spray-painted messages, including signatures, that are important to the community. A Valdez mural thus continues to interact dynamically with its community long after the mural has been "completed." It is a characteristic that suits the artist fine—"It's their wall, after all."

Matachines from Roy Lozano's Ballet Folklórico dance group, Austin. Photo by Jesse Herrera.

337

Seis celebration, Fiestas Patrias, is celebrated at Fiesta Gardens-West (2101 Bergman, east of IH 35) each year, also on the weekend closest to September 16. Founded in 1978, the fiesta features conjunto music, an El Grito ceremony, and ballet folklórico. Over 17,000 people attend the festival, which is sponsored by Fiestas Patrias, Inc. Another celebration, on the day of September 16, has been held for over a decade in the State Capitol rotunda.

Festival Cinco de Mayo. Weekend closest to May 5, at Fiesta Gardens, 2101 Bergman, just E of IH 35. Austin's Mexican-American community has been celebrating Cinco de Mayo for at least sixty years. Today, the city's largest celebration of the event is organized by the Comité Festival Cinco de Mayo, a group composed of representatives of the Austin Hispanic Chamber of Commerce, LULAC, and the Austin Parks and Recreation Dept. An opening ceremony commemorates the Battle of Puebla, with proclamations by Texas and Mexican officials, and the singing of the U.S. and Mexican national anthems. Concerts of traditional music, ballet folklórico and other dance performances, dozens of food booths, and a custom car show are part of the celebration. For information contact Comité Festival Cinco de Mayo, P.O. Box 6105, Austin 78762.

Diez y Seis at Zaragoza Park, Austin. Photo by Jesse Herrera.

BASTROP AND VICINITY, Bastrop County

Bastrop (pop. 4,044), originally known as Mina, was platted by Mexican land commissioner Miguel Arciniega in 1832. In 1837, when the town was chartered by the Republic of Texas, the name was changed to Bastrop, in honor of Felipe Enrique Neri, Baron de Bastrop. The flamboyant "baron" served as land commissioner of Austin's colony and as a member of the Congress of Coahuila and Texas. Bastrop, known as one of the oldest settlements in Texas, attracts visitors to its historic sites and to nearby Bastrop State Park, where "lost pines" are found in an area far from the woodlands of East Texas. The city also is the county seat of Bastrop County.

Bastrop County Historical Society. 702 Main St. The society has records dealing with the original settlement of the Bastrop area during the 1820s and 1830s.

El Camino Real. Marker, commemorating Bastrop County and El Camino Real, 1.5 mi. E of Bastrop on SH 71. El Camino Real north from San Antonio crossed the Colorado River at this locale. This crossing was the site of a short-lived Spanish stockade, called Puesta del Colorado, where troops were stationed in 1806 to protect commerce on the road. Lands in Bastrop County were part of Austin's 1821 colony in Mexican Texas. *CM 1936.*

Felipe Enrique Neri (Baron de Bastrop). Marker, Bastrop State Park, 1 mi. NE of Bastrop on SH 21. The Baron de Bastrop (1770–1829; real name, Philip Hendrik Nerig Bogel), was a pioneer empresario and land commissioner of Austin's colony during the Mexican period. He served as representative to the Mexican state of Coahuila and Texas, and in his honor the county and county seat were named. *CM 1936.*

St. Peter's Church, Boerne. Photo by Cathryn Hoyt, THC.

BOERNE, Kendall County

Boerne (pop. 4,274), founded in the 1850s by pioneer German settlers, is a livestock center and county seat of Kendall County. Visitors are attracted to hunting and recreational opportunities in the area, including nearby Cascade Caverns and Guadalupe State Park.

St. Peter's Church. 805 S. Main. The first church in the Boerne area was built about 1860 and served both Spanish- and German-speaking residents of the county. The present church in this predominantly German-Texan town is an impressive native stone structure constructed in 1923 and showing Spanish Revival stylistic influences.

339

BRACKETTVILLE, Kinney County

Brackettville (pop. 1,740) is located near Las Moras Springs, an important water source during the period of Spanish exploration. The settlement grew up around Fort Clark, a frontier outpost established here in 1852. Today, this small town is noted primarily as the locale of the historic fort (now a resort community open to the public) and for Alamo Village, located north of town. Brackettville is the county seat of Kinney County.

Alamo Village. 7 mi. N of Brackettville. The village was built around a replica of the Alamo façade constructed as a movie set for John Wayne's movie *The Alamo*. Over 1.25 million adobe bricks were made on the site to build the Alamo and the nearby reconstruction of 18th-century San Antonio with its whitewashed Old San Fernando Church. Chato Hernández, ranch foreman for J.T. Shahan, the entrepreneur who developed the village, also served as foreman of the replica project. John Wayne fans or Western Americana buffs are particularly attracted by the movie connection and the fact that country singer Johnny Rodríguez began his career here.

Brackettville High School. Ann (FM 674) and Fulton St. This charming Pueblo Revival school, with its exposed vigas and painted tile detailing around the door, was built in 1930.

Seminole-Negro Indian Scout Cemetery. Off US 90, on FM 3348 (693 on some maps) ca. 3 mi. S of Brackettville. When the Spanish and other Europeans arrived in the New World they set in play inexorable forces that, in Texas, led to the expulsion or eradication of most indigenous peoples. The displacement of populations that occurred throughout North America as a result of colonization and settlement set not only European against Indian, but Indian against Indian in a struggle for territory and survival. The Seminoles of Florida, who had intermarried with Negro refugees from Southern slavery, moved to Oklahoma following the second Seminole War (1835–42), and many sought refuge in Mexico. About 150 were hired by the U.S. Army to serve as scouts in the Indian wars of the frontier. A group settled in Brackettville around Fort Clark after the Indian scouts were disbanded, and the descendants who remain in the area as farmers and ranchers maintain an old cemetery nearby. Buried here are four who received Congressional Medals of Honor for service in campaigns against the Indians from 1873 to 1881. *SM 1971*.

Scenic Drive. FM 674 N to Rocksprings; or FM 334 NE to intersection with SH 55. Two routes lead north from Brackettville through scenic landscapes of the Hill Country and rocky pastureland. Especially in late afternoons, travelers may glimpse white-tailed deer and wild turkeys. The turkey and the dog were the only domesticated animals that Spanish explorers found among the Indians of the Southwest. The turkey was domesticated by New Mexico Puebloan groups primarily for its decorative feathers, not as a food source. The Indians of Texas seem to have preferred the hunt to the chores of domestication, but they may also have used the wild bird's feathers for ceremonial purposes or as items of adornment.

BUDA, Hays County

Buda (pop. 1,795), established in 1880 as a railroad depot in north-western Hays County, is believed to have derived its name from the Spanish word *viuda,* meaning widow.

Santa Cruz Catholic Church. E side of IH 35, on access road. This is one of three churches established by the Community of Holy Cross in 1941 to serve Mexican-Americans in the Austin to Buda area. Built of fieldstone, these rural churches were designed by Francis Kervick, then head of the School of Architecture at Notre Dame. The Spanish Mission style and fieldstone construction of Santa Cruz is particularly appropriate to the Texas Hill Country. Originally a mission church, Santa Cruz, which celebrated its 50th anniversary in 1991, was established as a parish in 1988.

CALDWELL AND VICINITY, Burleson County

Caldwell (pop. 3,181) is the county seat of Burleson County, which was organized in 1846. Although earlier travelers crossed through the area on El Camino Real, settlement began in the 1820s, and a short-lived Mexican military post was established in the area in 1830.

Burleson County Historical Museum. Buck and Main Sts. Located in the Burleson County Courthouse, the museum focuses on items and relics of area pioneers, including exhibits related to Fort Tenoxtitlán, which was established in 1830 to promote Mexican settlement of the area. Open Fri. 2–4:30.

El Camino Real. Marker, in rest area on SH 21, 9 mi. SW of Caldwell. Here, as in some other areas, SH 21 follows the route of historic El Camino Real, which was used as early as 1691 as the "Trail of the Padres." *SM 1968.*

Fort Tenoxtitlán Site. Marker, roadside park, 5 mi. E of Caldwell on SH 21, ca. 8 mi. NE of site. Fort Tenoxtitlán, located about eight miles southwest of the marker location, was named for the ancient Aztec capital Tenochtitlán. The fort was founded in 1830 by Mexico as a bulwark against Anglo-American immigration, but soldiers were withdrawn in 1832. The fort and its nearby settlement were twice proposed for the capital of Texas, but these efforts failed and the fort was again abandoned in 1841. José Francisco Ruiz, the Mexican commander, eventually took up the cause of independence from Mexico and was a signer of the Texas Declaration of Independence. *CM 1936; SM 1976.*

CAMERON, Milam County

Cameron (pop. 5,580), settled in the 1840s, is an agricultural center and the county seat of Milam County. The small city's residents reflect the typical ethnic mix of the Hill Country—German, Czech, Hispanic, and Anglo.

Milam County Historical Museum. 203 E. Main St. The museum focuses on the history of Milam County and Texas with exhibits that feature a few items relating to Hispanic heritage, including a Spanish military sword. Open Tues.–Sat. 1–5.

Cinco de Mayo. May 5, at Cameron Fiesta fairgrounds. Celebrations of Cinco de Mayo are an old tradition in Cameron and have been held throughout the 20th century. The annual event features music, evening dances, traditional foods, and speeches, including historical reminiscences.

Diez y Seis Celebration. September 15–16, at Cameron Fiesta fairgrounds. In 1990 Cameron held its 98th Diez y Seis celebration. Diez y Seis is celebrated in the same manner as Cinco de Mayo.

CAMP WOOD VICINITY, Real County

Camp Wood (pop. 595) is in the southwestern part of Real County. For seven years, in the mid 1700s, a Spanish mission was located in the area. The modern community grew up around a U.S. Army post established here in the late 1850s.

Mission San Lorenzo de la Santa Cruz Site. Marker, 0.3 mi. N of Camp Wood, on SH 55. Founded by Franciscan missionaries in 1762 for Lipan Apaches, the mission was not successful and never received the approval of the viceroy. After about seven years of precarious existence, it was abandoned. Following abandonment of Presidio San Sabá, the San Sabá garrison moved to San Lorenzo and remained for several months, but a presidio was not established there. *CM 1936.*

Scenic Drive. A series of highways to the northeast of Camp Wood offer beautiful Hill Country scenery in this area where Lipan Apaches and Spanish padres once lived: north on SH 55 and FM 335, east on SH 41, south on FM 336 and US 83 to Leakey, then west on FM 337 to return to Camp Wood.

DEVINE VICINITY, Medina County

Devine (pop. 3,928) was created as a stop on the International and Great Northern Railroad in 1881. The second largest town in Medina County, it is the trade center for the irrigated districts of the county.

Spanish Exploration in Medina County. Marker, 3 mi. N of Devine on SH 173 right-of-way. Among the routes of Spanish explorers and padres that have been traced through this area are those of Alonso de León, Manuel de la Cruz, Juan Larios and Fernando del Bosque, Domingo Terán de los Ríos, and Isidro de Espinosa. Place names throughout the county, including names of streams such as the Frio, Seco, Hondo, and Medina, serve as reminders of the rich Spanish heritage of the area now known as Medina County. *SM 1989.*

Cross Mountain, Fredericksburg. Photo by Cathryn Hoyt, THC.

FREDERICKSBURG VICINITY, Gillespie County

Fredericksburg (pop. 6,934) is predominantly German-Texan, but even here and in other small towns in the German-Texas Hill Country one finds reminders of an earlier American Indian and Hispanic presence. Fredericksburg, a tourism and trade center, is the county seat of Gillespie County.

Cross Mountain. Off FM 965 and Cross Mountain Dr., N of Fredericksburg. The first wooden cross at the summit of Cross Mountain is said to have been erected by Spanish missionaries, and was first described by an early settler in 1847. St. Mary's Catholic Church erected a substantial cross on the site in 1921 and then rebuilt the monument in 1940. In 1951 the Gillespie County Historical Society acquired the Cross Mountain property, which now plays a leading role in Fredericksburg's Easter Fires pageant. Cross Mountain also offers a panoramic view of the city.

GEORGETOWN, Williamson County

Georgetown (pop. 14,842) was established in 1848 as a trade center for the farms and Hill Country ranches that surround it. The city is home to Southwestern University, founded in 1840, and is the county seat of Williamson County.

Double File Trail. Marker, SH 29, 3.2 mi. E of Georgetown. The Delaware Indians, like many other American Indian groups, were displaced by European and Anglo-American settlement in North America. Migrating ahead of expanding settlement, they carved this trace about 1828 as they moved from East Texas to Mexico near Nuevo Laredo. Early settlements in Williamson County were located where this trail crossed waterways. The trail was called "Double File" because two horsemen could ride the track side by side. *SM 1978.*

Old Georgetown High School (Williams Middle School). 507 E. University Ave. Built in 1923, this brick and stone building exhibits Spanish Revival stylistic elements in its clay-tile roof, parapets flanking the building's center section, and an elaborate fan motif adorning the main entrance. *NR 1986; RTHL 1988.*

Residence. 1204 E. University Ave. This private residence, built in 1926, is particularly interesting because of the roof, which appears to be Mexican tile but is actually constructed of tin painted to resemble tile.

Shrines of San José and Santa María. The Shrine of San José (San Jose and 23d Sts.) was rebuilt in 1989 by the parishioners of St. Helen's Catholic Church following loss of an earlier shrine in a street widening project. San José is the patron saint of one of Georgetown's two Hispanic neighborhoods, and Our Lady of Guadalupe is the other. Santa María Shrine (at the corner of Hart and Stone Circle) was built in the late 1950s.

Fiesta San José. Labor Day weekend in September, at San Gabriel Park, Park Rd. and Stadium St. Sponsored by Los Unidos Club for the past 10 years, the festival features traditional food, music, and entertain-

Old Georgetown High School, Georgetown. Photo by Cathryn Hoyt, THC.

ment, as well as a cultural booth exhibiting photographs and historic items from the community.

HONDO, Medina County

Hondo (pop. 6,018) is located in an area rich in multicultural heritage, as reflected in its place names: Hondo and Hondo Creek, Medina River, and Seco and Verde creeks (Spanish); Castroville and D'Hanis (Alsatian); and numerous Anglo-American place names such as the towns of Devine and Yancey, and Squirrel Creek. Spanish explorer Alonso de León crossed the Medina County area in 1689 and gave the Medina River its name. Many other Spanish expeditions passed through the area (*see* Devine entries), and the Old San Antonio Road (San Antonio to Laredo) ran through the southern part of the county. Despite the early Spanish exploration of the area and the sizable modern Hispanic population, historic settlement in the county began with the Alsatian settlement at Castroville in the 1840s. Hondo is the county seat of Medina County.

Christmas in God's Country. Second Saturday of December, in downtown Hondo on 18th St. between Aves. K and M. The Hispanic component of this area celebration includes mariachi music and visits with "Pancho" Claus for children. For information contact Hondo Chamber of Commerce, P.O. Box 126, Hondo 78861.

Diez y Seis de Septiembre. Weekend closest to September 16, at the American Legion grounds. The celebration features traditional music and live entertainment.

Fiesta Fest. Second Saturday of October, on 16th St., around City Hall. This area celebration features traditional foods and music, a fiesta queen contest, and a dance with live band music. For information contact Hondo Chamber of Commerce, P.O. Box 126, Hondo 78861.

HUNT VICINITY, Kerr County

Hunt (pop. ca. 700), founded in 1913 at the junction of the North and South forks of the Guadalupe River, is a small town that serves the guest ranches and summer camps in this beautiful section of Kerr County.

MO Ranch. FM 1340, 11 mi. W of Hunt. Built by Dan Moran, president of Continental Oil Company, the MO Ranch complex served both as a vacation home for Moran and as a retreat for company employees. Spanish Revival architectural influence is evident in the red tile roofs, ornamental ironwork grilles, and decorative tilework of the buildings, which are built of native stone. Hand-painted tiles, a typical Mexican or Spanish architectural adornment, have here been adapted to some typically *Norteamericano* themes; for example, in the dormitory, large tile murals depicting scouting themes are set in recessed wall niches; in the pool area is a tile depicting Dan Moran wearing a Mexican sombrero. A more traditional influence is seen in other interior features, including exposed-beam ceilings and a winding stairway with a different tile pattern in brilliant blues

Shrine of San José, Georgetown. Photo by Cathryn Hoyt, THC.

Ceiling detail, St. Joseph's Catholic Church, Mason. Photo by Martha Peters, THC.

and earth tones on each tread. A chapel with striking stained glass windows also is part of the complex. Purchased by the Presbyterian Church in 1949, the complex is now a conference center and is open to visitors year round except the last two weeks in December. Open Mon.–Fri. 9–5.

KERRVILLE, Kerr County

Kerrville (pop. 17,384) was made county seat when Kerr County was created in 1856. Historic settlement in the county dates to the 1840s, but the resistance of Indians to the incoming Anglo-Americans was a barrier to rapid population growth until the 1870s. Ranching is the chief industry in this scenic Hill Country county. Major visitor attractions in Kerrville are the annual folk and country-western music festivals, usually held on Memorial Day and Labor Day weekends.

Cowboy Artists of America Museum. 1550 Bandera Highway. Designed by architect O'Neil Ford, the building that houses the museum was patterned after the walled haciendas of Mexico. The museum is a showcase for the works of contemporary cowboy artists.

MASON, Mason County

Mason (pop. 2,041). Historic Indians in this area included the Comanche, Lipan-Apache, Tonkawa, and Wichita, and their resistance to settlement in the area continued through the mid-19th century. Anglo-Americans and Germans began settling in the area in the 1840s, and the Hispanic population of today is largely a result of 20th-century population changes. Frontier Fort Mason, abandoned in 1869 and now in ruins, is now a local visitor attraction. The economy of Mason, the county seat of Mason County, is largely based on ranching.

St. Joseph's Catholic Church. 210 Ave. B. Built in 1876 by Irish and German immigrants, the church today has a largely Hispanic membership. A significant find was made here in 1989, when the tin roof of the historic wooden church was torn off by a storm. Repair workers found paintings of angels blowing trumpets and harp-strumming cherubs on the original vaulted ceiling. These folk-art treasures had been covered by a drop ceiling installed in the mid-1960s. The brilliant paintings were still in excellent condition and only minor restoration has been necessary. The decorative angels, characteristic of church paintings found in Mexican provinces 70 years ago, were executed in 1916 by Manuel López, then a resident of Mason. They are now a highlight of the Mason Historic Tour, sponsored by the local chamber of commerce.

MENARD, Menard County

Menard (pop. 1,606) is the locale of a 1757 Spanish mission and presidio. The mission was established to convert the Apache but the effort failed, and Indian resistance to settlement continued for a hundred years. Today the area's historic Indian and Spanish presence is reflected largely in the presidio site and in the names of the San Saba River and Las Moras Creek. Menard is now a ranching center and the county seat of Menard County.

Bevins Hotel. On San Saba St. This four-story, buff-brick structure shows Spanish Revival elements in the use of red tile at the roof, cast-stone detailing (especially the water spouts), wrought-iron balcony railings, and arches. The hotel now houses the Menard Hospital.

Frisco Depot. US 83. Built in 1911, this charming little depot is a stuccoed building in Spanish Revival style, featuring stepped parapets and a red tile roof. The depot displays a sign with the original town name, Menardville, and has housed a museum since 1972. The museum focuses on local and regional history. Open Mon.–Wed. 9–12, 1–5.

Mission Santa Cruz de San Sabá Site. Marker, 2 mi. E of Menard on FM 2092. Mission Santa Cruz de San Sabá, established in 1757, was burned by a force of Comanche and other Indians in 1758. A depiction of this event, one of the oldest non-Indian historic paintings in Texas, is still in existence, but its current ownership is in dispute. The exact locale of the mission site is not known. *CM 1936.*

Presidio de San Sabá Ruins. 2 mi. W of Menard, off SH 29. This Spanish fort, also known as Presidio San Luis de las Amarillas, was established in 1757 for the protection of the ill-fated Mission Santa Cruz de San Sabá. The presidio, unable to overcome Indian control of the territory, was abandoned little more than a decade later. A 1936 public works project reconstructed the presidio's northwest corner and the ruins are now managed as a county park. *CM 1936; NR 1972.*

MONTELL VICINITY, Uvalde County

Presidio de San Sabá ruins, Menard.
Photo by Robert Mallouf, THC.

Montell (pop. ca. 10) was established in the late 1800s near the site of Mission Nuestra Señora de la Candelaria. Today this tiny community serves the ranches in the area.

Mission Nuestra Señora de la Candelaria Site. Marker, in turnout of SH 55, at Montell. The third mission named Nuestra Señora de la Candelaria to be founded in Texas was established near here on the Nueces River in 1762. About 400 Lipan Apaches lived at the mission until it was abandoned about 1769. Stones from the ruins were taken by settlers in the 1800s to build houses, and now only historical markers can be seen at the site. *CM 1936; SM 1968.*

MOUNTAIN HOME VICINITY, Kerr County

Mountain Home (pop. ca. 100) was established in 1890 by a shopkeeper who supplied the large ranches in the area with food and other staples. The role of the small community remains much the same today.

Y.O. Ranch. Entrance 15 mi. W of Mountain Home on SH 41. A substantial herd of Longhorn cattle can be viewed at this ranch, which is a commercial venture open for daily tours.

Grotto at Holy Family Catholic Church, New Braunfels. Photo by Cathryn Hoyt, THC.

NEW BRAUNFELS AND VICINITY, Comal County

New Braunfels (pop. 27,334) is located in an area where Hispanic heritage dates from Alonso de León's naming of the Guadalupe River in 1689. In 1718 Martín de Alarcón, identifying the Comal River as the Little Guadalupe, claimed for Spain the lands where the Comal and Guadalupe rivers join. In the mid-1700s a mission was established near here, on the route of El Camino Real. In the early 1800s both the Baron de Bastrop and Juan Martín de Veramendi received grants of lands in the area. The post–World War II increase in Mexican-American population in predominantly German-Texan New Braunfels is reflected in the growth of Our Lady of Perpetual Help Parish and the creation of a second predominantly Mexican-American parish in the 1960s. The western part of the city, known as the "Barrio Seco," is predominantly Mexican-American in population. New Braunfels is a tourism and trade center and the county seat of Comal County.

El Camino Real. Markers, Seguin Ave. at Nacogdoches St.; FM 482 in Stratemann Ln. area S of New Braunfels. Private markers commemorate the route of El Camino Real and mark the way to the historic crossing at the junction of the Guadalupe and Comal rivers.

Guadalupe and Comal Rivers Junction. Marker, 246 E. Lincoln. The Guadalupe River was named by Alonso de León in 1689 in honor of Our Lady of Guadalupe. This site was claimed May 8, 1718, for the king of Spain by Martín de Alarcón and soon became an important crossing for priests and army units en route to East Texas. In the 19th century, the junction became an important ferry crossing site for German immigrants. *SM 1968.*

Holy Family Catholic Church. 245 S. Hidalgo St. Holy Family Parish, created in 1964, was the second Catholic church established in New Braunfels for a predominantly Mexican-American neighborhood. Of special interest here is the shrine at the right side of the church.

Hotel Faust. 240 S. Seguin St. This four-story masonry structure with brick veneer has Spanish Revival stylistic elements. The building's symmetrical façade is divided by slightly projecting pilasters, an elaborate stepped parapet, and ornate cast-concrete panels over the two main entrances. Originally called the Travelers Hotel, it was renamed in 1936 to honor Walter Faust and his family, who had been instrumental in the hotel's development. The hotel was restored in 1982. *RTHL 1984; NR 1985.*

Mission Nuestra Señora de Guadalupe Site. Marker, 2.5 mi. NW of New Braunfels on SH 46. Site of Mission Nuestra Señora de Guadalupe, a mission established in 1756 for the Tonkawas, Mayeyes, and associated Indians who were formerly at Mission San Francisco Xavier on the San Gabriel River. This Guadalupe mission was abandoned in 1758. *CM 1936.*

Our Lady of Perpetual Help Catholic Church. Austin and Union Sts. This parish was established in 1926 to meet the needs of the rapidly growing Mexican-American neighborhood in this area. The first church was built that year, but two years later a fire partially destroyed the interior, and a larger church was built. The parish was divided in 1964 and Holy Family Parish was created. Still, Our Lady of Perpetual Help needed a larger facility, and the present modern structure was completed in 1969. Of particular interest is the church's shrine to Our Lady, which faces Austin St. In keeping with Mexican-American traditions, mariachis perform on Sundays, and the Las Posadas procession is performed at Christmas.

Fiesta Histórica Mexicana. Date near September 16, at New Braunfels Civic Center, 390 S. Seguin. This celebration, sponsored by the New Braunfels Mexican-American Heritage Society, was initiated in 1986. Events include a Saturday night dance and Sunday heritage display with delicious foods and live performances by regional mariachi bands and local ballet folklórico groups.

ROUND ROCK, Williamson and Travis Counties

Round Rock (pop. 30,923) was once a small town famous primarily as the place where outlaw Sam Bass was killed. Round Rock grew rapidly in the 1970s and 1980s as Austin's population expanded into the area.

Fiesta Amistad. In May, usually Memorial Day weekend, on Main St. downtown. Sponsored by El Amistad Club, this celebration of friendship has been held since 1981 and now attracts about 12,000 visitors. The fiesta features musical entertainment ranging from conjunto to country and western. The emphasis is on family entertainment, including events such as races and tortilla-rolling and tamale-eating contests. In addition to games, music, and food, the fiesta also includes a queen contest and a Memorial Day observance.

Detail, Hotel Faust, New Braunfels. Photo by Cathryn Hoyt, THC.

SAN GABRIEL VICINITY, Milam County

San Gabriel (pop. ca. 100), a small agricultural community, is located in the eastern part of the county. Three Spanish missions were located near here in the 18th century.

Spanish Mission Sites. Marker, 6 mi. E of San Gabriel on FM 487. Five archeological sites from the mid-1700s, related to Spanish colonization in Central Texas, are located in Milam County and have been listed on the National Register of Historic Places as the San Xavier Mission Complex. Three of the sites have been identified as missions San Francisco Xavier de Horcasitas, San Ildefonso, and Nuestra Señora de la Candelaria. The other sites may be the remains of an associated presidio (San Francisco Xavier de Gigedo) and an Indian village. The San Xavier missions lasted only a few years and the sites, almost invisible now, are on private land and not open to the public. *CM 1936; NR 1973.*

SAN MARCOS AND VICINITY, Hays County

San Marcos (pop. 28,743) is located at the edge of the main Spanis route from San Antonio to East Texas. Several Spanish expeditions crosse this area in the late 17th and early 18th centuries. In 1755 three missions were removed from the banks of the San Gabriel River (near Georgetown) and located on El Camino Real on the San Marcos River. Only four years later the mission personnel were reassigned to San Sabá and San Antonio. Anglo-American settlement was initiated by Thomas G. McGehee's 1835 land grant from Mexico. The county was created in 1848 and San Marcos was designated the county seat. In addition to its historic homes from the late 19th and early 20th centuries, the city is well-known for its annual chili cook-off in the third week of September.

Don Felipe Roque de la Portilla. Marker, near the San Marcos de Neve marker, 3.7 mi. NE of San Marcos, off SH 21. Felipe Roque de la Portilla established a colony here on El Camino Real, founding San Marcos de Neve in April 1808. He later helped found a colony at Refugio, near Copano Bay. For his colonizing efforts, which preceded those of Stephen F. Austin and Martín de León, he is sometimes called the first empresario. *SM 1976.*

San Marcos de Neve. Marker, near crossing of San Marcos River on FM 266 (El Camino Real), about 2 mi. SE of San Marcos. The village of San Marcos de Neve was established in 1808, but Comanche raids and the brewing Mexican Revolution led to the abandonment of the villa in 1812. At the crest of the hill above the marker is the approximate location of a picket fortification where Spanish troops were stationed along the route of El Camino Real. *CM 1936.*

San Marcos Telephone Company. 138 W. San Antonio St. The two-story, stuccoed brick structure, built in 1928, is the only example of Spanish Revival style among the many designated historic buildings in San Marcos. *NR 1983.*

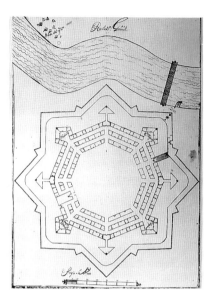

Eighteenth-century plan of the Spanish mission and presidio sites on the San Gabriel River. THC photo.

Southside Community Center. 518 Guadalupe. Spanish stylistic influence in this modern Mexican-American neighborhood center is exhibited in the red tile roof, painted tile, and wrought-iron details.

Veramendi Plaza. C.M. Allen Pkwy at Hopkins St. The plaza is named for Juan Martín Veramendi, a governor of Mexican Texas, who received a two-league grant here in 1831. His land later became the heart of the town of San Marcos as it presently exists. Accessible from the plaza is the San Marcos River Walkway, which unites three picturesque, lushly landscaped city parks along the river.

Cinco de Mayo in San Marcos. Weekend closest to May 5, at the Hays County Civic Center (IH 35S) and on the courthouse square downtown. Founded in 1975, the celebration features the annual State Menudo Cook-off, a street dance, the Tejas Softball Tournament, performances of ballet folklórico, mariachi music, and the Miss Cinco de Mayo contest. The event is sponsored by several city businesses and civic organizations, including the Hispanic Chamber of Commerce, LULAC, and the City of San Marcos. For information contact San Marcos Hispanic Chamber of Commerce, P.O. Box 1051, San Marcos 78666.

Scenic Drive. FM 12 NW to FM 32 to US 281. Parts of this route from San Marcos to near Blanco, in Blanco County, follow a ridge called the Devil's Backbone, now a peaceful, scenic aspect of the Hill Country where white-tailed deer are often seen. The name is said to derive from the Spanish *Cordillera del Diablo,* for the hills' having been used as a retreat by the Comanches.

SEGUIN AND VICINITY, Guadalupe County

Seguin (pop. 18,853) is named for Juan N. Seguín, Texas independence hero who commanded a group of Mexican-Texans at the Battle of San Jacinto. Guadalupe County received its name from the Guadalupe River, which was named by Alonso de León in 1689. In the 1820s and early 1830s, land grants in the area were made to settlers through the DeWitt Colony and directly from the Mexican government. Among the early ranch owners in the county was José Antonio Navarro, of Texas revolutionary fame. In the mid-1830s Indian resistance called a halt to further settlement, but land grants given to veterans of the Texas war for independence brought in hundreds of people in the last years of the decade. The county was created in 1846 and Seguin, founded in 1838, was named the county seat. In the second half of the 19th century, German immigrants and Anglo-Americans entered the county, introducing their traditions and customs.

Los Nogales. River St. and Liveoak. Surviving examples of structures utilizing indigenous adobe construction are rare in Central Texas. This adobe building, which now houses a museum, was built in 1849 for German immigrant Justus Gombert. The original one-room adobe structure was later stuccoed and enlarged. The name Los Nogales is derived from the Spanish word for walnuts. *RTHL 1962; NR 1972; SM 1989.*

Our Lady of Guadalupe Church. 409 W. Krezzorn. The first Church

Los Nogales, Seguin. Photo by
Cathryn Hoyt, THC.

of Our Lady of Guadalupe in Seguin was established in 1908 to serve the
Mexican-American Catholics of Guadalupe County. A second church was
built in the 1950s, and the present brick church was constructed in 1967.
Although the church is modern, the establishment of Our Lady of
Guadalupe Parish reflects the historic presence of Hispanics in the area.
This church served Mexican-Americans throughout Guadalupe County
until Immaculate Conception Church was built in Marion in 1954.

Juan Nepomuceno Seguín. Marker, City Hall, 205 N. River St. Juan
Nepomuceno Seguín, soldier in the Texas war for independence, led a contingent of Mexican-Texans at the battle of San Jacinto and later served as
mayor of San Antonio. In the backlash of hostility against Mexico that followed independence, Seguín was suspected of being a Mexican sympa-
thizer. He moved to Mexico in 1842, later returned to Texas, and returned
again to Mexico, where he died in Nuevo Laredo in 1890. *SM 1970.*

Juan Seguín's Burial Site. S. Saunders Ave. and Nelda St. In recog-

352

Juan Seguín's burial site, Seguin.
Photo by Cathryn Hoyt, THC.

nition of Seguín's role in Texas independence, Mexico returned his remains to Seguin for reinterment in 1974. The grave, marked with a granite slab, is located in a peaceful park setting.

Texas Theater. 400 block of N. Austin St. The small but ornate Texas Theater is one of several theaters in the state that survive from the golden age following the 1915 Panama-California Exhibition in San Diego, California, when entertainment and tropical Spanish decorations were synonymous. The exterior and much of the interior of the theater remains unchanged, but the auditorium, which originally seated 500, was modified in the 1960s to seat 300.

Cinco de Mayo. Weekend nearest May 5, at Central Park, on Austin St. The local Hispanic Chamber of Commerce sponsors a Cinco de Mayo festival with food, dances and fun.

Fiestas Patrias Mexicanas. Weekend nearest September 16, at Central Park, on Austin St. Organized by the Teatro de Artes de Juan Seguín, the fiesta promotes Mexican-American culture throughout the community and provides a traditional, family-oriented Diez y Seis celebration for the city's large Hispanic population. Major events include performances of traditional dance and music, a menudo cook-off, puppet shows for young visitors, and demonstrations of traditional arts and crafts. Over 8,000 visitors attend annually. For information contact Teatro de Artes de Juan Seguín, 1717 Westview, Seguin 78155.

Seguin Vicinity

El Capote Ranch Site. Marker, on FM 466, 14 mi. E of Seguin. El Capote Ranch was founded late in the Spanish Colonial period by French army officer José de la Baume, who came to the United States with the Marquis de Lafayette, of American Revolutionary War fame. La Baume later joined the Spanish army and received land in 1806 for his services. His grant was reaffirmed after Mexican independence. By 1810 El Capote was one of fourteen private ranches reported in the general area of San Antonio. The Capote Ranch land changed hands several times during the 19th century, and among its well-known owners was Theodore Roosevelt's second wife, who owned the ranch in the 1870s. *SM 1976.*

José Antonio Navarro Ranch Site. Marker, NE of Seguin, 1 mi. S of Geronimo on SH 123 right-of-way. José Antonio Navarro, a signer of the Texas Declaration of Independence, held several offices in Mexican government before becoming an active participant in the movement for Texas independence. Navarro possessed numerous landholdings in this part of the state. He purchased land along Geronimo Creek in 1832 and owned the ranch until 1853. *SM 1986.*

SOMERVILLE AND VICINITY, Burleson County

Somerville (pop. 1,542) was founded as a railroad town in 1883. Still known today as a railroad center, Somerville is also a gateway to Somerville Reservoir, a major recreational area in southern Burleson County.

Somerville Historical Museum. SH 36 and 8th St. Most of the museum's collections relate to German, Polish, and Czech settlers, but there are a few exhibited items relating to American Indian groups of the area and to Hispanic heritage. Open Sat. 10–4.

Yegua Creek. Marker, ca. 0.25 mile S of SH 36 bridge in Somerville. This creek lies in an area of early Spanish exploration. Originally named San Francisco in 1690, the stream was marked on an 1822 map made by Stephen F. Austin as Yegua. This second name derives from the Spanish word for mare, probably because mustang mares and foals then grazed along the timbered creek. Flooding of this area was common until the construction of Lake Somerville in 1967. *SM 1976.*

STONEWALL VICINITY, Gillespie County

Stonewall (pop. ca. 300) is known primarily for the peaches grown in the surrounding area and for the nearby historic park.

Lyndon B. Johnson State Historic Park. On US 290 near Stonewall. This historic site park was created to honor a native Texan who achieved the nation's highest office. In addition to being a historical facility, with mementos of the former president, the park features a nature trail (including a Hill Country botanical exhibit) that winds past wildlife enclosures stocked with buffalo, white-tailed deer, wild turkey, other native wildlife, and Longhorn cattle. This is one of the few parks that offers an opportunity to see both buffalo and Longhorns, living reminders of Texas' Indian and Hispanic heritage. Recreational facilities are available in the park.

UVALDE, Uvalde County

Uvalde (pop. 14,729) was named for a Spanish soldier of the late 18th century, Capt. Juan de Ugalde. In the 1760s Nuestra Señora de la Candelaria (see Montell entry) was founded to serve the Lipan Apaches who lived in the area. Although early explorers as well as countless pioneers and soldiers traveled through the area, Indian resistance delayed settlement until the 1850s. In 1849 a U.S. infantry camp was established on the Leona River, and this later became the site of Fort Inge. The military presence encouraged settlement, and in 1853 Encina was begun at the head of the Leona. The name of the town was changed to Uvalde in 1856, when Uvalde County was organized.

Cactus Jack Festival. Second weekend in October, at Memorial Park. Family-fun fall festival featuring continuous live entertainment, Saturday parade, arts and crafts, contests and games, country fair, auction, and dances. The Hispanic component includes traditional music (including mariachis) and foods, ballet folklórico, and an evening dance with live band music. For further information, contact Uvalde Chamber of Commerce, P.O. Box 706, Uvalde 78802.

Cinco de Mayo. Weekend closest to May 5, at West End park (Jardín de los Héroes). Music, fun, and food mark this traditional celebration. For information contact American Legion Post 479, 583 W. Main, Uvalde 78801.

Diez y Seis de Septiembre. September 15 and 16, at West End park (Jardín de los Héroes). The celebration features traditional dances, music, and food and includes the crowning of a queen and an evening dance with live band music. For information contact American Legion Post 479, 583 West Main, Uvalde 78801.

Scenic Drive. Some of the most spectacular scenery in the Texas Hill Country, once the home of the Lipan Apaches, can be seen in the Uvalde area. Take US 83 north to Leakey, then west on FM 337 and south on SH 55. Or, from Leakey, drive east on FM 337 to Vanderpool (near Lost Maples Natural Area) and south on FM 187 to Sabinal.

REGION 5

Houston and Southeast Texas

The Southeast Texas region includes the southern portion of the Piney Woods country and the upper reaches of the Gulf Coastal Plains. Caddoan Indian groups inhabited the East Texas woodlands at the time of the earliest European contacts, and the Karankawa and Orcoquisacs were living in the southern and coastal areas of the region. The Luis de Moscoso party in 1542 found the Caddoan bands along the Red River unfriendly, but other Spaniards (and later the French and Anglos) were more successful in dealing with the original inhabitants of the region. Spaniards soon began calling the Caddoan Indians—particularly the Hasinai tribe that lived near the Sabine, Angelina, and Neches Rivers—the Tejas Indians. This name is said to have evolved from the Indian greeting "tayshas," meaning "hello, friend" or "ally." Soon the Spaniards began using the word "Tejas" to refer to all of the lands east of the Trinity River. Later, after the San Antonio missions were founded, lands extending to the Medina River were so called, and ultimately the name, as Texas, was given to the state.

As early as 1536 Spanish authorities were receiving explorers' reports about the northern territories, but Spanish colonization of southeastern and southern coastal Texas did not begin until over 150 years later. The Spaniards' eventual attempt to establish a stronger presence in the region was a result of French exploration in East Texas during the 1680s. The Spanish established their first outpost in East Texas, Mission San Francisco de las Tejas, in 1690, and thus began eighty years of competition with the French in this region. Between 1690 and 1756, nine Spanish missions were established in this region (including Mission San Miguel de Linares de los Adaes just east of the Sabine River).

The East Texas missions had to be temporarily abandoned in 1719 because of the threat of French invasion, and the missions that were reestablished in the 1720s were later permanently relocated and renamed. The political necessity for maintaining the mission-presidio system in East Texas decreased after 1763, when the French ceded Louisiana to Spain in payment for assistance in fighting England during the French and Indian War. In response, Spanish authorities ordered the East Texas missions abandoned, and in 1773 the provincial capital of Texas was moved from Los Adaes to San Antonio de Béxar.

When the missions were abandoned, many settlers who had come to

Opposite: **St. Francis of the Tejas Catholic Church, Crockett. Photo by Cathryn Hoyt, THC.**

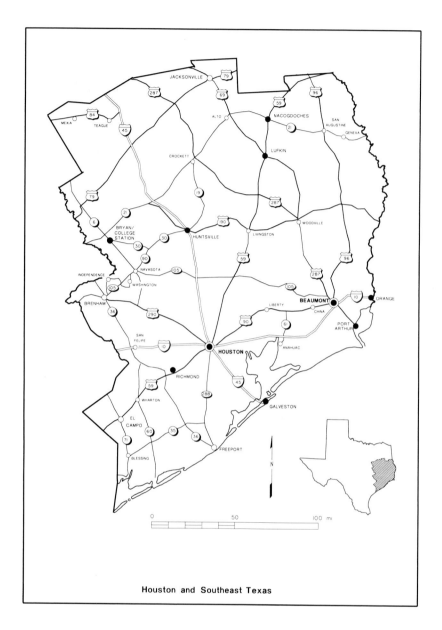

Houston and Southeast Texas

Guidebook Region 5. Map by Greg Miller.

live in the area were forced to leave also. Some of the more adventurous or determined returned without official permission to Nacogdoches and lived there illegally until 1779, when the crown recognized and permitted their presence. The independence shown by the early Nacogdoches returnees was but a hint of things to come. Nacogdoches became a center for adventurers and revolutionaries, including those of the Gutiérrez-Magee expedition (1812–13), and later with the Fredonian Rebellion (1826).

During this period, the Louisiana territory, which had been ceded back to France in 1800, was sold to the United States. When illegal immigration from the United States became noticeable, Mexican Governor Félix Trespalacios authorized American Indian settlement in Texas in hopes

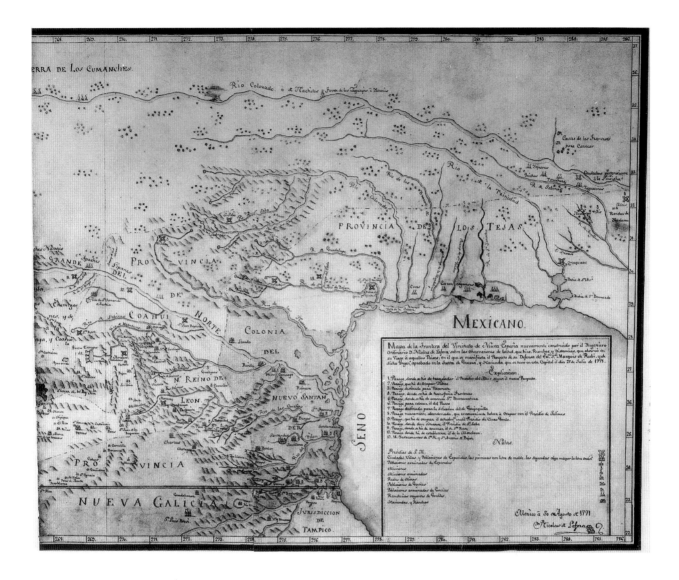

of discouraging the Anglo-Americans. American Indians from the southeastern United States were being forced westward by Anglo-American expansion into their homeland. Under the new Mexican policy they found temporary homes in East Texas, but they were not able to obtain title to lands they occupied. During the Texas war for independence from Mexico, Sam Houston promised them land titles in exchange for support, but his promise was later refuted. Indian involvement in the Córdova Rebellion of 1838 resulted in the expulsion of nearly all Indians from East Texas. Of those that had been in East Texas before the Texas Revolution, only the Alabama-Coushatta ultimately succeeded in legally obtaining lands from the State of Texas.

Two of the most famous events associated with Texas independence took place in this region of the state: the signing of the Texas Declaration of Independence at Washington-on-the-Brazos in Washington County,

Map, dated 1771, showing the region known as the Seno Mexicano and the Provincia de los Tejas. THC photo.

359

and the Battle of San Jacinto in Harris County. Prominent Mexican-Texans were involved in both of these historic events. Lorenzo de Zavala, José Francisco Ruiz, and José Antonio Navarro signed the declaration. Navarro also helped draft the 1836 Constitution, and De Zavala became the ad interim vice-president of the new republic. José Antonio Menchaca and Juan N. Seguín joined Sam Houston's forces at San Jacinto in April 1836, where Seguín commanded the only unit of Mexican-Texans.

Most of this region is sparsely populated today by Texans of Hispanic descent, but it nevertheless offers a number of important historic sites and one of only two American Indian reservations that currently exist in Texas. In the northern portion of this region El Camino Real is roughly paralleled by modern SH 21 from San Antonio to the Gaines Ferry site in Sabine County, at the Louisiana-Texas state line. Through the area of East Texas where this historic route passed are located the old mission sites of the Spanish Colonial period and early settlements such as Nacogdoches. This region has produced one of the state's most valuable collections of documents for the study of the Spanish and Mexican periods of Texas history, the Nacogdoches Archives. Houston, the largest city in the area, is also the largest city in Texas. There, as in other parts of the region, Mexican-American community churches, fine examples of Spanish-influenced architecture, and a number of traditional festivals attest to the continuance of Hispanic traditions and influence into the 20th century.

HOUSTON AND VICINITY, Harris County

Houston (pop. 1,630,553), the largest city in Texas, developed from an 1836 settlement promoted by John and Augustus Allen, brothers from Brooklyn, New York. They purchased several thousand acres in the area of Harrisburg, a settlement burned during the Texas war for independence, and sold real estate to the general public. The city was named for Sam Houston, the first president of the Republic of Texas. Anti-Mexican feelings after the battle continued to run strong, and several decades passed before substantial numbers of Hispanics moved into the city.

Hispanics moved to Houston as early as the 1880s, but the largest population increase came after the beginning of the 1910 revolution in Mexico. In 1911 the Catholic Church sent Oblate priests to found a parish, Our Lady of Guadalupe, to administer to the spiritual needs of the community. A second wave of immigration in the 1920s led to the expansion of Our Lady of Guadalupe, the establishment of the second and third Mexican-American Catholic churches (the Immaculate Heart of Mary and Our Lady of Dolores) and the formation of a distinct Mexican-American barrio, "la colonia mexicana" or "el pueblo mexicano." Through periods of prejudice, economic hardship, and war, Houston's Hispanic community continued to grow and cohere; theater troupes, dance groups, social clubs, and church organizations nurtured the community's *mexicanidad,* while civic organizations, business associations, and, later, political groups were organized to confront the social, economic, and political issues Houston's Hispanics faced in a plural society.

Today, Houston's Hispanic community is large, diverse, and well established. The community, which makes up about 28% of the city's population, is distributed throughout the city and has been called the least racially segregated population in Harris County. Eight out of every ten Hispanics in Houston are Mexican-American, but Spanish-Americans, Puerto Ricans, and Central Americans also contribute to the city's diversity. Houston Hispanics have been elected to office at many levels of government, and Hispanic businesses continue to organize through the Hispanic and Mexican-American chambers of commerce. The Hispanic media—now well over a dozen radio stations, television channels, and newspapers—expands to meet the growing concerns and needs of the Spanish-speaking community. Houston is home to one of the largest Hispanic communities in the nation and contains a large and representative sample of the Hispanic history, art, architecture, folklife, and foodways that contribute so profoundly to Texas' cultural diversity.

Information

Greater Houston Convention and Visitors Bureau. 3300 Main St. The Convention and Visitors Bureau provides maps, literature, and assistance to visitors.

Historic Sites

Lorenzo de Zavala (1789–1836). Marker, 3 mi. E of Channelview at Market St. and De Zavala Rd. The marker at this location recounts the achievements of De Zavala, a signer of the Texas Declaration of Independence and ad interim vice-president of the Republic of Texas. *SM 1968.*

Lorenzo de Zavala Home Site. Marker, Zavala Point at the Gulf Coast Portland Cement Company property, 16530 De Zavala Road (across Buffalo Bayou from the Battleship *Texas*). De Zavala's plank-covered log house, built in 1829, stood here and served as a hospital for the wounded after the Battle of San Jacinto. *CM 1936. See also* San Jacinto Battleground State Park.

San Jacinto Battleground State Park. 3800 Park Rd. (or Battleground Rd.), on SH 134 near Deer Park. Here Texas Army commander Sam Houston and 910 Texans defeated Mexican president Antonio López de Santa Anna and his 1200-man army at the Battle of San Jacinto on April 21, 1836. Among Sam Houston's troops were Mexican-Texans Lorenzo de Zavala, Jr., José Antonio Menchaca, and Juan N. Seguín, who commanded 25 Mexican-Texans in the Ninth Company of the Second Regiment of Texas Volunteers, the only Tejano unit. The 570-foot San Jacinto Monument, which stands 15 feet taller than the Washington Monument, was erected here in 1936–39 to commemorate the event. At the San Jacinto Museum of History, located at the base of this monument, visitors may view exhibits highlighting four hundred years of Texas history under six sovereign governments (open daily 9–5; closed Dec. 24 and 25). De Zavala

Plaza is a memorial to Lorenzo de Zavala (see entries above), and the De Zavala Cemetery, where Lorenzo de Zavala's headstone can be seen, is contained within the park. *NHL; RTHL 1964; SM 1970.*

Spanish Revival Architecture

Spanish Mission Revival architecture, as well as structures exhibiting other Hispanic stylistic influences, are numerous and well documented in Houston. Visitors wishing to view these structures in the context of other architectural styles in the city are advised to consult the invaluable *Houston Architectural Guide,* by Stephen Fox (1990).

Alamo Plaza Motor Hotel. 4343 Old Spanish Trail. A Pop Spanish Revival tourist court, the Alamo Plaza was built in 1948. The chain to which this motor hotel belonged is credited as being one of the earliest motel chains in the United States. First opened in 1929 in Waco, Texas, the Alamo Plaza Motor Hotels were characterized by their distinctive "Alamoesque" front façades.

Brennan's Houston. 3300 Smith St. This structure, designed by architect John F. Staub, was built in 1930 as headquarters for the Junior League of Houston. Staub based his design on an 18th-century Spanish Creole example from the French Quarter of New Orleans.

J.J. Burke House. 2158 Brentwood Dr. Built in 1933, the Burke House is one of two unique Spanish-style homes constructed of reinforced concrete by F. McM. Sawyer. Each features the traditional parapet, red tile roof, and arches.

Edd R. Campbell House. 2524 Wichita Ave. The Campbell House, designed by W.D. Bordeaux, was built in 1930. It is a two-story Monterey, California, style residence with arches, balconies, and red tile roof.

William A. Cooke House. 1724 Alta Vista Ave. Cooke & Co., architects, designed this 1912, Mission-style bungalow with parapets, red tile roof, and stuccoed exterior.

Carl Fleet House. 1911 Woodbury. Fleet House was built in 1946. C.D. Hutsell, architect, designed this idiosyncratic example of Spanish-style suburban design.

Guadalupe Plaza. Runnels St. at Jensen Dr. Hispanic Consortium, architects, designed this 1988 complex. The beautiful Mexican-theme plaza with its bright colors, fountains, and tropical plants shows the continuation of Hispanic stylistic influence in recent city architecture.

Gulf Publishing Company Building. 3301 Allen Pkwy. This large, Spanish Revival style printing plant was built in 1928. The entrance is framed by an elaborate cast-stone frontispiece. The tile roof, arched windows, and decorative wrought iron details enhance the Spanish Revival design.

Hermann Hospital (now Cullen Pavilion). 6411 Fannin, in Texas Medical Center Complex. Built in 1925 and restored during 1986–90, the structure shows Spanish Revival stylistic influences. The original Hermann Hospital carved-stone façade leads to the Cullen Pavilion Lobby, a Spanish-influenced courtyard (originally open-air, but now enclosed with

De Zavala headstone in San Jacinto Battleground State Park, Houston. Photo by Jane Ashley.

Left: Hermann Hospital, Houston. Photo by Jane Ashley.

Below: Courtyard of Brennan's Houston. Photo by Jane Ashley.

skylighting) with arched windows, fountains, and handmade tile floors.

Julia Ideson Building (Houston Public Library). 500 McKinney Ave. The Ideson Building housed the Houston Public Library from its completion and opening in October 1926 until 1976, when the new central library was constructed on an adjacent plot. Built in Spanish Revival style, the Ideson Building was designed by Boston architect Ralph Adams Cram. It was intended as a prototype in design for the rest of the public buildings in downtown Houston. Cram chose the Spanish Revival style because he felt that it best suited the needs and heritage of the Southwest. In the Ideson Building, Cram combined European Old World and Southwestern regional flavor with decorations appropriate to the building's location in Houston. Unfortunately, before the other public buildings could be built, the Depression interceded and the Ideson Building was the only example completed. The exterior walls of the building are buff-colored brick and concrete, ornately decorated with stone carvings and reliefs, and topped with red tile roofs. The interior of the Ideson Building is as distinctive as its exterior. Decorative elements range from a tile picture of Don Quixote of Talavera to murals painted by noted women artists as part of a Public Works Administration project in 1934–35. Three of the murals depict the New World's Spanish background. The building now houses the Houston Metropolitan Research Center. *NR 1977.*

Carl Fleet House, Houston. Photo by Jane Ashley.

364

Isabella Court. 1003–1005 Isabella Ave. W.D. Bordeaux was architect of this 1929 structure, which features a courtyard, stuccoed exterior, and red tile roof. Two floors of apartments top street-level commercial shops.

Dora Lantrip Elementary School. 100 Telephone Rd. Maurice J. Sullivan designed this 1916 school building. Spanish Revival style is reflected in the tile roof, arcaded loggias, and patios. This school, with its classrooms arranged in a series of pavilions, was the first in Houston to incorporate the "cottage plan" that is now so common.

Morris Levy House. 1215 Wrightwood Ave. Built about 1920, this Mission-style bungalow with its Alamo-style gable and stuccoed exterior is typical of the more modest Spanish-influenced houses of the early 20th century.

Our Lady of Guadalupe Church. *See* entry under Churches.

Rein Company Building (now houses a Savings & Loan). 3401 Allen Pkwy. Howell and Thomas, architects, incorporated Spanish details in this building in the late 1920s to conceal its commercial use.

St. Anne's Catholic Church. 2120 Westheimer Rd. Maurice J. Sullivan was the architect for this 1940 church. Santa Barbara Mission Revival stylistic influences can be seen in the bell tower, parapet, tile roof, stuccoed exterior, arches, and carved stone details. The interior of the church is decorated in neo-Byzantine style with a pink interior finish and rows of dark green columns. The church contains seven chapels, each representing one of the seven sacraments. Masses are given in English and Spanish.

Schlesser-Burrows House. 1123 Harvard St. This 1912 house shows Mission Revival stylistic influences, especially in the arched parapet. *NR 1983.*

Cleveland Sewall House. 3460 Inwood Dr. The Cleveland Sewall residence is an outstanding example of Spanish Revival architecture. Designed by noted Boston architect Ralph A. Cram in 1924, the house represents his most outstanding residential work. The interior features superb detailing in the use of decorative tiles from Spain, Churrigueresque plaster ornamentation, massive oak doors with iron plates, and heavily beamed ceilings. The large dining room is dominated by a fountain decorated with colorful tiles from Spain. The house was originally furnished with Spanish, Jacobean, and Mediterranean furnishings and tapestries from Europe, which are now in the collections of the Fine Arts Department at Rice University. The house was vacated in 1973 and, after almost ten years of neglect and vandalism, was restored to its present fine condition. *NR 1975.*

Star Engraving Company Building (now 3201 Allen Pkwy. Bldg). 3201 Allen Pkwy. R.D. Steele was the architect for this 1930 building, which features mission-style towers, parapets, carved stone details, and red tile roof.

Taggart Park Townhouses. 6402 Taggart Ave. Sensational colors and sensuous shapes give this 1984 row-house complex a definite Latin flair. The townhouses were designed by Laurinda Spear and Peruvian-born Bernardo Fort-Brescia, of the Miami architectural firm Arquitectonica. Their use of lyrical shapes and sensational colors can also be seen on other examples of modern architecture in the city.

Churches

Our Lady of Guadalupe Church. 2405 Navigation Blvd. In 1911 Oblate priests came to Houston to serve the growing Spanish-speaking Catholic community. The first Our Lady of Guadalupe Church, a wood frame structure, was built in 1912. The church was elevated to parish status in 1921 and, because its congregation kept growing, a second church structure was soon needed. Leo M.J. Dielmann served as architect for the new, brick structure, built in 1923 adjacent to the first church, and soon a parochial school was added. As late as 1925, Our Lady of Guadalupe was the only Catholic church for Spanish-speaking residents of Houston. Today, most masses are given in Spanish, but English and Vietnamese masses are included. A major devotional celebration is held on the Feast Day of Our Lady of Guadalupe, on December 12, and an annual October Fiesta is sponsored by the church. Both events include traditional Mexican music, dance, and foods. *SM 1991. See also* sidebar: Hispanic Catholic Ministry in Houston.

Sacred Heart Co-Cathedral. 1111 Pierce. The cathedral sponsors an annual diocesan procession commemorating the Feast Day of Our Lady of Guadalupe in December. The procession originates at the intersection of Texas and Crawford streets and proceeds to the cathedral. Over 1,000 parishioners and church leaders, accompanied by strolling mariachis, take part in this half-hour procession to Sacred Heart. The procession ends outside the cathedral, where an altar is prepared and a Spanish-language mass is given. After the mass, parishioners enjoy a *tamalada* and *buñelos*.

St. Anne's Catholic Church. *See* Spanish Revival Architecture.

Museums

Houston Museum of Natural Science. One Hermann Circle Dr. Permanent exhibits include a collection of prehistoric and 19th- and 20th-century Pueblo Indian ceramics, and 200 Mexican secular and religious Masks. Occasionally exhibited are collections of Spanish Colonial and Mexican ceramics and glass, and Mexican clothing. Permanent holdings include a collection of 29 retablos and santos, a small collection of Aztec ceramics and stone pieces, assorted Late Post-Classic (including Tarascan) ceramics and stone artifacts, a large collection (over 10,000 pieces) of Caddoan ceramics and stone tools from Louisiana and Arkansas, and a collection of Karankawa material. Open Mon.–Sat. 9–6; Sun. 12–6.

Jesse H. Jones Park. 3 mi. W of Humble, between US 59 and IH 45 on FM 1960, 1 mi. N of Kenswick community entrance. Visitors can learn about the natural environment and lifeways of the Akokisa (Orcoquisac) Indians who once lived at the site of this 225-acre park. The park's Nature Center and Pioneer Village provides exhibits on native plants and local history, as well as children's and adult classes on wild edible plants, animal tracks and signs, and pioneer crafts. A replica of an Akokisa lodge, an open-air summer shelter known as a Chickee (chá-kee), and a hollowed log used for grinding corn are on display in the park.

HISPANIC CATHOLIC MINISTRY IN HOUSTON

The heart of many Hispanic communities in Texas is the local Our Lady of Guadalupe Church. Churches named for the Virgin of Guadalupe, the patron saint of Mexico, are oftentimes the first churches established for Spanish-speaking Catholics in a Texas town, as is the case with Houston's Our Lady of Guadalupe Church.

According to Esther García, Director of Hispanic Ministry for the Houston-Galveston Catholic Diocese, Houston's Our Lady of Guadalupe Church has become the spiritual home not only of many of the city's earliest Hispanic residents, but also its most recent. Because of the strong devotion to *la virgen* that exists throughout Latin America, many recent Mexican and Central American immigrants will identify this church as a "home away from home" during the period of their transition into Houston life.

In addition to Our Lady of Guadalupe, Immaculate Heart of Mary (7539 Ave. K) and Our Lady of Sorrows (3006 Kashmere) are located in areas traditionally associated with Houston's Hispanic population. However, Hispanic residents (totaling about 450,000) are now distributed throughout the metropolis, and attending one of these churches is often a "rite of passage" for newcomers. Like those who came before them, recent immigrants soon establish themselves in other areas of town and become members of other churches.

Ms. García notes that changes in the geographic distribution of Houston's Hispanic Catholics is causing some interesting variations in the concept of the traditional Hispanic church. For example, because of changes in the makeup of neighborhoods, some churches that originated for Anglos have since become almost totally Mexican-American. Others have become the spiritual home of recent Central American immigrants, particularly recent immigrants from El Salvador, Guatemala, and Nicaragua. And others, located in neighborhoods that are still predominantly Anglo (or Polish or Italian) now have significant numbers of Mexican-Americans in attendance. The priests of such churches find themselves incorporating into their church decor images of *la virgen*, as well as favorite Mexican saints in the form of *santos* (carved three-dimensional images of saints) and

Museum of American Architecture and Decorative Arts. Houston Baptist University, 7502 Fondren Rd. Museum collections include Mexican folk retablos, which are occasionally exhibited. Open Mon.–Fri. 10–4; Sun. 12–4.

Museum of Fine Arts, Houston. 1001 Bissonnet. The museum's Gallery of Africa, Oceania, and the Americas includes permanent exhibits of materials from Mexican, Panamanian, Peruvian, and Ecuadorian (Salango Island) prehistoric cultures. Permanent museum collections include American Indian materials from the Anasazi, pre-Hopi, and Hopi cultures of the American Southwest, Caddoan material from Texas, Spanish Colonial and Mexican fine art and furniture, and Mexican-American art. Open Tues.–Sat. 10–5; Thurs. evenings 5–9; Sun. 12:15–6; closed on major holidays.

Museum of Texas History. 1100 Bagby (in Sam Houston Park). Operated by the Harris County Heritage Society, the museum includes permanent exhibits on Texas history since Spanish exploration. Included is a display of Spanish Colonial and Mexican coins. Open Mon.–Sat. 10–4; Sun. 12–5.

San Jacinto Museum of Texas History. *See* San Jacinto Battleground State Park.

Public Art

América, by Rufino Tamayo. 1955–56. Bank One Building, 910 Travis St. This mural, depicting the confluence of the peoples inhabiting the American continent, is a major work by one of Mexico's greatest 20th-century artists.

Julia Ideson Building (Houston Public Library) murals. *See* Spanish-Revival Architecture: Ideson Building.

The Rebirth of Our Nationality, by Leo Tanguma. 1972–73. 5801 Canal (exterior of the Continental Can Co. Bldg.). Images in the mural reflect the condition of poor Mexican-Americans in Houston.

A United Community, by Sylvia Orozco and Pio Palido. 1985. At Sixth Ward Community Park, Kane and Trinity Sts. Images in the mural reflect the cultural diversity of this multiethnic area.

Untitled Bas-relief, by Octavio Medellín. 1952. Front of the Houston Police Administration, Jail, and Municipal Courts Building, 101 Preston Ave. The stone relief panel depicts three striding figures.

Vaquero, sculpture by Luis Jiménez. 1978. Moody Park, 3725 Fulton St. The sculpture, constructed of fiberglass, depicts a Mexican cowboy riding a bucking horse.

Festivals and Events

Día de la Raza Festival Folklórico. October 12, at Miller Outdoor Theater in Hermann Park. Sponsored by the Institute of Hispanic Cultures, this event is Houston's largest celebration of Columbus Day. The

retablos (painted two-dimensional images of saints).

These intriguing developments are directly related to the immigration patterns of the eighties. For the Hispanic ministry during the nineties, awareness of the rapid changes that can occur in neighborhoods will be as important as bilingualism and social-service assistance, something the Houston-Galveston Diocese is learning firsthand.

Replica of Indian shelter, Jesse H. Jones Park, Houston. Photo by Jane Ashley.

A United Community, by Sylvia Orozco and Pio Pulido, Houston. Photo by Jane Ashley.

Bas-relief by Octavio Medellín, Houston vicinity. Photo by Jane Ashley.

festival was established in 1983 to provide an opportunity for Pan-American ethnic groups to share their cultures through costume, music, and dance. Performers representing fourteen countries come for this evening of traditional dance and music. Each year one participating country is honored, with the evening dedicated to, and featuring, several of its most famous performers.

Festival Chicano. Week-long event starting the first weekend in October, at Miller Outdoor Theater in Hermann Park, Guadalupe Park, Sam Houston Park, and other locations. Festival Chicano was founded in 1980 to promote and preserve the Hispanic cultural experience through music, dance, theater, and the visual and graphic arts. All events directly relate to Mexican-American culture: Mexican and Tejano folklórico dances (both historic and contemporary) are performed by dancers in traditional costumes; Tejano orchestra, conjunto, and mariachi groups play, with many musicians in traditional costume; and Mexican and Tejano foods are served. To encourage the participation of all of Houston's Hispanic families, the event is offered free of charge, and over 80% of the festival's 100,000 participants are Hispanic. For more information contact Daniel Bustamante, 2719 Morrison, Houston 77009.

KLAT Hispanic Festival. September 16, at a different location each year. Since 1979, Spanish-language radio station KLAT has sponsored this Diez y Seis festival, which features performances of different types of Mexican music, a trade show, and food booths. For more information contact KLAT, 1415 N. Loop West, Suite 400, Houston 77008.

ALTO AND VICINITY, Cherokee and Houston Counties

Alto (pop. 1,027) was once the site of a ceremonial and political center of the Early Caddo Mound Builder culture (ca. A.D. 800 to 1300). Caddoan descendants of these prehistoric people inhabited East Texas at the time of European contact. Mission Nuestro San Francisco de los Tejas was relocated six miles west of Alto and reestablished as Mission San Francisco de los Neches in 1721 among the Caddoan Neches bands. El Camino Real passed through this area and the Spaniards named the place Alto ("high" in Spanish) because it is situated at the highest point between the Neches and Angelina Rivers.

Caddoan Mounds State Historic Park. On SH 21, 6 mi. SW of Alto. The Early Caddo Mound Builder culture built this ceremonial mound about A.D. 800. The village became the political and ceremonial center of the most advanced and powerful prehistoric culture in Texas. Life centered on the religious, political, and economic practices of the ruling class, who lived on or around the ceremonial temple mounds. The common people lived on surrounding farms, growing food for the settlement and providing labor for mound construction. The Caddo had far-reaching trade connections, possibly as far away as Florida, Illinois, and the Great Lakes, and with their farming and trade success remained the dominant native group in Texas until about A.D. 1300. The park contains the remnants of this center, including two temple mounds, a burial mound, and a large portion of the adjacent village area. A Caddoan house has been reconstructed here, and visitors may take a self-guided walking tour. On display in the Visitors Center are Early and Middle Caddoan ceramics, stone tools, and exotic trade goods, and an interpretive audio-visual program is also featured. The park and Visitors Center are open Wed.–Sun. 8–5; group tours by appointment.

Mission San Francisco de los Neches Site. Marker, 6 mi. SW of Alto on SH 21. Mission San Francisco de los Tejas, the first Spanish mission in East Texas, was originally founded in 1690 near Weches. The mis-

Marker commemorating Mission San Francisco de los Tejas, placed near the site in 1934. Adina de Zavala Papers, courtesy Barker Texas History Center, General Libraries, University of Texas at Austin.

sion was reestablished at this site in 1721 as Mission San Francisco de los Neches after Mission Tejas was abandoned. Mission Neches operated in East Texas for nine years. In 1730 it was relocated to the Austin area, where it remained for several months, and in 1731 it was reestablished in San Antonio, where it ultimately became Mission Espada. *CM 1936.*

Mission Santísimo Nombre de María. Marker, about 11 mi. SW of Alto on SH 21. This mission was founded among the Hasinai, or Tejas, Indians in 1690 and was destroyed by flood in January 1692. *SM 1971.*

Mission Tejas State Historic Park. About 10 mi. SW of Alto on SH 21, near Park Rd. 44. Mission San Francisco de los Tejas, the first Spanish mission in East Texas, was established in 1690 for the conversion of the Caddoan Indians living in this area. The mission was abandoned in 1693, then twice relocated and renamed. Mission Tejas is often called the first mission in Texas because El Paso, where there are older missions, was originally part of New Mexico. A commemorative structure representing Mission Tejas now stands in the park. The historical park is open daily 8–5. *SM 1968.*

Neches Indian Village Site. Marker, 5 mi. SW of Alto on SH 21. The marker commemorates a village site of one of the Caddoan Neches bands, for whom the San Francisco de los Neches mission was established in 1721. *CM 1936.*

Anniversary of the Consecration of Mission San Francisco de los Tejas. Usually on the first weekend in June, at Mission Tejas State Historical Park. A bilingual Celebration Mass sponsored by the Tyler Diocese is given. Contact the park for annual scheduling information.

Annual Pilgrimage. Usually the first weekend in October, at Mission Tejas State Historical Park. Sponsored by the Houston County Historical Commission, this event's main focus is on Anglo-American settlement, but events include Alabama-Coushatta folklife presentations.

Scenic Drives. The forested hills and streams of Caddo country can be seen along US 69, SH 21 (El Camino Real), and several local roads in the Alto area.

ANAHUAC AND WALLISVILLE VICINITY,
Chambers County

Anahuac (pop. 1,993) is located in an area occupied, at the time of European contact, by Karankawa, Coapite, and Copane Indian tribes. In response to French exploration in the region, and the establishment of the Blancpain trading post in 1754, the Spanish built a mission-presidio outpost here in 1756. Anahuac is best known as the site of a Mexican garrison at which occurred events that contributed to Texas' declaration of independence from Mexico. Today, Anahuac is the county seat of Chambers County.

Fort Anahuac Site. Marker, in Fort Anahuac Park, Front Ave., 1 mi. S of Anahuac on Trinity Bay. In 1830 the Mexican government established Fort Anahuac to collect customs duties and limit unauthorized East Texas settlements. Anahuac was the center of disturbances when Col. John D. ("Juan") Bradburn, the local Mexican authority, arrested William Travis, an act which precipitated a series of confrontations between troops and colonists, resulting in the troops' removal from the post. Local colonists adopted the Turtle Bayou Resolutions, precipitating the Battle of Velasco, where the Mexicans were forced to surrender when they ran out of ammunition. Further disturbances occurred in 1835 when Travis and a force of 25 men gained control of the fort, an event that was a precursor of the Texas revolution. Today, the ruins of the fort are protected as an archeological site. *CM 1936; SM 1976; NR 1981.*

Mission Nuestra Señora de la Luz del Orcoquisac and **Presidio San Agustín de Ahumada Sites.** Marker, 0.25 mi. E of the Trinity River Bridge on IH 10. The mission and presidio were established in 1756, on the site of the Blancpain trading post. Though the presidio was moved twice and the mission three times within the immediate vicinity, the outpost was occupied until 1771. Small Indian villages were located in the vicinity of the mission and presidio. Archeologists have found evidence of contact between the two groups, particularly in the Indian adaptation of Spanish pottery-making technology. *CM 1936; NR 1971.*

Wallisville Heritage Park. 13 mi. E of Baytown on IH 10 at Trinity River, exit 807. Museum collections include artifacts and documents pertaining to the Spanish outpost El Orcoquisac, which included Mission Nuestra Señora de la Luz and Presidio San Agustín de Ahumada, occupied between 1756 and 1771. Spanish *reales* coins dating to 1813–15 from Anahuac are on permanent exhibit. Archival materials include the papers of the late John V. Clay, who discovered the remains of the mission and presidio in 1965, and a collection of books and archeological reports relating to the sites. The Alan Probert Collection of papers relates to the careers of John Davis Bradburn, 1830s commander of the Mexican fort at Anahuac, and

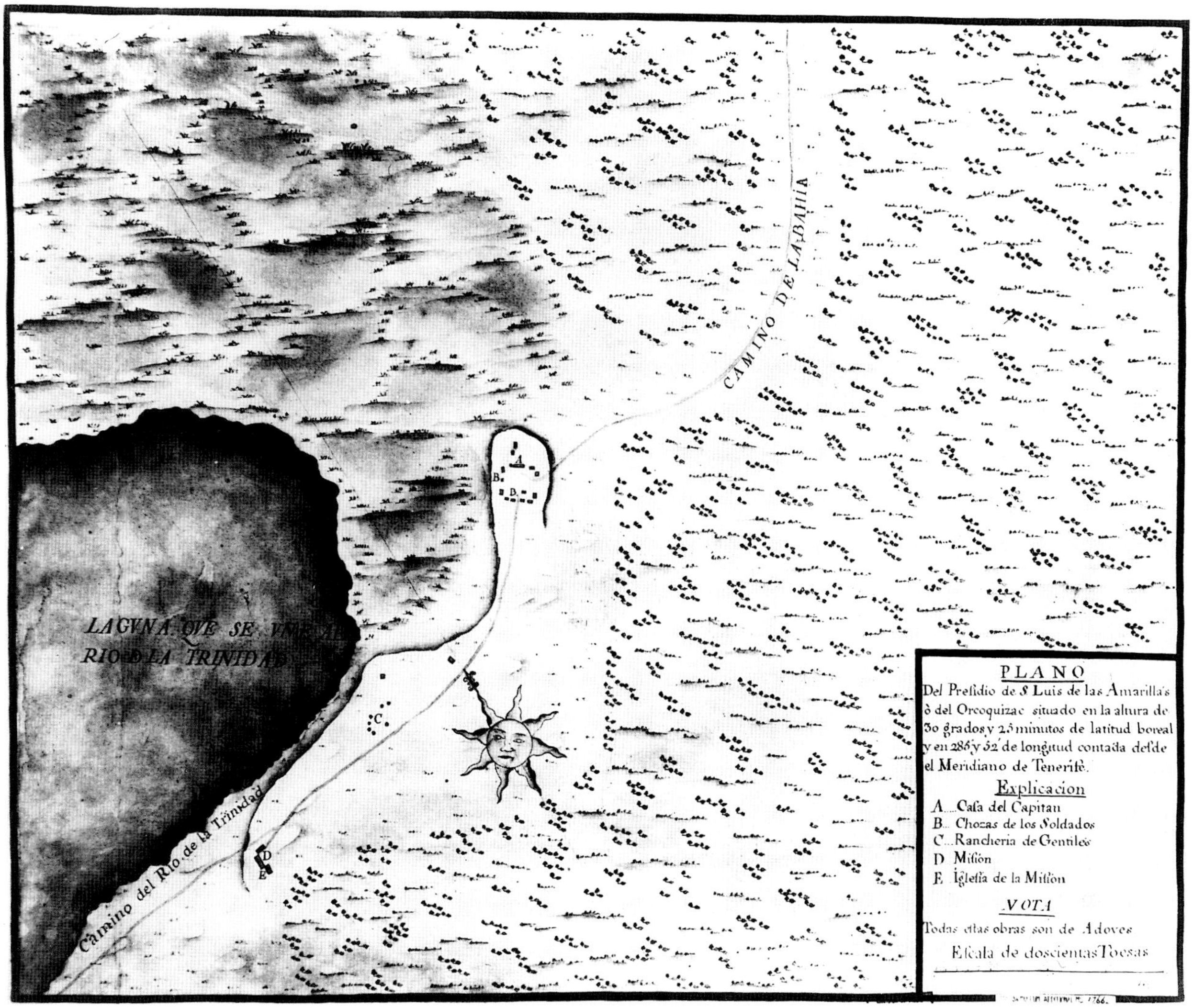
CAMINO DE LA BAHIA
LAGUNA QUE SE
RIO DE LA TRINIDAD
Camino del Rio de la Trinidad
PLANO
Del Presidio de S Luis de las Amarillas
ò del Orcoquizac situado en la altura de
30 grados y 25 minutos de latitud boreal
y en 286 y 52 de longitud contada desde
el Meridiano de Tenerife.
Explicacion
A....Casa del Capitan
B... Chozas de los Soldados
C...Rancheria de Gentiles
D Mision
E Iglesia de la Mision
NOTA
Todas estas obras son de Adoves
Escala de doscientas Toesas

Eighteenth-century map showing location of Mission Nuestra Señora de la Luz del Orcoquisac and Presidio San Agustín de Ahumada, Anahuac. THC photo.

Dr. James Grant, an early Texas filibuster, and to the history surrounding mining in the del Monte and Pachuca area of Mexico (including primary Spanish documents with English translations). The museum also possesses several rolls of microfilm of the Wagner Collection from the Beinecke Library at Yale University. The Wagner Collection includes primary documents relating to the Spanish Colonial and Mexican periods in Texas, such as the papers of Philip Nolan, the Berlandier papers, letters, and pamphlets, and broadsides about the Texas Revolution. Open Mon.–Sat. 8–5.

BEAUMONT, Jefferson County

Beaumont (pop. 114,323), an inland port, is the county seat of Jefferson County. This area was part of the municipality of Liberty in the Lorenzo de Zavala empresario grant of 1829. French and Spanish fur trappers and explorers had earlier established a trading post here, but the first permanent settlers were Anglo-Americans in the 1830s.

Alamo Plaza Hotel Courts. College Ave. The Alamo Plaza is credited with being one of the earliest motel chains in the United States. The first motel in the chain opened in 1929 in Waco, and the initial tourist court design combined Mission Revival and other Spanish Revival styles. The one-story office structure and flanking entrances were marked by a large "Alamoesque" false-front façade. The Beaumont Alamo Plaza, built about 1933, was the fourth court complex constructed.

Beaumont YMCA Building. 934 Calder Ave. Built in 1929, the building exhibits Spanish Revival features such as wrought-iron, tile, cast-stone details, open patio, stuccoed walls, and arched openings. *SM 1979; NR 1979.*

Mildred Buildings. 1400 block of Calder Ave. The Mildred Building complex consists of an apartment building, a commercial structure, and a garage. This beautiful Spanish Revival style complex is an excellent example of the elegant structures erected in Beaumont in the late 1920s and 1930s following the oil discovery at Spindletop. The exterior walls are terra-cotta and brick with molded decorative concrete lintels, bronze and wood *rejas* (grilles), and balustrades. Draperies, hand-carved furniture imported from Spain, and artwork original to the structures remain in the public areas. *NR 1978.*

St. Anne's Catholic Church and School. 11th and Calder Sts. This striking pink stucco church features ornate terra-cotta stonework, a central marble inset with a replica of Michelangelo's *Pieta,* and an ornate square belltower with colored tile roof. The downturned trident, seen on the tower and under the windows, is a motif taken from Mission San José in San Antonio and used to regionalize the otherwise Italian Baroque design.

Shopping Center. 2590 Calder Ave. This one-story, brick, Spanish Revival shopping center was built about 1930.

Scenic Drives. US 69/287 from Beaumont to Woodville runs through forested land. Although little virgin forest remains in East Texas, the big timber along this route is a reminder of the Piney Woods as they were in the long-ago days when Spain and France struggled for supremacy in the region. The route passes through Kountze, where information is available on visiting the Big Thicket National Preserve, located about 20 mi. N of Beaumont on US 287. The Big Thicket is a wilderness treasure, containing not only forest but swamplands that offer abundant plant life and exotic beauty. Here one may truly wonder at this land as it existed when Indians were its only inhabitants and imagine the barrier that the forest presented to early exploration and settlement. Undertake your journey into this eerie and legendary woodland with care.

BLESSING, Matagorda County

Blessing (pop. ca. 950). Thankful for the arrival of the Southern Pacific Railroad in 1903, Jonathan E. Pierce, founder of the town, named it Blessing (after the railroad rejected "Thank God" as a name).

Alamo Plaza Hotel Courts, Beaumont. Photo by Cathryn Hoyt, THC.

Hotel Blessing. 900 block of Ave. B. Built in 1907, the hotel is one of the earliest and most unusual expressions of Mission Revival architectural style in the state. Soon after founding the town, Jonathan Pierce decided to construct a hotel that expressed Spanish Mission design in wood-frame construction. The result was a two-story, wood-frame building with mission-style towers and parapets. The interior of the hotel remains essentially intact, with original finish on the woodwork, unaltered floor plan, and many of the original furnishings and accessories. *RTHL 1965; NR 1979.*

Mildred Buildings, Beaumont. Photo by Cathryn Hoyt, THC.

BRENHAM, Washington County

Brenham (pop. 11,952) lies in an area that was inhabited by small Indian tribes such as the Tamique and the Xarame at the time of Spanish contact. Though the La Bahía Trail passed through this area, the first European settlers were not Spanish, but rather Anglo-American colonists who obtained Mexican land grants in what was then known as the State of Coahuila and Texas. Brenham, located on land originally granted to Mrs. Arabella Harrington by the Mexican government, is now the county seat of Washington County.

Hotel Blessing, Blessing. THC photo.

La Bahía Road. Marker, intersection of SH 36 and FM 390, 7 mi. N of Brenham. La Bahía Road was originally an east-west Indian trail in southwestern Louisiana and southeast Texas. Alonso de León traveled the route in 1689 in his search for La Salle, and the Gutiérrez-Magee expedition traveled it in 1812–13 during its revolt against Spain. *SM 1971.*

St. Mary's Catholic Church. 701 Church St. The structure, built in 1936, is Romanesque in style with a Spanish Mission Revival bell tower. The congregation of St. Mary's originally was predominantly Polish-American but now includes a significant Mexican-American contingent. It is the only Catholic church in Brenham, and Spanish-language masses have been held here periodically in the past. *NR 1990.*

BRYAN AND COLLEGE STATION, Brazos County

Bryan (pop. 55,002) and neighboring **College Station** (pop. 52,456) are located in an area where, for over a hundred years, Spanish explorers, traders, and missionaries passed through on El Camino Real. Anglo-Americans in Stephen F. Austin's second colony, who received land grants here in the early 19th century to colonize Northern Mexico for the Mexican government, established the first permanent settlements in Brazos County. In Bryan, the county seat, and in neighboring College Station, subtle Hispanic influences may be seen today, particularly as expressed in the architecture of several structures dating from the first half of the 20th century.

R.C. Stone House, Bryan. THC photo.

Allen Academy Memorial Hall. 1100 block of Ursuline, Bryan. Built in 1924, the Mission Revival style, two-story structure features stucco finish, mission parapets, and tile roof. *NR 1987.*

Bryan Ice House. 107 E. Martin Luther King, Bryan. This single-story masonry building with flat roof and mission parapet is an outstanding local example of Mission Revival commercial architecture. The building was put into service as the Bryan Ice Company in 1912. In 1930 the Gulf States Utilities Company purchased the building, and the structure has housed various other commercial establishments since that time. *NR 1987.*

El Camino Real. Marker, 8 mi. SW of Bryan on SH 21. This famous Spanish Colonial route linked Rio Grande communities, San Antonio de Béxar, and the East Texas missions. Spanish explorers, missionaries, and traders traveled it as early as 1690. Historic markers placed at 5-mile intervals along SH 21 approximate its path. *CM 1936.*

Old Sinclair Service Station. 507 S. Texas, Bryan. This "Spanish Style" service station, built about 1933, is an excellent example of a once common service station type that featured tiled, shed roof parapets separated by piers over service bays, drive-through bay with tiles, and mission parapets at the corners. *NR 1987.*

R.C. Stone House. 715 E. 31st, Bryan. Built about 1925, the Stone House is one of the few local examples of the regionally popular Spanish Revival style. The house is an eclectic mixture of Spanish Colonial, Mission, and Pueblo Revival elements, including tiled shed roofs over windows and entries, arched openings, wrought-iron detailing, a Mission style parapet, and paired vigas. *NR 1987.*

CHINA, Jefferson County

China (pop. 1,144) was established in the late 19th century on the Texas and New Orleans Railroad. Rice and oil are the major economic bases in this small town.

Our Blessed Lady of Sorrows Catholic Church. US 90. This beautiful Spanish Mission Revival church was constructed in 1935 of bricks and lumber that the congregation salvaged from the old Thompson Ford Hardwood Sawmill. The style of the church was influenced by San Gabriel Mission in California. The "Seven Sorrows" for which the church is named are reflected in the seven stations of the cross, the seven windows on the north side of the building, and the seven bells in the campanile. The church serves a predominantly Cajun-French parish.

CROCKETT, Houston County

Crockett (pop. 7,024) is located where bands of Caddoan Indians lived at the time of the Spanish exploration. In response to La Salle's presence in the area in the 1680s, Alonso de León founded the first mission in the area now known as Houston County in 1690. El Camino Real, which linked the Spanish settlements along the Rio Grande with the new East Texas missions, was blazed in 1691, and Spanish explorers, missionaries, and traders traveled through the vicinity. Anglo-Americans received land grants from the Mexican government to colonize the area as early as 1828. In 1837 A.E. Gossett donated land for the founding of Crockett, finding it particularly suited for a townsite because of its proximity to El Camino Real. Crockett is the county seat of Houston County.

Discover Houston County Visitors Center and Museum. 303 S. First. The museum includes a permanent exhibit on Spanish missions. Collections include Caddoan artifacts, but these are infrequently exhibited. Open Mon.–Fri. 1–4 , or by appointment; contact the museum c/o 629 N. 4th, Crockett 75835.

El Camino Real. Markers, along SH 21. Crockett originated as a stop on this historic Spanish route. Look for the historical markers placed at 5-mile intervals along SH 21, which approximates the path of El Camino Real. *CM 1936.*

St. Francis of the Tejas Catholic Church. 609 Forrest St. Dedicated to St. Francis of Assisi, the church was built in 1931 and features a replica of the Mission Espada façade. The parish includes a significant number of Hispanics, and Spanish-language masses were begun here in 1985.

U.S. Post Office. An elegantly proportioned building constructed in 1932, the Crockett Post Office is an outstanding example of Spanish Revival architecture. The single-story, brick structure with limestone details has a low-pitched, red tile roof and an arched entry loggia. It is accented by a classic-influenced brick diamondwork frieze with decorative stone shields and low-relief carved-stone insets.

Scenic Drives. In Davy Crockett National Forest; nearest entrance ca. 10 mi. E of Crockett on SH 7. The national forests offer an opportunity

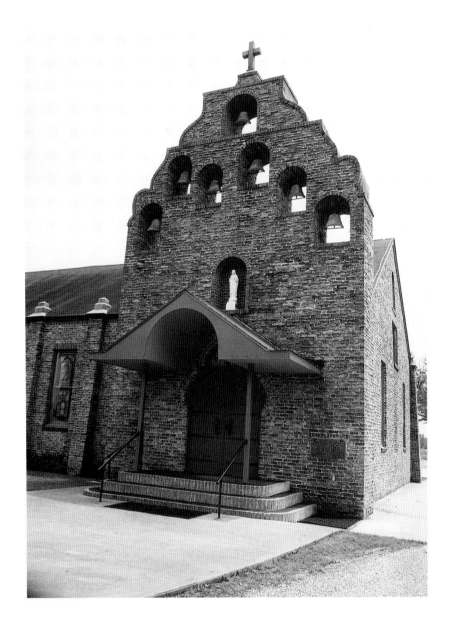

Our Blessed Lady of Sorrows
Catholic Church, China. Photo by
Cathryn Hoyt, THC.

to view the Piney Woods of East Texas and to imagine the even deeper forests that existed when Indian groups lived here and when the French and Spanish struggled for control of the region. Davy Crockett National Forest encompasses 161,497 acres, primarily in Houston and Trinity counties.

EL CAMPO, Wharton County

El Campo (pop. 10,511), the largest town in Wharton County, originated in 1881 as Prairie Switch, a stop on the New York, Texas, and Mexican Railway. In 1890, after becoming a camping place for the cattlemen of

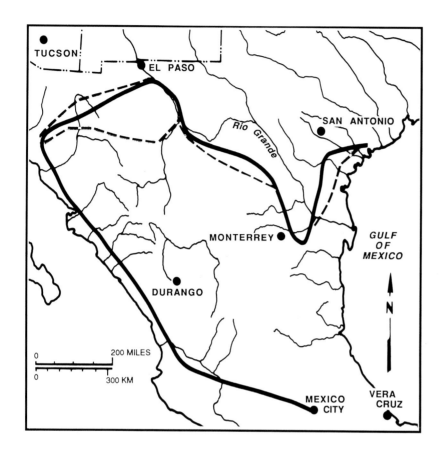

Map by Hector Meza adapted from Krieger, "The Travels of Alvar Nuñez Cabeza de Vaca in Texas and Mexico, 1534–1536" (1961).

the area who rounded up herds here, its name was changed to El Campo, Spanish for "the camp."

St. Philip's Catholic Church. 304 W. Church St. Sts. Peter and Paul Catholic Church, the first church in what is now St. Philip's Parish, was destroyed by a storm in 1909. Parishioners built their second church, named simply St. Philip's, the following year. The present church was constructed in 1931. The building has the distinctive twin bell towers that are characteristic of Spanish Mission Revival style.

St. Robert Bellarmine Catholic Church. 512 Tagner St. Built in 1948, the church exhibits Spanish Mission stylistic influences, and Spanish-language masses are given here.

FREEPORT, Brazoria County

Freeport (pop. 11,389) was founded in 1912 by New York investors interested in developing sulphur deposits in the area. Freeport has remained primarily an industrial center and is located in a community of nine cities known collectively as Brazosport—the world's largest basic chemical complex. Brazosport is the major urban center in Brazoria County.

Battle of Velasco. Markers, in Velasco City Park and at the U.S. Coast Guard Station. Eighty years before Freeport's founding, the Battle

380

of Velasco took place in the area on June 26, 1832. Texans on the way to the battle at Anahuac engaged in a nine-hour battle here with Mexican forces under Lt. Col. Domingo de Ugartechea. However, those involved soon discovered that the Battle of Velasco had been unknowingly fought after the dispute at Anahuac had been peaceably settled. After the Battle of San Jacinto in 1836, Velasco served as temporary capital of the Republic of Texas and was the site of the signing of the Treaty of Velasco, which ended hostilities between Texas and Mexico. *CM 1936; SM 1965.*

GALVESTON, Galveston County

Galveston (pop. 59,070). In 1770 Spanish surveyors christened Galveston Bay the Bay of Gálvez for Bernardo de Gálvez, the acting governor of Louisiana between 1777 and 1783. The first European settlement on Galveston Island was started by pirates Jean and Pierre Laffite in 1817, and Mexican troops in the 1830s guarded a customs house here. Anglo-American settlement dramatically increased during the Republic of Texas period. The city's original name, Galveztown, was an anglicization of its namesake, which has been further anglicized now to Galveston. The city is the county seat of Galveston County.

Cabeza de Vaca. *See* sidebar: Cabeza de Vaca in Texas.

Galvez Hotel. 2024 Seawall Blvd. The Galvez Hotel, built in 1910–11, is the oldest luxury beach hotel in Galveston. Designed by the St. Louis architectural firm of Mauran and Russell, the impressive six-story structure displays characteristic Spanish Revival features and is one of the few examples of this style in Galveston. Named Galvez in honor of Count Bernardo de Gálvez, the hotel was equipped with the most modern facilities and was regarded by *Hotel Monthly* (1912) as one of the "best arranged and most richly and tastefully furnished seaside hotels in America." The construction of the hotel was instrumental in reestablishing Galveston as a major resort area after the devastating hurricane of 1900. *NR 1979; RTHL 1980.*

Daniel Webster Kempner House. 2504 Ave. O. Built in 1907, the structure has Spanish Revival elements, including a stuccoed frame, tile roof, and rose window motifs. The house is outfitted with a ship's bilge pump, reflecting the owner's concern for hurricanes in low-lying Galveston. Once known as Las Palmas for the surrounding palm trees, the house is now overshadowed by live oaks. *NR 1979.*

Mission Reina de la Paz Church. 706 51st St. This church, now under the Diocese of Galveston-Houston, was founded in 1935 to serve the Spanish-speaking residents of Galveston. It contains a crucifix and image of Our Lady of Guadalupe brought to Galveston in 1935 by immigrants. Major annual celebrations held at the church include a Fiestas Patrias bazaar celebrating Diez y Seis de Septiembre; the Feast of Our Lady of Guadalupe, on December 12, with Spanish-language mass and mariachi music; Las Posadas, a Christmastime folk drama, presented in Spanish; and Christmas Eve Midnight Mass, which features mariachi music. All parish meetings are conducted in Spanish.

CABEZA DE VACA IN TEXAS

The story of Cabeza de Vaca's wanderings in Texas and northern Mexico is well known, but the route he followed across Texas has long been the subject of historical controversy. The island called Malhado on which his barge was wrecked is commonly identified as Galveston Island in school textbooks, but most recent historians believe that the island on which he landed is now a peninsula that parallels the mainland just west of Galveston Island. After living with Indians on the island and nearby mainland, Cabeza de Vaca ventured westward along the coast to the locale of Indians known as the Mariames. For most of each year, these Indians lived along a "river of nuts," which historians generally agree is the Texas river now known as the Guadalupe. However, this may be the last place on the wanderer's route in Texas that is not controversial. The many interpreters of Cabeza de Vaca's route have him crossing nearly all of the major regions of the state. Only two of the proposed routes are given serious consideration: a route that proceeds from the lower Guadalupe River westward and a route that proceeds from the same locale southwestward to the lower Rio Grande, where the route enters northeastern Mexico and turns westward toward the Pacific coast. This southwestward route, as interpreted by Alex D. Krieger and originally published in 1961, is the one most widely accepted today (see map).

As visitors travel across Texas, they will encounter in guidebooks, historical markers, and local historical brochures numerous references to the possibility of Cabeza de Vaca's presence in the area. Many of these references are based on the trans-Texas route, which crosses Texas at its widest point. Visitors who wish to retrace the routes and enjoy the historical controversy will find that much has been written on this topic. Well-known Texas ethnohistorian T.N. Campbell and his daughter, T.J. Campbell, propose a refined southwestern route in *Historic Indian Groups of the Choke Canyon Reservoir and Surrounding Area, Southern Texas* (1981). Equally useful and easier to find is Donald E. Chipman's "In Search of Cabeza de Vaca's Route across Texas," *Southwestern Historical Quarterly* 91 (October 1987), which provides maps of the many proposed routes.

Our Lady of Guadalupe Church. 45th St. and Ave. L. This church had its beginnings in St. Peter's School for Spanish-speaking children, which opened in 1917. In 1927 a mission church was established here to serve Galveston's Mexican-American Catholics, and a new church was built on the site in 1948. Since 1980, the Franciscans have operated it as a parish church of the diocese of Galveston-Houston. The congregation remains predominantly Hispanic. Each spring the church sponsors a pilgrimage to the Shrine of Our Lady of Guadalupe, in Mexico. The church's May Bazaar features Mexican foods and music, and the Christmastime folk-drama Las Posadas is performed annually in Spanish.

Rosenberg Library. 2310 Sealy. Permanent exhibits include Spanish Colonial and Mexican ceramics, glass, and clothing. Collections additionally include Mexican coins and military items, and Karankawa pottery sherds. Open Mon.–Sat. 9–5. *SM 1970.*

Sacred Heart Church. 14th St. and Broadway, Ave. L. This Spanish- and Moorish-influenced structure dates from 1903–04. When the storm of 1900 destroyed the original Sacred Heart Church, Jesuit Brother Jiménez based his design for the church's reconstruction on the Church of the Immaculate Conception in New Orleans (1857), which itself was modeled after the Moorish-built Port Santa María chapel in Spain.

Cinco de Mayo. On or near May 5, usually at the Moody Civic Center. Two public dances are held, and the celebration includes mariachi and conjunto performances, folklórico dancers, and Mexican food.

Fiestas Patrias. On or near September 16, usually at the Moody Civic Center. Mariachis, conjunto music, folklórico dance, and children's games are featured.

GENEVA AND VICINITY, Sabine County

Geneva (pop. ca. 100). Early French and Spanish explorers utilized traces of a Caddoan Hasinai Indian trail in this area. That trail became the eastern leg of El Camino Real when it was lengthened to reach the Spanish

Above: Mission bell on display at the Rosenberg Library, Galveston. THC photo.

Above left: Galvez Hotel, Galveston. THC photo.

mission at Los Adaes across the Sabine River—the Spaniards' eastern frontier—around 1714. Despite the Mexican government's discouraging settlement within twenty leagues of the Texas boundary, squatters came to the area. Geneva later became an attractive site for Anglo-American colonists because of its location near the important ferry crossing on the Sabine River.

El Lobanillo. Marker, in Geneva on SH 21 near the post office. El Lobanillo Ranch has been continuously occupied since the mid-1700s. It was established by Antonio Gil Ybarbo, the son of Spanish colonists from Andalusia, and his wife María Padilla. The Gil Ybarbos lived here until 1772, when Spain recommended abandonment of the presidios and missions of East Texas. His mother and other refugees remained here after the evacuation, but the Gil Ybarbos went on to settle Bucareli and, later, to reestablish the settlement of Nacogdoches. Rancho Lobanillo was granted to Juan Ignacio Pifermo in 1794 and inherited in the early 1800s by his adopted son, John Maximillian. *SM 1972.*

Sabine River Crossing of El Camino Real. Marker, on SH 21 near Gaines Memorial Bridge. Early travelers along El Camino Real first crossed the Sabine River here in dugout canoes made by Caddo Indians, then by Michael Crow's ferry (established in 1797), and later by the Gaines Ferry (established in 1812). James Gaines, for whom the ferry was named, participated in the Gutiérrez-Magee Rebellion of 1812–13. *CM 1936.*

Scenic Drives. In Sabine National Forest; 7 mi. S of Geneva on SH 87. The town of Hemphill is located at the western boundary of the forest. Sabine National Forest encompasses 188,220 acres, primarily in Sabine and Shelby counties. Excellent forest scenery can be seen along highways in all directions from Hemphill. One of the finest stands of longleaf pine is at a scenic roadside park on SH 184 about 5 miles west.

Gaines Ferry, ca. 1920s, at the Sabine River crossing of El Camino Real, Geneva. Adina de Zavala Papers, courtesy Barker Texas History Center, General Libraries, University of Texas at Austin.

HUNTSVILLE, Walker County

Huntsville (pop. 27,925) originated as an Indian trading post in the 1830s. During the Mexican period, Anglo-American colonists Pleasant and Ephraim Gray settled here near Bidai Indian camps. Anglo settlement of the area soon followed, and Sam Houston became the town's most famous resident. Today, Huntsville is the county seat of Walker County and the home of Sam Houston State University.

Sam Houston Memorial Museum Complex. 1836 Sam Houston Ave. The memorial is located on 15 acres originally belonging to Sam Houston. The historic Anglo-American structures and exhibits are the museum's main focus, but also to be seen here are Spanish Colonial and Mexican artifacts including clothing, documents, household items, military items, and information relating to individuals from the early periods of Texas history. The museum's collections include many artifacts that belonged to Santa Anna when he was captured at San Jacinto. Some of these artifacts are on permanent exhibit. Open Tues.–Sun. 9–5.

Scenic Drives. In Sam Houston National Forest; Huntsville is located at the northwestern boundary of the forest. Sam Houston National

383

Forest encompasses 160,443 acres, primarily in San Jacinto and Walker counties. FM 1374 and FM 1375 offer scenic drives through the forest.

INDEPENDENCE, Washington County

Independence (pop. ca. 150), located on the site of a Mexican land grant crossed by the old Bahía Trail (now FM 390), was originally known as Coles Settlement. In 1836 the name was changed to Independence in recognition of the recently issued Texas Declaration of Independence, which was signed at nearby Washington-on-the-Brazos.

Toalson House. Off FM 390, two blocks east of the FM 50–FM 390 junction. This two-room adobe structure, which has two-foot-thick walls and a stone fireplace, reputedly was built during the 1820s by Mexican officials and used as a jail. It was subsequently used as a schoolhouse, residence, and law office. Though its original use has never been documented, the building is remarkable because of its adobe construction, which is much more common in drier areas of the state. The Toalson House is also noteworthy for its age and the variety of purposes for which it has been used. It is now privately owned by a local family.

JACKSONVILLE, Cherokee County

Jacksonville (pop. 12,765). Bands of Caddoan Indians inhabited this area during the time of European contact. The Spanish established Mission San Francisco de los Neches at a locale south of Jacksonville in 1721, and El Camino Real passed near the mission. The Mexican government gave 54 land grants in Cherokee County to Anglos, but few actually moved to this region until the 1840s, when the Republic of Texas offered free land. The history of the modern town of Jacksonville begins during this period, in 1848, when its post office was established.

Vanishing Texana Museum. In the Jacksonville Public Library, on NE corner of W. Larissa and N. Bolton Sts. Spanish Colonial and Mexican artifacts in the collections that are frequently exhibited include ceramics and glass, clothing, coins, furniture, personal and household items, and documents and materials relating to historic individuals and events. Open Mon., Wed., Fri. 9:30–5; Sat. 9:30–2.

Scenic Drives. Although altered by man-made lakes, beautiful hill and forest scenery can still be seen in this historic countryside both north and south of Jacksonville on US 69, and a particularly striking view can be seen from Love's Lookout Park, 5 miles north on US 69.

LIBERTY, Liberty County

Liberty (pop. 7,733). At about the same time that the Orcoquisac mission-presidio complex on the Trinity River was built to prevent French encroachment in southeastern Texas (1756), the Spanish established the outpost of Atascosito (meaning "boggy" in Spanish) in this area. The

Saddle and bridle used by Santa Anna, on display at the Sam Houston Memorial Museum, Huntsville. Courtesy of Sam Houston Memorial Museum.

Mexican government later encouraged settlement here, and in 1831 J. Francisco Madero, general land commissioner for the Mexican state of Coahuila and Texas, changed the town's name to Villa de la Santísima Trinidad de la Libertad. The new name signaled Mexico's hopes of forthcoming independence from Spain. Madero also designed the town layout, and four of the town's original plazas remain today. Liberty, now an oil center, is the county seat of Liberty County.

Atascosito. Marker, 3 mi. N of Liberty on SH 146. The Spanish outpost Atascosito was established on the Atascosito Road in the mid-1750s to prevent French trade with the Indians. *CM 1936.*

Historic Plazas. J. Francisco Madero's 1830s design for the central section of town originally consisted of 49 squares, of which five were allocated for public use. Four of the five plazas remain public squares today, and all are commemorated with historical markers.

Plaza Constitucional (Municipal Square). Marker, on Travis St. at Sam Houston St. *SM 1968.*

Plaza de Casa Consistatorial (Courthouse Square). Marker, 400 block of Travis St. This square has been the site of four courthouses since 1831. *SM 1968.*

Toalson House, Independence.
Photo by Cathryn Hoyt, THC.

385

Street markers commemorating the original Spanish street names, Liberty. Photo by Cathryn Hoyt, THC.

Plaza Iglesia Parroquial (Parish Church Square). Marker, 1700 Sam Houston St. This square, originally the site of a Methodist log church which stood from 1846 to 1853, was granted to the Catholic Church in 1853. The first Catholic church of Liberty, the Immaculate Conception Church, has been rebuilt here four times. *SM 1968.*

Plaza de Carcel y Casas de Corrección (Square of Jail and Houses of Correction). Marker, on Main St. *SM 1968.*

Plaza de Mercado (Market Place). Marker, 418 Main St. This square has been the hub of commercial activity in Liberty since its founding. *SM 1968.*

Historic Streets. Downtown Liberty. Small markers at the corners of the downtown streets around the plazas indicate the original Spanish names of the streets. *PM.*

Sam Houston Regional Library and Research Center. FM 1011. Originally sponsored by the Atascosito Historical Society, the center was constructed to house records of the ten southeast Texas counties whose areas originally made up the Atascosito District of Mexico. The center sits on a league of land granted by the Mexican government to B.W. Hardin in 1831, and the Hardin Cemetery adjoins on the north side. The site is on the original road from Atascosito to Nacogdoches. Archival and artifact collections include Spanish Colonial and Mexican coins, Atascosito district archives, Mexican documents, and Karankawan and Alabama-Coushatta artifacts. Open Mon.–Fri. 8–5; Sat. 9–4.

La Bahía Trail. Marker, 2 mi. E of Liberty on SH 90 (near Ames Hill). Traveled by Europeans since at least 1690, La Bahía Trail (also known as the Lower Road) was originally an east-west Indian trail between southwestern Louisiana and southeastern Texas. *CM 1936.*

Mexican Hill Monument. Marker, 2315 Santa Anna St. (SH 90). After the Battle of San Jacinto, 60 Mexican prisoners, including General Martín Perfecto de Cós and Ten. Coronel Pedro Delgado, were held on William Hardin's property at Liberty from August 28, 1836, until April 25, 1837. According to Delgado, who wrote an account of his time at Liberty, the Mexicans were treated well and given the best care available during their stay. Descendants of some of these Mexican soldiers remain in the area today. *CM 1936; SM 1985.*

Scenic Drive. SH 146 N to Moss Hill. Several herds of Longhorns can be seen on this drive between Liberty and Moss Hill.

LIVINGSTON AND VICINITY, Polk County

Livingston (pop. 5,019) arose from Anglo-American settlement in the late 1830s and was established in the late 1840s. Development has centered around the lumber and oil industries and the town's position as the county seat of Polk County.

Alabama-Coushatta Indian Reservation. On US 190, approx. halfway between Livingston and Woodville. The Alabama-Coushatta Indians were the first permanent settlers in this area during the historic period. Pressured by Anglo-American settlement westward, the Alabama moved from their village Alibamo (in northern Mississippi) to East Texas around 1807. At that time the Spaniards were encouraging American Indian settlement of East Texas to discourage Anglo-American settlement. The Alabama were soon joined by the Coushatta, with whom they had long been closely affiliated. During the Texas-Mexican War, when the Alabama-Coushattas temporarily relocated to Louisiana, they lost their Texas lands and were homeless for sixteen years. In 1854, the group successfully obtained from the State of Texas a tract of land twelve miles east of Livingston, which they continue to maintain. The Alabama-Coushatta Indian Reservation is one of only two reservations in the state (the other is that of the Tigua, in El Paso; a third, for the Kickapoo of West Texas, is planned). Visitors may experience tribal dances, living history, arts and crafts, and museum exhibits at the Indian village. Open daily 10–6.

Alabama-Coushatta Annual Pow-Wow. First weekend in June, at the Alabama-Coushatta Indian Reservation on US 190, halfway between Livingston and Woodville. The Pow-Wow features ceremonial dances and traditional Indian crafts and foods.

Scenic Trails. N of Livingston, 1 mi. S of Moscow on US 59 is the entrance to the Moscow Woodland Trail, which winds beside Long King Creek, said to have been named for an Indian chief. Two trail segments, 1.5 and 0.5 miles, give access to an area of tall pines and other forest growth. About 5 miles north of Moscow on US 59 and 8.5 miles west on US 287 is the Bull Creek Trail, which parallels the spring-fed stream among large magnolia, white oak, maple, holly, dogwood, and other trees, all identified. Both trails offer walkers excellent opportunities to experience the forested landscape of East Texas.

LUFKIN, Angelina County

Lufkin (pop. 30,206) is the largest town and county seat of Angelina County. The county's name, which means "Little Angel" in Spanish, is derived from the name given to a member of the Hasinai tribe who served as an interpreter and guide for Spanish and French explorers (*see* sidebar: Angelina, the "Little Angel" of East Texas). Among the Indians who occupied this region before and during the Spanish Colonial period were the Caddo proper, Hasinai, and Bidai bands. Only one Spanish land title was granted here, that to Vincente Micheli in 1797. The Bedias Trail, a prehistoric Indian trail, passed through this region and was later used by Spanish explorers and colonists. During the Mexican period, the area encompassing Angelina County was part of the municipality of Nacogdoches. As Anglo-American settlement in the southeastern United States pushed American Indians westward, the Shawnee, Cherokee, and Biloxi Indians found temporary homes in this area until the mid-19th century.

Don Joaquín Crossing on Bedias Trail. Marker, on US 59 near the Angelina River bridge, 9 mi. N of Lufkin. This Indian trail was forged in prehistoric times to connect the Bidai Indian village on Santo Thomas Creek with other Indian settlements near Nacogdoches. The trail was later used by Spanish explorers, traders, and missionaries. Joaquín de Orobio y Bazterra, captain of the presidio at La Bahía, led troops along the trail in 1746. *SM 1979.*

Statue of Angelina, by Jim Knox. In front of Civic Center, downtown between First and Second Sts. The sculpture depicts Angelina in her role as interpreter in a scene in which a Spanish priest aids an Indian warrior. *See also* sidebar: Angelina.

Scenic Drives. In Angelina National Forest; nearest entrance, 14 mi. SE of Lufkin on US 69. Angelina National Forest encompasses 154,916 acres of woodland, primarily in Angelina and San Augustine counties.

MEXIA, Limestone County

Mexia (pop. 6,933) has both Hispanic and historic American Indian associations. The town is named for General José Antonio Mexía, and land for the town was donated by his children in 1871. Nearby Fort Parker State Historic Site is associated with the Comanche, who during the 19th century extended their range into most of Texas. Cynthia Ann Parker, Comanche captive and mother of the last great Comanche chief, Quanah Parker, is remembered at the historic fort (8 mi. SW of Mexia on SH 14 and Park Rd. 35). During the early 1920s oil boom, the population of Mexia reached 40,000. Although the boom faded, Mexia is still the largest town in Limestone County.

General José Antonio Mexía. Marker, General Mexia Hospital. Mexía, a Cuban-born linguist, came to the province of Texas as an interpreter between the Cherokee Indians and Mexicans. Mexía later served in the Mexican Senate and staunchly supported Mexican Federalism. He

ANGELINA, THE "LITTLE ANGEL" OF EAST TEXAS

Angelina, a member of the Hasinai band of Caddoan Indians, was baptized by the early Spanish missionaries who entered the forests of East Texas almost three centuries ago. Perhaps for her willingness to accept Christianity or her eagerness to learn, the padres must have recognized unusual potential in the young Indian girl and she was sent to Mission San Juan Bautista on the Rio Grande. She later returned to her East Texas homeland, where she served as an interpreter for both Spanish and French soldiers and explorers. Legend says that she helped to rescue at least one French explorer and that in 1713 she assisted Louis Juchereau de St. Denis, who had been appointed by the French to open an overland trade route with the Spanish in Mexico and who is best known as the founder of Natchitoches, Louisiana. She later accompanied the Caddoan chiefs who met with the Marqués de San Miguel de Aguayo, who in 1721 reestablished the abandoned missions of East Texas. Angelina later lived at one of those missions, Nuestra Señora de la Purísima Concepción de los Hasinai. The Angelina River, Angelina County, and Angelina National Forest bear the name of the "Little Angel" who was associated with many of the historic events of early-18th-century Texas.

Statue of Angelina, Lufkin. Photo by Cathryn Hoyt, THC.

fought Santa Anna and the Centralists during the 1830s and was captured and executed by Centralists after the defeat at Puebla in 1839. *SM 1967.*

NACOGDOCHES, Nacogdoches County

Nacogdoches (pop. 30,872) is named for the Nacogdoche band of Caddoan Indians who originally inhabited this area. French exploration of East Texas during the late 1600s spurred the Spanish to establish three missions in 1716 in this area, including Mission Nuestra Señora de los Nacogdoches. The mission was finally abandoned in 1773 when Spanish authorities evacuated East Texas during the years following French cession of Louisiana to Spain.

Many Texans who lived in East Texas were not satisfied with their choice of resettlement in San Antonio or along the Rio Grande, and Antonio Gil Ybarbo, who had formerly resided near Geneva in Sabine County, became the leader of the dissidents. After establishing a settlement at Bucareli (in Waller County) in 1774, Gil Ybarbo moved farther east to Nacogdoches in 1779 and built his settlement around the deserted mission buildings. Nacogdoches became significant as the gateway between the United States and New Spain, and smuggling between the town and Natchitoches (in Louisiana) flourished. Smuggled goods reputedly were stored in Gil Ybarbo's house, known as the Old Stone Fort. The independence demonstrated by the early settlers proved to be prophetic, for Nacogdoches was to become the site of several rebellions against the government. For more than 25 years in the early 1800s, the Nacogdoches area was the scene of revolution. The settlement was nearly destroyed by Spanish Royalist forces in 1813 after the suppression of the Gutiérrez-Magee expedition, an early Mexican revolt against Spain. After Mexico gained its independence from Spain, Nacogdoches experienced another revolution, the Fredonian Rebellion, in December 1826. At that time two Anglo-American settlers seized the Old Stone Fort and proclaimed it the Republic of Fredonia after Mexican authorities refused to evict long-time Spanish settlers from lands the Anglos claimed to have received through an empresario contract. After the Fredonians failed to gain the support of Texas colonists and Indians, Mexican officials and Stephen F. Austin's colonists marched on Nacogdoches and the Fredonians fled. A decade later, Nacogdoches became a center for financing the Texas Revolution and the site of the Battle of Nacogdoches. After independence, a Mexican settler named Vincente Córdova led an unsuccessful attempt to overthrow the new government in August of 1838 by seizing an island in the Angelina River and announcing secession. Indian participation in the event led to Mirabeau B. Lamar's expulsion of all of the Indians from East Texas.

In 1840, visiting Father John Mary Odin reported the presence of at least 300 Mexican-Texan families in the Nacogdoches area. The wooden church they had worshipped in had been destroyed and they had been holding masses in the vicinity of the Old Stone Fort. A new church was built as a result of Odin's visit and survived into the 1930s. Today, not only historic sites but an annual festival foster Hispanic heritage in Nacogdoches. Nacogdoches is the county seat of Nacogdoches County.

Historic Sites

Caddoan Mound. 1516 Mound St. This location was occupied by local Caddoan groups from A.D. 1200 to 1400. A small mound remains to mark the site. *SM 1966.*

El Atascoso Ranch. 8 mi. E of Nacogdoches on SH 21. This late-18th-century hacienda, established by J. María Mora of Spain, is typical of

Spanish ranches of the period and once had several log structures and a Catholic meeting place. It is still a working ranch, not open to the public. *SM 1973.*

El Camino Real. Marker, intersection of North and Power Sts. El Camino Real traversed Texas from the Rio Grande, in the area of Eagle Pass, to Louisiana. The sector of this historic route in East Texas is roughly paralleled by modern SH 21 from San Antonio to the Gaines Ferry site at the Louisiana-Texas state line. *CM 1936.*

Antonio Gil Ybarbo Home Site. Marker, 317 E. Main. Gil Ybarbo, a leader of early Texas dissidents, settled in Nacogdoches in 1779. *CM 1936. See also* Old Stone Fort Replica.

La Calle del Norte. North St. This modern street in Nacogdoches is believed to follow part of a prehistoric trail that connected the Indians of the Nacogdoches area with other Indian villages to the north. This trail later became a street in the 18th-century Spanish settlement.

Los Ojos de Padre Margil (The Eyes of Father Margil). Marker, Park St. Bridge over La Nana Creek. Father Antonio Margil de Jesús was the Franciscan missionary who established Mission Nuestra Señora de Guadalupe at Nacogdoches in 1716. According to legend, during the drought of 1717–18 he had a vision that led him to a point near here on the dry Lantana Creek. Upon his arrival, two springs burst forth with water.

Old Stone Fort about 1885, Nacogdoches. Adina de Zavala Papers, courtesy Barker Texas History Center, General Libraries, University of Texas at Austin.

Named Los Ojos de Padre Margil, the springs symbolized the faith of the Spanish missionaries. *SM 1978.*

Mission Nuestra Señora de Guadalupe Site. Marker, intersection of North and Muller Sts. This mission was founded for the Nacogdoche Indians in 1716, and Father Antonio Margil was placed in charge. The mission was abandoned because of the threat of French invasion of East Texas in 1719. In 1721 the mission, which had fallen into ruins, was restored, and it continued to function until 1773, when Spanish authorities ordered the East Texas missions abandoned. *CM 1936.*

Mission Nuestra Señora de la Purísima Concepción de los Hasinai Site. Marker, 15 mi. W of Nacogdoches, off FM 225 near Stripling Farm Rd. This mission, founded in 1716, also was abandoned in 1719 and reestablished in 1721. In 1730 it was moved to the Austin area and shortly moved again to San Antonio, where it was rededicated as Mission Nuestra Señora de la Purísima Concepción de Acuña. *CM 1936.*

Old Spanish Cemetery. Marker, courthouse grounds. Many Spaniards who settled in Nacogdoches, including Gil Ybarbo, were buried here. *SM 1964.*

Old Stone Fort Replica. On Vista Dr., Stephen F. Austin University campus. The original Old Stone Fort, built by Antonio Gil Ybarbo in 1779 as a storeroom and jail, was the site of numerous historic events. Members of Philip Nolan's group, suspected of being U.S. agents, were jailed there in 1801; the Gutiérrez-Magee expedition's green Republic of Texas flag flew over it in 1813; the Fredonians declared it the Capitol of their republic during their rebellion of 1826–27; and Mexican colonel José de las Piedras took refuge there during the Battle of Nacogdoches. *CM 1936.*

Juan Antonio Padilla Home Site. Marker, intersection of North and Power Sts. Juan Antonio Padilla served as secretary of the state of Coahuila and Texas and as land commissioner for the colony of Martín de León. In 1830 Padilla and Thomas Chambers received a contract to settle 800 families in Texas. During the revolutionary period, Padilla sided with the Texans, fought in the army, and served on the General Council until November 1836. *CM 1936.*

Presidio Nuestra Señora de los Dolores de los Tejas. Marker, 14 mi. W of Nacogdoches on FM 225. Originally established in 1717, one-fourth league away from Mission San Francisco de los Tejas, Presidio de los Dolores was abandoned in 1719 and reestablished and relocated in 1721 one league from Mission Nuestra Señora de la Purísima Concepción de los Hasinai. In 1729, the recommendation was made that the presidio be abolished because of the peaceful state of the Indians. Following abandonment of the presidio, its neighboring missions (Purísima Concepción, San José de los Nazonis, and San Francisco de los Neches) were reestablished and relocated first to Austin in 1730, and then to San Antonio the following year. *CM 1936.*

Sacred Heart Catholic Church. Mims Ave. and North St. Simplified Mission Espada influence is evident in this vernacular brick church. *See also* Festival entries.

Sacred Heart Catholic Church, Nacogdoches. Photo by Cathryn Hoyt, THC.

Archives

Ralph W. Steen Library. Stephen F. Austin State University. The Special Collections Department of the library contains material on Hispanic Texas history. For information contact Ralph W. Steen Library, SFA State University, P.O. Box 13055, Nacogdoches 75962.

Festivals and Events

Sacred Heart Multicultural Fest. In May (date varies), at the Exposition Center. This event, which celebrates the multicultural heritage of the Nacogdoches area and of Sacred Heart Parish, offers a variety of ethnic foods and entertainment, including Mexican and Mexican-American offerings. Another regional feature of the celebration is a dance performance by Alabama-Coushatta Indians. Sponsored by Sacred Heart Catholic Church, the festival is in its third year at the present location but has its beginnings in earlier parish celebrations.

Spanish/Tejas Rendezvous. In May (date varies), in downtown Nacogdoches. This event originated to foster Hispanic culture in Nacogdoches and to serve as a homecoming for descendants of the early Hispanic settlers of the area. The festival features southwestern American Indian folklife demonstrations, Spanish flamenco dance, Mexican ballet folklórico, and classical Spanish guitar performances, as well as traditional arts and craft exhibits.

NAVASOTA, Grimes County

Navasota (pop. 6,296) is the largest town in Grimes County. The area was known to Spaniards as early as 1690, when they were drawn into East Texas because of the French explorer La Salle's presence in the region. A statue of La Salle can be seen on the median of SH 6, near the business district, in Navasota. The first permanent settlers in Grimes County were Anglo-American colonists who received Mexican land grants during the early 1820s.

La Bahía Trail. Marker, off SH 6, one block N of Washington Ave. Originally an Indian trail, this route was used by Spaniards as early as 1690 when the De León expedition traveled from Mexico to East Texas to found Mission San Francisco de los Tejas among the Hasinai band of Caddoan Indians. *SM 1967.*

ORANGE, Orange County

Orange (pop. 19,381) lies in an area that was once inhabited by Atakapan Indians. Few Spanish explorers ventured into the area, though Joaquín Orobio y Basterra investigated French activity in East Texas and explored the area in 1748. During the early 1800s, when Anglo settlements

Southern Cheyenne moccasins,
Stark Museum of Art, Orange.
Courtesy of Stark Museum of Art.

in the southeastern United States increased, many Indian groups were displaced from their homelands. Choctaw, Alabama-Coushatta, Biloxi, and Cherokee Indians stopped briefly in the Orange County area as they were pushed westward. Today, Orange is an industrial center and the county seat of Orange County.

Stark Museum of Art. 712 Green Ave. The museum features a fine collection of western American art, including material crafted by the American Indian tribes of the Great Plains and Southwest. The collection includes examples of Plains clothing, body ornaments and beadwork, and baskets; Puebloan materials include pottery, Zuñi and Hopi kachina dolls, and Navajo rugs and blankets. Open Wed.–Sat. 10–5; Sun. 1–5; closed major holidays.

PORT ARTHUR, Jefferson County

Port Arthur (pop. 58,724). Part of Jefferson County originated as part of the municipality of Liberty in the Lorenzo de Zavala empresario grant. As early as 1840, the town of Aurora existed here but was abandoned in 1890. Port Arthur was founded as a port and railroad town in 1895 and later became a major oil-refining center.

Fourth of July All-American Ethnic Heritage Festival. July 4, at the Port Arthur Civic Center on Cultural Dr. at SH 73. This multicultural event features booths offering traditional foods of the many ethnic groups—including Mexican-Americans—that live in Port Arthur. Different entertainment is offered each year, and the evening concludes with a fireworks display. For information contact American Heritage Society, 4616 13th St., Port Arthur 77642.

International Holiday Festival. December 6, downtown. This multicultural holiday celebration begins at 6:00 p.m. with a Las Posadas procession from the Ramada Inn on SH 73 to the Public Library, where an outdoor Christmas tree is lit. Inside the library, many Christmas trees are decorated according to the traditions of the different ethnic groups—including Mexican-Americans—living in Port Arthur, and at each tree a traditional sweet of the ethnic group is featured. The trees remain on display through December. For more information contact Mexican American Heritage Society, 4616 13th St., Port Arthur 77642.

Mexican Heritage Festival. Weekend preceding September 16, at the Port Arthur Civic Center on Cultural Drive at SH 73. This fun-for-all-ages celebration features performances by the Heritage Society's own Mexican Heritage Folkloric Dancers, as well as traditional foods and music, historical displays, crafts, and piñatas. Contestants, dressed in traditional Mexican costumes, compete for a scholarship in the queen's pageant, and an evening dance with live entertainment concludes the celebration. For information contact Mexican Heritage Society, 4616 13th St., Port Arthur 77642.

RICHMOND and ROSENBERG, Fort Bend County

Richmond (pop. 16,700); **Rosenberg** (pop. 27,099). Karankawa Indians inhabited the area now occupied by these two neighboring cities when members of Stephen F. Austin's "Old Three Hundred," led by William Little, journeyed from the mouth of the Brazos River into this area in 1821. The modern town of Richmond was built on land granted by Mexico to Mrs. Jane Long in 1824. Santa Anna and 550 troops crossed the Brazos three miles north of Richmond on the way to Harrisburg in the spring of 1836. Today, Rosenberg is the larger of these two major cities, and Richmond is the county seat.

Fort Bend County Museum. 500 Houston St., Richmond. Exhibits focus on Stephen F. Austin's settlements. The museum's permanent collections include several of Austin's original Spanish land grants, a pair of Spanish spurs, and a copper pot recovered from the San Jacinto Battleground. Open Tues.–Fri., 10–4; Sat.–Sun. 1–5.

George Ranch Headquarters. SW of Richmond on FM 762. The origins of the George Ranch lie in the Longhorn cattle business run by J.H.P. Davis in the 1890s. Today, the George Ranch is a living history project administered by the Fort Bend Museum Association and the George Foundation. The ranch's Longhorns—the distinctive cattle breed originally brought to North America by the Spaniards—reflect the Spanish influence on this and other Anglo-American cattle ranches in Texas. For information contact the ranch at Route 1, Box 577, Richmond 77469.

Holy Rosary Catholic Church. 1416 George, Rosenberg. Spanish Mission Revival style with stucco exterior, this church was built in 1925, one year after the original Holy Rosary Church burned. A shrine to Our Lady of Lourdes was built at the church in 1937.

Our Lady of Guadalupe Church. 514 Carlisle St., Rosenberg. The first Spanish-speaking masses in Rosenberg were given in an old dance hall in 1937. In 1939 Our Lady of the Holy Rosary Church in Rosenberg constructed a mission, Our Lady of Guadalupe, to serve the Mexican-American members of the diocese. Our Lady functioned as a mission until 1966, when it was elevated to parish status. Its congregation remains predominantly Mexican-American today.

St. John Fisher Church. 410 Clay, Richmond. A tilework shrine here depicts the Virgin of Guadalupe's appearance to Juan Diego.

Thompson's Ferry Site. Marker, 3 mi. N of Richmond. Santa Anna and 550 troops crossed the Brazos here on the way to Harrisburg before the Battle of San Jacinto. *CM 1936.*

SAN AUGUSTINE, San Augustine County

San Augustine (pop. 2,337). Ais bands of Caddoan Indians were still present in this area during the French and Spanish exploration of East Texas. The Spanish established Mission Nuestra Señora de los Dolores de los Ais for these bands in 1716. The Dolores de los Ais mission was permanently abandoned in 1773 after the French ceded Louisiana to Spain. The mission's empty buildings drew Antonio Leal and his wife, Gertrudis de los Santos, to settle near the mission site in 1794, where they built corrals to accommodate wild mustangs. Leal, with the assistance of Philip Nolan, gathered the mustangs and sold them in Louisiana. In 1801 the Leals were apprehended by Spanish authorities for their participation in Nolan's insurrection. They sold their land title to Edmund Quirk, and Anglo settlement of the area commenced. San Augustine now is the county seat of San Augustine County.

Civic and Tourism Center. 611 W. Columbia. The center contains large fiberglass plaques depicting the history of San Augustine, including El Camino Real and the Spanish missions. At the Court of Nine Flags outside, the nine flags that have flown over the town, including the Spanish flag, are displayed.

El Camino Real. Marker, along SH 21. This historic trail linked Spanish settlements in East Texas to those along the Rio Grande and passed through San Augustine. Look for the historic markers at 5-mile intervals along SH 21. *CM 1936.*

Mission Nuestra Señora de los Dolores de los Ais Site. Marker, 0.5 mi. SE of the city center on FM 147. Mission Nuestra Señora de los Dolores de los Ais was established in 1716 to counteract French influence on the local Ais Indians through religious conversion. The mission was abandoned in 1719 but was restored in 1721 and remained in use until 1773, when all the East Texas missions were finally abandoned following France's cession of Louisiana to Spain. Today, the site is owned by the San Augustine Historical Foundation and the Texas Department of Transportation. Remnants of the original jacal and palisade structures, trash pits, and a well are evident. *CM 1936; NR 1977; SAL 1990.*

San Augustine County Courthouse Archives. County courthouse, in the Town Square (formed by Broadway, Columbia, Main, and Harrison Sts.). Included in the county archives are original deeds and legal records from the Spanish period, many with modern transcripts.

Scenic Drives. Both Angelina and Sabine National Forests are accessible from this area. The nearest entrance to Angelina National Forest is about 11 miles south on SH 147. The entrance to Sabine National Forest is about 5 miles east on FM 353.

SAN FELIPE, Austin County

San Felipe (pronounced "San Fillip"; pop. ca. 600) was founded by Stephen F. Austin in 1823 at the site of the Brazos River crossing of the Atascosito Road, which connected Goliad and Refugio to the Spanish missions of East Texas. As decreed by the Mexican government, it became the capital of the Austin Colony.

San Felipe de Austin. Marker, roadside park on FM 1458, 2 mi. N of IH 10. The original settlement of San Felipe is commemorated in this historical marker. *SM 1936.*

Stephen F. Austin State Historical Park. FM 1458 to entrance. The old ferry crossing site, where the Atascosito Road crossed the Brazos, is located in the park.

TEAGUE, Freestone County

Teague (pop. 3,268), which began as a machine and car shop for the Trinity and Brazos Valley Railroad Depot, was incorporated in 1906 and is the second largest town in Freestone County.

Trinity and Brazos Valley Railroad Depot (B-RI Depot Museum). 208 S. Third Ave. Built in 1907, the structure reflects Spanish influence in its architectural style. Predating the heyday of the Mission Revival style in Texas by about a dozen years, it demonstrates the early popularity of Spanish-style architecture in its red tile roof, arched entryways, and mission-style belfry. In 1906 a local newspaper reported that the roof was being covered with brick tiles "something durable and entirely new to this part of the country. This is, however, only in keeping with everything the T. & B.V. does—in the newest and best style." The townspeople took extraordinary pride in their new railroad depot, noting that it was one of the prettiest passenger stations in Texas. Today the depot houses a small general museum containing exhibits relating to the railroad and the history of Teague. Open Sat.–Sun. 1–5. *NR 1979; SAL 1981.*

WASHINGTON, Washington County

Washington (pop. ca. 300), also known as Washington-on-the-Brazos, was founded in 1821 when the Andrew Robinson family settled

permanently at La Bahía crossing. The Provisional Government of Texas designated Washington as the site of the 1836 General Convention, where Texas' future relationship with Mexico was decided. On March 1, 1836, while Santa Anna laid siege to the Alamo, delegates elected from each municipality in Texas convened here to declare Texas independence, establish a constitution, and organize an interim government. Three Mexican-Texans, all representatives of Béxar, signed the Texas Declaration of Independence. They were Lorenzo de Zavala, José Francisco Ruiz, and José Antonio Navarro. Navarro also served on the 21-member special committee that drafted the 1836 Constitution of the Republic. Today, Washington is recognized as a major state historic site.

Star of the Republic Museum. *See* Washington-on-the-Brazos State Historical Park.

Washington-on-the-Brazos State Historical Park. FM 1155 at Washington. The signing of the Texas Declaration of Independence took place here on March 2, 1836, and this event is celebrated in the park an-

Trinity and Brazos Valley Railroad Depot, Teague. Courtesy B-RI Railroad Museum, Teague.

José Antonio Navarro, one of three Mexican-Texans who signed the Texas Declaration of Independence in Washington-on-the-Brazos in 1836. Courtesy of Daughters of the Republic of Texas Library, San Antonio.

nually on the weekend closest to March 2. Much of Washington's old town, including Independence Hall, has been reconstructed in the park. The Star of the Republic Museum, located in the park, has exhibits relating to Texas history. Collections not on permanent exhibit include Spanish Colonial and Mexican documents and maps, as well as Mexican retablos, pistols, and ranching-related items. Park open daily, 8–sundown. Museum open daily 10–5.

WHARTON, Wharton County

Wharton (pop. 9,011), during the period of early statehood, was settled mainly by Southern planters, but Swedish, German, and Czech immigrants settled here in the 1890s. Wharton is the county seat of Wharton County.

Our Lady of Mount Carmel Church. 506 S. East Ave. In the 1940s, priests from the Basilian Fathers' Mexican Mission Center began commuting to Wharton to serve the Spanish-speaking community, giving masses at the Holy Family Church. In 1948, Wharton Mexican-Americans were able to build their own church, Our Lady of Mount Carmel.

Fiesta Hispano Americano. In September (date varies), at the courthouse square. This event features mariachis, folklórico dancers, traditional foods, and a carnival. Proceeds raised go to a scholarship fund for Wharton County students. For information contact Wharton Chamber of Commerce, 225 N. Richmond, Wharton 77488.

WOODVILLE, Tyler County

Woodville (pop. 2,636) was established in the late 1840s as the county seat of Tyler County. The town is a livestock and lumber-industry center, and is located in a heavily forested area. The Alabama-Coushatta Indian Reservation and several units of the Big Thicket National Preserve are accessible from Woodville.

The Alabama-Coushattas of Texas. Marker, FM 2097, Kirby Memorial Museum. The Alabama-Coushattas visited this area of Tyler County briefly in 1816, during the period when the Spaniards were encouraging Indians to settle in East Texas—in hopes of discouraging Anglo-Americans. During the Texas war for independence, the Alabama-Coushatta fled to Louisiana, but they returned and occupied this locale between 1836 and 1844. In adjacent Polk County the Alabama-Coushatta Indian Reservation, the first Indian reservation in Texas, was established in 1854. *SM 1964.*

Scenic Drive. US 69/287 to Beaumont offers an excellent opportunity to view the big timber for which the Piney Woods region of East Texas is named, but almost any highway in the Woodville area provides scenic views of Alabama-Coushatta country.

REGION 6

Dallas and North Texas

The broad expanse of land that constitutes the North-Central and North-east Texas region is made up of 75 counties whose diverse landscape changes from west to east from grassy plains to pine forests. The Dallas–Fort Worth Metroplex is located in the heart of the area, which is bounded on the north by the Red River and on the east by the Louisiana-Texas state line. On the south and west somewhat arbitrary boundaries separate the Central Texas and Plains regions.

Caddoan and Wichitan tribes were the dominant American Indian groups in the region well into the Historic period. Caddoan groups had occupied the great bend of the Red River in northeastern Texas and south-western Arkansas for centuries before the arrival of the first Spanish explorers. French explorer La Salle encountered Caddoan groups in East Texas in 1687 and the French presence here renewed Spain's interest in the area. In 1689 explorer Alonso de León traveled into Northeast Texas in search of La Salle's fort. By 1691 the Domingo Terán de los Ríos expedition had explored the Caddo settlements as far as the Red River, and the first mission-presidio complexes in East Texas were established to counteract French influences among the Caddoan tribes.

During the period when the East Texas missions were struggling to survive, the Spanish and French competed for influence among the Wichitan tribes in North-Central Texas. They were drifting southward from the Great Plains into Texas during this period and were soon followed by the Comanches. In 1759, in retaliation for Wichita and Comanche participation in the sacking of Mission San Sabá (in Menard County), Colonel Diego Ortiz Parilla, commandant of Presidio San Sabá, retaliated with an attack on a major Taovaya village subsequently known as Spanish Fort. The attack resulted in the first major victory of Indians over Spaniards in Texas, and it effectively blocked further Spanish colonization in North Texas.

By the late 1770s Spain had English traders as well as French competing for influence with the Taovayas. Tragically, neither trade policies, military, nor force were ultimately responsible for resolving the problem of the Taovayas. In a few decades the Taovaya population was decimated by diseases, notably smallpox, that had inadvertently been introduced by Europeans.

Opposite: Pre-Columbian figurines and incense burner from the W.O. Gross, Jr., collection at the Old Jail Art Center, Albany. Photo by Ken Ellsworth, courtesy of The Old Jail Art Center.

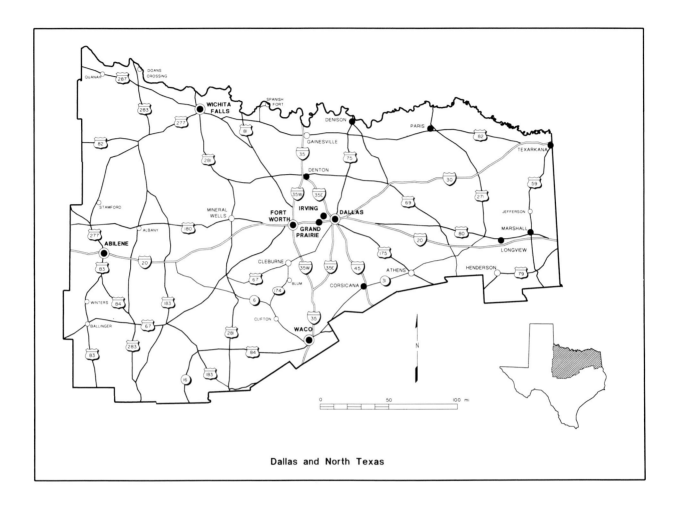

Dallas and North Texas

As Taovaya concerns ceased, problems with the Anglo-Americans and the Mexicans began. Early in the 19th century, power struggles in Mexico's interior took attention away from the outlying areas of Texas and, eventually, resulted in Mexico's independence from Spain. Under the Mexican Constitution of 1824, the Mexican State of Coahuila and Texas was formed, but Mexican dominion in Texas was shortlived. Anglo and Mexican Texans alike, enraged by the conservative centralist shift in President Santa Anna's policies, declared and won independence in 1836.

Spanish exploration of northern Texas was early and ephemeral, and the lands here were mostly granted to absentee landlords. Consequently, many counties lack the historic material evidence (such as Spanish Colonial buildings or museum collections of Spanish and Mexican period artifacts) that occurs in Texas counties farther south. Nevertheless, many natural landmarks in the region bear Spanish names bestowed upon them during the earliest years of exploration. The small museums of Northeast Texas are more likely to contain material relating to the indigenous peoples the Spaniards encountered than Spanish artifacts, since this is Caddo country. The prairie lands and cross timbers country to the west of Dallas–Fort

Guidebook Region 6. Map by Greg Miller.

Worth, like Northeast Texas, have traditionally been less than 10% Hispanic, although percentages increase to the west, especially in the Abilene area.

Permanent settlement in the Dallas–Fort Worth Metroplex area began with the Peters' Colony, a grant made by the Republic of Texas to W.S. Peters and associates for the introduction of colonists into the area. Despite controversies arising from the settlement scheme, population of the area increased steadily, and both Dallas and Tarrant counties were established in the 1840s. By 1890, Dallas had become the most heavily populated county in Texas, and the metroplex remains the largest urban area in the state.

Hispanic communities in this region today originated relatively recently during the late 19th and early 20th centuries, in response to the economic opportunities found here and the turmoil of the Mexican Revolution, and the population of most of the region is still less than 10% Hispanic.

DALLAS, Dallas County

Dallas (pop. 1,064,000) began as an 1841 trading post and small settlement established by Anglo-Americans from Tennessee. Today it is the second largest city in Texas and the county seat of Dallas County. Most of the county's 1,873,600 residents live in "Big D," which physically is sprawled over most of the county.

Though Dallas County remains a predominantly Anglo-American city, about 20% of its residents are Hispanic. Small numbers of Hispanics moved to Dallas soon after the city's founding, but not until the coming of the railroads in the mid-1870s did they begin to move into the city in significant numbers. Because Hispanics came in search of railroad jobs, the first Spanish-speaking neighborhood in town developed near McKinney St. and the Missouri-Kansas-Texas (M-K-T) railroad track. This area—where workers and their families lived in company housing made of converted railroad cars—became the nucleus of Dallas' "Little Mexico" barrio. The next wave of immigration occurred during the Mexican Revolutionary years after 1910, and the barrio continued to grow. As Hispanic population increased, other enclaves developed, including the Pike Park neighborhood, Cement City at Eagle Ford, and Juarez Heights. By 1935, the Hispanic population of Dallas had reached 6,650.

The social and cultural life of the Hispanic community flourished from the start. Many community organizations were founded to ease new residents' immigration transition; Cinco de Mayo, Diez y Seis, and Christmas *pastorelas* were celebrated annually; outdoor markets, newspapers, social clubs, small businesses, labor groups, and artisans' studios were established; and in 1949 the Mexican-American Chamber of Commerce was founded. In the late 1960s, in the wake of the Civil Rights movement, Dallas Hispanics increased their political power as well, winning elected offices for the first time.

Today, Hispanics live in many areas of the city and Hispanic culture is a vibrant part of the cultural makeup of Dallas. Many events, exhibitions, and historic sites offer an opportunity to experience Hispanic heritage that is unique in the region.

Pike Park fiesta, ca. 1939. THC photo.

Information Centers

Dallas Convention & Visitors Bureau. Renaissance Tower, 1201 Elm St., Suite 2000. Provides information on Dallas attractions and events, free maps, directions, literature, and information on accommodations and dining. Open Mon.–Fri. 8:30–5.

Union Station. 400 S. Houston St. Offers maps and brochures on Dallas attractions. Open daily 9–5.

West End Market Place. 603 Munger. Provides free maps, information on accommodations and dining, and brochures on local attractions can be found here. Open Mon.–Sat. 11–8; Sun. noon–8.

Historic Neighborhoods and Churches

Eagle Ford. Marker, 5300 Singleton at Clymer. The Eagle Ford community's early residents were Anglo-American farmers who settled in the area during the 1840s. After the coming of the railroads, Eagle Ford became a train stop west of Dallas. In 1907 the Southwestern States Portland Cement Company was established here, and the company built frame houses and operated a store to attract cement workers. Many Mexican immigrants moved into the area and obtained employment, settling in this neighborhood, which came to be called Cemente Grande, and in a smaller barrio, Cemento Chico, to the east. The oldest extensively Mexican cemetery in Dallas County is located in the area. *SM 1989.*

El Camposanto de Cemente Grande de la Compañía Trinity Portland (Trinity Portland Cement Company Cemetery). Marker, 3333 Fort Worth Ave. In 1918 the Trinity Portland Cement Company (formerly the Southwestern States Portland Cement Company) donated this land for use as a cemetery by its Hispanic employees who lived in a company town referred to as Cement City. The first interments were in 1918, when many residents fell victim to an influenza epidemic. The last occurred in 1945 when Eladio R. Martínez, killed in action in the Philippines during World War II, was buried here. The cemetery is on private property, but appointments for visits may be made through Henry Martínez, c/o Ledbetter Neighborhood Association, 3619 Tumalo Trail, Dallas, 75212. *SM 1989.*

Cathedral Santuario de Guadalupe (formerly Sacred Heart Cathedral). 2215 Ross Ave. Established in 1869, the original Sacred Heart Church, a wood-frame structure, was the first Catholic church in Dallas. When the Diocese of Dallas was established, a larger Gothic structure was built on this site to serve as the mother church of the diocese. In 1977 Sacred Heart Cathedral officially changed its name to Cathedral Santuario de Guadalupe when Our Lady of Guadalupe Parish, founded in 1913 in Dallas' "Little Mexico," merged with Sacred Heart. Now the cathedral serves a predominantly Hispanic parish. Two shrines have been erected here: the shrine to Our Lady of Guadalupe, the patron saint of Mexico, includes a replica of the *tilma* enshrined in Mexico City; the shrine to Our Lady of Charity reflects the devotion of Cuban parishioners. Spanish-language masses are held daily.

Our Lady of San Juan and St. Theresa Catholic Church. 2601 Singleton Blvd. Mexican-American residents of Cemente Grande and Cemento Chico barrios completed construction of St. Theresa Church in 1925. Several years later that wood-frame church was destroyed in a fire but was replaced. In 1940 the congregations of St. Theresa and Our Lady of San Juan Chapel merged, and, since 1954, the church of Our Lady of San Juan and St. Theresa has functioned as a mission church of Our Lady of Lourdes Parish church (5605 Bernal). Currently meeting in a brick structure that originally was a Baptist church, the congregation is wholly Hispanic. All masses except one are held in Spanish. The English mass primarily serves younger members of the congregation who are learning Spanish as a second language.

Pike Park. Marker at the park, 2807 Harry Hines Blvd. The City of Dallas bought this site for a play park in 1912, and by the 1920s it served a predominantly Hispanic community. During World War II, the park was a gathering place for Mexican-American servicemen and residents of "Little Mexico." The park has become the focal point of the community's cultural, recreational, and political interests. Its recreation center, renovated in 1978, exhibits Southwestern-style architecture, with stucco walls, a red tile roof, a row of arched windows, and a curved parapet. A *kiosco,* or Mexican-style bandstand, also stands in the park, which is enclosed within a decorative wrought iron fence. *SM 1981.*

Spanish Revival Architecture

DeGolyer Estate. 8525 Garland Rd. This magnificent Spanish Revival mansion was built in 1940 for oil man Everett DeGolyer. The one-story structure is constructed of random ashlar limestone and features arched breezeways and tile floors (*NR 1978*). The house is located on the grounds of the Dallas Arboretum, which also offers the Lyda Bunker Hunt Paseo de Flores, a garden area with a wide walkway and benches, based on the Spanish boulevard concept. The gardens are open daily, except Monday.

No. 4 Hook & Ladder Company (Oak Lawn Fire station). Cedar Springs Rd. and Reagan St. Built in 1909, this two-story, brick structure with cast-stone detail shows Spanish Mission Revival stylistic influences. *NR 1981.*

South Boulevard–Park Row Historic District. Atlanta and South Blvd. This 20th-century suburb originated in 1913 as a predominantly Jewish neighborhood and since the fifties has been predominantly African-American. Many of its original residences, several of which are Spanish Revival style structures, have been preserved by the community. *SM 1981.*

Museums and Archives

Dallas Diocese Archives. 3915 Lemmon Ave. Contains archives on the Catholic history of Dallas, including the city's Hispanic Catholic population. Hours by appointment.

Dallas Historical Society, Research Center Library and Archives. Hall of State, Fair Park. The research center houses Spanish Colonial documents. For further information contact the society at P.O. Box 26038, Dallas 75226.

Dallas Museum of Art. Ross Ave. at N. Harwood. The museum's collections include a number of Pre-Columbian artifacts. Open Tues.–Sat. 10–5; Thurs. 10–9; Sun. and holidays noon–5. Closed Dec. 25.

Dallas Public Library's Texas/Dallas History Division. 1515 Young St. The papers of Anita Martínez, the first Hispanic to be elected to the Dallas City Council, are contained in the Texas/Dallas archives. The collection consists of city council papers, personal papers, media clippings, and

Loggia of the DeGolyer mansion, patterned after the veranda at Mission San Juan Capistrano. Courtesy of the DeGolyer House archives, Dallas.

other materials relating to her long career as a political and cultural leader in Dallas. The collection also has original 16th-, 17th-, 18th-, and 19th-century editions of works relating to Spanish and Spanish-American law (including mineral, naval, and Mexican law), history, religion, and general culture, as well as historic Spanish Colonial maps.

International Museum of Cultures. 7500 W. Camp Wisdom Rd. The museum includes exhibits on contemporary indigenous cultures in Ecuador and Peru, displaying examples of pottery, clothing, and tools. Open Tues.–Fri. 10–5; Sat.–Sun. 1:30–5.

Meadows Museum of Art. Owens Fine Art Center, Southern Methodist University Campus, 6101 Bishop at Binkley. The museum has an outstanding collection of Spanish art that includes works by Goya, Míro, Murillo, and Picasso, as well as Mexican muralist Diego Rivera. Open Mon.–Sat. 10–5; Sun. 1–5.

Mexican American Cultural Heritage Center. Davy Crockett School, 401 N. Carroll. The center's permanent exhibits include a Spanish-Mexican room (18th and 19th centuries) and a Spanish Texas room, which features an exhibit entitled "Life and Art of the Times" (17th and 18th centuries). Other acquisitions include oral histories related to the Mexican-American heritage of the Dallas–Fort Worth area from 1850 to 1976. Mexican folk arts and crafts exhibits include toys, dolls, paper art, piñatas, masks, and much more. The museum contains a model of a Spanish presidio and mission and displays special collections of Spanish Colonial artifacts on loan from various institutions. Also in the museum's holdings are some Pre-Columbian, Southwestern, Midwest, and Northeast North American Indian collections, including a model of a Caddo house. Open Mon.–Fri. 8–4.

South American mantle (450–400 B.C.), Dallas Museum of Art, Dallas. Courtesy of Dallas Museum of Art, The Eugene and Margaret McDermott Fund in memory of John O'Boyle.

The Investiture of Saint Ildefonsus, by Juan de Borgoña (ca. 1470–1534). Algur H. Meadows Collection (accession number 69.03), Meadows Museum, Southern Methodist University, Dallas.

Southern Methodist University, Fikes Hall of Special Collections and DeGolyer Library. Third Floor, Science Information Library, Southern Methodist University Campus. Collections contain Spanish Colonial documents.

University of Texas at Arlington Library, Division of Special Collections. The library's special collections contain Spanish Colonial documents. For further information, contact the library at P.O. Box 19497, Arlington 76091.

Public Art

Texas Hall of State Mural. In the Hall of State at Fair Park. This mural depicts scenes from Texas history and includes panels on American Indian, Spanish, and Mexican contributions.

411

Es Todo, mural by Thomas Edison students, directed by Raúl Valdez. 1981. Thomas Edison Elementary School, 2940 Singleton Blvd. This mural features images that Thomas Edison students chose as representative of their lifestyle and identity, such as the Dallas skyline and lowriders, pyramids, corn, and the Virgin of Guadalupe.

Ignacio Zaragoza Statue. In Jaycee-Zaragoza Park, 3114 Clymer. Ignacio Zaragoza, the Goliad native who led Mexican troops to victory over the French in the 1862 Battle of Puebla, is honored here with this statue, a gift from Mexico.

Festivals and Events

ACAL's Annual Christmas Posada. In early December; location varies each year. Sponsored by ACAL de México (Alianza Cultural de Artes y Letras/Cultural Alliance of Arts and Letters), a nonprofit organization founded in 1973 to promote the fine arts and rich heritage of Mexico in the Dallas–Fort Worth Metroplex. For information on the Christmas Posada, as well as current activities, contact ACAL at 7208 Hillwood Lane, Dallas 75248.

Cinco de Mayo. May 5 or weekend closest to May 5, in several locations. Cinco de Mayo has been celebrated at historic Pike Park (2807 Harry Hines Blvd.) in the heart of Dallas' Little Mexico for decades. In Texas Fair Park, the festival is a two-day event featuring mariachi and conjunto music, folklórico dance, traditional foods, a pageant, international trade show, and carnival rides; it is the largest Cinco de Mayo festival in Dallas with over 150,000 people attending each year. The festival at Jaycee-Zaragoza Park (3114 Clymer St.) is organized by residents of the Ledbetter Neighborhood, and the entertainment varies each year, although it is always typically Mexican; about 800 people attend annually.

Diez y Seis. September 16, at Pike Park. Diez y Seis celebrations have been held at this historic park in the heart of Little Mexico since 1926, making this the oldest Diez y Seis celebration in Dallas. Also celebrating Diez y Seis, the Hispanic Heritage Festival, a two-day event, is held at various locations (contact Dallas Chamber of Commerce for location); this festival features conjunto and tropical music, ballet folklórico, and traditional foods, and over 50,000 people attend each year.

Mex-Fest. Mid-June, at Lee Park, 3400 Turtle Creek Blvd. Features traditional Mexican food and drink, music, and dance.

Teatro Dallas. 222 S. Montclair Ave. Teatro Dallas presents four or five plays a year by Latin American authors and playwrights. *See* sidebar: Teatro Dallas.

ABILENE, Taylor County

Abilene (pop. 106,654), a prairie town, is located in a transitional area between central West and North-Central Texas, with strong ties to the plains. When Anglo settlement of the area began about 1840, Comanches

TEATRO HISPANO IN DALLAS

Dallas is the home of Teatro Dallas, a nonprofit professional theater organization dedicated to producing plays that reflect the diverse cultural experiences of Hispanic communities throughout the world.

In the four or five plays produced by the company each year, there is something to please just about everybody. Classic works of tragedy and *amor* by writers such as Spain's Garcia Lorca share the bill with a contemporary play on gangs by an emerging playwright or an unconventional Día de los Muertos adaptation of the legendary Don Juan, who in *Don Juan Vampire* appears as a street-wise musician from Dallas' Deep Ellum. Each play is presented in both Spanish and English.

"Fostering understanding and promoting a sense of community while celebrating our diverse traditions" are the goals of Teatro Dallas. The group's level of commitment is evident not only onstage, but also "behind the scenes." Teatro Dallas' playwrights, actors, and technicians come from diverse ethnic backgrounds and become involved in the company through open auditions. The troupe also sponsors a community outreach program, taking one show a year on the road to Dallas schoolchildren and distributing theater tickets to groups of citizens and students who might not otherwise be able to attend theater performances.

The House of Bernarda Alba performed by Teatro Dallas, Dallas.
Photo by David Moynihan, courtesy
of Teatro Dallas.

Paramount Theatre, Abilene. THC
photo.

still dominated the area as they followed the winter buffalo migration
southward. Delaware, Kiowa, and Kiowa Apaches also were present here
until the buffalo were slaughtered for hides and the Plains Indians finally
were forced from Texas. Abilene, established in 1881, was a railroad center,
and cattle, wool, and buffalo bones were shipped from here in the late 19th
century. The city, which is the county seat of Taylor County, is still a major
distribution center, but today oil also plays a large part in the local economy.

Paramount Theater. 352 Cypress St. Cited by Carla Breeze as an out-

413

Sacred Heart Catholic Church, Abilene. Courtesy of Sacred Heart Church.

standing example of Pueblo Deco in her book of the same name, the Paramount Theater, built in 1929, is a unique blend of Spanish Revival and Art Deco styles. The exterior parapets are trimmed with terra-cotta panels depicting conquistador paraphernalia. The interior features vigas painted with Spanish and Indian motifs, enameled stuccoed walls, and arched entryways. *NR 1982.*

Sacred Heart Catholic Church. 1633 S. 8th St. Sacred Heart began as a mission church in the 1880s to serve the Catholics of Abilene, who were primarily of German, Irish, and Mexican descent. In 1926 the original church was moved to Cottonwood St., to serve the city's Spanish-speaking Catholics. The new Sacred Heart, completed in 1931, was designed by noted San Antonio architect Leo M.J. Dielmann. Spanish Revival in style, the structure also exhibits Moorish architectural influences, especially in the treatment of the arches. Sacred Heart is the best-preserved, pre-1940s religious structure in the city and is the mother church of Catholicism in the Abilene area. It still serves both Euroamericans and Mexican-Americans, and includes among its 450 families a number of more recent Vietnamese immigrants. *RTHL 1990; NR 1989.*

St. Francis Catholic Church. 8th and Treadway (US 83) Sts. St. Francis, established in 1906 as a branch of Sacred Heart Church, is the oldest Hispanic community church and the second-oldest Catholic church in the city. Until 1980 St. Francis was still housed in the old Sacred Heart church that was moved to Cottonwood St. in 1926. This old church, built in 1895, is still used as classroom space. The new St. Francis Church is modern in style, but the statues of Our Lady of Guadalupe and St. Francis were retained from the old church. Also prized by the church is a replica of the crucifix that is said to have played a role in the conversion of St. Francis; the bronze replica was made in Mexico and purchased especially for the new church. St. Francis Church still serves a predominantly Mexican-American parish.

Vicinity of Coronado's Camp. Marker, on US 277 at FM 2928, 15 mi. SW of Abilene. Coronado is thought by some students of his route to have camped here in 1541 on his way to Quivira. *SM 1968.*

Cinco de Mayo. Weekend closest to May 5, at St. Vincent Catholic Church (2525 Westview). At this weekend Jamaica celebrating Cinco de Mayo, the church's ballet folklórico group performs and other musical entertainment, a carnival, and traditional foods are available.

Scenic Area. Abilene State Recreation Area, about 21 mi. SW of Abilene on FM 89. The 490-acre park is located near Buffalo Gap, named for the thousands of buffalo that once migrated through the area. The park has been preserved in a natural state, and visitors may experience the habitat in which Tonkawa and Comanche Indians, nomadic tribes who followed the buffalo herds, once lived.

ALBANY, Shackelford County

Albany (pop. 1,962) was established in the early 1870s and became the seat of Shackelford County in 1874. The town developed as a supply point for cattle drivers en route to Dodge City on the Western Trail, and when the Texas Central Railroad arrived in 1881, the town became a cattle shipping point. The discovery of oil here in 1926 diversified Albany's economy, but the town's slogan, "Albany, Home of the Herefords" attests to the importance of ranching in the development of this Texas town.

Albany Theatre. US 180. This charming, stucco-covered theater, built in 1927, is an example of the Hollywood approach to Spanish Revival architecture. The balconies and mezzanine are a whimsical representation of a small Spanish village. The theater was restored in 1991.

Old Jail Art Center. 211 S. Second. The museum's collections include Pre-Columbian artifacts from Mexico, Central America, and Peru. Open Tues.–Sat. 10–5; Sun. 2–5.

Texas State Longhorn Herd. At Fort Griffin State Historical Park on US 283, 15 mi. N of Albany. A part of the Texas State Longhorn herd can be viewed here at this historic park, which encompasses the ruins of Fort Griffin, established in 1867 (*CM 1936; NR 1971*).

ARCHER CITY, Archer County

Archer City (pop. 1,748). While the Spaniards were attempting to influence American Indians in other areas of Texas through the mission-presidio system during the mid-1700s, French traders in this vicinity used trade—including supplies of guns and ammunition. The French were so successful with their approach that Taovaya Indians, armed with French weapons, defeated Spaniards handily at Spanish Fort in 1759 (*see* Spanish Fort, Montague County). Spanish explorer José Mares passed through the area on a road mapping expedition in 1787, but no permanent Spanish settlements were established. Comanches and Kiowas prevented Euroamerican settlement here until the 1870s. Archer City was established as the seat of Archer County in 1880. Originally a ranching center, the city's economy diversified with grain processing and oil production in later years.

Confluence of Brazos, Trinity, and Red River Watersheds. Marker, SH 79, 3 mi. N of Olney. This natural landmark guided many explorers, surveyors, and soldiers throughout Texas history, including Captain Diego Parilla, who passed this place in 1759 on the way to Spanish Fort. *SM 1976.*

French Trading Area. Marker, roadside park at the intersection of SH 25 and FM 210, 2 mi. W of Archer City. The trade in arms between American Indians and the French helped to defeat Spanish attempts to control this outlying area. *SM 1974.*

ATHENS, Henderson County

Athens (pop. 10,967) is located on lands that were part of an empresario grant made by the Mexican government to David Burnet in 1826, but there were no permanent settlements in the area until the late 1830s. Athens was established in 1850 and is the county seat of Henderson County.

Henderson County Historical Museum. 217 N. Prairieville St. The museum exhibits Caddoan materials including pottery, stone tools, and a beaded necklace. Open Fri.–Sat. 10–3.

BALLINGER AND VICINITY, Runnels County

Ballinger (pop. 3,975) is located near the site of the first Spanish outpost east of the Pecos River. Established in 1684 by the Mendoza-López expedition, the outpost, sometimes called a mission, did not result in a permanent Spanish presence in the area. In 1886, Ballinger was established as the county seat of Runnels County.

San Clemente Site. Marker, on US 83, 7 mi. S of Ballinger; Centennial Marker on FM 2134, 12 mi. N of Millersview. The Mendoza-López expedition stayed six months at a place called San Clemente, but the exact site of the encampment, which has sometimes been called a mission, has not been determined. This expedition was aimed at founding missions in western Texas, but La Salle's landing at Matagorda Bay diverted the attention of the Spanish eastward. *CM 1936; SM 1968.*

Festival of Ethnic Cultures. Last weekend of April, at the county courthouse grounds, intersection of US 67 and US 83. The culture of the city's significant Hispanic population is represented in this celebration of Ballinger's ethnic diversity. The event features food booths, a parade, live entertainment, and arts and crafts.

CLEBURNE, Johnson County

Cleburne (pop. 25,823), the county seat and largest city of Johnson County, is a rail shipping terminal and dairy center and offers access to lakes and a state recreation area.

Layland Museum. 201 N. Caddo St. This museum, housed in the 1905 Cleburne Carnegie Library (*NR 1976; RTHL 1981*), has permanent collections that include stone and wooden implements, pottery, and other artifacts of Southwest, Plains, and Northwest Coastal Indian tribes. Open Mon.–Fri. 10–12, 1–5; Sat. 9–1.

CORSICANA, Navarro County

Corsicana (pop. 25,189), established in 1849, is the county seat of Navarro County, which is named for José Antonio Navarro, a signer of the Texas Declaration of Independence. Corsicana is named for the birthplace of Navarro's father, the Isle of Corsica.

José Antonio Navarro Statue, by Allie Tenant. 1936. Courthouse grounds, US 287 and SH 31. This monumental bronze statue of José Antonio Navarro was designed for the Texas Centennial.

Pioneer Village Park. On Park Ave. In 1831, at the location of the old Watering Hole, or Indian Spring, Sam Houston ordered a trading post built to serve local tribes and visiting Indians. The Wichitan Kichai and Yscani, the Tehuacanas, and the Wacos lived in the area at the time of its establishment, and occasionally groups of Cherokees and Kickapoos traversed the area as well. The park's focus is on Anglo-American settlement of Navarro County, but the old trading post, now located within the park, houses American Indian artifacts from the Archaic to Historic periods. Open Mon.–Sat. 9–5; Sun. 1–5.

DENISON, Grayson County

Denison (pop. 21,505) originated in 1858 as a stop on the Butterfield Overland Trail Route and is the second largest city in Grayson County. Texoma Lake, northwest of Denison, and Hagerman Wildlife Refuge on the Big Mineral Arm of the lake, are major tourist attractions in the county.

Old Denison High School. 701 E. Main St. This Spanish Revival

school, built in 1914 with additions in 1939, has multiple curvilinear parapets that define receding bays, a red tile roof, and a projecting arcaded entrance with exposed rafter ends. The tower contains the bell from the first free school in Texas, which once occupied the site. *NR 1983.*

Statue of José Antonio Navarro, Corsicana. Photo by Curtis Tunnell, THC.

DENTON, Denton County

Denton (pop. 66,270) was established in 1857 and is the county seat of Denton County. The city is best known as the home of the University of North Texas and Texas Woman's University.

Denton County Historical Museum. 110 W. Hickory. Collections include Denton County abstracts denoting Hispanic land ownership between 1847 and 1876. Open Mon.–Sat. 1–4:30; closed on holidays.

Texas Woman's University, Blagg-Huey Library. Texas Woman's

University campus. The library's special collection, Texas Women: A Celebration of History Resources Collection, includes information relating to Hispanic women in Texas. For information on exhibits and collections contact the library at P.O. Box 23715, Denton 76204-1715.

Doan's Adobe House, Doan's Crossing. THC photo.

DOAN'S CROSSING, Wilbarger County

Doan's Crossing (pop. ca. 20), a tiny community in northeastern Wilbarger County (on FM 2916 at FM 924), originated as a stop on a cattle trail and at its height consisted of fourteen structures. It is said that six million head of cattle crossed the Prairie Dog Town Fork of the Red River at this point.

Doan's Adobe House. On FM 2916, Doan's Crossing. This simple structure, built in 1881, was a trading post at the Western Texas–Kansas

Trail Red River crossing. It is the oldest building in the county and is remarkable for its adobe construction, which is unusual for North Texas. *CM 1936; RTHL 1962; NR 1979.*

FORT WORTH, Tarrant County

Fort Worth (pop. 472,600) grew up around a military post established in 1849 and in 1860 was designated the county seat of Tarrant County. In 1850 a stage line was initiated between Fort Worth and Yuma, Arizona, but it was Anglo-American commercialization of the cattle industry that sparked Fort Worth's growth. By the 1860s cowboys had discovered the profits that could be made from selling their beef to northern markets, and the small town of Fort Worth became the last stop for the cowboys who headed north with their herds on the Texas extension of the Chisholm Trail. The cattle lost so much weight during the treks that they needed to be fattened up in feed lots at the end of the trail, and the railroads soon realized that it would be advantageous to run lines into Texas and eliminate the need for the long drives. When the Texas & Pacific Railroad made Fort Worth a new stop in 1876 (just after Dallas' Eagle Ford), Fort Worth became a major shipping point for beef, prompting the construction of the city's stockyards. The city subsequently became a stop for six more railroads. As in Dallas, Fort Worth's Hispanic community is fairly recent, dating to the coming of the railroads. The influence of Spanish Revival style—perhaps boosted by the Fort Worth Stockyards—is repeated over and over in homes, apartments, and commercial buildings in the north, south, and west sides of Fort Worth.

Information

Fort Worth Visitor Information Center. 123 E. Exchange Ave. Located in the Stockyards district and open seven days a week.

Spanish Revival Architecture

City of Fort Worth Water Works (North Holly Treatment Plant). 1500–1608 Eleventh Ave. The first Mission Revival style building in the water works complex was built in 1891–92. Subsequent buildings, featuring red tile roofs, stuccoed exteriors and Alamoesque façades, were erected in 1917, 1931, 1932, and 1952. The interiors of several of the buildings have unusual appointments such as marble table tops and tile mosaics.

Elizabeth Boulevard Historic District. 1000–1616 Elizabeth Blvd. In this historic neighborhood (developed between 1911 and 1929) are several residences typifying Spanish, Mediterranean, and Mission Revival architectural styles, including the Dulaney House at 1001 Elizabeth Blvd. (1923) and the Fuller House at 1400 Elizabeth Blvd. (1923). *NR 1979; SM 1981.*

Fort Worth Stockyards Historic District. 131 E. Exchange at N.

Main. When the railroad arrived in 1876, Fort Worth became a major shipping point for beef, prompting the construction of the Union Stockyards Company. The Fort Worth Stockyards Company was chartered in 1893 and bought out Union Stockyards' property. In 1902 Armour & Company and Swift & Company built meat-packing plants here, and the Livestock Exchange Building was constructed. This Spanish Mission Revival complex now houses restaurants, shops, musical entertainment, and a weekly cattle auction. *RTHL 1967; NR 1976.*

Lacy Tourist Courts, Fort Worth. Photo by L. Standifer, courtesy of Tarrant County Historical Commission.

Horse and Mule Barns. 122–24 E. Exchange Ave. The horse and mule barns, built in 1911, are made of red brick, with the E. Exchange St. façade sheathed in rough-cast tan stucco. A pair of two-story towers with red-tiled pyramidal roofs flank the entrance to Mule Alley. Mission Revival parapets occur at intervals on both sides of Mule Alley. The barns are being restored and adapted for shops, restaurants, and amusements.

Northside Coliseum. 123 E. Exchange Ave. Built in 1907-08, the coliseum and ticket-office building continue the Mission Revival architectural style of the stockyards area. The world's first indoor rodeo was held at the coliseum.

Stockyards National Bank. 118–120 E. Exchange Ave. The bank, built in 1910, features a diagonal entrance at the corner, arched windows along E. Exchange St., and an Alamo-influenced parapet above the main entrance.

Gethsemane Presbyterian Church. 408 Lexington. This lovely church was built about 1923 as a Baptist mission church. The main building is of frame construction, as is the tapered bell tower. The front and side entrances are built of native limestone. Spanish Revival influence is evident in the arched openings that frame the front windows and entrance.

Lacy Tourist Courts. 4500 block of Surfside Dr. N. Built about 1937, these buildings are a combination of Mission Revival style and Mexican stonework construction. Seven stone duplex cottages with mission parapets and recessed carports make up the complex. This is a unique example of roadside architecture of the 1930s.

Mary Elizabeth Court Apartments. 2008–12 Hemphill St. Built about 1929, the building exhibits Spanish stylistic influences in its courtyard, mission-style parapets, arched windows, and wrought-iron details.

Matthews Memorial Methodist Church (University United Methodist Church). 2416 W. Berry St. at McCart Ave. Built in 1939–40, this Spanish Revival church features a stuccoed exterior, red tile roof, and ornate front entrance and bell tower. The church was altered and restored in 1948–49 and 1954–55.

Montgomery Ward. 2600 W. 7th St. This large building of monolithic construction, the first of its kind in Fort Worth, was built in 1928. The construction method known as "continuous pour" was employed, and concrete was poured around-the-clock until all concrete work was finished. The Spanish Revival style is now most evident in the top story, which retains arched windows and Mission Revival parapets.

North Hi Mount Elementary School. 3801 W. 7th St. The buff-

Our Mother of Mercy Catholic Church, Fort Worth. Photo by Cathryn Hoyt, THC.

brick school, built in 1937, reflects a combination of Spanish Revival styles in its arched windows, mission parapet at the front entrance, and decorative use of wrought iron.

Our Mother of Mercy Catholic Church (formerly Holy Name Catholic Church). 1003 E. Terrell Ave. at New York St. This charming Spanish Revival church, built in 1909–10, features stuccoed walls, arched windows, buttresses at the sides and front, and rear parapets that are suggestive of the Alamo.

Park Hill Neighborhood. Medford Court. This elegant neighborhood offers excellent examples of residences built in the Spanish Revival style during the 1920s. Of particular interest is the Shaw House (2404 Medford Ct. E.), which reflects a California architectural style known as Monterrey Colonial Revival. The arched windows, red tile roof, stucco exterior, and second-story porch are typical of Spanish-influenced structures built in California during the early 1900s.

Museums

Amon Carter Museum. 3501 Camp Bowie Blvd. The Amon Carter Museum, renowned for its collection of Western American art, also has outstanding photography collections. Its permanent holdings include Mexican photographs, lithographs, and illustrated books, as well as 19th- and early-20th-century photographs of American Indians. Open Tues.–Sat. 10–5; Sun. 12–6.

Fort Worth Museum of Science & History. 1501 Montgomery St. 1 mi. N of IH 30. Permanent exhibits and collections include Mexican art, secular and religious festival artifacts, and personal items of the 19th and 20th centuries. Frequently exhibited Mexican-American materials include ceramics and glass, clothing, festival artifacts, folk art, and foodways-, household-, and music-related items. Pre-Columbian and Aztec pottery from Mexico are on permanent exhibit, as are examples of Puebloan pottery from the American Southwest. Open Tues.–Sun. 9:00 a.m.–9:30 p.m.

Fort Worth Nature Center and Refuge. 2 mi. past Lake Worth Bridge on SH 199. This 3,500-acre refuge is home to a herd of American buffalo. Open daily except holidays.

Kimball Art Museum. 3333 Camp Bowie Blvd. Included in the art museum's permanent collections are materials from the Aztec, Maya, Olmec, and Xochipala cultures of Mexico, and the Incan Conte of Peru. Contact the museum for information on current exhibits. Open Tues.–Sat. 10–5; Sun. 11–5.

GAINESVILLE, Cooke County

Gainesville (pop. 14,256) became a prosperous cattle center in the late 19th century and is now a manufacturing and agribusiness center, as well as the county seat of Cooke County.

Santa Fe Passenger Depot. 505 Broadway. Built in 1902 by the Gulf, Colorado, & Santa Fe Railway, this one- and two-story building is typical of the creative eclecticism of the late Victorian period, combining vastly different architectural styles in one building. In the depot, the influences of the Jacobethan Revival are seen in the fenestration details, while Spanish Revival style is apparent in the curvilinear gable parapets and red tile roof. *NR 1983.*

GRAND PRAIRIE, Dallas County

Grand Prairie (pop. 99,616), established as a post–Civil War railroad village, is now a metroplex suburb. Located mostly in Dallas County, about halfway between Dallas and Fort Worth, it extends southward into Ellis County.

Cross Timbers. Marker, 2602 Mayfield. The one-million-acre area of sandy timberland that separates the topographical regions of Blackland Prairie and Grand Prairie was in centuries past an Indian camping ground. The nearby plains supported large herds of buffalo and horses, natural resources were plentiful, and the climate mild. During the 1700s, Caddoan and Wichita Indians roamed the area to the west, frequently encountering Southern Plains tribes such as the Kiowa and Comanche who wintered here. The French at that time attempted to establish trade networks with the Indians, while the Spaniards were interested chiefly in counteracting the influence of the French in Spanish territory. Neither established any major, permanent settlements in the area. The Indians ultimately were forced out of the state by Anglo-American settlers. *SM 1979.*

Cinco de Mayo. Weekend closest to May 5, at Traders Village, 2602 Mayfield. Cinco de Mayo has been celebrated here since the mid-1970s. This event features musical entertainment from Mexico, a queen's pageant, and many booths with Mexican foods, arts, and crafts. Over 70,000 people attend annually.

National Championship Indian Pow-Wow. Second weekend in September, at Traders Village, 2602 Mayfield. This event began in the early 1960s when local Boy Scout troops invited members of the metroplex's American Indian population to collaborate on a cultural event. Now one of the largest pow-wows in the country, Indians from all over the United States attend the event. The largest tribal delegations represented are Cherokee, Kickapoo, Kiowa, and Comanche. Featured events are dance and drumming competitions, and Indian crafts and foods are sold at many booths.

HENDERSON, Rusk County

Henderson (pop. 12,151), designated the county seat of Rusk County in 1843, is a commercial center in an oil and agricultural area. According to local legend, nearby Hendricks Lake was the site of a battle between Mexican soldiers and French pirates during the early 19th century. Apparently in 1816 the Spanish ship *Santa Rosa,* carrying $2 million worth of bar silver, was seized by Jean Laffite's men off Galveston Island. The pirates attempted to transport the silver to St. Louis by wagon but were intercepted by Spanish authorities near Hendricks and Black lakes. The story says that the pirates' leader ordered that the wagons be cut loose from the mules and rolled into the lake. As with most treasures, it has never been recovered— but it makes a wonderful story.

Depot Museum Complex. 514 N. High St. The museum is located in the waiting room and office of a restored 1901 Missouri Pacific Railroad depot. A permanent exhibit is devoted to Jean Laffite and his stolen Spanish treasure. Open Mon.–Fri. 9–5; Sat. 8–1.

IRVING, Dallas County

Irving (pop. 137,660), established at the turn of the century as a railroad town, is now a metroplex suburb. It is located roughly halfway between Dallas and Fort Worth (north of Grand Prairie) in Dallas County.

The Mustangs of Las Colinas Sculpture, by Robert Glen. 5215 N. O'Connor Rd. in Williams Square. This bronze is the largest equestrian sculpture in the world. The design, which features nine wild mustangs running through water, symbolizes freedom. Mustangs, the descendents of horses introduced into North America by the Spaniards, were running free on the Great Plains by the early 1700s. An exhibit located in the Williams Square Plaza tells about the making of the sculpture. Open Mon.–Sat. 10–6; Sun. 2–6.

JEFFERSON, Marion County

Jefferson (pop. 2,199) was a major 19th-century river port for steamboats on the Big Cypress. The city, which is the county seat of Marion County, is famous for its historic homes, associated primarily with the city's 19th-century Anglo-American population.

Jefferson Historical Museum. Located in the old federal courthouse. Collections on permanent display include Mexican documents and some Mexican-American materials (such as kitchenwares), barbed wire and branding irons, and the Hobart Key Collection of Caddoan stone and ceramic artifacts. Open daily 9:30–5.

Caddo Lake. 13 mi. SE of Jefferson off SH 43. Caddo Lake covers 25,400 acres in Louisiana and Texas. The Caddo Indians believe that the lake was formed at night by earthshaking spirits that were angered by a Caddo chief. The legend may be partly true, as some believe that the lake was formed during the great New Madrid (Mo.) earthquake of 1811.

LONGVIEW, Gregg County

Longview (pop. 70,311). Explorer Pedro Vial reported the presence of a Bidai Indian settlement in this area in 1788, and in 1809 the presence of a Nadaco village between the Sabine River and Cherokee Bayou was reported. Cherokees, displaced from the southeastern United States, were present (in southwestern Gregg County) during the Mexican period. After 1827 much of the area's land was distributed in Mexican land grants, but no permanent settlements developed. Planters from the Old South began to settle here after 1850, and Longview, the county seat of Gregg County, was named in 1870.

Caddo Lake was named for the Caddo Indians, who were forced from Texas in 1835. Courtesy of Texas Memorial Museum (accession no. pc-e204).

Cherokee Trace. Marker, 7.3 mi. W of Longview on US 80. During the 1820s, Cherokee Indians blazed this trail that ran from near Nacogdoches to their home reservation in White River, Arkansas. According to legend, they marked the trail by slashing marks in trees and planting "Cherokee" roses along the way. The trail was later used by Sam Houston on his way to Texas, by Davy Crockett and other soldiers joining the Texas Revolution, and by early settlers moving into the region. The Cherokees also followed this trail when they were expelled from Texas in 1839. *SM 1967.*

Old Fredonia Townsite. Marker, 4.9 mi. W of Longview at intersection of FM 2087 and IH 20. Old Fredonia was the town founded by former empresario Haden Edwards in 1843 after his return to Texas. He had been expelled in 1827 by Mexican officials and Mexican and Anglo-American colonists for his organization of the Fredonian Rebellion of 1826–27. Early advertisements for the town mentioned that it had recently been occupied by the "Northern Indians" and had been in "forty years constant cultivation in corn." The town was abandoned about 1870 when the railroad passed it by. *SM 1967.*

MARSHALL, Harrison County

Marshall (pop. 23,682), located in Caddoan Indian country, was founded in 1842 and was settled primarily by planters from the southern United States. The city is noted historically for its importance as a Confederate center for the Trans-Mississippi West during the Civil War. Today Marshall is a petrochemical, lumber-processing, manufacturing, and tourism center and the county seat of Harrison County.

Marshall Hotel. Lafayette and Houston Sts. Built in 1929, this eight-story brick building with decorative stonework and blue tile banding is the second oldest hotel in Marshall. It is distinguished by an elaborate penthouse expressed on the exterior with stone balconies, arched windows, a Mediterranean influenced parapet, and a green, Spanish tile roof.

Old Courthouse Museum. On the Square. The library's archival resources include early maps and original Spanish land grants from the area. Among the numerous exhibits is a collection of Indian arrow points, tools, beads, moccasins, and pottery. Open Tues.–Sat. 9–5; Sun. 1:30–5.

St. Joseph Catholic Church. Alamo and Grand Sts. This red brick church combines an Alamoesque parapet with twin towers reminiscent of Mission San José.

Texas & Pacific Railroad Depot. 800 N. Washington, in the Ginocchio Historic District. The two-story, red brick depot with white trim was built in 1908. Spanish Mission Revival in style, the depot has a low pitched tile roof with overhanging eaves and curvilinear gables on three sides. *RTHL 1979; NR 1974.*

MINERAL WELLS, Palo Pinto County

Mineral Wells (pop. 14,870) is located in a rough, hilly area of Palo

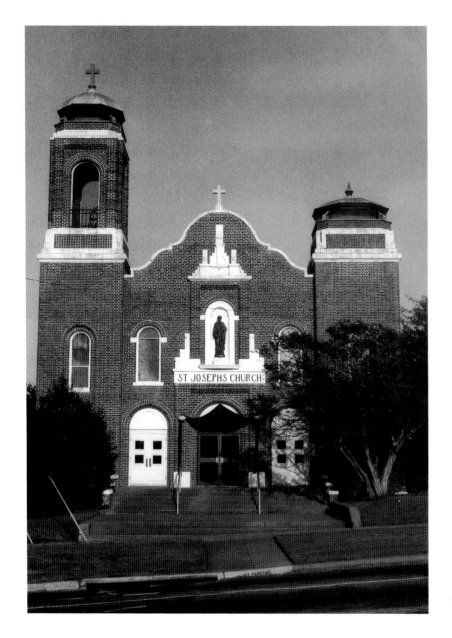

St. Joseph Catholic Church,
Marshall. Photo by Cathryn Hoyt,
THC.

Pinto County that remained an Indian stronghold even after many of the
early communities in the county were organized. In the early 20th century
the town was known worldwide for its mineral water and became a famous
health spa. Among the city's attractions are its beautiful Spanish Revival
buildings and its annual chili cook-off, usually held in February. Mineral
Wells is now the largest town in Palo Pinto County.

Baker Hotel. 200 E. Hubbard St. This eleven-story, reinforced-
concrete structure, built in the late 1920s and renovated in 1949, exhibits
Spanish Revival features, including cast-stone details and a three-story
cupola-tower. *NR 1982.*

Corner detail of the Baker Hotel, Mineral Wells. Photo by Cathryn Hoyt, THC.

Our Lady of Lourdes Catholic Church. N.W. 3d Ave. at N.W. 1st St. This charming church is an interpretation of Mission Espada in San Antonio, but the use of rough stone reflects the influence of the Our Lady of Lourdes Grotto in France.

Palo Pinto Community Service Building. N.W. 4th St. and N.W. 2d Ave. This is an excellent example of Spanish Revival style municipal buildings from the 1930s. The Community Service building is notable for the sophisticated detail in the cast-stone decoration around the three top floors and the quality of the metalwork and woodwork.

Our Lady of Lourdes Catholic Church, Mineral Wells. Photo by Cathryn Hoyt, THC.

PARIS, Lamar County

Paris (pop. 24,699), founded in 1839, grew in importance after it became a railroad center in the late 19th century. It is now a manufacturing, medical, and educational center and the county seat of Lamar County.

Paris Public Library. 326 S. Main St. The library houses a collection of original pen-and-ink drawings by renowned Texas artist José Cisneros.

Trammel's Trace. Marker, on SH 121, E side of Hughes Springs. This pioneer trail was named for Nicholas Trammel, who traded horses

Untitled drawing by José Cisneros, Paris Public Library, Paris. Courtesy of the Paris Public Library.

along the route in the early 19th century. Trammel's Trace originated in St. Louis and linked the "Southwest Trail" with El Camino Real to Mexico. The route crossed the North Sulphur River at Epperson's Ferry, continuing south and west in an arc that passed through Chalybeate Springs (Hughes Springs). *PM*.

QUANAH AND VICINITY, Hardeman County

Quanah (pop. 3,413) is named for the last chief of the Comanches, Quanah Parker, who led the Plains Indian tribe in pursuit of buffalo and in defense of their plains stronghold. Medicine Mounds, believed to have been an important ceremonial site for Quanah Parker and the Comanches, can be seen east of Quanah, south of US 287. The town is the county seat of Hardeman County.

Copper Breaks State Park. About 15 mi. S of Quanah on SH 6. The park is located on lands once occupied by the Comanche Indians, who moved into North Texas around 1700. The park's interpretive center offers an opportunity to learn not only about the Comanches, but about the prehistoric Clovis, Folsom, and Plainview peoples who hunted here thousands of years before. At the park, visitors will likely see also a more recent historical reminder—part of the official Texas Longhorn herd.

Quanah, Acme & Pacific Railroad Depot. 100 Mercer St. This Spanish Revival style depot, built in 1909, features cupolas, an interior central rotunda, red tile roof, and arched entryways. The Quanah, Acme & Pacific Railroad was originally built to serve the gypsum deposits and plaster manufacturer at Acme, and gypsum hauled from Acme by railroad was used for the plaster-detailed buildings at the 1893 Chicago World's Fair, which stimulated interest in Spanish Mission Revival architecture. Quanah Parker visited the town of Quanah many times and called the train, "My engine, my railroad." Thus, the railroad was nicknamed the Quanah Route and the cars and depot bear the emblem of an Indian inserted in the Q of the name Quanah. *NR 1979*.

SPANISH FORT, Montague County

Spanish Fort is little more than a ghost town today. In 1982 fifty residents still lived in the town, which then sported a combination pool hall, general store, and single-pump gas station. Yet, its historical significance continues to captivate many. Five thousand Taovaya Indians lived here in what was the largest Indian village in Texas during the historic period. The Taovaya at Spanish Fort, using French weapons, gave Spain its first defeat in Texas in 1759.

Taovaya Victory over Spain. Marker, in Spanish Fort on FM 103, across from the General Store. Site of the Taovaya Indian village and the 1759 Indian victory over Spanish forces. *CM 1936; SM 1976*.

STAMFORD, Jones County

Stamford (pop. 3,817), founded at the turn of the century, is best known as the site of the Texas Cowboy Reunion, a celebration of cowboy culture held here every July 4th weekend since 1930.

Bryant-Link Building. 120 S. Swenson. This flat-roofed, Spanish Revival structure was built in 1928; the concrete façade was made in San Antonio.

West Texas Utility Company. 127 E. McHarg St. This one-story, Spanish Revival structure was built in 1928 and features a flat roof, gabled tile parapets, and decorative cast-stone panels. *NR 1986*.

TEXARKANA, Bowie County

Texarkana (Texas pop. 31,656) straddles the Texas-Arkansas state line in the northeast corner of the state. A Caddo Indian village originally occupied the site of Texarkana, and many mound sites are located in the area. Texarkana has historically been a gateway to the Southwest, first via historic trails and later by railroad. Although not the county seat, Texarkana is the largest town in Bowie County.

Texas Travel Information Center. On IH 30, from Arkansas. This is one of 12 centers at key highway entrances to Texas; open daily except major holidays.

Ace of Clubs House. 420 Pine St. The Ace of Clubs House was formerly owned by Olivia Smith Moore, a local high-school Spanish teacher, and her husband. The house's glassed-in porch was restored to represent 1940s decor, and in it are exhibited items collected in Mexico by the Moores over a forty-year period. Displays include copper, silver, and brass household items, some of which are inlaid with turquoise and abalone, and Spanish textbooks. Hand-painted terra-cotta religious figures are displayed at Christmastime. Open Wed.–Fri. 10–3; Sat.–Sun. 1–3.

Texarkana Historical Society Museum. 219 State Line Ave. Permanent exhibits include Caddoan pottery and stone tools. Open Tues.–Fri. 10–4; Sat.–Sun. 12–3.

Trammels Trace. Marker, 4.5 mi. N of Texarkana on US 59/71. Trammel's Trace, in use by 1813, entered Texas at this point. From here the road connected with Nacogdoches, linking the "Southwest Trail" with El Camino Real. *SM 1965.*

WACO, McLennan County

Waco (pop. 103,590), near the confluence of the Bosque and Brazos rivers, is located in an area occupied historically by the Waco Indians and, in the 1830s, the Cherokees. The land was included in a grant made by the Mexican government to Thomas J. Chambers in 1832. The townsite was laid out in 1849, and the newly incorporated city became the county seat in 1850. Waco enjoys a diversified economy based on manufacturing, agribusiness, education, and tourism.

Baylor University Library, Texas Collection. Baylor University campus. The Texas Collection, through the Institute for Oral History, includes oral histories concerning the history of Mexican-American Baptists in Texas and the development of the Raza Unida political movement in South Texas.

Hippodrome (Waco Theater). 724 Austin Ave. The 1929 renovation of the original façade incorporated Spanish Revival elements in this 1913 structure. *RTHL 1981; NR 1983.*

Latin American United Methodist Church. 15th St. and Webster. This charming white stucco church with a single bell tower is an interesting combination of the architectural styles of both Mission Espada and Mission Socorro.

St. Francis Church. 301 Jefferson. The first Sunday School classes for Waco's Mexican-American community were held in the basement of Assumption Church in 1921. Until their own church was built, a priest from Austin commuted to Waco once a month to give mass to this group. Benefactor Fannie G. Smith donated the historic home of Dr. W.R Clifton for the establishment of a mission church and the building was completed in

St. Francis Church interior, Waco. Photo by Cliff Shelley, courtesy of the Franciscans.

1925. That frame structure was destroyed by fire in 1927. The present St. Francis Church, built in 1931, is patterned after Mission San José in San Antonio, complete with Rose Window, and was dedicated to the memory of the Franciscan missionaries who served in Texas. The architect, Roy E. Lane, made several trips to San Antonio to study San José and to adapt the model to the Waco site. The interior was designed in an adaptation of Spanish Renaissance style. In the 1950s St. Francis Church was instrumental in the establishment of Sacred Heart Catholic Church to serve the

Spanish-speaking residents of South Waco, reflecting the growth of the Mexican-American community in the city. *See also* Fiesta de la Raza.

Strecker Museum. Baylor University Campus. An interpretive exhibit traces the entrance of American Indian groups into Central Texas and the development of their cultures from prehistoric times to the pioneer settlement period. Open Mon.–Fri. 9–4; Sat. 10–1; Sun. 2–5.

U.S. Post Office. Franklin and 8th Sts. This buff-brick post office features Spanish Mission Revival influences in its red tile roof, canales, intricate cast-stone decorative motifs around windows and doors, and Alamo-esque façade.

Veterans Administration Medical Center. Memorial Blvd. and New Rd. In the early 20th century, Veterans Administration architects in Washington, D.C., put together a set of standardized designs and plans for veterans facilities throughout the United States. Although the plans were the same, the exteriors of the buildings reflected regional traditions. Spanish Revival was selected as appropriate to the southwestern states and is seen in the Veterans Administration Medical Center in Waco. The complex was constructed in three major building campaigns between 1931 and 1945.

Veterans Administration Medical Center, Waco. Photo by Cathryn Hoyt, THC.

434

Fiesta de la Raza. In October (date varies), at St. Francis Church. For over 50 years, the church has sponsored this fiesta to honor Columbus' arrival in the New World. In addition to religious observances, the celebration features a Grand Jamaica, or carnival, with traditional music, dance, and foods, the coronation of a queen, and games for all ages. *See also* St. Francis Church.

WICHITA FALLS, Wichita County

Wichita Falls (pop. 96,259) is located in an area inhabited by Wichita and Taovaya Indians in the early 18th century, and later by Comanches and Kiowas. The first recorded Europeans in the area were Pedro Vial and José Mares, who were seeking to establish a route from Santa Fe to San Antonio in the 1780s. An attempt at Anglo-American settlement was made in the mid-19th century, but population remained sparse until 1882, when Wichita County was organized and the railroad arrived. Wichita Falls became the county seat of Wichita County in 1883.

Texas Travel Information Center. In the northern part of the city on IH 44. This is one of 12 centers located at key highway entrances to Texas; open daily except for major holidays.

Cinco de Mayo. In early May (date varies), sponsored by Our Lady of Guadalupe Church (606 Homes). The Jamaica held to celebrate Cinco de Mayo features the coronation of a queen, traditional music and foods, and ballet folklórico performances. This is primarily a parish and Hispanic community observance.

Diez y Seis de Septiembre. Mid-September, sponsored by Our Lady of Guadalupe Church (606 Homes). Observed in the same manner as the Cinco de Mayo Jamaica.

Wichita Falls Museum and Art Center's Spring Fling. Last full weekend in April, at the museum, 2 Eureka Circle. International in flavor, the Spring Fling art show features hand-crafted, one-of-a-kind items, as well as international entertainment and food booths. The ethnic components of the event vary from year to year, but Mexican food is always included among the international food offerings. Spring Fling is attended by about 20,000 people.

WINTERS, Runnels County

Winters (pop. 2,905) was established in 1880 and is primarily a farming center.

Z.I. Hale Museum. 242 W. Dale. Permanent collections include Spanish Colonial and Mexican coins and military items. The Mexican materials, which also include Christmas items, date from the 19th through 20th centuries. Open Mon.–Thurs. 12–5; Fri. 2–4.

REGION 7

Lubbock and the Plains

The Plains region encompasses the Panhandle and all of western Texas except for the region west of the Pecos River. Here the wide open spaces for which the American West was famous still exist, and large urban centers are few and far between. The Panhandle, the northernmost region of the state, is the southernmost extension of mid-America's Great Plains, known regionally as the High Plains or the Llano Estacado. The vast expanses of prairie are interrupted in an east-west swath by the breaks of the Canadian River and in the southeastern part of the region by the rough country of the Cap Rock. The contrast between the plains' level expanse and the Canadian Breaks, and the even more abrupt contrast of the chiseled canyons in the Cap Rock country, often are a surprise to the first-time visitor, just as they must have been to the first explorers. Below the Cap Rock lie the Rolling Plains, noted for their abundance of wildlife and once the home of vast herds of buffalo.

Long before the fabled adventures of the Coronado expedition, the Panhandle was home to settled farmers and nomadic groups of buffalo hunters. The Antelope Creek culture was one of the three major prehistoric groups in Texas that cultivated corn and settled in permanent villages. Their villages were abandoned before the first Spanish explorers arrived. At the time of the earliest Spanish exploration, both the Llano Estacado and the Lower Plains are believed to have been occupied by nomadic tribes of buffalo hunters, probably ancestors of modern groups such as the Apaches and the Wichita. The history of the intervening centuries until the 1800s is largely one of Plains Indian dominance, made possible by horses and weapons first introduced by the Spanish. The Apaches, last of the indigenous people of the Texas Plains, ultimately were pushed farther south by the Comanches. The Comanches appeared in the region in the early 1700s and ruled the plains here and in eastern New Mexico for almost two centuries. The American Indian heritage of the plains is reflected primarily in museum collections, including those of the Panhandle-Plains Museum in Canyon, one of the finest museums in the state.

In the southern portion of this region, Hispanic heritage dates from at least the early 17th century, when a mission was briefly established for the Jumano Indians. Despite this early presence and later exploration of the Concho and Pecos rivers, no permanent settlements were established,

Opposite: Hutchinson County Library, Borger. Photo by Cathryn Hoyt, THC.

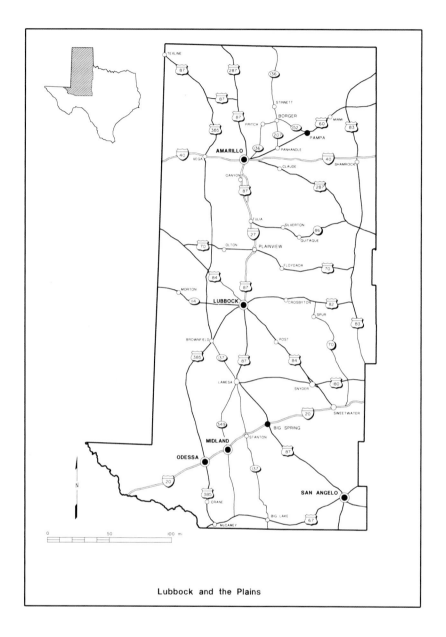

Lubbock and the Plains

Guidebook Region 7. Map by Greg Miller.

in part because the Plains Indians ruled the region. When Plains Indian dominance of the region had ended, the first settlers were Hispanic shepherds—*pastores*—from New Mexico. The period of settlement by the pastores was too brief to leave an abundant material legacy, but these sheepherders and their predecessors, the *ciboleros* and *comancheros,* are an important part of the region's history. The ruins that remain are largely inaccessible, and this era, too, is represented primarily by exhibits in the major museums of the region.

Late in the 19th century came the Anglo-American buffalo hunters, soldiers, and ranchers, and agricultural settlements soon followed. The

coming of the railroad in the 1880s, the development of large-scale farming and ranching, and the discovery of oil have contributed to the growth of the economy and population of the area's cities and towns. The plains, part of Texas' last frontier, have now been tamed to the hand of the farmer, the rancher, and the oilman. In only a few areas can one see the former, trackless majesty of native grasslands and rugged canyons relatively undisturbed. Yet areas of historic importance and majestic beauty remain, drawing an increasing number of visitors to major tourist attractions such as Alibates Flint Quarries National Monument and Palo Duro Canyon.

Hispanic communities in many areas of the region date from the arrival of the railroads, but in most areas contemporary population increases are largely related to agribusiness. Although designated historic sites of the twentieth century are rare for all ethnic groups, including Hispanics, the culture of the region nevertheless reflects their presence. Churches such as San José in Lubbock and Our Lady of Guadalupe in Amarillo are focal points of the social and cultural life of Hispanic communities, and well-established festivals celebrate Diez y Seis de Septiembre, Cinco de Mayo, and other special occasions. And here, as elsewhere in the state, fine examples of Spanish and Pueblo Revival architecture reflect both the reality and the myth of the Spanish and American Indian legacy in Texas.

Indian encampments such as this were once common on the Great Plains. Courtesy Barker Texas History Center, General Libraries, University of Texas at Austin.

439

LUBBOCK, Lubbock County

Lubbock (pop. 186,206). The Lubbock area was settled in the 1880s with two communities called Lubbock and Monterey. In late 1890 a new town site was chosen and named Lubbock. The town soon became a ranching center, and its economic base expanded with the arrival of the first train in 1909 and the development of regional agriculture. Lubbock is the county seat of Lubbock County and a major commercial and wholesale center for West Texas. The residential and commercial architecture of Lubbock has been heavily influenced by the Spanish Revival style of the Texas Tech University buildings, and many fine Spanish Revival buildings can be seen around the city.

Information

Lubbock Convention and Visitors Bureau. 14th and Ave. K. Offers information on tours, local attractions, dining, hotels, and entertainment in the Lubbock area. Mailing address: P.O. Box 561, Lubbock 79401.

Spanish Revival Architecture

Baker Building. 1211 13th St. This two-story, Spanish Revival style building is one of the few 1920s commercial buildings remaining in Lubbock.

Fort Worth and Denver South Plains Railway Depot. 1801 Ave. G. Built in 1928, this Spanish Revival style depot provided the city with a second rail connection and an expanded trade area. The depot was designed by Fort Worth architect Wyatt C. Hedrick, who was responsible for the design of Texas Tech buildings from the 1930s to the 1950s. The depot was restored in the 1970s and now houses a restaurant.

Holden Home (Casa Grande). 3109 20th St. Casa Grande is the oldest of three Pueblo-style houses built by Dr. and Mrs. W.C. Holden during the 1930s. Each was built with adobe bricks made on the site. Dr. Holden, a noted anthropologist and historian who worked in Texas, New Mexico, and Mexico, conducted pioneering expeditions to study the Yaqui Indians of Sonora, Mexico (during 1934–50). He was instrumental in the establishment of the Museum at Texas Tech and the Ranching Heritage Center in Lubbock.

St. Elizabeth's Catholic Church. 2305 Main St. Built in 1935, this Spanish Revival style church was designed by local architect O.R. Walker and is architecturally compatible with the Texas Tech buildings to the west. The church now serves the university parish.

Texas Tech University. The central campus, built in the 1920s, features beautiful examples of Spanish Revival architecture. William Ward Watkin, designer of the original buildings, chose the Spanish Revival style to reflect the early architectural history of the state as embodied in the Spanish missions. The geographic location of the university also played a

Home Economics Building, Texas Tech University, Lubbock. Photo by Cathryn Hoyt, THC.

role in his selection of architectural style, since the broad, flat plains of the Llano Estacado reminded him of the plains of central Spain. Brick and fine gray stone from Leuters, Jones County, were the dominant building materials, with red ceramic roof tiles adding color and a finishing touch to the Spanish theme. Five major buildings that formed the original core of the university are described below. Several later buildings on the campus (1930s–50s) were designed by Fort Worth architect Wyatt C. Hedrick. For other, nonarchitectural resources of the university, see the Texas Tech entry under Churches, Museums, and Archives below. *NR 1993.*

Administration Building. Completed in 1925, the Administration Building is reminiscent of mid-16th-century Spanish city halls, with its salle-porte leading to an interior courtyard and the monumental stairways and vaulted ceilings of the interior. The northern exposure of the Administration Building was modeled on the 1534 University of Alcalá de Henares in Spain.

Chemistry Building. The design of the Chemistry Building was influenced by the Palacio Monterey of Salamanca, Spain, and features a long arcade embellished with carved stone columns attached to the piers. The building is heavily decorated with carved stone alchemical symbols and inscriptions.

Home Economics Building. Originally, the Home Economics Building was a modest structure with little ornamentation. Later expansion, which maintained the Spanish Revival style, has resulted in a beautiful complex with carved stone decoration and a simple Alamo façade.

Textile Engineering Building. The design of the Textile Engineering Building was based on the mission buildings of the American

Southwest. Beautiful, carved stone detailing, some resembling the detailed carving of Mission San José in San Antonio, surrounds the entrance portal in the center of the building. An interesting adaptation of the mission theme is seen on the second level where carved stone cotton bales occupy the statuary niches.

West Engineering Building. The West Engineering Building features examples of pierced stone carving, another very traditional Spanish design element. The cupids and finials located above the entrance were modeled after the Archives Building in Salamanca, Spain.

Churches, Museums, and Archives

Lubbock Lake Landmark State Historical Park. Near the intersection of Loop 289 and US 84 (Clovis Rd.). Lubbock Lake Landmark currently is the only known site in North America that contains archeological evidence related to all of the major American Indian cultures that existed on the Southern Plains over the past 12,000 years. The park includes an interpretive center that houses museum exhibits, three interpretive trails, and picnicking facilities. *SM 1970; NR 1971; NHL 1977.*

San José Catholic Church. 102 N. Ave. P. There are several Hispanic-community Catholic churches in Lubbock, including San José and Our Lady of Guadalupe. The oldest is San José, in the old Guadalupe area. The parish was established in 1924 and the present, contemporary church building was completed in 1962. The feast day of Our Lady of Guadalupe is an important devotional celebration, usually observed on the Sunday preceding December 12. San José's Jamaica is celebrated annually, on the last Sunday in June, in nearby Guadalupe Park. The family-oriented event features arts and crafts, games, and traditional foods.

Texas Tech University. Texas Tech is one of the state's four major comprehensive universities. The following university divisions include materials relevant to several aspects of Hispanic heritage in the state.

Institute for Hispanic Studies. In 1978 the Department of Classical and Romance Languages of the university established the Institute for Hispanic Studies for the study and promotion of the works of important Spanish-American writers of the late 19th and 20th centuries. The institute's holdings are especially strong in the period of Modernism and in Mexican and Chilean materials.

Library. The library's archival Southwest Collection holds more than 16.5 million manuscript leaves as well as books, photographs, maps, and other materials relating to the history of the American Southwest.

Museum of Texas Tech University. Fourth and Indiana Ave. The museum has permanent exhibits featuring Spanish, Mexican, Mexican-American, and American Indian artifacts. Of special interest are the Pre-Columbian and Taos-Southwest galleries.

Ranching Heritage Center. Fourth and Indiana Ave. More than 30 historic ranching structures have been relocated to the center as au-

Mexican devil masks in the collections of the Museum of Texas Tech University, Lubbock. Photo by Julie Kinzelman, courtesy of Texas Tech University News and Publications.

Picket and Sotol House, Ranching Heritage Center of the Museum of Texas Tech University, Lubbock. Photo by Cathryn Hoyt, THC.

thentic demonstrations of how life really was on the western frontier. The Picket and Sotol House was built in 1904 on a ranch southwest of Ozona for Mr. and Mrs. D.B. Kilpatrick. The walls of the house are formed of cedar pickets and sotol stalks, and the roof is thatched with Sacahuiste grass. The structure demonstrates the ability of ranchers to adapt to their environment and shows how ranchers in the Ozona area used indigenous construction methods and materials originally employed by Mexican residents of the region. Also in the center is the Matador Half Dugout (built about 1891), an example of a shelter type used by many early settlers on the plains, including the pastores of

New Mexico. Exhibits in the interpretive center further tell the story of ranching, including the role of vaqueros. Recent special exhibits have depicted the history and development of saddles, spurs, wagons, and branding irons. Open Mon.–Sat. 10–5; Sun. 1–5.

Festivals

Cinco de Mayo. On or near May 5; locations vary. Local Spanish radio and television stations join with Hispanic organizations in sponsoring Cinco de Mayo observances each year at one or more locations. The celebrations include traditional music and dance.

Fiesta del Llano. Mid-September, at Lubbock Memorial Civic Center. Fiesta del Llano is the major annual Hispanic community celebration in Lubbock. The three-day celebration honors Mexico's independence (Diez y Seis de Septiembre) and features ethnic foods, entertainment, and evening dancing to the sounds of popular Hispanic bands. For information contact the Lubbock Convention and Visitors Bureau.

AMARILLO, Potter and Randall Counties

Amarillo (pop. 157,615) was named for Arroyo Amarillo. The Spanish name Amarillo was given to a nearby arroyo, or creek, by early Hispanic sheepherders and traders (the pastores and comancheros) because of the yellow color of the soil along the creek banks. The nucleus of the original community was a railroad construction camp located at a place known as Ragtown, which consisted of a collection of tents and buffalo-hide huts. The town moved to a new site one mile to the southeast, which was renamed Amarillo when it became the county seat of Potter County in 1893. Farming and ranching are the historic economic bases of the area, joined in the modern era by gas and oil, and the city is the commercial center of the Texas Panhandle.

Information Centers

Amarillo Convention and Visitors Bureau. 1000 Polk St., P.O. Drawer 9480, Amarillo 79105. Maps and other tourist information can be picked up at the visitors bureau.

Amarillo Hispanic Chamber of Commerce. 714 S. Tyler, Amarillo 79101. The chamber can provide information on local Hispanic community festivals and events.

Texas Travel Information Center. IH 40/US 287 just east of Amarillo. This is one of 12 centers that are located at key highway entrances to Texas; open daily except for major holidays.

Painted tile *retablo* depicting the Virgin of Guadalupe, Our Lady of Guadalupe Catholic Church, Amarillo. Photo by Cathryn Hoyt, THC.

Historic Sites and Museums

Amarillo Art Center. 2200 S. Van Buren. Housed in a three-building complex, the center focuses on twentieth-century art and has occasional exhibits featuring Mexican and Mexican-American art. Open Sat.–Sun. 1–5; Tues.–Fri. 10–5; Thurs. 10–9:30.

Atchison, Topeka, and Santa Fe Railway Company Depot. 307 Grant. This large two-story structure, built in 1909–10, features Spanish Revival stylistic elements, including load-bearing masonry walls with

445

Potter County Courthouse, Amarillo. Photo by Cathryn Hoyt, THC.

stucco veneer and a gabled, red tiled roof. Spanish influence is particularly evident in the detailing, such as the hood moldings and the trefoil.

Our Lady of Guadalupe Church. 1210 E. 11th St. at S. Houston. When a new church was built and dedicated as Sacred Heart Cathedral in 1918, the building of Amarillo's first Catholic church was moved to 11th and Arthur and renamed Our Lady of Guadalupe. The church, serving the Spanish-speaking Catholics of Amarillo, was moved again, to 11th and Houston, in 1927. In 1948 the parish bought a small factory for $65, and the members of the parish produced 6,000 cement blocks for construction of a new church. The first mass was held in the Spanish Mission Revival style church on December 12, 1949, the feast day of Our Lady of Guadalupe. The church's statue of Our Lady, retained from the old church, was originally purchased in 1916 with funds donated primarily by Spanish-speaking railroad workers. The Spanish Mission style architecture, with its twin bell towers, is particularly appropriate to the church's role as the major Hispanic community church in Amarillo. Its parishioners are active in educational, cultural, religious, and civic affairs. *See also* Las Fiestas de Amarillo.

Potter County Courthouse. 511 Taylor. Built in 1931, this well-preserved courthouse is one of several buildings in the state that have been described by Carla Breeze in her book *Pueblo Deco* as outstanding examples of Pueblo Deco architecture, a Southwestern Art Deco style inspired by regional Hispanic and Indian influences. The courthouse features relief decorations, such as the heroic figures of a frontiersman and an American Indian and a frieze of prickly pear cactus pads, that evoke Amarillo's western heritage.

Festivals and Events

Diez y Seis de Septiembre. Mid-September, at El Alamo Park, 1300 block of E. 16th Ave. at S. Houston. This Hispanic community festival features traditional foods and music, ballet folklórico, games, and entertainment. The Amarillo Hispanic Chamber of Commerce is one of the sponsors of the event.

Kwahadi Indian Winter Show. Weekend following Christmas, at the Kiva, Plains Blvd. and Bellaire St. In their winter show, the nationally known performers of Kwahadi Boy Scouts Explorer Post 80 feature Plaza dances of the Pueblo Indians of New Mexico. In the fall, the troupe also performs Indian ceremonials and dances in Palo Duro Canyon. The performance group takes its name from the Kwahadi, or Quahada, a Comanche group that once inhabited the Llano Estacado.

Las Fiestas de Amarillo. In July, at various locations. Las Fiestas de Amarillo was initiated in 1981 by Our Lady of Guadalupe Booster Club. The club combined with a local civic group, Los Barrios al Este de Amarillo, to form Mexican-Americans in Action. The first fiesta was intended as a reunion for everyone who had ever attended Dwight Morrow and Our Lady of Guadalupe schools. Since that first successful event, the celebration has grown to include a parade, coronation of a queen, mariachis and other musical entertainment, children's programs, ballet folklórico and traditional costumes. A wide variety of traditional foods are offered, including tacos, fajitas, tostadas, gorditas, beans and rice—and even hamburgers. For additional information, contact Our Lady of Guadalupe Church, 1210 E. 11th St., Amarillo 79102.

447

BIG LAKE, Reagan County

Big Lake (3,672) received its name from an important water source between the Concho River—the scene of early Spanish exploration in this region—and the springs at Fort Stockton. The town of Big Lake was established in 1912 when the Santa Fe Railroad was constructed. Big Lake is now the county seat of Reagan County and a center for oil activities and ranching trade.

Martín-Castillo Expedition. Marker, Downtown Park (US 67 at corner of Main and 2d Sts.). The Martín-Castillo expedition departed from Santa Fe in 1650, explored the Concho River, and traveled eastward to the edge of the Tejas nation. This expedition sparked interest in further exploration of East Texas. *SM 1970.*

BIG SPRING, Howard County

Big Spring (pop. 23,093) is named for a spring south of town that was an important water source from prehistoric to recent times. Located on the Comanche War Trail, the town was a typical, rough frontier town by the time the railroad came here in the 1880s. Big Spring is the county seat and major town of Howard County.

Heritage Museum of Big Spring. 510 Scurry. Focusing on local and pioneer history, the museum features a collection of artifacts attributed to the Comanche Indians and exhibits related to early exploration and ranching in the area. Open Tues.–Sat. 9–5.

Municipal Building. 400 E. Third St. Built in 1932 and designed by architects Peters, Strange, and Bradshaw, the Big Spring Municipal Building combines city offices and an auditorium. Featuring classic twin bell towers, it is one of the finest examples of Spanish Mission Revival architecture in the area. *PM.*

Diez y Seis de Septiembre. Mid-September. The event features traditional foods, games, arts and crafts, music (including mariachis), dancers and a queen contest. For further information contact Big Spring Chamber of Commerce, P.O. Box 1391, Big Spring 79721-1391.

Scenic Drive. FM 669 N to Post reaches the edge of the Llano Estacado and ascends through vistas of steep cliffs and colorful canyons.

BORGER, Hutchinson County

Borger (pop. 15,675) developed as an oil boomtown in the 1920s. It is the largest town in Hutchinson County, although Stinnett is the county seat. Both Alibates Flint Quarries National Monument and Lake Meredith are accessible from Borger.

Hutchinson County Library. 625 Weatherly at Sixth St. The library, built in 1936 by the WPA, is a Pueblo Revival adobe building. It is one of the few remaining adobes in the region.

Hutchinson County Museum. 608 N. Main St. at Sixth St. Exhibits

focus on area history from Coronado to the present and include an exact-scale replica of Adobe Walls. The museum also displays a WPA Post Office Mural, entitled *Big City News*, by artist José Acevez. Open Mon.–Fri. 11–5; Sat. 11–4:30; Sun. 2–5. *See also* Stinnett Vicinity: Adobe Walls.

Big Spring Municipal Building, Big Spring. Photo by Cathryn Hoyt, THC.

CANYON AND VICINITY, Randall County

Canyon (pop. 11,365), founded in 1889 as a ranch-country town, is the county seat of Randall County, an educational and recreational center, and one of the most charming small cities in the Panhandle. West Texas State University is located here, and the Panhandle-Plains Museum is one of the finest museums in the state. Historic Palo Duro Canyon is accessible from Canyon.

Borquez Adobe House. Sixth St. and Second Ave. Built by Luis and Lena Borquez in 1925, this is one of the few remaining adobe structures in the area. The house originally had a flat roof; the pitched, shingled roof is a later addition. Luis Borquez was a sheepherder who came to the area from New Mexico in 1918. He later worked as a ranch hand and for the railroad, and he and his wife reared their family of three girls in this house.

Palo Duro Canyon State Park, near Canyon. Photo by Cathryn Hoyt, THC.

The house was abandoned as living quarters in the 1950s and is now used for storage.

Palo Duro Canyon State Park. About 12 mi. E of Canyon via SH 217 and Park Rd. 5. Palo Duro Canyon was formed by the erosional action of a branch of the Red River. From the high plains, the canyon walls plunge over a thousand feet to the canyon floor. The name Palo Duro (literally meaning "hard wood") was derived from the strong Mountain Juniper tree that the Indians used to make their arrows. The canyon also provided shelter and food for Indians for thousands of years. The first European to enter the canyon is believed to have been Francisco Vásquez de Coronado in 1541. Historic Plains Indians—Apache, Cheyenne, Kiowa, and Arapaho—visited the canyon until the Comanches claimed it as a stronghold in the 19th century. Later, comancheros also lived or camped in parts of the canyon. Today, the state park covers 15,103 acres and has facilities for camping and picnicking. Other activities and facilities available include horseback riding, hiking trails, an interpretive center (closed in the winter), and an amphitheater where shows are staged during the summer.

Panhandle-Plains Historical Museum. On West Texas State University campus, 2401 Fourth Ave. Built in 1932, the museum is one of several buildings in the state described by Carla Breeze in her book *Pueblo Deco* as outstanding examples of Pueblo Deco architecture, a Southwestern style inspired by regional Hispanic and Indian influences. This is the oldest and largest state-supported museum in Texas, and it has extensive exhibits relating to the history of the Panhandle. Spanish materials from the periods of exploration through colonization include coins, spurs, helmets and armor, crucifixes, and trade items. Especially popular is the Hall of the Southern Plains Indians, which includes authentic materials of the Comanche (including the feathered headdress of famed Comanche war chief Quanah Parker), Southern Cheyenne, Arapaho, Kiowa, Kiowa Apache, and Apache tribes. The Ranching Hall traces the story of ranching from the arrival of cattle in North America to the present. Paleontology and geology exhibits place the history of the region in an environmental context. Open September through May: Mon.–Sat. 9–5, Sun. 2–6; June through August: Mon.–Sat. 9–6, Sun. 2–6; closed on major holidays.

Santa Fe Depot. 911 Second Ave. Built in 1924, this steel and concrete depot reflects Spanish Revival style in its stucco finish and red tile roof.

Kwahadi Indian Ceremonials. Last Saturday in September and first Saturday in October, in Pioneer Amphitheatre, Palo Duro Canyon State Park. Traditional Indian ceremonials and dances are performed by the nationally known Kwahadi Boy Scouts Explorer Post 80. Performances include Plains and Southwestern Indian dances, as well as Aztec and Yaqui Indian dances of Mexico. The troupe also presents an annual winter show in Amarillo.

CLAUDE, Armstrong County

Claude (pop. 1,199) is located in an area believed to have been on the route of Coronado in the 1540s. The town developed as a railroad stop in 1887, and agriculture is the basis of the town's economy. Claude is the county seat of Armstrong County.

Route of the Coronado Expedition. Marker, located on the courthouse lawn. The marker commemorates the route of Coronado across the Panhandle, to Tule Canyon, then north to Palo Duro Canyon and beyond. *SM 1969.*

Scenic Drive. SH 207 south toward Silverton provides an excellent view of vast stretches of plains that plunge suddenly to the scenic grandeur of Palo Duro Canyon and, farther south, Tule Canyon. This is one of the most striking scenic drives in the Panhandle, through country that is rich in both Spanish exploration and American Indian history.

CRANE, Crane County

Crane (pop. 3,533), a commercial center for local oil and ranching industries, is the county seat and only town in Crane County. A well-known historic site in the area is the Horsehead Crossing of the Pecos River, for centuries a major crossing into the Trans-Pecos. The crossing is located on private land where the river crosses the Pecos–Crane County line and is not open to the public.

Juan Cordona Lake. Marker, county courthouse lawn, 11 mi. NE of the site. Juan Cordona Lake is a natural salt deposit that has been known for at least 300 years. Spanish explorers encountered Apaches here in the 1680s. The name of the lake derives from its location on Juan Córdova's Mexican land grant, but the name was misprinted as Cordona on early maps of the area. *SM 1965.*

Spanish ring bit found near Quitaque. In the collections of the Panhandle-Plains Historical Museum. Courtesy of Panhandle-Plains Historical Museum, Canyon.

451

CROSBYTON AND VICINITY, Crosby County

Crosbyton (pop. 2,026) lies in an area that was frequented by 19th-century ciboleros and comancheros from New Mexico, who used nearby Blanco Canyon as a travel route in the era before Anglo-American settlement. Both the canyon and the White River that flows through it were called Blanco ("white") by these early Hispanic inhabitants. Crosbyton, an agribusiness center, is the county seat of Crosby County.

Crosby County Pioneer Memorial Museum and Community Center. Intersection of US 82 (SH 114) and FM 651 in Crosbyton. This fine small museum features murals depicting individuals and cultures that have influenced the development of Crosby County and the Llano Estacado. One exhibit depicts the region's Plains Indian history. Open Tues.–Sat. 9–12, 1:30–5; closed on major holidays.

FLOYDADA, Floyd County

Floydada (pop. 3,896) is located in an area once occupied by Plains Apaches and Comanches. Several important sites in the area have yielded archeological remains of both of these important historic Indian groups, including evidence of trade with the New Mexico pueblos. Anglo-American settlement began late in the 19th century, and the coming of the railroad was a major inducement to development. Floydada was established on a rail line and became the county seat of Floyd County in 1890.

Zimmerman House. 516 S. First St. Built in 1930 for farmer-rancher Fred Zimmerman, the house was designed by Wichita Falls architect Ray Arnhold. The Pueblo Revival structure, built of stuccoed brick and tile, was designed to resemble the adobe houses of New Mexico. Noteworthy architectural elements include vigas, hewn beams, and the interior fireplace. *RTHL 1990.*

FRITCH AND VICINITY, Hutchinson County

Fritch (pop. 2,335), incorporated in 1959, is the gateway to recreational areas around Lake Meredith and to Alibates Flint Quarries National Monument.

Alibates Flint Quarries National Monument. Off SH 136, ca. 6 mi. S of Fritch. The flint quarries at Alibates National Monument were used by Indians of the region for thousands of years, beginning about 10,000 B.C. to the historic period. The multihued stone was favored by the Antelope Creek peoples whose village ruins are major archeological sites all along the Canadian River. This prized resource was traded over a wide area of Texas and across the Southern Plains. Entry to the monument is by ranger-guided tours only.

Lake Meredith Aquatic and Wildlife Museum. 104 N. Robey. Exhibits focus on natural history, especially fish found in the lake, and a series of wildlife dioramas depict typical plains animals. The National Park Service display shows examples of Alibates flint and devices that the Indians used to fashion stone tools and weapons from the colorful stone.

LAMESA AND VICINITY, Dawson County

Lamesa (pop. 10,809) is located at the southeastern edge of the High Plains. The city's name is from *la mesa,* Spanish for "the table," which accurately describes the flat terrain. Once buffalo country, then ranchland, the area yielded to farming as cotton fields took the place of pastures, and the area economy now is based primarily on the oil industry and agriculture. Until the second half of the 20th century, most of the area's Hispanic residents were migrant workers.

Dal Paso Museum. 310 S. First. The museum is housed in a restored, 1925 building that was originally the Dal Paso Hotel. Focused on local and pioneer history, the museum is currently engaged in documenting the role various ethnic groups have played in the settlement of Dawson County. Noteworthy among the museum's permanent exhibits is the Veterans Room, which includes photographs, uniforms, medals and other materials relating to area veterans, including Mexican-Americans. The Mexican-American materials in the exhibit were assembled with the assistance of the G.I. Forum. Open Tues.–Sun. 2–5.

Los Ybañez, formerly known as Lamesa Farm Workers Community, is a tiny town about 1.5 mi. SE of Lamesa. The community originated as a model migrant-labor camp operated by the Farm Security Administration, a New Deal program of the Depression era. The camp was designed for 125 families in 25 houses and 25 quadruplexes, and included a gate house, a manager's residence, and a community center, all of frame construction. The administrative offices of the camp were located in the gate house, and the community-center building served also as a church. Israel and María Ybañez purchased the community from the Dawson County Farm Labor Association in 1980, with the intention of providing low-rent housing to Hispanic families. Los Ybañez, renamed for its new owners, was incorporated as a city in 1983, when it had 300 residents. Many of the original migrant-community structures still remain.

McCAMEY, Upton County

McCamey (pop. 2,493) developed during the Panhandle oil boom of the 1920s and, like many towns in the region, is an oil and ranching center. It is the major town of Upton County, although Rankin is the county seat.

Mendoza Trail. Marker, in front of Mendoza Trail Museum (SH 67). The marker commemorates the route followed by Lt. Gen. Juan Domínguez de Mendoza in 1683–84. Mendoza's purpose was to explore the Pecos plains, obtain pearls from Texas rivers, and christianize the Jumano Indians. *SM 1967.*

MIAMI, Roberts County

Miami (pop. 675) is famed as the location of one of the first major Clovis Paleoindian sites discovered in Texas, providing evidence of prehistoric peoples in the region as much as 12,000 years ago. Miami began as a railroad construction camp in the late 1880s, and the small town's economy is now based on ranching and oil-industry activities. Miami is the county seat of Roberts County.

Roberts County Museum. US 60E, Old Santa Fe Depot. The focus of the museum is on the history of Roberts County and the surrounding region. The Paleontology and Native American rooms include several exhibits of special interest. The Dare and Betty Lock Collection of Art features 36 limited-edition silk-screen prints by Kiowa and other tribal artists of the 1920s, as well as 15 watercolors by other American Indian artists. Another exhibit contains rare Mimbres, Moundbuilder, and Tularosa pottery, as well as rugs, baskets, and blankets of Southwestern Indian groups. The Jack Mead Paleontology Exhibit contains material relating to the Miami Clovis site. Open in winter Tues.–Fri. 1–5, Sun. 2–5; summer, Tues.–Fri. 10–5, Sat. 2–5.

MIDLAND AND VICINITY, Midland County

Midland (pop. 89,443), in what was once buffalo country, is located on the route of the Chihuahua Road. Prehistoric occupation spanning thousands of years is documented in numerous archeological sites, including the well-known Midland Paleoindian site (inaccessible). Midland, originally settled by ranchers and farmers, was a community by 1880. The city developed rapidly during the 1920s oil boom, and the local economy is now largely based on the petroleum industry. Midland is the county seat of Midland County.

Information Centers

Midland Convention and Visitors Bureau. 109 N. Main, P.O. Box 1890, Midland 79702. The bureau supplies information on local events and accommodations.

Midland Hispanic Chamber of Commerce. P.O. Box 11134, Midland 79702. Contact the chamber for additional information on local events and celebrations.

Spanish Revival Architecture

Midland Historic District. Several fine examples of Spanish Revival architecture can be found in the Midland Historic District, bounded on the north by Texas Ave., on the south by College Ave., and on the west by Garfield Ave. Of particular interest are the Boy Scouts of America Build-

Tularosa pottery from New Mexico (ca. A.D. 1250) and a Navajo chief's blanket from the Roberts County Museum, Miami. Photo by Rex Holland, courtesy of the Roberts County Museum.

ing, at North D and Texas Sts.; the Mission Revival bungalow on Missouri at K St.; and the West Elementary School, located at 2200 Missouri.

Boy Scouts of America building, Midland Historic District, Midland. Photo by Cathryn Hoyt, THC.

Museums and Archives

Midland County Historical Museum. 301 W. Missouri. This small museum features exhibits on local and pioneer history, as well as the natural history and archeology of the area. The museum maintains an archival collection of early photographs, interviews, and unpublished histories of the Midland area. Open Mon.–Thurs. 11–5; Sat. 9–4.

Museum of the Southwest. 1705 W. Missouri. The museum focuses on the art and culture of the American Southwest. Exhibits feature historical and contemporary Southwestern art, paintings, sculpture, and ceramics, along with Indian artifacts and special exhibits. Open Mon.–Sat. 10–5; Sun. 2–5.

Nita Stewart Haley Memorial Library. 1805 Indiana. In the library's collections is one of four bells from Mission San Antonio de Valero (the Alamo). In addition to manuscripts and books focusing on the range-cattle industry and the history of the American cowboy, the Haley Library

displays western art and artifacts and a varied collection of saddlery, bits, and spurs, and South American gaucho materials. A bronze statue of a Longhorn cow and her calf titled *Old Maude* (by Veryl Goodnight, 1982) stands outside the entrance. Open Mon.–Fri. 9–5.

Permian Basin Petroleum Museum. 1500 IH 20W, exit 136. Although primarily concerned with the history and technology of the oil industry, the museum collections also include historic Indian, Spanish Colonial, Mexican, and Mexican-American items. Open Mon.–Fri. 9–5.

Veryl Goodnight statue of a Longhorn cow and calf in front of the Nita Stewart Haley Memorial Library, Midland. Photo by Cathryn Hoyt, THC.

Festivals and Events

Ballet Folklórico of Midland. This established dance group, performing traditional dances in appropriate costume, is a highlight of local Hispanic community celebrations.

Celebration of the Arts. Early May, at Centennial Plaza. A Cinco de Mayo parade and traditional music are features of the Mexican-American component of Midland's multicultural Celebration of the Arts. The Mexican-American events are sponsored by the Hispanic Chamber of Commerce and other community organizations, while the Celebration of the Arts is sponsored by the Arts Assembly of Midland.

Diez y Seis de Septiembre. September 16, at various locations. Diez y Seis is commemorated with a parade followed by celebrations at various locations. Bazaars at several Hispanic community churches are traditional aspects of this celebration in Midland.

Mex-Tex Menudo-Fajita-Chili Family Festival. Second week in July, at Midland County Exhibition Building. This three-day festival attracts thousands of people and is the major Hispanic community celebration in Midland. In addition to traditional foods, music, and dance, the festival features a carnival, arts and crafts, and a scholarship beauty pageant. A high point is the charreada held by the Miguel Hidalgo Charro Association.

MORTON VICINITY, Cochran County

Morton (pop. 2,597), an oil and agriculture center, is the major town and county seat of Cochran County. Cochran County was created in 1876 but was so sparsely populated—having a population of only 25 cowboys as late as 1900—that the county was not organized until 1924, when the village of Morton became the county seat.

C.C. Slaughter Ranch Headquarters. 2 mi. S of Morton on SH 214, 1 mi. W on FM 1169 (not shown on most maps). Adobe buildings, placed to form a quadrangle, were part of the extensive Slaughter Ranch headquarters complex. The early use of adobe in the Panhandle indicates that here, as elsewhere in the state, early ranchers and settlers used indigenous construction materials and methods to build their first structures. Visitors are welcome.

ODESSA, Ector County

Odessa (pop. 89,699), the county seat of Ector County, was established in 1881 as a farming community on the Texas and Pacific Railroad but had become a typical cow town by the time the county was organized in 1891. The town became an oil center in the 1930s with the discovery of the Permian Basin oilfields.

Ballet Azteca. Odessa's ballet folklórico group gives performances at local schools and celebrations. The group is sponsored by the Odessa LULAC organization.

Cinco de Mayo. On or near May 5, usually on Lions Club grounds. Cinco de Mayo is celebrated with a parade on the city's south side and with entertainment and other events, including traditional music and foods, in the evening. Sponsored by the local Lions Club and Spanish-language radio stations.

Diez y Seis de Septiembre. Mid-September, usually on Lions Club grounds. Diez y Seis is celebrated in the same manner as Cinco de Mayo and is sponsored by the same local groups. Both of these celebrations offer

Fiesta queens at the Olton Mexican Festival, Olton. Photo by Sue Cannon, courtesy of Olton Mexican Festival.

excellent opportunities to experience events that are central to Hispanic community life in Odessa.

OLTON, Lamb County

Olton (pop. 2,116) is a small farming community located in northeastern Lamb County. The town, originally completely surrounded by the vast holdings of the C.C. Slaughter ranch, was settled about 1900 and named for an early preacher in the area. Between 1908 and 1946, Olton served as the county seat of Lamb County, but Littlefield is now the county seat.

Olton Mexican Festival. Weekend preceding September 16 (Diez y Seis de Septiembre), in Olton Town Square. The Olton Mexican Festival, organized by the Olton Chamber of Commerce and St. Peter's Catholic Church, was begun in 1982 as an educational and ethnic heritage event. For the Fiesta Queen title, young women compete with Spanish-language presentations on Mexican history. Other events include ballet folklórico performed in traditional dress, narrative displays about Mexican independence, traditional games including lotería mexicana and piñatas, conjunto and mariachi music, and Mexican and Tejano foods such as enchiladas, tamales, Mexican rice, refried beans, tripitas, and menudo. As many as 2,000 visitors attend the event annually.

PAMPA, Gray County

Pampa (pop. 19,959) area economy is largely based on ranching and oil-industry activities. The town was established on the Santa Fe Railroad in 1881 and takes its name from the American Spanish word *pampa,* meaning plain. Two fine examples of Spanish-influenced architecture dating from the 1920s oil boom can be seen here. Pampa is the county seat of Gray County.

U.S. Post Office. 120 E. Foster. As a result of the 1920s oil boom, Pampa's postal needs jumped. This large, impressive post office, built in 1933–34, is an example of the federally funded response to that growth and anticipation of continued economic prosperity. Built in Spanish Revival style, the Post Office is a one-story reinforced-concrete structure with limestone veneer and a hipped tile roof. Large, round-arched window openings have ornate hand-forged metal grilles. The cornice and frieze are elaborately carved. The beautiful lobby features marble floors, coffered ceiling, and decorative bronze doors and grilles. *NR 1986.*

Schneider House. 120 S. Russell and Atchison Ave. The Schneider House, built in 1927 during the Panhandle oil boom, was the major hostelry in the region and served as the social center of Pampa during the 1920s and 1930s. The hotel features Spanish Revival influences such as the mission-style parapet, the five-bay arcaded portico, the use of decorative brick, and the cast-stone detailing. *NR 1985.*

PANHANDLE AND VICINITY, Carson County

Panhandle (pop. 2,353) was named for its location in the Texas Panhandle. The probable routes of several of the earliest explorers through Texas pass through this area of the Llano Estacado, including Francisco Vásquez de Coronado in 1541. Juan de Oñate followed in 1601, Pedro de Villasur in 1720, and Facundo Melgares in 1807. The earliest European settlers in the area were pastores from New Mexico in the early 1800s. Today the area economy, typical of the region, is based largely on agribusiness and oil-industry activities. Panhandle is the major town and county seat of Carson County.

"Buffalo Hunt" by Stephen Mopope (Kiowa name: Painted Robe). Watercolor in the collections of the Carson County Square House Museum, Panhandle. Photo by David L. Hoover, courtesy of Carson County Square House Museum.

Atchison, Topeka, and Santa Fe Railroad Depot. US 60 and Main St. Built in response to the traffic increase caused by the 1920s oil boom, this structure exemplifies the eclectic mix of styles common to the area. Features include Spanish Revival stepped parapets and curvilinear brackets as well as other design features that reflect Prairie School and Tudor influences. The building has served as the city hall since 1985. *RTHL 1988.*

Carson County Square House Museum. Fifth and Elsie Sts. The Square House was constructed as a ranch manager's headquarters in the 1880s. The museum now housed in the building has both indoor and outdoor exhibits, and collections include Hispanic materials from the Spanish Colonial period to the present, as well as native American artifacts from ca. A.D. 1400 to 1700. The Senator Grady and Andrine Hazlewood Education Center exhibits feature artifacts "made in America," from the period of the Plains Indians through pioneer settlement. Open Mon.–Sat. 8:30–5:30; Sun. 1–5:30.

Panhandle Inn. Third and Main Sts. Built in the 1930s, this Pueblo Revival building once housed an inn and several commercial establishments.

Scenic Drive. FM 293 to SH 136 leads through agricultural land into the rolling grasslands of the broad Canadian River valley. SH 136 leads north to the popular recreational areas of Lake Meredith, an area once inhabited by the prehistoric Antelope Creek people.

PLAINVIEW, Hale County

Plainview (pop. 21,700) is located in the central Llano Estacado, which was buffalo and Plains Indian country until the late 19th century. A military trail made by Ranald S. Mackenzie's troops was long the only

460

road across the plains in this area. Hackberry groves, said to be the only trees on the plains, were a landmark on the trail, and Plainview grew from an 1880s homestead site among the groves. Today the American Indian and Hispanic heritage of the area is preserved primarily in collections and exhibits at the Llano Estacado Museum. Plainview is the county seat of Hale County.

Llano Estacado Museum. 1900 W. 8th St. The museum maintains 80 exhibits describing the geological, prehistoric, cultural, and economic development of the Llano Estacado, including permanent displays relating to Plains Indians, Spanish exploration, comancheros, and pastores. The museum also maintains an archeological research laboratory and an archival collection that concentrate on the region. Open in summer, Mon.–Fri. 9–5, Sat.–Sun. 1–5; winter, Sat.–Sun. only, 1–5.

QUITAQUE VICINITY, Briscoe County

Quitaque (pop. 513) was named for the Quitaque Ranch and Quitaque Creek. José Tafoya established a trading post in the area during the

Detail, Panhandle Inn, Panhandle. Photo by Cathryn Hoyt, THC.

461

mid-1800s and by the 1890s the location was a stage stop. The town of Quitaque was organized in 1940.

Caprock Canyons State Park. 3.5 mi. N of Quitaque on FM 1065. As you drive north on SH 86 in the Panhandle, a long row of distant hills marks the Cap Rock, which separates the high plains from the rolling prairies to the east. On closer inspection, the hills are seen to be remnants of rock, not yet weathered away by winds or the occasional flash flood that are the chief creators of the landscape. Caprock Canyons State Park preserves about 14,000 acres of this rugged canyon country. The park provides an opportunity to view remnants of wild Texas as it existed for the earliest Americans, the Spanish explorers, and the 19th-century pioneers. Buffalo can be seen in the park, although the area is accessible only by a strenuous hike. A historical marker (*SM 1978*) commemorating the earliest Americans, the Paleoindians, has been placed near the Lake Theo Folsom Bison Kill site on FM 1065. Camping, fishing, swimming, and hiking are the most popular activities in the park.

José Tafoya and Other Comancheros. Marker, roadside park 7 mi. NW of Quitaque on SH 86. Comanchero trading in this area was at its peak in the 1860s. José Tafoya was arrested by the U.S. Army for trading with the Indians and later enlisted as a frontier scout. *SM 1969*.

SAN ANGELO, Tom Green County

San Angelo (pop. 84,474), established by pioneer Bart DeWitt in the 1870s, grew up around Fort Concho and is believed to have been named Santa Ángela for DeWitt's wife, Ángela de la Garza. The name officially became San Angelo in the 1880s. The first nonmilitary settlers in the region were sheep and goat ranchers, and the city is still a major wool and mohair center. The oldest Mexican-American neighborhood is the Santa Fe barrio, north of the Santa Fe railroad in the Miles Addition, which was well established by the turn of the century. The Oriente barrio, west of Fort Concho, was attracting new residents by 1910 and eventually became the center of the city's Hispanic population. In either area are still to be found examples of small vernacular houses dating from the early twentieth century, as well as numerous Hispanic community churches, both Catholic and Protestant. The annual celebration of Fiestas Patrias reflects an important and on-going cultural tradition. Arnoldo De León, in his book *San Angeleños* (1985), says that by "the mid-1980s, members of San Angelo's Hispanic community could accurately be labeled 'Mexican-American,' for they had assimilated important parts of both cultures. . . . Equipped with this dual identity, San Angeleños—as they had been doing for more than a century—were able to enrich both themselves and the life of the entire community." San Angelo is the county seat of Tom Green County.

Information

San Angelo Convention and Visitors Bureau. 500 Rio Concho Dr.

The bureau distributes free brochures and maps. Open Mon.–Fri. 8:30–5; on weekends the Fort Concho Museum provides visitor information.

Historic Sites and Topics

Concho Pearls. Freshwater pearls known as Concho pearls are found only in the branches of the Concho River of this region. Several types of river mussels are found here and were once a staple food source for Indians of the area. Only one of the mussels produces pearls, which are pinkish to lavender in color. Spanish explorers as early as the 17th century traded with the Indians for these treasures, which are still highly prized. Pearls, loose or in jewelry, are available in several jewelry shops in San Angelo.

Fort Concho. *See* Festivals and Events.

Iglesia Santa María (St. Mary's Catholic Church). 7 W. Ave. N. The Catholic church has been active in the San Angelo area since the 1870s. The growth of the city and of the Hispanic community led to the construction of this church in the Oriente barrio in 1930. It is a focal point of the social and cultural life of the community. The Mission Revival style brick church

Iglesia Santa María, San Angelo. THC photo.

features a curvilinear gable and small belfry with a convex roof; also noteworthy is the Spanish quatrefoil rose window.

Jumano Indian Mission. Marker, Rio Concho Dr. at Bell St. A historical marker commemorates a mission that served the Jumano Indians for about six months in the 1630s. The marker also relates the story of the "Lady in Blue"; the Jumanos told the Spanish that the vision had appeared to them and requested that they seek mission protection. *PM.*

Spanish Revival Architecture

Cactus Hotel. 36 E. Twohig. Built as a Hilton Hotel in 1928, this fourteen-story, buff-brick building is capped with a red tile roof. The building reflects sensitivity to both classical and Southwestern regional influences.

Commercial Building (originally Aztec Cleaners and Laundry). 119 S. Irving. This two-story, buff-brick building is Spanish Eclectic in style and features stone accents at its porch and a Spanish clay tile roof. *NR 1989.*

Commercial Building. 113–119 E. Concho. This one-story, buff-brick building, which covers an entire block, was built in 1928 for a Packard and Terraplane auto dealership. Mission Revival influence is evident in the curvilinear parapet and arched entryway with statuary niche. *NR 1989.*

Hagelstein Commercial Building. 618 S. Chadbourne. Constructed in 1927, this one-story, buff-brick building is triangular in shape to fit its railside lot. The structure has a characteristic Mission style parapet and tile roof. *NR 1989.*

Household Furniture Company. 11 N. Chadbourne. A two-story building with characteristic curved parapet, this commercial building is a good example of Spanish Revival style buildings in San Angelo. It was built during the city's commercial and residential boom of 1927–30. *NR 1989.*

Iglesia Santa Maria. *See* Historic Sites and Topics entries above.

Santa Fe Railroad Station. 702 S. Chadbourne. This early-twentieth-century station is one of the outstanding examples of Spanish Revival style architecture in the region. Established as divisional headquarters of the Kansas City, Mexico, and Orient Railroad in 1909, it was a major locale of San Angelo trade.

Texas Sheep and Goat Raisers Association Headquarters. 233 W. Twohig. The one-story, stucco-on-adobe house features a parapeted, flat roof, Spanish clay tiles, an arched main entry, and decorative ironwork. Built as a residence for a local physician in 1925, this structure is unusual in that adobe was rarely used for more expensive homes in this area. The residence became the Texas Sheep and Goat Raisers Association Headquarters in 1962 when San Angelo was selected in recognition of its role as a primary sheep and wool market. *NR 1989.*

West Texas Utilities Building. 15 E. Beauregard. The one-story, brick structure was built in 1924, and one- and two-story additions were constructed in 1927. The building, featuring arched windows, an elaborately carved cornice, and four circular medallions, is a good example of Spanish Revival style in this area. *NR 1989.*

Festivals and Events

Christmas at Old Fort Concho. First weekend in December, at Fort Concho, 213 E. Ave. D. In this multicultural celebration, the fort buildings are decorated and participants are costumed to represent various themes, including Mexican Christmas. A musical pageant depicting San Angelo's colorful beginnings is held nightly, and artisans and merchants display and sell their wares.

Fiesta del Concho. June, at Fort Concho, 213 E. Ave. D. This week of special events for all ages features a parade, foods, arts and crafts, and other events; the Hispanic community participates in various aspects of the fiesta. *See also* Frontier Day at Fort Concho.

Fiestas Patrias. Mid-September, at Fort Concho, 213 E. Ave. D. Las Fiestas Patrias has been celebrated by San Angeleños since their arrival in the Concho Valley during the late 1800s. The city's fiesta tradition, institutionalized under organizer Estalislado Sedeño for thirty years, continues today at Fort Concho. After Sedeño's death in 1974, the Southside Lions and Lionesses began organizing Diez y Seis de Septiembre fiestas, which have been celebrated at this historical landmark since 1984. All festival events directly relate to Mexican-American culture, and today the celebration focuses on the contributions of Mexican-Americans in West Texas. "Viva Mexico, Viva America," a historical pageant written by Dr. Arnoldo De León, scholar of Tejano history, presents Mexican history from the Aztecs, to the Grito de Dolores, to Mexican settlement in the Concho Valley. Other festival events include a reception honoring dignitaries from San Angelo and other cities, ballet folklórico performed by dancers in traditional dress, a style show of modern dress designed by local Hispanic seamstresses and designers, live mariachi music, and an exhibit of Mexican folk art, retablos, and Mexican toys. Another significant event is "La Perla de las Fiestas Patrias" scholarship pageant, a competition based on students' knowledge of Mexican-American culture, language, and history. Over 20,000 people participate in the annual fiestas held on September 15 and 16.

Frontier Day at Fort Concho. Third Saturday in June, at Fort Concho, 213 E. Ave. D. This celebration of West Texas heritage includes the Texas state sheep-shearing contest and sheepdog trials, an excellent opportunity to observe skilled Mexican-American sheep shearers perform—and usually win the competition.

SHAMROCK, Wheeler County

Shamrock (pop. 2,286) was established as a railroad stop in the opening years of the 20th century. The Wheeler County area was home to

School children dancing during the Fiestas Patrias celebration, San Angelo. Reprinted by permission of the *San Angelo Standard-Times*.

Plains Indians and buffalo until the hide hunters killed off the buffalo in the 1870s and the region was opened to Anglo-American settlement. Shamrock is the major town of Wheeler County, although Wheeler is the county seat.

Pioneer West Museum. 204 N. Madden. Collections include a few 19th-century military artifacts from Mexico. Open daily: in summer, 9–12, 1–5; winter 10–12, 1–4.

SILVERTON VICINITY, Briscoe County

Silverton (pop. 779) is an agribusiness center and, small town though it is, the major town and county seat of Briscoe County. The county lies partly on the High Plains, and the broken country of the Cap Rock escarpment provides a scenic drive on SH 207 north toward Claude. Archeological sites (inaccessible) in the Mackenzie Reservoir area to the west have provided evidence of American Indian occupation in the Tule Creek drainage from the Paleoindian through the historic periods. A historical marker *(SM 1979)* commemorating important archeological sites in the Tule Canyon and Mackenzie Reservoir areas has been placed on SH 207, 11 mi. NW of Silverton.

SNYDER, Scurry County

Snyder (pop. 12,195) is located in an area that was visited by nomadic Indian tribes, Spanish explorers, military expeditions, and buffalo hunters before permanent settlement began with early ranchers in the 1870s. The town began as a camp for buffalo hunters at the end of the frontier period. The discovery of a major oil field in 1948 has contributed to the prosperity of the area. Snyder is the county seat of Scurry County.

Scurry County Museum. SH 350S, Western Texas College. The museum features a permanent exhibit and collections of Mexican artifacts, as well as Mexican-American clothing and ranching items. A display depicts the era of the buffalo hunters. Open Mon.–Fri. 10–4.

SPUR, Dickens County

Spur (pop. 1,300), laid out as a townsite in 1907, is located on lands that were owned by the Spur Ranch, one of the largest and best-known ranches in West Texas in the late 19th century. Spur is the major town of Dickens County, although Dickens is the county seat.

St. Mary's Catholic Church. E. 6th St. St. Mary's was originally established in Jayton, in Kent County, in a frame church built in 1929. The frame church was moved to Spur in 1948, and it served as the church hall after the new Spanish Revival style church was built in 1950–54.

STANTON, Martin County

Stanton (pop. 2,576) was originally settled by German farmers and named Mariensfield. The name was changed to Stanton in 1890. Stanton is the county seat of Martin County and petroleum production and agribusiness now dominate the economy.

Martin County Historical Museum. 207 E. Broadway. The museum's collections include Mexican-American household items as well as oral histories of Martin County settlers of Hispanic descent. A permanent exhibit on Hispanic history in the area is planned. Open Tues.–Sat. 9–5.

Sisters of Mercy Convent. Convent St. Built in 1882 by Mexican craftsmen from Ysleta, this two-story adobe structure is the only surviving building of the original complex. The convent is significant because of its role in the early history of the county and its adobe construction, which is rare in this area.

467

STINNETT VICINITY, Hutchinson County

St. Mary's Catholic Church, Spur. Photo by Ann Worley-Shrimpton, courtesy of *Texas Spur*.

Stinnett (pop. 2,166) is located in an area that was probably crossed by Coronado on his way to Quivira in the 1540s and by Juan de Oñate in 1601. Numerous Indian villages were once located on the Canadian River, which crosses the county from southwest to northeast, and an Indian trading post (known as Adobe Walls) was located on nearby Bent's Creek by the late 1830s. An 1870s camp established by Indian traders and buffalo hunters, also known as Adobe Walls, was the scene of a famous battle between buffalo hunters and others against Plains Indians led by Quanah Parker. Stinnett was established as the county seat of Hutchinson County in 1901.

Adobe Walls. Ca. 12 mi. N of Stinnett off SH 207. The trading post known as Adobe Walls was a major supply center for late-19th-century hunters who eventually destroyed the region's vast herds of buffalo and thus contributed to the final expulsion of Plains Indians from Texas. The site contains the ruins of sod and picket structures, a well, grave markers, and foundation remains. Adobe Walls was the scene of two Indian battles, and one of the historical markers at the site commemorates the Indians

Sweetwater Auditorium–City Hall, Sweetwater. Photo by Cathryn Hoyt, THC.

who fought for the land they considered to be theirs. On private land; permission required for entry to site. Historical markers (*CM 1936* and *SM 1964*) have been placed at the site.

Scenic Drive. The 25-mile drive south and east to Borger crosses through the canyon-cut landscape of the Canadian River breaks and leads across the dam of Lake Meredith. This drive, south on FM 687, FM 1319, and east on SH 136, crosses through country once occupied by the prehistoric Antelope Creek people. Nomadic Plains Indians inhabited this area when Coronado crossed the Panhandle in 1541.

SWEETWATER, Nolan County

Sweetwater (pop. 11,967) had its beginnings in a dugout store established for buffalo hunters in 1877. The village that eventually developed became the county seat and was moved two miles to the newly completed Texas and Pacific Railroad right-of-way in 1882. During the boom years of the 1920s many significant commercial and public structures were erected, including several in Spanish Revival style. Sweetwater is the county seat of Nolan County.

469

Sweetwater Commercial Historic District. City Center. The historic district includes parts of 17 blocks downtown. The commercial and governmental buildings, primarily of brick construction, reflect early-20th-century construction materials and styles, including Spanish Revival. Of particular interest are the two-story, brick-veneer Municipal Auditorium–City Hall and the Central Fire Station, both Spanish Revival style buildings constructed in 1926 and located at the E. Fourth and Locust Sts. intersection. They were designed by the well-known firm of Page and Page, Architects, of Austin. *NR 1984.*

TEXLINE VICINITY, Dallam County

Texline (pop. 425), established in the 1880s, is named for its location on the Texas–New Mexico state line. The national grassland is accessible on FM 296 east from Texline.

Rita Blanca National Grassland. Made part of the national forest system in 1956, the grassland encompasses 77,000 acres in Texas and thousands of acres in Oklahoma and New Mexico. The area fosters rejuvenation of 30 or 40 species of grass, especially the shortgrasses such as blue grama, side oats grama, and sand dropseed. The grasslands offer an opportunity to experience the vast prairie that once was the habitat of countless herds of buffalo, home to the Plains Indians, and an almost insurmountable challenge to the earliest explorers and settlers.

TULIA AND VICINITY, Swisher County

Tulia (pop. 4,699) area history begins with the Coronado expedition in the 1540s, but Hispanic heritage here is scarcely reflected in the modern built environment. However, the drive on SH 86 east of Tulia, toward Caprock Canyons State Park near Quitaque, provides spectacular scenery through a historic landscape. Tulia, a farming center, is the county seat of Swisher County.

Swisher County Archives and Museum. Swisher Memorial Building, 127 SW 2d St. Focusing on pioneer and local history, the museum has a special exhibit devoted to Comanche leader Quanah Parker, as well as stone artifacts related to prehistoric Indian occupation in the area. Open Mon.–Fri. 9–5.

Tule Canyon. E of Tulia on SH 86. Tule Canyon, although not marked by monuments or historic ruins, is nevertheless rich in history. It is believed to have been visited by Coronado in the 1540s and was on the route of late-18th-century explorers seeking a route between the Spanish settlements in Texas and Santa Fe in New Mexico. Plains Apaches probably occupied this area at the time of Coronado and remained in control here until about 1700, when the Comanches appeared on the scene. Comanche dominance of the area ended in 1874, when Col. Ranald Mackenzie, just after his victory at Palo Duro, destroyed about 1,500 Indian mustangs in Tule Canyon.

Quanah Parker as a young man. Photo by W.S. Soule, courtesy Barker Texas History Center, General Libraries, University of Texas at Austin.

470

VEGA VICINITY, Oldham County

Vega (pop. 840) is situated in an area where sites of major historic and archeological significance exist but are not open to the public. During prehistoric times, Antelope Creek people lived along the Canadian River, and one of their village sites, Landergin Mesa, is a National Historic Landmark. In the late 19th century, major pastores settlements were established in the area. Historic remains of the pastores include Tascosa and an archeological site (inaccessible) known as the Chávez City Ruins, or Chávez Plaza, which contains the ruins of eight stone-slab structures *(NR 1984)*. The plaza once boasted two mercantile establishments and a saloon. The largest town in the area today is Vega, which is the county seat of Oldham County.

Tascosa. On US 385, about 32 mi. N of Vega. Now a ghost town, Tascosa originated as a pastores plaza called Atascosa, settled by Casimero Romero in 1875. The town was bypassed by the railroad in the late 1880s and was eventually abandoned. By 1939 the site had been acquired as a boy's ranch headquarters. The boy's ranch has turned the Old Tascosa courthouse into a small museum and is actively working on the restoration of the original adobe schoolhouse. For information on visiting the site contact Cal Farley's Boys Ranch, P.O. Box 1890, Amarillo 79174-0001.

Abbreviations

CM	Centennial Marker
FM	Farm or Ranch to Market Road
IH	Interstate Highway
ITC	Institute of Texan Cultures, San Antonio
NHL	National Historic Landmark
NR	National Register of Historic Places
PM	Private Marker
RTHL	Recorded Texas Historic Landmark (includes SM)
SAL	State Archeological Landmark
SH	State Highway
SM	Official Texas State Historical Marker
TFLHR	Texas Family Land Heritage Registry
THC	Texas Historical Commission, Austin
US	US Highway

References

**Hispanic Imprints on the Texas Landscape,
by Félix D. Almaráz, Jr.**

Almaráz, Félix D., Jr. 1989. *The San Antonio Missions and Their System of Land Tenure*. University of Texas Press, Austin.

———. 1991. "Spain's Cultural Legacy in Texas." In *The Texas Heritage*, edited by Ben H. Procter and Archie P. McDonald. Harlan Davidson, Arlington Heights, Ill.

Branda, Eldon S. (Editor). 1976. *The Handbook of Texas: A Supplement*. Texas State Historical Association, Austin.

Castañeda, Carlos E. 1936–58. *Our Catholic Heritage in Texas, 1519–1936*. 7 vols. Von Boeckmann-Jones, Austin.

García, Clotilde P. 1984. *Captain Blás María de la Garza Falcón: Colonizer of South Texas*. San Felipe Press, Jenkins Publishing Co., Austin.

Jordan, Terry G., J.L. Bean, and William M. Holmes. 1984. *Texas: A Geography*. Westview Press, Boulder, Colo.

Jones, Oakah L., Jr. 1979. *Los Paisanos: Spanish Settlers on the Northern Frontier of New Spain*. University of Oklahoma Press, Norman.

Stephens, A. Ray, and William M. Holmes. 1989. *Historical Atlas of Texas*. University of Oklahoma Press, Norman.

Texas General Land Office. 1988. *Guide to Spanish and Mexican Land Grants in South Texas*. Austin.

Webb, Walter P. (Editor). 1952. *The Handbook of Texas*. 2 vols. Texas State Historical Association, Austin.

**Riches, Religion, and Politics: Early Exploration in Texas,
by Cathryn A. Hoyt**

Bolton, Herbert E. 1949. *Coronado, Knight of Pueblo and Plains*. University of New Mexico Press, Albuquerque.

———. 1952. *Spanish Explorations in the Southwest 1542–1706*. Barnes & Noble, New York.

Cabeza de Vaca. See Covey, Cyclone.

Campbell, Thomas N. 1988. *The Indians of Southern Texas and Northeastern Mexico: Selected Writings of Thomas Nolan Campbell.* Texas Archeological Research Laboratory, University of Texas at Austin.

Castañeda, Carlos E. 1936. *Our Catholic Heritage in Texas,* Vol. 1: *The Mission Era: The Finding of Texas.* Von Boeckmann-Jones, Austin.

Covey, Cyclone (Translator and Editor). 1984. *Cabeza de Vaca's Adventures in the Unknown Interior of America.* (Translation of *La relación y comentarios del gouernador Aluar Núñez Cabeça de Vaca de los acaescido en las dos jornadas que hizo a las Indias,* first published in 1542.) University of New Mexico Press, Albuquerque.

Hammond, George P., and Agapito Rey (Editors and Translators). 1953. *Don Juan de Oñate: Colonizer of New Mexico, 1595–1628.* Coronado Historical Series, Vols. 5 and 6. University of New Mexico Press, Albuquerque.

Hodge, Frederick W., and Theodore H. Lewis. 1984. *Spanish Explorers in the Southern United States, 1528–1543.* Texas State Historical Association in cooperation with the Center for Studies in Texas History, University of Texas at Austin.

John, Elizabeth A.H. 1975. *Storms Brewed in Other Men's Worlds: The Confrontation of Indians, Spanish, and French in the Southwest, 1540–1795.* Texas A&M University Press, College Station.

Manguel, Alberto, and G. Guadalupi. 1980. *The Dictionary of Imaginary Places.* Macmillan, New York.

Martire d'Anghiera, Pietro. 1555. *The Decades of the Newe Worlde or West India.* Facsimile reprint, 1966, Readex Microprint, London.

Newcomb, W.W., Jr. 1961. *The Indians of Texas: From Prehistoric to Modern Times.* University of Texas Press, Austin.

Weddle, Robert S. (Editor). 1985. *Spanish Sea: The Gulf of Mexico in North American Discovery.* Texas A&M University Press, College Station.

Weddle, Robert S., Mary Christine Morkovsky, and Patricia Galloway (Editors). 1987. *La Salle, the Mississippi, and the Gulf: Three Primary Documents.* Texas A&M University Press, College Station.

Cross and Crown: The Spanish Missions in Texas, by Robert S. Weddle

Bolton, Herbert Eugene. 1970. *Texas in the Middle Eighteenth Century: Studies in Spanish Colonial History and Administration.* Paperback reprint of 1962 ed. University of Texas Press, Austin.

Brinckerhoff, Sidney B., and Odie B. Faulk. 1965. *Lancers for the King: A Study of the Frontier Military System of Northern New Spain, with a Translation of the Royal Regulations of 1772.* Arizona Historical Foundation, Phoenix.

Moorhead, Max L. 1975. *The Presidio: Bastion of the Spanish Borderlands.* University of Oklahoma Press, Norman.

Weddle, Robert S. 1964. *The San Sabá Mission: Spanish Pivot in Texas.* University of Texas Press, Austin.

———— 1968. *San Juan Bautista: Gateway to Spanish Texas.* University of Texas Press, Austin.

———— 1973. *Wilderness Manhunt: The Spanish Search for La Salle.* University of Texas Press, Austin.

Weddle, Robert S., and Robert H. Thonhoff. 1976. *Drama and Conflict: The Texas Saga of 1776.* Madrona Press, Austin.

Weddle, Robert S., Mary Christine Morkovsky, and Patricia Galloway (Editors). 1987. *La Salle, the Mississippi, and the Gulf: Three Primary Documents.* Texas A&M University Press, College Station.

Hispanic Heritage on the High Plains:
The Panhandle Perspective,
by Patricia A. Mercado-Allinger

Archambeau, Ernest R. 1946. "Spanish Sheepmen on the Canadian at Old Tascosa." By José Ynocencio Romero as told to E. R. Archambeau. *Panhandle-Plains Historical Review* 19: 45–72.

———. 1950. "The First Federal Census in the Panhandle, 1880." *Panhandle-Plains Historical Review* 23.

———. 1971. "Lieutenant Whipple's Railroad Reconnaissance across the Panhandle of Texas, 1853." *Panhandle-Plains Historical Review* 44.

Armstrong County Historical Association. 1965. *A Collection of Memories: A History of Armstrong County, 1876–1965.* Pioneer Book Publishers, Hereford, Tex.

Baker, Inez. 1940. *Yesterday in Hall County, Texas.* Book Craft, Dallas, Tex.

Brown, Lorin W., with Charles L. Briggs and Marta Weigle. 1978. *Hispano Folklife of New Mexico.* University of New Mexico Press, Albuquerque.

Cabeza de Baca, Fabiola. 1954. *We Fed Them Cactus.* University of New Mexico Press, Albuquerque.

Carlson, Alvar Ward. "New Mexico's Sheep Industry, 1850–1900: Its Role in the History of the Territory." *New Mexico Historical Review* 44 (1): 25–49.

Carter, Capt. R.G. 1935. *On the Border with Mackenzie; or Winning West Texas from the Comanches.* Enyon Printing Co., Washington, D.C.

Fehrenbach, T.R. 1974. *Comanches: The Destruction of a People.* Knopf, New York.

Gregg, Josiah. 1844. *Commerce of the Prairies: The Journal of a Santa Fe Trader.* Reprint ed., 1954, edited by M.L. Moorhead, University of Oklahoma Press, Norman.

Haley, J. Evetts. 1935. "The Comanchero Trade." *Southwestern Historical Quarterly* 38 (3): 157–76.

———. 1953. *The XIT Ranch of Texas and the Early Days of the Llano Estacado.* University of Oklahoma Press, Norman.

———. 1967. *Lore of the Llano Estacado.* Publications of the Texas Folklore Society 4. Southern Methodist University Press, Dallas.

Hunter, Lillie Mae. 1969. *The Book of Years: A History of Dallam and Hartley Counties.* Pioneer Book Publishers, Hereford, Tex.

Kenner, Charles L. 1969. *A History of New Mexican–Plains Indian Relations.* University of Oklahoma Press, Norman.

Key, Della Tyler. 1961. *In the Cattle Country: History of Potter County, 1887–1966.* Nortex Press, Quanah, Tex.

Levine, Frances, and Martha Doty Freeman. 1982. A Study of Documentary and Archeological Evidence for Comanchero Activity in the Texas Panhandle. Report on file at Texas Historical Commission, Austin.

Loomis, Noel M., and Abraham P. Nasatir. 1967. *Pedro Vial and the Roads to Santa Fe.* University of Oklahoma Press, Norman.

Newcomb, W.W., Jr. 1961. *The Indians of Texas: From Prehistoric to Modern Times.* University of Texas Press, Austin.

Oldham County Historical Commission. 1981. *Oldham County.* Craftsman Printers, Lubbock, Tex.

Rathjen, Frederick W. 1973. *The Texas Panhandle Frontier.* University of Texas Press, Austin.

Stephens, A. Ray, and William M. Holmes. 1989. *Historical Atlas of Texas.* University of Oklahoma Press, Norman.

Taylor, Anna Jean. 1983. New Mexican Pastor Sites in the Texas Panhandle. National Register of Historic Places nomination, on file at Texas Historical Commission, Austin.

Wallace, Ernest, and E. Adamson Hoebel. 1952. *The Comanches: Lords of the South Plains*. University of Oklahoma Press, Norman.

Worcester, Donald E. 1986. *The Spanish Mustang: From the Plains of Andalusia to the Prairies of Texas*. Texas Western Press, University of Texas at El Paso.

Hispanic Ranching Heritage,

by Jack Jackson

Ahlborn, Richard E. (Editor). 1980. *Man Made Mobile: Early Saddles of Western North America*. Smithsonian Studies in History and Technology 39. Smithsonian Institution Press, Washington, D.C.

Jackson, Jack. 1986. *Los Mesteños: Spanish Ranching in Texas, 1721–1821*. Texas A&M University Press, College Station.

Lea, Tom. 1957. *The King Ranch*. 2 vols. Little, Brown, Boston.

Slatta, Richard W. 1990. *Cowboys of the Americas*. Yale University Press, New Haven.

Tinker, Edward L. 1967. *The Horsemen of the Americas and the Literature They Inspired*. University of Texas Press, Austin.

Worcester, Donald E. 1986. *The Spanish Mustang: From the Plains of Andalusia to the Prairies of Texas*. Texas Western Press, University of Texas at El Paso.

The Built Environment in South Texas: The Hispanic Legacy,

by Joe S. Graham

Applegate, Howard E., and C. Wayne Hanselka. 1974. *La Junta de los Ríos del Norte y Conchos*. Texas Western Press, El Paso.

Barbee, W.C. 1981. *A Historical and Architectural Investigation of San Ygnacio, Texas*. Unpublished master's thesis. University of Texas at Austin.

Bunting, Bainbridge. 1976. *Early Architecture in New Mexico*. University of New Mexico Press, Albuquerque.

Connally, E.A. 1955. *The Ecclesiastical and Military Architecture of the Spanish Province of Texas*. Unpublished Ph.D. dissertation. Harvard University, Cambridge, Mass.

Crawford, P.P. 1925. *The Beginning of Spanish Settlement in the Lower Rio Grande Valley*. Unpublished master's thesis. University of Texas, Austin.

De la Cajiga, D.I. 1944. *La casa rural en México*. Publicaciones del Comité Permanente de la Segunda Conferencia Interamericana de Agricultura. Mexico, D.F.

García, R.O. 1970. *Dolores, Revilla, and Laredo: Three Sister Settlements*. Texian Press, Waco.

George, Eugene. 1975. *Historic Architecture of Texas: The Falcon Reservoir*. Texas Historical Commission and Texas Historical Foundation, Austin.

Graham, Joe S. 1978. "Folk Housing in South and West Texas: Some Comparisons." In *An Exploration of a Common Legacy*, edited by Marlene Heck, pp. 36–53. Texas Historical Commission, Austin.

———. 1986. "Southwestern Hispanics." In *America's Architectural Roots*, edited by Dell Upton and Diana Maddex, pp. 91–98. National Trust for Historic Preservation, Washington, D.C.

———. 1988. "The *Jacal* in the Big Bend: Its Origin and Evolution." In *Contributed Papers of the Second Symposium on Resources of the Chihuahuan Desert Region*, edited by Robert J. Mallouf, 28 pp. Chihuahuan Desert Research Institute Publication No. 20. Alpine, Tex.

————. 1988. "Mexican-American Lime Kilns in West Texas: The Limits of Folk Technology." In *Hoein' the Short Rows,* edited by Francis E. Abernethy, pp. 73–92. Texas Folklore Society Publications No. 47. Southern Methodist University Press, Dallas.

Hierro, Fray Simón del. 1942. *Diario que Hizo el Padre Fray Simón del Hierro en el Seno Mexicano Año de 1749.* Apendia, Documento 6, in *Conquista Espiritual del Nuevo Santander,* edited by Fidel P. de Lejarza. Instituto de Santo Toribio de Mogrovejo, Mexico.

Hinojosa, Gilberto M. 1983. *A Borderlands Town in Transition: Laredo, Texas, 1775–1870.* Texas A&M University Press, College Station.

Hoffman, David. 1972. *Roma.* San Antonio Conservation Society and Texas Architectural Foundation, Austin.

Jackson, Jack. 1986. *Los Mesteños: Spanish Ranching in Texas, 1721–1821.* Texas A&M University Press, College Station.

Lea, Tom. 1957. *The King Ranch.* 2 vols. Little, Brown, Boston.

Lehmer, Donald J. 1939. "Modern *Jacales* of Presidio." *El Palacio* 46: 183–86.

McVey, Lori Brown. 1988. *Guerrero Viejo: A Photographic Essay.* Occasional Papers of the Nuevo Santander Museum Complex, Vol. 3, No. 1. Dept. of Education, Laredo Junior College, Laredo, Tex.

Newton, Ada Louise. 1964. *The History of Architecture along the Rio Grande as Reflected in the Buildings around Rio Grande City, 1749–1920.* Unpublished master's thesis. Texas A&I University, Kingsville.

————. 1973. "The Anglo-Irish House of the Rio Grande." *Pioneer America* 1: 33–38.

Paredes, Américo. 1958. *With His Pistol in His Hand: A Border Ballad and its Hero.* University of Texas Press, Austin.

Prieto, Valeria, et al. 1978. *Vivienda campesino en México.* Secretaría de Asentamientos Humanos y Obras Públicas, Mexico.

Robinson, W.B. 1979. "Colonial Ranch Architecture in the Spanish-Mexican Tradition." *Southwestern Historical Quarterly* 83: 123–50.

Sanford, Trent Elwood. 1947. *The Story of Architecture in Mexico.* W.W. Norton, New York.

Texas Historical Commission. Nuestra Señora de los Dolores National Register Nomination. On file, Texas Historical Commission, Austin.

Torres Balbas, L. 1931. *La Vivienda Popular en España.* Vol. 2 of *Folklore y Costumbres de España,* edited by F. Carreras Candi. A. Martin, Barcelona.

West, Robert C. 1974. "The Flat-Roofed Folk Dwelling in Mexico." In *Man and Cultural Heritage: Papers in Honor of Fred B. Kniffen,* edited by H.J. Walker and W.G. Haag. Louisiana State University Press, Baton Rouge.

Exploring the West Texas Borderlands, by Curtis Tunnell and Enrique Madrid

Heck, Marlene E., and Frances M. López-Morillos (Compiler and Translator). 1978. *An Exploration of a Common Legacy: A Conference on Border Architecture.* Texas Historical Commission, Austin.

Hudson, Wilson M. (Editor). 1951. *The Healer of Los Olmos and Other Mexican Lore.* Facsimile ed., 1966, Southern Methodist University Press, Dallas.

Jordan, Terry G. 1982. *Texas Graveyards: A Cultural Legacy.* University of Texas Press, Austin.

Langford, J.O., and Fred Gipson. 1955. *Big Bend: A Homesteader's Story.* University of Texas Press, Austin.

Mallouf, Robert J. 1985. *A Synthesis of Eastern Trans-Pecos Prehistory.* Unpublished master's thesis, University of Texas at Austin.

Maxwell, Ross A. 1968. *The Big Bend of the Rio Grande: A Guide to the Rocks, Land-scapes, Geologic History, and Settlers of the Area of the Big Bend National Park.* Bureau of Economic Geology Guidebook 7. University of Texas at Austin.

Mullen, A. Kirsten, and Candace M. Volz (Compiler and Editor). *Texana I: The Frontier.* The Proceedings of a Humanities Forum Held at Round Top, Texas, May 1–3, 1980. Texas Historical Commission, Austin.

Tunnell, Curtis. 1981. *Wax, Men, and Money: A Historical and Archeological Study of Candelilla Wax Camps along the Rio Grande Border of Texas.* Office of the State Archeologist Report 32. Texas Historical Commission, Austin.

Tunnell, Curtis, and Enrique Madrid. 1990. "Making and Taking Sotol in Chihuahua and Texas." In *Proceedings of the Chihuahuan Desert Research Institute 1990.* Chihuahuan Desert Research Institute, Alpine, Tex.

Tyler, Ronnie C. 1975. *The Big Bend: A History of the Last Texas Frontier.* National Park Service, U.S. Department of the Interior, Washington, D.C.

Wulfkuhle, Virginia A. 1986. *The Buttrill Ranch Complex, Brewster County, Texas: Evidence of Early Ranching in the Big Bend.* Office of the State Archeologist Report 34. Texas Historical Commission, Austin.

Spanish Mission Revival in Twentieth-Century Architecture, by James W. Steely

Robinson, Willard B. 1974. *Texas Public Buildings of the Nineteenth Century.* University of Texas Press, Austin.

———. 1981. *Gone from Texas.* Texas A&M University Press, College Station.

Steely, James W. (Compiler). 1984. *A Catalog of Texas Properties in the National Register of Historic Places.* Texas Historical Commission, Austin.

Sunset Publications. 1981. *The California Missions.* Lane Publishing Co., Menlo Park, Calif.

Weitze, Karen J. 1984. *California's Mission Revival.* Hennessey & Ingalls, Los Angeles.

Whiffen, Marcus. 1969. *American Architecture since 1870: A Guide to the Styles.* MIT Press, Cambridge, Mass.

Churches, Chapels, and Shrines: Expressions of Hispanic Catholicism in Texas, by Helen Simons and Roni Morales

Anonymous. 1980. *Virgen de San Juan Shrine.* Custombook, Hackensack, N.J.

Branda, Eldon S. (Editor). 1976. *The Handbook of Texas: A Supplement.* Texas State Historical Association, Austin.

Brown, Angel Sepulveda, and Gloria Villa Cadena. n.d. *San Agustín Parish of Laredo: Marriage Book I, 1790–1857.* Laredo, Tex.

Driskill, Frank A., and Noel Grisham. 1980. *Historic Churches of Texas: The Land and the People.* Eakin Press, Burnet, Tex.

Hinojosa, Gilberto M. "The Enduring Hispanic Faith Communities: Spanish and Texas Church Historiography." *Journal of Texas Catholic History and Culture* 1 (1): 20–41.

Jasper, Pat, and Kay Turner. 1986. *Art Among Us/Arte entre Nosotros: Mexican-American Folk Art of San Antonio.* San Antonio Museum Association, San Antonio, Texas.

Kauffman, Christopher J. (Editor). 1990. *Hispanic Catholics: Historical Explorations and Cultural Analysis.* Special issue of *United States Catholic Historian* 9 (1 and 2).

Oblate Fathers. n.d. *The Story of La Lomita Chapel.* Booklet published by Oblate Fathers, Mission Tex.

Sandoval, Moíses. 1983. *Fronteras: A History of the Latin American Church in the U.S.A. since 1513.* Mexican-American Cultural Center, San Antonio, Texas.

Wangler, Rev. Msgr. Alexander C. (Editor). 1974. *Archdiocese of San Antonio, 1874–1974.* Privately published, Archdiocese of San Antonio, Texas.

Webb, Walter Prescott (Editor). 1952. *The Handbook of Texas.* 2 vols. Texas State Historical Association, Austin.

Tejano Festivals: Celebrations of History and Community, by Ann Perry

Black, Laura. 1990. "Viva Charreada." *Texas Highways* 37 (July): 7.

Brandes, Stanley. 1988. *Power and Persuasion: Fiestas and Social Control in Rural Mexico.* University of Pennsylvania Press, Philadelphia.

Bryant, Bruce W., and Joe Torres. 1975. "The Charreada." *Reflejos del Barrio.* Video, 21.05 min., December 16, 1975. Videocassette No. 10, Benson Latin American Collection, University of Texas at Austin.

Brock, Virginia. 1966. *Piñatas.* Abingdon Press, Nashville, Tenn.

Campa, Arthur L. 1979. *Hispanic Culture in the Southwest.* University of Oklahoma Press, Norman.

De León, Arnoldo. 1978. *Las Fiestas Patrias: Biographic Notes on the Hispanic Presence in San Angelo, TX.* Caravel Press, San Antonio.

Del Villar, José Alvarez. 1979. *Men and Horses of Mexico: History and Practice of "Charrería."* Ediciones Lara, Mexico City.

Geijerstam, Claes af. 1976. *Popular Music in Mexico.* University of New Mexico Press, Albuquerque.

Graham, Joe S. (Compiler). 1989. *Hispanic-American Material Culture: An Annotated Directory of Collections, Sites, Archives, and Festivals in the United States.* Greenwood Press, Westport, Conn.

Guerra, Carlos R. 1989. "The Unofficial Conjunto Primer for the Uninitiated Music Lover, Revised." *Tonantzin* 6 (2): 6–7.

Jasper, Pat, and Kay Turner (Editors). 1986. *Art among Us/Arte entre Nosotros: Mexican-American Folk Art of San Antonio.* San Antonio Museum of Art, San Antonio, Tex.

Johnston, Edith. 1974. *Regional Dances of Mexico.* National Textbook Co., Skokie, Ill.

Luevanos, Carmen. 1990. "Ocho Años de Cambio/Eight Years of Change." *Tonantzin* 6 (2): 14–15.

Madsen, William. 1973. *The Mexican-Americans of South Texas.* Holt, Rinehardt and Winston, New York.

Melville, Margarita B. 1978. "The Mexican-American and the Celebration of the Fiestas Patrias: An Ethnohistorical Analysis." *Grito del Sol* 3: 107–18.

Meyer, Michael C., and William L. Sherman. 1987. *The Course of Mexican History.* Oxford University Press, New York.

Muñoz, Luis Luján. 1987. *La Lotería de Figuras en Guatemala.* Serviprensa Centroamericana, Guatemala.

Muñoz, Sergio. 1980. "Cinco de Mayo: Looking beyond the Margaritas." *COMEXAZ News,* May 4, pp. 116–17.

Peña, Manuel H. 1985. *The Texas-Mexican Conjunto: History of a Working-Class Music.* University of Texas Press, Austin.

Pugh, Grace Thompson. 1944. "Mexican Folk Dances." In *Workshop in Inter-American Education: Southwest Texas State Teachers College of San Marcos, TX. Summer Session 1944.* Curriculum Service Bureau for International Studies, New York.

Reyna, José R. 1989. "Tejano Music as an Expression of Cultural Nationalism." *Tonantzin* 6 (2): 24–25, 35.

Salinas-Norman, Bobbi. 1987. *Folk Art Traditions I*. Piñata Publications, Oakland, Calif.

Thonhoff, Robert H. 1981. *The Texas Connection*. Eakin Press, Burnet, Tex.

Toor, Frances. 1947. *A Treasury of Mexican Folkways*. Mexico Press, Mexico, D.F.

West, John O. 1988. *Mexican-American Folklore: Legends, Songs, Festivals, Proverbs, Crafts, Tales of Saints, of Revolutionaries, and More*. August House Publishers, Little Rock, Ark.

Wolff, Len. 1985. "Charreada: Rodeo Mexican-Style." *Texas Highways* 32 (April): 12–15.

The Tex-Mex Menu,
by Helen Simons

Bayless, Rick, and Deann Groen Bayless. 1987. *Authentic Mexican Regional Cooking from the Heart of Mexico*. William Morrow, New York.

Brittin, Phil, and Joseph Daniel. 1982. *Texas on the Halfshell: Tex-Mex, Barbecue, Chili and Lone-Star Delights*. Doubleday, Garden City, N.Y.

Covey, Cyclone (Translator and Editor). 1984. *Cabeza de Vaca's Adventures in the Unknown Interior of America*. (Translation of *La relación y comentarios del gouernador Aluar Núñez Cabeça de Vaca de los acaescido en las dos jornadas que hizo a las Indias*, first published in 1542.) University of New Mexico Press, Albuquerque.

Crosby, Alfred W., Jr. 1972. *The Columbian Exchange: Biological and Cultural Consequences of 1492*. Contributions in American Studies No. 2. Greenwood Press, Westport, Conn.

Graham, Joe S. 1983. "Foodways of Pioneer Texas-Mexicans." In *Texana I: The Frontier*. Proceedings of a Humanities Forum Held at Round Top, Texas, May 1–3, 1980. Texas Historical Commission, Austin.

———. 1990. "Mexican-American Traditional Foodways at La Junta de los Rios." *Journal of Big Bend Studies* 2: 1–27.

Kraig, Bruce. 1982. *Mexican-American Plain Cooking*. Nelson-Hall, Chicago.

Linck, Ernestine Sewell, and Joyce Gibson Roach. 1989. *Eats: A Folk History of Texas Foods*. Texas Christian University Press, Fort Worth.

Sokolov, Raymond. 1989. "Before the Conquest." *Natural History*, August, pp. 76–79.

———. 1989. "Insects, Worms, and Other Tidbits." *Natural History*, September, pp. 84–87.

———. 1989. "The Well-Traveled Tomato." *Natural History*, June, pp. 84–88.

Tolbert, Frank X. 1972. *A Bowl of Red*. Doubleday, Garden City, N.Y.

West, John O. 1988. *Mexican-American Folklore: Legends, Songs, Festivals, Proverbs, Crafts, Tales of Saints, of Revolutionaries, and More*. American Folklore Series. August House, Little Rock, Ark.

The Written Word,
by Jesús F. de la Teja

Beers, Henry Putney. 1979. *Spanish and Mexican Records of the American Southwest*. University of Arizona Press, Tucson.

Cummins, Light Towsend, and Alvin R. Bailey, Jr. 1988. *A Guide to the History of Texas*. Greenwood Press, Westport, Conn.

Guidebook

NOTE: This section of the References does not repeat works listed above that were also used in the preparation of the guidebook. However, we wish to acknowledge here our special indebtedness to the *Handbook of Texas* (Branda 1976, Webb 1952), which was used extensively for general historical background on Texas cities and towns.

Almaráz, Félix D., Jr. 1979. *Crossroads of Empire: The Church and State on the Río Grande Frontier of Coahuila and Texas, 1700–1821.* Center for Archaeological Research, Archaeology and History of the San Juan Bautista Mission Area, Coahuila and Texas Report 1. University of Texas at San Antonio.

Big Bend Area Travel Association. 1986. *Getting the Most from Your Big Bend Area Vacation* 1 (2). Alpine, Tex.

Big Bend National Park. 1990. *Alvino House.* Pamphlet distributed by Big Bend National Park, Tex.

Breeze, Carla. 1990. *Pueblo Deco.* Rizzoli, New York.

Byfield, Patsy Jeanne. 1966. *Falcon Dam and the Lost Towns of Zapata. Texas Memorial Museum Miscellaneous Papers 2.* University of Texas at Austin.

Calleros, Cleofas. 1951. El Paso's Missions and Indians. Booklet, privately published, El Paso, Tex.

———. 1952. *The Mother Mission: Our Lady of Mount Carmel.* Booklet, privately published, El Paso, Tex.

———. 1969. *San Elizario Presidio-Mission.* Booklet, privately published, San Elizario, Tex.

Carson, Chris, and William McDonald (Editors). *A Guide to San Antonio Architecture.* San Antonio Chapter, American Institute of Architects, San Antonio.

Carson, Mrs. Ira. 1966. *Ozona, Texas.* Crockett County Historical Society, Ozona, Tex.

Casey, Clifford B. 1972. *Mirages, Mystery, and Reality: Brewster County, Texas, of the Big Bend of the Rio Grande.* Pioneer Book Publisher, Hereford, Tex., for Brewster County Historical Survey Committee.

Chabot, Frederick C. 1937. *With the Makers of San Antonio.* Privately published, San Antonio.

Chipman, Donald E. 1987. "In Search of Cabeza de Vaca's Route across Texas: An Historiographical Survey." *Southwestern Historical Quarterly* 91 (2): 127–48.

Crockett County Historical Society. 1976. *A History of Crockett County.* Anchor Publishing Co., San Angelo, Tex.

Cummings, Joe. 1990. *Texas Handbook.* Moon Publications, Chico, Calif.

Downie, Alice Evans (Editor). 1978. *Terrell County, Texas: Its Past and Its People.* Anchor Publishing, San Antonio, for Terrell County Heritage Commission.

Fehrenbach, T.R. 1968. *Lone Star: A History of Texas and the Texans.* Macmillan, New York.

Ferguson, Bobbie, and George Agogino. 1979. *Tracing John Reed's 1914 Desert Route: The Haciendas.* Eastern New Mexico University Contributions in Anthropology, Vol. 10, No. 1. Portales, N.M.

Foster, Nancy Haston, and Ben Fairbank, Jr. 1989. *San Antonio.* 3d ed. Texas Monthly Guidebooks. Texas Monthly Press, Austin.

Fox, Stephen. 1990. *Houston Architectural Guide.* American Institute of Architects, Houston Chapter, and Herring Press, Houston.

Franciscan Missionaries of the T. O. R. of Waco, Texas. 1931. *Dedication Souvenir: Church of St. Francis.* St. Francis Church, Waco.

Giles, Robert C. 1972. *Changing Times: The Story of the Diocese of Galveston-Houston in Commemoration of Its Founding.* Diocese of Galveston-Houston.

González, Fidencio. 1985. *Mexican-American Heritage*. Privately published, El Paso, Tex.

Gordon, Alice, Jerry C. Dunn, Jr., and Mel White. 1990. *The Smithsonian Guide to Historic America: Texas and the Arkansas River Valley*. Stewart, Tabori & Chang, New York.

Greene, Shirley Brooks. 1987. *When Rio Grande City Was Young: Buildings of Old Rio Grande City*. Pan American University, Edinburg, Tex.

Gregory, H.F. (Editor). 1986. *The Southern Caddo: An Anthology*. Garland Publishing, New York.

Greth, Carlos Vidal. 1990. "Radio Español." *Austin American-Statesman*, Tuesday, October 2, p. B6.

Gunter, Ellen. 1987. *Dallas: Your Complete Guide to a Vibrant Texas City*. Texas Monthly Press, Austin.

Harry, Jewel Horace. 1981. *A History of Chambers County*. Chambers County Historical Commission, Chambers County, Tex.

Heritage Museum of Big Spring. 1989. "Historical Commission and the Municipal Auditorium." *Howard County Historian*, Fall Issue, p. 1.

Hester, Paul, and Peter C. Papademetriou. 1979. *La Architectura: Spanish Influences on Houston's Architecture*. Houston Public Library, Houston.

Hispanic Beginnings of Dallas Project. 1990. *Hispanic Beginnings of Dallas: Into the 20th Century, 1850 to 1976*. Exhibition booklet. Dallas Independent School District, ACAL de Mexico, Hispanic Beginnings of Dallas Project, Dallas.

Historic Preservation Council for Tarrant County, Texas. 1986. *Tarrant County Historic Resources Survey: Phase III, Fort Worth's Southside*. Fort Worth.

Hoefer, Hans Johannes (Project Director). *Insight Guides: Texas*. APA Productions, Singapore.

Hodge, Larry D. (Editor). 1990. "The Little Winery That Could, Does." *Traveling Historic Texas,* June 1990, pp. 1–2, 5.

Horgan, Paul. 1954. *Great River: The Rio Grande in North American History*. Holt, Rinehart, and Winston, New York.

Hughes, Jack T., and Patrick S. Willey. 1978. *Archeology at Mackenzie Reservoir*. Office of the State Archeologist Survey Report 24. Texas Historical Commission, Austin.

Ivey, James E. 1990. *Presidios of the Big Bend Area/Los Presidios del Area de Big Bend*. Spanish text translated by Carlos Chavez. Southwest Cultural Resources Center Professional Papers 31. National Park Service, Santa Fe, N.M.

Kreneck, Thomas H. 1989. *Del Pueblo: A Pictorial History of Houston's Hispanic Community*. Houston International University, Houston.

Krieger, Alex D. 1961. "The Travels of Alvar Núñez Cabeza de Vaca in Texas and Mexico, 1534–1536." In *Homenaje a Pablo Martínez del Río en el XXV aniversario del primera edición de "Los orígines americanos."* Instituto Nacional de Antropología e Historia, Mexico City.

Leavenworth, Geoffrey, and Richard Payne. 1985. *Historic Galveston*. Herring Press, Houston.

Lowery, Jack. 1990. "Save the Alamo." *Texas Highways* 37 (3): 40–41.

Lubbock Heritage Society. *Historic Homes and Buildings Tour, Lubbock, Texas*. Pamphlet published by Lubbock Heritage Society, Lubbock.

McIlvain, Myra Hargrave. 1985. *Texas Auto Trails: The South and the Rio Grande Valley*. University of Texas Press, Austin.

McWhorter, Eugene. 1989. *Traditions of the Land: The History of Gregg County*. Gregg County Historical Foundation, Longview, Tex.

Mallouf, Robert J., Barbara J. Baskin, and Kay L. Killen. 1977. *A Predictive Assessment of Cultural Resources in Hidalgo and Willacy Counties, Texas*. Office of the State Archeologist Survey Report 23. Texas Historical Commission, Austin.

Meinig, D.W. 1969. *Imperial Texas: An Interpretive Essay in Cultural Geography*. University of Texas Press, Austin.

Metz, Leon C. 1980. *City at the Pass: An Illustrated History of El Paso.* Windsor Publications, Woodland Hills, Calif.

Miller, George Oxford, and Delena Tull. 1984. *Texas Parks and Campgrounds: North, East, and Coastal Texas.* Texas Monthly Press, Austin.

Miller, Ray. 1979. *Eyes of Texas Travel Guide: San Antonio/Border Edition.* Cordovan Corporation, Houston.

———. 1988. *The Eyes of Texas Travel Guide: Dallas and East Texas.* Lone Star Books, Houston.

Newell, H. Perry, and Alex D. Krieger. 1949. *The George C. Davis Site, Cherokee County, Texas.* Memoirs of the Society for American Archaeology, No. 5. Society for American Archaeology and the University of Texas, Austin.

Neyland, Rev. Malcolm. 1977. *St. Mary's and Missions.* Published by Parish Councils of St. Mary's, Spur; Our Lady of Guadalupe, Matador; and Epiphany Church, Jayton, Tex.

O'Malley, Nancy, Lynn Osborne Bobbitt, and Dan Scurlock. 1976. *A Historical and Archeological Investigation of Roma.* Office of the State Archeologist Special Report 20. Texas Historical Commission, Austin.

Osborne, Lynn, T. Moriarty, S. Spence, and K.P. Almond. 1976. *Texas Border Architecture: Report on the Architectural Survey of Villa Guerrero, Coahuila, Mexico, and Eagle Pass, Texas, United States.* School of Architecture, University of Texas at Austin.

Our Lady of Guadalupe Church, Amarillo. 1990. *Our Lady of Guadalupe Parish: Nuestra Historia a Través de los Años, 1918–1990.* Privately published, Amarillo, Tex.

Our Lady of Guadalupe Church, Austin. 1975. *Golden Jubilee of the Oblate Fathers in Our Lady of Guadalupe Church, Austin, Texas, 1925–1975.* Privately published, Austin.

Our Lady of Guadalupe Church, Laredo. 1979. *Our Lady of Guadalupe: February 1929–1979.* Privately published, Laredo, Tex.

Panhandle-Plains Museum. Archival Collections: newspaper clippings relating to structures in Canyon and vicinity. Canyon, Tex.

Pagès, Pierre Marie François. 1782. "A Journey Through Texas in 1767." Translated by Corinna Steele. *El Campanario* 16 (1): 1–28.

Papademetriou, Peter C. (Editor). 1972. *Houston: An Architectural Guide.* Houston Chapter of the American Institute of Architects, Houston.

Pinkard, Tommie. 1983. "Hop a Ferry to Mexico." *Texas Highways* 30 (1): 32–35.

Ragsdale, Kenneth Baxter. 1976. *Quicksilver: Terlingua and the Chisos Mining Company.* Texas A&M University Press, College Station.

Robertson, Brian. 1985. *Rio Grande Heritage: A Pictorial History.* The Donning Company, Norfolk, for the Hidalgo County Historical Museum.

Roseman, R., and B. Sanderson with J. Dycus. 1985. *Annually in Texas.* Tumbleweed Productions, Dallas.

Ruff, Ann. 1986. "Angel of Goliad." *Texas Highways* 33 (8): 18–19.

St. Joseph's Catholic Church, Fort Stockton. 1975. *St. Joseph Catholic Church, Fort Stockton.* Privately published, Fort Stockton, Tex.

San Antonio Conservation Society. 1990. "Society To Present Las Posadas." *San Antonio Conservation Society News* 27 (2): 1.

Sánchez, Mario, and Aura Nell Ranzau Jr. (Editors). 1991. *A Shared Experience: The History, Architecture and Historic Designations of the Lower Rio Grande Heritage Corridor.* Los Caminos del Rio Heritage Project and Texas Historical Commission, Austin.

Sauvageau, Juan. 1976. "The Junipero Serra of Texas (Father Peter Keralum)." In *Stories That Must Not Die,* Vol. 2. Oasis Press, Austin.

Scott, Florence Johnson. 1966. *Historical Heritage of the Lower Rio Grande.* Texian Press, Waco.

Shiffen, Marcus. 1969. *American Architecture since 1870: A Guide to the Styles*. Cambridge, Mass.

Simpson, Amy. 1981. "Pike Park: The Heart and History of Mexican-American Culture in Dallas." On file, Los Barrios Unidos Community Clinic, Dallas.

Stambaugh, J. Lee, and Lillian J. Stambaugh. 1974. *The Lower Rio Grande Valley of Texas*. Jenkins, Austin.

Syers, Ed. 1988. *Backroads of Texas*. 2d ed. Lone Star Books. Gulf Publishing Co., Houston.

Texas Department of Agriculture. 1974–present. *Texas Family Land Heritage Registry*. Annual vols. of the registry published by Texas Department of Agriculture, Austin.

Texas Historical Commission. Cultural Resource Survey Files. Austin.

———. National Register of Historic Places Files. Austin.

———. Office of the State Archeologist Files. Austin.

———. Official Texas Historical Marker Files. Austin.

Texas Historical Commission, Division of Architecture. 1991. *Endangered Historic Properties of Texas*. 2d ed. Texas Historical Commission, Austin.

Texas Monthly. 1991. "Texas Tropical Trail." Special promotional supplement in *Texas Monthly* 19 (2): 75–85.

———. 1991. "Texas Brazos Trail." Special promotional supplement in *Texas Monthly* 19 (5): 72–83.

Texas Parks and Wildlife Department. 1970 to present (magazine established 1943). *Texas Parks and Wildlife*. Magazine published monthly, Austin.

Texas Department of Transportation. 1990–91. *Texas Events Calendar*. Published quarterly, Austin.

———. 1975 to present. *Texas Highways*. Magazine published monthly, Austin.

———. n.d. *Texas*. Guidebook issued and revised periodically by the department, Austin.

Texas State Library and Archives Commission. "Midland's Haley Library." *Texas Libraries* 51 (2): 57.

Thompson, Celia. 1985. *Marfa and Presidio County, Texas, 1535–1946*. Nortex Press, Austin, for Presidio County Historical Commission.

Thompson, Jerry. 1986. *Laredo: A Pictorial History*. Donning Co., Norfolk, Va.

Thybony, Scott. 1991. "Against All Odds, Black Seminole Won Their Freedom." *Smithsonian* 22 (5): 90–101.

Tidwell, Laura Knowlton. *Dimmit County Mesquite Roots*, Vol. 1. Wind River Press for Dimmit County, Tex.

Timmons, W.H. n.d. "A History of the San Elizario Jail." Copy on file, Office of the State Archeologist Library, Texas Historical Commission, Austin.

Tucek, James. 1990. *A Century of Faith: The Story of the Diocese of Dallas*. Taylor Publishing, Dallas, for Diocese of Dallas.

Tunnell, Curtis, and W.W. Newcomb, Jr. 1969. *A Lipan Apache Mission: San Lorenzo de la Santa Cruz, 1762–1771*. Texas Memorial Museum Bulletin 14. University of Texas at Austin.

Wedel, Mildred Mott. 1988. *The Wichita Indians 1541–1750: Ethnohistorical Essays*. Reprints in Anthropology Series, Vol. 38. J & L Reprint Company, Lincoln, Neb.

Wooldridge, Ruby A., and Robert B. Vezzetti. 1982. *Brownsville: A Pictorial History*. Donning Co., Norfolk, Va.

Wylie, Rosa Lee. 1973. *History of Van Horn and Culberson County, Texas*. Pioneer Book Publishing, Hereford, Tex., for Culberson County Historical Survey Committee.

Notes on Contributors

FÉLIX D. ALMARÁZ

Dr. Félix D. Almaráz, Jr., is professor of history at the University of Texas at San Antonio. The author of numerous books and articles, including *Tragic Cavalier: Governor Manuel Salcedo of Texas, 1808–1813* (Texas A&M University Press, 1992) and *The San Antonio Missions and Their System of Land Tenure* (University of Texas Press, 1989), he is a frequent speaker on the lecture circuit. He also has hands-on preservation experience, having served for nearly twenty years as an active member of the Bexar County Historical Commission (five as chairman and eleven as vice-chairman, the latter a position he currently holds).

JESÚS F. DE LA TEJA

Dr. Jesús F. de la Teja is currently assistant professor of history at Southwest Texas State University. He formerly was archivist with the Texas General Land Office, where he was engaged in reorganizing the Spanish Collection in the office's archives. He is the author of numerous articles relating to Texas' Spanish and Mexican heritage and of the recently released *A Revolution Remembered: The Memoirs and Selected Correspondence of Juan N. Seguín* (published by State House Press), and he served as managing editor of *Guide to Spanish and Mexican Land Grants in South Texas* (published by the Texas General Land Office, 1988).

T.R. FEHRENBACH

T.R. Fehrenbach, one of the best-known historians in Texas, is a member and former chairman of the Texas Historical Commission. His major historical works include *Lone Star,* the most widely read history of Texas, *Comanches: The Destruction of a People,* and *Fire and Blood: A History of Mexico.*

JOE S. GRAHAM

Dr. Joe S. Graham is a professor in the Department of Psychology and Sociology and a research associate with the John E. Conner Museum at Texas A&I University in Kingsville, where he recently received a university award for research excellence. He is a recognized authority on vernacular (or folk) architecture in the Hispanic tradition. His publications include *The Dream Mine: A Study in Mormon Folklore* (1977), *Hispanic-American Material Culture: An Annotated Directory of Collections, Sites, Archives, and Festivals in the United States* (1989), and *Hecho en Tejas: Texas-Mexican Material Culture* (1991). He also has recently cooperated with the Office of the State Archeologist in a major oral history project covering the border area of Trans-Pecos Texas.

CATHRYN A. HOYT

Cathryn A. Hoyt is a staff archeologist with the Office of the State Archeologist, Texas Historical Commission. She formerly was with the Institute of Maritime History and Archaeology in Bermuda, where she was engaged in collecting and analyzing archival and marine archeological data relating to the age of exploration. She has directed the archeological investigation of two pre-18th-century shipwrecks and is the author of several articles dealing with the material culture of the period of exploration, including "Bermuda in the Age of Exploration: The Re-examination of the *San Pedro*," in *Underwater Archaeology Proceedings from the Society for Historical Archaeology Conference* (1988).

JACK JACKSON

Jack Jackson, author and artist, is widely known for his knowledge of Spanish ranchos and ranching practices and for his commitment to better understanding of our Hispanic heritage. His publications include *Los Mesteños: Spanish Ranching in Texas, 1721–1821,* published by Texas A&M University Press in 1986, and a comic book history of Juan N. Seguín.

ENRIQUE MADRID

Enrique Madrid is a dedicated avocational archeologist and preservationist. He is a member of the Texas Archeological Stewardship Network, a select group of avocationals who work with the Texas Historical Commission's Office of the State Archeologist to promote archeological preservation and protect important archeological sites. In addition to previous articles coauthored with Curtis Tunnell, he has transcribed and translated a major oral history project undertaken in the La Junta de los Ríos area and has translated *Expedition to La Junta de los Ríos, 1747–1748: Captain Commander Joseph de Ydoiaga's Report to the Viceroy of New Spain* (scheduled for publication by the Texas Historical Commission).

PATRICIA A. MERCADO-ALLINGER

Patricia A. Mercado-Allinger is a staff archeologist with the Office of the State Archeologist, Texas Historical Commission. She formerly conducted archeological investigations in Arizona, on National Park Service properties, and in Texas, where she participated in a field season at the Lubbock Lake site, served as park archeologist at Caprock Canyons State Park, and worked in various areas across the state and in southwestern Missouri as a field archeologist with Prewitt and Associates in Austin. She is the author of several monographs on Texas archeology, including *Ar-*

cheological Investigations at Site 41B1452, Caprock Canyons State Park, Briscoe County, Texas (1982). She is an active member of a number of archeological organizations and served as president of the Texas Archeological Society in 1990.

RONI MORALES

Roni Morales heads the Texas Historical Commission's Publications Department and is editor of the agency newsletter, *The Medallion*. In her staff capacity at the commission, she has written numerous articles on historical and preservation topics and has produced special issues of the newsletter devoted to American Indian, Mexican-American, and African-American history.

ANN PERRY

Ann Perry is a former staff member of the Texas Historical Commission's Local History Programs, where she assisted in the review and writing of historical marker texts. Her experience also includes researching and drafting U.S.–Mexican trade legislation. She has studied Spanish in Mexico and is particularly interested in the archeology and folkart of the Southwest and Mexico. She is currently attending the University of Texas School of Law in Austin.

HELEN SIMONS

Helen Simons, editor and administrative assistant with the Office of the State Archeologist, Texas Historical Commission, formerly was a freelance editor of scholarly books and a staff member of the University of Texas Press. Her technical editing experience covers a period of 25 years and books in many fields, especially archeology, Texas history, and folklore. Her publications include *Archeological Bibliography for the Northern Panhandle Region of Texas* (1988) and (as co-author) *The Years of Exploration* (1984), an overview for young readers of the archeology and history of the Spanish Contact period in Texas.

DEBORAH SMITH

Deborah Smith, former archeological assistant in the Archeological Planning and Review Department of the Texas Historical Commission, has worked on numerous archeological projects in Texas and is currently working in Guam. While with the Texas Historical Commission, she assisted William A. Martin in the compilation of *Archeological Bibliography for the Northeast Region of Texas* (1990). She is an active member of several professional organizations and has recently served as editor of the *Council of Texas Archeologists Newsletter*.

JAMES W. STEELY

James W. Steely is director of the National Register Programs, Texas Historical Commission, and, in the course of his duties, has undertaken extensive studies of Spanish Colonial architecture and its preservation. He has published numerous articles in books, magazines, and journals, and his interests include Texas history as well as architecture. Both these interests are reflected in his booklet on the Civilian Conservation Corps, published by the Texas Parks and Wildlife Department, and he is currently working on a history of Texas state parks and their historic structures. He also is the compiler of *A Catalog of Texas Properties in the National Register of Historic Places* (published by the Texas Historical Commission, 1984).

CURTIS TUNNELL

Curtis Tunnell is executive director of the Texas Historical Commission and was formerly state archeologist. In addition to his distinguished career in historical preservation, he is the author of numerous monographs, articles, professional papers, and reviews. He has directed archeological investigations across the state in sites dating from the Paleoindian period through the Spanish Colonial era to settlers' cabins dating from the 19th century. His publications reflect the depth of his experience, ranging from *A Description of Enameled Earthenware from an Archeological Excavation at Mission San Antonio de Valero (the Alamo)* (1966) to *Wax, Men, and Money: A Historical and Archeological Study of Candelilla Wax Camps along the Rio Grande Border of Texas* (1981). In addition to archeology, architecture, historical preservation, and Texas history, his interests include oral history and folklife along the border and in northern Mexico.

ROBERT S. WEDDLE

Robert S. Weddle is the author of several books concerning the period of Spanish exploration and colonization in Texas, including *San Juan Bautista: Gateway to Spanish Texas* (1968), *The San Sabá Mission: Spanish Pivot in Texas* (1964), and *Wilderness Manhunt: The Spanish Search for La Salle* (1973), all published by the University of Texas Press. He also is the author of *Spanish Sea: The Gulf of Mexico in North American Discovery* (1985) and *The French Thorn: Rival Explorers in the Spanish Sea, 1682–1762* (1991), and editor of *La Salle, the Mississippi, and the Gulf: Three Primary Documents* (1987), all published by Texas A&M University Press.

Index

(Italic page numbers indicate a reference to an illustration.)